The New Century Handbook

Third Edition

CHRISTINE A. HULT
Utah State University

THOMAS N. HUCKIN
University of Utah

PEARSON
Longman

New York   Boston   San Francisco
London   Toronto   Sydney   Tokyo   Singapore   Madrid
Mexico City   Munich   Paris   Cape Town   Hong Kong   Montreal

About the Cover

The cover of this new edition of *The New Century Handbook* features a photograph of Walt Disney Hall in Los Angeles, widely recognized in periodicals across the country as the 2003 New Building of the Year. The spirit of innovation typified in this groundbreaking structure is mirrored in the content of *The New Century Handbook*.

Senior Vice President and Publisher: *Joseph Opiela*
Development Manager: *Janet Lanphier*
Senior Development Editor: *Judith Fifer*
Executive Marketing Manager: *Megan Galvin-Fak*
Senior Supplements Editor: *Donna Campion*
Media Supplements Editor: *Nancy Garcia*
Production Manager: *Donna DeBenedictis*
Project Coordination, Text Design, and Electronic Page Makeup:
    Nesbitt Graphics, Inc.
Cover Design Manager: *Wendy Ann Fredericks*
Cover Designer: *Kay Petronio*
Cover Photo: © *Lara Swimmer-Esto*
Senior Manufacturing Buyer: *Alfred C. Dorsey*
Printer and Binder: *Von Hoffmann Corporation*
Cover Printer: *Phoenix Color Corporation*

For permission to use copyrighted material, grateful acknowledgment is made to the copyright holders on pp. C-1–C-3, which are hereby made part of this copyright page.

Library of Congress Cataloging-in-Publication Data

Hult, Christine A.
    The new century handbook/Christine A. Hult, Thomas N. Huckin.—3rd ed.
        p. cm.
    ISBN 0-321-23392-1
    1. English language—Rhetoric—Handbooks, manuals, etc. 2. English language—Grammar—Handbooks, manuals, etc. 3. Report writing—Handbooks, manuals, etc. I. Huckin, Thomas N. II. Title.
PE1408.H688 2004
808'.042—dc22
                                                                                    2003028087

Please visit us at http://www.ablongman.com/hult

ISBN 0-321-23392-1

3 4 5 6 7 8 9 10—VH—07 06 05

Contents

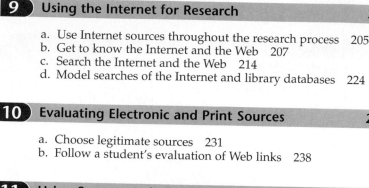

Part 6 | Sentence Grammar 639

Part 10 | Punctuation 837

Part 11 | Mechanics   889

57   Capital Letters and Italics   889

58   Abbreviations and Numbers   899

Part 12 | ESL Issues   912

Preface

The New Century Handbook, Third Edition, is a comprehensive resource for college writers. It shows students how to plan, compose, and revise; how to do research and formulate arguments; and how to write for different disciplines and special purposes. At a time when many students arrive at college without adequate grounding in "the basics," this handbook provides thorough coverage of grammar, style, diction, and punctuation, as well as a special section on ESL challenges. In an increasingly visual world, it shows students how to apply principles of document design and visual rhetoric. The handbook repeatedly emphasizes both the conventional and the rhetorical aspects of good writing, pointing out how even small details should reflect the writer's consideration of audience, persona, genre, field, and goals.

We are delighted and deeply gratified by the positive response to earlier editions of *The New Century Handbook,* the first college handbook developed with computer users in mind. Its success confirms our conviction that students can benefit from a handbook that includes instruction in using a computer in the writing and research processes. Most students today do their writing on a computer, taking advantage of the unique features afforded by word-processing programs. Most also use the Internet, gathering information on the World Wide Web and communicating via email with their peers. Since students today often turn first to the World Wide Web to conduct research, it is vital that they learn how to define a search and how to evaluate and document their findings, as well as how to utilize resources both in a library and on the Internet.

We are confident that our users will appreciate the additions and improvements to this new edition, which we have attempted to make even better while retaining the book's primary emphases on sound rhetorical principles and on an accessible, useful treatment of computer technology and online resources.

CONTENT

Writing

While retaining a general focus on the rhetorical principles that underlie effective writing, this handbook is unique in that it shows students how to tap the power of computers to become more effective and more confident writers. The first part of the handbook shows students how to become critical thinkers, how to analyze visual as well as written communications, and how to apply critical thinking principles to their own work. Accompanying boxes explain how to use the computer as a powerful writing tool.

Part 1 opens with an overview of how communication has changed in the new century, and how these changes affect reading, writing, and viewing in a variety of media (Chapter 1). In the following chapters, student writers learn about critical thinking, critical viewing, and the reading process (Chapter 2). They discover how to prepare for writing assignments (Chapter 3). They find out how to make the best use of the organizational possibilities computers offer for storing work in directories and folders. They also learn how to explore topics through Internet searches; how to brainstorm potential topics using email or newsgroups; and how to harness the power of computers to focus, develop, and organize ideas.

Chapter 4 introduces students to the many ways to compose. They learn techniques for combining prewriting and outlining documents, building a first draft from an electronic outline, and composing with documents in two separate windows. The chapter encourages students to collaborate online with other student writers, sharing drafts via computer networks and responding to each other's writing through document comments or email. Chapter 5 guides students through the steps in efficiently and effectively rewriting their work—from comparing and revising drafts of their texts to editing for more effecting wording and sentence structure.

The next two chapters are devoted to two fundamental issues in writing academic papers: structuring paragraphs and formulating arguments. Chapter 6 explains how to devise an appropriate thesis, support it with compelling evidence, and construct paragraphs that guide readers through the text. Using a student essay on cybercensorship to illustrate its main points, Chapter 7 emphasizes the importance of audience analysis, sound reasoning, and considering alternative points of view.

Research

This handbook provides unparalleled coverage of the research process. The six chapters in Part 2 detail the steps in the research process; each chapter addresses the ways in which computers can facilitate researching and writing.

In addition to describing traditional library catalogs and print indexes, Chapter 8 covers innovations such as computerized notebooks and note cards, document comments and annotations, computerized footnote and bibliography programs, Boolean keyword searching, and online databases. Then, because the Internet is so radically changing the research process, two complete chapters explain using sources on the World Wide Web. Chapter 9 shows students how to use the Internet to find and explore topics, conduct background and focused research, and collaborate and exchange feedback with peers. It also illustrates the range of information available via the Internet and the use of search tools to find that information. Perhaps most importantly, Chapter 10 helps students assess the credibility and reliability of sources they find in print and on the Internet. Both Chapters 9 and 10 include model student searches.

An entire chapter (Chapter 11) covers using sources appropriately and effectively. The chapter offers helpful guidance on avoiding plagiarism and on quoting, summarizing, and paraphrasing source information. In Chapter 12, students learn to harness the power of computers as they plan and organize, draft, review and revise, and format research papers. Chapter 13 includes an overview of the MLA documentation style; Chapter 14 covers APA style; Chapter 15 includes CMS, CBE, and COS styles. In addition to supplying explanations and illustrations of how to document conventional sources, this handbook provides unprecedented coverage of how to document electronic sources. The latest information from the 2003 editions of the *MLA Style Manual* and *The Chicago Manual of Style* is included, as well as extensive and up-to-date tips on electronic citation formats across the disciplines.

Writing in the Disciplines

In Part 3, students get advice on writing papers for literature classes, as well as for other courses in the humanities, social sciences, and natural sciences. A new chapter provides an overview of writing and researching in academic disciplines. Each of the following writing-across-the-curriculum chapters introduces students to the major

types of writing in the disciplines and to the most important technological resources available. The extensive list of sources provides
Web sites selected by professors in the different disciplines and
include only those sites they found most useful to themselves and
their students.

Design in Print and on the Web

With the increased availability of computer graphics programs, the
"look" of documents has become more important. Part 4 covers
designing documents of all types.

Chapter 20 describes three basic design principles and then
explains how various formatting tools (such as itemized lists,
frames, and columns) can be used to put these principles into practice. The chapter also discusses common types of graphical displays.
In all cases, students are encouraged to use design elements not simply for decoration but as a way to enhance their readers' engagement
with and understanding of the document.

Because so many of today's writers are required to "publish"
their work using the word-processing software available for personal computers, this handbook includes a chapter on designing
print documents. In Chapter 21, students learn how to write and
publish both a brochure and a newsletter. Instructors may wish to
suggest these types of desktop publishing as alternative ways to format traditional essays.

Chapter 22 teaches students how to apply basic design principles when designing Web pages. In this chapter, students learn the
important ways in which Web texts differ from print texts and proceed through the process of designing their own Web pages. In
Chapter 23, students learn about writing for the Web. They are introduced to HyperText Markup Language (HTML) and receive step-by-
step instruction in constructing a Web page. The "Global Warming"
newsletter from Chapter 21 is used to show students how they can
publish a paper as both a newsletter and a Web document.

Writing for Different Purposes

Part 5 covers special types of writing that students encounter,
including writing email and writing resumes. Chapter 24 introduces
the many ways students can use computer networks to enhance
their writing. Students need to become familiar with all of these
resources—email and listservs, bulletin boards and newsgroups,
IRCs, MOOs, instant messaging, and collaborative software. The
chapter also explains how to use electronic media to write better

papers. In particular, the chapter encourages students to become involved with online communities as a way to collaborate with other writers.

Writing in college offers an excellent opportunity to practice writing for the workplace. Chapter 25 provides basic instruction in writing letters, résumés, reports, memos, and other forms of business correspondence. With more and more business communication taking place electronically, the chapter devotes special attention to email, scannable résumés, and homepage résumés. Chapter 26 is a new chapter on oral presentations. In addition to standard advice on how to prepare and deliver an oral presentation, the chapter includes tips and illustrations on how to prepare and use overhead transparencies and *PowerPoint* slides. Chapter 27 covers essay exams. It includes both excellent and poor student responses for comparison. A new chapter, Chapter 28, guides students toward developing effective writing portfolios.

Grammar and Style

Parts 6–12 of the handbook provide comprehensive coverage of grammar and style, including traditional topics such as sentence structure, pronoun case, agreement, consistency, conciseness, parallelism, word choice, spelling, and punctuation. Because students are likely to use this material selectively, discussions and explanations are concise and various devices (consistent formatting, FAQs at the beginning of each chapter, frequent cross-references, and a comprehensive index) make it easy for students to look up a particular topic. More than 100 exercise sets are sprinkled throughout these chapters, giving students hands-on practice in analyzing grammatical forms and correcting errors.

The handbook's unique emphasis on computers continues in this section. Warnings about the shortcomings of grammar checkers are accompanied by suggestions about special ways to make good use of these checkers. Help boxes explain how to customize a grammar checker, search for particular grammar problems, use an electronic thesaurus, customize and streamline spell checking, and identify punctuation problems. The text includes many references to helpful Web sites. Students who need basic instruction in using grammar checkers and other computerized word-processing tools can turn to Chapter 29 for help.

ESL students will benefit as much as native-speaking students from the material presented in this handbook. Four chapters address specific ESL concerns: the use of definite and indefinite articles

(Chapter 60), verb problems (Chapter 61), word order (Chapter 62), and vocabulary (Chapter 63).

New to This Edition

In writing this third edition, we listened to feedback from users of the earlier editions to make *The New Century Handbook* even more useful. An exciting change to this edition is the inclusion of annotated CD and Web site icons within the book, indicating to students where additional material that is both supplementary and complementary to the book can be found in these multimedia components. Additional material includes video clips, audio clips, interactive exercises, assessment tests, links to useful Web sites, and further explanations and examples.

Here are other major changes listed by chapter:

- Chapter 1, "Writing in the New Century," has been completely rewritten to include an extended discussion of the implications of visual communication on literacy and rhetoric and the various tools, media, genres, discourses, and conventions of writing in an electronic age.
- Chapter 2, "Critical Thinking, Reading, and Viewing," includes new coverage of engaging actively and critically in the viewing process. This coverage is particularly crucial when so much information comes to students in visual form, whether via photos, advertisements, movies, or streaming video on the Internet. News photographs and an advertsement illustrate the process of learning to analyze and reflect on images as well as writing about them. A new essay on Title IX illustrates critical reading.
- Chapters 3, 4, and 5 on the writing process have been revised to incorporate more cautions about plagiarism and to encourage collaboration through the new "For Collaboration" exercises.
- Chapter 6, "Structuring Paragraphs," includes more information on how to write effective introductory and concluding paragraphs.
- Chapter 7, "Formulating Arguments," now includes coverage of visual argument, with illustrations that show how arguments are presented in visual media such as advertising; and how graphics can be used to support an argument. The section on electronic argument covers new forms of interactive arguments

such as email, newsgroups, list servs, and Internet relay chats (IRCs).

- Chapters 8, 9, 10, 11, and 12 on the research process have similarly been revised to incorporate clearer examples regarding plagiarism and to encourage collaboration. New to this section as well is an extended model of searching via library subscription databases such as Lexis/Nexis and EBSCOHost.

- Chapters 13, 14, and 15 on documentation styles have been totally updated to reflect the updated style manuals for the Modern Language Association (MLA), the American Psychological Association (APA), and the Chicago Manual of Style (CMS), with a particular emphasis on the documentation of electronic sources.

- Chapter 16, "Disciplinary Discourse," is a new chapter that introduces the subsequent writing in the disciplines chapters (17, 18, and 19). It explores the typical research questions asked and evidence used in the disciplines, as well as disciplinary discourse, including format, style, and vocabulary.

- Part 4, "Design in Print and on the Web," outlines the most recent understandings of design for both print and Web documents. All of the chapters in Part 4 have been updated to include visual literacy as well as textual literacy.

- Chapter 20, "Design Principles and Graphics," includes updated coverage of creating and using graphics, including how to use a scanner to save and edit images, and digital editing of photographs.

- Part 5, "Writing for Different Purposes," has been updated and expanded and two completely new chapters have been added: Chapter 26, "Oral Presentations," and Chapter 28, "Writing Portfolios."

- Chapter 24, "Email and Electronic Communication," includes expanded coverage of building community online, including a new discussion of instant messaging.

- New Chapter 26, "Oral Presentations Using *PowerPoint* and Other Tools," shows students how to organize, prepare for, and present an oral presentation, including how to select an appropriate format for graphics—whether overhead transparencies, flip charts, or *PowerPoint* slides.

- Chapter 28, "Writing Portfolios," guides students through writing and compiling portfolios for a variety of purposes, from large-scale writing assessment, to career portfolios for job searches.

- Chapter 29, "Word-Processing Tools for Improving Sentences," includes cautions to be applied in using grammar- or sentence-checkers, and how to use these computer tools to best effect.
- Chapter 46, "Language and Power," has been fundamentally revised to address how language affects identity and how society shapes our expectations for "correct" usage. The chapter also covers avoiding language bias regarding sex or sexual preference, race and ethnicity, age, disabilities, and other differences.

Additional exercises, including new "For Collaboration" exercises, updated Web links and screen shots, and new Help boxes can be found throughout the book.

PEDAGOGY

The New Century Handbook is an easy-to-use yet comprehensive reference. It contains both extensive writing instruction and a complete guide to grammar and style issues. The grammar coverage is authoritative. Tom Huckin, a leading applied linguist, brings to these sections of the handbook an important understanding of grammatical systems. The examples, illustrations, and exercises that appear throughout the handbook will help students to write correctly and to understand the principles, both grammatical and rhetorical, on which good writing is based. The effectiveness of this handbook is extended via the Web links in the handbook and at the book's companion Web site. These Web links, designed to connect students to the many important writing resources found on the Internet, will be updated regularly to ensure their currency.

Help Boxes

A unique pedagogical feature throughout the handbook is the Help boxes. These boxes provide students with key computer-related information in an accessible, succinct form. Because the instructions are compartmentalized in Help boxes, they do not interrupt the flow of the text; instructors and students can use them as appropriate. The Help boxes are generic—the advice they provide will work across different operating systems and with a variety of computer software. An explanatory note points to any advice that is platform-specific.

The companion Web site offers specific instructions to supplement many of the Help boxes found in the handbook.

FAQs and Other Informational Boxes

In addition to the Help boxes, other types of boxes highlight information throughout the handbook. FAQs, which introduce each chapter, cite frequently asked questions about the chapter's topic. Some boxes contain checklists, which guide students through a process or concept; other boxes summarize key information in a succinct format. All boxes work as reference aids for students providing a concise representation of the information in the handbook.

Sample Student Papers

Student models and examples, which appear throughout the handbook, illustrate both the writing process and written products. Part 1 follows a student through the process of developing an essay on Net theft, from prewriting through revising. Chapter 7 uses a second student essay, on cybercensorship, as its model for argumentation. Chapters 8–12 follow one student's research process, including Internet research. The resulting research paper on cybershopping appears in Chapter 12. A number of student models appear in Chapters 25 and 27. Finally, four model research papers from different disciplines appear in Chapters 17–19. All student models were chosen for their accessibility, their lively and interesting topics, and their usefulness to students as examples for their own work.

Engaging Exercises

The exercises in this handbook provide students with practice at every step in the writing process. The handbook includes individual, collaborative, and computer-based exercises, thus providing instructors and students with a number of helpful options. All exercises are designed with students in mind. The exercises are not busy work, but rather provide students with additional practice in important skills that they can put to use in their own writing. Additional exercises that can be self-scored and emailed to the instructor can be found at the companion Web site.

Glossaries

Separate glossaries are provided for grammatical and rhetorical terms and usage.

SUPPLEMENTS

An extensive package of supplements for both instructors and students accompanies *The New Century Handbook,* Third Edition. Please see your representative for details.

For the Instructor

- *Instructor's Manual and Media Guide to Accompany The New Century Handbook,* written by the handbook's authors, presents a wealth of material to help instructors, including chapter highlights, teaching suggestions, classroom activities, collaborative activities, computer activities, usage notes, linguistic notes, computer novice notes, ESL notes, connections (cross-references to the handbook and connections to related literature in composition), additional exercises, and exercise answers.

- *The New Century Handbook Web Site* <http://www.ablongman/hult> enables instructors to post and make changes to their syllabi; receive the scores of objective tests in the areas of grammar, punctuation, and mechanics; and receive email and essay assignments directly from students. In this edition, the Web site now more extensively supplements and complements the book. In addition, a special version of Blackboard, called *CourseCompass,* accompanies *The New Century Handbook,* Third Edition. Please contact your sales representative for details.

- *Teaching Writing with Computers,* developed by Eric Hoffman and Carol Scheidenhelm, both of Northern Illinois University, offers a wealth of computer-related classroom activities. It also provides detailed guidance for both experienced and inexperienced instructors who wish to make creative use of technology in a composition environment.

- *The Allyn & Bacon Sourcebook for College Writing Teachers,* Second Edition, compiled by James C. McDonald of the University of Louisiana at Lafayette, provides instructors with a varied selection of readings written by composition and rhetoric scholars on both theoretical and practical subjects.

- *Diagnostic and Editing Tests and Exercises* includes two diagnostic tests, keyed to the relevant handbook sections, for analyzing common errors. The additional exercise sets on grammar, punctuation, and mechanics topics supplement those found in the handbook. (It is also available in computerized Windows and Macintosh formats.)

For the Student

- *Interactive Edition of The New Century Handbook* is a valuable resource and learning tool that brings instruction on writing, research, and grammar to a new and exciting level. This CD-ROM contains all pages from the text, with icons providing instant Web links, audio and video explanations of key concepts, and interactive exercises. Special CD icons appear in the book itself to indicate where additional material that complements and supplements the book appears on the CD.

- *The New Century Handbook Web Site* offers a wealth of added material that is integrated with the book and designed to supplement and complement its content. Special Web site icons appear in the margins of the book pages to indicate where additional related material can be found on the Web site.

- *The Exercise Book to Accompany The New Century Handbook* contains seventy additional exercise sets that supplement and parallel the exercise sets found in the handbook. A separate answer key is available.

- *Researching Online*, Fifth Edition, by David Munger and Shireen Campbell, gives students detailed, step-by-step instructions for performing electronic searches; for researching with email, discussion groups, and synchronous communication; and for evaluating online sources.

ACKNOWLEDGMENTS

We wish to acknowledge and thank the many people who helped to make *The New Century Handbook* a reality—both in earlier editions and in this further evolved third edition. In addition to those specifically mentioned below, we owe a debt of gratitude to the many researchers and writers in the fields of rhetoric, composition, and linguistics whose work informs our own. In particular, we are indebted to the following colleagues who have contributed in countless ways to the shaping of this handbook: Kenneth W. Brewer, Kathy Fitzgerald, Keith Grant-Davie, Joyce Kinkead, Lynn Meeks, Jeff Smitten, and William Strong, Utah State University; Barrett M. Briggs, University of Arizona; Louise Bown and Clint Gardner, Salt Lake Community College; Julie Simon, Southern Utah University; and Jeanette Harris, Texas Christian University. For their technical expertise and innovative ideas for online teaching and learning, we thank David Hailey, Chris Okelberry, and Kevin Watson, Utah State University;

and Judith Kirkpatrick, Kapi'olani Community College. For the model papers, exercises, and assignments we thank Sonia Manual-Dupont, Jana Kay Lunstad, Kristine Miller, Fayth Ross, Anne Shifrer, and Alice Lindahl, Utah State University; Phil Sbaratta, North Shore Community College; Gail Forsyth; Doug Downs, Daniela Liese, and Iris Salazar, University of Utah; Bumpy Johnson and Glenn Sacks.

We owe a debt of gratitude to the entire team at Longman Publishers, who supported this handbook from the beginning. Specifically, we would like to thank Joseph Opiela, whose vision for this book both inspired its early beginnings and has continued to shape it. Many others of the Longman Publishers team also helped with both direct and indirect support. These include, among others too numerous to name individually, Nancy Garcia, Beth Strauss, Quinn Perkson, and Mike Coons. To our developmental editors, whose hands-on, in-the-trenches writing feedback made us write better and work harder, we owe our thanks as well: Judy Fifer, Ellen Darion, Marlene Ellin, Allen Workman, and Donna de la Perriere. And finally, to the production editors, Bob Ginsberg and Donna DeBenedictis, and their supporting staff, including many designers, copyeditors, and proofreaders, we are grateful for the careful attention to design and details that make this handbook unique.

Throughout the handbook, we stress the principle that writing is not a solitary act, but rather is collaborative in the best sense of the term. Writers need feedback from readers in order to communicate better. We benefited tremendously from the timely feedback of the many reviewers who read our drafts. In particular, we would like to thank John Clark, Bowling Green State University; Ray Dumont, University of Massachusetts, Dartmouth; Todd Lundberg, Cleveland State University; and Bill Newmiller, United States Air Force Academy. We are grateful to Kathy Fitzgerald, Utah State University, for help with a computer cross-platform review; Eric Hoffman, Northern Illinois University, for help with the Web links in the handbook; and Joe Law, Wright State University, for help with the documentation chapters.

We would also like to thank reviewers of the first and second editions: J. Robert Baker, Fairmont State College; Kelly Belanger, University of Wyoming; Anne Bliss, University of Colorado; H. Eric Branscomb, Salem State College; Susan Brant, Humboldt State University; Deborah Burns, Merrimack College; Hugh Burns, Texas Woman's University; Joseph Colavito, Northwestern State University; Linda Daigle, Houston Community College; Carol David, Iowa State University; Michael Day, Northern Illinois University; Kitty Chen

Dean, Nassau Community College; Keith Dorwick, University of Louisiana at Lafayette; Scott Douglass, Chattanooga State College; Raymond Dumont, University of Massachusetts, Dartmouth; John W. Ferstel, University of Louisiana at Lafayette; Bob Funk, Eastern Illinois University; Casey Gilson, Broward Community College; Gordon Grant, Baylor University; Richard Harrington, Piedmont Virginia Community College; Erin Hughey-Commers, Piedmont Virginia Community College (student); Gary Hatch, Brigham Young University; Joseph Janangelo, Loyola University of Chicago; Michael Keller, South Dakota State University; Thomas P. Klammer, California State University at Fullerton; Christine Leichliter, The College of New Jersey; Richard Louth, Southeastern Louisiana University; Barry Maid, Arizona State University; Richard Marback, Wayne State University; Caroline Maun, Morgan State University; Lawrence Millbourn, El Paso Community College; Michael Morgan, Bemidji State University; Webster Newbold, Ball State University; Nicole Oechslin, Blue Ridge Community College; Kevin Parker, Orange Coast College; Joe Pellegrino, Eastern Kentucky University; Alison Regan, University of Utah; Donna Reiss, Tidewater Community College; Susan Romano, University of New Mexico; Paula Ross, Gadsden State Community College; Jack Scanlon, Triton Community College; Allison Smith, Louisiana Technical University; Max Smith, Normandale Community College; Nancy Stegall, DeVry Institute of Technology; Todd Taylor, University of North Carolina; Nancy Trachsel, University of Iowa; Alice Trupe, Bridgewater College; Lynda Vannice, Umpqua Community College; Audrey Wick, University of Texas at Arlington; Donna Winchell, Clemson University; and Donnie Yielding, Central Texas College.

Thanks to reviewers who offered valuable suggestions for the third edition: Kaye Adkins, Missouri Western State College; Cathryn Amdahl, Harrisburg Area Community College; Laura N. Black, Southern Wesleyan University; Alison Cable, North Carolina State University; Douglas Capps, Midlands Technical College; Dennis Chepurnov, Missouri Western State College; Patrick Christle, University of Tennessee; P. J. Colbert, Marshalltown Community College; Lynn Crabtree, Somerset Community College; Rosemary B. Day, Albuquerque TVI Community College; David Elias, Eastern Kentucky University; Judith G. Gardner, The University of Texas at San Antonio; Keith Hale, South Texas Community College; Betty Fleming Hendricks, University of Arkansas at Monticello; A. Wesley Jones, University of Mary; Cathlena Martin, University of Florida; Caroline Maun, Morgan State University; Margaret McCampbell, Community College of Baltimore County, Catonsville; Brett J. Millàn, South Texas Community College; Mark James Morreale, Marist

College; Samantha A. Morgan-Curtis, Tennessee State University; Arnold R. Oliver, Eastern Shore Community College; Jeff Olma, Florida Community College at Jacksonville; JoAnn Pavletich, University of Houston, Downtown; Kamala Platt, The University of Texas at San Antonio; Allison Smith, Middle Tennessee State University; and Frank D. Walters, Auburn University.

We were fortunate to have in our classes student writers who were willing to share their fine work with us—and with the larger readership of this handbook. Student writers whose work appears in these pages include the following: Brandy Blank, Heidi Blankenship, Jennifer Bodine, Ron Christensen, Annie Gabbitas, Janevieve Grabert, Eric Horne, Allan Johnson, Abbey Kennedy, Myndee McNeill, Jeff Meaders, Wensdae Miller, Benjamin Minson, Angela Napper, Chris Nelson, Wyoma Proffit, Heather Radford, Kirsten Reynolds, Sarah Smith, Tim Syndergaard, DeLayna Stout, Jon Weber, Bryce Wilcox, and Adam Whitney.

Lastly, we say thanks to our friends and families who supported us in our personal lives so that we could free up the time, and the energy, to work on this challenging project. Specifically, we wish to thank our respective spouses, Nathan Hult and Christiane Huckin, and our children, Jen and Justin Hult and Jed and Neil Huckin.

CHRISTINE A. HULT
THOMAS N. HUCKIN

CHAPTER **1**

Writing in the New Century

FAQs

▸ Why is writing a vital skill in today's high-tech world? (1a)

▸ How can learning to write help me in college and at work? (1a)

▸ What are the principles of rhetoric and how do I apply them to different writing situations? (1b)

▸ How has technology changed the way we write? (1c)

▸ How can I use new technologies in my writing process? (1c-2)

You may be majoring in law and constitutional studies, wildlife biology, geology, literature, interior design, landscape architecture, mechanical engineering, German, history, business information systems, or mathematics. Your hobbies may include reading, listening to and playing music, watching movies and TV, traveling, running, swing dancing, ping-pong, tennis, contact sports, horseback riding, hiking, biking, swimming, fly-fishing, skiing, or backpacking. You may also be enrolled in a college writing course. Why do you need to learn to write well, in a world that is continually developing new technologies for communication?

Writing is both a mode of learning and a way of constructing knowledge. Through writing, you learn to think critically and to solve problems. Writing is a skill that everyone can improve—and it is a skill that can make all the difference to your success in college and beyond.

1a   Why do we write?

People are motivated to write for all sorts of reasons, but most writing falls into a few basic categories, each reflecting a different underlying motivation. One important purpose for writing is to share information. Another is to clarify your thinking on a topic. A third purpose is self-expression—writing to express what you think or feel about something meaningful to you. Another purpose is persuasion—to present your ideas to others in a convincing way. Whatever your specific purpose for writing, the ability to write well will help you succeed in college and in the workplace and become an effective participant in your community. Each purpose for writing assumes communication, sometimes just with yourself (as in some expressive writing that is never publicly shared) but more often with an audience of readers.

1   Writing to communicate

Every day you communicate with others using various channels or media. For example, in a typical day, you talk and listen to friends and acquaintances in person or over the telephone. You will most likely also communicate with others through writing and reading. You may jot down a note to your roommate, compose a paper for a class assignment, read a novel or magazine, write and send an email message, or read messages from friends.

AUDIO
Writing to connect in communities.

WWW

1.1
Connecting with discourse communities.

In many cases, writing is used to build a sense of *community* and to connect you with others who share some of your interests. Groups of writers who share a common set of interests and assumptions may also be called "discourse communities." You may already belong to several discourse communities, through school, work, or other settings. Think about the people with whom you communicate in writing every day. These may include online discussion groups, study groups, or groups collaborating on a project at work. As you begin to use this book, reflect on how writing permeates your daily life. Today, more than ever, writing is vital for communicating with others.

(EXERCISE 1.1)

In a journal or notebook, keep track of all the writing you do in one day. At the end of the day, look back at the writing and categorize the types of writing you did. How many different types of writing do you do in a typical day? What are your discourse communities?

(FOR COLLABORATION)

In an email message or a post to a class discussion forum, introduce yourself to your classmates, telling them a bit about your background and your hobbies and interests, as Chris Nelson has done in Figure 1.1 on page 4.

2 Writing as a way of knowing

In addition to allowing you to communicate with others, writing helps you get in touch with your own ideas. It is often said that people write what they know in order to know what they think. Writing about something can help you clarify your thinking about it. When beginning an essay for a course assignment, you probably have had the experience of not knowing exactly what you were going to say. As you wrote, you explored your own ideas and in a sense "discovered" what you really thought (see Chapters 3–4). This discovery function is an important reason to write. Sometimes writing not only reveals what you already know but also uncovers things you do not yet know but would like to learn. Thus, writing has an intimate connection with both reading (see Chapter 2) and research (see Part 2) because it encourages you to seek further knowledge by those means. In addition, through your writing, you can make the knowledge you have acquired available to others, thus completing the communication circle.

AUDIO

Writing to find out what you think.

3 Writing to be creative

In addition to expanding knowledge, writing has an important creative dimension. Writing is an inherently creative act. In the process of writing, you explore what truly motivates you as you sort through your own thoughts and impressions. As you generate ideas for writing, you may work from intensely personal notes in journals to create a focused piece of writing that meets the goals of a particular course assignment (see Chapter 3). Writing an essay is essentially as creative as writing a story or poem, because any piece of writing evolves from your vision of the world (see Chapter 4). Having written something that conveys your own personal vision or values is both emotionally and intellectually satisfying. For example, Jeff Meaders is able to share his creative vision by placing his poem on a Web site (see Figure 1.2).

My name is Chris Nelson. This is my first year
here at Utah State. I am majoring in mathematics. I
am from Ogden, Utah, where I attended Ben Lomond
High School. In high school I enjoyed being a member
of the wrestling team for four years. Nowadays I
enjoy jump-roping, lifting weights, listening to
music, running, and watching TV. My favorite book is
Green Eggs and Ham by Dr. Seuss. My favorite movie
is Teen Wolf. My favorite song is "Born to Run" by
Bruce Springsteen. My favorite band is Radiohead. My
favorite TV show is The Simpsons. My favorite cereal
is Fruity Pebbles, although I usually end up buying
the generic kind. My favorite musical instrument is
the cowbell. My favorite color is green. My favorite
number is 71, although 25 comes in at a very close
second. My favorite word is humdinger. My favorite
color of shoe is blue, although you can't go wrong
with black. I like long walks on the beach.
That's me.

FIGURE 1.1 Here is first-year student Chris Nelson's response to an introductory writing assignment, asking him to describe himself and his hobbies.

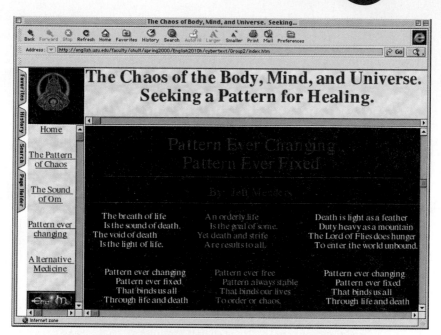

FIGURE 1.2 A Student's Poem Published on an Internet Web Site

4 Writing to succeed in college

Much of the communication that occurs in an academic setting takes place through writing. Although you may talk with, and listen to, your instructors, you will almost certainly convey your mastery of the subject matter through writing. Think about the number and types of written assignments that are required of you. You are asked to write term papers, essays, and lab reports (see Figure 1.3) and to complete written exams of all types, from multiple choice to short essay.

Clearly, knowing how to write well is one of the keys to success in college. This handbook is designed to help you with a variety of college writing tasks, from essays (Part 1) to research papers (Part 2) to writing in the disciplines (Part 3). Other chapters included in this handbook will help you desktop publish your writing (Chapter 21) or design and write for the Web (Chapters 22–23). Additional help for college student writers comes in Chapter 24 on Email and Electronic Communications, Chapter 27 on Essay Exams, and Chapter 28 on Writing Portfolios.

Tim Synder

Biology 1210

Lab Sec. 927 Thursday 6:30

Enzyme Specificity

I. Introduction

Enzymes are very specific as a result of a lock and key relationship between the substrate and the enzyme. If a particular enzyme's tertiary structure (shape and charge distribution) "fits" a substrate, the enzyme will be able to bind to the substrate and catalyze the reaction.

We will determine if a reaction occurs using specific enzymes (α- and β-galactosidase) that break down melibiose or lactose into glucose. Indirect measurement of glucose will be determined by the amount of CO_2, which is a product of cellular respiration of yeast when it utilizes glucose.

II. Method

Table 1 shows the 9 test conditions. Tests 1-4 will test for the specificity of the enzymes. Tests 5-9 test assumptions of the experiment design.

Each set (conditions) was mixed in clean 50-ml beakers. The conditions were then placed in fermentation tubes and were marked to identify each condition. The tubes were then placed in a water

FIGURE 1.3 Short, Informal Biology Lab Report

Table 1. Test Conditions for Specificity of Enzymes

Treatment	Sugar or Control (4 ml)	Enzyme or Control (2 ml)	Yeast (10 ml)
HYPOTHESIS			
1	Lactose	β-galactosidase	Yeast
2	Melibiose	β-galactosidase	Yeast
3	Lactose	α-galactosidase	Yeast
4	Melibiose	α-galactosidase	Yeast
ASSUMPTIONS			
5	H_2O	α-galactosidase	Yeast
6	Melibiose	H_2O	Yeast
7	Lactose	H_2O	Yeast
8	H_2O	H_2O	Yeast
9	Glucose	H_2O	Yeast

bath set at 37°C. Volume of CO_2 was measured every 5 minutes for 25 minutes.

III. Results

The overall trends show what conditions break down the sugars into glucose.

IV. Discussion

Table 2 shows the amount of CO_2 produced in each condition. Conditions 5, 6, and 8 had no production of CO_2. Conditions 1, 4, and 9 show the most production of CO_2. Conditions 1 and 4 indicate that there is specificity for enzyme.

FIGURE 1.3 (*continued*)

Table 2 Amount of CO_2 Produced in Each Condition

Condition	CO_2 volume (ml)				
	Time (min)				
	5 min	10 min	15 min	20 min	25 min
1	3.5	7.2	8.1	8.4	8.7
2	1	1.5	1.7	2	2.2
3	0.5	1.3	1.7	2.1	2.3
4	0	0.7	1.9	3	3.6
5	0	0	0	0	0
6	0	0	0	0	0
7	0.8	1.3	1.5	1.7	1.9
8	0	0	0	0	0
9	1.8	4	5.8	6.7	6.9

Condition 9 indicates that it is glucose that the yeast is metabolizing.

Conditions 2, 3, and 7 indicate that there is some glucose produced. This may be due to the enzymes not being completely specific, or possibly the melibiose and lactate sugars breaking down for some unknown reason, such as high temperature.

Conditions 5, 6, and 8 support the assumptions that yeast in the presence of enzymes alone, the lactose alone, or the absence of both, does not produce any CO_2 and therefore shows the specificity of the product glucose.

FIGURE 1.3 (*continued*)

5 Writing to function in the workplace

Writing also plays a key role in success on the job. It is certainly true that technology has altered the workplace with the advent of communication tools such as email, fax, and the Internet. However, all these technologies depend on the written word. In fact, the information explosion has increased the demand for good writing, not decreased it. When communicating on the job, you must be able to write your thoughts clearly and succinctly so they can be understood and acted on appropriately. The wide range of communication tools makes it essential that you make appropriate choices for your on-the-job writing. (Should I send my message via fax, email, or voice mail? Do I use a formal salutation or just say "Hi"?) The writing skills you will need in the workplace include the ability to analyze your audience and your purpose, called your *rhetorical stance* (see 3b-2). This handbook emphasizes the importance of adapting your style and tone to the task at hand. Specific guidance for communicating on the job is provided in Chapter 25 on business writing and Chapter 26 on oral presentations, and a sample business email message is shown in Figure 1.4.

AUDIO
Reading and writing are integral parts of most jobs.

1.2
Statistics about writing in the workplace.

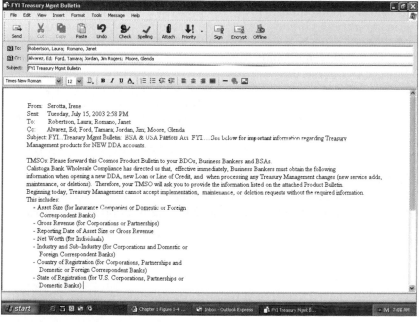

FIGURE 1.4 Business Email Memo

1b   How do we communicate effectively?

WWW

1.3

More on
rhetoric.

In the ever-changing communication arena of the twenty-first century, it is crucial that writers understand the basic principles of effective communication, also called the *principles of rhetoric*. If you understand these key rhetorical principles (which are covered extensively in this handbook), you will be a successful communicator, regardless of evolving technology.

The principles of rhetoric, as used to persuade an audience through spoken and then written language, have been studied extensively, beginning as far back as ancient Greece with the writings of Aristotle. The early teachers of rhetoric recognized an important principle: to persuade other people, you need to appeal to their sense of logic (through reasoning and evidence), their belief systems (through their emotions), and their sense of ethics (through your credibility as a writer or speaker). These three appeals evolved over time into what we now call the *rhetorical triangle* (see 3b-2). The three sides of the rhetorical triangle (purpose, readers, persona) correspond to the persuasive appeals of the ancient Greeks. What we now call *purpose* is analogous to using logic, or *logos,* in your argument; understanding your *readers* is analogous to knowing the emotional appeals, or *pathos,* that will sway an audience; and *persona* is analogous to putting yourself forward in an ethical and credible manner, or *ethos.*

There are some major differences between the rhetorical situations of writers of the past and those of the current technologically rich environment. For example, today's writing is frequently public. In times past it was more likely that one writer communicated directly with one reader, through a note or letter, perhaps. Today, a single email message may grow "legs" and be forwarded to hundreds or even thousands of people without the knowledge of the original author. Today's writing is also an extremely rapid form of communication; where it used to take weeks or months for a letter to reach its recipient, now an instant message can be read within seconds of its composition. You need to keep these factors in mind as you write in these new media.

(EXERCISE 1.2)

Select one of the pieces of writing you did in Exercise 1.1. Using the elements of the rhetorical triangle, determine your purpose for writing that particular piece or message; decide who the intended audience was or could be; and analyze your persona—how you presented yourself—in that particular piece of writing. Now list some alternatives: how could you have changed your writing to reflect a different purpose, audience, and persona?

(**FOR COLLABORATION**)

Working with a group of your peers, discuss your analysis of the rhetorical situation for your writing. Share thoughts on how you might change the rhetorical elements in order to shape your writing for a different situation.

1 Writing for various audiences and purposes

In today's cyberculture, it is possible to communicate with a wide range of people simultaneously, as with a Web site or an online newsletter. Writers have many choices of media available to them (from a notebook or journal to a multimedia *PowerPoint* presentation). But they still need to think through who their audience is likely to be and what their ultimate communication purpose will be. Writers may find that they have multiple audiences with conflicting points of view or multiple purposes in the same widely broadcast message. The savvy writer of the new century has learned how to negotiate these seemingly conflicting and often contradictory demands. More information about audience and rhetorical stance can be found in 3b-2.

2 Writing with various tools, media, and genres

Today's writers use a range of writing tools and technologies. They haven't discarded their pencils and pens in favor of keyboard and mouse. Instead, new tools and technologies are added to the old, thereby increasing the choices in a writer's toolkit. Today's writers also produce a wide range of types of writing (from letters and memos to user manuals and press releases), using a variety of available media (text, graphics, audio, and video, for example). Different types of writing are also called genres. A **genre** is simply a particular type of writing that follows specified conventions. For example, poetry and short stories are both genres of creative writing. Similarly, memos and reports are genres of business writing.

What happens, though, when a traditional genre such as a memo is written in a new medium such as email? Do the discourse conventions remain the same, or do they change? Do you address a business letter sent via email the same way as one that is typed and mailed (*Dear Sir or Madam,* for example)? In some ways, conventions of writing are changing rapidly. Informal genres of online writing, including email and online chats such as instant messaging, seem closer to informal speech than to formal writing.

Even if you are writing in a new medium such as an email message or a Web page, however, some conventions—such as correct spelling, punctuation, and mechanics—reflect on your persona as a writer. If there are misspelled words or ungrammatical phrases in your email message or chat room posting, you may inadvertently present yourself as less educated or less informed than you really are. This handbook can help you identify errors, understand correct construction, and improve your spelling and vocabulary (see Parts 6–11). Your writing in almost any genre, and particularly writing done for the workplace, needs to be clear, direct, error-free, and to the point in order to communicate your message effectively to your audience.

3   Using visual rhetoric

In addition to the challenges of writing in the new millennium, added to the mix is the ability to communicate not just in words but also with images (pictures, photos, graphics, and even video). Writers in the new century need to learn how to use pictures and graphics together with texts in a complementary mix of words and images. The term *visual rhetoric* refers to the effective use of visuals to communicate with specific audiences for specific purposes. Parts 4–5 in this handbook discuss the many ways in which writers can communicate successfully with visual information. Chapter 7 discusses the use of visuals in argumentation and specifically how to make an electronic argument.

1c   How has technology changed the way we write?

AUDIO

The impact of computers on communication.

Some of the underlying stages and basic processes of writing have remained the same throughout the technology revolution. You still need to analyze your writing situation, determine your topic, provide data to support your position, and draft, edit, and revise your work. However, technology has given us some additional tools and some alternative means of communicating. The "information explosion" has dramatically increased the demand for good writing, making learning to write effectively more crucial than ever.

Think for a moment about how just one writing technology, email, has changed communication practice. Many of you are more likely to communicate with your parents and friends via email or instant messaging than through a phone call or letter. Many businesspeople are more likely to send out an email memo than a printed one. Everyone who has come to rely on email knows that it is different in substantive ways from letters and phone calls. There is an immediacy to email that letters or memos do not have. But, at the same time, email is more distant than face-to-face or phone conversations. Because email cannot readily convey emotions through tone of voice, there is always the possibility that messages will be misunderstood.

Each of the many Internet communication forums that are now available—chat rooms, instant messaging services, bulletin boards, newsgroups, MUDs, and MOOs (see Chapter 24)—has its own customs and protocols that writers need to know in order to communicate effectively. In some of these forums, it is even possible to adopt a persona other than your own. Since it may not always be clear who your audience is, you must take pains to avoid offending someone with a careless remark. It is also important to realize that your message may be read by someone in a different culture, with a different background and set of assumptions. Learning how to communicate effectively in these new forums is a tremendous challenge for writers in today's cyberculture.

1   Viewing critically

To the skills of critical thinking, reading, and writing has been added a new skill, critical viewing. Another term for this skill is *visual literacy*. What is meant by visual literacy is the ability to critically interpret, analyze, or evaluate visual images. Our culture is becoming increasingly more visual as we turn to media such as television for a great deal of our news and other information, as opposed to using primarily print media as a source. Furthermore, much of the information we receive even in print media has now become much more visual. Compare the two newspaper examples in Figure 1.5. Today the front page of most newspapers features a rich array of fonts, headings, and color photographs; in the past a newspaper was almost exclusively black ink text with a few black-and-white photographs. This handbook will help you analyze and interpret visual images, as well as understand the effects of different types of visual arrangement of your papers and other writing.

FIGURE 1.5 Newspaper front pages from the Ogden, Utah, *Standard,* later called the Davis County *Standard-Examiner,* from July 22, 1890 and November 14, 2003.

2   Using new technologies in the writing process

Writing is not a neat or orderly process but instead is often very messy. Your writing may proceed in fits and starts, with repeated cycles of writing, researching for information, rereading what you have written, revising and editing, and so on. Technology—specifically, the use of the computer—now gives you some additional tools for compiling information, creating and saving drafts of your work, checking your spelling, incorporating illustrations, and even publishing your own work. This handbook provides guidance in using the computer in each of these stages of the writing process, from generating ideas and choosing a topic to revising your work to producing your work as a Web page. Throughout the text, Help boxes provide detailed guidance for using new technologies in your writing process.

3 Using the computer for research

The computer, and specifically the Internet and the World Wide Web, provides access to millions of pages of information. However, this information needs to be carefully weighed and evaluated. Much of the information that is available on the World Wide Web is provided by commercial sources; much of it, too, is driven by a particular agenda, either political or one individual's unique perspective. Thus, the cyberculture has made critical thinking even more crucial than it was before. You need to sharpen and hone your critical thinking skills to deal with this cascade of information. You need to be able to distinguish quickly and accurately between what information is reliable and what is not; learn what types of information can be used in conducting academic research; and understand how to incorporate that research appropriately, by crediting and documenting your sources. We discuss critically evaluating both electronic and print sources at length in Chapter 10, incorporating sources in Chapter 11, and documenting sources in Chapters 13–15.

1d How can this handbook help you with your writing?

This handbook will equip you with the basic skills you need to become a good writer. Because this handbook emphasizes the use of rhetorical analysis, regardless of the particular medium (from print to email to Web pages), you will learn how to adapt your writing to any situation you encounter. Just as effective writing principles cross media, they also cross genres, or types of writing. As you write, either with or without computer assistance, keep in mind that the lessons you learn about the writing process (planning, researching, drafting, and rewriting) apply to any genre of writing—from essays and research papers to business reports and memos to email messages and chat room conversations.

CHAPTER 2

Critical Thinking, Reading, and Viewing

FAQs

▶ What is critical thinking? (2a)
▶ How do I read critically? (2b)
▶ Should I take notes while reading? (2b-3)
▶ How can I view images critically? (2-c)

Throughout your life, you have been reading and writing—formally at school and work, informally with family and friends. The processes of reading and writing are closely interrelated. We read and write to understand our world, to communicate with others, and to share our thoughts and ideas. Everyone can improve both reading and writing abilities through practice.

AUDIO
Writing, reading, and thinking are related.

As a college student, you have a unique opportunity to practice your reading and writing skills. Much college work revolves around the processes of reading and writing. Academic knowledge is both created and shared through these processes. Whether your course of study is mathematics or sociology or engineering, reading and writing are intimately involved in learning. You read to understand what others think and say about a topic; you write to share what you learn or understand about a topic. This is how knowledge progresses.

2a   Think critically

A term often used to describe the way in which educated people approach knowledge building is *critical thinking*. To think critically is to make a conscious effort to delve beneath the surface of things. Much of the process of obtaining a college education is designed to help you become a more critical thinker. The term *critical* in this case does not mean "criticize." Critical thinking does not imply a negative attitude; rather, critical thinking involves the ability to contemplate, question, and explore ideas in depth without accepting easy answers. When you identify the political propaganda as you listen to a political speech on your campus, you exhibit critical thinking. When you recognize the overblown claims for a product in an advertisement in the local newspaper, you also exhibit critical thinking.

The processes involved in thinking critically are the same for all aspects of communication—speaking and writing as well as listening and reading. They include (1) establishing your purpose and raising questions, (2) analyzing the topic, (3) synthesizing, (4) making inferences, and (5) evaluating. Although they tend to occur in the order given, this is not always the case. Critical insight can sometimes be gained by doing some of these processes simultaneously, or by redoing previous steps.

1 Establishing your purpose and raising questions

The key first step in critical thinking is to have a clear sense of purpose. *Why* are you interested in this topic? Why do you want to learn about it in depth? What specific aspects of the topic most concern you? What is your goal? Having a clear sense of purpose is crucial, because it will guide you through the entire process of critical thinking. Among other things, knowing your purpose will allow you to formulate more specific questions about the topic. And these questions will help focus your exploration.

For example, let's say you're in the market for a used (or "pre-owned," as they say in the trade) car. If you're a careful buyer, you won't just head for the nearest used-car lot and let yourself be talked into the first car that catches your eye. It's more likely that you'll do some research—by reading *Consumer Reports*, talking to your parents or knowledgeable friends, showing the car to a trusted mechanic, and so on. And if you know what kind of car you're looking for and why, you'll probably ask the right kinds of questions to elicit the kind of information you need to make a wise decision.

2 Analyzing the topic

Analyzing something means mentally dividing it into its parts. Sometimes, when the subject being analyzed has obvious component parts, this division is straightforward. For example, a music reviewer will conventionally analyze a symphonic performance according to its different movements, and a drama critic will conventionally analyze a play according to its acts and scenes.

But critical analysis usually goes beyond such obvious procedures. Guided by particular purposes and questions (see 2a-1), a critical analyst will often see *other* ways to dissect a subject. For example, the music reviewer may choose to analyze the symphony according to the different instruments, and the drama critic may decide to focus on the acting, the costumes, or the sets. The mode of analysis, in short, is not necessarily predetermined by the object of analysis; more often it is governed by the purposes and interests of the analyst.

The purposes and interests of your sources of information should also be taken into account. Analysis often depends to some degree on information provided by other people, who have their own interests, biases, beliefs, and assumptions. As a critical thinker, you should always be aware of other people's orientations and try to keep them in mind as you absorb their information. Information from any source can be lacking in objectivity, so it's a good idea to routinely gather your information from multiple, independent sources and compare them.

(EXERCISE 2.1)

The used car case offers a good illustration of how different interests will cause people to analyze something in different ways.

1. How would a used-car salesperson or other seller likely analyze (describe) a car?

2. How would an auto mechanic likely analyze that same car?

3. How would *you* analyze a car, if you were shopping for one today?

4. In each of the above cases, explain how a particular set of purposes gives rise to a particular basis of analysis.

3 Synthesizing

Synthesizing is the opposite of analyzing. Instead of taking something apart, synthesis puts things together. But this does not mean that synthesizing merely restores something to the way it was before analysis. Rather, synthesis seeks to find *new* ways of assembling things, *new* relationships among the parts, *new* combinations. Like analysis, this process is governed by the critical thinker's purposes.

For example, let's say you live in the north and you're looking for a car that will get you back and forth to school through the winter. You have looked at various cars and analyzed them in various ways, but you're uncertain which one is best for you. As you sit back and ponder the situation, you realize that what matters most to you is not the purchase price or the fuel efficiency or the looks of a car but rather how suitable it is for winter driving. You want a reliable car that has a good heating/defrosting system, a good ignition system, solid traction (either four-wheel or front-wheel drive), and all-weather tires in decent shape. Also, it should be a dark color (for better visibility in snow). A combination snowboard/ski rack would be a plus. This set of features is not one that would emerge from any standard analysis. Rather, it is the result of synthesizing, guided by your own purposes and needs.

4 Making inferences

Another important critical thinking skill is the ability to make inferences or "read between the lines." People often do not say exactly what's on their mind. Sometimes their lack of candor is just an effort to be tactful; sometimes it's more deceptive than that. When you interpret what people don't say, or don't say fully, you are making inferences. For example, if a used-car salesperson evades your question about a car's heating system, and you thereby infer that something is wrong with the heating system, you are exhibiting an important kind of critical thinking. (Note how *purpose* once again plays a key role—in this case, the purpose or intent of the message producer.)

Many of the logical fallacies discussed in 7g—such as the *non sequitur*, either/or reasoning, and begging the question—invite the listener or reader to make *faulty* inferences. The ability to detect such fallacies is also a type of critical thinking.

5 Evaluating

Once you've determined your purpose, analyzed your topic, synthesized new ideas, and made appropriate inferences, you are ready to evaluate the results. Evaluation involves examining everything you have done up to this point and determining what it all adds up to. In the case of buying a used car, you would want to review what you have learned from going through the first four steps; in particular, you would check to see if the information you have gathered consistently points to the same conclusion. If not, you would want to identify the contradictions and try to resolve them. Perhaps your sources of information are not as knowledgeable as you had thought, or perhaps you haven't asked them the right questions. In any case, this activity itself is a form of critical thinking—the willingness to confront and resolve inconsistencies in your reasoning and information gathering.

If at this point there are still troubling inconsistencies in your thinking about the topic, you may want to "change the playing field"—that is, broaden your inquiry. This can be done in either of two ways. One, you can use additional sources of information: talk to more people, consult other publications, gain some more firsthand experience. Or two, you can reexamine the initial premises of your investigation. It could be that these have changed in the course of your inquiry—or were never quite accurate in the first place. For example, in your search for reliable transportation that would beat the winter weather, perhaps you went too quickly for a used car when public transit might be just as good or even better. Sometimes it is only at this evaluation stage that nagging discrepancies and uncertainties are resolved and critical thinking is fully rewarded.

WWW

2.1

Critical
analysis.

WEBLINK

http://www.drury.edu/
faculty/Ess/critthink
.html

Good advice on how to do
critical analysis

2b   Engage actively and critically in the reading process

A good reader reads actively. As you read, your mind must be actively engaged with what your eyes see on the page or on the computer screen. You need to see the text on multiple levels—the words, the sentences, the paragraphs, the text as a whole—and you need to think about how it relates to things *outside* the text, such as where it was published, what you know about the author, who its target audience might be, other readings, and your own life experience. In short, you need to situate the text, and make sense of it, in a larger context.

A good reader also reads critically; that is, he or she reads with an open mind and a questioning attitude. To be a critical reader, you need to go beyond understanding what the author is saying; you need to challenge or question the author. You may question the validity of the author's main point or ask whether the text agrees or disagrees with other writings on the same topic and with your own experience.

VIDEO

Analyzing
the writing
situation.

1 Reading on three different levels

To fully understand a text, you should read it on three different levels: literal meaning, interpretation, and criticism. As you move from one level to the next, you increase your "resistance" to the text and thereby construct, in your mind, an alternative text. This three-step process is illustrated with reference to the following essay by Glenn Sacks.

Title IX Lawsuits Are Endangering Men's College Sports
Glenn Sacks

1   In one of UCLA's proudest moments, UCLA-trained swimmers and gymnasts dominated the 1984 Summer Olympics. Half of the gold-medal winning men's gymnastic team were Bruins. Yet, despite producing 22 Olympic swimming competitors and dozens of world-class gymnasts, these UCLA men's teams were eliminated less than a decade later. In fact, over the past five years more than 350 men's collegiate athletic teams have been eliminated nationwide, and the number of men's gymnastics teams has fallen from 200 to just 21. What happened?

2   These athletic programs were not felled by mismanagement, drugs, or rules violations. They were destroyed by Title IX.

3   Title IX of the Education Amendments Act of 1972 barred sex discrimination in any educational program or activity which receives federal funding. In the decades since, women's athletics have burgeoned in high schools and colleges. Title IX was and remains an important and laudable victory for the women's movement.

4   More recently, however, misguided feminist lawsuits and political lobbying have changed Title IX from a vehicle to open up opportunities for women to a scorched earth policy whereby the destruction of men's athletics has become an acceptable substitute for strengthening women's athletics.

Margin notes:
High-profile, specific example makes for an attention-getting intro.

Basic background info sets the stage.

Exaggerations like "scorched earth" and "destruction" undermine the writer's objectivity. Implies that feminists are out to "get men."

5   Feminists have used an obscure, hastily prepared bureaucratic action—known now as the 1979 Policy Interpretation—to mandate that the number of athletes in college athletic programs reflect within a few percentage points the proportion of male and female students on campus. The problem is, as studies have shown, fewer women than men are interested in playing organized sports, even though the opportunity is available.

Even if true (which needs to be shown), this could change.

6   The fact that women now outnumber men in college 57%–43% nationwide makes it even harder for schools to achieve the numerical gender balance demanded by the 1979 Policy—an interpretation never reviewed or approved by Congress. Time and again the Federal Department of Education's Office of Civil Rights (OCR) has investigated schools and allowed them only two options to meet Title IX—create new women's teams for which there often are neither funds nor interested female athletes, or cut men's teams.

A key claim! Needs supporting evidence.

7   Thus women have gained a little but men have lost a lot. According to the National Collegiate Athletic Association (NCAA), for every new women's athletics slot created between 1992 and 1997, 3.6 male athletes were dropped. Kimberly Schuld, director of the Independent Women's Forum's Title IX Play Fair! Project, calls this "clear, government-sanctioned sex discrimination."

Discrimination? Or fairness?

8   Critics of modern Title IX point out that its equity calculations are misleading in part because they count college football's athletes and dollars without considering football's money-making ability. USC, for example, has been hit hard by feminist legal action based on its greater number of male athletes and higher men's athletic budget. What's not considered is that USC's men's teams—largely football— are responsible for over 99% of the near $20 million total

Okay, but how typical is this?

How big a profit? And what about the other divisions?

revenue of the Athletic Department. In fact, over 70% of Division I-A football programs turn a profit.

9   Thus schools are caught in a vise. Because schools need football's revenue yet must also equalize gender numbers, they are forced to cut men's non-revenue sports.

Neatly summarizes the gist of his argument.

10   Todd R. Dickey, USC's general counsel, Schuld, and many others argue that football should simply be taken out of the gender equity equation because no other sport earns as much revenue, has such a large number of athletes or staff, and needs as much equipment. "You can't spend as much on women's sports as you can on men's, because there is no women's equivalent for football," Dickey says.

Maybe football is the problem. (Maybe it should be professional-ized.)

11   Title IX's modern application has struck hardest at minority men. Lawsuits brought to balance the number of athletic scholarships awarded to men and women have decreased the number and value of men's scholarships, upon which minority men often rely to finance their educations. Black colleges and universities, where female students outnumber males 60%–40% and money is usually tight, have been particularly wounded by feminist lawsuits. And when Title IX forces schools to drop their football programs, as San Francisco State did in 1995, it is black athletes who are hurt disproportionately.

Very effective! Pits one historically disadvantaged group (women) against another (blacks).

12   While modern Title IX has been devastating for male and particularly for minority male athletes, it has also hurt female athletics. By allowing the destruction of men's teams to substitute for increasing the number of women's teams, universities have been stripped of the incentive to build more and better female squads. A school that has six female teams and nine male teams may find it much easier to cut men's teams than to provide the new money and resources to create more women's teams.

The metaphors of violence (struck, hurt, wounded, stripped, destruction) have emotional power but are out of place here.

Assumes there 13   The situation cries out for a flexible athletics policy
is no
flexibility   based on student interest levels instead of rigid propor-
now —which   tionality. Title IX states "no person . . . shall, on the basis of
remains to be   sex . . . be subjected to discrimination under any education
shown.
                       program or activity receiving federal financial assistance."

Continues to   Misguided women's advocates have used a bureaucratic
demonize   obscurity to undermine these simple yet high-minded
women's   words, and turn Title IX from an instrument used to fight
advocates and
feminists.   sex discrimination into a policy mandating it.

Reading for literal meaning

The literal meaning of a text is its explicit meaning as determined by the words on the page and their conventional meanings. Put
another way, it is the "surface" meaning of a text. It comprises all those
aspects of a text that are available to anyone who reads that text. Literal
meaning does not include insinuations, satire, irony, subjective impressions, tone, or other implicit meanings that must be inferred by the
reader. (This type of meaning is discussed below.)

When readers start reading a novel, a magazine article, a textbook, or another published text, they expect to move from sentence
to sentence in a smooth flow of literal meaning. (Certain kinds of
poems might be an exception to this.) Authors, of course, are aware
of this and work hard to provide readable texts. Indeed, there seems
to be an implicit understanding among readers and authors that the
linguistic surface of a text should be coherent, meaningful, and accessible to all. Since the deeper meanings of a text (see below) are deriv-
ative of this literal meaning, before you can engage in interpretive or
critical reading you must fully understand the literal meaning of a
text. Use a good dictionary to help you with any words you don't
know (see 48b). At this stage, you should be a *compliant* reader trying
to understand the text on its most basic terms. This is no different
from a moviegoer enjoying a sci-fi film as sheer entertainment,
rather than analyzing it as a movie critic would.

In "Title IX Lawsuits Are Endangering Men's College Sports,"
essayist Glenn Sacks makes an explicit argument that Title IX of the
federal Education Amendments Act of 1972 is discriminating against
male athletes in colleges and high schools. He acknowledges that
Title IX has been an enormous boon to women's athletics, but he
claims that a 1979 policy interpretation has caused it to be very damaging to men's athletics. Specifically, he accuses feminists of using

this 1979 provision to embark on a "scorched earth" campaign against men's athletics, to the point where schools and colleges are being forced to drop hundreds of men's programs in order to comply with federal law and accommodate women's sports. In short, Sacks claims that Title IX has become an instrument of sex discrimination against male athletes in high school and college. This literal meaning of Sacks's essay is plain for all to see.

Reading for interpretation

Once you have grasped the literal meaning of a text, you should go beyond it to the realm of interpretation. At this level, you are seeking a deeper understanding of the author's ideas, point of view, and attitude. You become more conscious of the author's role in constructing the text, giving it a certain "spin," and manipulating the reader. In short, you become a more detached, "resistant," and analytical reader. You look for clues as to what the author has implied rather than overtly stated, what assumptions the author is making, what audience the author seems to be addressing, and what the author's attitude seems to be as revealed by the tone of his or her writing.

This interpretive work should start with certain words, expressions, and statements found in the text, but instead of taking these textual details at face value, you contrast them with alternative words, expressions, and statements that the author opted *not* to use. For example, if an author consistently used the term *fetus* where he or she could have used the alternative term *unborn child*, you might infer that he or she supports reproductive freedom. These two terms have the same denotation but differ in connotation (see 45a–45b); in choosing one term over the other, the author would probably be revealing something about his or her stance on abortion. In reading for interpretation, you should always ask yourself questions such as "In what other way(s) could the author have said this?" or "What *didn't* the author say here that he or she could have?"

Usually the easiest way to get started in such an analysis is with those words and phrases that draw attention to themselves, for example, because they are loaded terms (as in *fetus* vs. *unborn child*), are emphatic (see 43), are deliberately "off-register" (45c) or figurative (45g), or are punctuated with "scare" quotation marks (55b–55c). Sacks's "Title IX Lawsuits Are Endangering Men's College Sports" contains several such examples. In general, Sacks uses a dignified, formal level of diction. However, there are several places in his essay where he uses charged language to add emphasis and establish a more dramatic tone. For example, the word *endangering* in the title is a form of hyperbole (43d), suggesting that men's college sports, like endangered species, are facing extinction. A more accurate term would be *restricting* or *undercutting*. This theme is continued in paragraph 4 with reference to the *destruction* of men's athletics and is now linked to a *scorched earth policy* being pushed by *misguided feminists*. *Scorched earth* is a vivid metaphor (45g), as is the expression *caught in a vise* in paragraph 9; both phrases are likely to catch the reader's attention. In paragraph 11, Sacks employs an extended metaphor to depict Title IX's effects in militaristic terms. He states that Title IX's modern application has *struck hardest* at minority males, has *wounded* black colleges and universities, and has *hurt* black athletes. The metaphor continues in paragraph 12 where Title IX is claimed to have *hurt* female athletics and led to the *destruction* of men's teams. In that same paragraph we see another use of charged language, the use of *stripped* instead of, say, *deprived*. Indeed, rather than saying that "universities have been stripped of the incentive to build . . . ," it would have been more accurate, and more in keeping with the next sentence, for Sacks to have said that "universities have *less* incentive to build. . . ." But that would have been less vivid!

The combined effect of this charged language is to exaggerate and thereby emphasize a polarization of the two sides in this conflict: aggrieved males versus "feminists" and "misguided women's advocates." Although this word choice gives the essay more dramatic power, it also undermines, to some degree, the author's objectivity and credibility.

(EXERCISE 2.2)

1. In the topic sentences of paragraphs 4 and 5, Sacks prominently uses the word *feminist*. Whom is he referring to? Is this an accurate depiction of the situation, in your view? What other term could he have used? Why didn't he?

2. Sacks uses the term *sex discrimination* several times in his essay, but to different ends and from different perspectives. Analyze these, and describe how you interpret the term differently according to the context in which it is used.

Reading critically

Finally, you want to read beyond the literal and interpretive meanings to evaluate the worth of the writing and the validity of the author's ideas or argument. In this mode, you should be even more detached, resistant, and analytical than you were in the interpretive mode. Critical evaluation should be done on two levels, internal and external. With *internal evaluation*, you restrict your attention, as before, to the text itself. This time, though, you focus on the overall logic of the text. Does it hang together? Does it make sense? If the author is making an argument, does it have enough supporting evidence (see 7c)? Does it consider alternative views (7d)? Is it appealing mainly to logic, to authority, or to emotion (7f)? Does it have any fallacies (7g)? With *external evaluation*, you go a step further. Here you evaluate the text against other texts and against your own experience. These other texts could include other writings by the same author—to get a sense of his or her general views or interests—or other writings on the same topic by other authors. Engaging in this kind of comparative analysis allows you to see the text in a larger perspective. This in turn enables you to make an informed guess as to any agenda the author might have, and should give you insight into the author's purpose in writing the text. A comparative analysis will also make it easier for you to guess what's been *left out* of the text. Most writers who are trying to persuade readers to a particular point of view will tend to avoid mentioning facts that might damage their cause. As a critical reader, it is important that you not allow yourself to be manipulated in this way. By looking at other texts and considering your own life experience, you can often make an educated guess as to what's been left unsaid in a particular text.

AUDIO
Finding alternative views.

2.2
Apply your critical reading skills.

Internal evaluation

Look again at "Title IX Lawsuits Are Endangering Men's College Sports." Starting with *internal evaluation*, does Sacks's argument hold up under close scrutiny? Let's start with the overall logic of his argument. According to Sacks, Title IX demands "rigid proportionality" by gender in athletics according to overall college enrollment. Women outnumber men in college enrollment and thus are allowed more places in athletic programs; but men are more interested in playing sports, so men are forced to sacrifice their athletic interests to a far greater degree than women, which is unfair. Is this a sound argument? If his facts are right and if he hasn't left out any relevant information, then yes, his argument would appear to be quite solid. But it rests on at least two claims that are worth examining. First, is it true that Title IX demands strict proportionality? Since 1979 there have been three optional ways, not one, for a school to establish nondiscrimination in college athletic programs: (1) substantial proportionality, (2) evidence of "a history and continuing practice of program expansion for the underrepresented sex," or (3) evidence that a school is "fully and effectively accommodating the interests and abilities of the underrepresented sex." Sacks focuses only on the first of these and misrepresents it as "rigid proportionality," not the *substantial* proportionality called for in the 1979 Policy Interpretation. It's true that since 1992 the vagueness of options 2 and 3 has caused many colleges to restrict their nondiscrimination cases to option 1. However, most complaints filed with the Office of Civil Rights since then have been resolved using options 2 or 3, not 1.

Second, are men in fact more interested in playing sports than women? In paragraph 5, Sacks says that "studies have shown" this to be the case, but he fails to cite any. Even if numbers do support his contention, one could point out that interest in women's athletics has "burgeoned," to use his term, from 300,000 at the high school level in 1972 to 3 million today, and from 32,000 at the intercollegiate level to more than 150,000 today. In other words, increased opportunities for women have apparently led to increased interest, a trend that could end up erasing the claimed gender difference altogether.

Sacks's argument appeals to logic and factuality more than to emotion or authority, so it should be evaluated on this basis. In general, he does a good job of supplying factual details (data, names, examples) to support his generalizations. But there are places where one would want even more evidence. For example, is it true that the cutback in men's collegiate athletic teams (paragraph 1) is due solely to Title IX, as implied in paragraph 2? Is it true that the 1979 Policy Interpretation mandates proportionality (paragraphs 5–6)? To what extent do "schools need football's revenue" (paragraph 9)? How is Sacks defining "feminists," and to what extent are they to blame for Title IX's modern application? Such questions could all use concrete evidence or at least reference to appropriate sources.

Are there any fallacies (7g) in Sacks's argument? Putting the blame entirely on "misguided women's advocates" appears to be a case of *overgeneralization* (7g-1), and impugning the character of such women, by accusing them of pursuing a "scorched earth" campaign against men, exemplifies the *ad hominem* fallacy (7g-3). And the author's simplification of this complex issue to two sides, with schools "caught in a vise," is an example of *either/or reasoning* (7g-4).

EXERCISE 2.3

1. Sacks argues that "the destruction of men's athletics has become an acceptable substitute for strengthening women's athletics" (paragraph 4) and gives an example in paragraph 12, citing "misguided feminists" as the architects of this "destruction." Does his logic hold up? Can you imagine a situation in which a school may opt to cut men's teams yet not find that action fully "acceptable"?

2. Sacks's argument is based on several major assumptions, both stated and unstated, for which he offers no evidence. What are they?

(FOR COLLABORATION)

With one or two other students, consult the list of logical and emotional fallacies in 7g and see if any of them apply to "Title IX Lawsuits Are Endangering Men's College Sports."

External evaluation

Using *external evaluation*, try to consider this text against other texts and against your own experience. Normally a good starting point for this aspect of critical reading is to note the company it keeps, that is, other texts with which it is grouped. In this case, however, the text was published simply as an opinion piece in the *Los Angeles Times* and then posted separately on the Web. Is this text similar in ideology to the author's other writings? Yes, it would appear so. A quick search of the Web reveals that Glenn Sacks is a staff writer for a conservative political journal called *The American Partisan*, where he is described as "the only regularly published male columnist in the US who writes about gender issues from a perspective unapologetically sympathetic to men" (see http://www.american-partisan.com/about.htm). Other topics he has written on include domestic violence (specifically, battered men), adoption (specifically, notification of the biological father), and child custody (specifically, rights of the natural father). "Title IX Lawsuits Are Endangering Men's College Sports" falls in the same vein. Consistent with conservative ideology, it supports a traditional view (whereby athletics are mainly a male domain) against further encroachment by women. This would explain also his clear animus against feminists and "misguided women's advocates."

Authors who consistently follow one philosophy—of any kind—tend to downplay or overlook ideas or facts that are not compatible with that philosophy. Thus, to broaden your horizons as a critical reader, it is important that you not restrict yourself to that one author's view but consult a range of opinions. In this case, you could search the Web for writings by other authors, using *Title IX* as your search term. Such a search would turn up some interesting facts not mentioned by Sacks. For example, although more than 400 men's programs have been cut in the past three decades, even more men's programs have been *added*. Indeed, since 1980 for every 2 women's sports programs added, 1.5 men's programs have been added. A Web search would also turn up a variety of perspectives on this

2.4

Other sources of information on Title IX.

whole issue. For example, there are those who argue that the OCR does *not* mandate proportionality, that Title IX enforcement already *is* flexible. There are those who claim it is the gargantuan size of football programs that's to blame and that either downsizing or professionalizing college football would take the pressure off other (both men's and women's) programs.

Sacks hardly acknowledges any of these facts. They are "textual silences" that can be filled in only by a critical reader familiar with different points of view on the topic. Like most editorialists in the public media, Sacks wants to promote his own point of view and is less interested in presenting all sides of the issue. The burden is on you, the reader, to educate yourself on the issue, which can best be done by reading widely and critically and then weighing others' ideas against your own experience.

Checklist for Critical Reading

Internal evaluation

1. Is the text coherent? Does its logic hang together and make sense?
2. If it constitutes an argument, is it appealing mainly to logic, to authority, or to emotion (7f)?
3. Does it have enough supporting evidence (7c)?
4. Are there any fallacies in the author's reasoning (7g)?
5. Does the author consider alternative views (7d)?

External evaluation

6. Where was this particular piece of writing published? Does this suggest an ideological slant of any kind?
7. Judging from the author's other writings, what are his or her general views or interests?
8. What purpose or "agenda" might the author have had in writing about this topic?
9. What do other writers have to say about this topic?
10. What might the author have *left out* of the text? Why?
11. How well does the author's representation of the world fit with your own experience?

EXERCISE 2.4

1. Using *Title IX* as your search term, search the Internet for other writings on this subject by other authors. Be sure to look for various points of view, not just those opposed to it.

2. On the basis of what you found in question 1, what other textual silences do you think there are in Sacks's essay? That is, in arguing for one point of view, what has he left out?

2 Structuring your reading process

Reading thoroughly on all three levels is crucial to understanding a text well enough to discuss it intelligently and write about it knowledgeably. If you structure your reading process according to the three steps of previewing, reading, and reviewing, you will understand what you read more completely.

Previewing

Begin any reading session by previewing the material as a whole. By looking ahead, you gain a general sense of what is to come. This will help you to predict what to expect from the text as you read and to better understand what you are reading. Jot down in a journal or notebook any questions that occur to you during previewing.

As you approach a textbook for the first time, look closely at the table of contents to preview the book's main topics. You can also learn the relative importance of topics by scanning the table of contents. Next, preview one chapter. Page through the chapter, reading all chapter headings and subheadings in order to gain a sense of the chapter's organizational structure. Look also at any words that are in boldface or italic print. These words are highlighted because the author considered them to be especially important. Finally, preview any graphs, charts, or illustrations. These visuals are included to reinforce or illustrate key ideas or concepts in the chapter.

WEBLINK

http://www.yorku.ca/
cdc/lsp/downloads/
reading_brochure.PDF

Tips on effective reading strategies, including SQ3R, from York University

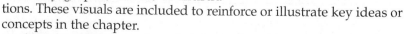

2.5

Tips and strategies for academic success.

You should also preview shorter works, such as magazine or journal articles, prior to reading them. An article may include subheadings, which provide an idea of the article's structure. Again, look for highlighted words or graphics in the article, since these can provide clues about key ideas. You should read any biographical information about the author, both to note his or her credentials and to determine whether he or she might have a particular bias on the subject. For example, an author who is a leader in the National Rifle Association will probably express a particular bias about gun control. As a final step in previewing an article, read the opening and closing paragraphs to get an idea of the author's thesis and conclusion.

Reading

After you preview the text, read it carefully and closely. Pace your reading according to the difficulty of the material—the more difficult the material, the more slowly you should read it. You may find that you need to take frequent breaks if the reading is especially dense or contains a lot of new information. You may also find that you need to reread some passages several times in order to understand their meaning. Material assigned for college classes is often packed with information and therefore requires not only slow reading but also rereading. As you read, pay attention to the three levels of meaning (see 2b-1).

AUDIO
Reading topic
sentences.

Reviewing

Once you have completed a thorough reading, go back to the text and review. Pay particular attention to those areas of the text that you previewed. Have the questions you had when previewing been answered? If not, reread the relevant passages. It may also help to review with a classmate or a study group; discuss the text with your peers to be sure that your understanding conforms with theirs. Talking about the text with others will also help communicate your understanding in a meaningful way. If your class has a computer bulletin board or online discussion group, post any questions that you still have about the reading. Like discussing the text in groups, writing about the text in such forums will help you articulate your ideas, which will serve you well when you are asked to write about the material more formally, in an essay or exam. To gain a thorough understanding from your reading, plan to review the material several times.

3 Converting your reading into writing

Reading invariably stimulates thought. To get the most out of reading, you may find it helpful to record these thoughts in writing. There are a number of ways to do this, including (1) annotating the text while reading, (2) summarizing, (3) keeping a journal, and (4) using a double-column notebook.

Annotating the text while reading

One way to ensure that you are reading actively and critically is to annotate the text as you read. **Annotating** a text means making summary notes in the margins, as well as underlining or highlighting important words and passages. Typi-cally it is best to preview the material before annotating it. Your annotations should summarize the key ideas in the text. Take care, however, not to over-annotate. You need to be selective so that you do not highlight everything in the text. The following excerpt illus-trates a student's annotation of a pas-sage from an article on creativity in science and art.

AUDIO

Using anno-tations in studying.

WEBLINK

http://karn.ohiolink.edu/
~sg-ysu/process.html

A Web page that breaks the writing process down into a series of steps, one leading to the next

What is the relationship between science and art?
There must be a link, as so many scientists are also artists.

<u>What is the kinship between these seemingly dissimilar species, science and art?</u> Obviously there is some—if only because so often the same people are attracted to both. The image of Einstein playing his violin is only too familiar, or Leonardo with his inventions. It is a standing joke in some circles that all it takes to make a string quartet is four math-ematicians sitting in the same room. Even Feynman plays the bongo drums. (He finds it curious that while he is almost always identified as the physicist who plays the bongo drums, the few times that he has been asked to play the drums, "the introducer never seems to find it necessary to mention that I also do theoretical physics.")

Art and science cover the same ground— several examples.

<u>One commonality is that art and science often cover the same territory. A tree is fertile ground for both the poet and the botanist.</u> The relationship between mother and child, the sym-metry of snowflakes, the effects of light and color, and the structure of the human form are studied equally by painters and psychologists, sculptors and physicians. The origins of the universe, the nature of life, and the meaning of death are the subjects of physicists, philosophers, and composers.

—K. C. Cole, *The Scientific Aesthetic*

(EXERCISE 2.5)

One more paragraph from Cole's article is included below. Annotate this paragraph, underlining important ideas and noting key points in the margin.

There are, of course, substantial differences between art and science. Science is written in the universal language of mathematics; it is, far more than art, a shared perception of the world. Scientific insights can be tested by the good old scientific method. And scientists have to try to be dispassionate about the conduct of their work—at least enough so that their passions do not disrupt the outcome of experiments. Of course, sometimes they do: "Great thinkers are never passive before the facts," says Stephen Jay Gould. "They have hopes and hunches, and they try hard to construct the world in their light. Hence, great thinkers also make great errors."

—K. C. Cole, *The Scientific Aesthetic*

Summarizing

A critical thinker is able to abstract or summarize the gist of information read or heard. When you summarize something, you boil it down to its essence, picking out the major points or ideas and restating them in a succinct way. For example, if you had just attended a lecture by a history professor, you might summarize the lecture by writing down the three or four major points made by the speaker. In summarizing, you generally stick to the literal meaning of what you've read or heard (see 2b-1). The ability to summarize effectively is discussed at length in Chapter 11.

Keeping a journal

Many people find it helpful to jot down thoughts while reading, and keep them in a journal. Like a diary, a reading journal requires you to put your thoughts into words, an activity that can clarify your thinking about a topic. It allows you to "converse" with yourself, thereby setting up an internal sounding board for your own thoughts. In addition, if you later decide to include these thoughts in an essay or other formal writing, the fact that you have already formulated them will give you a head start. Finally, and most obviously, a reading journal is simply a valuable way to remember things that you might otherwise forget.

What makes journal keeping special is the fact that it is a private activity, meant for your use only. You are free to think and write whatever you want, in whatever style you want, without worrying about what other people might think of it. You should take advantage of this freedom and use your journal to explore and play with all sorts of ideas, even seemingly crazy ones. As Francis Bacon once said, "Write down the thoughts of the moment. Those that come unsought for are commonly the most valuable."

Using a double-column notebook

A double-column notebook is a special kind of reading journal that has become increasingly popular in recent years. It combines summarizing and journal keeping. Using a notebook, you draw a vertical line down the middle of each page (or use the notebook spine itself as the dividing line), thus creating two columns. In the left-hand column, you summarize your reading as you go along. In the right-hand column, you record your interpretations, evaluations, and other thoughts about the left-hand items. The left-hand column is for literal meaning, the right-hand column for interpretation and criticism. Here is an example from a reading of Sacks's "Title IX Lawsuits Are Endangering Men's College Sports."

SUMMARY	COMMENTS
• Sacks says that between 1992 and 1997, 3.6 men's athletic slots had to be dropped for every women's slot created.	• I wonder what the ratio was before 1992. Should check on this. Might provide a different perspective.
• He seems to assume that football occupies a sacrosanct position in college sports.	• Has anyone thought about making college football semiprofessional? It already seems to be that anyway.
• Sacks says that Title IX demands "rigid proportionality" between the sexes according to overall school enrollment (last paragraph).	• Check on this. It doesn't seem plausible.
• "Over 70% of I-A football programs turn a profit."	• How big a profit? And how many of these programs are there? What about all the others?

HELP

Can I create a double-column notebook on my computer?

Yes, by simply setting up a two-column table.

1. Open a new file (FILE > NEW).
2. On your desktop, select TABLE.
3. Click on INSERT > TABLE.
4. For "Number of Columns," insert "2." For "Number of Rows," insert "8" (you can add more rows later, if you need them).
5. Set AUTOFIT to FIXED COLUMN WIDTH.
6. Click OK.
7. At the top of the left-hand column, write "SUMMARY." At the top of the right-hand column, write "COMMENTS." You now have your double-column notebook.
8. Hit SAVE and give your table an appropriate name.

2c Engage actively and critically in the viewing process

In today's world, especially with the growth of the Internet and cable TV, much of what we know (or think we know) about the world comes to us through visual images. Images are everywhere, and we are drawn to them because they are so accessible. Their "meaning" usually seems straightforward, unmediated, plain for all to see. Our enchantment with the visual is longstanding, captured in stock phrases such as "seeing is believing" and "one picture is worth a thousand words." Indeed, criminal trials often hinge on *eyewitness* testimony, which is given more credence than any other form of evidence (except now perhaps DNA).

Traditionally, the major source of ideas for writing has been reading. But as visual imagery becomes more and more ubiquitous in our modern world, the viewing of images is taking its place alongside reading as a source of input. And as in reading, viewing can be done on three different levels: literal meaning, interpretation, and criticism. We will illustrate this three-step process using a sequence of two photos of the famous pulling down of a statue of Saddam Hussein during the Iraq War, and an ad for a sport-utility vehicle, or SUV.

FIGURE. 2.1 A statue of Saddam Hussein was pulled down in Baghdad. (Associated Press)

FIGURE 2.2 Iraqis swarmed over the hollow torso, hitting it with sticks. Men dragged the torn-off head through the street with ropes, while children rode it and beat it with shoes. (Associated Press)

FIGURE 2.3 Saturn VUE ad (Used with permission of General Motors Corp.)

Viewing for literal meaning

The literal meaning of an image is its "surface" meaning, the meaning that anyone with a minimal knowledge of the context would attribute to it at first glance. For example, the literal meaning of Figure 2.1 on the previous page is that a statue of Saddam Hussein is being pulled down by an attached cable in front of a small group of photographers. The caption provides enough context to make sense of the photo for those readers who are not already familiar with this historic event. Additional context can be found in the accompanying photo (Figure 2.2), which has its own literal meaning as described in the caption. Since the two photos form a sequence of actions, each draws contextual meaning from the other. The literal meaning of the SUV ad (Figure 2.3) is simply that a Saturn VUE sport-utility vehicle is parked in an evergreen forest, surrounded by a variety of wildlife.

Viewing for interpretation

Like written texts, visual images can be manipulated to favor a certain perspective. When viewing for interpretation, you should try to detect ways in which this is done. Consider, for example, the *composition* of the image. How is the image structured? How are its parts arranged? Which parts are given prominence, and which are not? How does this affect your interpretation of the image? Consider also the *point of view*, or perspective. From what angle and distance are you viewing the scene? Would a different point of view make a difference in your interpretation, and if so, how? Consider next the *tone* of the image, including color and clarity. Do these qualities affect your reaction?

Let's illustrate these points with regard to Figures 2.1 and 2.3. In terms of *composition*, Figure 2.1 is structured so that the statue of Saddam is the focus of attention. It's only slightly off center, and its darker hues contrast vividly with the lighter hues of the dome behind it (which serve to frame it). The statue contrasts also with the group of bystanders below it. This positioning mirrors the long-standing power structure in Iraq—a powerful Saddam dominating the weak Iraqi population—a relationship that of course plays a central role in the modern history of Iraq and in the drama enacted in this sequence of photographs. As for *point of view*, the sideways angle of the photo maximizes the sense of a falling statue. Taken from a close distance, the photo also has a sense of involvement. Together, the angle and the distance convey the perspective of someone who is caught up in the action, someone who might even be a participant.

Thus, the photo presents itself as a simple snapshot taken perhaps by a local Iraqi. If the photo had been taken from more of a distance, it would have seemed to be more detached, taken perhaps by a foreign observer. Finally, the *tone* of the photo is that of objective realism. The relative clarity of the photo and the bright if slightly muted colors depict a midday scene captured with little artifice. The downward movement of the statue contrasted with the transfixed spectators in the foreground and the building in the background captures the tension of a historic moment.

In Figure 2.3, the *composition* of the ad is such that it draws our attention mainly to the SUV and certain of the animals, especially the largest of them, the moose. The other animals and birds that compete for our attention include the skunk, puma, red crossbill, goshawk, porcupine, fox, and bear. All of these benefit from having contrasting colors, being of larger size, or being in the foreground. They are all depicted as larger than they would be in real life, making the SUV appear smaller—and therefore less intrusive. The forest itself is pristine—there are no tree stumps or fences, for example. And the vehicle appears to be in some kind of forest clearing; there are no signs of a road. The *point of view* is that of an observer, possibly the driver, standing in the forest and enjoying this Disney-like scene. As for *tone,* the artist has rendered the scene as a painting, thus capturing the kind of tranquility found in paintings by Audubon, Bateman, and other naturalists. The happy tone of the scene is further enhanced by the use of warm, earthy colors. (Just imagine how different it would be in black and white!) And the keys in the upper-left and lower-left corners are reminiscent of a nature book for children, with the SUV being labeled along with the other animals as if it were just another species of "wildlife."

(EXERCISE 2.6)

I   Analyze Figure 2.2 for composition, point of view, and tone.

Viewing critically

Finally, as with reading, you want to go beyond interpretation and engage in critical evaluation of the image. Except for purely aesthetic evaluation, this stage of viewing requires a consideration of factors external to the image itself. Since images often are accompanied by words, such words are among the external factors that need to be examined. Other factors include the site where the image is viewed, the "story" it supports, the rhetorical purpose(s) behind use of the image, the rhetorical purpose(s) behind the construction of the image (see previous section), the veracity of the image in terms of what it purports to represent, and deliberate or unwitting omissions.

To illustrate these points, consider the two photos in Figures 2.1 and 2.2. These photos were taken by an Associated Press photographer and made available to newspapers throughout the world. They were taken in Baghdad in mid-April 2003 during the War in Iraq. Although there were hundreds of Saddam statues throughout Iraq, the pulling down of this particular one was widely publicized in the mass media as symbolic of the fall of the Iraqi dictator's regime. Hence these photos were viewed by millions around the world, and were interpreted by most as illustrating the Iraqi people's rage against despotic rule and their euphoria about its downfall. In a war that was highly controversial both at home and especially abroad, these photos were seen as vindication of the decision by President George W. Bush to invade Iraq. A primary rhetorical purpose in showing them, therefore, would be to support the Bush policy (which predicted that Iraqis would "dance in the streets" when Saddam fell); those media outlets that supported the war would be expected to show these photos more than those media outlets that did not. Since the war was more popular in the US than anywhere else, the photos would have their best chance of being published in the US, the most lucrative market for photojournalism. The AP photographer almost certainly would have been aware of these political

Checklist for Critical Viewing

1. Where does this image appear?
2. What "story" does it support?
3. What purpose does the image serve in that story?
4. Why did the artist construct the image the way he or she did?
5. How closely do the words accompanying the image, if any, fit with the image itself?
6. How truthful is the image in what it purports to represent?
7. What has been left out of the image that should be there?

and economic facts, and he chose to highlight those features of the scene that fit the standard account disseminated by US officials and the US mass media.

How truthful are these images in what they purport to represent? Has anything been left out that should be there? A search of the Web indicates that there is considerable controversy surrounding these photos. In particular, photos from the BBC Web site showing the entire square in Baghdad during this event indicate, for example, that less than two hundred people were there, and reports from the scene suggested that many were US soldiers or journalists. Without actually having been there or having other photos by other photographers, it is difficult to know the truth. But these alternative accounts should serve as a good reminder to be skeptical in your interpretation of visual images, even those that purport to be objective.

As for the SUV ad in Figure 2.3, it appeared as a two-page spread in upscale magazines. The ad's designers apparently targeted consumers who might want an SUV but who are sensitive to accusations that SUVs are harmful to the environment. They apparently wanted to counter those accusations by promoting the idea that SUVs can peacefully and harmlessly co-exist with the environment. This theme is reiterated in the slogan at the bottom of the page, "At home in almost any environment." It is not a truthful image; rather, it is a romanticized one. Not only does it portray a scene that could never exist in real life, but it fails to include any of the ways in which SUVs are accused by critics of damaging the environment.

(EXERCISE 2.7)

Go to *Yahoo! News* at *<http://news.yahoo.com/>* and click on Slideshows. Select one of the images and use the Checklist for Critical Viewing to critically analyze both the text and the photo.

(FOR COLLABORATION)

Together with one or two classmates, find a current news story featured in the major weekly newsmagazines (*Time, Newsweek, US News & World Report*). (You could divide this up so that each has only one magazine.) Using the Checklist for Critical Viewing, analyze the photos and other visual images (graphs, diagrams, and so on) in these accounts.

Preparing

Novice and experienced writers tend to devote different amounts of time and attention to preparing. Novice writers often dive right into drafting a final version of their paper. Rather than experimenting, inventing, and planning, they spend most of their time struggling with the writing itself. Many experienced writers, however, report that they spend a great deal of time thinking about what they want to say before they actually begin to write a piece. Learn from these experienced writers—take time to prepare prior to drafting.

Your computer can help you as you prepare for writing. You can designate folders on your computer's hard drive or on a floppy disk to organize your work. Many operating systems permit you to create a treelike hierarchy of directories, folders, and document files. Using this capability, you can group related documents in the same location on the hard drive or disk, much as you might store related papers within a folder in a file cabinet. Using the power of computers, you can store the following kinds of information, each in its own folder: the experimental ideas you generate, the prewriting you do, and the preliminary information you gather. The screen in Figure 3.1 shows the structure one student selected for organizing files.

HELP

How do I organize my files?

1. Using a file management program (such as *Windows Explorer*) or opening the FILE MENU, create a directory or folder for each course in which you have written assignments (for example, English and history).

2. Within each directory or folder, create subdirectories or additional folders in which to store the work for each assignment.

3. Each time you begin a new writing assignment, save all the work in the appropriate assignment directory or folder.

NOTE: Be sure to keep backup files of important work.

3.1
Step-by-step instructions for using folders.

FIGURE 3.1 Screen Showing Directory Structure in *Windows Explorer*

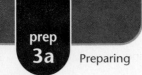

3a An overview of the writing process

3.2

Online help in understanding the writing process.

As a college student, you should be developing your writing skills. Although there are certainly writers who exhibit unique talent, everyone can improve his or her writing.

Thinking critically is just as important to the writing process as it is to the reading process (see Chapter 2). To make sense out of the seeming jumble of ideas floating around in your head, you need to engage critically and actively with your own writing. The mental processes involved in writing are enormously complex. To even try to describe these processes is to oversimplify. However, we can make some generalizations about the writing process based on the accounts of experienced writers.

3.3

An introduction to the writing process.

WEBLINK

http://cctc2.commnet
.edu/grammar/
composition/
composition.stm

A great introduction to the writing process

Writing involves three stages, each of which includes a number of tasks. The diagram in Figure 3.2 will help you envision the writing process. The preparing stage encompasses experimenting and exploring, inventing and prewriting, gathering information, and

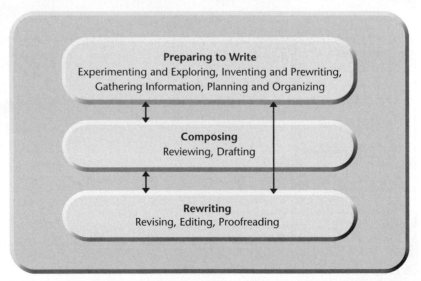

Preparing to Write
Experimenting and Exploring, Inventing and Prewriting, Gathering Information, Planning and Organizing

Composing
Reviewing, Drafting

Rewriting
Revising, Editing, Proofreading

FIGURE 3.2 The Writing Process

AUDIO
How stages of
writing vary.

Stages of the Writing Process

Preparing

Experiment and explore. Decide on a topic, and consider
your rhetorical stance, genre, and language choice.   3b
Invent and prewrite. Inventory your knowledge on a
topic, prewrite on the topic, and narrow the topic.   3c
Gather information. Work with peers to brainstorm
and to discuss your topic. As necessary, find
credible sources to support your own ideas.   3d
Plan and organize. To guide your writing, compose a thesis
and construct an organizational plan or outline.   3e
Try computer prewriting software. Let your computer's
prewriting program help you with the
preparation process.   3f

Composing

Review. Before you compose, review your prewriting,
thesis statement, and outline, and use them as raw
material for your paper.   4a
Draft. Either flesh out your outline by building your
text in blocks, or compose from the top down,
using your thesis as an advance organizer and
writing the piece in a linear sequence.   4b
Collaborate. Work with your peers as you compose
and gather feedback on drafts.   4c
Try composing with a computer. Use your computer to
help you compose effectively.   4d

Rewriting

Shift from writer to reader. Become a skilled reader—
think critically and evaluate your own writing.   5a
Revise. As you revise, add, delete, and rearrange your
text, checking for focus, coherence, organization,
development, tone, and format.   5b
Edit. Edit to make your text easier to read.   5c
Proofread. Proofread to correct errors in punctuation,
spelling, and usage.   5d
Collaborate. Peer review each other's texts.   5e

3.4

Details for finding a topic with search engines.

HELP

How do I use the Internet to find a topic?

1. Use your Internet browser to access a search directory such as *Yahoo!* that has hierarchical subject categories.

2. On the subject tree, look for categories that interest you or that are related to your assignment (for example, "entertainment" or "politics").

3. Within each category, search for possible topics. (For example, under "society," you might find the topic "environment" interesting.)

4. Each time you go one level deeper in the subject tree, jot down other categories that might provide possible topics for you to write about.

NOTE: Not all search tools use subject trees. Some use only keyword searching. For some commonly used search engines, see 9c.

---

planning and organizing. The composing stage requires reviewing and then drafting. The rewriting stage incorporates revising, editing, and proofreading. These stages are often described as *recursive,* as writers typically move freely among them as they plan, shape, compose, and revise their texts.

Thus, writing is often a messy process involving much cycling back and forth between stages: planning and drafting, and then revising and rewriting, and then more planning. If you slow the process down and really look at each stage, you will better understand what happens as you write. If you understand the process better, then you will also be able to control it better. It will seem less mysterious and more workable.

AUDIO

The importance of experimentation.

3b Experiment and explore

During the first phase of the first stage of the writing process, you experiment and explore in preparation for writing. There are many ways of experimenting with language and exploring ideas.

1 Deciding what to write about

It is important that you choose a topic you are interested in, can develop an interest in, are somewhat familiar with, or have questions about. You will write much better if your interest level is high. If you choose a topic that you have absolutely no interest in, you may find yourself bored before you even begin. However, do not close your mind to topics that are not immediately appealing to you. It is possible to develop interest in something once you know a bit more about it. Following are some ways to explore ideas to write about.

- Watch educational programs on television (PBS or Discovery).
- Converse with friends, family members, or teachers.
- Think about your own hobbies and interests.
- Think about your employment experiences.
- Think about your college major or other courses you have taken.
- Surf the Net.
- Browse through current periodicals in the library.

In workplace writing, the topic is often predetermined: an engineer might write a report describing a new piece of computer hardware, a nurse might write a case history of a patient's illness, and so on. Often college writing assignments do not appear to have any inherent purpose, and thus you may feel that your writing is out of context. One of your major tasks when given a writing assignment is to assess what the instructor is asking you to do. Does your instructor want you to analyze or discuss something you have been reading about in class? Does she or he expect you to choose your own topic and write an argumentative essay? How the assignment is phrased will help you to determine how to approach the choice of a topic.

WEBLINK

http://writing.colostate
.edu/references
An introduction to the writing process, focusing on developing ideas and writing strategies

3.5

A detailed resource for developing a topic.

(EXERCISE 3.1)

Using one of the search tools available on your Internet browser, explore possible topics of interest to you. Make use of the directory structure to search on topics in different categories (for example, "education," "entertainment," or "politics"). If you do not have access to the Internet, browse through the magazines in the current periodicals section of your library.

Discuss the list of possible topics with a group of your classmates. Which of the topics do they find interesting or intriguing? What questions about each topic would they be interested in finding out an answer to? Keep a list of the most promising topics in your writing journal or in a computer file. Add to this list as more topics occur to you.

2 Considering your rhetorical stance

Once you have selected an area of interest to write about, you can begin to consider the approach that you will take toward your topic, called your **rhetorical stance.** The term *rhetoric* refers to written or spoken communication that seeks to inform or convince. The rhetorical stance you adopt for a particular writing assignment reflects the way you define the components of the rhetorical situation: your purpose for writing the piece, your persona (how you wish to come across as a writer), and your readers (audience). You can visualize the rhetorical stance in terms of a triangle, as shown in Figure 3.3. We will discuss each component of the rhetorical triangle in turn.

Purpose

At the top of the rhetorical triangle is your paper's purpose. You need to decide on some general goals for the piece of writing and some strategies for accomplishing these goals. For example, for a newspaper

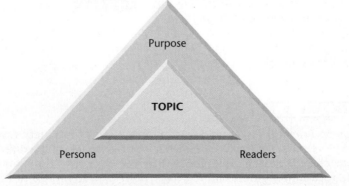

FIGURE 3.3 Rhetorical Triangle

Considering Your Rhetorical Stance

Considering Your Purpose

- Is a problem suggested by the topic?
- What are your writing goals?
- What is your intent—persuasive, argumentative, informative?

Considering Your Persona

- How do you want to sound to your readers?
- What kind of language will you use—formal or informal?
- What role or identity will you assume?

Considering Your Audience

- Who are your readers?
- Are your readers experts or novices on your topic?
- Are your readers likely to agree with you or not?

reporter covering an automobile accident, the goal might be to describe the scene clearly for the newspaper's readers. For each writing task, you should determine your purpose. Is it to inform your readers of the current state of knowledge on a subject, to persuade them to accept a particular point of view, to illustrate or describe a scene?

In Chapters 3–5, we will illustrate the writing process by following the progress of Kirsten Parsons, a college student assigned to write a paper on a computer topic that interests her. The instructor wants the piece to be written largely from the students' own experiences, from a brief Internet search, and from the class text. After thinking about several possible topics, Kirsten finally settled on the topic of Net theft. Her purpose in the piece would be to persuade her fellow students that petty Net crimes were not much different from other petty crimes, such as shoplifting; they were simply easier to commit.

Persona

Next you need to consider your **persona**—how you will present yourself to your readers. Do you want to sound objective and fair, heated and passionate, sincere and persuasive, informative and impartial? The term *persona* is used to describe the identity that a speaker or writer adopts and the credibility that the speaker or writer

establishes. Just as you play many roles in life, depending on the situation, you can be flexible about how you portray yourself in your writing, changing your persona with your purpose and readership. For example, a scholarly audience demands a rather formal persona, whereas an audience of your peers probably does not. The language you choose goes a long way toward establishing your persona.

Kirsten decided to take a somewhat lighthearted approach to her topic to maintain the interest of her peers. She would attempt to play the role of a knowledgeable student, but one with a sense of humor and an understanding of other college students' experiences of the Internet.

Readers or audience

VIDEO
Considering
your audience.

Finally, try to identify as best you can your readers or audience. A piece of writing is often judged by how effectively it reaches its intended audience. Defining your potential audience will help you make appropriate decisions about what to include in and exclude from your writing. Although your instructors are ultimately the audience for most writing you do in college, you may find yourself writing for others as well. Here are some questions about audience that you need to think through.

- Who are your readers likely to be? (Consider age, sex, income, belief systems, and potential biases.)
- Are your readers likely to be novices or experts on the subject you are writing about?
- Are they likely to agree with you, or will you need to persuade them of your point of view?
- What are your readers likely to know? (Consider educational level and prior knowledge.)

After pondering this list of questions, Kirsten decided that her readers would probably be her peers—that is, other college students on her own campus. From talking with other students, she had learned that most seemed to think that it was acceptable to "borrow" material from the Internet. She wanted to alert students that this practice was unethical, if not illegal. She felt that it was important for her fellow students to realize that unattributed use of Internet sources was a form of plagiarism, not unlike stealing.

3 Considering genre and language choice

WWW

3.6
How genre
affects lan-
guage choice.

The **genre** of a piece of writing refers to the kind of writing, such as essay, poem, song lyrics, or report. Once you have identified a genre for a piece of writing, you can consider conventional ways in which that genre is typically written. For example, a convention of the fairy tale genre is to begin with "Once upon a time." Most of the writing you will do in college falls under the broad genre called *academic discourse.* The characteristics of academic discourse include the use of Standard Edited English; that is, academic writers pay close attention to the conventional uses of grammar, spelling, punctuation, and mechanics as described in later sections of this handbook. Other characteristics are a standard format (such as a report or essay format), clear presentation and organization of information, and a formal tone.

The tone of your writing is established through the language choices you make—the words you include in your sentences. A formal tone is conveyed by formal language; for example, you generally would not use contractions in formal writing. Similarly, you typically would not use jargon or slang in formal academic writing. You might, however, use technical terminology if the particular terms would be known by your target audience.

Your tone contributes to your rhetorical stance by revealing the attitude you have adopted toward your topic and the audience you are writing for. In addition to a formal or informal tone, language can be used to convey an ironic tone, a scornful tone, or a distasteful tone. Take care that the tone you adopt reflects the rhetorical stance you have chosen.

(EXERCISE 3.2)

Using the guidelines given in Considering Your Rhetorical Stance on page 49, outline a rhetorical stance for one of the topics you listed in Exercise 3.1. Describe the rhetorical stance in a brief paragraph.

(FOR COLLABORATION)

Draft a one-paragraph audience profile for an essay you plan to write. Describe your intended audience. After you have written a first draft of the essay itself, exchange papers with another student in your class and write an audience profile for that student's essay. Discuss with your peer how well you each were able to identify the writer's intended audience. Give each other suggestions that might help target the audience better.

3c   Invent and prewrite

Writing begins with thinking. The words that appear on your computer screen are the result of the thinking you do prior to and during the writing process. In the prewriting stage, you invent or discover what you want to say about your subject. As the words *invent* and *discover* imply, during this period you delve into your subject, come up with new ideas, connect these new ideas with prior experiences and knowledge, read about and research your subject, and generally allow your thoughts to take shape. All of these activities will help you to decide what you will write. In the prewriting stage, you retrieve from your memory the experiences and information that will allow you to accomplish your writing task. Prewriting also helps you decide what additional information you need to discover (through conversations, reading, and research) in order to write knowledgeably about your subject.

3.7

The process of topic discovery.

> **WEBLINK**
>
> http://www.powa.org/discover/index.html
>
> Prompts to help you discover what to write about, from *Paradigm Online Writing Assistant*

As you prewrite, you can use several techniques to tap your own inner resources and knowledge. Many of these techniques also work well when you begin writing with a partner or a small group. As we look at each technique, we will suggest ways to use it both on your own and with others.

1   Brainstorming

Brainstorming refers to generating random ideas or fragments of thought about a topic. You are probably familiar with brainstorming from writing classes you have taken in the past. It is possible to brainstorm as a group, calling out ideas to the instructor, who writes them on the blackboard. It is also possible to brainstorm at a computer, either individually or with another classmate. Or you may write brainstorming ideas in your writing journal.

KIRSTEN'S BRAINSTORMING

Taking information from the Net. Is it legal? Can we swipe graphics? People copying CDs from each other. Napster? What is Net theft like? Maybe shoplifting? Copyright laws. Hackers and other Net criminals. What is a criminal? If I copied a graphic, was that a crime? Who are hackers? Do I know any? Are they always criminals? Maybe they're just having fun.

EXERCISE 3.3

Following the steps in the Help box, brainstorm at a computer on the topic you selected in Exercise 3.2. If you do not have a computer available, brainstorm in your writing journal instead.

2 Freewriting

Freewriting is like brainstorming in that it involves writing down thoughts as they come to mind. However, unlike brainstorming, freewriting is typically formulated in connected sentences rather than lists. The idea is to write rapidly in an informal style without conscious regard to details of usage, spelling, and punctuation. Using either your word-processing program or a writing journal, you can freewrite on a topic to generate ideas and to discover information stored in your mind. After freewriting on a particular topic for five or ten minutes

HELP

How do I brainstorm on a computer?

1. Open a new document in your word-processing program, and make a list of any ideas that occur to you about your topic.
2. Type what you know about your topic, what information you want to cover, and what you still need to find out about.
3. Review your list, and move items into logical groupings.
   a. Convert important items into headings, and group other items under them.
   b. CUT items that do not fit and PASTE them at the end of the list.
   c. DELETE items that seem irrelevant.
   d. Expand ideas by moving your cursor to the appropriate position and inserting new phrases or sentences.
4. Save the brainstorming document on your hard drive or disk.
5. Update the brainstorming document as you come up with new ideas.

3.8
Step-by-step
instructions for
brainstorming
on a computer.

without stopping, read over your freewriting. As you read it, you may see relationships between ideas that you had not seen before. If you were freewriting at the keyboard, you can CUT and PASTE in order to group related ideas. If you were freewriting with pen and paper, circle important ideas and use arrows to show relationships.

KIRSTEN'S FREEWRITING

I think that my topic will be about Net theft. Wondered about the legalities of copying stuff off the Net. A friend asked me the other day if he could copy my CD. Is that the same kind of crime? What about downloading a CD from the Net? Lots of people are worried about giving out their Visa number over the Internet. Is it really secure? Or I wondered, too, about when we use graphics in our other writing. It is so easy now to just go out on the Net, find a graphic, grab it, and paste it into your own paper. Can we do that? I'm concerned about copyright laws. Maybe that graphic is copyrighted, but I don't know that it is. I remember when I was little, I got caught shoplifting. Maybe stealing on the Net is the same kind of petty crime as shoplifting. But it's sure much easier to get caught in a store than on the Net. People can get away with a whole lot more in cyberspace.

MAIN IDEAS FROM KIRSTEN'S FREEWRITING

1. "Borrowing" information from the Internet: CDs, graphics, others? Is this legal? Are there copyright restrictions?

2. Comparisons of Net theft to other petty crimes: shoplifting, copying software, tapes, or CDs. Is it easier to steal on the Net?

(EXERCISE 3.4)

Using one of the ideas generated by your brainstorming session in Exercise 3.3, freewrite for ten minutes nonstop at the keyboard or in your writing journal. Print out your freewriting session for review, or read over your freewriting from your journal.

Share your freewriting with a peer or small group of classmates. Identify together the best ideas in each of your freewriting sessions. Pinpoint what seem to be the logical connections among the ideas generated by freewriting.

3 Invisible writing

Invisible writing is a computer freewriting technique designed to release you from the inhibitions created by seeing your own words on the computer screen (see the Help box on writing invisibly). Compulsive revisers find it difficult to ignore the errors they see on the screen and so are unable to write freely at the computer. When you write invisibly, your words do not appear on the screen, so you are free to generate ideas without interruption. You can concentrate on the emerging thoughts rather than on the form those thoughts are taking. You may wish to alternate sessions of invisible writing and regular freewriting.

(EXERCISE 3.5)

After turning the computer monitor off or turning down the contrast, begin a ten-minute invisible freewriting session, either on the topic you selected in Exercise 3.2 or on another topic.

HELP

How do I write invisibly?

You can reduce your anxiety about writing by turning off the computer's monitor.

1. On your computer, open a document in which to store your invisible freewriting.

2. Close any other open windows or applications on your computer. (You do not want to lose valuable data if you should accidentally hit the wrong key.)

3. Turn down the contrast or turn your monitor off altogether, thus making your writing invisible.

4. When you have finished freewriting, turn the monitor back on and read what you have written.

3.9
Step-by-step instructions for writing invisibly.

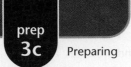
> (FOR COLLABORATION)
>
> Discuss the experience of invisible writing with your peer group.
>
> 1. How did it compare with regular freewriting?
> 2. Did you feel it freed you from editing constraints?
> 3. Was it more or less frustrating than regular freewriting?

4 Clustering

Clustering is a prewriting technique that can help you see relationships among the ideas you have generated in brainstorming or freewriting exercises. You begin a clustering session by putting your topic, in the form of a word or a phrase, in the middle of a sheet of paper. Then, attach to the word or phrase other words or phrases that come to mind, linking and connecting related ideas or subtopics. When you cluster, you free associate from one word or phrase to another, allowing your mind to trigger related ideas that may not have occurred to you before. Because clustering helps you to see relationships among ideas, it is useful for planning the structure of a paper. When you have finished your clustering activity, look at the results closely for any new insights you might have uncovered. Perhaps a string of subtopics will indicate to you a line of argument on the topic. Through clustering, you can focus on one area of interest to pursue in your paper. Although it is possible to do clustering on a computer, it is easier to do with pencil and paper. The results of Kirsten's clustering session on her topic of Net theft are shown in Figure 3.4.

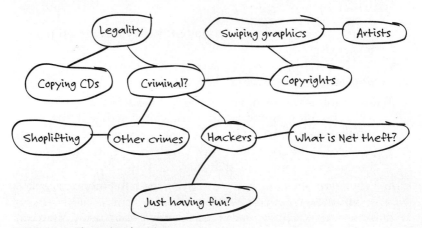

FIGURE 3.4 Clustering by Kirsten

(EXERCISE 3.6)

Try clustering your ideas on one of the topics you generated in Exercise 3.1. Make an effort to free associate rather than consciously thinking through the ideas and the relationships among them. This activity should free you for creative thinking.

5 Debating

Debating is a prewriting technique that can help you explore a controversial issue from all sides. You might begin by writing down all the generalizations you can think of about the topic—either handwriting them in your journal or typing them into a computer file. Since Kirsten's Net theft topic has both pro and con arguments, she decided to write contrasting general statements that could then be supported through examples and evidence.

PRO

1. Using other people's work from the Net is just another form of sharing.

2. The Internet should be "free." To regulate it goes against its very nature.

3. When people put their ideas out on the Internet, they should just assume they're public.

CON

1. Authors and artists who publish on the Internet should not have their work "stolen."

2. "Borrowing" creative ideas, texts, and graphics from the Net is a form of stealing.

3. Net theft is the same thing as shoplifting.

Under each general heading or statement, you then can insert examples or evidence to support the generalization. In this way, you build your arguments and counterarguments. (If your examples or evidence are drawn from outside sources, you must make sure to credit those sources appropriately; see Chapter 11 on using sources.) Once you have constructed a list of generalizations supported by

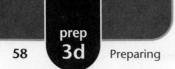
evidence, look over the arguments with an eye toward taking a side and defending it. Begin to think about how your arguments could be arranged to best advantage and how you could refute arguments on the other side. Examine areas where you need further evidence or additional information. Debate your pro and con lists with your classmates.

If you generate your lists using a word-processing program, you can add to, delete, replace, and rearrange the information. The general statements and evidence you accumulate while debating the topic can be used to start an outline or an exploratory draft of your paper.

(EXERCISE 3.7)

Pick one of the broad topics you listed in Exercise 3.1, and type into a document all the generalizations you can think of on the topic. Order your generalizations, perhaps by pro and con positions. Then, for each generalization, list two or three specific examples or pieces of evidence. Save and print your prewriting. If you do not have access to a computer, complete this exercise in your writing journal.

(FOR COLLABORATION)

Working with a small group of your classmates, share your prewriting generalizations. Discuss the pro and con positions and/or the specific examples or evidence you have thought of with your group. Are there additional arguments or evidence that you should consider? Have you thought of all the arguments on the other side of your position?

3d   Gather information

Particularly if your assignment is to write a research paper, you will need to supplement whatever prewriting techniques you use by gathering information from external sources. The first stage of your research may be informal and *ad hoc:* discussing the idea with friends and peers, talking to a professor, reading a few journal articles, or surfing the Net. The ideas you read about and formulate will lead you into a more systematic and extensive search that is focused on a specific topic. When searching in a focused way, you will likely consult library databases and the Internet and use CD-ROMs and online sources. Formal researching is discussed extensively in Part 2, particularly Chapters 9–11. If your writing task involves significant research, refer to those chapters for guidance.

AUDIO

Gathering preliminary sources.

1 Engaging in informal discussions

Informal discussions with classmates, friends, family members, and professors can provide valuable information on your topic. Start with informal discussions before moving to more formal searching. Collaborating with your peers to brainstorm a topic is a good idea. Talking to others about your topic may help you to pose the right questions before beginning a systematic search.

2 Browsing through periodicals

Your library most likely has a section devoted to current periodicals—that is, recently published magazines, newspapers, and journals. You can browse through these to see if your topic is currently being discussed in the media. As you browse, look for articles related to your topic. If you find one, read it for background information.

3 Surfing the Net

A preliminary Internet search can serve much the same purpose as browsing through current periodicals. You can try out several Internet search tools, using a variety of keywords, to see what kinds of information are available on the Internet (see Chapter 9).

4 Taking notes

As you begin your preliminary research on a topic, you will want to take notes. If you are reading, you should read actively and critically and annotate your readings (see 2b-3). If you are listening to a lecture, you should listen attentively and take accurate notes. Record the most important points the lecturer makes, rather than trying to write down everything. Be selective. Finally, always identify the source of the lecture notes completely (course, professor, date, and time of the lecture).

3e Plan and organize

Once you have explored your topic, done some prewriting, and consulted a few sources, you are ready to begin thinking about a logical order in which to present the ideas you have developed. The struc-

www

3.10

Specific help on how to organize your writing.

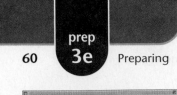

WEBLINK

http://www.powa.org/
organize/index.html

Several organizational strategies, from *Paradigm Online Writing Assistant*

ture of your paper will be influenced by all of the items shown in the rhetorical triangle in Figure 3.3 (purpose, persona, readers). For example, if your purpose is to report on a scientific experiment, the structure of your paper most likely will be the one conventionally used by scientists in professional journals (see 18a).

No matter how good your information, if your paper is not organized, your readers will not be able to understand what you are trying to say.

1 Narrowing your topic

Through prewriting, you develop an awareness of what you do and do not know about a topic. As you look back at your prewriting, think about ways in which you could narrow your topic to a manageable size. Think of any subdivisions there might be within the topic. Try to write down in one sentence what you take to be your specific, narrow topic.

For example, through brainstorming and clustering, Kirsten discovered that her broad topic of Net theft could be subdivided into legal issues, ethical issues, crimes on the Net, computer hackers, and so on. Out of all the possible subtopics, Kirsten decided to narrow the focus of her topic to the practice of "borrowing" information from the Internet.

2 Formulating a working thesis statement

AUDIO

Develop a working thesis statement.

Once you have written down your narrow topic, try to state in one or two sentences the main point you want to make about that topic. This will be your working **thesis statement.** A thesis statement concisely identifies the topic and main point of a piece of writing. Many writers like to formulate a working thesis statement early in the writing process (see 7a). Your working thesis should ideally have two parts: the first part defines the specific topic to be covered in the essay and the second part makes a strong point about the topic.

For her working thesis, Kirsten wrote a two-part sentence that defined the specific topic and articulated her main point.

KIRSTEN'S WORKING THESIS

When it comes to "borrowing" information from the Internet, we are gradually becoming a people that can accept lawbreaking as long as we can participate, too.

Evaluating a Working Thesis

Below are three important questions to ask regarding your working thesis.

1. Does the thesis define a specific topic?
2. Does the thesis make a strong point about the topic?
3. Does the thesis provide a blueprint for the paper's development?

Kirsten's Working Thesis: When it comes to "borrowing" information from the Internet, we are gradually becoming a people that can accept lawbreaking as long as we can participate, too.

Q1. The specific topic is borrowing information from the Internet.

Q2. The main point is that people accept lawbreaking if they can participate, too.

Q3. This thesis implies that the paper will explain how we have accepted lawbreaking in the Internet arena. We expect it to explain how easy it is for everyone to "participate" in this kind of lawbreaking.

An effective thesis statement defines the specific topic and makes a strong point about it. An effective thesis also provides the reader with a blueprint for the direction the paper will take. In other words, the thesis not only states the writer's opinion on the topic but also indicates how the writer intends to support that opinion. Kirsten's thesis implies that her essay will explain how borrowing information from the Internet is a kind of lawbreaking that society has begun to accept.

3 Evaluating and revising your working thesis

To evaluate your working thesis, ask yourself the three questions outlined in Evaluating a Working Thesis. Your answer to each of these three questions should be "yes." If it is not, you will need to revise your thesis accordingly. You may need to revise your working thesis several times as you draft your paper. This is why it is called a "working thesis": it can be clarified, modified, or even completely rewritten during the course of the writing process. Allow your thesis to evolve with your understanding of the topic.

3.11

Examples of revised thesis statements.

EXERCISE 3.8

Draft a few working thesis statements for one of the topics you identified in Exercise 3.1, either typing them into a computer document or
writing them in your journal. Evaluate your working thesis statements using the questions in Evaluating a Working Thesis on page 61.

FOR COLLABORATION

Share your working thesis statements with a peer or a small group. Use
the questions in Evaluating a Working Thesis to frame your discussion.

4 Organizing your information

In addition to constructing an effective thesis, another step in
coming up with a blueprint for your paper's structure is to revisit your
rhetorical stance, since your persona, purpose, and readers will also
influence how you arrange information in your text.

There is no one right way to organize material. However, since
we habitually organize experience on the basis of time, space, and
logic, these factors often influence the organization of written work.

Organizing by *time* usually implies imposing a chronological
order of information—that is, relating one thing after another in
sequence. If you are telling a story in your paper, you will most likely
present information in the order in which events occurred. In Kirsten's
essay on Net theft, for example, the section in which she tells the story
of her own shoplifting experience is organized by time (see 4e). Similarly, you would probably use a chronological organization when
describing how to carry out a process.

Organizing by *space* implies providing a visual orientation for
your readers. If you are describing something, you need to orient your
readers spatially for them to be able to follow your writing. Spatial
description will most likely proceed in an orderly fashion from a given
vantage point. For example, if you are describing your college dorm
room, you might begin at the far corner of the room and work your
way across the room to the doorway.

By far the most frequently used principle of organization in college writing is *logic*. (See 6b for a discussion of the typical patterns for
logical organization.) With any logical organizational pattern, you are
providing your reader with a familiar way of ordering experience,
whether through cause and effect, problem and solution, or some other
logical pattern. Reviewing possible patterns at this point in your prewriting will help you construct an organizational plan.

Consider what organizational principles might govern a paper on the topic you selected in Exercise 3.8. Type your ideas into a computer document or write them in your journal.

(**FOR COLLABORATION**)

Work with a peer or a small group to write a possible thesis statement that reflects the organizational principles you have chosen.

5 Writing an outline

Once you have decided which organizational pattern best suits your working thesis, you may find it useful to construct an outline for your paper. You need not be overly concerned with formal outline structure at this point, unless your instructor stipulates a particular outline format. An outline should serve as a guide as you write—not a constraint that confines and limits your thinking. You may need to change your outline several times as you make new discoveries during drafting.

AUDIO
Outlines are flexible writing tools.

Formal outlines

A formal outline is typically structured in a conventional hierarchy, with numbered and lettered headings and subheadings. A formal outline can be either a topic outline, in which words or phrases are used, or a sentence outline, in which complete sentences are used.

Formal Outline Pattern

Thesis Statement
I. First main idea
    A. First subordinate idea
        1. First example or illustration
        2. Second example or illustration
            a. First supporting detail
            b. Second supporting detail
    B. Second subordinate idea
II. Second main idea

VIDEO
How to use a computer's outline feature.

Informal outlines

Informal outlines are not structured as rigidly as formal outlines. For example, in a formal outline, you are not allowed to have a num-

HELP

How do I use a word-processing program's outline feature?

1. With your word-processing program in OUTLINE mode, enter the outline.

2. Be sure to use the OUTLINE feature to set the levels within your outline, as well as the outline style (for example, bullets, numbers).

3. Use the outliner's COLLAPSE and EXPAND features to view your work at different levels of detail.

4. Rearrange major sections as needed. Your outliner will make sure that subpoints move automatically with the major headings.

5. When you have finished, end the OUTLINE feature and save your work.

NOTE: Programs differ in the ways they change levels and add text. Check your online HELP for details.

3.12

Step-by-step
instructions
for outline
formatting.

ber one subheading unless there is also a number two subheading. Informal outlines allow you to create any hierarchies you like, without paying close attention to issues of format.

Informal Outline Pattern

Thesis Statement
First main idea
    Subordinate idea
        First example or illustration
        Second example or illustration
Second main idea
    Subordinate idea

In constructing an outline that would guide her through her paper, Kirsten used her thesis statement as a blueprint.

KIRSTEN'S NET THEFT OUTLINE

Thesis: When it comes to "borrowing" information from the Internet, we are gradually becoming a people that can accept lawbreaking as long as we can participate, too.

I. Introduction

    A. Scenario

    B. Definition of Net theft

II. Different medium, same crime

III. Standards of honor

    A. Describe what is legal

    B. Describe what is not legal

IV. Redefining a criminal

(EXERCISE 3.10)

If you have a word-processing program with an OUTLINE feature, generate a preliminary outline for a paper based on the working thesis and organizational plan you generated in Exercises 3.8 and 3.9. If you do not have a computer outlining program, outline on paper.

3f   Try computer prewriting software

You may find that your computer lab or writing center has prewriting software that can help you think through and prewrite on a topic. Such programs generally include a series of open-ended questions that allow you to generate ideas systematically. Your ideas are recorded in a computer file for later use. If you have access to commercial prewriting software, it is worth your while to give it a try. It may help you come up with ideas that would not have occurred to you while prewriting on your own.

In this chapter, you have learned about the first stage in the writing process—preparing. We suggest that you try several of the prewriting techniques with various writing assignments from your courses. You may find that combining them in some unique way works best for you. Return to these prewriting techniques at different times during the writing process, whenever you need fresh ideas or feel that your writing is blocked in some way. Remember that all of the techniques we have discussed may be useful as you draft and revise your papers as well. Chapter 4 focuses on the second stage of the writing process—composing.

Composing

FAQs

▶ Why should I review my prewriting before I compose a first draft? (4a)

▶ How do I get over writer's block? (4b-3)

▶ Can a computer help me collaborate? (4c)

▶ Are there different ways to compose with computers? (4d)

After paying conscious attention to prewriting and planning, you are ready to begin composing—that is, writing a first draft of your text. Of course, you have already done considerable writing—through your brainstorming and freewriting, for example, and through your planning and outlining. But when we talk about composing a draft, we are speaking more specifically about the stage in the writing process when you put your ideas down in the form of connected sentences and paragraphs. You can write your first draft using pen and paper, a typewriter, a word processor, or some combination of these tools. Your first draft will be tentative and exploratory. It is important to understand that an effective piece of writing goes through a number of drafts, each of which is improved through revision. We discuss the revision process at length in Chapter 5.

4.1

Thorough introduction to the writing process.

WEBLINK

http://web.uvic.ca/wguide

An introduction to various elements of the writing process, from one of the best writing resources on the Net

HELP

How do I work with word-processing files and documents?

The FILE menu of many word-processing programs is used to work with documents (sometimes called "files"). Listed below are some of the options provided within the FILE menu. Many of these options are also included as icons on the standard toolbar.

4.2
Step-by-step instructions for managing files.

1. NEW—begin a blank document or document template.
2. OPEN—open an existing document.
3. CLOSE—close an open document.
4. SAVE—save a new document with an appropriate name.
5. SAVE AS—save an existing document with a new name.
6. SAVE AS A WEB PAGE—save a word-processing document as a Web page.
7. PAGE SETUP—format a document's margins, paper size, page orientation, and so on.
8. PRINT PREVIEW—view the page as it will look when printed.
9. PRINT—send the document to the printer.
10. SEND TO—email or fax the document.
11. PROPERTIES—identify the document's writer, track its length, and so on.
12. LIST OF FILES—the most recent documents worked on will be listed here following the other menu items.

NOTE: The above listing is from *Microsoft Word 2000*. Your FILE options may differ from these, depending on which word-processing software you are using.

4a Review

When composing your first draft, you use the information and ideas you generated in your prewriting, as well as your working thesis and outline. In the composing stage of the writing process, your concern shifts from experimenting with ideas and gathering infor-

mation to expanding on your ideas and structuring them into effective, coherent prose.

1 Reviewing prewriting, thesis, and outline

You can use your prewriting as the raw material for your first draft. If you recorded your prewriting in an electronic journal, begin by printing it out. Reading your prewriting in a printed format may spark fresh thoughts about the ideas you have generated. If your prewriting is in a handwritten journal or notebook, reread the entries. As you read, jot down notes in the notebook margin or enter notes at the bottom of the page in your computer journal. If one idea stands out, you may want to highlight it using a marker or the highlighting function on your computer.

Next, review your working thesis and outline. Add any new ideas you discovered while reading through your prewriting. If you think the main idea has shifted since you wrote your working thesis, rewrite it and adjust your outline. Finally, revisit your rhetorical stance—your purpose, persona, and readers—and make any needed adjustments to your plans.

When Kirsten read over her brainstorming and freewriting, she decided that her best topic ideas involved a focus on various kinds of "borrowing" from the Internet: copying files, graphics, CDs, and so on. She also found that she was interested in exploring why such Net crime seemed so accepted.

When Kirsten first wrote her working thesis, it reflected the focus she had decided on after her prewriting review.

ORIGINAL Gradually, we are becoming a people that accept lawbreak-

     ing as long as we can participate, too.

As she reviewed her thesis, she decided that it was too broad to give her a specific direction in the paper because it did not specify what kind of lawbreaking the paper would discuss. She revised it to more specifically describe the Net crimes she wanted to cover in the paper.

AUDIO
Crime on the
Internet.

REVISED When it comes to "borrowing" information from the

     Internet, we are gradually becoming a people who can

     accept lawbreaking as long as we can participate, too.

Kirsten's outline provided a broad plan for her paper. As she reviewed the outline, she added several more subheadings (in blue on the next page) to make it more specific.

    I. Introduction

        A. Scenario

        B. Definition of Net theft

        C. Thesis

   II. Different medium, same crime

        A. Compare to shoplifting

        B. Compare difficulty of each crime

  III. Standards of honor

        A. Describe what is legal

        B. Describe what is illegal

   IV. Redefining a criminal

        A. Why Net theft is accepted

        B. What should we do about it?

(EXERCISE 4.1)

Review the brainstorming you did for Exercise 3.3. Think again about
the rhetorical stance you adopted in Exercise 3.2. If you can, identify
one main point, highlight it, and then review your working thesis
statement and outline. Adjust your thesis and outline to reflect any
new ideas you discover.

2 Copying prewriting and outline documents

It is a good idea to copy your prewriting and outline documents
before you begin composing. Or, you can create a new document that
contains both earlier documents (see the Help box on page 70). You
can use this new document to manipulate the text and rewrite it into
a finished product. If you change your mind about where your writing
is headed, you will still have your original prewriting and outline
documents to go back to.

If you prefer, you can use your prewriting and outline documents
for reference and begin composing from scratch in a new document.
The WINDOW feature of many word-processing programs allows you to
work on two or more documents simultaneously. Multiple windows
are useful for keeping track of your ideas as you work—you can keep
your prewriting and/or outline document in one window and your

HELP

How do I combine my prewriting and outline documents?

Word-processing programs provide multiple ways to accomplish the same task. Here are two ways to combine documents.

1. Inserting the two documents into a blank document using the INSERT command from the menu bar:
   a. Create a blank document.
   b. INSERT the contents of your prewriting document (INSERT > FILE).
   c. INSERT the contents of your outline document (INSERT > FILE).
   d. Move appropriate information from the prewriting document to the outline document (using COPY and PASTE).
   e. Save the combined document as a first draft with an appropriate new name.
2. Combining the two documents using multiple windows (see Figure 4.1):
   a. Open your prewriting document and your outline document, each in its own window (FILE > OPEN).
   b. Moving between the windows, COPY and PASTE appropriate information from the prewriting document to the outline document.
   c. Save the combined text as a new document with an appropriate name.

4.3

Instructions for adding notes to an outline.

draft in another. Otherwise, because computer screens provide you with a limited view, it is easy to lose a sense of the flow of your document. With multiple windows, you can either switch back and forth from one window to the other or tile the windows so that they all appear on the screen at once.

EXERCISE 4.2

Using the directions provided in the Help box on page 71, open a new document in one window (for your draft) and open your prewriting and outline documents (from Exercises 3.7 and 3.10) in two other windows. Arrange the three windows so that they will all be available on your screen when you begin composing (see Figure 4.1).

How do I open documents in separate windows?

If you want to work on more than one document at a time, you can do so by using separate windows.

1. Open a document containing a text you have written.
2. Open another document containing another text.
3. View your documents simultaneously by selecting the VIEW or WINDOW feature.
4. Arrange your documents on the screen for better viewing (select TILE or ARRANGE ALL, MINIMIZE, or click and drag).

TIP: It is also possible to use separate windows to display different parts of your document at the same time. For example, you could insert your thesis into one window and your draft into another.

NOTE: Your operating system must support windows.

4.4

Step-by-step instructions for opening documents in separate windows.

4b Draft

When you are ready to begin composing, you can choose from a number of different approaches. Two possible approaches are the building-block technique and the top-down method.

1 Using the building-block technique

One approach to composing is to create a group of building blocks that you can use to construct your text a piece at a time. Many writers first compose a skeleton of the finished text and then expand it by adding new arguments, supporting examples and evidence, or illustrative details—the "building blocks" of a text. Word processing is particularly effective for this approach. Some writers like to write their central paragraphs—the middle blocks of a text—first and add the introductory and concluding blocks later. You can decide which blocks will be easiest and write those blocks first, saving the more difficult parts for last. Once you have a preliminary draft, you can return to your text to amplify sections, one block at a time. To create blocks, you can use the new document you made from copies of your prewriting

and outline documents. Use the headings in your outline to expand and build your text. CUT and PASTE text from your prewriting to place under the headings; then rewrite and amplify the text to create blocks. You can also COPY information from your prewriting window and PASTE it into your document in the other window. In this way, you avoid having to retype information from your prewriting document as you compose.

Below is an illustration of how Kirsten built one section of her paper by copying and pasting information from her prewriting file into her outline file; the blocks are in blue.

COMPOSING FROM OUTLINE WITH BUILDING BLOCKS

   I. Introduction

      A. Scenario

"Look at this new CD I bought!" Jane exclaims to her friend. Interested, Michael eagerly looks at it. "Wow he says! These guys are my favorite group! Mind if I make a copy of it?"

      B. Definition of Net theft

In spite of laws that prohibit the unlicensed copying of music, written materials, and movies, it has become an accepted practice. Graphics, quotes, articles, and many other various things can be copied for personal use, but often no credit is given to the original author.

      C. Thesis

When it comes to "borrowing" information from the Internet, we are gradually becoming a people who can accept lawbreaking as long as we can participate, too.

2 Using the top-down method

Instead of composing from building blocks, you may prefer to work from the beginning of your paper straight through to the end, thus moving from the top down. You can use your working thesis statement and the corresponding organizational plan to compose in

Suggestions for Overcoming Writer's Block

- *Gain some distance.* Set your writing aside for a few days or hours. Take a coffee or snack break before coming back to your writing task.
- *Keep at it.* When your writing is flowing well, try to avoid interruptions so that you can keep the momentum going.
- *Stop when you know what's next.* This will make it easier to pick up where you left off.
- *Try freewriting.* Often, the act of writing itself will stimulate those creative juices.
- *Use visualization.* Picture yourself writing or picture some aspect of the topic you are writing about. Then describe what you see.
- *Change your point of view.* Try writing from another person's point of view. Or try writing in a different form such as a letter or a memo.
- *Write what you know first.* Rather than beginning with an introductory paragraph, start by writing the portion of your paper that you know the most about.
- *Change your mode of writing.* If you normally type at a computer, try using pencil and paper, or vice versa.

4.5

How other writers overcome writer's block.

this way. Type or COPY and PASTE your working thesis statement into a new document. As discussed in 3e, your thesis statement can provide a blueprint for composing. With the thesis statement at the top of your screen, begin writing your draft, following the blueprint suggested by your thesis. Save your draft into the appropriate folder on your hard drive so that you can return to it for more work at a later time. Remember, your working thesis is just that—working. You can revise it at any time (see 3e). Be flexible and open to new directions that may occur to you as you write.

3 Avoiding writer's block

Each writer develops his or her own writing rhythms. You need to discover what your rhythms are. If you find yourself "blocked" as a writer, set your work aside for a few hours or even a few days. If you can't put the work aside for this long, at least get up and stretch;

make yourself a cup of coffee or grab a soft drink before returning to your draft. Coming to it again fresh may give you renewed energy. If you find the writing is flowing well, try to keep at it—writing often takes on a life of its own and generates its own momentum. Finally, do not expect perfection from a first draft. Remember that writing is essentially rewriting: everything you write should undergo extensive revision in a continuous cycle of writing, revising, editing, and writing again.

(EXERCISE 4.3)

Using either the building-block technique or the top-down method, begin drafting in the new document you opened in Exercise 4.2. As you compose, refer often to your prewriting and outline documents. Remember to take advantage of the text-building capabilities of your word-processing program, including the WINDOW and CUT, COPY, and PASTE features.

4c   Collaborate

AUDIO

Keep an open mind about group projects.

As you compose, you might find it helpful to collaborate with others either face to face or via a computer network. In college classes, as in the workforce, writers often work on projects in writing groups or writing teams. Your teammates can serve as a sounding board for your ideas and arguments. You can compose together at the keyboard, with one team member acting as the scribe. Or you can compose separately and then turn to each other for responses. Your peers can read early drafts and provide you with valuable feedback on your work. (See 5e for more information on giving and receiving feedback.) Take advantage of the help that can be found in such collaborative writing groups.

4.6

The benefits of collaborative learning.

1   Working with a group

Working with a group may be something you enjoy or something you dread, depending on whether your prior experience with group projects was positive or negative. In some group projects, one or two students may end up feeling that they are doing all the work. In other group projects, a few students may be bossy or controlling rather than cooperative. But if you pay attention to group dynamics and role assignments from the start of your collaborative project, you should all get along just fine and together produce an outcome that none of you could have achieved alone.

When you first receive a collaborative assignment, meet with your group to begin brainstorming the possibilities. One person can act as

How do I collaborate on a computer?

If your instructor or lab supervisor has designated a common location (drive) on a local area network for your class, you can use it to share work with your classmates (step 1). Other ways to collaborate include using Web pages and email.

1. Post your work to the common drive by using the SAVE AS function in your word-processing program.
   a. Read and comment on the work that has been posted by your classmates (use italics, boldface type, or your word-processing program's COMMENT feature).
   b. On a PC, use SAVE AS to save your classmates' work plus your comments in a new document under a new title.
2. If possible, post your work to a class Web site for others to read and review.
3. Use email to send your work to a peer.

(See also Chapter 24.)

4.7
Three ways to collaborate using computers.

the scribe, typing into the computer all of the ideas generated by the group. Do not cut off creative avenues; brainstorm with the intention of both understanding and opening up the assignment for your group. Once you have a brainstorming list, begin to divide it into component parts, in an effort to outline a plan of action. You might want to "story-board" your piece—that is, put the components of the overall piece onto 3" x 5" note cards and then work together to arrange the pieces to best advantage.

2 Writing collaboratively

Once you have come up with an overall plan of action for your writing project, you can assign specific tasks or roles to group members. One writing class was assigned the task of developing a group Web site on a topic related to cyberspace. The students in each group brainstormed together the possibilities for their site, first deciding on the nature of the content their Web site would present. They agreed to each write independently a two- to three-page piece that would be incorporated as a page at the site. Then, they assigned each person in the group one of the following roles: *group leader* (organized group meetings, set deadlines, reported progress to the instructor), *group librarian* (recorded

relevant Web sites, produced a bibliography, ensured that all links in the site were operational), *group publisher* (took responsibility for the "look" of the site, importing graphics and deciding on appropriate fonts, colors, backgrounds), *group Webmaster* (took responsibility for placing all of the group's writing onto the server, making sure that the site was both functional and readable). Because each student in the group knew exactly what his or her contribution would be, group members were able to work together cooperatively. Please remember that if you use any source material for your group project it must be incorporated appropriately to avoid plagiarism (see Chapter 11).

(FOR COLLABORATION)

This exercise will provide you with practice in composing collaboratively in a computer classroom. First, exchange keyboards with the person sitting beside you so that your writing appears on the other person's screen. Next, decide who will be writer 1 and who will be writer 2. Writer 1 begins to freewrite on the topic "Why I chose my college major." Writer 2 begins to write when writer 1 types a series of question marks (???). When writer 2 runs out of ideas, she or he types a series of question marks. Continue to exchange ideas for about ten minutes.

3 Collaborating via network

If you are involved in a joint writing project, forming an email discussion group can facilitate collaboration with others in the group. Students collaborating to write material for a Web site they were creating, for example, used a study group address so that they could email the first draft of each Web page to the entire writing group for review. Most email software offers the option INCLUDE EMAIL MESSAGE IN REPLY. That option places the entire message—in this case, the draft of a Web page—into the reply window. Members of the writing group could add their comments and suggestions in capital letters or italics to make them stand out from the draft itself. Then, by selecting the REPLY TO ALL option, they could send the reply message to everyone in the group, or, by selecting the REPLY TO SENDER option, they could send their reply to only the writer.

AUDIO
Using email for
collaboration.

You can also use the email software's ATTACHMENT capability to facilitate collaboration with a writing group. This feature allows you to include a document (file) with the email message. In this way, you can send your actual word-processed document to the others in the group for their review. Group members can use the word-processing program's COMMENT feature (found in the INSERT menu) to insert their comments and suggestions for revision. The paper and comments can then be sent back to the writer, again as an email attachment. (See the Help box on page 75 for specific advice on using COMMENTS.)

4 Presenting with your group

Once you have completed your collaborative project, in addition to preparing a written product of your group's work, you may be asked to share it publicly as an online document, a poster presentation, or an oral or multimedia presentation. As you think about making your presentation, consider both the content and the logistics of the presentation itself.

The content of the presentation

Make sure that what you are presenting (the content) is interesting and logically sequenced so that your audience can easily follow your train of thought. Visuals must be appropriate to the content. Everything you present needs to be readable by your entire audience no matter where they are in the room. Make sure that if you are using overheads or a *PowerPoint* presentation, all of your slides can be read easily by everyone.

The logistics of the presentation

It will be important that everyone hear all of your group members, so you must make good use of voice as well as making eye contact with your audience. To do this well requires several practice sessions with appropriate group feedback. Consider, too, how you can divide the allotted time appropriately among group members and still stay within the time limits. Work together with your group so that you are all sharing responsibility for the presentation and the burden doesn't fall on one or two group members. (For more information about making oral presentations, see Chapter 26.)

4d Try composing with a computer

Although some students who do not have computers readily available may still be writing out rough drafts by hand, most students (with computers of their own or liberal access to computer labs) now compose their papers directly at a computer keyboard. In this section, we will examine the ways in which computers have affected composing and suggest strategies for adapting to the changes.

1 Adapting your writing habits

If you are accustomed to writing with pen and paper, you may find that your old writing habits do not translate directly when you use a computer. Old habits are difficult to break, and some writers steadfastly resist the new technology. Others stick to their old habits because they are comforting. For example, a friend of ours reports that before each writing session, he takes a dozen pencils and sharpens them to neat points. He then puts all the pencils in a pencil holder and sits down to type at the computer, not using the pencils at all! You too may find that it helps to observe some of the rituals you developed for writing with pen and paper. But the more familiar you become with writing at the computer, the more you will see its value to you as a writer. Most writers eventually move to composing at the keyboard once they get beyond the initial learning stages.

2 Changing your notion of text and draft

Changing to a new writing tool may subtly alter your relationship with your own words. At first, the words on the screen may seem distant to you—somehow foreign and strange—unlike the words you

HELP

How do I save my work in a series of drafts?

1. Each time you begin a new draft, use the SAVE AS feature and name your drafts in sequence: draft1, draft2, and so on. Then, if you decide that your revisions have not been successful, you can always return to an earlier draft.

2. When working on a draft, do not discard work too hastily by using the CUT or DELETE functions of your word-processing program.

3. Instead, use the COPY or CUT and PASTE functions. PASTE any information you decide to cut out of your draft at the end of the document so that you can retrieve it later if needed.

TIP: Because you may be revising frequently while you write, be certain that you periodically save your work. You can set an AUTOSAVE feature on your word-processing program that will automatically save at regular intervals.

4.8

Step-by-step instructions for saving your work in a series of drafts.

produced with paper and pencil. One of our students remarked that the words seemed like phantoms that could disappear at the touch of a key. However, this sense of distance that word processing creates also allows you to see your writing as more fluid and changeable. It will probably make you more willing to experiment and to abandon text that is not working. In fact, the very notion of a draft changes when you compose at a computer. Each time you open a document to make changes in the text, you are in essence creating a new draft, whether or not you print it out for review. Dozens of drafts may appear and disappear as you continue to revisit your text while composing.

3 Using the computer wisely

When you begin to use a computer for composing, do not get carried away. Some writing—such as a short note to a friend—is still better done with pen and paper. If you compose in a computer lab where access is limited, you might want to write your first draft on paper, saving your computer time for a later draft and for revisions. Even if you have a computer of your own, unless it is portable you may want to keep a notebook handy for on-the-spot composing. If you own a laptop computer, it probably has a NOTEPAD or SCRAPBOOK feature, which you can use to record notes and organize your ideas. Work on developing a writing system that uses the computer—and your time—to best advantage. Remember, you need to attribute appropriately all ideas taken from the Internet that are not your own.

4 Working effectively in a lab environment

If your only access to a computer is in a lab, try to be flexible about your writing process. Schedule work at the time that best suits your own writing habits. However, if the lab is not open at 2:00 a.m., when you work best, you may need to write a draft on paper and then transfer it to the computer for revision later. Most lab directors try to accommodate students by opening the lab some evenings or weekends, but during those times the lab may be overly busy or some computers may not be functioning. Plan ahead and leave time to compensate for these potential problems.

You can help your lab coordinator improve the environment by making suggestions and providing feedback on your lab experience. If a lab assistant is surly and unhelpful, say so. If other writers in the lab are noisy or disruptive, ask the lab assistant to quiet them down. In most cases, the lab coordinator and assistants will be genuinely inter-

ested in helping you write successfully, and your suggestions will help improve the lab environment for everyone.

Write a brief paragraph describing your own writing process, paying particular attention to any composing habits that you have developed over the years. For example, do you have particular tools that you use or a special place where you are comfortable composing? Do you like to have music playing in the background, or is quiet better for you?

(FOR COLLABORATION)

Share your paragraph with a group of your classmates. Discuss the similarities and differences in composing habits among your group.

4e Review a student draft

Following is the first draft of a persuasive paper by Kirsten Parsons, the student introduced in Chapter 3. The assignment was to write an essay on a computer topic of interest. The piece was to be written largely from the students' own experiences, from a brief Internet search, and from the class text. Kirsten thought through several possible topics, but she settled on Net theft.

Notice the format of this essay. Kirsten has used the standard format as recommended by the Modern Language Association (MLA), according to her teacher's specifications. Her identifying information is in the left-hand corner, 1 inch down from the top margin. Her last name and the page number are listed in a header on the upper right-hand side of each page, spaced $1/2$ inch from the top margin. Everything in the essay is double-spaced, including between the title and the first line of the text.

There is much that is good about this draft. Kirsten has identified a real problem that many students face—that is, being uncertain of the "rules" when it comes to using the Internet. The topic is compelling, and her comparisons to shoplifting are insightful. But there are things about the paper that can be improved. We have included the instructor's comments (directed at global revisions) on this early draft (in blue) to highlight some of the areas that need work. Because it is an early draft, the instructor has chosen not to comment on specific grammar, usage, and spelling errors until later in the writing process. A revision of this paper is included at the end of Chapter 5.

Kirsten Parsons

Professor Hines

English 101-35

15 September 2003

Net Theft

"Look at this new CD I bought!" Jane exclaims to
her friend. Interested, Michael eagerly looks at it.
"Wow he says! These guys are my favorite group! Mind
if I make a copy of it?"

Unfortunately, this is a common request within
our society today. In spite of laws that prohibit the
unlicensed copying of music, written materials, and
movies, it has become an accepted practice to
reproduce another's work without paying for it.
Similarly, this has spread to the Internet where
access to software, phone cards, and other products
is convenient and fast. It has become a situation
where "legality collides with practicality" (Meyer
and Underwood 113). When it comes to "borrowing"
information from the Internet, we are gradually
becoming a people who accept lawbreaking as long as we
can participate, too.

I'm sure all of us once glimpsed a tempting item
in a store and after getting no for an answer from

*I'm not certain what the reference to phone cards and other products is in the above paragraph.
There are many kinds of computer theft. It's not really clear what the focus of this paper will be
because of all the different examples in this opening paragraph, although your thesis is quite good.*

Mom or Dad, took matters into our own hands. Sneaking the treasure into a hidden pocket, it probably took only a few moments for your parents to notice something was up. With available technology, Net theft is commonplace. Flowers, phone cards, magazines, books, and software all are vulnerable to cybershoplifting and plagiarism.

Part of the problem is that the physical element involved in actually traveling to a store, and taking something is not necessary for these Net crimes. Imagine walking down the aisle of the local Walmart with the intention of stealing a Hobbes doll, your favorite cartoon character. This scenerio is only possible in a physical world. Because the Net is so unphysical, the risk of being caught, which may deter many thieves in a store, is minimal. Because Net crimes often go ignored, and "everyone" is guilty, more and more people engage in them.

Information about copyright laws, what is legal, and what isn't is available on the Net as well. "Web Issues" at the Copyright Website <www.benedict.com> provides information about what can be copied from the Net and how to do it properly. Another page

I really liked this comparison to other petty crimes, like shoplifting. Again, I wasn't sure about your Net comparison, however (flowers, phone cards, magazines, books—how are these vulnerable to Net theft?). Maybe it would be better to just focus on one kind of petty theft—like copying software or "borrowing" materials such as graphics from someone else's Web site.

Parsons 3

specifically discusses using graphics (PageWorks at
<http://www.snowcrest.net/kitty/hpages>). Those who
decide to break these "laws" run the risk of being
ostracized by a group such as Netbusters! This
vigilante group seeks to prevent what they call
"bandwidth robbery" by informing Net users about its
devastating results.

If the definition of a criminal is one who has
committed a crime, then in the world of the Net,
perhaps we all need to serve some time.

*I'm not certain of the relevance of the Netbusters example. It needs to be tied in with the rest of
the paper. You seem to be going further astray here at the end. You need a strong conclusion that
sums things up and returns you to your thesis.*

Parsons 4

Works Cited

Meyer, Michael, and Anne Underwood. "Crimes of the
    'Net'." CyberReader. Ed. Victor Vitanza. 2nd ed.
    Boston: Allyn, 1999. 111-13.

*You will need to cite your Internet sources here as well as your print source. Please check MLA
style for the correct format used with Internet sources. We will work on editing for correct
grammar and usage on your next draft.*

CHAPTER 5

Rewriting

FAQs

▶ Can I be an objective reader of my own writing? (5a)
▶ How can the computer help me revise my writing? (5b)
▶ What is the difference between revising and editing? (5b–5c)
▶ How do I proofread onscreen? (5d)
▶ How do I give effective feedback to my peers? (5e)

This chapter discusses three rewriting skills—revising, editing, and proofreading. As you think about rewriting, imagine that you are viewing your writing through a camera lens. The first view is panoramic (revising): you look globally at the entire piece of writing with the goal of revising its focus, coherence, organization, development, tone, and format. The second view is at normal range (editing): you look locally at specific sentence-level features with the goal of eliminating wordiness, repetition, and ineffective or awkward language. Finally, you zoom in for a close-up (proofreading): you look for any distracting errors that might interfere with a reader's understanding, including grammar, punctuation, and mechanics.

AUDIO

The three phases of rewriting.

5a   Shift from writer to reader

To be a skillful reviser, you must put yourself in the place of your reader. When you read your own work, however, you may have trouble seeing what you have actually written. Instead, you may see only what you *intended* to write. This section offers some strategies to help you shift roles from writer to reader when you review your writing.

84   Rewriting

1 Allowing time to review your draft

If possible, allow at least a day between the time you finish a draft and the time you read it over to revise, edit, and proofread. You will be astonished at how much more clearly you can view your writing if you take a break from working on it. If you are facing a tight deadline, even several hours away from the work can be helpful. Also, try to schedule more than one session for revising. When your writing is stored electronically, it is much easier to revise because you do not need to retype or recopy the entire text after each change.

2 Reading critically

As you read your work critically, pay attention to different major elements during each subsequent reading. These elements are focus, coherence, organization, development, tone, and format. (See page 87 for Critical Reading Questions for Revision.)

Focus

Focus refers to how well you adhere to your topic and your purpose throughout a piece of writing. As you reread a draft, check that

---

HELP

How do I manipulate my text to make revising easier?

1. Change the way your text looks in any of these ways.
    a. Change the spacing of your text lines from double to triple.
    b. Change the font size from 12 points to 15 points.
    c. Insert a page break after each paragraph.
    d. Change the margin width from 1 inch to 2 inches.
2. Save the reformatted text under a different name.
3. Print out the reformatted text.
4. Read each paragraph of the printed text carefully, using the Critical Reading Questions for Revision (see page 87).
5. Write suggestions for revisions in the margins.

5.1
Formatting tips to make revising easier.

each paragraph relates in some way to the thesis. Is each of your examples and supporting details needed for your argument? It is more important to maintain focus than to add length. Your readers expect you to fulfill the commitment made by your thesis. If you go off on a tangent, they may lose interest.

Coherence

The various components of a piece of writing should "stick together," from sentence to sentence and from paragraph to paragraph. This writing glue is known as **coherence.** Make certain that your sentences and paragraphs are linked through transitional words and phrases. Your goal is to make your writing *cohere*—that is, form a unified whole. (See also 6b on structuring paragraphs.)

Organization

If your piece is well organized, it follows a direction set by the thesis and the opening paragraphs. If you have decided on a particular pattern of **organization,** check to be sure you followed through with that pattern. For example, if you decided to use the cause-and-effect pattern, make certain that you covered both causes and effects. You may find as you reread a draft that some paragraphs would be more effective in a different order or that your closing argument is not your most persuasive and so should not be last. (See also 6b.)

Development

Development refers to the depth of coverage given key ideas. As you reread the text, you may identify points that are underdeveloped. Look particularly for ways in which you have supported your thesis and developed each part of your organizational pattern. For example, if you decided on a problem and solution pattern (see 6b-6), have you developed each alternative solution sufficiently, arriving at a best solution? Be certain that each of your main points is backed up within its own paragraph by supporting details, illustrations, or examples.

Tone

The language you chose to use conveys the **tone**—that is, your attitude toward your topic and your readers. Your tone may be formal or informal, perhaps even humorous. Revisit your rhetorical stance to determine whether the tone you adopted is appropriate to your persona, purpose, and readers (see 3b-2). If you are writing on a serious

Critical Reading Questions for Revision

- Do I have a clearly stated thesis?
- Do all the major points refer to and support my thesis?
- Are all of the examples and illustrations relevant?
- Are the transitions the best ones available?
- Are the major points arranged in the most effective order?
- Are my strongest arguments placed near the end?
- Have I followed through with the organizational pattern?
- Are my major points backed up with specific details?
- Are my paragraphs developed proportionately?
- Have I eliminated contractions or first-person pronouns?
- Is the font I have used readable and appropriate?
- Are the headings descriptive and helpful?

topic, you are likely to use a formal tone. Your sentences and paragraphs will be relatively long; your word choices may be abstract; you will use very few personal references and contractions—in general, you will establish a considerable distance between yourself and your readers. If, however, you are writing on a less solemn topic, you may wish to strike an informal tone. Your sentences and paragraphs will be shorter; you will use less abstract language; you may include contractions and perhaps first-person pronouns—your readers will feel a closeness to you, the writer. (See also 3b-3.)

Format

If your draft is more than a page or two long, consider using the **format** to help the reader navigate the text. By using headings to delineate the major parts, you can help the reader recognize the organizational structure. However, if a piece is relatively short, headings are usually more distracting than helpful. Note, too, that using headings is more common in some fields than in others. For example, papers written in APA format tend to have headings, while those in MLA format may not. Also, pay attention to the font (type style) you have used. It is important that the font be appropriate to the final product; that is, a font that is suitable for a brochure might not be appropriate for a research paper. Standard fonts for all types of writing

include Times New Roman and Courier. (See 20b-7 for more information on fonts.)

3 Outlining your draft

One technique that may help you evaluate a piece of writing is preparing a revision outline. When you have a first draft and perhaps some peer or instructor comments on it, you can create a revision outline by updating the original outline for the piece to reflect the weaknesses of the draft. To begin to plan for revising, add comments in brackets to the revision outline concerning items you need to change in your draft.

Kirsten used this revision outline to plan changes to her first draft on Net theft.

KIRSTEN'S REVISION OUTLINE

Net Theft

Thesis: When it comes to "borrowing" information from the Internet, we are gradually becoming a people who can accept lawbreaking as long as we can participate, too.

    I. Introduction

        A. Scenario

        B. Definition of Net theft [I need to focus this better to correspond with my thesis.]

        C. Thesis

   II. Different medium, same crime

        A. Compare to shoplifting

        B. Compare difficulty of each crime

  III. Standards of honor

        A. Describe what is legal [I really didn't do this very well. Need to expand this section to show where the law stands now.]

        B. Ten commandments for computers [This section doesn't really fit the focus of the paper. Maybe just mention it.]

IV. Redefining a criminal

    A. Why Net theft is accepted [I need to eliminate examples
       that don't fit the focus. Concentrate on why it's so
       widely accepted.]

    B. What should we do about it? [I need a strong conclusion
       that restates the problem with Net theft and what--if
       anything--should be done about it.]

(EXERCISE 5.1)

Reread the rough draft of a paper you are working on. Using the
Critical Reading Questions for Revision (page 87), come up with an
overall plan for revising your draft. Prepare a revision outline, and
add comments about those items you intend to revise.

5b Revise

Critical reading can highlight problems of focus, coherence,
organization, development, tone, and formatting in your paper.
Revising involves adding to the text, deleting from the text, and rearranging information within the text to fix those problems. Using a
word-processing program makes these tasks easy. Knowing what to
add, delete, and rearrange is the tricky part.

AUDIO
One student's
revision
process.

1 Revising for focus

Revisit your working thesis, and revise it to more accurately
reflect the overall point of your text. Then revise each paragraph, one
by one, to ensure that it is focused on
only one idea, which supports the thesis. Try changing the format of your
text to help you revise each paragraph. Delete any paragraphs that are
not related to the thesis.

Kirsten revised her second paragraph to focus more clearly on the
idea of "borrowing" from the Internet.
Notice how she eliminated references

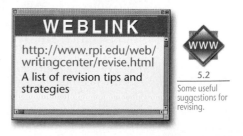

WEBLINK

http://www.rpi.edu/web/
writingcenter/revise.html
A list of revision tips and
strategies

WWW

5.2

Some useful
suggestions for
revising.

to phone cards and other products and included music, software, written texts, and graphics instead.

How do I rewrite my word-processed text?

Your word-processing program will help you to rewrite your text by using the CUT, COPY, PASTE, and move or drag text options. Many of these options are also included as icons on the standard toolbar.

1. CUT—Highlight the text that you want to CUT from your document by using the mouse. When the text is highlighted, click on the scissors (CUT) icon or choose EDIT > CUT from the menu. The cut text will be transferred to the word-processing program's clipboard until you decide to PASTE it somewhere else in the document or in another document or application, such as an email message.

2. COPY—Highlight the text to be copied and click on the double page icon (COPY) or choose EDIT > COPY from the menu. The text to be copied will still appear in your document, but a copy of it will also be transferred to the clipboard until you decide where to PASTE it. Use COPY when you want to preserve your original document intact.

3. PASTE—Move the cursor to the location in the document where you want the cut or copied text to appear. Click on the clipboard icon (PASTE) to paste the text from the clipboard into your document or select EDIT > PASTE from the menu.

4. Move or drag text—You can also "click and drag" highlighted text to a new location in a document instead of using CUT and PASTE. After highlighting the text, click on the selected text with your mouse and, while still holding down the mouse button, drag the text to the new location. You will see a small square next to the cursor arrow to indicate that text is being dragged. When you release the mouse button, the text will be pasted into the new location.

NOTE: The above listing is from *Microsoft Word 2000*. Your rewriting options may differ slightly from these, depending on which word-processing software you are using.

VIDEO
How to rewrite text on a word processor.

5.3
Specific suggestions for revising text.

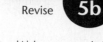
Unfortunately, this is a common request ~~within our society~~
today. In spite of laws that prohibit ~~the~~ unlicensed copying ~~of~~
~~music, written materials and movies.~~ _in some circles_, it has become an accepted
practice to reproduce another's work without paying for it.
Similarly, this _practice_ has spread to the Internet where access to _music,_ software,
~~phone cards, and other products~~ _written texts, and graphics_ is convenient and fast. ~~Graphics,~~
~~quotes, articles and many other various things~~ _These items_ can be copied for
personal use with ease, but often no credit is given to the
original author.

HELP

How do I compare drafts of my text to track my changes?

Here are three ways you can use your word-processing program to track changes you have made to a draft.

1. When you begin to revise a document, turn on TRACK CHANGES (REVISION MARKING) from the TOOLS menu. This feature will mark any changes you make in the document. (Note: Not all word-processing programs offer this feature.)

2. If you forgot to turn on TRACK CHANGES, you may still be able to compare two versions of a document by selecting the DOCUMENT COMPARE or COMPARE VERSIONS feature of the word-processing program.
   a. Select the files that you want to compare (for example, draft1 and draft2).
   b. Look closely at the changes you have made between the two documents. (Revisions will be indicated with markings in the text.)
   c. Check to see that your revisions were substantive; that is, you did not merely tinker with the text but actually added, deleted, and rearranged materials.

3. If your word-processing program does not have DOCUMENT COMPARE, open both files concurrently in two windows and scan for differences.

5.4
Step-by-step instructions for tracking changes.

2 Revising for coherence

5.5

An example of revising for coherence.

Wherever you notice that sentences do not flow smoothly in your draft, add appropriate transitional words and phrases. Look particularly at the links between paragraphs. Insert transitions to help the reader follow the flow of the text. Words or phrases such as *however, on the one hand/on the other hand, but,* and *in addition* can help the reader see the relationships between ideas. Add these words to your text at appropriate places. If you are using one transitional word too frequently, check the thesaurus in your word-processing program for alternatives. (See also 6c-1.)

3 Revising for organization

Once you have decided how to improve the organization of your text, use the CUT, COPY, and PASTE commands to move parts of your text. Rearrange the words, sentences, and paragraphs into the most effective order. Be sure to check for coherence after rearranging.

4 Revising for development

Your argument is stronger if you include many concrete examples or details. If you are writing an informal piece, do not hesitate to add anecdotes or narratives of personal experiences to give life and personality to your writing. If you are writing a formal paper, you can add information from sources that support your arguments. Using the INSERT command of your word-processing program, place the cursor where additional explanatory details, evidence, examples, or illustrations from your notes need to be inserted into your text.

While working on her revision outline, Kirsten discovered that she needed to focus and develop her discussion of the legalities of the Internet (item IIIA in her outline). She rewrote the paragraph as follows:

ORIGINAL PARAGRAPH

Information about copyright laws, what is legal and what isn't is available on the Net as well. Web Issues at the Copyright Website (www.benedict.com) provides information about what can be copied from the Net and how to do it properly. ~~Another page specifically~~

~~discusses using graphics (PageWorks available at http://www.snowcrest~~
~~.net/kitty/hpages). Those who decide to break these "laws," run the~~
~~risk of being ostracized by a group such as Netbusters! This~~
~~vigilante group seeks to prevent what they call "bandwidth robbery"~~
~~by informing Netusers about its devastating results. The Netbusters~~
~~homepage has a place to report clandestine computer activities if you~~
~~know of any perpetrators.~~

REWRITTEN PARAGRAPH

Organizations and individuals have tried to establish standards of
conduct for Internet use. For example, the Computer Ethics Institute
wrote its Ten Commandments for Computer Ethics, which includes such
obvious "rules" as "Thou shalt not use the computer to steal" (Roach).
But what is stealing when it comes to materials found on the Internet?
The Copyright Website asserts that any texts or graphics that you find
on the Internet are by their very nature published and thus are
"copyrighted" (O'Mahoney). This means that in order to use anything
from someone else's Web site, you need their permission. If you put a
comic strip such as Calvin and Hobbes onto your homepage, you run the
risk of being sued for violation of copyright.

5   Revising for tone

In rereading, you may decide that
your tone is either too formal or too
informal. To revise your tone to be
more formal, expand contractions into
their full forms, combine some short
sentences to make longer sentences,
and change informal diction or slang
into more formal wording. The Help
box on page 94 offers guidance in
using the SEARCH function of your
word-processing program as you revise for tone.

WEBLINK

http://www.powa.org/
revise/index.html
Extensive advice on revising
the style and tone of your
essay, from *Paradigm Online
Writing Assistant*

WWW

5.6

Advice on
revising style
and tone.

HELP

How do I use the search function to revise for tone?

5.7

Step-by-step instructions for using the SEARCH function to revise for tone.

1. Activate your word-processing program's SEARCH function. (Note: It may be called EDIT > REPLACE.)

2. Instruct the computer to search your document for a troublesome word, phrase, or punctuation mark (for example, the apostrophe in contractions).

3. As the computer moves to each case of the word, phrase, or punctuation mark in succession, you can decide whether to change it or not.

4. Revise any other troublesome words, phrases, or punctuation marks by initiating further searches.

6 Revising for format

To convey your information in a more visual way, you may want to add formatting more commonly found in a brochure or a newsletter (see 21a or 21b). You can import and insert graphics to illustrate your text at appropriate points. Try using different fonts by selecting them from the FORMAT menu. Remember, though, that readability of your text is the most important goal; choose fonts accordingly. (See 20b-7 for more information on fonts.)

7 Writing effective openings, closings, and titles

VIDEO

Composing introductions.

Openings

Writers have very little time in which to grab the reader's attention—usually only a few seconds. That is why a piece's opening, or lead, is so important. But do not let concern over how you will begin become a stumbling block. Many writers find that leaving the opening for the last stages of revision works best.

5.8

The power of effective openings.

If appropriate for a particular writing assignment, you can be inventive in your opening paragraph. To grab a reader's attention, try starting your lead with an anecdote or story, quotation, dialogue, or descriptive scene. For example, Kirsten decided to begin with dialogue. Note that in her revised opening, Kirsten also corrected the punctuation for dialogue.

Revision Checklist

Your response to each question should be "yes." If not, you need to go back and revise in that area.

Focus

- Do my thesis, paragraphs, and topic sentences all work together and deal with the same topic?

Coherence

- Have I used transitional words and phrases to provide the glue that holds various parts of the paper together?

Organization

- Does each part of the paper flow logically from the pre-ceding part?
- Have I reserved my strongest arguments for last?

Development

- Have I used examples, facts, and source support to rein-force each major point in the paper?

Tone

- Is my tone consistent throughout the paper?

Format

- Is the format appropriate to the content?

"Look at this new CD I bought!" Jane exclaims to her friend. Interested, Michael eagerly looks at it. "Wow," he says. "These guys are my favorite group! Mind if I make a copy of it?"

Although some academic writing, by tradition, demands it, most experienced writers will not begin a piece with the thesis, or statement of purpose, such as "This paper will explore the pros and cons of drilling an auxiliary well in Smithfield Canyon." The following example illustrates a traditional academic lead.

This essay examines issues of diversity and literacy education primarily in terms of the concept of *difference* via a new term: *non-*

negotiable difference. It argues that networked classrooms provide writing instructors with unique extra-linguistic cues (body language) that can help teachers and students become more responsive to racial difference.

—Todd Taylor, "The Persistence of *Difference* in Networked Classrooms: *Non-Negotiable Difference*"

(See also 6h-1.)

Closings or conclusions

A conclusion usually takes the form of a summary, which points the reader back to the text itself, or speculation, which points the reader outside of the text.

A SUMMARY CONCLUSION

Few Interneters would disagree that stealing and reselling software or credit cards is wrong. But fewer still would feel guilty about copying the latest game version of Doom, or some such, rather than forking out $39.95. Unfortunately, that often admirable ethos makes it easier for genuine crooks to perpetrate—and justify—their crimes.

—Michael Meyer and Anne Underwood, "Crimes of the 'Net'"

A SPECULATIVE CONCLUSION

Nevertheless, in the litigations and political debates which are certain to follow, we will endeavor to assure that their electronic speech is protected as certainly as any opinions which are printed or, for that matter, screamed. We will make an effort to clarify issues surrounding the distribution of intellectual property. And we will help to create for America a future which is as blessed by the Bill of Rights as its past has been.

—John Perry Barlow, "Crime and Puzzlement"

Do not feel obligated to limit yourself to a summary conclusion. Sometimes a speculative conclusion will work better. This type of conclusion is most appropriate for papers that point the reader in a new direction, that reflect on the implications of some topic, or that suggest the need for further research. (See also 6h-2.)

Titles

Because the title is the first thing a reader sees, it must spark interest in the reader. The title helps the reader anticipate the topic and perhaps the writer's particular point of view. Kirsten's title, "Net Theft," is

descriptive and intriguing, if not particularly clever. It is more important that the title be related to the content than that it be cute or funny.

EXERCISE 5.2

> Try out several titles and openings for your piece. Be inventive and
> playful. To catch your reader's attention, write an opening scene,
> describe a character, tell a story, give a startling fact or statistic, or make
> an outrageous claim. Then try out several possible conclusions for your
> piece. Write both a summary conclusion and a speculative conclusion.

FOR COLLABORATION

> Share your titles, openings, and closings with a peer or a small group
> of classmates. Which titles and openings do they find most effec-
> tive? Do they prefer the summary conclusion or the speculative con-
> clusion? Write down any suggestions you receive from your peers.

5c Edit

When editing a text, the writer's goal is to make it easier to read.
During revision, you concentrate on making the piece focused, organized, and well developed. During editing, you concentrate on refining
words and sentences. Like a car buff putting the final finish on a classic automobile, an editor "finishes" a piece of writing—in general,
refining what has been done and making it aesthetically pleasing as
well as functional.

As with revising, it is important for writers to distance themselves
from their words before editing and become objective readers of their
own writing. Listening to the words as the text is read aloud helps you
to see where you need to clarify an idea or where you may have used
too many words or expressed thoughts awkwardly. The Editing
Checklist on page 98 refers to sections that can help you correct specific problems.

1 Checking sentence structure

As you edit your draft, make sure that your sentences are structured according to the conventions of academic writing. Over the
years, scholars have developed a standard formal English used for academic writing. Following the conventions of Standard Edited English
will mark you as an educated, careful writer.

Editing Checklist

Sentence Structure

- Are all of my sentences complete? (Ch. 35)
- Have I avoided both comma splices and run-on sentences? (Ch. 36)
- Do paired elements have parallel structures? (Ch. 42)

Wordiness

- Have I avoided using unnecessary words, such as *in order to* instead of simply *to*? (Ch. 40)
- Have I replaced two-word and three-word phrases, such as *new innovation* and *repeating recurrence*, where one word is sufficient? (Ch. 44)

Repetition

- Have I avoided excessive use of a single word? (Ch. 44)
- Have I avoided repetition of a single idea that is not the thesis? (Ch. 44)

Verb Usage

- Have I primarily used active rather than passive voice? (32g)
- Have I replaced overused, general verbs with more vivid, specific verbs where possible? (45a)

Other Errors

- Is my end punctuation correct? (Ch. 50)
- Is my internal punctuation correct? (commas, Ch. 51; semicolons, Ch. 52; colons, Ch. 53)
- Have I used quotation marks appropriately? (Ch. 55)
- Have I used other punctuation marks appropriately? (Ch. 56)
- Is my spelling correct? (Ch. 44)
- Are my mechanics correct? (capitals and italics, Ch. 57; abbreviations and numbers, Ch. 58; hyphens, Ch. 59)

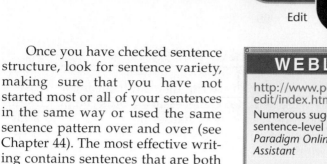

Once you have checked sentence structure, look for sentence variety, making sure that you have not started most or all of your sentences in the same way or used the same sentence pattern over and over (see Chapter 44). The most effective writing contains sentences that are both clear and varied. Adding an introductory phrase to one sentence or moving a clause in another will help you achieve variety. Notice how Kirsten revised these sentences.

WEBLINK

http://www.powa.org/edit/index.html

Numerous suggestions for sentence-level editing, from *Paradigm Online Writing Assistant*

5.9

Specific suggestions for sentence-level editing.

Blood rushes to your ears and your heart begins to pound, as your body reacts to the rush of adrenaline. Casting a nervous glance around the nearby aisles,ₐ *you decide that* the coast is clear.ₐ E̶x̶t̶e̶n̶d̶i̶n̶g̶ *You extend* your arm, y̶o̶u̶ grab the orange tiger, -a̶n̶d̶ place it in your backpackₐ *, and* then walk nonchalantly towards̶ the exit.

HELP

How do I check sentence structure?

1. Scroll up from the end of the document, reading it backwards sentence by sentence.
2. Use the SEARCH function.
   a. Ask the computer to search for each period in the document (begin either at the start or at the end of the document).
   b. Each time you stop at a period, look carefully at the group of words that precedes it to be sure they form a complete sentence. If you are not sure, see Chapter 30 on sentence structure.
   c. Use the SEARCH function to review the other punctuation by locating first the commas and then the semicolons. See Chapters 50–56 for advice on punctuation.

5.10

Step-by-step instructions for checking sentence structure on a computer.

2 Checking for wordiness

Many writers tend to overwrite their drafts, using a phrase or clause when a word will do. Unnecessary words can obscure the meaning or make the reader work harder than necessary to understand it. These three examples show how Kirsten edited sentences in her draft for wordiness.

Unfortunately, this is a common request ~~within our society~~ today.

[Kirsten omitted three words that convey no additional meaning.]

Not only ~~are these~~ *is this* ^practices~~ wrong from a moral^, *standpoint* ~~viewpoint~~, but legally, ~~they are~~ *it is* forbidden as well. [By using pronouns to refer back to the previous sentence, Kirsten eliminated wordiness.]

Walking into a store and taking something without paying for it is obviously not^ *legal.* ~~encouraged in our society.~~ [Again, Kirsten omitted words that convey no additional meaning.]

5.11
How to use a computer to check for unnecessary repetition.

3 Checking for repetition

Repeating words is not necessarily a bad thing. Using a key term more than once in a text may help you achieve coherence (see 6c-2). However, you do not want to use nonessential words repeatedly. Notice that Kirsten deleted the nonessential word *society* twice as she edited her draft sentences (see 5c-2).

4 Checking for verb usage

Weak verbs can lead to ineffective writing. Review your verbs to be certain that they are appropriate and effective. Kirsten edited the verbs in one of her final paragraphs as follows:

The problem, as Meyer and Underwood also point out, is that the "Wild West culture of the Internet promotes an anything goes attitude in Net surfers" (113). Most Internet users^ *would agree* ~~think~~ that stealing

HELP

How do I check for overuse of specific words or terms?

1. Make a list of words that you suspect you may have overused.
2. Use the SEARCH function of your word-processing program to find each instance of each word in your document.
3. Use the THESAURUS function to help you think of alternative wording.
4. Be sure you are familiar with any word you decide to use from the thesaurus so that you use it appropriately for the context.

5.12
Step-by-step instructions for checking for overuse of words or terms.

phone card numbers and selling them is wrong. However, many would not
agree
~~think~~ that sharing a pirated copy of a game was illegal or even
find
wrong. Similarly, many would not ~~think~~ that using a cool graphic
from
~~found on~~ someone else's page was unethical or illegal. The
considers
freewheeling world of the Internet ~~finds~~ capitalist rules like
to be
"copyright" offensive.

5 Checking for other errors

In addition to editing for *style*, you will want to edit your text for usage, punctuation, spelling, and mechanics. To be acceptable in college courses as well as in most work settings, your writing must conform to the conventions of Standard Edited English. As the writer, you are responsible for making the text comprehensible as well as technically correct. Use the Editing Checklist on page 98 to help you as you edit your work.

(EXERCISE 5.3)

Edit your text, using a combination of strategies outlined in this section. Refer to the sections of the handbook referenced in the Editing Checklist for help; see also Chapter 29. When you have finished editing, run your word-processing program's grammar checker. Consider its advice carefully before making changes to your text.

5d   Proofread

AUDIO
Proofread for
accuracy and
correctness.

Proofreading is the final phase in rewriting. At this stage of the process, writers look closely for distracting punctuation and mechanical errors that will interfere with the reader's understanding. Proofreading prematurely, before there is a final, edited draft, may cause you to overlook important revision and editing issues, in addition to wasting a lot of time. By proofreading after revising and editing, you can concentrate on details related to manuscript preparation, such as typographical errors, missing words, and irregular spacing, as well as errors in punctuation that you may have missed in earlier stages.

WWW

5.13
Additional
suggestions for
proofreading.

WEBLINK

http://www.ualr.edu/
owl/proofreading.htm

Tips on proofreading,
including a useful list of
suggestions

Some writers prefer to proofread on the computer screen. However, recent studies have shown that writers who read their texts onscreen may not see them as clearly or read them as carefully. Also, proofreading requires reading each word carefully, and doing so on a computer screen can be tiring to the eyes. If you choose to proof-

HELP

WWW

5.14
Step-by-step
instructions
on using a
computer to
proofread.

How do I use the computer to become a more effective proofreader?

1. When proofreading onscreen, use the cursor arrow to scroll down one line at a time, forcing yourself to read each line slowly before reading the next one.
2. Use the VIEW menu to see the text one full page at a time by selecting the FULL PAGE option.
3. View the text two pages at a time, displayed side by side on the monitor.
4. Move the cursor to the end of the text, and read the sentences in reverse order.
5. Read the text aloud from the screen, slowing down as necessary to attend to the text more closely.
6. If you have a text-reading program, instruct the computer to do the reading aloud, and then listen for errors.

Proofreading Strategies

1. Scroll rapidly through your text to check for spacing, margins, indents, widows and orphans (single lines and words left alone at the top or bottom of a page), page numbering, and so on.

2. Print the text; wait several hours, or longer if possible, before proofreading it.

3. Use a pointer or ruler to force yourself to read slowly and deliberately.

4. Proofread the text several times; each time, you will pick up additional errors.

5. Change your reading technique to a proofreading one. Normal reading involves skimming; a typical reader "reads" only two or three words per line. In contrast, proofreading requires that you look carefully at every word and punctuation mark.

6. Ask someone else—a friend, a relative, or a classmate—to proofread the printed text as well.

read onscreen, take frequent breaks. Experiment with your own proofreading technique, which may be a combination of onscreen and printout proofreading.

EXERCISE 5.4

Proofread your text, using the suggestions in the Proofreading Strategies box above to read it both onscreen and in print. Evaluate which method seems to work better for you. Were you able to identify more errors or different errors with either method?

WEBLINK

http://www.lynchburg.edu/writcntr/guide/drafting/proofing.htm

A good plain-text handout on proofreading strategies

5.15

Tips for proofreading.

5e Give and receive feedback

When you participate in peer response groups, you are taking part in a writing tradition that is as old as writing itself—writers helping fel-

low writers. We (the authors of this handbook) also participate in writing groups in which we share work with our colleagues, giving and receiving feedback on our professional writing. In fact, we are so much in the habit of gathering feedback on our written work that we feel uncomfortable with the idea of sending anything for publication before it has received a reading from at least one other person, whether that person is a member of our writing group, a coauthor, or an editor. Preferably we would gain reader responses from a number of readers for each piece of writing we do. When gathering other opinions remember that, ultimately, the piece of writing is your own and the feedback that you receive should be taken in the spirit of help offered. Comments from readers should not dictate to you the "right" way to write a piece.

The actual processes used to exchange drafts within a writing group or a peer response group will vary. For example, in our professional writing group, we share our work first with the group via email attachments. Then, before we meet in person, we all read and comment on the written drafts, using handwritten notes in the margins or typed document comments (see the Help box on page 105). Some instructors will follow a similar model by using the Internet to have peers share their drafts, either via email or local area networks (LANs; see the discussion in 21b-4). Other instructors prefer to have students use read-around groups during class time. In read-around group sessions, groups of three or four students sit in a circle and read their drafts out loud to each other one at a time. While a draft is being read, group members take notes about what they are hearing (for some suggestions on how to respond, see 5e-1).

The instructor may also comment on early drafts and make revision suggestions. Or students may be asked to take their papers to a writing center, where a tutor will read them and offer suggestions. As a writer, you will find it helpful to receive feedback on your work from a variety of sources. Such feedback allows you to become increasingly sensitive to the needs of your readers.

1 Giving feedback

Peer review gives students in a writing class a sense of audience. A peer reviewer can tell you whether he or she understands the purpose, whether the thesis is clear, and whether the supporting evidence is sufficient. But a peer's response is only as helpful as it is sincere. Just telling a peer that the writing is "good" is not particularly useful. As a peer reviewer, you can be most helpful by showing interest in and enthusiasm for the work and by questioning and constructively commenting on the piece.

HELP

How do I insert comments into a word-processed document?

Most word-processing programs will allow you to insert comments into a document that you are reading.

1. Commenting in *Microsoft Word:*

To establish your identity, choose OPTIONS from the TOOLS menu. Under the USER INFORMATION tab, fill in your name and your initials. These will show up along with your comments. Make sure that SHOW HIGHLIGHT and SCREEN TIPS are both checked on the VIEW tab on the OPTIONS screen.

To insert a comment, choose COMMENT from the INSERT menu. A comment box will appear at the bottom of your screen. Type in your comment and close the comment box when finished. Your comment will not interfere with the text itself; rather, the presence of a comment will be indicated by highlighted words in your text. The comment inside a box will open when the mouse is held over the highlighted words. You can EDIT or DELETE your comments by using a mouse click (right click for PCs). You can also view all comments by selecting VIEW > COMMENTS from the VIEW menu or print the comments by selecting COMMENTS from the "print what" line on the print dialogue box.

2. Commenting in *WordPerfect:*

To establish your identity, choose TOOLS > SETTINGS>ENVIRONMENT. You can include your name and initials, and you can also select a color in which your comments will appear in the document. Choose CREATE COMMENT from the INSERT menu and type your comment in the window. When you close the window, your comments appear as marginal icons that will open when you click on them. As with *Word,* comments can also be edited, viewed, and printed.

NOTE: Your commenting options may differ slightly from these, depending on the word-processing software you are using.

VIDEO

Inserting comments into documents.

5.16

How to insert comments into a document.

In order to respond appropriately, you should first read the entire draft, looking for global (general) features of organization and development. In a first reading, try to establish what you take to be the

VIDEO
Peer reviews.

writer's rhetorical stance (see 3b-2). During a second reading, make specific comments on the finer points (such as style and mechanics). Comments should be phrased as praise, suggestions, and questions, not as barbed criticisms. Learning to be a sensitive peer reviewer will help you to be a better writer; to respond appropriately, you must put yourself in the writer's shoes.

The instructor may provide a list of questions or prompts to use as you read a peer's paper. If so, try to address each item completely and candidly. Here are some ways in which you can respond generally (globally) and specifically (locally) to a peer's writing.

Responding globally

On the first reading, respond to the overall piece of writing, looking for the writer's rhetorical stance and global features of development and organization.

1. The writer's purpose, persona, and audience seem to be . . .
2. I identify with . . .
3. I like . . .
4. I wonder about . . .
5. I suggest . . .

Guidelines for Giving Peer Feedback

1. Read the piece through carefully, noting first what you take to be the writer's rhetorical stance: his or her intended purpose, persona, and audience.

2. Formulate your comments, phrasing them as suggestions and questions, not as criticisms. Remember, you are reading a draft, not a finished product.

3. Respond globally and then locally with both general and specific suggestions for revisions. It is not helpful to the writer if you just say "this is good" without saying why you think so.

4. Give positive feedback and praise where appropriate. It is important that you be sincere in your comments.

5. Respond completely to any prompts provided by the instructor. Follow the specified process for commenting: handwriting comments in the margins, typing document comments, or making verbal comments in a read-around group.

Responding locally

On the second reading, respond to specific features of the text.

1. Are the ideas understandable, and is the logic clear?
2. Is the writing style appropriate and the tone consistent?
3. Is the sentence structure correct?
4. Is the writing concise?
5. Are the verbs vigorous and active?
6. Are the sentences clear and easy to read?
7. Is the punctuation correct?
8. Is the format appropriate and the font readable?

2 Receiving feedback

Prior to exchanging drafts, list any specific concerns you have about the draft on which you would like some reader feedback. When comments are returned to you, read them with an open mind. Just as you need to criticize the work of peers with a generous spirit, you also need to receive criticism without becoming defensive. Remember that

Guidelines for Receiving Peer Feedback

1. Provide your peer reviewer with a list of any specific concerns you have about your draft on which you would like some reader feedback.
2. Read your peer's comments with an open mind, without becoming defensive.
3. Some comments may be confusing or ambiguous. If you don't understand your peer's comments, ask for an explanation before revising.
4. Accept only those comments that will help you to improve your piece. Remember that you retain the ownership of your writing.
5. Reject any comments that seem to be leading you off in a direction that you did not intend.
6. Write down a specific plan for revising your draft and/or write a revision outline.

5.17

Step-by-step instructions for reviewing a peer's work.

you can learn a great deal from others who read your work. Try to get enough distance from your own writing so that you do not take comments personally. Your peer is reviewing your *writing*, not you personally. Not all feedback you receive will be useful. Take it with a grain of salt—another's opinion may simply differ from yours. Once you have read and absorbed the peer comments, write down a specific plan for revising your draft. (See 5a-3 on preparing a revision outline.)

FOR COLLABORATION

Exchange drafts with a peer, either on paper, by email, or via your class's LAN. Read your peer's work straight through once, with an eye toward global features such as purpose, audience, and tone. Then, read it again carefully before commenting. If you are reading onscreen, use the word processor's commenting feature (see the Help box on page 105).

5f Review a model student paper

5.18

View two model student essays.

Consider the revised version of Kirsten's essay on Net theft. Kirsten followed her revision outline as she rewrote this piece (see pages 88–89). As you compare the first draft (in Chapter 4) with this draft, notice that Kirsten worked hard to better organize and focus her piece. She worked particularly hard on parts II and IV of her outline, where the paper had begun to fall apart in her earlier draft. She also edited sentences to make them clearer and proofread carefully to catch grammatical and mechanical errors.

It is a truism in the writing field that there are no finished pieces of writing, only deadlines. Any piece can be revised and improved. In what ways do you think this draft is an improvement over Kirsten's first draft? Are there elements Kirsten could still work on to make them more effective?

Parsons 1

Kirsten Parsons

Professor Hines

English 101-35

15 September 2003

Net Theft

"Look at this new CD I bought!" Jane exclaims
to her friend. Interested, Michael eagerly looks at
it. "Wow," he says. "These guys are my favorite
group! Mind if I make a copy of it?"

Unfortunately, this is a common request today.
In spite of laws that prohibit unlicensed copying,
in some circles it has become an accepted practice
to reproduce another's work without paying for it.
Similarly, this practice has spread to the Internet,
where access to music, software, written texts, and
graphics is convenient and fast. These items can be
copied for personal use with ease, but often no
credit is given to the original author. Not only is
this wrong from a moral standpoint, but legally, it
is forbidden as well. It has become a situation
where "legality collides with practicality" (Meyer
and Underwood 113). In other words, breaking the law
is more convenient than obeying it, and since we
know we can get away with doing it, our conscience
gives in. When it comes to "borrowing" information

Student and course identification

Opening scenario

Introduction

Print source: authors and page number

Thesis

from the Internet, we are gradually becoming a people who accept lawbreaking as long as we can participate, too.

Compare to shoplifting

I'm sure all of us once glimpsed a tempting item in a store and, after getting "no" for an answer from Mom or Dad, took matters into our own hands, sneaking the treasure into a hidden pocket. It probably took only a few moments for your parents to notice something was up. I remember well a discussion about why taking the package was wrong. Then my Dad took me back to the store, where an apology was made and my Strawberry Hubba Bubba Bubblegum was paid for.

Definition of Net theft

Walking into a store and taking something without paying for it is obviously not legal; ironically, this principle seems to break down where the Net is concerned. With available technology, Net theft is commonplace. Written texts, software, graphics, and music all are vulnerable to cyber-shoplifting. Though it is not encouraged per se, it is not really discouraged either. Isn't this just stealing masked by softer adjectives such as "sharing" or "borrowing"? Granted it is less noticeable, but that doesn't change the fact that you didn't pay for it.

Parsons 3

Part of the problem is that the physical element involved in actually traveling to a store and taking something is not necessary for these Net crimes. Imagine walking down the aisle of the local Wal-Mart with the intention of stealing a Hobbes doll, your favorite cartoon character. Blood rushes to your ears and your heart begins to pound, as your body reacts to the rush of adrenaline. Casting a nervous glance around the nearby aisles, you decide that the coast is clear. You extend your arm, grab the orange tiger, place it in your backpack, and then walk nonchalantly toward the exit. Then the alarm goes off and you are caught holding the goods!

Compare difficulty of each crime

This scenario is only possible in a physical world. Because the Net is so unphysical, the risk of being caught, which may serve to deter many thieves in a store, is minimal. Net theft is committed within the reach of the refrigerator! Imagine that while Net surfing you find a "Calvin and Hobbes" cartoon on a commercial Web site. You think it would look great on your homepage. With a click of the mouse, you grab the graphic and paste it onto your own page. Who has ever heard of someone being arrested for copying a graphic? Because Net crimes often go ignored, and "everyone" is guilty, more and

Net theft is easy to commit

Parsons 4

more people engage in them. The consequences seem to be less punitive, and thus we give in to the influence of the Wild Net.

Organizations and individuals have tried to establish standards of conduct for Internet use. For example, the Computer Ethics Institute wrote its Ten Commandments for Computer Ethics, which includes such obvious "rules" as "Thou shalt not use the computer to steal" (Roach). But what is stealing when it comes to materials found on the Internet? The Copyright Website asserts that any texts or graphics that you find on the Internet are by their very nature published and thus are "copyrighted" (O'Mahoney). This means that in order to use anything from someone else's Web site, you need their permission. If you put a comic strip such as "Calvin and Hobbes" onto your homepage, you run the risk of being sued for violation of copyright.

The problem, as Meyer and Underwood also point out, is that the "Wild West culture of the Internet promotes an anything goes attitude in Net surfers" (113). Most Internet users would agree that stealing phone card numbers and selling them is wrong. However, many would not agree that sharing a pirated copy of a game was illegal or even wrong. Similarly, many would not find that using a cool graphic from

Standards of conduct

Online source without page number

Summary of the conflict

Parsons 5

someone else's page was unethical or illegal. The
freewheeling world of the Internet considers
capitalist rules like "copyright" to be offensive.

In the tangled world of the Internet, not all   Conclusion
of the new dilemmas that have surfaced will be
solved immediately. However, if the definition of a
criminal is one who has committed a crime, then in
the world of the Net, perhaps we all need to serve
some time.

Parsons 6

Works Cited

Meyer, Michael, and Anne Underwood. "Crimes of the   Print source
    'Net.'" CyberReader. Ed. Victor Vitanza. 2nd ed.
    Boston: Allyn, 1999. 111-13.

O'Mahoney, Benedict. The Copyright Website. 2002.   Online
    1 Sept. 2002 <http://www.benedict.com>.   source:
                                                        Web site

Roach, Kitty. PageWorks. 2 Jan. 2001. 1 Sept. 2002   Online
    <http://www.snowcrest.net/kitty/hpages>.   source:
                                                        Web site

Structuring Paragraphs

AUDIO

Chapter overview.

6.1

Writing paragraphs from start to finish.

A **paragraph** is a sentence or group of sentences that develops a main idea. Paragraphs serve as the primary building blocks of essays, reports, memos, and other forms of written composition. In Shakespeare's time, a single paragraph could go on for pages, but English paragraphs have evolved into shorter and shorter units. This trend seems likely to continue, as it is now common to find paragraphs of only one or two sentences in news reports, advertisements, memos, and Internet communications.

WEBLINK

http://www.uottawa.ca/academic/arts/writcent/hypergrammar/paragrph.html

An excellent Web guide to writing and revising paragraphs

Well-written paragraphs facilitate quick skimming and help readers stay focused on the main ideas so that they can understand and evaluate the text. To promote this kind of readability, paragraphs should be unified, coherent, and adequately developed, while flowing from one to the next as smoothly as possible.

6a Write unified paragraphs

A **unified paragraph** focuses on and develops a single main idea. This idea is typically captured in a single sentence, called a *topic sentence*. The other sentences in the paragraph, the *supporting sentences*, should elaborate on the topic sentence in a logical fashion.

VIDEO
Achieving para-
graph unity.

1 Using a topic sentence

A **topic sentence** gives readers a quick idea of what the paragraph as a whole is about. It is a good idea to place the topic sentence at the beginning of a paragraph, where it provides a preview of the rest of the paragraph. A topic sentence should, if possible, do four things: (1) provide a transition from the preceding paragraph, (2) introduce the topic of the paragraph, (3) make a main point about this topic, and (4) suggest how the rest of the paragraph will develop this point.

> During the past decade or two, children have slipped into poverty faster than any other age group. One of six white U.S. children, two of every five Latino children, and almost one of every two African-American children are poor. These figures translate into incredible numbers—approximately *18 million* children live in poverty: 9 million white children, 4 million Latino children, and 5 million African-American children.
>
> —James M. Henslin, *Sociology*

The opening sentence of this paragraph establishes the topic (child poverty in the United States), makes a main point about it (the percentage of individuals living in poverty is growing more quickly for children than any other age group), and allows the reader to guess that the rest of the paragraph will provide evidence supporting this point.

In a series of paragraphs, the first sentence of each paragraph should serve as a transition from the preceding paragraph. Often, you can make the first sentence both a topic sentence and a linking sentence, as it is in this example (a continuation of the preceding example).

> According to sociologist and U.S. Senator Daniel Moynihan, this high rate of child poverty is due primarily to a general breakdown of the U.S. family. He points his finger at the sharp increase in births outside marriage. In 1960, only 5 percent of U.S. children were born to unmarried mothers. Today that figure is *six times higher;* and single women now account for 30 percent of all U.S. births. The relationship to social class is striking, for births to unmarried mothers are not dis-

tributed evenly across the social classes. For women above the poverty line, only 6 percent of births are to single mothers, while for women below the poverty line this rate jumps to 44 percent.

—James M. Henslin, *Sociology*

The expression "this high rate of child poverty" restates the main topic of the preceding paragraph and thus links the two paragraphs. The topic sentence immediately expresses a new idea ("is due primarily to a general breakdown of the U.S. family"), which represents the main point of this paragraph. The rest of the paragraph supports this point with relevant statistics.

2 Placing the topic sentence

The paragraph opening is not always the best location for a topic sentence. Sometimes writers use the first sentence of a paragraph to provide a transition, making the second sentence the topic sentence.

The new knowledge that civilization is much older and more widespread than was previously believed is understandably producing much new scholarly writing, with massive reassessment of earlier archeological theories. But the centrally striking fact that in these first civilizations ideology was gynocentric has not, except among feminist scholars, generated much interest. If mentioned by nonfeminist scholars, it is usually in passing. Even those who, like Mellaart, do mention it, generally do so only as a matter of purely artistic and religious significance, without probing its social and cultural implications.

—Riane Eisler, *The Chalice and the Blade*

The topic of this paragraph ("in these first civilizations ideology was gynocentric") is introduced not in the opening sentence but in the second sentence. The first sentence serves a transitional function, connecting this paragraph to the one preceding it. The goal here, as always with paragraphing, is to help the reader stay focused on the flow of the main ideas. This is as important in the brief paragraphs of a typical email message as it is in longer paragraphs like the examples above.

Occasionally a topic sentence falls at the end of a paragraph, either as a summary or as a restatement of a topic sentence appearing earlier in the paragraph.

Analytical, creative, and practical thinking often are used together. For example, consider the question of why people become depressed. You would use analytical thinking to evaluate the quality of a theory of why people become depressed. You would use creative thinking to come up with your own theory of why people become depressed. But because you would draw on other people's thoughts, you would necessarily combine analytical and creative thinking. You would use practical thinking to decide how to help someone who is depressed come out of his or her depression. But in order to help the person, you would need to analyze which theory of depression to use and you would have to formulate your own ideas about how to help the person. <u>So, in thinking as a student of psychology and helping someone, you would combine the three kinds of thinking: analytical, creative, and practical.</u>

—Robert J. Sternberg, *Pathways to Psychology*

Sometimes no topic sentence is needed. If a paragraph continues the topic covered in the preceding paragraph or simply narrates a series of events or a set of details whose common theme is obvious, you may decide that an explicit topic statement is unnecessary. In Internet messages, especially email, using short topic sentences and tightly linked paragraphs will help you to avoid the conversational tendency to ramble on with an unfocused message.

(**EXERCISE 6.1**)

Open one of your textbooks to the beginning of a section and examine the first five paragraphs. Do they all seem unified? Does each paragraph have a topic sentence? If so, where is it located?

(**EXERCISE 6.2**)

1. Examine the paragraphs in Kirsten Parsons's paper (pages 109–113). Do they all have topic sentences? Are the topic sentences properly positioned? Are they well worded? Could some of them be improved? If so, how?
2. See how paragraphs appear in Internet settings. Start by looking at how a topic that interests you is presented in listserv messages; then compare these messages with Usenet discussions on the same topic. Is the topic sentence or main idea more obvious in the Usenet discussions or the listserv messages?

6b Write coherent paragraphs with clear patterns of organization

All paragraphs should be *coherent:* each sentence should connect logically with those preceding and following it. Readers are able to move smoothly from one idea to the next when writers construct coherent paragraphs. One way to create coherent paragraphs is through the use of organizational patterns.

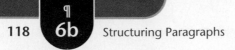

HELP

How do I connect my ideas in a coherent way?

If you have problems connecting ideas and making paragraphs, try outlining the topics and subtopics within a section of your first draft (see 5a-3).

1. From within the first-draft document, open the function that provides numbered or lettered lists (usually called OUTLINE).

2. Find your first topic idea, and list it as main heading 1. If you have a second and third main idea following the first, list them as main headings 2 and 3.

3. Find ideas that support or expand on each main heading. List these as subheads a, b, and so on. Ideas subordinate to these subtopics can be listed as (1), (2), and so on.

4. Survey the outline for connections between the main items. How can you use the subheads to build a phrase or sentence that will connect to the next main heading?

5. Finally, write full paragraphs based on your outline, constructing or combining sentences so that they flow in the order of the outline.

6.2

Paragraph patterns graded by difficulty and utility.

Among the countless ways to organize paragraphs, certain patterns are especially common: general to specific, cause and effect, comparison or contrast, definition, classification, problem and solution, narrative or process description, exemplification, and physical description. These organizational patterns mirror typical ways people categorize experience. Readers look for familiar patterns, so the more explicitly you signal those patterns, the easier it will be for readers to see the logic connecting your ideas.

1 Organizing by general to specific

The sample paragraphs in 6a-1 both illustrate general-to-specific organization, in which a general statement is followed by specific supporting details. This is one of the most common paragraph patterns, and the general statement serves effectively as a topic sentence. Here is another example of general-to-specific ordering.

Every society creates an idealized image of the future—a vision that serves as a beacon to direct the imagination and energy of its people. The ancient Jewish nation prayed for deliverance to a promised land of milk and honey. Later, Christian clerics held out the promise of eternal salvation in the heavenly kingdom. In the modern age, the idea of a future technological utopia has served as the guiding vision of industrial society. For more than a century utopian dreamers and men and women of science and letters have looked to a future world where machines would replace human labor, creating a near-workerless society of abundance and leisure.

—Jeremy Rifkin, *The End of Work*

This paragraph leads off a chapter in Rifkin's book called "Visions of Techno-Paradise." Rifkin uses the general-to-specific pattern to first situate his discussion in universal terms ("every society") and then narrow his focus to the "near-workerless society" that will be the subject of the chapter.

It is possible, though much less common, to organize a paragraph in the reverse order—that is, from specific to general. The specific details grab the reader's attention, and are followed by increasingly more general comments culminating in a summarizing statement.

2 Organizing by cause and effect

Many pieces of writing link phenomena through cause-and-effect relationships. The cause-and-effect organizational pattern is especially appropriate for explaining why something happened the way it did or predicting some future sequence of events. Paragraphs organized with this pattern usually include transitional words and phrases such as *therefore, thus, as a result, since, because, consequently, for this reason,* and *thereby.* Two of these are italicized in this example.

Fetal alcohol syndrome (FAS) occurs when alcohol ingested by the mother passes through the placenta into the infant's bloodstream. *Because* the fetus is so small, its blood alcohol concentration will be much higher than that of its mother. *Thus,* consumption of alcohol during pregnancy can affect the infant far more seriously than it does the mother. Among the symptoms of FAS are mental retardation, small head, tremors, and abnormalities of the face, limbs, heart, and brain.

—Rebecca J. Donatelle and Lorraine G. Davis, *Access to Health*

3 Organizing by comparison or contrast

Many writing situations call for comparing or contrasting two or more ideas, issues, items, or events. Comparison focuses on similarities; contrast focuses on differences. In either case, the writer evaluates two or more subjects on the basis of one or more criteria. Transitional words and phrases commonly found in comparison or contrast paragraphs include *however, on the one hand/on the other hand, similarly, in contrast, just as, while, but,* and *like.*

A paragraph based on the comparison or contrast pattern should be structured either (1) by evaluating one subject completely and then turning to the other or (2) by focusing on each criterion, one at a time. For example, in a comparison of the two sociological theories known as structural functionalism and conflict theory, arrangement by *subject* might look like this:

> *Subject A:* Structural functionalism
>> *Criterion 1:* How it views society
>> *Criterion 2:* What it emphasizes
> *Subject B:* Conflict theory
>> *Criterion 1:* How it views society
>> *Criterion 2:* What it emphasizes

Arrangement by *criteria,* on the other hand, would look like this:

> *Criterion 1:* How it views society
>> *Subject A:* Structural functionalism views society as . . .
>> *Subject B:* Conflict theory views society as . . .
> *Criterion 2:* What it emphasizes
>> *Subject A:* Structural functionalism emphasizes . . .
>> *Subject B:* Conflict theory emphasizes . . .

AUDIO

Multiple paragraph patterns working together.

Which type of structural arrangement is better? It depends on where you want to focus the reader's attention—on the subjects or on the criteria.

The following paragraph is organized according to subject. The liberal view of affirmative action is contrasted to the conservative view, and the criteria used (such as group fairness and individual fairness) are secondary. (Italics are added.)

> The role of affirmative action in our multicultural society lies at the center of a national debate about how to steer a course in race and ethnic relations. In this policy, quotas based on race (and gender) are used in hiring and college admissions. Most liberals, both white and minority, defend affirmative action, saying that it is the most direct way to level the playing field of economic opportunity. If white males are passed over, this is an unfortunate cost we must pay if we are to make up for past and present discrimination. Most con-

servatives, *in contrast,* both white and minority, agree that opportunity should be open to all, but say that putting race (or sex) ahead of people's ability to perform a job is reverse discrimination. They add that affirmative action stigmatizes the people who benefit from it because it suggests that they hold their jobs because of race (or sex), rather than merit.

—Adapted from James M. Henslin, *Sociology*

4 Organizing by definition

In academic writing, defining important new terms sometimes requires a complete paragraph. The term is usually introduced in a topic sentence at the beginning of the paragraph and elaborated on in the sentences that follow. Here is a typical example of a paragraph organized by definition, from an introductory biology textbook.

Nucleic acids are large complex organic molecules composed of carbon, oxygen, hydrogen, nitrogen, and phosphorus atoms. Nucleic acids are polymers of individual monomers known as *nucleotides*. Nucleotides are molecules built up from three basic parts: a special 5-carbon sugar, a phosphate group, and a molecule generally known as a nitrogenous base. Individual nucleotides can be linked together by covalent bonds to form a polynucleotide. There are two basic kinds of nucleic acids: *ribonucleic acid (RNA),* which contains the sugar ribose, and *deoxyribonucleic acid (DNA),* which contains the sugar deoxyribose. Despite their name, nucleic acids are not strongly acidic.

—Kenneth R. Miller and Joseph Levine, *Biology*

A paragraph organized by definition should include a formal definition—that is, a statement "*X* is a *Y* that _____," where *X* is the *term* being defined, *Y* is the *class* it belongs to, and _____ is a set of *distinguishing features*. In the above example, such a definition is found in the first sentence: "Nucleic acids are large complex organic molecules composed of carbon, oxygen, hydrogen, nitrogen, and phosphorus atoms."

(EXERCISE 6.3)

Search the Web to find an interesting article of at least 300 words in a newspaper or other source. Download it. Then use the SEARCH function of your word processor to locate all instances of *however, on the one hand/on the other hand, similarly, in contrast, just as, while, but,* and *like.* In each case, identify the subjects that are being compared.

5 Organizing by classification

To make sense of the world, people routinely classify things according to their characteristic parts. Classification is an essential part of the analytic work you do in school. Whenever you search the Internet or a library, for example, you focus your quest by using a search system that classifies topics in helpful categories. In academic writing, an entire paragraph is often devoted to classifying some concept. Paragraphs organized by classification normally introduce the topic in the first sentence and the various subtopics in the following sentences. Using these subtopics as the grammatical subjects of their respective sentences, as in this example, creates grammatical parallelism (see 6e), which makes it easy for readers to see the structure of the paragraph.

The United States Army traces its origin to the American Continental Army of 1775. The Army has primary responsibility for military operations on land. Its basic combat units are infantry, armor, and artillery. *The infantry* remains the Army's backbone. Transported to the front lines by helicopter or personnel carrier, foot soldiers engage the enemy in direct small-arms combat in order to seize and hold ground. *Armor* is the cavalry of the modern army, except that the armored soldiers today move into battle in tanks instead of on horseback. *Artillery* operates the cannons of the battlefield and antiaircraft missile installations.

—Robert L. Hardgrave, Jr., *American Government*

6 Organizing by problem and solution

In the problem and solution organizational pattern, a particular problem is identified and one or more solutions are proposed. Usually the writer states the problem explicitly, though sometimes it is only implied. Posing the problem in the form of a question is especially attention-getting.

What can be done about drug abuse among students? First, we should distinguish between experimentation and abuse. Many students try something at a party but do not become regular users. The best way to help students who have trouble saying no appears to be through peer programs that teach how to say no assertively. The successful programs also teach general social skills and build self-esteem (Newcomb & Bentler, 1989). Also, the older students are when they experiment with drugs, the more likely they are to make responsible choices, so helping younger students say no is a clear benefit.

—Anita E. Woolfolk, *Educational Psychology*

EXERCISE 6.4

An Internet or library research project is frequently a search for a solution to a problem—finding specific information on an issue that the researcher wants to explore and clarify. Such a search often turns up key words and ideas that suggest an even more interesting issue.

Choose an issue to research. Write it down as the problem, and then list two or three "solutions," or pieces of information you hope or expect to find in your search. This list could be the outline for a descriptive paragraph with a problem and solution pattern.

Conduct the search, and list the information you actually discover in a second column. Do you need to revise your problem statement in light of what you found? Write a coherent problem and solution paragraph using the information.

7   Organizing by narrative or process description

Narratives and process descriptions present events in a time-ordered sequence. A **narrative** tells a story; a **process description** depicts a step-by-step procedure. In either case, the writer recounts events in chronological order, using verb tenses consistently and not jumping from one time frame to another.

When narrating the plot of a literary work, you normally use the present tense, as in this brief description of Ibsen's *Enemy of the People*.

> The play is set in a little town which makes its living from the tourists who come to take its famous baths. Dr. Stockmann discovers that the waters have been contaminated by the local sewage system. He insists that the facts must be revealed, and expects that the city authorities will be grateful for his discovery. To his astonishment he finds that he has become an enemy of the people because he insists that the truth be known and the evil corrected. Doggedly he decides to fight on for truth even though the whole community is against him.
>
> —Vincent F. Hopper and Bernard D. N. Grebanier,
> *Essentials of European Literature*

When writing a process description, keep the verb tenses consistent (see 32e), and use an occasional transitional word such as *first, second, finally, after, then,* or *while.* Notice the transitional words in this process description paragraph.

> Land reclamation is the careful burying and grading of refuse that is dumped into prepared sites, such as deep trenches, swamps, ponds, or abandoned quarries. *After* the refuse has been dumped, it is sprayed with chemicals to kill larvae and insects. *Then* it is compacted

by heavy equipment, covered with a thick layer of clean earth, and graded so that it blends with surrounding land.

—*The New Book of Knowledge*

8 Organizing by exemplification

Examples are a powerful way to make difficult concepts understandable. A paragraph organized by **exemplification** often follows a general-to-specific pattern. The concept to be explained is introduced in general terms at the beginning, and then one or more specific examples are offered to make it meaningful, as in this paragraph.

The importance of equality is often contrasted with that of liberty. Indeed, someone's position in the alleged conflict between equality and liberty has often been seen as a good indicator of his or her general outlook on political philosophy and political economy. For example, not only are libertarian thinkers (such as Nozick 1974) seen as anti-egalitarian, but they are diagnosed as anti-egalitarian *precisely because* of their overriding concern with liberty. Similarly, those diagnosed as egalitarian thinkers (e.g., Dalton 1920, Tawney 1931, or Meade 1976) may appear to be less concerned with liberty precisely because they are seen as being wedded to the demands of equality.

—Amartya Sen, *Inequality Reexamined*

9 Organizing by physical or spatial description

A descriptive paragraph paints a picture of a person, place, or object by appealing to the reader's senses (sight, sound, touch, taste, or smell). It emphasizes details, which should be carefully selected to give the reader a vivid sense of what is being described. The following example brings to life something that most people can only imagine— the microscopic structure of ordinary soil.

The spaces between the soil grains offer a variety of habitats. The smaller pores and channels are filled with water, the larger ones mostly with air. Clay soils have narrow, threadlike channels that twist and taper downward; in sand, as might be imagined from seeing it on the beach, there are air pockets in the tiny spaces between the grains. Draped upon the skeleton of the soil are the sinews and flesh of a teeming life: each particle, even the finest, has a tight-fitting film of oxides, water, bits of organic matter. This skin is what gives life to the soil underfoot.

—Peter Farb, *Living Earth*

FOR COLLABORATION

Textbooks make heavy use of the organizational patterns described above. Working with a classmate, each of you take a textbook from one of your other courses and open it randomly to any page containing three or more whole paragraphs. Together, analyze and discuss these paragraphs in terms of their organizational patterns.

10 Organizing by mixing patterns

Although many paragraphs can be structured using one of the organizational patterns just described, you may sometimes want to express ideas in a way that does not conform to any one pattern. In such cases, do not be afraid to mix two or more organizational patterns. Just make it clear what pattern you are following at any one time. Here is an example of a paragraph that mixes patterns.

Popular music has never been a stranger to controversy or opposition. Herman Gray has noted three periods of particularly strong opposition: the response to jazz in the early part of the century, the reaction against rock 'n' roll in the 1950s and 1960s, and the most recent wave of controversy associated with heavy metal and rap. No matter what the genre, certain themes such as a fear of the connection between music and sexuality tend to run through all three periods. Such concerns may be expressed either as the fear that sensual rhythms can overcome rationality or that lyrics that push the boundaries of decorum can undermine moral values. Because of these fears, each genre has been linked at various times to drug abuse, lawless behavior, and general moral decline. In turn, all of these problems have been projected to some degree onto race.

—Reebee Garofalo, *Rockin' Out*

This paragraph basically follows the exemplification pattern, with sentences 2–6 exemplifying the generalization stated in the first sentence. But sentence 2, describing "three periods," is a classification statement. And sentences 5–6, marked by "Because . . .," follow the cause-and-effect pattern. As long as pattern shifts are clearly marked, mixed paragraphs can be comprehensible and coherent.

EXERCISE 6.5

Examine the first four paragraphs in this chapter, and determine what patterns of organization they exemplify. (Remember that a paragraph may use more than one pattern.)

FOR COLLABORATION

The topic sentence often suggests the organizational pattern that governs the rest of a paragraph. Try to guess what pattern might follow each of these topic sentences. Then compare and discuss your answers with those of a classmate.

1. *Self-disclosure* is the sharing of personal information with others. _____
2. Self-disclosure can be a double-edged sword, for there is risk in divulging personal insights and feelings. _____
3. Self-disclosure can affect our dealings within health-care settings. _____
4. Stores are exploiting your senses and sentimentality in order to make you comfortable, happy, and willing to spend more money. _____
5. In *Ties That Stress: The New Family Imbalance*, David Elkind writes that in today's postmodern family, the needs of hurried children have been sacrificed to the needs of their harried parents. _____

6c Write coherent paragraphs with sentence-linking techniques

6.3

Details on developing an argumentative essay.

WEBLINK

http://www.utoronto.ca/writing/parag.html

Guide to composing coherent paragraphs

In addition to conforming to organizational patterns, writers increase the coherence of their paragraphs by developing connections between sentences through the use of transitional expressions, repetition of words or phrases, or references to earlier information.

1 Using transitional words and phrases to link sentences

Transitional words and phrases are useful for linking sentences. The various expressions listed under Common Transitional Expressions (page 127) differ somewhat in degree of formality. For example, *furthermore* and *consequently* are more formal than *besides* and *so*. Being aware of these differences will help you strike a consistent tone in your writing (see 39c).

Common Transitional Expressions

To show cause and effect	*therefore, thus, consequently, as a result, for this reason, so, so that*
To compare	*similarly, likewise, in like manner, also*
To contrast	*however, on the one hand/on the other hand, in contrast, conversely, but, yet, nevertheless, nonetheless, on the contrary, still*
To show addition	*and, in addition, also, furthermore, moreover, besides*
To indicate time	*before, now, after, afterwards, subsequently, later, earlier, meanwhile, in the meantime, while, as long as, so far*
To give examples	*for example, for instance, specifically, namely, to illustrate, that is*
To conclude or summarize	*in conclusion, to conclude, in summary, to summarize, in short, in other words, therefore, thus, in reality*
To generalize	*in general, for the most part, as a general rule, on the whole, usually, typically*
To emphasize a point	*indeed, in fact, as a matter of fact, even*
To signal concession	*of course, naturally, although it is true that, granted that*

Notice how effective the transitional expressions are in making this paragraph more readable.

In many cultures, if not all, touching between adults can indicate sexuality; *however*, the conditions under which it does vary greatly. *For instance*, in the United States, men do not walk around holding each others' hands, unless one is blind or otherwise infirm and the other appears to be helping him get around. *Otherwise* this is seen as a strong indication of homosexuality. This is true of female pairs *as well*. *Yet*, in some countries, such as Egypt or at least some of Latin America, same-sex hand-holding or arms around the waist or shoulder indicates sol-idarity only. In those cultures, *typically*, one wouldn't touch a decent woman in public.

—Elaine Chaika, *Language: The Social Mirror*

2 Repeating key words to link sentences

A paragraph almost always has key words. Repetition of these words helps the reader focus on the topic at hand. Exact repetition can become tiresome, however, so good writers use synonyms or paraphrases. (The THESAURUS feature of your word processor can help you choose synonyms.)

Exact repetition can also be used for special effect. In this example, repetition of the word *growth* acts like a drumbeat, emphasizing the authors' skepticism about the virtues of economic growth.

Modern economics worships *growth*. *Growth* will solve poverty, the theory goes. *Growth* will increase our standard of living. *Growth* will reduce unemployment. *Growth* will keep us apace with infla-tion. *Growth* will relieve the boredom of the rich and the misery of the poor. *Growth* will bolster the GNP, boost the Dow and beat the Japanese. A rising tide lifts all boats.

—Joe Dominguez and Vicki Robin, *Your Money or Your Life*

After introducing the key word *growth* in the first sentence, the writers repeat it six times in the next six sentences. The reiteration of *growth* keeps the reader's focus on the main topic of the paragraph and thus increases its coherence.

Pronouns allow you to refer to the main topic without repetition. If one sentence after another has the same topic, you can often refer to it with a pronoun without confusing the reader. For example, the writers could have substituted *It* for *Growth* at the start of the third sentence. Using pronouns can also help reduce wordiness (see Chapter 40). Just make sure the pronouns always have clear referents (see Chapter 37).

3 Using old information to link sentences

Another way to link sentences is to refer to "old information," something readers are already familiar with, at the beginning of the new sentence. These references to old information usually consist of repeated words, pronouns, or words marked by *the* or *this*, inserted into the subject position (see 30b). Here is an example from a textbook on public speaking.

In a classic study, Ralph Nichols asked both good and poor listeners what their listening strategies were. *The poor listeners* indicated that they listened for facts such as names and dates. *The good listeners* reported that they listened for major ideas and principles. *Facts* are useful only when you can connect them to a principle or concept. In speeches, *facts* as well as examples are used primarily to support major ideas. *You* should try to summarize mentally the major idea that the specific *facts* support.

—Steven A. Beebe and Susan J. Beebe, *Public Speaking*

Notice how the grammatical subjects of sentences 2–5 repeat concepts that are mentioned earlier and that two of these repetitions include the article *the*. The concepts "good [listeners] and poor listeners" are first mentioned in the first sentence. Both of these concepts are then referred to as old information in sentences 2 and 3. The concept "facts" is new information in sentence 2 but old information in sentences 4–6. In all cases, the reference to the old information occurs at the beginning of the sentence. Even the pronoun *you* starting off sentence 6 refers to old information; it acknowledges the ongoing existence of the reader and is preceded by the *you* in sentence 4.

Keeping the sentence subject fairly short makes it easier for readers to understand the sentence and see how it fits into the paragraph as a whole. Using repeated words or pronouns to refer back to old information should help you keep sentence subjects short. Notice how short the sentence subjects are in the preceding example paragraph: *Ralph Nichols, The poor listeners, The good listeners, Facts, facts, You, facts*.

AUDIO
An explanation of the "Light before heavy" principle.

(EXERCISE 6.6)

Photocopy a page from one of your textbooks. Underline the grammatical subject of each sentence. (The subject is usually that part of the main clause that precedes the verb; see 30b if you need help.) What is the average length of the sentence subjects? How many of them refer to old information?

6d Be consistent with verb tense, person, and number

Verb tenses help create a time frame for readers (see 32e). When you jump from one verb tense to another within a paragraph, you disrupt the paragraph's coherence and risk confusing the reader. Conversely, maintaining a consistent point of view in the use of pronouns helps readers. After using the first-person plural (*we, us, our*), do not switch to the singular (*I, me, my*) or to second or third person (*you, they, . . .*) unless there is a good reason to do so (see Chapter 39).

> Watching Monday Night Football on ABC has become a ritualistic practice for countless American sports lovers. Every Monday night during the NFL season, ~~we would~~ *millions of fans* gather to watch the "old pigskin" being thrown around. This activity can be experienced in the comfort of ~~your~~ *one's* own home, at parties, or in popular sports bars. ~~A typical viewer will~~ *Viewers* especially enjoy the opening segment of the program, with all its pyrotechnics and special effects. ~~They~~ *The producers* really know how to put on a show at ABC! ~~If you~~ *For those who* like football, MNF is not to be missed.

6e Use parallelism to make paragraphs coherent

Many paragraphs contain embedded "lists"—that is, sets of sentences that have equivalent values and roles. In such cases, it is important to establish **parallelism** between the sentences by giving them the same grammatical structure. This helps the reader to easily see the relationship between sentences. (Chapter 42 discusses parallelism *within* sentences.) Notice how the two parallel sentences in this paragraph set off the contrast between two living situations.

> [Centuries ago,] divorce was common and easy for most Native American women. *If a woman was living with her husband's family, she simply took her belongings and perhaps the children and went home to her parents. If the couple was living with the wife's parents or if the dwelling was considered hers, she told the man to leave, throwing his clothes and paraphernalia out after him.* Common grounds for divorce were sterility, adultery, laziness, bad temper, and cruelty.
>
> —Carolyn Niethammer, *Daughters of the Earth*

To make it easy for the reader to spot the two situations she is talking about, Niethammer describes them in separate, grammatically parallel sentences (*If a woman was living with. . . . If the couple was living with . . .*).

(EXERCISE 6.7)

1. Pick three paragraphs from one of your textbooks, and identify the techniques (such as use of an organizational pattern, sentence links, repetition, or parallelism) that give them coherence.

2. From a Web page, copy three interesting paragraphs that use repetition. Put them into a new document, and use the SEARCH function to locate all occurrences of key words. If there seems to be too much repetition or not enough, rewrite the paragraphs to better use repetition and other techniques that improve coherence.

6f Decide on appropriate paragraph length

Each paragraph should be long enough to adequately develop its main point. Thus, paragraph length depends mainly on how complicated the topic is. The important thing is to make paragraphs complete and unified. As long as you do this, your paragraphs are not likely to be excessively long or excessively short.

Also, bear in mind that desirable paragraph length can vary from one type of writing to another. In college essays, most paragraphs are likely to be three to six sentences long. In contrast, email messages often have short paragraphs, sometimes with only one or two sentences, like a conversation. Similarly, newspaper reports usually have very short paragraphs (one to two sentences), in part to grab the reader's attention. But newspaper editorials aim for more reflective reading and so have somewhat longer paragraphs (two to three sentences). Paragraphs in the *Encyclopaedia Britannica* may contain twelve or more sentences.

6g Link paragraphs with key words

In any series of paragraphs, a reader should be able to move easily from one paragraph to the next. If a paragraph picks up where the pre-

When Is It Appropriate to Start a New Paragraph?

- When you have adequately covered one topic and are shifting to a new one.
- When the current paragraph is getting too long and you want to give the reader some "breathing space."
- When you want to emphasize a point by using it as the opening sentence of a new paragraph.
- When you want to set off a contrasting point.

ceding one left off, provide at least one link in the first sentence of the new paragraph. Links can be transitional words and phrases or expressions referring to old information and preceded by terms such as *this*, *these*, or *such*. Notice that the first sentence of the second paragraph contains a phrase that continues a theme from the first paragraph.

> Economic recovery after the war was especially strong in West Germany. Between 1950 and 1958, West Germans doubled their industrial output. The people of West Germany who were facing starvation in 1945 enjoyed one of the highest standards of living by the late 1950s.
>
> There were several reasons for *this "economic miracle."* The Marshall Plan provided crucial financial aid toward recovery. Under the Marshall Plan, the United States channeled almost $1.4 billion in aid to Germany. Also, since many industrial plants had been destroyed during the war, the Germans rebuilt modern, much more efficient ones.
>
> —Burton F. Beers, *World History*

EXERCISE 6.8

1. Select an essay from a book you have used in one of your courses or an editorial from a daily newspaper, and choose one section of four or five paragraphs. In the first sentence of every paragraph except the first, identify all the words and phrases that help connect that paragraph to the one preceding it.

2. Look again at a single topic as presented in listserv messages and in Usenet discussions. What differences do you see in the way the two presentations make connecting links between paragraphs or parts?

6h Construct effective introductory and concluding paragraphs

The beginning and the end of a document are the two places where readers are most likely to give full attention to what they are reading. Thus, it is particularly important that you write effective opening and closing paragraphs (see 5b-7).

1 Writing an introductory paragraph that will draw the reader's attention

When readers start to read a piece of writing, they want to know what it will be about and whether it will be interesting—and they want to know quickly. Therefore, you should write an opening paragraph that is informative and interesting. The opening paragraph should always be appropriate to the genre: an academic essay requires a different sort of opening than, say, a letter of complaint. In all genres, however, an introductory paragraph should accomplish four things.

6.4
Some examples of effective opening paragraphs.

1. Identify the topic of the piece.
2. Stimulate reader interest.
3. Establish a tone or style.
4. Enable readers to anticipate what comes next.

Here is an example of an ineffective introductory paragraph. It comes from a student paper on how the media can affect our behavior.

ORIGINAL

> Some people think that watching TV or seeing movies is only entertainment, that it doesn't affect their behavior. Are you one of them? If so, you will be surprised to learn that media effects are extremely powerful. This paper will talk about those effects. It will describe how the media contributed to the Nazi hate that killed so many Jews and fueled Ted Bundy's killing spree. We should, as a nation, stand up to the tyranny of violent media.

This is a weak introduction for several reasons. First, it's unlikely to stimulate reader interest. Few readers, even if they are media addicts, will let themselves be put in the role laid out in the opening sentences. Second, we don't have a clear sense of what's to come, other than a description of Nazi propaganda and Ted Bundy's killing spree. Finally, there's no clear tone or style to this introduction. It jumps from a direct appeal to the reader to a description of media effects to, finally, an exhortation about media "tyranny."

Consider now the revised version:

REVISED

> Reese's Pieces candies played only a small role in the popular film *ET*, but sales of the candy were boosted by 65 percent after the movie. A similar effect was seen in an episode of *Happy Days*. Fonzi decides to get a library card and mentions that the library is cool: "Anybody can get one of these suckers [library cards] and you can meet chicks there, too." After the show aired, there was a 500 percent increase nationally in library card registration. If the media affect little decisions such as what candy we buy or whether or not we decide to register for a library card, could they affect the big decisions that we make? How much are the media to blame for some of the problems that we have in society?

This version is much more compelling. It starts with two vivid examples of the topic under discussion—examples that a college audience can relate to. Thus, it not only identifies the topic but does so in a way almost sure to stimulate reader interest. The next two sentences then nicely raise the stakes, from candy selection to "big decisions" and "problems that we have in society." We can guess what's likely to come next—a discussion of media effects and how they have a strong effect not just on individual decision making but on our society as a whole. All of this is carried off in an engaging style that is likely to encourage the reader to read on.

While some types of writing, such as business letters and memos (see Chapter 25), have fairly conventional openings, other types of writing give you more latitude in ways to draw reader interest. For example, if you are writing an exploratory essay, you have some freedom in how you construct your opening paragraph. You can adopt a relaxed style, and you can hint at your thesis instead of stating it explicitly. If you are writing an argumentative essay, your readers will expect you to use a more formal style and tighter structure, and they will look for an explicit thesis in the first paragraph.

2 Writing a concluding paragraph that creates a sense of completeness

The concluding paragraph of an extended piece of writing should not leave the reader hanging but, rather, should neatly tie things up. Except in a very short essay, the concluding paragraph should reiterate your main point, preferably not by simply restating it but by adding something to it. Ideally, it should also stimulate the reader to think beyond what you have already said. See Some Effective Devices for Concluding Paragraphs; sometimes two or more of these techniques work well together.

Here are "before" and "after" versions of a concluding paragraph from a student essay titled "The Human Genome Project: Ethical, Social, and Legal Considerations."

ORIGINAL

The genetic revolution brings us breathtaking new technology that calls for extreme caution. The ability of genetic science to determine our birth and predict our future health is increasing at an amazing pace, and the overwhelming amount of new information puts government under increasing pressure to pass legislation.

Although this version reiterates the main theme of the essay, it fails to introduce anything new or stimulate the reader to think beyond what's already been said. The revised version is much more engaging.

REVISED

> "Without adequate safeguards, the genetic revolution could mean one step forward for science and two steps backward for civil rights. Misuse of genetic information could create a new underclass: the genetically less fortunate" (Jeffords 1252). A Gallup poll by the Institute for Health Freedom found that 93 percent of adults questioned want their permission to be obtained before their genetic information is used. Under current practice those 93 percent would have their constitutional right to privacy taken away. This is a breathtaking new technology we have, and extreme care should be taken. The ability of genetic science to determine our birth and predict our future health is increasing at an amazing pace, and the overwhelming amount of new information should tell our government representatives that it is time to enact new legislation regulating it.

This revised version is far better than the original for several reasons. First, it draws the reader in with a powerful quotation. Second, it presents new information in the form of survey data, underscoring the political explosiveness of this topic. And finally, it concludes with a clear call for action.

(**EXERCISE 6.9**)

1. In light of the above discussion, evaluate the introductory paragraph and the concluding paragraph of Kirsten Parsons's essay on Net theft (pages 109–113). For practice, construct an alternative version of each paragraph, using one or more rhetorical devices not used by Kirsten.
2. Apply the same procedure to an essay found in one of your course readings, in a newsmagazine or newspaper, or on the Internet.

CHAPTER 7

Formulating Arguments

FAQs

▶ How can I get people to understand my point of view?

▶ How can I get people to respect what I am proposing?

▶ What is the difference between a convincing argument and a personal opinion?

▶ What makes a good, arguable thesis? (7a)

▶ If I'm presenting an argument online, do I need to do anything special? (7i)

▶ How can I use visuals to support an argument? (7j)

AUDIO

Chapter overview.

A natural outcome of the critical thinking you are expected to do in college (see 2a) is speaking or writing in which you formulate and defend your own point of view. This is called **argument.** Argument in this sense does not mean quarreling; rather, it means taking a position on an issue and supporting it with evidence and good reasoning.

> **WEBLINK**
>
> http://www.englishbiz.co .uk/mainguides/argue.htm
>
> From Britain, an authorative guide to writing argumentative essays

Argument is essential to a democratic society. Unless people can discuss their differences in a rational, intelligent manner, they cannot make well-informed decisions about how to govern themselves. An important part of a college education is learning how to contribute, as a citizen, to the public discourse. Whether through writing a letter to a legislator, attending a PTA meeting, discussing public issues with a neighbor, or participating in a newsgroup on the Internet, life beyond college will call on you to act as an informed member of the civic community. Skill at argumentation is indispensable for most professional careers. Doctors, managers, teachers, social workers, lawyers, engineers, sales-people—indeed, all people whose work involves taking a point of view and then persuading others to agree with it—depend on argumentation to accomplish their goals. In short, the ability to formulate coherent, well-supported arguments will enhance your ability to persuade people in your community or workplace to see your viewpoint or think and act in the ways you advocate. College courses are designed to give you the critical thinking and arguing skills you will need to achieve these goals.

7a Formulate an arguable thesis

The first step in developing an argument is to formulate a good thesis, or claim (see 3e-2). In argument, as in exposition, a thesis is a statement in which the writer or speaker takes a supportable position on an issue—for example, "Voting rights can be extended safely to most of the mentally ill." In some college assignments, the thesis is given. For example, many standard-ized tests and final exams have essay questions on a preset thesis. In other cases, however, students are expected to formulate a thesis themselves. Many instructors give students complete freedom to select their own topics for course papers. The critical reading you do (see 2b) in preparation for an

WEBLINK

http://www.powa.org/argument.htm
Thorough treatments of how to formulate and develop an arguable thesis

VIDEO
Finding arguable topics.

assignment may raise the kinds of questions that lead to an appro-priate thesis, as may encounters with others' ideas on the Internet or exchanges with others in a network. (See Chapters 9 and 10 for help in finding and evaluating evidence from networks and the Internet.) Whether the thesis is assigned or one that you have created yourself, try to shape the thesis and develop the argument so that they become an expression of your own point of view.

1 What constitutes an appropriate thesis?

To have an influence on others, a thesis should be *open to debate*. That is, it should not make a claim that everyone would already agree with. "Smoking is harmful to your health" is not an effective argumen-

An Arguable Thesis or Claim

- Is debatable. Not everyone will automatically agree with it.
- Can be supported with evidence available to everyone.
- Can be countered with arguments against it.
- Is a clearly stated claim of fact, value, or policy, with terms defined.
- Is not based just on personal opinion or subjective feelings.

tative thesis because almost no educated person would disagree with it. A more interesting, more arguable thesis would be "Smoking should be prohibited in all public places, including bars."

Second, an appropriate thesis is *open to evidence and counterevidence*—you can gather and present evidence for and against this claim. For the smoking example, you could search the research literature, Web sites, or newsgroups for scientific evidence about the effects of secondhand smoke; you could look for health statistics on communities that have already enacted such a prohibition; or you could try to locate results of public opinion surveys. If a thesis merely expresses your own opinion about something ("I think smoking is cool"), without citing evidence beyond your own feelings, it offers no claim that can be objectively assessed by others.

Third, a thesis should be *clearly stated.* It should leave no confusion in the mind of the reader as to what you are claiming. Provide definitions or paraphrases of any terms that may be unclear. In the example about smoking in public places, readers would need to know exactly what is meant by the term *public places.* Indeed, the entire argument could hinge on how this term is defined.

A thesis can be a claim of fact, a claim of value, or a claim of policy. A claim of fact asserts that something is true ("Smoking is harmful to your health"). A claim of value asserts that something is or is not worthwhile ("People should make efforts to protect their health by avoiding smoke"). A claim of policy argues for a course of action ("Smoking should be banned in all public places"). Your thesis should make clear to the audience which type of claim you are making (see 3e-2).

2 Using inductive and deductive reasoning

If you have to develop your own thesis, there are two kinds of reasoning that should help you get there. **Inductive reasoning** begins with particular evidence and arrives at some general conclusion. For example, if your mail has been delivered three hours late for the past four days (particular evidence), you might conclude that a substitute carrier is now working your route (generalization). Or let's say the front tire on your bike needs frequent pumping but your rear tire doesn't; you might reasonably infer that your front tire has a small leak. As you can see from these examples, inductive reasoning is something we use routinely, every day. We use inductive reasoning to try to make sense of things and to come up with new ideas. Inductive reasoning relies on experience; it is sometimes referred to as "educated guesswork." Inductive reasoning deals with probability, not absolute truth or validity. Thus, the conclusions it arrives at are not necessarily "true"; rather, they are only probable or plausible.

NO **Deductive reasoning** goes in the opposite direction, from general to particular. You start with some generalization—a general claim, principle, or belief—and then you apply it to some specific fact and arrive at some specific conclusion or prediction. Deductive reasoning relies on a strict form of logic, conventionally expressed in a **syllogism**. A syllogism contains a major premise (the generalization), one or more minor premises (the facts), and a conclusion.

MAJOR PREMISE   People who work hard are usually successful.

MINOR PREMISE   Kevin works hard.

CONCLUSION   Kevin will probably be successful.

In deductive reasoning there is a difference between *validity* and *truth.* When a deductive argument conforms to the rules of logic, it is said to be *valid.* In the example above, the minor premise fits logically the condition set up in the major premise ("People who work hard"), and so the conclusion logically follows. A deductive argument can be *true,* however, only if its premises are true, so if any premise is false, the argument itself is false. For example, if it turns out that Kevin does *not* work hard, the above argument, although valid, would be false.

In everyday use, deductive reasoning often leaves its major premise unstated. This is because major premises are often widely accepted assumptions in a particular culture. Thus, the syllogism given above might be expressed in everyday language as "Kevin works hard—I think he'll be successful some day." Such abbreviated syllogisms (or **enthymemes**) are commonplace in daily life because they convey logical reasoning in shortcut fashion. Unfortunately, the convenience of enthymemes makes them easy to misuse for deception. Here is an example from a political campaign: "The Congressman clearly supports family values. He has five children."

MAJOR PREMISE, UNSTATED	Anyone who has five children supports family values.
MINOR PREMISE	The Congressman has five children.
CONCLUSION	The Congressman supports family values.

By leaving the major premise an unstated assumption, the speaker avoided subjecting it to public scrutiny. If he had stated it explicitly, people in the audience might have raised questions about its truth, about the vagueness of the term *family values*, and so on. (This example illustrates the fallacy of begging the question; see 7g-2.)

Of course, there is no guarantee that induction and deduction by themselves will lead to good, arguable theses. The claim that "Kevin will probably be successful" would not make a good thesis, as it is not open to evidence and counterevidence and is not a claim of fact, value, or policy. The claim that "the Congressman supports family values" works better as a thesis, especially if it is a public issue in the Congressman's district. But it would first need to have the term *family values* defined in a way that allowed for evidence to be marshaled for and against it.

Inductive and deductive reasoning often work together, and the combination has a better chance of producing a good, arguable thesis. For instance, you might use inductive reasoning to formulate a generalization from particulars, and then use that same generalization as your major premise in deductive reasoning. Here is an example.

INDUCTIVE REASONING

PARTICULARS	You keep reading or hearing news reports about mass shootings in southern and western states.
PARTICULARS	You have read in several places that there are more guns per capita in southern and western states than in other states.
GENERALIZATION	More gun ownership leads to more gun-related violence.

DEDUCTIVE REASONING

MAJOR PREMISE	More gun ownership leads to more gun-related violence.
MINOR PREMISE	The new concealed weapon ordinance in our city is causing more people to buy guns.

CONCLUSION   The new concealed weapon ordinance will cause the rate of gun-related violence in our city to increase.

This conclusion would serve as a good thesis for an argument because it is an important public issue, is debatable, can be supported or refuted with evidence, is a clearly stated claim of fact (which, in this case, can be converted to a claim of policy), and is not just based on personal opinion. Note also how the underlying premises themselves satisfy these requirements.

3 Working through a thesis

Not every claim, or thesis, ends up the way it began; most writers develop a thesis somewhat by trial and error, refining their ideas as they gather more information. For an essay in her composition class, Angela Napper decided to write about cybercensorship. She had heard that administrators at her college were considering new rules that would prohibit students from accessing certain Web sites in the school's computer labs. She felt this would be an infringement on academic freedom, so she decided that her thesis would be something like "Censoring Internet usage is inappropriate in a college environment." But this was only her *working thesis*. As she explored the subject and worked through her ideas, she realized that the issue of cybercensorship was far broader than just its effect on college students. She also decided that she should make her thesis more specific, more open to evidence—that is, more arguable. After further research and brainstorming, Angela decided to focus not on the inappropriateness of cybercensorship in college but on the constitutionality of such censorship in the broader public sphere. This resulted in a *revised thesis:* "Citizens need to take a stand to protect their rights to privacy and freedom of information on public computers as these rights are guaranteed to them in the Constitution under the Bill of Rights."

Angela's thesis is a good one. First of all, it is not a statement that everyone would automatically agree with. In fact, after the terrorist attacks of September 11, 2001, many people would argue that citizens must sacrifice some of these rights for the sake of greater national security. Second, the thesis can be debated with evidence and counterevidence. Angela could cite the relevant parts of the Constitution and court decisions that either support or undermine her thesis. Third, the thesis is a clearly stated claim of policy, alluding to several of the key subissues (the right to privacy, freedom of information, the use of public computers, constitutional rights).

Although a thesis should be stated early, it should be preceded by any background information the reader needs to make sense of it. Delayed presentation of the thesis is especially appropriate if the audience is either ignorant of the subject or likely to disagree with or be skeptical about the thesis. Delaying the thesis tells the reader that you are not "jumping to conclusions" but instead are thoughtfully and impartially working through the issue. Since readers in college are trained to be skeptical, you should not feel that you have to state your thesis up front (unless, of course, your instructor tells you to).

(EXERCISE 7.1)

Analyze each of the following claims to decide (a) whether or not it expresses a clear and arguable thesis and (b) what kinds of evidence and counterevidence would be relevant to it. In cases where the claim is not an arguable thesis, reformulate it into one.

1. U2 is the best musical group in the world.
2. The National Park System would be better off if it were privatized.
3. Overpopulation is threatening our quality of life.
4. It is a bad idea for governments to attempt to regulate delivery of information via the Internet.
5. Within a decade, soccer will replace baseball as our national pastime.

7b   Consider your purpose and audience

At some point early in the process of developing an argument you need to carefully consider your purpose and audience (see 3b-2). In general, the reason for making an argument is to persuade other people to your point of view. But depending on the situation, you may have any of the following more specific purposes.

- To persuade those who are undecided to agree with you.
- To reinforce the views of those who already agree with you.
- To change the minds of those who disagree with you, or at least deter them from acting against you.
- To test your *own* commitment to this point of view.

Notice how each of these purposes has a distinctly different audience. It is extremely unlikely that one argument presented one way to all of these audiences will be successful with each of them. Different people with different backgrounds, beliefs, and so on will often respond differently to the same argument. Thus, you'll have a better chance of succeeding if you shape your argument to address the interests and values of each audience.

A good time to start this process is while working through your thesis. Angela did this when she conducted extra research on her initial topic and found it to be broader in scope than she had realized. Kirsten Parsons revised her original thesis while reviewing her first draft (4a-1). In all cases, you should try to develop a thesis that (1) defines a specific topic, (2) makes a strong point about the topic, and (3) provides a blueprint for the paper's development (see 3e-3). As for positioning your thesis, if you have an audience that you think will be either skeptical or uninformed on the issue, you should build up to your thesis by first presenting appropriate background information. Conversely, if you have a knowledgeable, supportive audience, you can proceed more quickly to your thesis.

7c Generate good supporting evidence

Central to the strength of an argument is the evidence cited to support it. There are five main types of evidence: factual data, expert opinion, personal experience, examples, and statistics.

Factual data include any information presented as representing objective reality. Factual data most often consist of measurable, or quantitative, evidence such as distances, amounts, and ratios. But factual data can include historical events, longstanding assessments, and other widely attested observations about the world. Objectivity makes factual data difficult to refute. Therefore, in most academic disciplines, factual data are considered to be the most powerful form of evidence you can present.

Expert opinion can also be persuasive, because it represents the studied judgment of someone who knows a great deal about the subject at hand. If a famous literary critic said that *Twelfth Night* was one of Shakespeare's finest plays, quoting this expert's statement would strengthen any argument you made along those lines. But expert opinion has its limitations. First, a quotation taken out of context may not convey what the expert really meant. Second, experts sometimes fall prey to the influence of some special interest. Not long ago, experts employed by the tobacco industry testified that tobacco was not addictive. Finally, experts can simply be wrong in their judgments and predictions.

VIDEO
Investigating
assumptions.

Personal experience is less objective than either factual data or expert opinion, but it can be highly compelling. Personal experience is especially effective when presented in the form of a narrative. The story you tell may represent only your own experience—and thus lack generalizability—but since it is coming directly from you it has a certain vividness that is missing from more detached accounts. Personal experience is not the same as personal opinion: the former is an account of an experience—something you have personally tested against reality—while the latter may be nothing more than a snap judgment. Arguments do not go far on opinion alone.

Examples are effective because, like personal experience, they are concrete, vivid, and therefore easy for readers to relate to. (Just think of how much you appreciate good examples in the textbooks and other instructional materials you read!) Unlike personal experience, examples are supposed to be generalizations about a larger category. That is, they are good only to the extent that they are typical of an entire class of phenomena. If you present an odd case as a "typical example," you may justifiably be criticized for giving a misleading example.

A collection of numerical data, statistics are usually compressed in a way that points to a certain interpretation. Because statistics typically represent a large body of data, they can be compelling as evidence. But they can also be manipulated in deceptive ways. If you gather your own statistics, be sure you know how to analyze them correctly. If you take statistics from other sources, try to use only sources that are considered reliable (for example, the US government or prestigious academic journals).

7.1

Background documents on cyber-censorship.

Angela's essay on cybercensorship is printed on the following pages. Note what kinds of evidence she used to support her thesis.

Napper 1

Angela Napper

Professor Hult

English 101

13 October 2003

Cybercensorship

With more and more regulations being formed
about what citizens are allowed to view on the
Internet, concerns as to the constitutional rights of
these citizens are being raised. At public libraries,
at colleges and universities, and at businesses the
debate rages as to how much privacy users should have
and whether censorship of certain materials is needed
to protect the public welfare. More and more it is
becoming clear that citizens need to take a stand to
protect their right to privacy and freedom of speech
on public computers as these rights are guaranteed to
them in the US Constitution, specifically the First,
Fifth, and Fourteenth Amendments.

Recently, the Board of Supervisors in
Chesterfield County, Virginia, passed a law to
prohibit access to any material deemed by the
community to be pornographic or obscene. This
includes any information on sex education and any
Web sites containing prohibited words. Consequently,
a site containing a recipe for chicken breasts would
be banned. The local chapter of the American Civil
Liberties Union (ACLU) is expected to challenge the

> Introduces the issue in attention-getting terms: "the debate rages. . . ."

> Presents her thesis.

> Gives an example as background information.

legislation. However, the new policy seems to be popular with some local residents. They have even started a Liberty Watch group in which citizens make a point of monitoring what those around them are accessing on the Web. Anything they deem illegal by the new standards is reported to the local authorities (Oder and Rogers).

Presents main supporting evidence for her thesis.

With this type of system in place, citizens' right to access information--as guaranteed in the freedom of speech and freedom of press clauses of the First Amendment and the equal protection clause of the Fourteenth Amendment--is greatly infringed upon. The morals and beliefs of those in power have been forced upon everyone. It is exactly this type of regulation that the Founders were trying to escape when they created the United States, a country where everyone would be free to live their lives as they chose, assuming they were not hurting others. I fail to see how attempting to access a recipe for chicken is hurting anyone. For that matter, gaining information on sex education is not infringing on the well-being of the community. Rather, it is likely improving the overall well-being by preventing unwanted pregnancies and diseases. Educator David Thornburg points out, "Libraries in schools and communities should be the last places to use censorship of any kind. Once the

Uses quotation from authority to reinforce her point.

Napper 3

door to censorship is opened, how do we ever get it
closed again?"

The debate between freedom of speech and
censorship is also raging at a number of
universities. At Snow College in southern Utah,
administrators added software that blocked student
access to all information deemed nonacademic. They
said the motivation behind their actions had nothing
to do with moral censorship. Rather, they claimed
that students playing games and viewing pornography
were using up too much computing time and power.
Students who needed to use campus computers for
homework had to wait in long lines and deal with
slower computers. With the new policy in effect, the
rate of hits on blocked sites (versus approved
sites) dropped from thirty-five percent to less than
five percent per day. This reduction speeded up the
computers for those who used them for academic
purposes. Students complained that they were never
asked about their opinion beforehand and were not
told about the decision after it had gone into
effect. When asked what they would do if the student
body voted against the new policy, school officials
said the policy would be removed (Madsen).

Similarly, Indiana University banned the
downloading of MP3s on school computers because it
was using up too much of the school's bandwidth.

Shifts to another locale that has the same issue. Should resonate with other students.

Another example of students being victimized.

Napper 4

Opposition came from a group called Students Against
University Censorship who began circulating a
petition around the nation with the goal of gaining
popular support as well as legal representation in
their fight against these censorship policies. Their
aim was to gain public support so as to have more
power in a court of law or in negotiations with
officials who could strike down censorship at
universities nationwide (Ferguson).

This more
reasonable
approach
provides
support for
her
argument.

   However, some universities are in favor of giving
students free rein. The University of Nevada, Las
Vegas, refuses to put limits on what students can
access on school computers or in the dorms. Officials
state that they respect the students' rights and they
want to make them feel at home when they are living in
the dorms, which means allowing them access to all
sites. If anyone on campus is offended by what another
student is viewing, the offending student is simply
asked to relocate to a more private computer. This
type of policy respects the rights of all involved. It
does not infringe on the freedom of speech rights of
the students, while at the same time students who feel
uncomfortable by material being viewed around them are
accommodated appropriately (Ferguson).

   More and more the battleground is moving into the
workplace. Employers are looking to monitor what their
employees access during work hours so as to prevent

Napper 5

them from wasting company time on personal
entertainment. Currently, over two thousand companies
have begun using Cyber-Patrol, software that filters
out any Web sites the company does not want its
employees to access. Microsystems Software, Inc., the
company that designs this software for corporations,
claims it is not censoring anything but only filtering.
It allows managers to personally inspect Web sites that
have been accessed by company employees. Since every
Web site Cyber-Patrol blocks has been viewed by a
person, there is not blanket censorship based on what
words a site may contain. All sites are placed into one
of three categories: CyberYes, CyberNo, and
Sports/Entertainment. With this system, any company can
choose whether it wants its employees to be able to
access sports and entertainment sites during work
hours. It can also restrict any sites that have been
deemed pornographic or violent. (Markels).

This counter-example serves nicely to restrict her thesis; gives her more credibility.

　　This type of restriction seems less in violation
of citizens' rights because it is designed to be used
only in the workplace. Most would agree employers
have the right to monitor what their employees are
doing during office hours because the employers own
the machines and are paying the employees for their
time. Similarly, it might be argued that public
libraries and universities also own their computers
and consequently should have the right to censor

Highlights the public vs. private dimension of this issue, setting up the next section.

them. It must be kept in mind, however, that those computers were purchased using taxpayers' money, so in reality they belong to the public. Cyber-Patrol is also improved in its format in that each Web site is individually viewed. Web sites with recipes for chicken breasts would consequently not be banned.

These same issues of the public's right to privacy have become a point of controversy in recent government hearings. There is a push by the Bush administration led by Attorney General John Ashcroft to allow government officials access to private citizens' Web use and emails. New technology called Carnivore would allow officials access to the records of any Internet provider. "In order to find specific emails, Carnivore must sort through all the email of an Internet service provider. That opens up all the people using that provider to government surveillance without judicial review" (Puzzanghera). This same system has the ability to record all people who have hit on any given site, or all of the sites accessed by any given computer.

This example adds complexity to the issue, making it even more interesting.

Ashcroft is pushing to have the legislation passed quickly. He claims that such laws are necessary to gain ground against further terrorist attacks in the United States. Opposition to proposed laws such as this is led by Jerry Bermann, the executive director of the Center for Democracy and Technology in

Napper 7

Washington. He and his supporters claim that the
government is moving too fast, not stopping to
consider the long-term effects that this legislation
would have. The Attorney General's response to this
claim is that Americans do not have time on their side
if further attacks are to be prevented (Puzzanghera).
This seems to be a scare tactic on the part of the
government to pass legislation quickly before it can
be debated and, if necessary, modified. Although we
may need new laws to stop future attacks by terrorists
in the United States, it is also vital to ensure that
citizens' rights are not crushed in the process. As
one human rights researcher has said, "If allowed to
be controlled by a government, instead of a tool for
democracy, the Internet may be employed as a tool by
which more modern dictatorships can monitor and
control their citizens" (Hansen).

> Refutes the counter-example, making her argument stronger.

   With the debate raging as to how much privacy
Americans are entitled to when it comes to the
Internet and what information they should be able to
access, it is the citizens' job to take a stand and
fight for their rights. It is only by doing so that
the ideals of freedom of speech and right to privacy
that the Founders so highly valued will be
preserved. As Supreme Court Justice William O.
Douglas once said, "The right to be let alone is
indeed the beginning of all freedom."

> Concludes with a concise summary of the main points.

Napper 8

Works Cited

Ferguson, Kevin. "Net Censorship Spreading on
    University Campuses." <u>Las Vegas Business Press</u>
    28 Feb. 2000: 20.

Hansen, Stephen A. <u>The Unhindered Use of the Internet
    in Human Rights Work</u>. Speech to the American
    Academy for the Advancement of Science, 1999. 9
    Oct. 2003 <http://shr.aaas.org/Cybercensorship/
    Hansen.htm>.

Madsen, Grant. "Snow College Officials Defend Net
    Censorship: Blocking Pornography Was Not for
    Moral Reasons." <u>Salt Lake Tribune</u> 16 Jan.
    1999: D3.

Markels, Alex. "Screening the Net; Microsystems
    Cleans Up Web for Kids, Workers: Screening the
    Internet for Nudity, Profanity." <u>Salt Lake
    Tribune</u> 5 May 1997: B1.

Oder, Norman, and Michael Rogers. "VA County Public
    Library to Filter All Access." <u>Library Journal</u>
    126 (2001): 15.

Puzzanghera, Jim. "Privacy Advocates Argue Anti-
    Terrorism Plans Harm Free Society." <u>San Jose
    Mercury News</u> 27 Sept. 2001: 17.

Thornburg, David. <u>Children and Cybercensorship</u>. PBS
    Teacher Source. 22 Aug. 2002. 6 Oct. 2003
    <http://www.pbs.org/teachersource/thornburg/
    thornburg1098.shtm>.

What kinds of evidence does Angela use to support her argument? Mainly, she relies on a number of extended examples in which citizens' rights to privacy and freedom of speech are being eroded through the use of cybercensorship. By using a broad selection of settings (libraries, colleges, businesses, government surveillance), she conveys a sense of how widespread the danger is. She also cites the opinions of experts ranging from US Attorney General Ashcroft to Jerry Bermann, the executive director of the Center for Democracy and Technology. She also gives source information for many of the statements in her paper. Angela uses factual data as well, in the form of objective accounts of the different cases and of the applicability of the US Constitution to them.

(EXERCISE 7.2)

Of the different kinds of evidence that Angela used, which—in your opinion—is most compelling? Why? What other evidence could she have used?

(FOR COLLABORATION)

Together with a classmate, find a written argument that one of you finds persuasive but the other does not. (The opinion page in the campus newspaper or local city newspaper would be one place to look.) Then analyze— dispassionately!—why you differ in your reactions. As noted above, people with different backgrounds, beliefs, and values will often respond differently to an argument as well as to the evidence used to support it; this may explain why you and your classmate have the different responses you do.

7d Take note of evidence for alternative views

In gathering evidence, do not go looking just for evidence that supports your case; take note of evidence supporting other positions as well, including evidence that argues directly against your case. On issues that are of any interest or value, the evidence will not be entirely one-sided; there will be evidence supporting alternative views. When you acknowledge the counterevidence, you gain credibility as a careful, conscientious thinker, thereby strengthening your argument rather than weakening it. (This is especially true in academia.) Conversely, readers may interpret your failure to present a full spectrum of evidence either as an indication of a less than full effort to address

VIDEO
Accommodating
opposition.

the issue or an attempt to hide negative evidence. Remember, you do not have to make an overwhelmingly lopsided argument in order to prevail; you simply have to show that there is more support *for* your thesis than against it. In most college writing, an awareness of the complexity of an issue is considered a sign of intellectual maturity. Do not be afraid to bring forth counterevidence. (See 7e for more information on how best to deal with counterevidence.)

Another advantage of gathering counterevidence early on is that it forces you to review your thesis and, if necessary, modify it. In formulating your thesis, you may have overlooked some arguments against it. Maybe you overgeneralized, used either/or reasoning, or committed some other fallacy (see 7g). If so, this is a good time to reformulate your thesis and make it more defensible. (Getting your fellow students involved in this effort can be helpful; see 5e for more on collaborating.)

Angela's essay includes two different kinds of counterevidence against her thesis. First, she notes that some college administrators have been restricting students' Internet access not to censor their access to inappropriate material but to save on computing resources, thus ultimately giving students more access to appropriate uses of the schools' computer systems. Second, she says that private companies have a legitimate right to restrict employees' use of company computers because these computers are owned by the company and the employees are paid to do the company's work, not to entertain themselves. She also acknowledges the government's desire to promote greater security against terrorism as a reason for its increased cybersurveillance of American citizens.

EXERCISE 7.3

What other counterevidence could Angela have used? How could she have responded to it?

EXERCISE 7.4

Log on to a newsgroup, chat room, or other Web site where arguments are taking place (see 24b). (Some interesting newsgroups are *talk.politics, ab.politics, alt.society.resistance, alt.fan.rush-limbaugh,* and *alt.politics.radical-left.*) Print out two conversational threads, each involving several exchanges: one in which the participants make some concessions to each other's point of view and another in which they do not. Do the threads differ in tone, argumentative force, or intellectuality? Write a short paper describing the differences you find.

7e Develop and test your main points

Once you have formulated an appropriate thesis and compiled enough information to make a case for it, you need to develop and test the main points you want to make. This is the heart of an argument, where you lay out your reasoning in step-by-step fashion.

1 Deciding what your strongest points are

In any argument, some points are stronger than others: they are more central to the issue at hand, they make more sense in terms of logical reasoning, they have more evidence supporting them, and they have less counterevidence opposing them. In constructing your argument, you need to try to identify those points that seem to be strongest. You might start by simply listing all the points you can think of to support your thesis. Then ask yourself this question: Which of these points are most central to the issue I am addressing? Any controversial topic will give rise to a hierarchy of concerns, which will vary from one person to another. If you ignore a concern that is of overriding importance to a particular reader, you will lose the argument with that reader. For example, in the debate over abortion, the stated overriding concern of most pro-life adherents is the sanctity of human life. No amount of arguing in terms of freedom of choice, population control, or women's rights is likely to sway such an audience if the sanctity of human life issue is ignored. These readers will just say that you are missing the point. Thus, an important step at this stage is to analyze your audience and determine how they rank their concerns about the topic under discussion.

AUDIO
Talk with a friend to test your argument.

What do you do if your strongest points do not coincide with the main concerns of your audience? One strategy is to *redefine* their concerns and your points so that there is a closer fit. For example, if you were writing about abortion from the pro-choice side, you could argue that the sanctity of human life encompasses individual freedom, including the freedom of women to decide what happens to their own bodies. Another strategy is to accept the differences between yourself and your audience and prepare to make your argument anyway. Even a losing argument can have value, so long as it is a strong argument. It may gain the respect of your opponents, temper their views, resonate unexpectedly among disinterested parties, "plant a seed," or have other beneficial results. But for these good things to happen, you must at least acknowledge your opponents' point of view. Indeed, in some cases, your strongest points will be refutations of your opponents' strongest points.

2 Developing and checking your points

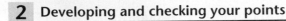

WEBLINK

http://www.engl.niu.edu/
wac/reason.html

Expanded discussion of
Toulmin logic

Starting with your strongest point, use careful step-by-step reasoning to develop each point. Your main goal is to make sure that your points are logically sound by analyzing their structure according to a method devised by the philosopher Stephen Toulmin. This structure consists of six parts: claim (or point), data (supporting reasons), warrant (general principle connecting data to claim), backing (for the warrant), qualifier (of the claim), and possible rebuttal (or counterargument, with a response). Here is an illustration of how Toulmin logic can be used to check one of Angela Napper's claims, namely, that the Constitution guarantees citizens the right to access information.

POINT OR CLAIM | American citizens have the right to freely access information.

DATA | The Constitution guarantees freedom of speech and freedom of the press.

WARRANT (implied) | Freedom of speech and freedom of the press imply a freedom to *listen* to speech and *read* the press, that is, to access information.

BACKING | The Founders believed that people should be free to live their lives as they choose, provided they do not hurt others.

QUALIFIER | The right to access information does not include the right to make others uncomfortable or waste company or university computing resources.

REBUTTAL | People should not be allowed to use public computers to view immoral material. (Response: People have a constitutional right to access whatever information they please, and no one else has the right to impose their own standards of morality on them.)

Notice that in both cases the validity of Angela's argument depends on some implied warrant. Are these two warrants valid? Many people in our culture might think so.

When careful readers judge your arguments, they will be scrutinizing your chain of reasoning. Thus, be aware of the warrant you use

---

Checking Your Argument for Sound Reasoning

1. Have I arrived at a clearly stated, arguable thesis (7a)? What is it?
2. What is the evidence for my thesis, and how does it function as support for the thesis (7c)?
3. What are the main underlying assumptions—or *warrants*—that logically connect my claims to my evidence (7e)?
4. If these warrants are unstated, will they be obvious to everybody in my audience?

---

for each point you make. Often, the warrant is assumed rather than actually stated. But if critical readers do not share your assumptions, they will say that your claims are *unwarranted.* Any assumptions that might not be shared by your readers should be stated explicitly.

EXERCISE 7.5

Identify a point in Angela's essay other than the one analyzed above. Using the same data-warrant-claim structure, analyze this point.

7f   Build a compelling case

The primary goal of any argument is to make the best case you can. The three basic ways to make a case are by using logical reasoning, asserting your and others' authority, and appealing to the readers' emotions.

AUDIO
More on how
to make a case.

1   Appealing to logic

In college, certainly the most important type of support you can give an argument is logical reasoning. Indeed, one of the main purposes of education is to promote the ability to communicate effectively with a broad, skeptical audience (in both professional and public life), and logical reasoning is the primary tool for doing so. In particular, you should avoid logical fallacies (see 7g). In whatever field of study you undertake—sociology, history, mathematics, or biology—your instructors will pay close attention to the logical reasoning you use (see Chapters 16–19). They will want to know that you can develop an argument step by step, laying out a chain of reasoning that compels skeptical readers to respect your thinking.

www
7.2
Some terms
used in formal
logical
reasoning.

WEBLINK

http://commhum.mccneb
.edu/argument/summary
.htm

A tutorial in critical reasoning and argument

There are many effective patterns for developing an argument. They include linking cause and effect, making comparisons and contrasts, defining and classifying, narrating a series of events, generalizing from particulars (*induction*), drawing particular inferences from general rules (*deduction*), and providing relevant examples and analogies. (Some of these approaches underlie the paragraph patterns discussed in Chapter 6; see also 7a-2.)

2 Appealing to authority

People are usually greatly influenced by the credibility or reputation of the person trying to persuade them. That is why advertisers like to use highly esteemed celebrities such as Tiger Woods and Jennifer Lopez to push their products. The appeal to authority takes advantage of people's natural desire to simplify their lives. If Tiger says that Nike golf balls are the best, it is easier to take his word for it than to go to the local library and look up the research findings in *Consumer Reports*.

More discerning readers are not so likely to be influenced by celebrity endorsements, but they are often influenced by expert judgments. Thus, you can support an argument by invoking the authority of true experts. In doing so, it is important to (1) find experts who are addressing an issue within their field of expertise, (2) use actual quotations rather than paraphrasing, (3) include enough context to make the quotation an accurate reflection of the expert's statement, and (4) provide a reference so that skeptical readers can look up the quotation for themselves.

An even more important type of authority is your own. Since you are the person who has gathered the information and assembled the argument, your own credibility (or *ethos*) will be under scrutiny. If readers have any reason to doubt your honesty, fairness, or scholarly integrity, they will treat what you say with a good deal of skepticism. Here are some things you can do to safeguard and enhance your credibility.

1. Avoid making exaggerated or distorted assertions.
2. Acknowledge opposing points of view and counterevidence.
3. If you use other people's ideas or words, give them explicit credit.
4. If appropriate, mention your credentials (without bragging).
5. Use good reasoning throughout.
6. Maintain a respectful, civil tone.
7. Pay attention to details of writing such as grammar, style, spelling, and punctuation.

3 Appealing to emotion

A third powerful way of supporting an argument is by enlisting the readers' emotions. Although this type of persuasion is generally not emphasized in academic and technical writing, it can be highly effective so long as it is used in conjunction with a more logical appeal. In many other kinds of writing (such as political discourse, journalism, and advertising), emotional appeals are used frequently.

Here are some ways to add emotional power to an argument.

1. Describe the issue in a way that relates it to the readers' values or needs.
2. Include examples that readers can identify with, such as stories featuring sympathetic human beings.
3. If you use other people's ideas or words, give them explicit credit. Avoid plagiarism (see 11a-3).

7.3

Details on five major case-building strategies.

(EXERCISE 7.6)

In your opinion, what type of support does Angela's essay rely on most heavily? In her essay, identify examples of a logical appeal, an appeal to authority, and an emotional appeal, and evaluate, in writing, the effectiveness of each.

7g Avoid logical and emotional fallacies

A **fallacy** can be either a false statement or a false line of reasoning. As a critical reader and a careful writer, you should always be on guard against both types of fallacies. With regard to false statements, your best defense is good, solid factual knowledge. For example, if someone claims that Mexico is a monarchy, the best way to expose

VIDEO

Recognizing familiar fallacies.

such a fallacy would be to state knowledgeably that Mexico has not been a monarchy since the nineteenth century.

Lines of reasoning pertain more to the formal aspects of argument. Here, you should be on the lookout for any logical or emotional errors. Such errors can all be classified as *non sequiturs*—that is, claims that "do not follow" logically from the premises on which they are based. Some of the most common fallacies are discussed below.

1 Overgeneralization and oversimplification

When you make a broad statement on the basis of too little evidence, overlooking important differences, you are *overgeneralizing* or *oversimplifying*. Usually the tip-off to this fallacy is the use of absolute qualifiers such as *all, every, none,* or *never.*

EXAMPLES   All Democrats are liberals.

Corporations never look beyond quarterly profits.

Everyone knows about the ozone layer.

Examples are also vulnerable to oversimplification, because an example, by definition, is a claim for generality. If you present something as an example of a broad category, make sure it truly represents that entire category. Otherwise, you will be guilty of overgeneralizing.

EXAMPLE   American cars are bigger gas-guzzlers than import cars. For example, the Ford Explorer gets only 16 miles per gallon while the Toyota Corolla gets 30.

The first sentence may be correct, though it should be qualified by a term such as *on average.* But the example used to support it is misleading. The Explorer is not a typical American car (in terms of gas mileage) and the Corolla is not a typical import car. Furthermore, they are different types of vehicles, so comparing the two is like comparing apples and oranges.

2 Begging the question

When you make an argument at too superficial a level and leave the underlying issue(s) unaddressed you are *begging the question.* This is also known as "assuming what needs to be proved," or *circular reasoning.* Often, begging the question involves unstated but controversial warrants (see 7e-2). In some cases, the unstated warrant is the missing premise of an enthymeme (see 7a-2).

EXAMPLE   Sex education should be eliminated from the public schools. We shouldn't be encouraging our young people to engage in sex.

This is a fallacious enthymeme.

MAJOR PREMISE, UNSTATED   Sex education encourages students to engage in sex.

MINOR PREMISE   We do not want to encourage students to engage in sex.

CONCLUSION   Sex education should be eliminated.

The unstated warrant in step 1 is unproven and indeed highly controversial. By using it as an unstated assumption, the speaker is guilty of begging the question.

3 Attacking the person instead of the evidence (*ad hominem*)

Also called the *ad hominem* (Latin for "to the man") fallacy, this tactic is commonly practiced in public discourse. It tries to divert attention from the real issue by discrediting the opponents' character.

EXAMPLE   My opponent wants you to believe that she will give you good representation in Congress, but can you really trust someone who admits to having smoked marijuana?

A candidate's personal life, past or present, may have little to do with how she performs as a public servant, yet this is a ploy commonly used in political campaigns and elsewhere to sway people.

4 Using either/or reasoning

This fallacy results from assuming that there are only two ways of looking at a particular issue. Psychologists call it the *black-or-white syndrome*. Also called the *false dilemma*, this fallacy is commonplace in the media (with its predilection for getting "both sides of the story"), in our adversarial system of justice, and in our two-party political system. But reality teaches us that there are typically *many* sides to a story. To be a good thinker, avoid falling into the either/or trap.

EXAMPLE   Bill is an avid hunter and gun collector. He is opposed to any gun control legislation, saying, "You're either in favor of the Second Amendment or you're against it."

Bill's statement constitutes a false dilemma, because it ignores any middle ground where gun ownership could be maintained as a constitutional right yet regulated in the way that other rights, such as freedom of speech, are regulated.

(Note) Many gun advocates deliberately reject any such middle ground, believing that it would result in a gradual chipping away of their rights. This is known as a *slippery slope argument:* "Once you start down that slope, there's no stopping."

5 Using faulty cause-effect reasoning

Just because two events occur closely in time does not necessarily mean that one caused the other. As statisticians are careful to point out, correlation is not always causation.

EXAMPLE   Tax cuts can lead to higher economic growth. From 1990 to 1995 the ten states that raised taxes the most created zero net new jobs, while the ten states that cut taxes the most gained 1.84 million jobs, an increase of 10.8 percent.

It could be that it was the lack of new jobs that caused the first group of states to raise taxes (to pay unemployment compensation, for example), not the other way around.

A special case of faulty cause-effect reasoning is the *post hoc* fallacy (for Latin *post hoc, ergo propter hoc,* or "after this, therefore because of this"). In this fallacy, an assumption is made that because one event occurred after another, the first event caused the second. It could be, however, that the two events are unrelated.

EXAMPLE   Two days ago I signed up with a new Internet service provider, and now my computer is acting up. Maybe I should go back to my old provider.

It is of course *possible* that one action caused the other, but it is by no means certain. Any of a number of things unrelated to the Internet service could be causing those computer problems.

6 Using false analogies

False analogies start with true analogies and then try to extend them beyond reason, claiming similarities that do not exist.

EXAMPLE   Just as the Founders said that a well-regulated militia was necessary to the security of a free state, modern-day militias like the Montana Freemen are the best guardians of our freedom.

Such a statement may seem reasonable at first reading, but analysis of its logic reveals serious flaws. Contemporary "militias" such as the Montana Freemen are sectarian groups with no official standing; thus, they are very different from the militias of the late 1700s, which more closely resemble today's National Guard.

7 Using the bandwagon appeal (*ad populum*)

This is a common emotional ploy that tries to pressure you into going along with the crowd. The *bandwagon appeal* plays on people's natural urge to belong to a group.

EXAMPLE   Everyone agrees that a free-market economy is best.

The general consensus is that Pearl Buck was not as great a writer as Toni Morrison.

Since "everyone agrees," if you don't agree too, there must be something wrong with you! Remember, though, that the hallmark of a well-educated person is the ability to think critically, which requires an independent mind (see Chapter 2).

8 Using a red herring

Anything that draws attention away from the main issue under discussion is a *red herring* (in the way that the scent of a fish might distract hunting dogs). Politicians are notoriously adept at using this type of evasive tactic, as are advertisers.

EXAMPLE   At a press conference, Senator Gladhand is asked about campaign contributions he has received from X Corporation and how they will affect his votes in the Senate. He responds by saying that X Corporation is a "good citizen" and that "American business contributes greatly to America's prosperity."

By shifting attention to American business and away from this particular corporation, the Senator is guilty of using a red herring.

Red herrings can be seen in much modern advertising (especially on TV), where instead of addressing the merits of the product, the ad diverts attention to something else (a beautiful landscape, beautiful people, funny dogs, and so on).

9 Assuming that two wrongs make a right

Another way to deflect attention away from an issue is by using the "two wrongs make a right" fallacy. In this ploy, the arguer defends an accusation of wrongdoing on his or her part by claiming that the other side is guilty of similar or worse wrongdoing. For example, if a local politician defends the city's high crime rate by saying that crime is even worse in other cities, she would be diverting attention away from the real issue, her own city's crime rate.

10 Appealing to bias

Using words with strong positive or negative connotations can exploit the biases of an audience. As with other emotional fallacies, the appeal to bias disregards rational thought but can still be effective in influencing readers or listeners. A bumper sticker saying "Your kids and my taxes go to St. Pedophile's" might be effective with readers who have an anti-Catholic bias. More fair-minded readers, however, would notice its loaded language ("St. Pedophile's") and gross overstatement and quickly dismiss it.

EXERCISE 7.7

The Internet, like other media, is fertile ground for logical and emotional fallacies. Log on to one of the political newsgroups (see 24b–2) and find two examples of fallacious reasoning. Analyze each according to the principles discussed in this chapter.

7h Structure the argument

There are numerous ways to structure an argument. After looking at four of the most common ones, we will consider ways to decide which method to select and whether to use an inductive or a deductive arrangement.

1 Using the classic five-part method

The classic method, which dates back to antiquity, has five parts.

WEBLINK

http://www.philosophy
.eku.edu/williams/
rhetsum/default.htm
Detailed description of the classic method of argument

1. Introduce the topic, explain why it is important, and state or imply your thesis.

2. Provide enough background information so that readers will be able to follow your argument.

3. Develop your argument. If you did not state your thesis in step 1, state it here. Support it with appropriate evidence, compelling appeals, and sound reasoning.

4. Acknowledge and refute possible objections and counterarguments, using good evidence and reasoning. Various objections can be dealt with in different parts of the paper. For example, you may want to cite one or more counterarguments early in the paper in order to introduce some of your main points as refutations.

5. Conclude by reemphasizing the importance of the issue and the main points of your argument.

2 Using the problem and solution method

The problem and solution method involves describing a problem and then proposing one or more solutions to it. This pattern is common in reports, memos, and other forms of business and technical writing. For example, a memo might state, "Some people can't get here in time for our 10:00 a.m. meetings. Do you think we could change the starting time to 10:10?" The key to this method is to clearly identify the problem before stating the solution. The problem and solution method is a good choice when (1) the audience agrees on the nature of the problem and (2) the possible solutions are few in number. In situations where these conditions do not exist, you are likely to have to spend too much time defining the problem and discussing the various solutions.

3 Using the Rogerian method

The aim of the Rogerian method is to defuse a hostile audience. The arguer begins by characterizing the opponent's position in terms the opponent can accept and then presents his or her own position in a form that respects both the opponent's and the arguer's views. Once a dialogue has been established, the differences between the two sides can be explored. For example, in her essay on Net theft (5f), Kirsten Parsons begins by noting that unlicensed copying off the Internet "has become an accepted practice," one that "we know we can get away with." By framing the issue in this way (in particular, by using the collective pronoun "we"), she establishes common ground with her readers before going on to argue against Net theft.

WEBLINK

http://www.winthrop.edu/wcenter/handoutsandlinks/rogerian.htm

Good advice on Rogerian argument, from Winthrop University

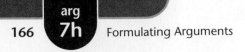
4 Using the narrative method

Storytelling is a powerful and persuasive form of presentation, especially if the narrator has a lot of credibility with the audience. But because a skeptical reader may not be willing to generalize from the experience of the narrator, the personal narrative is not effective in college writing unless it is backed up by other kinds of support.

Kirsten Parsons's essay (5f) uses two stories in making her argument. She starts off with a brief narrative illustrating a common instance of unwitting Internet theft. Written in the form of a dialogue, it is likely to engage readers' interest. Then, on pages 2–3, she tells how as a little girl she was caught shoplifting, using this story to argue that Net theft is no different than shoplifting.

5 Selecting a method

Which method works best? The answer depends mainly on how your audience is likely to react to what you have to say. In any argument, your readers are likely to agree with you on some issues and disagree on others. The usual strategy is to structure the argument so that the agreed-upon parts come first and the more contentious parts later. This way, you can establish common ground with your readers before going on to more difficult matters.

If you know, for example, that your readers are concerned about the same problem you are, the problem and solution method would be a good choice. If your readers know you personally and respect your experience and knowledge, you could start out with a personal narrative. If you and your readers have broadly divergent viewpoints, the Rogerian method is useful because you start out by stating the readers' position—something you know you can agree on. The classic method is popular in college writing because all it presumes about the readers is that they will take the time to read the entire paper carefully; thus, the first few paragraphs can be devoted to introducing the topic and providing whatever background information the readers need.

Although each of these four patterns can be used in its pure form, they can also be combined in different ways. For example, you could tell a personal narrative in the first part of the problem and solution method, or you could take a Rogerian approach in the first part of the classic method to establish common ground with a hostile reader. Indeed, expert writers often combine techniques in interesting ways.

HELP

How do I keep track of my argument?

1. Analyze your audience and topic, and then select an appropriate argument structure.
2. Open the outlining feature of your word-processing software.
3. List your main points from most important to least important, and plug them into the outline according to the argument structure you have selected.
4. Under each point, indicate your supporting evidence and basic line of reasoning.
5. Check the hierarchical structure of your outline. Make sure each point is distinct and independent. If two points say similar things, select one as a main point and make the other a supporting point under it.
6. Draft your paper as you normally would, but shift to your outline occasionally to make sure you are staying on track.

(EXERCISE 7.8)

Outline Angela's essay, showing how it essentially follows the classic five-part structure.

7i Electronic argument

Traditional forms of argument, as described above, depend on a model of communication in which a writer (or speaker) produces a complete argument that is then read and evaluated by a passive, "captive" reader. With the advent of Internet-based forms of communication, however, argument itself has taken on new forms. Email, newsgroups, listservs, and Internet relay chat (IRCs) all use an interactive, dialogic form of communication that promotes an equally interactive form of argument. In this conversation-like environment, there is great pressure on participants to take turns, with no one dominating the floor. The interaction provides little opportunity for any one person to lay out an extended argument in its entirety; rather, one must be content to offer a quick, abbreviated argument or even, in some cases, just make a single point.

WWW

7.4

Three examples of effective electronic arguments.

The give-and-take nature of these electronic forms of argument calls for some adaptations.

1. If you want to contribute an argument to an ongoing discussion (for example, in a newsgroup or an IRC), make sure you are up to date on how the topic has been discussed up to that point. By reading previous posts, you can avoid simply repeating what has already been said (which might only irritate other participants).

2. Do provide enough context, however, so that the reader knows what you are referring to. One or two sentences should suffice.

3. Limit your response to whatever you can say on a single screen. In most cases, this means making only one or two well-supported points. Most people do not want to scroll through page after page of print.

4. Consider adding links (see 23b-3) to Web sites containing relevant supporting information.

5. Make your point concisely and precisely. Take time to edit and proofread.

6. Before hitting SEND button, read your message over and make sure you're comfortable with its content and tone. Remember that electronic postings are often read by a larger and more diverse audience than the writer anticipates.

HELP

How should I design an argument for a Web site?

1. Make the opening screen both visually and textually appealing, so as to capture the interest of your readers. Establish the issue that your argument addresses.

2. Decide on your main pieces of supporting evidence and put clearly labeled links to these items on the opening screen (see 23b-3).

3. Cluster your claims and your supporting evidence so that each page of your Web site has unified content.

4. Use graphics only as needed to support your argument, not for decoration (see 20).

5. Include a "For Further Reading" link to other Web sites dealing with the same topic as well as some that present alternative views. This material could enrich the reader's experience and, if nothing else, will enhance your credibility.

Another, albeit less interactive, form of electronic argument can be found on Web sites. Unlike either traditional arguments (laid out in one piece from start to finish) or the interactive types of arguments just described, Web site arguments are dispersed over hypertext links (see 22a-2). For example, the main claims may be on a single page, but the supporting evidence may be found on other pages or even at other linked sites. Visitors can navigate the site in any number of ways, and so a creator who wishes to present an argument has to somehow induce visitors to navigate the site in a way that brings out the full force of that argument. Following the general principles of good Web site design (see Chapter 22) should help, as should the more specific guidelines in the preceding Help box.

EXERCISE 7.9

Log on to a newsgroup, listserv, or other discussion forum and find a posting that adheres to the guidelines given in the Help box on page 168. Then find a posting that does *not*. Rewrite the latter according to the guidelines.

7j   Visual argument

Visual images can communicate ideas in powerful ways, and this power extends to argument. Consider, for example, the poster from *Adbusters.com* shown on the following page.

The image of what appears to be Joe Camel sitting in a hospital bed with his sunglasses off and a downcast look on his face (Figure 7.1) is highly attention-getting. Because it's so different from the standard Joe Camel ads we're used to seeing, we're inclined to look closely at it. This causes us to notice the words *Joe Chemo* and perhaps even read the "Surgeon General's warning" that "smoking is a frequent cause of wasted potential and fatal regret." We quickly understand that this is a parody of the Camel ads: the likable icon of smoking now undergoing chemotherapy (presumably against lung cancer) is meant to persuade viewers to stop smoking.

In this case and in countless others, the visual and the verbal work together; both are indispensable. And together they make what could be considered the *beginning* of an argument in that they implicitly express a thesis. The poster implicitly makes a claim about the danger of smoking. Visual images are often powerful in drawing attention to some issue, but visuals alone cannot present a full argument. That is, visuals cannot make a clearly stated claim (7a), cannot provide good supporting evidence (7c), cannot consider and refute

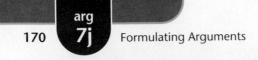

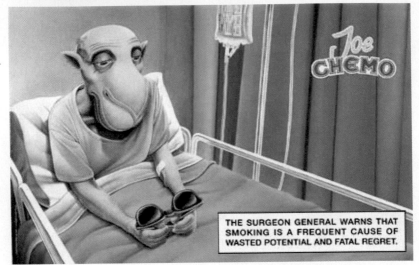

THE SURGEON GENERAL WARNS THAT SMOKING IS A FREQUENT CAUSE OF WASTED POTENTIAL AND FATAL REGRET.

FIGURE 7.1 Joe Chemo ad.
Source: www.adbusters.com

alternative views (7d), cannot build a compelling case (7f), and cannot avoid logical and emotional fallacies (7g); for all these things, you need language. But visual images and language together can form a very powerful combination.

Although argument is conducted mainly through language, it can be strongly supported by pictures, graphs, or other forms of visual representation. Consider, for example, the table below about the worldwide HIV/AIDS epidemic. Like most tables, this one presents words and numbers in a visual layout that suggests certain themes. If you were writing an argumentative essay about the global

TABLE 7.1 Global Summary of the HIV/AIDS Epidemic, 2002 (in millions)

	Men	*Women*	*Children*	*Total*
Newly infected in 2002	2.2	2.0	0.8	5
Living with HIV/AIDS	19.4	19.2	3.2	41.8
Died from AIDS in 2002	1.3	1.2	0.6	3.1
Died from AIDS since 1981	12.4	12.4	5.5	30.3

Source: Joint UN Program on HIV/AIDS, 2001. <http://www.unaids.org>.

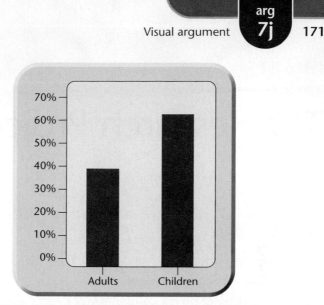

FIGURE 7.2 AIDS Mortality by Percentage of Those Who Have Contracted
the Disease, 1981–2002
Source: World Health Organization; UNAIDS. <www.unaids.org>.

HIV/AIDS epidemic, you could use Table 7.1 to support a claim that
adults have suffered far more from AIDS/HIV than children have.

Tables can provide an effective form of visual argument, but
they are not as rhetorically powerful as more visual types of graphics, such as line graphs, bar graphs, pie charts, maps, diagrams, and
photographs. For example, the bar graph in Figure 7.2 shows more
dramatically than a table the contrast between adults and children
with regard to AIDS mortality. The stark visual difference between
the two columns illustrates the enormous difference in degree of vic-
timization suffered by children. A graph such as this could add
vividness and memorability to an essay about the effects of HIV/
AIDS on children.

Whenever you are constructing an argument paper or oral presentation (Chapter 26), look for ways to enhance your argument with
visual support. (For further discussion of the use of graphics, see 20c.)

FOR COLLABORATION

Together with one or two classmates, find an argument essay that
lacks visual support. (Some suggestions: the essay by Glenn Sacks in
Chapter 2, the essay by Kirsten Parsons in Chapter 5, or an op-ed column in a newspaper.) Working separately, come up with ideas for
adding visual support. Then compare the results and discuss them.

CHAPTER **8**

The Research Project

FAQs

▶ What does it mean to do research? (8a)

▶ How will I ever get it all done? (8b)

▶ Can I take notes on my computer? (8c)

▶ What is a bibliography? (8d)

▶ What are background sources? (8e)

▶ How do I focus my search? (8f)

VIDEO

Drafting a research paper.

The process of writing a research paper does not differ markedly from the process of writing an essay, described in Part 1 of this handbook. The writing stages outlined in Chapter 3 (and discussed in Chapters 3–5)—preparing, composing, and rewriting—still apply. The difference is one of scope. A research paper is longer than most essays and contains more information from external sources, found by doing research. It would be a good idea to review the stages of the writing process briefly before you begin a research project.

WWW

8.1

Ideas and assistance for writing research papers.

WEBLINK

http://www.wisc.edu/ writing/Handbook/ PlanResearchPaper.html

Guide to planning and writing a research paper

AUDIO

Breaking research tasks into manageable parts.

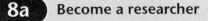

8a Become a researcher

Why research? Work in many academic and professional disciplines, including law, medicine, engineering, and psychology, depends heavily on research. In all fields, researchers conduct studies to answer important questions, to solve problems, to prove cases, and to argue positions. In college, your main reason for researching may be to carry out an assignment in a particular course. For example, in a literature course, you may be asked to research an author's life or critiques of literary texts; in a political science course, you may be asked to research a political campaign or a political trend. Whatever your motivation for researching, you need to become seriously engaged in the research process.

The ability to research—that is, to explore a problem systematically—is a crucial skill. A researcher is a careful, critical, systematic thinker who goes beyond memorizing facts on a subject to examine the bases on which claims and arguments rest. Although you may not realize it, you probably have already researched many subjects. Have you ever purchased a DVD player or an automobile? How did you decide which one to choose? If you read about DVD players in *Consumer Reports* or other magazines, talked to friends about them, compared several models, or shopped around, you researched your purchase. The thinking processes you used are similar to those used to research a subject in a college course.

WEBLINK

http://www.ipl.org/div/aplus

A+ Research and Writing, to help writers get started on their research paper projects

8.2
Getting started on a research paper.

1 Understanding the research assignment

When you receive a research assignment, first think through what you are being asked to do. Ask yourself questions such as these:

- What will my purpose be?
- How should I sound as a writer?
- Who will my readers be?
- Where will I get my authority?

Deciding on a rhetorical stance (see 3a-2) will help you determine a general approach to the assignment. If a rhetorical stance has not been specified by the instructor, you may want to discuss it with him or her.

The two main types of research are primary research and secondary research. **Primary research** entails generating information or data through processes such as interviewing, administering questionnaires, or observation (see 8f-6). **Secondary research** involves finding information in secondary, or published, sources (see 8f-1 to 8f-5). You need to decide which type or types of research your project demands. Can you find what you need in secondary sources, or will the research be primary in nature or some combination of the two? What kinds of sources does your instructor expect you to use? Today, secondary sources take a variety of forms: books in the library, articles in journals and magazines, newspapers and government documents, computerized hypertexts found on the Internet.

8.3

The process of research.

Does your assignment provide clues as to what your instructor expects from you? Look for key terms, such as *analyze, discuss, explain, define, evaluate, compare,* and *persuade,* in the assignment. These terms can help you decide how to approach your research project.

FOR COLLABORATION

Discuss the implications of the key terms *analyze, discuss, explain, define, evaluate, compare,* and *persuade* with a small group of your peers. How might each word lead to a different research paper?

---

2 Finding a topic

Once you have a sense of the assignment, you can begin to think about possible topics for your research. If your instructor left the choice of topic up to you, you have an opportunity to research a question that interests you or a problem that intrigues you. It is important to find a topic that you already know something about or that you would like to become more knowledgeable about. Because you will be spending a great deal of time on the topic, it is helpful if the topic provokes some kind of response from you, even if that response is a questioning or skeptical one.

Research typically begins with good questions. Experienced researchers do a great deal more than just find information in library books or encyclopedias and report it in the form of a research paper. You need to think about how to use the information you find in your research to answer a question that a particular subject has inspired in you. A good place to begin looking for a research question is in the textbooks you are currently using. Is there a debate that is discussed in the textbook that has not yet been resolved or that is arguable? For example, perhaps in your history textbook you read that there is a difference of opinion among historians concerning the nature of the interactions between Native Americans and the Pilgrims. Out of this debate might come a question for your research: "What was the relationship between the local indigenous population and the Pilgrims in the early colony of Plymouth Plantation?" Or, you might begin by browsing through a specialized encyclopedia, such as the *Encyclopedia of Psychology* or the *Encyclopedia of Educational Research,* for some ideas. Another place to begin looking for potential research questions is the Internet (see the Help box in Chapter 3, p. 46). For additional information on Internet searching, see Chapter 9.

Once you have some preliminary ideas for a topic, discuss your ideas with a reference librarian, your instructor, and other students in your class. They may have suggestions about your topic or may be able to direct you to aspects of the topic that you had not considered. Listen particularly to your instructor's advice on the appropriateness of topics. Although there are no "bad" topics *per se*, there are topics that may prove difficult, given the constraints of the assignment. Your instructor will be able to tell you if topics are overused (for example, capital punishment and abortion), too trendy (for example, rock stars, fads, and fashions), or too trivial or specialized (for example, family interaction in *The Simpsons*). Take your instructor's advice so that you do not find yourself struggling with an unworkable topic.

(**FOR COLLABORATION**)

Investigate a few possible topics. Discuss the options with peers, classmates, a librarian, and your instructor. Narrow your choices down to one or two workable topics that you can later investigate more thoroughly.

3 Selecting a specific topic

Kaycee Sorensen, the student whose research paper is included in Chapter 12 as a model, was given the assignment of writing a research paper on a technological subject. She was not sure what technological issue she wanted to write about, so she decided to surf the Net as a way of generating some specific topics (see 9c-1). After browsing in the *Yahoo!* search directory, Kaycee noticed the topic of "shopping and services" listed under the category "Business and Economy." She was curious about the prevalence of online shopping in our culture. Was the number of cybershoppers increasing? Was shopping via the Net a viable alternative for consumers? Was it safe to use a credit card for online shopping? These questions served as a starting place for Kaycee's research. Posing these questions allowed Kaycee to begin her background reading in search of answers, rather than reading aimlessly in an unfocused way.

4 Narrowing and focusing the topic

Search tools are useful not only for getting topic ideas but also for narrowing a general topic area or dividing a subject into several component parts, much as the subject directories on the Internet do. For example, under the broad topic of business and the economy, Kaycee selected the specific topic of cybershopping, passing over other possible technological topics such as intellectual property or ethics and responsibility. She then narrowed the topic of cybershopping to exclude sites related to retail sales since she was interested in the advantages and disadvantages of cybershopping but not in sites that promoted online retail sales. (See 3e-1 for more on narrowing topics.)

Asking research questions

Once you have identified a specific topic, the next step is to focus the topic by asking pertinent research questions that you will attempt to answer—your "starting questions." For the specific topic of cybershopping, Kaycee's starting questions were as follows:

```
Is the number of online shoppers increasing?

Is shopping via the Internet a viable option for consumers?

Is it safe to use a credit card for online shopping?
```

Developing a hypothesis

As you work through the research process, attempting to answer your starting questions, you should come up with a hypothesis—a tentative statement of what you anticipate the research will reveal. A working hypothesis specifically describes a proposition that research evidence will either prove or disprove. As you begin to gather background information on your topic, you should develop a hypothesis that will help you to focus your research. Kaycee moved from her starting questions to a working hypothesis as follows:

TOPIC

```
Cybershopping
```

RESEARCH QUESTIONS

```
Is the number of online shoppers increasing?

Is shopping via the Internet a viable alternative for consumers?

Is it safe to use a credit card for online shopping?
```

WORKING HYPOTHESIS

```
The number of online shoppers is increasing, which means that

cybershopping is becoming a convenient, affordable, safe option

for consumers.
```

A working hypothesis should be stated in such a way that it can be either supported or challenged by the research. Kaycee's research will either support or challenge her working hypothesis. The hypothesis is called "working" because you may find that you need to change or revise it during the course of the research.

5 Developing a search strategy

A search strategy is a plan for proceeding systematically with research. Once you have decided on your starting questions and working hypothesis, you are ready to outline your search strategy. Your first decision will be about the nature of your research. Will you be relying mostly on secondary (library and Internet) research or on primary (field) research? Secondary research is discussed in 8f-1 to 8f-5. Primary research is discussed in 8f-6.

8.4

Mastering
Internet search
techniques.

The goal of a search is to build a working bibliography—a list of possible sources that may or may not eventually be used in the final paper. A working bibliography is typically about twice as long as the final bibliography for a research paper (see 8d for more about working bibliographies), because many of the sources you identify will turn out not to be applicable to your paper or not to be available in time for you to use in your research. By searching for sources in a systematic way, you avoid aimlessly wandering around the library or surfing on the Internet. Figure 8.1 shows possible steps in a search strategy.

8b Schedule a time frame

If you have never done a research project before, you may be overwhelmed at the thought of such a large and complex task. If you break the job down into smaller parts, however, it will seem much more manageable. Formulating a time frame in which to complete your research project will also help. If your instructor has not given you deadlines, set your own dates for accomplishing specific tasks.

For a major project, allow at least three to four weeks for background research and a more focused search. As you begin to work in the library or on the Internet, you will see that searching and reading are time-consuming. Plan to spend one or two hours in the library and/or on the Internet each day for the first month of your research project. After that, you may find that you can spend less time in the library. If your project involves primary research, allow one to two weeks for designing, conducting, and analyzing the primary research.

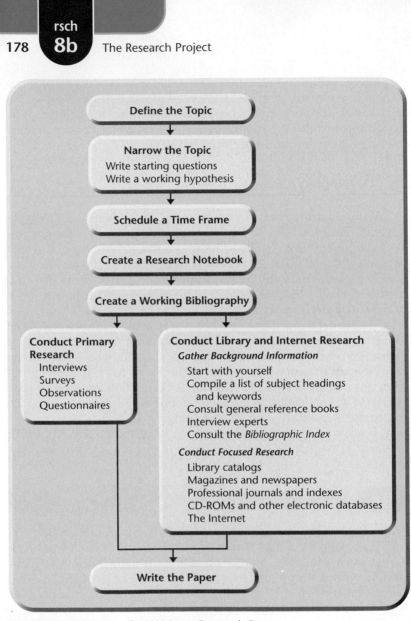

FIGURE 8.1 A Strategy for Writing a Research Paper

Schedule at least one to two weeks for preliminary writing. If you are a slow writer, you will need more time. To make sense of your subject and answer your starting questions, you will need to spend time studying and evaluating your sources, brainstorming, and prewriting. Eventually you should be able to express your understanding of the subject in a working thesis statement, which will control the shape and direction of the research paper and provide the readers with a sense of the paper's main idea or argument (see 3e-3).

Finally, give yourself enough time to plan, organize, and write a first draft and then several revisions. You need time to outline and con-

Sample Schedule for Writing a Research Paper

(Allow approximately one week for each step.)

Step 1. Select a preliminary research topic; articulate starting questions; begin background research; schedule a time frame; begin to focus the topic (see 8e).

Step 2. Build a working bibliography by using indexes, online catalogs, databases, and the Internet (see Chapter 9); begin to locate sources in the library and on the Net (see 8f).

Step 3. Read and evaluate sources; take notes on relevant sources; in a research notebook, comment on the importance of sources to the topic and their relationship to other sources (see 10a); print out information from the Internet; write down complete bibliographical information for each source and make a note of Web site addresses, or URLs (see 8d-2).

Step 4. Arrange and conduct any primary research; complete the reading and evaluation of sources; identify gaps in the research and find more sources if necessary (see 8f).

Step 5. Begin preliminary writing in a research notebook—summarize key information; begin brainstorming on the topic; write a few possible thesis statements designed to answer the starting questions (see 12a).

Step 6. Write a working thesis statement that will guide the direction of the piece; sketch a tentative outline or plan of the research paper (see 12a-2, 12b).

Step 7. Write a rough draft of the research paper; keep careful track of sources through accurate citations; take care to distinguish quotes and paraphrases and to document all source information appropriately (see Chapter 11); write a References or Works Cited list (see Chapters 13–15).

Step 8. Revise and edit the rough draft; spell check; check sentence structure and usage; check documentation of sources; solicit peer responses to the draft (see 5c, 5e).

Step 9. Print and proofread the final copy; have a friend or classmate proofread as well (see 5d, 5e).

struct your argument, using source information to reinforce or substantiate your findings in a clearly documented way (see Chapters 13–15). Most students need one to two weeks to organize and write a rough draft and an additional week to revise, edit, and proofread. As you can see from the sample schedule on page 179, most research projects take an entire college term to complete.

EXERCISE 8.1

Using the sample schedule on page 179, draw up a time frame for your own research, with specific target dates for each step in the research process.

8c Create a research notebook

It is important to create a notebook in which to record all the information relating to your research project. If you are using a word-processing program, you can take advantage of its storage capabilities to develop an electronic research notebook. Create a directory (see the Help box on page 43), and label it your research notebook directory. In this directory, you can create files to record your topic and your starting questions, notes from your background research and focused research, and your working bibliography (if you do not have bibliography software). In your electronic research notebook, you can also begin to articulate answers to your starting questions as your understanding evolves through research. As you investigate your topic, record not only what others have said on the subject, but also your own impressions and comments. You can also use research notebook files to develop your thesis statement and an informal outline or organizational plan for your paper, and to write all preliminary drafts of your paper.

If you do not have a computer, you might set up a ring binder with dividers for all of the files just described.

- Topic and starting questions
- Thesis statement and outline
- Research notes and comments
- Working bibliography
- Drafts 1, 2, 3, as needed

Many students like to record notes in their research notebooks, while others like to take notes on note cards.

1 Recording notes in a notebook

Whether your notebook is paper or electronic, be sure to keep your recorded notes separate from your comments in order to avoid inadvertent plagiarism (see Chapter 11). If your notes are handwritten, you might use two columns when recording information: one for notes taken from the source and the other for comments, analyses, and queries. If your notes are electronic, you can use your word-processing program's DOCUMENT COMMENTS (or ANNOTATIONS) feature to insert your comments and analyses into the notes taken from sources. Figure 8.2 shows a document comment on the screen.

AUDIO

Insert your comments into research notes.

2 Taking notes on note cards

Like notebooks, note cards can be either handwritten or computer generated. If you choose to handwrite notes on index cards, give each note card a descriptive title and take notes on only one side of each card to allow for easy sorting and scanning of information later on. Include a page reference on your note card for all notes, both quoted and para-

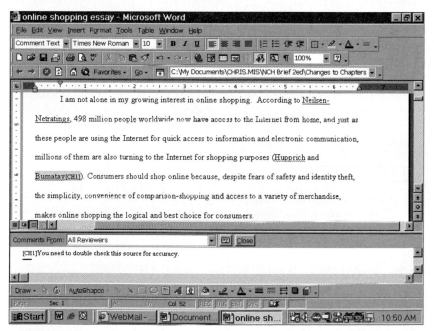

FIGURE 8.2 Example of a Document Comment in *Microsoft Word*

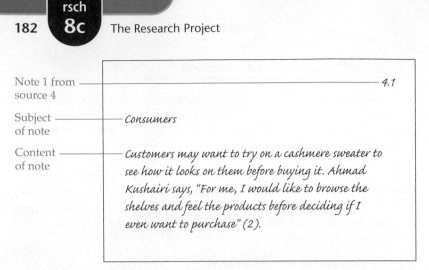

Note 1 from source 4 ———————————————————— 4.1

Subject of note ——————— *Consumers*

Content of note ——————— *Customers may want to try on a cashmere sweater to see how it looks on them before buying it. Ahmad Kushairi says, "For me, I would like to browse the shelves and feel the products before deciding if I even want to purchase" (2).*

FIGURE 8.3 Note Card

phrased (see Chapter 11). In the upper right-hand corner of the note card, include a control number that identifies the source. Then consecutively number your notes for each source. On the note card in Figure 8.3, the number 4.1 indicates that this note was the first one taken from source 4. It is important to use this system consistently, since you will be relying on these cards later when you cite your sources in your final paper (see Chapters 13–15).

Some computer operating systems and Internet browsers offer computerized note card systems. Or you can purchase software for a note card system. Such a system can be particularly useful if you own a laptop computer, which you can use while in the library taking notes. You can use the computer note cards just as you would use index cards: title each card by topic, and then type your notes onto the card provided by the computer. The computer note card system will sort the cards automatically by topic.

(**EXERCISE 8.2**)

Create a directory or folder to serve as your electronic research notebook. Divide it into subfolders to use as you pursue your search (a folder for your working bibliography, another for notes from sources, and so on).

3　Taking notes with photocopies and printouts

Photocopies and database printouts

With photocopy machines and computer printers now so readily available in libraries and computer labs, more researchers are making use of these tools to record source information. Making your own photocopies and printouts of sources has many advantages: first, you will have the actual wording of the authors at your fingertips, so you will not have to rely on your notes for accuracy when quoting (thereby reducing the chances for inadvertent plagiarism); second, you can highlight passages that are important to your own research for future reference; third, you can actually take notes on the photocopies or printouts (see Figure 8.4). Make certain that you record complete bibliographic information on all photocopies and printouts from books, newspapers, journal articles, or full-text library databases. You will make your life much more difficult if you have to retrace your steps because you neglected to write down the publication date from an article you photocopied, for example. Refer to Chapters 13–15 for the complete bibliographic information that needs to be listed for each type of source you use in your research.

Printing Internet sources

When you are researching on the Internet, it will most likely be easiest for you to print out copies of relevant Web pages rather than take notes by hand. If you wish to use a specific section of a Web page as a source, highlight that section using your computer's mouse and then choose PRINT/SELECTION from the PRINT dialog box. In this way, you will print only the parts you need, not the entire Web site. As with photocopies, printouts of sources from the Internet will also need to have complete bibliographic information. In addition to the usual information for all sources (the author, title, and publication data), for Internet sources you will need to note the complete URL of the page(s) you are referring to, the date you accessed the page, and the dates when the site was posted and last updated.

Downloading Internet sources

Another method of obtaining information is to download or save Internet pages directly into your own computer files (using FILE > SAVE AS). When downloading or copying and pasting files from the Internet, you need to be especially careful not to import information directly into your own work without citing the source appropriately. To keep from inadvertently plagiarizing from the Internet, always type into your computer notebook the complete bibliographic information from each source, and put quotation marks around any text that you COPY and PASTE from the Internet. Also, note for yourself the author of the quotation so that you can use that information in a *signal phrase* that introduces the quotation. (For

Need to learn more about this organization and its political motives

> **MoveOn.org**   Page 1 of 1
>
> **MoveOn.ORG**   **News Release**
> citizens making a difference
>
> **FOR IMMEDIATE RELEASE**   **Contact:**
> April 24, 2001   Joan Blades 510-701-0078 joan@moveon.org
>   Peter Schurman 202-669-2186 peter@moveon.org
>
> **Online Advocacy Group Takes on Energy Suppliers:**
> **Grassroots Campaign asks Feds to Restore Stable and Reliable Energy**
>
> San Francisco, CA - In an initial salvo declaring, "the energy market is broken," online advocacy group MoveOn.org urged its 250,000 members to support a bill Senator Dianne Feinstein is introducing today, which would limit wholesale energy prices.
>
> "Energy prices are skyrocketing across the nation, yet Washington is doing nothing," said MoveOn.org president Wes Boyd in his email message to supporters. "Energy producers are making huge windfall profits. Consumers and taxpayers are given the shaft."
>
> MoveOn.org members will ask US Senators to cosponsor the Energy Reliability and Stability Act of 2001. This bill, already cosponsored by Senators Feinstein (D-CA), Smith (R-OR), Lieberman (D-CT), Cantwell (D-WA), and Murray (D-WA), would direct the Federal Energy Regulatory Commission to set either a temporary cap on wholesale electricity prices, or temporary "cost-plus" rates allowing wholesalers to charge just a reasonable rate of profit, not the excessive premiums they are now charging in California.
>
> Today's energy action by MoveOn.org today kicks off the organization's campaign on energy, launched not only in response to the current crisis, but also because the group's members chose protection of the environment as one of their top priorities in an online forum conducted at its website last fall. Energy is a critical environmental issue.
>
> **About MoveOn.org**
>
> MoveOn.org is committed to helping its members be effective, informed citizens, and to broadening participation to counter the influence of monied interests and partisan extremes. MoveOn.org offers members a way to work together to be heard. The website, begun by Silicon Valley entrepreneurs Wes Boyd and Joan Blades, has inspired 500,000 Americans to lobby Congress.
>
> When those voices are not heard, the MoveOn.org PAC helps members engage in meaningful electoral action. Last election cycle, the MoveOn.org PAC served as a conduit for more than $2 million in small contributions to congressional campaigns across the nation.
>
>   ###
>
> http://www.moveon.org/release042401.htm   12/13/02

Need evidence to support this assertion

Need to find out the status of these bills

This explains the group somewhat

FIGURE 8.4 Example of Annotated Internet Printout

more information about citing electronic sources, see Chapters 13–15. For more information about avoiding plagiarism, see Chapter 11.)

8d Create a working bibliography

A **bibliography** is any listing of books and articles on a particular subject. When you submit a research paper, you include a bibliography to show readers what sources you consulted to find your information. As you begin your research, start a **working bibliography,** which will grow as your research progresses. This working bibliography will likely contain some sources that you ultimately will not use in your research paper, so entries need not be in final bibliographic form. However, be careful to accurately record all the information you will need on bibliography cards or in your research notebook so that you do not have to track down sources twice (8d-1). Include the author's full name, a complete title including subtitle and edition, the city and state where the work was published, the name of the publisher, and the date of publication. When you actually write your research paper, you will compile a **final bibliography.** It will include only the sources that you actually used in writing the research paper, and it will be formatted according to a particular documentation style. The final bibliography will be named according to the documentation format you are using: in the Modern Language Association (MLA) format it is called *Works Cited*; in American Psychological Association (APA) format it is called *References*; and in the Council of Biology Editors (CBE) format, it is called *Cited References* (see Chapters 13–15).

AUDIO
Keeping accurate records of sources.

1 Recording bibliographic information

You can prepare a working bibliography manually on index cards or electronically on a computer file. If you use index cards, record bibliographical information (author, title, and publication data) on one set of cards and content notes (see 11a-2) on a separate set. Figure 8.5 shows a sample bibliography card.

Using a computer to record bibliographic information is even more efficient because you can easily reformat the information later, when you prepare your final bibliography. Some word processors are

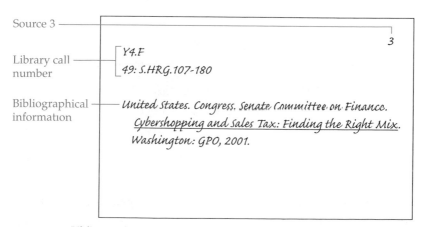

Source 3

Library call number

Bibliographical information

3

Y4.F
49: S.HRG.107-180

United States. Congress. Senate Committee on Finance.
  Cybershopping and Sales Tax: Finding the Right Mix.
  Washington: GPO, 2001.

FIGURE 8.5 Bibliography Card

HELP

How do I use a computer bibliography program?

8.5

Instructions for
using *TakeNote!*
software.

1. Open the bibliography software, such as *TakeNote!* from
   Pearson Education.

2. Follow the directions for entering data; usually you will be
   asked to enter information by category (author, title, publication data).

3. Wait for the bibliography program to generate your bibliography, based on the information you provide. It will format
   the information appropriately for a particular documentation
   style and place it in alphabetical order. Some bibliography
   programs will convert from one documentation style to
   another—for example, MLA (see Chapter 13) to APA (see
   Chapter 14) style.

4. Name and save your bibliography, as well as any Works
   Cited lists you may have generated from it.

NOTE: You still need to check your bibliography carefully to be certain the program has generated it in the correct format.

equipped with bibliographic software that automatically formats the
information. (See the Help box above.)

Here is Kaycee's working bibliography, which was generated
electronically.

Better Business Bureau Program. 2002. 22 July 2002 <www.bbbonline.org>.

Chan, Christine, et al. "Online Spending to Reach $10 Billion for
    Holiday Season 2001." *Nielsen/NetRatings*. 20 Nov. 2001. 28 Jul
    2002 <http://www.nielsennetratings.com/pr/pr_011022.pdf>.

Cox, Beth. "E-commerce: Color it Green." *Cyberatlas* 3 Aug. 2002. 12
    Aug. 2002 <http://cyberatlas.internet.com/markets/retailing/
    article/0,,6061_1364801,00.html>.

Frey, Christine. "Online Shopper: Advantages of Plastic." *Los Angeles
    Times* 18 Oct. 2001: T8.

Greenspan, Robyn. "E-shopping Around the World." Cyberatlas 5 Aug.

    2002. 23 Jul 2002 <http://cyberatlas.internet.com/markets/

    retailing/article/0,,6061_1431461,00.html>.

2 Writing an annotated bibliography

One type of bibliography that is frequently required by instructors is called an *annotated bibliography* because it includes annotations, that is, brief descriptive paragraphs about each source. You might also find it useful to compile an annotated bibliography for your own use, whether it is required or not, because it is an ideal way to keep track of what is contained in each source. Below are a few entries excerpted from an annotated bibliography for a research paper about acupuncture.

Annotated Bibliography

"Acupuncture." Fishbein's Illustrated Medical and Health

    Encyclopedia. 1983 ed.

    Good source of background information. Concentrates on an

    introduction, then provides specifics about anesthesia. Shows

    pictures of acupuncture being performed.

"Acupuncture." The New Encyclopaedia Britannica. 1992 ed.

    Not a specialized source, but provides some good background

    information. Tells the theory of how acupuncture works.

"Acupuncture Boom Punctured." Nature 318 (1985): 222.

    A short article with some general information about anesthesia,

    its acceptance, and its uses.

"Acupuncture for Craniofacial Pain." Geriatrics 40 (1985): 36.

    From a scholarly source; shows how acupuncture can be an

    alternative to surgery for certain problems.

"Acupuncture May Offer Hope for Alcoholics." RN 53 (1990): 113.

    Specific information on acupuncture being used on skid row

    alcoholics. Some statistics.

American Academy of Medical Acupuncture. General Information. 2001.

    AAMA. 9 March 2001 <http://www.medicalacupuncture.org/acu_info/

    generalinfo.html>.

    A Web site provided by the accrediting agency for physicians who

    wish to become trained and certified as medical acupuncturists.

    Includes lots of good information for consumers and physicians.

"Baltimore Tries Treating Substance Abuse with Acupuncture." <u>Public

    Health Reports</u> 105 (1990): 436.

    Scholarly source reporting on a clinic in Baltimore that uses

    acupuncture to treat people with drug addictions.

3 Printing or saving online sources

As mentioned in 8c-3, if you are using sources from online databases, you may want to print out copies for later review or download them onto your own computer disk using the FILE > SAVE AS command. In either case, be sure that complete bibliographic information appears on the pages or in the files. If it does not, make a bibliography card for the source, in addition to the printout. Include the following information: (1) author's name, if available; (2) publication information for print and online versions; (3) the URL; (4) the date of posting or updating; (5) the date you accessed the site. If you print material from the Web, your browser may automatically include source information, but be sure to check. If you cannot find the complete address, or URL, on your printed copy, record it by hand.

> (EXERCISE 8.3)
>
> Establish a consistent format for entering the bibliographic information on your research, either as bibliography cards or as a computerized working bibliography.

> (FOR COLLABORATION)
>
> Meet with a group of three or four classmates to discuss your working bibliographies. Share ideas about sources and databases that you found useful in your search. Suggest possible places to look for information that your classmates might not have thought about.

What leads were particularly helpful to you? What dead ends did you encounter? What search challenges are you still facing?

8e   Gather background information

Now is the time to gather background information, using your starting questions and working hypothesis as a guide. This information will help you conduct more focused research later on.

1   Starting with yourself

At the start of a research project, write down everything you already know about your topic. The list may be quite extensive or rather short. The important thing is to inventory your own knowledge first so that you can systematically build on that knowledge base. The more you know about your topic, the better you will be at judging the value of sources you read. Also check your biases and assumptions about the topic, asking yourself the following questions.

1. Do I already have a strong opinion about this topic?
2. Have I "rushed to judgment" about it without looking at all the facts?
3. Am I emotionally involved with the topic in some way that might bias my judgment?

If your answer to any of these questions is "yes," think seriously about whether you will be able to keep an open mind as you read about the topic. If not, you might want to choose another topic.

2   Compiling a list of subject headings and keywords

The cataloging system developed by the Library of Congress is the one most widely used for organizing library materials. In order to put information into related categories, the Library of Congress has developed a listing of subject headings. This listing is compiled in a multivolume set, called the *Library of Congress Subject Headings* (or *LCSH*), available in both printed and computerized form. Kaycee Sorensen, whose final research paper appears in Chapter 12, looked up the subject heading "online shopping" in the *LCSH*. Figure 8.6 shows what she found.

Notice that her topic was listed in the *LCSH* not as "online shopping" but as the related subject "teleshopping." In addition to the main headings, the *LCSH* lists related subject headings that may lead to other potentially useful sources. Additional subjects are listed in the *LCSH* under RT (related term), BT (broader term), and NT (narrower term). In Figure 8.6, UF means that the heading in bold is "used for" the other headings listed, which are *not* subject headings.

Researchers use the subject headings in the *LCSH* to find both books and periodicals (magazines and journals) related to their topics. Whether you are using a regular library card catalog or a computerized catalog, the subject headings are the key to locating information on your topic. Searching a library's catalog is discussed in 8f.

Related to subject headings are **keywords** (sometimes called descriptors or identifiers), which are used to identify the subjects found in electronic databases, including the Internet. The keywords used to search for electronic sources may not be exactly the same as the subject headings in the *LCSH*. So, it is important to compile a comprehensive listing of both possible subject headings and possible keywords for

This is the subject heading to use for online shopping	Online shopping Subject heading USE Teleshopping **Online stockbrokers** *(May Subd Geog)*
Used for	UF Electronic stockbrokers Internet stockbrokers Web Stockbrokers
Broader term	BT Stockbrokers
Related term	RT Electronic trading of securities Online trading of securities USE Electronic trading of securities

Subject heading	**Teleshopping** *(May Subd Geog)* — Indicates the presence of geographical subdivisions to follow the heading UF Home shopping Online shopping BT Shopping Telecommunication systems
A subtopic	**—Law and legislation** *(May Subd Geog)* **Teleshopping equipment industry** *(May Subd Geog)* *HD9696.T45-HD9696.T454* BT Telecommunication equipment industry

FIGURE 8.6 Library of Congress Subject Headings

Keyword Searching

1. *What is a keyword search for?* A keyword search allows you to search for the term or terms that you have identified as being most important for your project.

2. *Where does the computer search for the keywords?* The computer will locate all items in the database that include the particular keywords or terms anywhere in the work's record, from the title to the body to the bibliography.

3. *Can the computer supply other related words?* Typically the computer will not be able to supply synonyms for the keywords you have identified. You need to think of as many keywords as possible.

4. *What terms should I use as keywords?* You will have to use your knowledge of the topic, gained through background reading, to come up with keywords. For example, if you are searching the subject of UFOs, you might use *UFO* as a keyword. But you might also want to try *flying saucers* or *paranormal events.*

5. *Can I do a keyword search on the Internet?* The same kind of keyword searching discussed here can be done on the Internet. (See Chapter 9 on Using the Internet for Research.)

VIDEO
Narrowing a subject online.

AUDIO
Tips for keyword searching.

your topic at the outset of your research. In an electronic database search, keywords can be combined using what are known as **Boolean operators.** These operators, most commonly AND, OR, and NOT, tell the computer to combine keywords in ways that it recognizes. (See Tips on Using Boolean Operators for Internet Searching, on page 219.)

3 Doing preliminary background reading in general reference books in the library

We recommend that you begin your library search in the general reference section. Here you will find reference books that have condensed huge amounts of information into an accessible form. These sources can help you to define your subject area more clearly, to identify keywords and important authors, and to gain a general understanding of your topic.

8.6

Reference books and online reference resources.

Most of the reference works listed on the following pages are available both in book versions and in computerized versions (either on CDs or on the Internet). Many libraries provide access to computer-based dictionaries, encyclopedias, thesauruses and bibliographies. Such computerized reference sources often are more up to date and can be searched faster than the printed forms.

Dictionaries

Dictionaries typically provide concise information about words: definitions, pronunciations, usage, origin, and changes in meaning. It is essential to have a good desk dictionary to consult for all your writing. Some good ones include the following:

American Heritage College Dictionary. 4th ed. Boston: Houghton, 2002.
Random House Unabridged Dictionary. 2nd ed. New York: Random, 1993.
Webster's Dictionary and *Roget's Thesaurus,* searchable through *refdesk .com* <http://www.refdesk.com>.
Webster's Collegiate Dictionary. 11th ed. Springfield, MA: Merriam, 2003.

Figure 8.7 shows the homepage for *refdesk.com.*

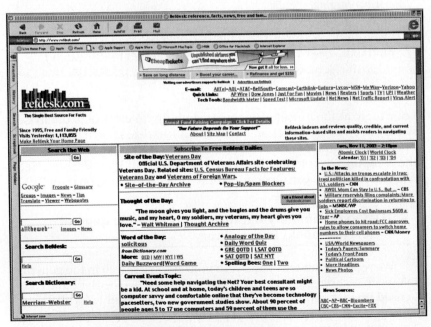

FIGURE 8.7 Homepage for *refdesk.com*

Encyclopedias

Encyclopedias provide concise information on people, places, subjects, events, and ideas. Encyclopedias are particularly useful for locating general background information on a subject or person. Look in the encyclopedia's index for references to related subtopics and articles within the encyclopedia. Some general encyclopedias include the following:

Academic American Encyclopedia. Rev. ed. Danbury: Grolier, 1998.
Encyberpedia: The Living Encyclopedia from Cyberspace <http://www .encyberpedia.com/cyberlinks/links/index.html>.
Encyclopedia Americana. Rev. ed. New York: Grolier, 2003.
Encyclopedia Britannica. Chicago: Encyclopaedia Britannica, 1997.

In addition to the general encyclopedias (print, CD, and online versions), there are also numerous specialized encyclopedias, such as the *Encyclopedia of American History* and the *Encyclopedia of World Art.* Listings of specialized encyclopedias by discipline can be found in Part 3 of this handbook.

Biographies

Biographies provide information on the lives and work of famous people. As with encyclopedias, there are both general and specialized biographies. General biographies include the following:

Current Biography: Who's News and Why. New York: Wilson, 1940 to present.
Dictionary of American Biography. New York: Scribner's, 1943 to present.

Bibliographies

Bibliographies are lists of books or articles about particular subjects. Some bibliographies appear at the end of an article or a book; others are entire books in themselves.

Guide to Reference Books. 11th ed. Robert Balay et al., eds. Chicago: American Library Association, 1996.

Other sources

The general reference section of a library contains many other sources that may be helpful in your research. Check with the reference librarian for the following types of sources, if they are relevant to your research: atlases, which contain maps; almanacs, which briefly present a year's events in government, sports, politics, and economics; yearbooks, which contain worldwide data; and handbooks, or fact books, which provide statistical data.

By reading about your topic in a number of general reference works, you can ascertain what is considered to be "common knowledge" about your topic. Common knowledge is information that is generally known and, therefore, need not be cited as the idea of one particular author. If you read the same information in three or more general sources, you can assume it is common knowledge. However, any facts or data found in general sources still need to be cited in your paper, and the reference source listed in your bibliography. (For information on citing sources, see Chapters 13–15; see also Chapter 11 on using sources.)

4 Interviewing experts or joining a discussion group

Even if your assignment does not specifically require primary research, it is a good idea to talk to experts in the field, if possible. You may know a professor or a family friend who is familiar with the topic. Make an appointment to talk to that person and get his or her views on the topic. It is not necessary to conduct a formal interview—an informal conversation is generally sufficient. If there are online discussion groups or listservs on your topic, join in on the conversation or follow others' exchanges to gain a better understanding of your topic (see Chapter 24).

5 Consulting the *Bibliographic Index*

After surveying your own knowledge on a topic, reading background sources, and talking to experts, you should be able to narrow the focus of your topic. At this time, you may wish to consult the *Bibliographic Index,* an annual listing of bibliographies, arranged by subject. This index lists all the bibliographies on a particular subject in a given year (a bibliography of bibliographies). Browsing through this index for several recent years will give you a sense of the subject and its subtopics; in addition, you may find some pertinent sources on your topic.

> (EXERCISE 8.4)
>
> Using the suggestions outlined above, investigate background sources on your topic and begin to focus your research. Cast a wide net as you begin your research; you can always revise and refine your focus based on the

information you locate. When you have completed your background reading and research, begin to search and read in a more focused way.

8f Conduct focused research

Once background reading has helped you understand your subject, narrow it to a manageable size, and formulate a hypothesis, you are ready to read in a more focused way on your topic. Conducting focused secondary research involves locating—through magazines, newspapers, journals, books, government documents, and the Internet—the specific information you need to write your paper. (For information on primary research, see 8f-6.)

AUDIO
Searching print and online sources.

1 Using library catalogs

Libraries have catalogs that list all the books and documents in the library. Although some libraries may still use card files (which include cards for authors' names, subjects, and book titles), either by themselves or in combination with *computerized catalogs,* most libraries today house their catalogs on computers. Computerized catalogs allow for ease of storage and searching (see Figure 8.8).

The computerized catalog is one of the most visible computer tools in libraries today. Computerized systems, which are replacing the traditional card catalog, are designed to handle various library functions, such as circulation, cataloging, and location of materials within the library collection. Like card catalogs, most computerized catalogs are searchable by author, title, and subject; in addition, computerized catalogs are searchable by keyword or by a combination of subject and keyword. (See Keyword Searching on page 191 and Tips on Using Boolean Operators for Internet Searching on page 219.)

When you log on to your library's computerized catalog, you typically will see a menu listing the various databases available for searching. In order to select the appropriate database from the computer menu, you need to know how the information in the library is organized. Many libraries offer instruction in the use of the computerized catalog. If yours does, take advantage of it, and spend the time you need to learn how to confidently use your library's computer system.

Typically, libraries divide their computerized catalogs into a general database, which indexes books, government documents, and audiovisual materials, and specialized databases, organized by discipline. Specialized databases found in many computerized library catalogs include the following:

Biological and Agricultural Sciences Index (lists articles from biology and
 agriculture journals)
Education Index (lists articles from education journals)
General Sciences Index (lists articles from journals related to science)
Humanities Index (lists articles from journals in the humanities)
Social Sciences Index (lists articles from social science journals)
Wilson Guide to Applied Science and Technology Index (lists articles from
 journals related to the applied sciences and technology)
Wilson Guide to Art Index (lists articles from art magazines and journals)
Wilson Guide to Business Periodicals (lists articles from business journals)

The articles that you find in a computerized catalog search may or
may not be available to you in your own library, as most libraries can
afford to subscribe to only a limited number of magazines, newspapers, and journals. Ask the librarian for a list of the periodicals your
library subscribes to. Sometimes this information will appear right
on the computer record when you locate the reference in the index. If
your library does not own a particular magazine, newspaper, or jour-

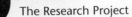

FIGURE 8.8 Library Catalog Entry

nal, do not despair. Through interlibrary loan or the Internet, you can often locate an article and obtain it for your own use. Check with the librarian to find out about such reciprocal services.

When you are using computerized catalogs, it is important to be familiar with the *Library of Congress Subject Headings (LCSH)* (see 8e-2). To search a computerized database by subject, you must provide the computer with the official subject headings used by the Library of Congress, as listed in the *LCSH*. You may also want to search by title, author, or keyword.

2 Using indexes to magazines and newspapers

In your library's general catalog, you'll find a listing of magazine and journal names, but you will not find a listing of specific articles within those publications. Private indexing services, such as the Educational Research Information Clearinghouse (ERIC), have taken on the job of listing (indexing) all of the individual articles found in specific journals on particular topics. In the case of ERIC, the articles indexed are related to the field of education. To locate articles in education journals on a particular topic, you would use the ERIC descriptors, which are keywords that ERIC uses to index the articles. As with the *LCSH* subject headings discussed in 8e-2, to make the best use of such indexes you need to first discover the keywords by which the subject has been indexed. These "controlled vocabularies" will vary by indexing service. Specialized subject indexes are often available both by computer searching and in print form.

8.7

Sites devoted to finding news.

Magazines

Magazines and other publications that come out at regular intervals (usually longer than one day) are called periodicals. Articles in periodicals can often provide specific and up-to-date information on a topic. You can locate magazine and newspaper articles both through computer searching and through print indexes. The most commonly used indexes to magazines are the *Readers' Guide to Periodical Literature* and the *Magazine Index*. In both sources, entries are arranged by subject and author.

Newspapers

Libraries generally store back issues of newspapers on microfilm. You will need to use a newspaper index to locate relevant articles. To gain access to articles in the *New York Times,* use the *New York Times Index,* which lists all major articles in the *Times* from 1913 to the present.

The *Newspaper Index* lists articles from the *Chicago Tribune, Los Angeles Times, New Orleans Times-Picayune,* and *Washington Post.* Both indexes are arranged by subject. For business news, use the *Wall Street Journal Index.* Newspaper indexes are available in both print and computerized formats.

WEBLINK

http://news.google.com/
Search and browse the
latest headlines

Many search engines now offer a feature to help patrons keep track of the news headlines. Such "news tracker" services can also be customized to search for news stories related to particular subjects or topics (see Figure 8.9). One of the best news tracker services is available from the *Google* search engine.

3 Using indexes to professional journals

If you are researching a technical or academic subject, you will want to refer to articles written by professionals in the field. Profes-

FIGURE 8.9 Screen from Google's *NewsPage*

sional journal articles are indexed in much the same way as magazine and newspaper articles. However, you will need to find a specialized index or database for professional articles in the particular discipline or subject area. For example, *Social Sciences Abstracts* lists articles from journals in the social sciences, and *General Science Abstracts* lists articles from science journals. Figure 8.10 shows the beginning of the "Internet + shopping" entry in the *Social Sciences Abstracts*. Discipline-specific indexes are available in most libraries, both in print and on computer. Some of the specialized indexes that can be searched through a computerized cataloging system are described in 8f-1.

4 Using CD-ROMs and other electronic databases

Locating specific information on a topic may require use of a variety of computerized search tools. In addition to your library's computerized catalog (8f-1) and computerized indexes to magazines, newspapers, and journals (8f-2, 8f-3), investigate any CD-ROM databases available to you.

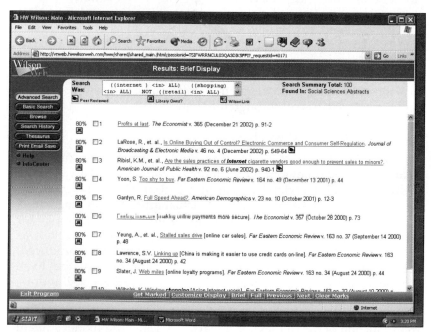

FIGURE 8.10 Excerpt from *Social Sciences Abstracts*

CD-ROM (compact disc–read only memory) databases make large amounts of information accessible by storing it digitally on compact discs. For example, the education index *ERIC* is available in this format, as is the business index *ABI-INFORM*. CD-ROM databases are subject-specific, so you need to find out just which journals or subjects they cover. Most CD-ROM databases provide an abstract of each work listed. By reading the abstract, you can get a good sense of whether the article contains information useful for your research.

As with any computerized searching, it is important in using CD-ROMs to know your keywords. Many CD-ROM databases use their own controlled vocabulary, which may vary slightly from the subject headings used in the computerized catalog. Ask a librarian whether there is a thesaurus or listing of subject headings for the particular database you are using. *ERIC* on disc, for example, uses the "ERIC Descriptors" as its method of cataloging by subject. To find the exact keyword for your search, you need to look up your topic in the Descriptors volume.

Figure 8.11 shows an example of an article listing from the *Environmental Periodicals Bibliography* CD-ROM. Notice the information that is listed for this article, including the keywords under which it has been indexed. You would need to use the information provided about the journal source—climate change; 1996 Vol 33. No. 2 (June), p 145—to find the specific journal in which this article can be found. First, find out if your library carries the journal by looking up its title in the computerized catalog; then, if the library subscribes to this journal, you can locate it either in the serials collection in your library stacks or in the current periodicals section (for a very recent issue). If your library does not subscribe to the journal, you may still be able to locate the journal in a full-text database or through interlibrary loan.

Electronic full-text databases

It is clearly impossible for libraries to own all magazines and journals in a world of rapidly exploding information. Many libraries subscribe to full-text database services that provide library patrons with Internet access to copies of the actual articles from magazines, newspapers, and professional journals. Your library has to pay for such services, and subscriptions may be expensive—but not as expensive as trying to purchase every publication that's produced! Check with your librarian to find out if your library subscribes to an online database service such as *Lexis-Nexis* or *EBSCOHost*. If it does, you may be able to search the database via the Internet by subject or keyword to find not just a listing of the article's title and source but a reproduction of the full text of the article itself. For a model student search using a library subscription service, see 9d-2.

```
* * * * * * * * * * * * * * * * * * * * * * * * * * * * * * * * * * * * * * * * * * * * * * * * * *
                         NISC REPORT
      ENVIRONMENTAL PERIODICALS BIBLIOGRAPHY    June 1997

* * * * * * * * * * * * * * * * * * * * * * * * * * * * * * * * * * * * * * * * * * * * * * * * * *
```

TITLE:	Uncertainties in global climate change estimates. An editorial essay.
AUTHOR:	Pate-Cornell, Elisabeth
SOURCE:	Climatic Change; 1996 VOL. 33, NO. 2 (June), page 145
KEY TERMS:	Climate change; Uncertainty analysis; Policymaking; Science role; Risk assessment; Probability model
MAJOR TOPIC:	AIR
NOTES:	Assessing Uncertainty in Climate Change and Impacts
RECORD ID:	1997-018516
TITLE:	Evaluating the implementation of state-level global climate change programs.
AUTHOR:	Feldman, David L.; Wilt, Catherine A.
SOURCE:	Journal of Environment and Development; 1996 VOL. 5, NO. 1 (March), page 46
KEY TERMS:	Climate change, global; Environmental policy, national and international; Government compliance, state; Policy implementation evaluation; Non-governmental organization role; Evaluation criterion
MAJOR TOPIC:	SOCIAL, POLITICAL AND PHILOSOPHICAL ISSUES
RECORD ID:	1997-015217

FIGURE 8.11 Listing from the *Environmental Periodicals Bibliography* CD-ROM

5   Using Internet resources

The Internet is becoming an increasingly important research tool in all fields of study. A biologist observed that he can locate information crucial to his research in minutes via the Internet, when it used to take days or even weeks of searching through print sources. Since the Internet has become so crucial to research, we devote an entire chapter in this handbook to the topic. In Chapter 9, we follow Kaycee Sorensen's use of the Internet to research her topic of cybershopping. Kaycee discovered extensive information related to her topic on the Internet. You can find out more about how to use the Internet to enhance your research project by reading Chapter 9.

6 Doing primary, or field, research

In all disciplines, researchers use primary research methods to gather information and search for solutions to problems. (The researchers who read the printed reports generated from the primary research are using secondary research methods.) For example, when a chemist performs an experiment in the laboratory, that is primary research; when an archaeologist goes on a dig, that is also primary research. For our purposes, *primary research* (8a-1), also called *field research*, will refer to the kind of field collection of data that you as a college undergraduate can do. Of course, there is a great deal to learn about the primary, or field, research methods commonly used in various disciplines; we will consider just a few field research techniques that can be adapted for use in a research project—observation, surveys, and interviews.

Observation

The general goal of observation is to describe and perhaps evaluate customary behaviors. Observation is best suited to the collection of nonverbal data. The observer watches people behave in customary ways in a particular environment or setting and takes notes. You might observe where people stand in an elevator, for example, or how they cross a street at an unmarked crosswalk. Through observation, you accumulate *field notes*, which are used to analyze trends and discern customary behaviors. The disadvantages of observation include lack of control over the environment, lack of quantifiable data, and small sample size. Also, whenever an observer enters the environment to observe people, the participants' behaviors may cease to be natural. For example, if you stand in an elevator taking notes about people's behavior, eventually they will notice you, and they may no longer behave the way they ordinarily would. As you think about your research project, consider whether observational data would enhance your report. Be sure to gather enough background information prior to the observation itself to ensure its usefulness to your research project.

Surveys

Ideally, an entire population would be studied to gain insights into its society. However, polling an entire population is seldom fea-

Guidelines for Effective Observations

1. Articulate a general goal for the observation.
2. Gather background information.
3. Plan your observation carefully so as not to unduly influence the behaviors of those you are observing.
4. Take accurate notes during your observation and accumulate them in a research notebook.
5. Analyze your observation notes for trends or patterns.

sible, so surveys are used to sample small segments of the population selected at random. The most frequently used sampling technique is random-digit dialing of the telephone. Researchers have refined sampling techniques to be extremely accurate. One common kind of survey is the questionnaire, a form that asks for responses to a set of questions. Designing questions is a science that has been developed over the years. Although the details are beyond the scope of this book, the basic principles are to be sure that the questions you write are clear and understandable and written in such a way that the responses will be easy to tabulate. Researchers generally agree that closed questions, which require checking a box or answering "yes" or "no," yield more usable data, but open-ended questions, which require a short written response, can provide valuable insights (though they are harder to interpret). Think through your research topic to see if a questionnaire might yield useful data. For an example of a paper that uses data from a student-generated questionnaire, see the social science paper in Chapter 19.

Interviews

Interviews are one particular type of survey. The advantages of the interview include flexibility (the questioner can interact with the respondent), speed of response (the questioner immediately knows the responses), and nonverbal behavior (the questioner can gather nonverbal as well as verbal responses). However, because interviews take time, fewer responses can be gathered. Another disadvantage is that the character of the interviewer him- or herself can influence the outcome of the interview. Here are some considerations in designing an interview.

Guidelines for Effective Interviews

1. Articulate a general goal for the interview and make an initial contact with the subject.
2. Confirm the appointment the day before.
3. Be prompt, have your questions ready, and stick with the time allotted for the interview.
4. Ask your questions exactly as you wrote them down.
5. Politely probe any unclear or incomplete answers.
6. Review your notes immediately following the interview.
7. Follow up with a thank-you note.

1. Be certain that the questions are written down in advance and asked exactly as worded.
2. Be certain that you probe any unclear or incomplete answers.
3. Be certain that inadequate or brief answers are not probed in a biasing (directive) way.

If you decide that an interview would enhance your research, be sure that you conduct the interview professionally. Be prompt, have your questions ready, ask permission before taping responses, and be careful not to take up more of the person's time than you indicated when setting up the interview. A follow-up letter thanking the person for the interview is a polite gesture. After the interview, take time to review your notes and to clarify or supplement them as needed while the information is still fresh in your mind.

EXERCISE 8.5

Using the suggestions and resources described in this section, conduct focused research on your topic. Include both secondary (print and Internet) sources and primary (field) sources, as appropriate to your topic.

FOR COLLABORATION

Interview a classmate using the interview guidance provided above. When you have completed your interviews, report to the class what you learned about your subject. Discuss with your classmates what makes an effective or ineffective interview.

CHAPTER 9

Using the Internet for Research

- ▶ How can the Internet help me with my research? (9a)
- ▶ What kind of information is available on the Internet? (9b)
- ▶ How can I find anything on the Web? (9c)
- ▶ What is a search tool? (9c-1)
- ▶ What does an Internet search look like? (9d)
- ▶ What does a search of a library subscription service look like?

One of the primary benefits of the **Internet** is that it connects computer users to information on computer networks around the world. People use the Internet for a variety of purposes, such as communicating with each other, playing games, sharing information, and selling products. We discuss the uses of computer networks for communication in Chapter 24. The Internet also has many educational uses. Much information published by educational institutions, libraries and service organizations, commercial and corporate providers, the public press, and the government can be located through an Internet search. Through the Internet you may also be able to search databases to which your library subscribes. This chapter introduces the ways in which the Internet can help with a research project.

9a	**Use Internet sources throughout the research process**

AUDIO
The importance of Internet research.

As mentioned in Chapter 8, the Internet is becoming increasingly important for research. Searching the Internet for information on a topic

9.1

Read this before starting an electronic search.

WEBLINK

http://www.lib.berkeley
.edu/TeachingLib/Guides/

Current information on electronic searching, from UC Berkeley librarians

is similar in many respects to researching in the library. When beginning to research on the Internet, you should follow a search strategy, as outlined in 8a-5. Use the Internet for finding and exploring research topics, for background and focused searching, and even for collaboration with your peers and feedback from your instructor.

However, as you begin searching the Internet, you need to realize that this process is not an exact science. Searching the Internet is time-consuming, messy, and often frustrating for students, with numerous dead ends and false starts. Sometimes you will find far too many sources and sometimes none at all. Searching smarter can help. We recommend persistence and also attention to using search tools wisely (see 9c).

1 Finding and exploring topics

You do not need to wait until you are well into your research to turn to the Internet. In fact, you can use the Internet in the preparing stage of the writing process, to help you find a topic. The Help box in 3a-1 explains how to use the Internet to explore topic choices. Because Internet search tools (see 9c) are often organized by topic and subtopic in subject directories, you can use them to explore topic options. For an example of how one student used the Internet to explore research topics, see 8a-3.

2 Conducting background and focused research

Once you have decided on a topic, you can use the Internet to find background information and to search in a more focused way. Many of the reference materials used in the library for background information (such as dictionaries, encyclopedias, and handbooks) are also available through the Internet. Internet libraries, online collections, and library subscription databases are discussed in 9c-2. Other sources of information available via the Internet include journals and magazines, newspapers, and government documents.

3 Collaborating and exchanging feedback

Email and online discussion forums are ideal for trying out your topic ideas on your instructor and your peers. These Internet tools are discussed in Chapter 24. As you research and write your paper, take advantage of the forums the Internet provides for sharing information—trade ideas, drafts, research sources, and revision feedback. For more information on collaboration, see also 3d-1, 4c, and 5e.

9b Get to know the Internet and the Web

The many helpful research tools on the Internet include communication tools (email and mailing lists, bulletin boards and Usenet discussion groups, real-time writing with *Instant Messenger* or MOO) and collaboration tools (such as Microsoft's *Netmeeting* or Netscape's *Collaborator*). All of these tools are discussed in Chapter 24 on Using Email and Computer Networks. But no doubt the main Internet tool that you will be using for research is the World Wide Web.

The **World Wide Web,** or the Web for short, is by far the easiest and most popular way of accessing information from the Internet. The Web provides a hypertext interface for "reading" Internet information. This means that information is presented in the form of a series of

> ### WEBLINK
>
> http://www.lib.berkeley .edu/TeachingLib/Guides/ Internet/FindInfo.html
>
> A tutorial for finding information on the Internet, from UC Berkeley librarians

9.2
A tutorial and Internet research guide.

hyperlinks, each leading to another document or another location on the Internet. Documents structured as a series of links are called **hypertexts.** You simply use a mouse to click on the link (usually a graphic or a word or phrase in colored type with underlining) to connect with the hyperlinked document. Researchers navigate the Web through the use of an Internet browser, such as *Netscape Navigator* or *Internet Explorer* (see 9b-1).

1 Surfing the World Wide Web: Browser tools and homepages

The World Wide Web, a huge spider web–like structure that encompasses computer networks throughout the world, seems to have been woven overnight. No one spider wove this web; anyone and everyone can contribute (see Chapters 22–23 for information on designing and writing for the Web). This is probably the Web's greatest strength as well as its greatest weakness. It is a strength because no single organization could have compiled the varied and vast amounts of information placed on the Web for anyone to access. It is a weakness because the lack of control creates an information hodgepodge, with the trivial alongside the profound. When looking for information on the Web, you may find everything from vanity homepages to the latest scientific information from a NASA space probe.

Though no entity controls the Web, the organization that establishes common standards for Web technology is the World Wide Web Consortium, or W3C. The Consortium consists of CERN, the organization in Geneva, Switzerland, that originated the Web; the Laboratory for Computer Science at the Massachusetts Institute of Technology (MIT); and INRIA, the European W3C center. The Consortium does not regulate information on the Web. Rather, the Consortium establishes technical standards that ensure that the Web will be accessible to people around the world.

Getting connected

You will probably be accessing the Internet either through a direct connection in a campus computer lab or through a dial-up modem, cable, or DSL service from home. Direct connections are much faster than dial-up modems. If you intend to use your home computer to access the Internet, ask your campus computing center to recommend the best way to connect to the campus computer network.

Internet browser tools

Once you have an Internet connection, you need an Internet **browser** in order for your computer to display Web pages. If you are using a computer in a campus lab, there will probably be icons on the opening screen for the two most popular browsers, *Netscape Communicator* or *Internet Explorer*. They have comparable features and are free. If you are using a recent version of *Windows*, you will find that *Internet Explorer* has already been installed on your computer. Upgrades for both of these browsers can be found at their respective Web sites and **downloaded** to your own computer. Be aware, however, that downloading software from the Internet via a dial-up modem can be extremely slow.

AUDIO

Take advantage of Internet browser tools.

WEBLINK

http://www.microsoft.com/ie, or http://www.netscape.com

To find out if upgrades to *Internet Explorer* or *Netscape* are available, go to the Web sites listed

Both *Explorer* and *Netscape* include many useful tools that will help you as you conduct your research on the Internet (see Figures 9.1 and 9.2).

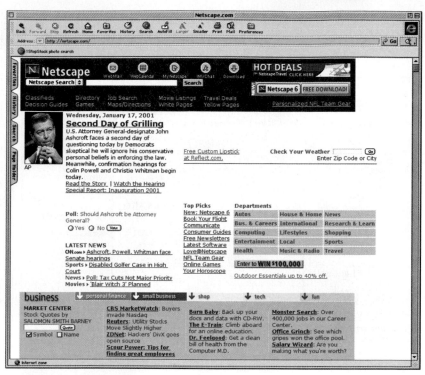

FIGURE 9.1 *Netscape* Browser

Keeping track of your search

Both *Netscape* and *Explorer* help you keep track of important Web sites and retrace the steps of your Internet search. The GO feature keeps a running list of the Web sites you have visited during your current Internet session. It will disappear when you close down your browser. The GO command is found on the menu bar in *Netscape* and within the VIEW menu in *Explorer*.

If you have found a page that you want to visit frequently, you can add this site's address to your list of bookmarks (*Netscape*) or favorites (*Explorer*). You can add a page to your bookmarks/favorites by visiting that page and then choosing ADD BOOKMARK or ADD TO FAVORITES from the bookmark menu or button. You can also arrange your bookmark/favorite sites into folders. (See the Help box on page 211.)

To retrace your steps after an Internet search, you can use the HISTORY feature of your browser (found as a button on the toolbar in *Explorer* and within the COMMUNICATOR > TOOLS command on the

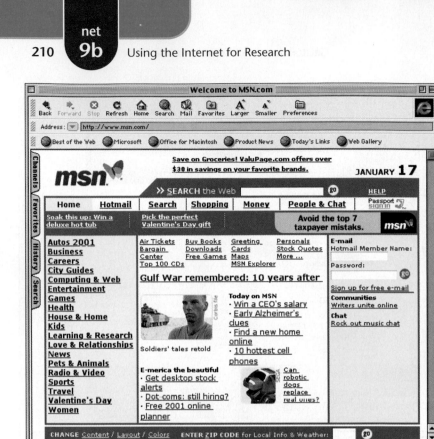

FIGURE 9.2 *Internet Explorer* Browser

menu bar in *Netscape*). You can customize your history to keep track of Web pages visited within a certain length of time. This is useful if you visited a site recently but can no longer recall its address or how you found it. (See the Help box on page 212.)

Designating a homepage on your browser

You will want to identify which page your browser will display when you first open it (your "homepage"). Both *Explorer* and *Netscape* allow you to determine that **homepage.** To do so in *Explorer*, you first open the page you want designated and then click on TOOLS > INTERNET OPTIONS. You should see the site's address displayed and click on CURRENT to select that homepage. In *Netscape* you select your homepage via the EDIT > PREFERENCES menu. You can click USE CURRENT PAGE if the correct page address is displayed, or you can browse until you find the page you wish to use as your homepage. You might want to designate your campus's Web page as your homepage or some other

How do I use the BOOKMARK and FAVORITES features?

Your Internet browser may have features that allow you to mark and organize sites for future use.

1. Marking Internet sites using *Netscape Communicator:*
   a. Add a site to your list of bookmarks by clicking on the BOOKMARK button. The browser will link this book-marked site so that all you need to do to launch the site is select it from the bookmark list.
   b. Check the list of bookmarks; the site you have just selected should now be listed.
   c. As you collect more bookmarks, take advantage of your browser's organization feature to sort your bookmarks into folders. If you work in a lab, you may wish to save your bookmarks to a disk.
2. Marking Internet sites using *Internet Explorer:*
   a. Add sites to your list of favorites by clicking the ADD TO FAVORITES button on the FAVORITES menu.
   b. Click on ORGANIZE FAVORITES to sort them into folders.

9.3

Step-by-step instructions on using BOOKMARK and FAVORITES.

page that you use frequently. You can get to your designated home-page quickly in either browser by clicking on the HOME icon.

2 Understanding URLs

To facilitate finding information on the Internet, a system of unique names was devised so that each resource on the Internet has a different name from any other resource. As long as you have the correct name of the resource, you should be able to locate it on the Internet. Names on the Internet are called **URLs** (Uniform Resource Locators). You can ask your browser to locate the resource by typing its URL into the browser's **address** bar. Or, you can go directly to the resource by clicking on a link found on another Web page. The link itself contains the URL as embedded code. A link on a Web page can be indicated by highlighted or colored text or by a graphical icon. Even without such signals, you can tell when your mouse is pointing to a link because, when it is over a link, the arrow will turn into a hand.

AUDIO

Tips for work-ing with URLs.

HELP

How do I use the HISTORY feature of my Web browser?

Your Internet browser has a feature that allows you to retrace the Web sites that you have visited over a specified length of time.

1. Checking your history in *Netscape:*
   a. The HISTORY feature is found within the COMMUNICATOR menu by clicking on TOOLS and then HISTORY.
   b. Here you will find a listing of all the sites you have visited, plus an indication of how long ago you visited them (e.g., 3 hours, 6 days, etc.).
   c. Use the HISTORY feature to retrace a prior search. You can customize the length of time your history is operating via the EDIT > PREFERENCES menu.

2. Checking your history in *Explorer:*
   a. You can check the history of your search by clicking on the HISTORY button found on the toolbar.
   b. *Explorer* will display a searchable history menu on the left side of your browser window.
   c. The HISTORY feature can be customized using the TOOLS menu from the menu bar.

9.4

Step-by-step instructions on using the HISTORY feature of a browser.

Each URL is divided into several parts that provide you with important information about the resource itself. The major parts are separated by periods (called "dots" in Internet shorthand). If you understand what each part of the URL means, you will be more likely to remember a specific URL and to type it accurately. The parts of a URL are illustrated below.

9.5

More on the anatomy of URLs.

protocol   host name   directory path

http://www.english.usu.edu/dept/index.htm

domain name domain type file name file extension

The first part, the **protocol,** indicates the type of link itself (ftp, http, gopher, etc.). The hypertext transfer protocol (http) is the protocol used by resources found on the World Wide Web. This abbreviation is followed by a colon and two slashes. Next comes the **host name** (which typically begins with *www* to indicate a World Wide Web site); the **domain name** is the part of the host name that is registered by the organization that "owns" the Web site, in this case the English Department at Utah State University. Part of the domain name is the **domain type,** in this case *edu*, which indicates the type of organization sponsoring the Web site. The domain type can give you important information about a site's purpose: whether it is a commercial (*com*), educational (*edu*), or nonprofit organization (*org*), and so on. After the domain type comes the **directory path,** in this case a directory named *dept* for department. There may be several directories or subdirectories within a directory path. Finally you will find a **file name** that the site author has used to identify a particular document located at the site. The **file extension** for a Web page will usually be *.htm* (hypertext markup) or *.html* (hypertext markup language). Your browser may allow for shortcuts on the address bar—that is, it is usually not necessary to type the *http://* at the beginning of a web address. The browser will fill it in for you. *Explorer* and *Netscape* also have an AUTO COMPLETE feature that recalls previous addresses and calls them up for you to select from. A **root URL,** that is, a URL without a specific file name, is the address used by an organization or company for its **index page** or **homepage.** For example, the root URL for Amazon books is simply <*amazon.com*>.

3 Respecting copyright and avoiding plagiarism

The amazing growth of the Internet has spawned numerous debates about censorship and freedom of information. At issue is the amount of control that governments should be able to exercise with regard to information found on the Internet. Because information that you access electronically is in the form of pixels and not print, everything from the Internet that you see on your screen is a copy of a file located on someone else's computer. Electronic sharing of information via the Internet is predicated on the copying of files—including files of digitized music, art, graphics, or films—from one computer to another. This ability to copy the work of others has led some people to ask legislators to place restrictions on copying, or "borrowing," information from the Internet.

Current legal interpretation of copyright law indicates that anything (such as text, graphics, or music) placed on the Internet by an individual or group is presumed to be copyrighted by its authors. However, the ease with which information can be copied and distributed via the Internet makes it nearly impossible to enforce such a rigid interpretation of copyright law. The debate over rights is likely to continue to rage, as commercial authors and publishers seek to receive just compensation for their work and Internet boosters try to preserve the free flow of Internet information. The *Copyright Website* at *<http://www.benedict.com>* provides detailed information on recent copyright controversies.

VIDEO

Understanding online citation.

As a student, you need to behave ethically and responsibly when using Web materials and when publishing your own work on the Web. In any piece of writing, including Web pages, be certain to cite all sources, including Internet sources, in such a way that readers can find the sources themselves (see Chapters 13–15 for guidelines for citing Internet sources). When writing your own Web pages, also be sure to download only images or texts that are considered "freeware," that is, they are offered by the site to users free of charge. If you are not certain, you should email the author or site sponsor for permission to either download the material or link to it from your own page. If you wish to use a portion of another's work on your Web page, the rule of thumb is that duplicating ten percent or less of the work constitutes fair use. Using more than this from a source requires you to secure permission. Be sure to include the statement "Reprinted by permission" when you have secured permission. Of course, you should include appropriate citation information for the original source, both for sources you have obtained permission from and for sources that do not require permission such as shareware and material used according to fair use copyright standards. (See the *Copyright Website* listed above.) See Chapter 11 for more information about using sources responsibly and avoiding plagiarism.

WWW

9.6

Learn more about Web ethics.

9c Search the Internet and the Web

AUDIO

Practice Internet searching.

Many corporations, nonprofit organizations, and special interest groups maintain information-rich Web sites. The purposes of these sites vary from disseminating information to peddling propaganda to luring customers into spending money. When you use information from an Internet source, remember that it probably has not been reviewed by anyone other than members of the organization that maintains the site. For example, a review of computers on Gateway Computer's Web site is likely to be biased in favor of Gateway products, and a discussion of gun control at the National Rifle Association's site will reflect that organization's views. (See Chapter 10 for guidelines on evaluating Internet sources.)

WWW

9.7

Different search engines and how to use them.

1 Using search tools to locate information on your topic

How do you go about finding specific information on a particular topic? The most reliable way is to use one of the Internet **search tools.** Search tools use different methods of sorting Web pages. Some search tools, often called **search engines,** use an automated system to sort pages based primarily on the use and placement of keywords. *AltaVista* and *Excite* are examples of search engines. Search engines automatically find and catalog new sites as they are added to the Web, indexing information by title and keywords. Other search tools, such as *Yahoo!*, are actually subject directories with a system of categories in a hierarchy. *Yahoo!* uses real people to screen sites and sort them into categories. There are also metasearch tools available, which search multiple databases at the same time. *Ixquick*, *Zworks*, and *ProFusion* are all examples of metasearch tools. You might wish to begin with a metasearch tool first and then choose one or two search engines or Web directories as you fine-tune your search. *Google, Excite, HotBot, Yahoo!, AltaVista*, and *Lycos* are some of the biggest Internet databases that index a large number of Web pages (see the list of search tools on page 218).

WEBLINK

http://sunsite.berkeley.edu/Help/searchdetails.html

Details about search tools, from the University of California at Berkeley

9.8
Using Search IQ for advanced searches.

Searching via subject directories

A **subject directory** is basically an organized index of topics and subtopics. The *InfoSeek* guide to information on the World Wide Web, for example, starts with the following subject areas on the opening screen: Arts & Entertainment, Business & Finance, Computers & Internet, Education, Government & Politics, Health & Medicine, Living, News, and Reference. Using this subject directory, you can narrow the scope of your search. For example, if you were interested in finding out about Brazil's form of government, you could select the "Government & Politics" subject list. Then, once you were in that subtopic, you could type in the keyword *Brazil. Yahoo!* is a popular subject directory because it is both fast and comprehensive, including listings from newsgroups in addition to links to thousands of Web pages. Other subject directories that offer both subject directories and keyword searching include *Lycos* and *HotBot* (see Figure 9.3).

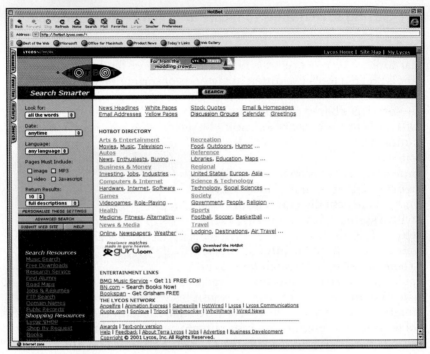

FIGURE 9.3 *HotBot* Subject Directory

Searching with keywords

VIDEO

Conducting online keyword searches.

Once you have selected a search tool and located an appropriate subject directory, you need to determine what search terms to try. If you searched your library's collection (see 8e-2), you may already have identified subject headings and keywords that you can use. Enter a **keyword** that identifies your topic and search for **hits** of that keyword—Web pages on which the word appears. Many search tools also permit more sophisticated, customized searches, but the options differ from one search tool to another. Check the search tool's HELP screen for ways to customize your search, particularly if you are getting hundreds or even thousands of hits for your search term.

Using Boolean operators

One of the ways in which search tools allow you to focus is by means of **Boolean operators**—for example, AND and NOT (see Tips on Using Boolean Operators for Internet Searching on page 219). The same principles used to search by keyword in a library database also apply to searching on the Internet. For example, if you type *childcare in Utah,* you may get all of the hits for *childcare* in addition to all of the hits for *Utah,* yielding thousands of sources. But if you combine the terms using the Boolean operator AND, you ask the search engine to find only those sources that include both *childcare AND Utah* in the same source (the AND limits the search). To limit the search even more, you could add the Boolean operator NOT: *childcare AND Utah NOT preschool.* Then, any sources mentioning preschool would be eliminated from the list.

Using quotation marks

Another way to focus the search is by using quotation marks, which indicate that the words must appear in a particular order in the text. For example, *"global warming"* would tell the search tool that you are not interested in *global* or *warming* by itself; you want only the two terms in combination, exactly as written inside the quotation marks. In a search on global warming, one student found that *Yahoo!* yielded over 1,000 hits for *global warming* without quotation marks and 37 hits for *"global warming."*

The only way to see if your search is yielding the results you are after is to browse through the listing of sites found by the search tool. Most search tools provide a brief description of the site, so you can quickly ascertain whether or not the search is finding relevant sources. If it is not, try again with new search terms, subject areas, or delimiters (such as Boolean operators). Make use of the search tool's HELP screen if you are not achieving the results you desire.

2 Using Internet library subscription databases and periodical collections

As discussed in 8f-4, many libraries now subscribe to database services so that their patrons can search Internet databases for articles. Full-text databases provide access to the complete text of an article. In 9d-2 we illustrate a student's search using such a database. Find out if your library subscribes to any of these services. Some common examples are *Lexis-Nexis* and *EBSCOHost.*

Searching virtual libraries

Many libraries make some of the information from their collections available via the Internet. For example, the online collection of the University of California is available at the site listed in *Internet Libraries and Collections.* You can also use *LibCat,* which provides links to hundreds of libraries with Web access, or *LibWeb,* which provides links to

Search Tools

About.com http://about.com	Information database for "what you need to know about," using human guides who are each experts in a particular field.
AltaVista http://www.altavista.com	Large, comprehensive database. Keyword searching only. Supports Boolean searching.
Excite http://excite.com	Subject directory and keyword searching available. Supports Boolean searching.
Google http://google.com	Subject directory and keyword searching available.
HotBot http://hotbot.com	Subject directory and keyword searching. Includes newsgroups and email. Supports Boolean searching.
Ixquick http://ixquick.com	One of the world's largest metasearch tools, searching 14 other tools simultaneously.
Lycos http://lycos.com	Subject directory and keyword searching available. Supports Boolean searching.
ProFusion http://www.profusion.com	Searches multiple tools simultaneously, using keywords (includes most search tools in this table). Supports Boolean searching.
Yahoo! http://yahoo.com	Subject directory and keyword searching available. Includes news, chat, and email. Does not support Boolean searching.
Zworks http://zworks.com	Searches multiple search tools simultaneously. Ranks the results of searches for relevancy by search tool. Also filters to be relatively child-safe.

9.9

Access to online search tools.

Tips on Using Boolean Operators for Internet Searching

Online databases use Boolean operators to combine two or more terms in ways that the computer recognizes. The Boolean operators most commonly used are AND, OR, and NOT.

1. Be sure to use the appropriate Boolean operator.
   a. AND (&) limits the search, because both keywords must be found in the search. For example, if you wanted to find information only on cats as pets, you could limit your search with the AND operator, typing in *pets AND cats*. The search would then be limited to those sources that included both words.
   b. OR (|) expands the search, because any text with either keyword will be included in the search results. For example, if you wanted to expand your search to include both dogs and cats, you would use the OR operator, typing in *dogs OR cats*. Both groups would then be included in your search.
   c. NOT (!) limits the search by excluding any text containing the keyword after the operator. For example, if you wanted to exclude dogs from your search of pets, you could do so with the NOT operator, typing in *pets NOT dogs*.

2. Enter Boolean operators in UPPERCASE letters (unless you use the symbols).

3. Leave a space before and after each Boolean operator.

4. If your phrase is complex, involving several Boolean operators, use parentheses: *(pets AND cats) AND (NOT dogs)*. The same search can be indicated using symbols: *(pets & cats) & (! dogs)*.

online document and image collections of libraries around the world. Once you connect with these sources, you will need to browse through an index much like the online catalog in your own library, using keyword and subject searches to locate specific information. Some libraries have special online directories that link researchers to resources in specific subject areas. For example, the University of California at Riverside sponsors the *Infomine Internet Library*. Its resources are divided topically into major subject disciplines, such as scientific and medical sources, government sources, and social sciences and humanities sources.

Searching government documents

The federal government maintains numerous sites that you may want to use for research. The White House Web site offers an online photographic tour of the White House and provides links to important information about the federal government, including pending legislation, recently produced government documents, and cabinet activities and reports. (See also the *Thomas* Web site for legislation.) At the site produced by NASA, you can find information on space flights, space research, and aeronautics. By using a search tool, you can locate specific information on hundreds of other government Web sites, including city and state sites.

Searching online periodicals

Journals and magazines that are published on the Web can be a good source for a research paper. Several publishers now offer online versions of their publications to consumers. Often you can access the full texts of articles that appear in the print version. For example, the *New York Times* is available online, as is *Time* magazine. Once again, there is no one quick and easy way to locate online periodicals. If you know the name of the publication, you can search for it using one of the search tools described in 9c-1. In addition, some Web sites will link you to major journals, newspapers, and magazines. For example, News Directory's twenty-four-hour *Newsstand* provides links to thousands of magazines and newspapers from around the world, cataloged by region and organized by topic (business, health, religion, sports, travel, social issues, and so on). Finally, you can use a search tool such as *Excite* or *Yahoo!* to search for news in magazines and newspapers by selecting "NewsTracker" or "Today's News" from the subject index.

Use Internet sources in combination with indexes in other media—print or CD (see 8f-4). Note that URLs change often. If the URL we have listed does not work, try shortening the address or searching by title. Also, go to <http://www.ablongman.com/hult> and click on the Web site for this handbook to get updates on URLs and additional sites to search.

Internet Libraries and Collections

Academic Info http://academicinfo.net	Gateway to quality educational resources categorized by discipline.
AskERIC Virtual Library http://ericir.syr.edu	Includes Internet resources on a variety of issues.
Educators' Reference Desk http://www.eduref.org	Includes the ERIC database with over 1 million abstracts on education topics.
Internet Public Library http://www.ipl.org	Reference site built by the University of Michigan.
LibCat http://www.metronet.lib.mn.us/lc	Links to hundreds of online libraries.
Librarian's Index to the Internet http://lii.org	About 11,000 links compiled by public librarians. Highest-quality sites included with annotations.
Purdue's Virtual Library http://thorplus.lib.purdue.edu/vlibrary	Lists many online journals by academic subject.
University of California—Berkeley LibWeb http://sunsite.berkeley.edu	Links to online documents and image collections around the world.
University of California—Riverside Infomine http://infomine.ucr.edu	Lists over 115,000 online sources by academic subject. Reliable annotations.
Virtual Information Center http://lib.berkeley.edu/Collections	Links to reference sites in many academic subjects.

9.10

Access to online libraries and collections.

Internet Sites for Government Documents

Bureau of the Census http://www.census.gov	Social, demographic, and economic information; index a–z; searchable by place, location, and word
Bureau of Justice Statistics http://www.ojp.usdoj.gov/bjs	Statistics on all criminal justice topics—law enforcement, drugs, crime, and so on
Bureau of Labor Statistics http://stats.bls.gov	Statistics by region, searchable by keyword; economy at a glance
Congressional Quarterly http://www.cq.com	World-class information and insight on government and politics
Department of Education http://www.ed.gov	Educational initiatives; news; publications; programs
Fish & Wildlife Service http://www.fws.gov	Information related to fish and wildlife
Library of Congress http://lcweb.loc.gov	Centralized guide to information services provided by the Library of Congress
National Institutes of Health http://www.nih.gov	Health information, grants, health news; database searchable by keyword
National Library of Medicine http://www.nlm.nih.gov	Free *Medline* searches; other medical databases
NASA http://www.nasa.gov	Tracking of current space flights and missions, including *Pathfinder* on Mars
Statistical Abstract of the U.S. http://www.census.gov/statab/www	Collection of statistics on social, economic, and international subjects
Thomas (congressional legislation) http://thomas.loc.gov	Full text of current bills under consideration by US House and Senate
White House http://www.whitehouse.gov	Information on federal government initiatives, tours, etc.

9.11

Access to online government documents.

Internet Sites for Online Periodicals

CNN Interactive
http://www.cnn.com

CNN news from around the world; includes audio and video clips

Electronic Library
http://www.elibrary.com

Keyword searching of online magazines and newspapers; subject directory

Excite NewsTracker
http://news.excite.com

News headlines from Excite (includes Reuters and UPI)

Google NewsTracker
http://news.google.com

News headlines by topic

London Times
http://www.timesonline.co.uk

Daily contents from the London Times

Lycos News
http://news.lycos.com/news

News headlines from Lycos news service (includes CNN, ABC, Reuters, and others)

New York Times
http://nytimes.com

Daily contents of the New York Times

Yahoo! Today's News
http://dailynews.yahoo.com

News headlines from Yahoo! news service (includes CNN, ABC, Reuters, and others)

9.12

Access to online periodicals.

EXERCISE 9.1

Open your Internet browser and explore several of the search tools described above, including library links, government links, and newspaper links. Take an online tour of the White House, try searching the New York Times database, or find an online version of a local or regional newspaper. (Search for the newspaper by title, using any available search tool.)

9d Model searches of the Internet and library databases

1 Follow a student Internet search

To show you how a search might work, in this section we follow the Internet search of Kaycee Sorenson. Her starting questions were these:

```
Is the number of online shoppers increasing?

Is shopping via the Internet a viable solution for consumers?

Is it safe to use a credit card for online shopping?
```

Her search strategy included looking for current sources on the Internet. She used the *Yahoo!* directory as a launching point for her Internet search.

When Kaycee opened the *Yahoo!* guide, she saw several potentially interesting subject categories listed. Kaycee noticed the topic of "Shopping and Services" listed under the category "Business and the Economy." Since she was interested in the online shopping topic, she decided to look for relevant sources listed in that category. She typed the words *online shopping* into the search screen and asked *Yahoo!* to search just "Shopping and Services" (see Figure 9.4).

That search yielded more than 15,000 hits for Web sources that contained either the word *online* or the word *shopping*. Kaycee also noticed that many of the sites were commercial businesses that offered consumers online shopping opportunities. Kaycee realized that her search terms were much too broad, so she needed to narrow her search further, especially since many of the links were irrelevant to her research topic. She first put the search terms in quotation marks so that *Yahoo!* would look for the keywords together in sequence. When she typed *"online shopping"* in quotation marks and clicked *Search just this category, Yahoo!* returned 744 hits, a more focused result, but still too broad. Kaycee then tried combining *ecommerce* and *+ security* to further focus her search. She used the + sign to indicate that all results must have both the term *ecommerce* and the term *security* in them. The result of this search was closer to what she was after—51 hits with a range of articles and Web sites that were both commercial and noncommercial (see Figure 9.5).

After browsing through the 51 sources, following the links, and reading some of them to evaluate the sites for their relevance to her research questions, Kaycee printed out a few for later use, including the *Cyberatlas* and the shopping guide from *Hypermart.net*. Kaycee then went to her library's database to find books, magazines, news-

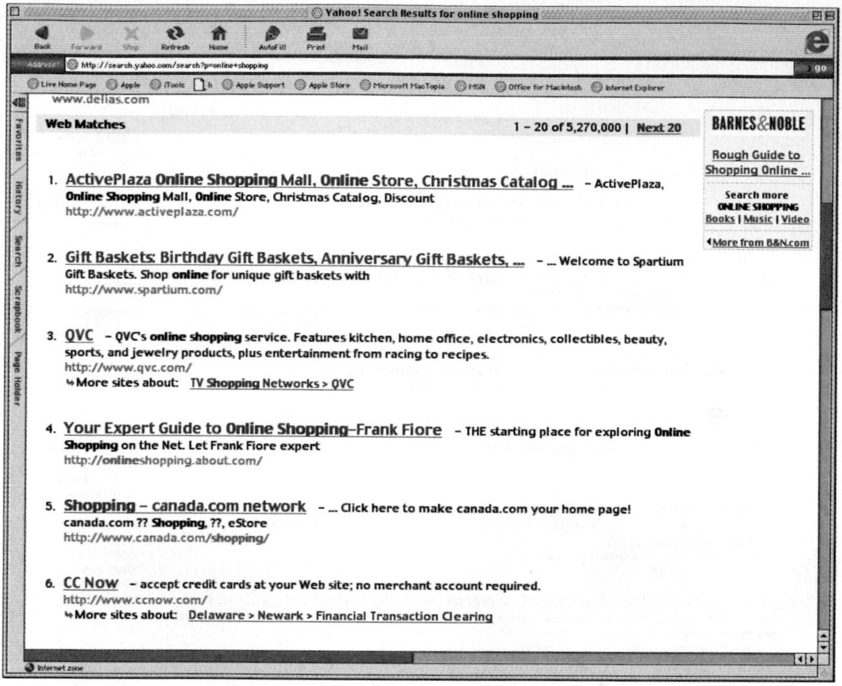

FIGURE 9.4 Searching the Shopping and Services Category of *Yahoo!*

papers, and journal articles. She located several more sources that were useful in her research, including *Money* magazine and *Capital Times*. Remember that you should be seeking a combination of different types of sources rather than relying exclusively on the Internet.

2 Follow a student search of a library subscription database service

One of the best ways to search for journal and newspaper articles that are academic in nature is through your library's subscription database services. You will need to check your library's Web site to find out which services it subscribes to. These databases will put journal and newspaper articles on your topic at your fingertips. Often they include the full text of the article itself. That is, you can actually read the article online rather than having to locate it within the paper-bound volumes in your library.

Kaycee used the library subscription databases extensively during her search for information on cybershopping. She first went to her

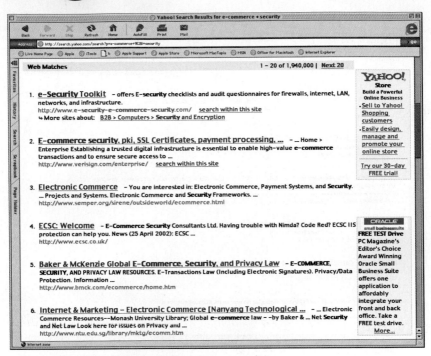

FIGURE 9.5 *Yahoo!* hits on *ecommerce + security*

library's homepage to find out which indexes (lists of articles by topic) were available. She found a long list of general indexes and specialized indexes by discipline (see Figure 9.6). Notice that the databases are listed by subject in the left-hand margin and alphabetically in the main window. A check mark indicates a database that is suitable for general research; a page icon represents a database that includes full-text articles. Kaycee's librarian recommended *EBSCOHost* as a comprehensive database to use for academic research.

When she clicked on *EBSCOHost,* it took her to a list of databases from which to choose. By checking a box in the margin, she could search several databases simultaneously. She decided to try the *Academic Search Elite* to see what kinds of articles would be listed there.

This link brought her to a search page where she could enter her keywords and other relevant information to limit her search results. Kaycee's librarian had recommended that she use the *advanced search* because it would allow her to combine terms such as *Internet* and *shopping.* Notice how Kaycee refined her search by asking the database to find *Internet AND shopping* but *NOT retail* (see Figure 9.7). She did this to avoid sites that promoted retail shopping, such as Old Navy's online

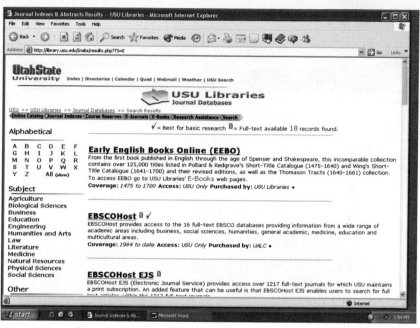

FIGURE 9.6 Library Subscription Databases

catalog. She also limited her results by asking for full-text journals that were peer-reviewed between the years 2000 and 2003.

She got 14 hits from these terms. A few of them looked promising, so she clicked the ADD button to add those to her personal citation folder (see Figure 9.8). By clicking on the links to either the PDF or HTML full-text version, she could read the article themselves. Once she had located an article, she could also download, print, or save it for future reference.

This brief tour through the *EBSCOHost* illustrates how valuable subscription databases through your library's Web site can be for your research.

⎛ E X E R C I S E   9 . 2 ⎞

Pick a topic that interests you and begin a search. First use a search tool with a subject directory to work your way down the database; then type in a keyword and see what results you achieve. Check out some of the links. Are you finding relevant sources? If not, try narrowing your search using AND or NOT; you can also combine terms in quotation marks.

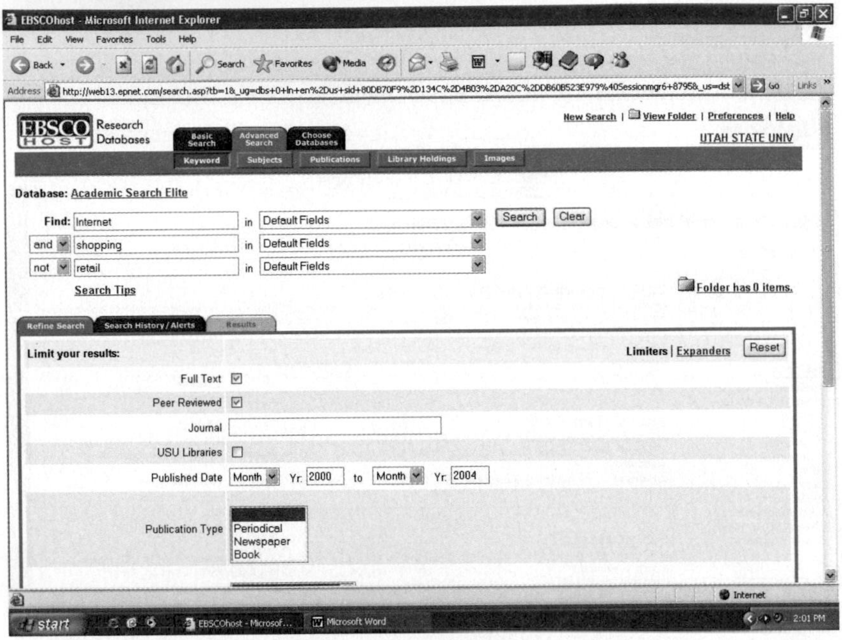

FIGURE 9.7 Searching by Keywords: *Internet AND Shopping NOT Retail*

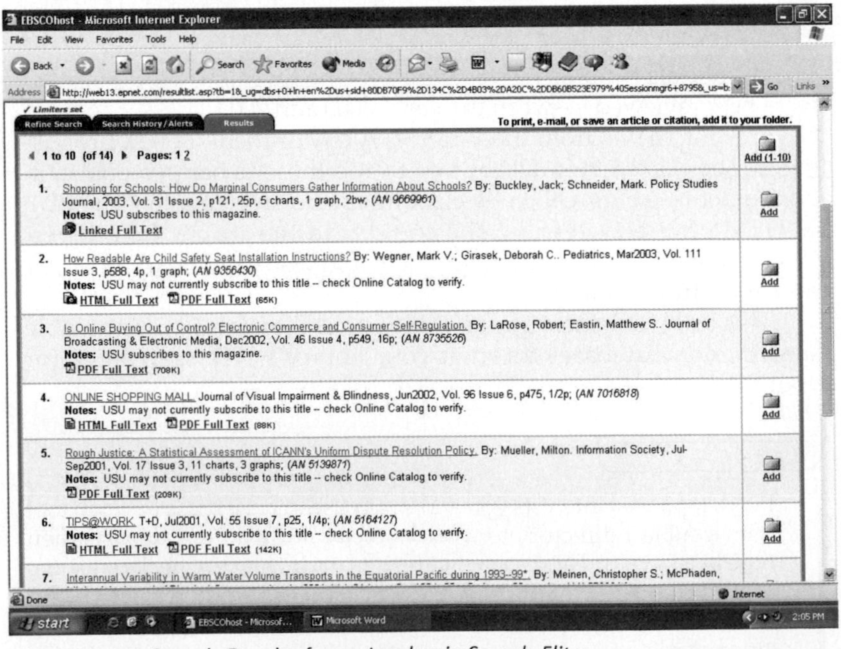

FIGURE 9.8 Search Results from *Academic Search Elite*

FOR COLLABORATION

Write a brief paragraph about your understanding of copyright as it applies to information (texts, graphics, photos) you find on the Internet. Share your paragraph with a small group of your classmates. Do you all agree on what is ethical and fair use of Internet materials? Share your collective understanding with the rest of the class in order to generate your own class standards of fair use.

EXERCISE 9.3

Search a full-text database to which your library subscribes. Use the keywords you have listed thus far in your research. Print out or save to a disk any relevant articles you locate.

CHAPTER 10

Evaluating Electronic and Print Sources

FAQs

▶ How can I tell if a Web site has reliable information? (10a)

▶ What makes a source worth reading? (10a-1)

▶ How important is the date something was published? (10a-1)

▶ Are there ways to evaluate an author's credibility when conducting an Internet search? (10a-1)

▶ What makes a source worth using? (10a-2)

AUDIO

The challenge of evaluating sources.

WWW

10.1

Guidelines for evaluating Web and print resources.

As a researcher in today's information environment, one of your most important tasks is to evaluate what you read. The tendency to believe everything you read is dangerous, especially with respect to Internet sources. Some, but by no means all, print sources undergo a process of peer review and evaluation before they are published. (Peer review refers to the practice of sending written material out to experts in the field for evaluation before it is actually published.) Peer reviewed sources can generally be trusted to present information accurately. In contrast, the screening process for Internet materials is usually determined by the author. Many people who create Web sites have a sense of personal integrity, but others are less than forthright in the ways they use the medium to promote themselves or their viewpoints. Reading with a critical eye is

WEBLINK

http://lib.berkeley.edu/
TeachingLib/Guides/
Internet/Evaluate.html

A fabulous collection of materials to help you evaluate all kinds of electronic texts

HELP

How do I find a site's homepage?

To locate a site's homepage, you can travel up the URL's directory path.

1. Open your browser and locate the site that interests you.
2. Look at the URL, listed on the LOCATION or ADDRESS line of your browser.
3. Back your way up the URL by deleting the last section of the address, following the last slash. Hit ENTER to retrieve the new page.
4. Look at the URL of the page you have now located.
5. Continue backing up in the URL until you reach the site's homepage.

NOTE: A well-designed Web page contains a link to the site's homepage.

WWW

10.2
Instructions for
finding a site's
homepage.

always important, but it is particularly crucial in dealing with Internet information (see 2b).

10a Choose legitimate sources

Because you will be relying on your sources to provide the evidence and authority to support your hypothesis, it is crucial that you choose legitimate sources. Your reputation as a researcher may be at stake. Choosing a legitimate source is a two-step process. First decide whether or not the source is worth reading. Then decide whether or not the source is worth using in the research paper.

WEBLINK

http://www.library.cornell
.edu/okuref/research/
skill26.htm
Another excellent source
evaluation page

WWW

10.3
Detailed steps
for critically
analyzing
sources.

1 Deciding whether the source is worth reading

To save yourself a great deal of time, quickly assess a source by skimming for a few key elements.

Relevance

Is the source relevant to your research? That is, does it address the topic you are researching? Sometimes a title will mislead you; a source will turn out to be on another topic entirely or on an aspect of the topic that does not interest you. If a source is not relevant, move on.

Publisher or sponsor

Who is the sponsoring organization or publisher? Is the article in a popular magazine, such as *Ladies' Home Journal*, or a professional journal, such as *Journal of Behavioral Sciences*? Depending on the nature of the research project, it may or may not be appropriate to use information from the popular press, which tends to be less scholarly than information found, for example, in a professional journal. For many college papers, however, the popular press—including major newspapers such as the *New York Times* and magazines such as *Time* and *Newsweek*—can certainly be useful. The publishers of newspapers and popular magazines are typically commercial publishers. The publishers or sponsoring organizations for professional journals are usually academic societies, such as the Modern Language Association or the Society for Engineering Educators. Generally you can rely on the information found in publications produced by these academic entities. But no information, regardless of its publisher or sponsoring agency, should be accepted at face value without critical evaluation (see 2a).

VIDEO

Comparing online sources.

Although determining the sponsoring organization or individual is no less important for an Internet site than for a print source, it may not be as easy to accomplish. One clue to the nature of the sponsoring organization is the URL itself. Internet conventions have been established to identify a standardized suffix for Web addresses, also called a *domain type* (see 9b-2). These domain types tell you something about the nature of the sponsoring organization. Looking at the domain type of a Web site will help you to understand the purpose behind the page—whether educational or commercial, for example. Common domain types include

- Education (*.edu*)
- Government (*.gov*)
- Nonprofit organization (*.org*)
- Commercial (*.com*)
- Network (*.net*)
- Military (*.mil*)
- Other countries (*.ca* for Canada; *.uk* for United Kingdom)

Guidelines for Distinguishing a Popular Magazine from a Scholarly Journal

Is the source a popular magazine or a scholarly journal? Here are some features common to each type of source to help you decide.

1. Does the cover have a picture or photo? (popular) *or* Does the cover have a table of contents list? (scholarly)

2. Is there a snappy title, like *Newsweek*? (popular) *or* Is the word *Journal* in the title? (scholarly)

3. Are there many colorful advertisements and photos? (popular) *or* Are there very few photos or ads, with none for commercial products? (scholarly)

4. Are the authors journalists or simply not named at all? (popular) *or* Are the authors scholars who are listed with their academic credentials? (scholarly)

5. Are the articles all fairly short with no abstracts? (popular) *or* Do the articles begin with short abstracts and run many pages in length? (scholarly)

6. Are there no listings of references or bibliographies? (popular) *or* Are there reference lists following every article? (scholarly)

7. Is the source found at newsstands and in the grocery store? (popular) *or* Is the source found at the library? (scholarly)

10.4

Distinguishing popular and professional journals.

Author

In addition to a sponsoring organization, is an individual author listed? Look carefully at both print and online sources to evaluate the author's credentials. Does he or she work for a government agency, a political group, a commercial industry, or an educational institution? Often the author's professional affiliation will be noted at the bottom of a journal or magazine article. A Web site may have an "About the author" page. Of course, the sponsoring organization itself may provide the author with credibility. We assume, for example, that anyone who writes for *Time* or *Newsweek* must have appropriate credentials.

HELP

How do I find out about an author through an Internet search?

10.5

A sample author search using *AltaVista*.

1. Open a search tool such as *AltaVista* or *InfoSeek*.
2. In the search box, type the name of an author about whom you want information.
3. Choose phrase searching if it is available. If not, put the name in quotation marks.

NOTE: By typing *"Nicholas Negroponte"* into the *AltaVista* search box, we found hundreds of columns in *Wired* magazine written by Negroponte. In addition, we found biographies, book reviews, speeches, interviews, and photographs. We learned that Negroponte is the director and founder of MIT's MediaLab.

National magazines are selective about their writers and extremely careful to provide authoritative information to their readers. Of course, this does not mean that sources written by authors in magazines should not be read critically (see 2b).

Timeliness

Be sure to check the date of any piece you encounter. In many fields, the timeliness of the information is as important as the information itself. For example, if you are researching a medical topic, you want to be certain that your sources include the most up-to-date research. One of the many benefits of the Internet is that it allows information to be updated continually, but unfortunately not all Web sites list the dates on which they were first posted and last updated. With print sources, you need to be especially careful about when a piece was written. Months or even years may go by between when something is discovered and when it finally appears in print. Thus, research conducted many months or years ago may just now be appearing in print. In fields where information is changing rapidly, such as medicine, access to current information can be crucial.

Although the instant access of the Internet compares favorably with the lag time often associated with print sources, the downside of the Internet is that it is sometimes difficult to know what information is reliable. Many ideas presented on the Internet have not stood the test of time or endured the rigors of peer review. Much of the information that appears in printed sources, in contrast, has been rigorously reviewed by peers, editors, and professional reviewers before it appears in print. Of course, there are exceptions. You need look no further than your local supermarket counter to find printed sources, such as the *National Enquirer* or the *Star,* that are not appropriate sources of reliable information for a research paper.

Cross-references

Is the source cited in other works? You can sometimes make decisions about a work's credibility by considering how it is cited by other sources. When you are researching a topic, sometimes one author's name will come up repeatedly in references and in discussions. This author is probably an expert on the topic; it would be worth your while to check into sources written by that person (see the Help box on page 236).

2 Deciding whether the source is worth using

Once you have decided that a source is worth reading, read and evaluate the source to determine whether or not you want to use it in your paper. First look at the author's rhetorical stance (see 3b-2). Then evaluate the content of the piece itself.

Rhetorical stance

Who is the intended audience for the piece? Does the title help you to understand which readers it is targeting? Is there evidence that the author has taken a particular stance in a controversy on his or her subject? Journals and magazines typically write for particular target audiences, whom they assume share certain biases and opinions. If you are aware of that bias before you read a piece, you will be able to keep the information in context. As well as considering the audience, think about the author's purposes for writing and publishing the piece. What are the author and sponsoring organization trying to accomplish? Are they trying to sell a product or market an idea? To persuade you to accept a particular point of view? Read the editorial policy of a magazine or newspaper to get an idea of the publication's purpose. Check to see if a Web site includes an "About our site" page, which describes its purpose or agenda. Regardless of the source, you need to exercise caution as an information consumer.

10.6
A sample site evaluation reveals a parody.

Elements to Examine to Assess a Potential Source's Appropriateness

Print Sources

Title and Subtitle: Check both the title and the subtitle for relevance to your topic. For example, you could not be sure that a book titled *Wishes, Lies, and Dreams* was appropriate without reading the subtitle: *Teaching Children to Write Poetry*.

Copyright Page: Check this page, just after the title page, to find out who published the book, where it was published, and when.

Table of Contents: Check the titles of parts, chapters, and sections. The outline of a book can show you the topics covered and the detail of that coverage.

Abstract: Read the abstract, if included. It will provide you with a concise summary.

Preface: Read the preface. This is where the authors generally set out their purpose.

Chapter Headings and Subheadings: Check the headings and subheadings to find out what specific subtopics will be discussed.

Electronic Sources

Title and Subtitle: Check the Web page title (found on the top line of your screen, above the browser window) and the title on the page itself for their relevance to your topic.

Copyright Information: At the bottom of the homepage, you should find information about who sponsors the site. Knowing the sponsor can give you clues to a site's reliability.

Major Links to Secondary Pages: Check to see if the site includes links to secondary pages that elaborate on subtopics.

Abstract: Read the abstract, if included. It will provide you with a concise summary.

Introduction: Read any introductory material on the homepage. It should tell you about the site's purpose.

Headings and Subheadings: Look closely at the major divisions on the homepage. They may tell you how detailed the site is.

(continued)

Elements to Examine *(continued)*

Print Sources	Electronic Sources
Conclusion: Read any conclusion or afterword. It may give you another sense of the authors' stance.	**Conclusion:** Read any concluding material on the final page of the site. It may give you another sense of the authors' stance.
Author Note: To evaluate credibility, read anything provided about the author.	**Author Page:** To evaluate credibility, read any "About the author" or "About our site" pages or information. Conduct a search on the author's name, using a search tool.
Index: If available, check the index for a listing of topics included in the book.	**Glossary:** If the Web site includes a glossary of terms, use it to help you understand the topics covered.
Bibliography: Look at the list of references at the end of the article or book. It can tell you how carefully an author researched and can lead you to other related information.	**Links to References or Related Sites:** Look at the links to related sites or to sources referenced. They can tell you about the site's research and can lead you to other related information.

Content

Pay close attention to the content itself. Does the language seem moderate and reasonable, or are there terms that might be considered inflammatory or prejudiced? Does the writer seem overly emotional? Is the tone strident or preachy? Other factors to consider as you read closely include how the piece uses source evidence, how logically the argument is developed, and how the content matches (or contradicts) what others have said on the subject.

Special criteria for Internet sources

As we have discussed, some Internet sources are more reliable than others. When evaluating a Web site, look to see what other sources are linked to it and what sites it links to. How useful and/or legitimate are the linked sites? What is the general tone of the Web site? If the Internet source is an online bulletin board or newsgroup, you should question its reliability. Because the online discussion medium is freeform by nature, it is difficult to evaluate the credibility of the information found there. Those who enter into newsgroup discussions are ordinarily people who have some kind of interest in the topic. Occasionally you will find an expert on the topic with professional credentials, but usually you will find others like yourself, with a variety of opinions to share. Newsgroup discussions can be helpful in pointing out interesting areas for further research, but they will not help much with the actual information you need for a research paper. When evaluating a newsgroup posting, you should be asking the same questions about the author, audience, and purpose that were discussed above. As a general rule, verify with another source any information you find in a newsgroup posting.

(E X E R C I S E 10.1)

Select for evaluation four Web sites. For each site, make note of the sponsoring organization, the author (if known), the target audience, the purpose, any apparent bias, and the timeliness of the information. Rank the sites in order of trustworthiness, from the most trustworthy to the least trustworthy.

10b Follow a student's evaluation of Web links

AUDIO
Conduct your
own Internet
search.

To give you a sense of how you might go about evaluating information you find via an Internet search, we will follow a student's search for information related to smoking. Mark Robb had been reading about the debate on smoking and addiction. He wanted to find out about both sides of the debate, in an effort to answer the question "Is smoking addictive?" Mark knew that the tobacco industry had argued recently that smoking was not addictive but rather habit-forming.

Mark began by turning to the *Lycos* search tool located at *<http://www.lycos.com>*. Browsing through the subject directory, Mark noted a category "Health" (see Figure 10.1 on page 240). He clicked on "Health" and found the subcategory "substance abuse" and under that, "smoking and other tobacco-related dependencies." He found 49 hits for his search term. These were mainly sites to help smokers quit. He wanted to find information on both sides of the question. One link caught his eye.

Checklist for Evaluating Information

The Sponsoring Organization

1. Where does the information appear—in the popular press, in a scholarly report, on a Web site?
2. Who is the sponsor of the source—an academic society, a publishing house, an organization?
3. For a Web site, what is the domain of the URL—educational, governmental, commercial?

The Author

1. Who is the author? Have you ever heard of this person? Have you run across the name in other sources?
2. What are the author's credentials?
3. What kind of language does the author use?
4. What kind of tone has the author adopted?

AUDIO

Evaluation checklist.

The Audience

1. Who is the intended audience for the publication?
2. Does the publication target obvious biases in its audience?
3. What are the characteristics of the audience members?

The Purpose

1. What are the author and sponsoring organization trying to accomplish?
2. Is an idea or product being marketed?
3. Are you being urged to adopt a particular point of view?

The Timeliness

1. When was the piece published?
2. When was the Web site posted and/or updated?
3. How important is it that your information be current?

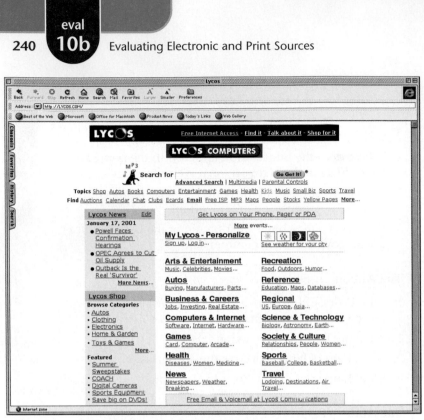

FIGURE 10.1 Homepage for *Lycos* Search Tool

Smoking from All Sides   I've tried to include links about all perspectives of smoking: Health Aspects Statistics Tobacco News Anti-Smoking Groups Smoking Cessation Tobacco History Commentary.

Mark clicked on the link to find out what this site was all about. He found page links to newsgroups, articles, and homepages that discussed smoking.

Mark wondered about the author of this page. He wanted to find out if the person who had collected the links at this site was reliable. He followed the link to the author's page and discovered that the author, Loring Holden, was a software engineer in the Brown University computer science department. Although Mark was not sure that these credentials related in any way to expertise on the tobacco industry, he decided to give the author the benefit of the doubt and read the site. He could not figure out from reading Holden's résumé why he was interested in tobacco issues or what rhetorical purpose was behind the creation of the "Smoking from All Sides" page. But since the site provided links without much editorial commentary, Mark decided that the site was probably intended to be informational.

Since Mark knew that he could find a great deal of anti-smoking information, he used Holden's page to locate pro-smoking sites. In addition to listings of organizations, magazines, and articles (e.g., *Smoke* magazine) there were about a half-dozen homepages, with names like *Smoke and Be Cool*, and *Smoker's Home Page*. *Smoke and Be Cool* was a diatribe by an individual smoker against anti-smoking regulation. The language used by the author of the site was strident and even offensive. The author's tone clued Mark in to the author's agenda of irritating those in the anti-smoking campaign. The site was timely, though; it had been updated just a month before Mark visited.

Smoker's Home Page, also updated recently, was a bit less strident in tone but equally militant in its arguments against any regulation by the government of the tobacco industry. On *Smoker's Home Page* was a category called "Issues," which included articles with such titles as "Secondhand Smoke: The Big Lie" and "Addiction." These articles were authored by Joe Dawson. Mark could not find any information at the site about Joe Dawson, but it was obvious from his arguments that he was extremely suspicious of all government-sponsored studies having to do with smoking. The main thrust of his arguments was to keep the government out of the lives of individuals. Mark printed out this article for later reference. It was the only article he found that explicitly argued that nicotine was not addictive.

Next Mark turned to the link for *Smoke* magazine, also on Holden's page. The magazine was touted as promoting the cigar-lover's lifestyle. Mark wondered just what type of journal this might be. He followed the link to the journal's Web page and glanced at the glitzy cover and the glossy photographs. He opened the site's page about the journal's sponsor and discovered that *Smoke* was a trade journal for the tobacco industry published by the Lockwood Publications Corporation. To find out more about Lockwood, he followed the links to the corporation's homepage. He discovered that the URL was *<http://tobaccointernational.com>* and its history page described the long-standing relationship between Lockwood and the tobacco industry. That relationship went back to Lockwood's 1872 publication of the weekly trade journal *Tobacco*, "published for the burgeoning cigar retailing business," according to the Web site. Mark knew that any information found in articles in this publication would have to be read with the magazine's obvious bias in favor of the tobacco industry in mind.

Mark now had information on the smoking and addiction issue. He proceeded to read the relevant sources carefully, taking notes in his electronic notebook file. In addition to taking notes, Mark wrote down evaluative information about each source's sponsor, author, purpose, and so on, to remind himself of the source's credibility.

Mark's brief researching tour through the Internet illustrates the importance of evaluating everything you read. In thinking critically about the sites he encountered in his search, Mark posed all of the questions on the Checklist for Evaluating Information (page 239). He considered the sponsoring organization, the rhetorical stance of the site (including author, audience, and purpose), and the timeliness of the site. By using these evaluative questions, Mark was able to get a sense of the reliability of the information he found.

EXERCISE 10.2

Make a chart in which you compare the sites you labeled "most trustworthy" and "least trustworthy" in Exercise 10.1. Use the questions in the Checklist for Evaluating Information (page 239) to help you construct your chart. Bring a copy of your chart to class for discussion.

FOR COLLABORATION

Share your charts of trustworthy and untrustworthy sites with a small group of your peers. What makes each of them either trustworthy or not? What were some clues as to obvious biases? Use the Checklist for Evaluating Information (page 239) to shape your discussion.

CHAPTER 11

Using Sources and Avoiding Plagiarism

FAQs

▶ What should I put in my notes? (11a)
▶ What is plagiarism and how do I avoid it? (11a-3)
▶ What is the difference between paraphrasing and summarizing? (11b–11c)
▶ How many quotations do I need, and how do I integrate them into my paper? (11d)

Writers gain credibility through the use of information from experts. It is the responsibility of research authors to be certain that any information from another author, whether paraphrased, summarized, or quoted, is accurately relayed and clearly acknowledged. Integrating source information into your own writing is a skill that takes practice. Being careless about your sources can lead to a serious academic offense called plagiarism—with serious consequences such as a failing grade for the course or even expulsion from school. *Plagiarism* is defined as the unauthorized or misleading use of the language and text of another author. Whenever you use exact words from a source, this must be indicated clearly through the use of a signal phrase, quotation marks, and an in-text citation at the point where the source information is quoted. When you paraphrase or summarize ideas, similarly you need to give proper attribution to the source (see Chapter 13 for information about in-text citations). It is not enough to list the authors in footnotes or bibliographies. Readers must be able to tell as they are reading your paper exactly what information came from which source and what information is your own contribution to the paper.

AUDIO
Using sources
accurately.

11a Use sources responsibly

11.1

Avoid plagiarism with these in-depth guidelines.

WEBLINK

http://www.wisc.edu/
writing/Handbook/
QuotingSources.html

Detailed explanations and examples of using quotations, paraphrases, and summaries

When writing a research paper, you must acknowledge any original information, ideas, and illustrations that you find in another author's work, whether it is in print or on the Internet. Acknowledging the work of other authors is called documenting sources. (The appropriate forms for documentation are discussed in Chapters 13–15.) When incorporating information from other authors into a research paper, you can present the source information in the form of a direct quotation; a paraphrase, in which you restate the ideas in your own words (see 11b); or a summary, in which you condense the information (see 11c). By incorporating source information appropriately, you will avoid plagiarism (see 11a-3).

1 Reading critically

Your main task as a researcher is to make sense of the subject you have chosen to research. To understand the subject and come to some conclusions of your own about it, you need to read widely and critically. If you rely on only one source throughout your paper, you immediately lose credibility with your readers. Readers will question the depth of your research and the level of your knowledge; your competence as a researcher will be called into question. On the other hand, if you use a number of authors to provide supporting evidence, you gain credibility with your readers. So, it is important to read and evaluate several sources.

Chapter 2 describes the process of reading critically, which involves previewing, reading, and then reviewing. When you read sources for your research paper, pay special attention to reading with a critical eye. It would be a good idea at this time to review the Checklist for Evaluating Information in Chapter 10.

Previewing

Preview the source first. As you preview, pay attention to key words or phrases and try to get a general idea of the work's purpose and structure.

Reading

Read the work a first time at a relatively rapid pace, either a section or a chapter at a time. This first reading should be more than skimming, however, as the goal is to understand in general what you have read. Then read the work again, carefully and slowly. When you are reading your own books or photocopied articles, use a highlighter or a pencil to underline key ideas. Stop frequently to take notes, either in your research notebook or on index cards (see 8c).

As you read, keep your working hypothesis in mind (see 8a-4). By providing you with a focus, your starting questions and hypothesis will prevent you from reading aimlessly. As you read various sources, decide both how the sources relate to your hypothesis and how they relate to each other. Read each one with your purpose clearly in mind—using the sources to reinforce your own opinion, as stated in your hypothesis.

Reviewing

As part of your review, assess and evaluate each source, including those you find as you search the Internet. As discussed in Chapter 10, assessment is a two-step process of deciding whether or not the source is worth reading and whether or not the source is worth using in your paper. Evaluating involves thinking carefully about key elements in the work.

Synthesizing

As you read your sources, you should also seek to determine relationships among them. What kinds of "conversations" are happening between the authors that you are reading? Does one source contradict another, or does it reinforce what you've read in other places? Does a particular source serve as an example of something explained in a more general source? Or perhaps one source gives an excellent definition of the topic you are researching while another describes something in more detail. In your research notebook, be sure that you not only summarize the individual sources but also look for relationships between the ideas in one source and those in another.

2   Taking accurate, usable notes

If you do not take good notes while you read, you may have to retrace your steps in an attempt to relocate a particular source. In the worst-case scenario, the source you need to reference will have been checked out by another library patron or the Internet site will be gone. So, it is important to take accurate, usable notes when you first encounter a source.

Taking content notes and bibliographical notes

Chapter 8 describes taking content notes and bibliographical notes. Content notes include source information; bibliographical notes provide documentation information (see 8d). Be sure to take both kinds of notes, either on note cards or in a research notebook.

Recording substantive and interpretive information

The most successful research papers incorporate information from several sources into the flow of the paper. The least successful papers tend to make one of the following major mistakes. Either they rely too heavily on just one source for support of the argument or they cobble together the opinions of three or four authors, one right after the other, without interpreting their meanings or relationships. To avoid these mistakes, make your notes both substantive and interpretive. That is, record in your notes both what the source author is saying and what you think about it (see 8c).

Deciding whether to quote, paraphrase, or summarize

When you record content notes from a source, you typically either paraphrase or summarize what you have read. If the information seems especially significant to your research topic or if it provides new insights or ideas that you have not encountered before in your research, you will probably want to paraphrase it. Paraphrasing is an almost line-by-line rewording of the source information. (See 11b for examples of appropriate paraphrasing.) If the information seems less crucial to your topic or if you need little detail to make your point, you may wish to summarize instead. A summary, in contrast to a paraphrase, condenses information. (See 11c for examples of appropriate summarizing.) Record information in the form of a direct quotation if it is impossible to put the information into your own words—for example, if the author expressed a thought so memorably that you could not possibly say it otherwise. (See 11d for examples of appropriate quoting.)

11.2

Recognizing and preventing plagiarism.

3 Avoiding plagiarism

If you use source information carefully and accurately, you will avoid any charges of plagiarism. **Plagiarism** is the unauthorized or misleading use of the language and thoughts of another author. By following the guidelines in this chapter when you paraphrase, summarize, and quote, you can avoid plagiarism.

VIDEO
How to avoid plagiarism.

Acknowledgment required

Any word, phrase, or sentence that you copied directly from a source must be placed in quotation marks, and complete bibliographic information must be given, including the page reference for the quotation. Similarly, you must acknowledge paraphrases and summary restatements of ideas taken from a source, even though you have cast them in your own words. (See Chapters 13–15 on Documentation Formats.)

If you find information on a Web site, it is a relatively simple matter to download it to a disk or to your computer's hard drive. However, you need to be careful to use the information fairly. When you summarize, paraphrase, or quote from a Web site, you must give proper acknowledgment to the source. It is not acceptable to CUT and PASTE text or graphics from the Internet without acknowledging the source. The same general principles about paraphrasing, summarizing, and quoting apply to other online sources found through the Internet.

Many online databases provide abstracts rather than complete works (see 8f-4). For example, when searching the *ERIC* database on CD-ROM, you will find abstracts that tell what an article or document is about, in addition to showing its location and source. What if you use information from the abstract but do not actually read the original? You need to acknowledge the abstract when paraphrasing, summarizing, or quoting information it contains. Note in your bibliography that you are quoting the abstract rather than the source itself.

No acknowledgment required

You need not document "common knowledge." This term refers to information that is generally known or accepted by educated people. Information that you can find readily in general reference works such as encyclopedias or in the popular media is probably common knowledge and need not be documented, though it must be stated in your own words. Common knowledge should be verified. Be certain that several sources provide the same information before assuming that it is common knowledge. Well-proven historical facts and dates need not be documented. As a general rule, it is better to overdocument than to underdocument and be accused of plagiarizing. When in doubt, document.

Unintentional plagiarism

Your notes should accurately record source information in your own words, when possible. You should be able to tell at a glance from your notes when information is from a source and when it is your own commentary or thoughts on a source.

AUDIO

Take accurate notes to avoid plagiarism.

Students taking notes from a source sometimes commit *unintentional* plagiarism by carelessly copying words and phrases from a source into their notes and then using these words and phrases without acknowledgment in a paper. One way to avoid this problem is to read a piece carefully and then set it aside while you write your notes. If you follow the reading and notetaking procedures outlined in this chapter, paraphrasing and summarizing in your own words what you have read, you are unlikely to use the author's exact wording inappropriately in a research paper. Unintentional plagiarism can occur even if you have kept a good record of your sources because of poor paraphrases or summaries of source information (see 11b–11c).

If you record your notes by hand in a research notebook, you can divide each page into two columns, one for notes and one for your comments. If you use note cards, you can label the cards, indicating which are notes from a source and which are your own commentary. If you use a computerized research notebook, you can use the ANNOTATIONS or DOCUMENT COMMENTS feature of the word-processing program to separate source notes from your own thoughts (see 8c-1).

Intentional plagiarism

WWW

11.3

Myths and excuses about plagiarism exposed.

Sometimes plagiarism is *intentional;* that is, a writer knowingly copies the work of another without proper acknowledgment of the source. A *Newsweek* article reported on a Stanford University business school lecturer who used several pages from an article by Greg Easterbrook in his book, word for word, without acknowledging the original author (G. Easterbrook, "The sincerest flattery: Thanks, but I'd rather you not plagiarize my work," *Newsweek*, 19 July 1991, pp. 45–46). When the plagiarism came to light, the Stanford author apologized to Easterbrook but insisted that he had not plagiarized because he had included Easterbrook's name in the book's footnotes. Easterbrook's response explains an important distinction: "Footnotes my foot. Footnotes mean the place a fact can be found; they do not confer the right to present someone else's words as your own work" (46).

The distinction being made here is that whenever you use words from a source, this must be indicated clearly through the use of quotation marks and documentation at the point in the text where the source information is used. It is not enough to list the author in the footnotes or bibliography. Readers must be able to tell as they are reading your paper exactly what information came from which source and what information is your contribution to the paper. Note that in the example we used signal phrases to indicate the information in the paragraph comes from a *Newsweek* article by Easterbrook ("A *Newsweek* article reported . . ." and "Easterbrook's response explains . . ."). We also included specific documentation regarding the source itself, along with quotation marks around the exact quotation from Easterbrook. This is an example of proper attribution of source information.

11b Paraphrase sources accurately

Instead of directly quoting from sources, writers have the option of paraphrasing source information. The objective of paraphrasing is to present an author's ideas clearly, using your own words and phrases. This important skill not only deepens your understanding of the author's ideas but also helps you avoid plagiarism (see 11a-3). Here are some suggestions to help you paraphrase.

11.4
Examples of paraphrasing sources.

1. *Place the information in a new order.* When paraphrasing, you must rework a passage. One way to do this is to reorder the information. In the following example, from an article titled "Finding Medical Help Online" that appeared in *Consumer Reports,* the good paraphrase inverts the sentence structure of the original, whereas the poor paraphrase copies both words and sentence structure from the source and hence leads the student to commit unintentional plagiarism. The source is identified by the author's last name and the page number on which the material appears. (Plagiarized text is underlined.)

ORIGINAL QUOTATION FROM "FINDING MEDICAL HELP ONLINE," SCHWARTZ, P. 28

> If you're coping with an illness or want to exchange views about a medical topic, you'll want to find your way to a newsgroup. Despite the name, these are not collections of news items. They are, in effect, virtual bulletin boards open to anyone who cares to participate. The messages generally consist of plain text.

GOOD PARAPHRASE [WITH INVERTED SENTENCE STRUCTURE AND DIFFERENT WORDS]

YES   In a recent *Consumer Reports* article, the author suggests finding a relevant newsgroup if you have a particular medical problem or if you want to talk with others about a medical subject. Newsgroups are online bulletin boards that are available to anyone; in spite of their name, they are not news reports. Anyone who wishes to may join in a newsgroup discussion (Schwartz 28).

POOR PARAPHRASE [COPIES WORDS AND SENTENCE STRUCTURE DIRECTLY FROM SOURCE RESULTING IN PLAGIARISM]

NO   If you're faced with an illness or want to exchange views about a medical topic, you'll want to find your way to a newsgroup. Despite the name, these are not news items. They are virtual bulletin boards open to anyone. The messages generally consist of ordinary text (Schwartz 28).

2. *Break the complex ideas into small units.* If the author has expressed him- or herself in a rather complicated way, paraphrasing gives you the opportunity to state the complex ideas of the source more simply. Here is the another passage from the same article.

ORIGINAL

The "perfect" search engine would guide users to every relevant location, ranked in order of usefulness, without leaving anything out and without including anything irrelevant. That engine doesn't yet exist.

GOOD PARAPHRASE [WITH SIMPLIFIED SENTENCE STRUCTURE]

Schwartz states that no Internet search tool is yet "perfect." If it were, it would lead you to all the appropriate locations on your topic. It would rank all the Web sites by how useful they were. It would never leave something out that was relevant. It would never include anything that was irrelevant (29).

3. *Use concrete, simple vocabulary in place of technical jargon.* If the author has used technical vocabulary, you can replace some of the technical jargon with more simple, familiar words as you paraphrase. Here are some examples of jargon from these examples that might be changed in a paraphrase.

newsgroup = online bulletin board

search engine = Internet search tool

users = those who are using the Internet

location = Web site found at a unique Internet address

4. *Use synonyms for words in the source.* Just as you can replace jargon with more familiar terms, you can use synonyms (words that mean roughly the same thing) in the place of words from the source. Here are some of the synonyms used in the paraphrases above.

illness = medical problem

exchange views = talk with others

medical topic = medical subject

available to = open to

despite = in spite of

news items = news reports

5. *For each important fact or idea in your notes, write down the source page number.* With paraphrases, as with quotations, you must indicate exactly on what page in the source you found the information. Ideally, anyone else reading your work should be able to locate the exact wording from which your paraphrase was taken. If the source has no pages, as is true of many Internet documents, provide the author's last name only. (See Chapters 13–15 for more information on documenting electronic sources.)

1 Recording paraphrases in your notes

As you take notes on sources, you will mostly be recording them in the form of paraphrases (or summaries). The following example shows a passage from an Internet newsletter and a student's paraphrased notes. In her paraphrase, notice how the words have been changed or reordered and the sentence patterns altered from the original in order to avoid plagiarism. Notice also that the information is fairly complete, with most of the ideas from the original source retained in the paraphrased version.

ORIGINAL

> Technologies to reduce CO_2 emissions and solve global warming are with us already. They work and they're cost effective. This isn't "rocket science". It starts with simple things like double-glazing of windows, better-insulated buildings, energy-saving lighting and household appliances, televisions and photocopiers which consume no power during "standby". And cars which use a fraction of the fuel used by today's gas guzzlers. Using less energy means less pollution. And renewable energy sources, like wind power and solar power, produce no global warming pollution at all. This combination won't just solve global warming, it also cuts other emissions that pollute city air, aggravate people's asthma and contribute to acid rain.

GOOD PARAPHRASE [FROM STUDENT'S COMPUTERIZED NOTEBOOK]

> We already possess effective and inexpensive technologies to solve the global warming crisis. Easy-to-implement solutions include replacing old windows, insulating buildings, using appliances and lights that save power, and buying fuel-efficient automobiles. When

consumers use less power, there is a corresponding reduction in air pollution. Furthermore, alternative, renewable power, such as wind and solar, do not result in any emissions that contribute to global warming. Changing energy policies will not only help with the global warming problem but will at the same time reduce pollution in the air we breath that contributes to poor health and to the problem of "acid rain."

From *Climate Change*. 2003. World Wildlife Fund (WWF). 1 Nov. 2003 <http://www.panda.org/about_wwf/what_we_do/climate_change/index.cfm>

2 | Integrating paraphrases smoothly into your paper

Paraphrases from notes should be integrated into a paper in much the same way as direct quotations. You should introduce them with signal phrases, place them in context for the readers, or perhaps use the author or title in the introduction. You need to provide documentation indicating the source of the information (see Chapters 13–15). The following example illustrates the successful paraphrase above, now effectively integrated into a paper.

GOOD PARAPHRASE [INTEGRATED INTO A PAPER WITH A SIGNAL PHRASE AND DOCUMENTATION FOR A WEB SITE]

According to an article published at the World Wildlife Fund Web site, we already possess effective and inexpensive technologies to solve the global warming crisis. Easy-to-implement solutions include replacing old windows, insulating buildings, using appliances and lights that save power, and buying fuel-efficient automobiles. When consumers use less power, there is a corresponding reduction in air pollution. Furthermore, alternative, renewable power, such as wind and solar, do not result in any emissions that contribute to global warming. Changing energy policies will not only help with the global warming problem but will at the same time reduce pollution in the air we breath that contributes to poor health and to the problem of "acid rain" (World Wildlife Fund).

(EXERCISE 11.1)

Select a short article on a topic of interest to you and print or photocopy it. Select a short paragraph from the article. Following the guidelines in this section, paraphrase that paragraph. Provide

Guidelines for Effective Paraphrasing

1. Place the information in a new order.
2. Break the complex ideas into small units.
3. Use concrete, direct vocabulary in place of technical jargon.
4. Use synonyms for words in the source.
5. Accompany each important fact or idea in your notes with the source author and page number.
6. Incorporate the paraphrase smoothly into the grammar and style of your own writing.

AUDIO
Three sets of guidelines.

appropriate documentation for the source, as if you were using the paraphrase in a research paper.

FOR COLLABORATION

Bring to class a passage that you have paraphrased as well as the paraphrase itself. Exchange passages and paraphrases with a classmate. Use the Guidelines for Effective Paraphrasing to evaluate the classmate's work, looking specifically for how effectively your peer has captured the original passage in his or her paraphrase without using the language or wording of the original source.

11c Summarize sources briefly

Summaries condense the information found in sources. Like paraphrasing, summarizing involves restating the author's ideas or information in your own words, but summaries are typically much briefer than the original information. To be sure that your summary accurately reflects the author's most important ideas, you must first read the source carefully in order to understand it thoroughly. Summaries typically leave out extended examples, illustrations, and long explanations. The goal of a summary is to record the gist of the piece—its primary line of argument—without tangential arguments, examples, and other departures from the main ideas. As with paraphrasing, you need to be sure that the summary is stated in your own words to avoid plagiarism.

11.5
Examples of summarizing sources.

1   Recording summaries in your notes

When you first preview a source to determine its relevance to your research, you can also decide how much of the source you are likely to use in your paper. You would not want to paraphrase an entire article, for example, if only the introduction related to your topic. Rather, you could simply summarize the relevant portion. On note cards or in a research notebook, record summary information in the form that will be most useful to you later on. As with paraphrasing, you should keep track of the page numbers covered by the summary, when they are available. Summarizing is the technique you will probably use most when recording information in your notes. A student summarized the original wording from the World Wildlife Fund Web site (quoted on page 251) as follows:

GOOD STUDENT SUMMARY IN RESEARCH NOTEBOOK

The World Wildlife Fund Web site outlines easy-to-implement solutions to the global warming problem. They suggest changes in both individual energy use and global energy policies as ways to tackle the problem. Changing energy policies will also reduce health problems related to pollution and acid rain (World Wildlife Fund).

Here are some additional suggestions to help you summarize effectively.

1. *Identify key points.* A summary must reflect the main ideas of the source accurately, so you need to read carefully before you write a summary. As you read your own books or photocopied articles, underline or highlight key ideas, words, or phrases. Ask yourself, "What is the central idea of this passage?" Try to articulate that idea in your own words, using just a sentence or two.

2. *Record information.* As you record the key ideas, be certain that you separate your own interpretive comments from the source information itself. You can do this by using a two-column notebook or document comments (see 8c-1).

3. *Create lists and tables.* When you are condensing ideas, sometimes it helps to write them down in the form of a list or a table. In this way, you can capture the most important ideas in the simplest form possible and present them to readers as a listing of key ideas. In the following example, the student has summarized an entire article in the form of a table of key ideas. Notice that the article headings, taken directly from the source, are placed in quotation marks to indicate a direct quotation.

GOOD STUDENT SUMMARY OF THE ARTICLE "FINDING MEDICAL HELP ONLINE"

In a recent Consumer Reports article titled "Finding Medical Help Online," Schwartz explains how to find the "good stuff" (27). The major parts of the article are summarized in the table below.

Summary of Schwartz Article

"Basic Information about the Internet" (27-28)	Discusses terminology, equipment, hardware and software issues.
"Newsgroups" (28)	Explains how newsgroups work and how they can provide forums for like-minded individuals to discuss issues.
"Search Engines" (29)	Describes some general search engines and explains how they work.
"Health Web Sites" (29)	Outlines general and specific medical sites that might be useful.
"Strategies for Searching" (30-31)	Walks through a model search, explaining what one is likely to find and how useful it is likely to be.

Source: Consumer Reports (Feb. 1997): 27-31.

4. *Check for accuracy.* Just as you did when quoting or paraphrasing from a source, you need to check your summaries to ensure their accuracy. Make sure that the words and phrases are your own. Place any of the author's unique words or phrases in quotation marks and include a page reference. Check to be sure that you have not been interpretive or judgmental about anything the author has said. When summarizing, you should restate the author's main ideas objectively in your own words, without interpretation. Record any interpretive judgments as document comments or clearly distinguish them in a two-column notebook. It is a good idea to reread the source after you have summarized it, just to be certain that you have not inadvertently altered the author's meaning.

2 Integrating summaries into your paper

Summaries are incorporated into a paper in much the same way as direct quotations and paraphrases. Introduce a summary with a signal phrase, place it in a context for the readers, or perhaps use the author's name or article title in the introduction. As with quoting and paraphrasing, you need to provide documentation indicating the source of the summarized information (see Chapters 13–15).

3 Avoiding plagiarism when summarizing

As mentioned above, using your own words and providing documentation for the source will produce a summary that avoids plagiarism. In the following examples, the unacceptable summary makes the mistake of using the same wording and sentence structure of the original source (underlined words are plagiarized) as well as failing to provide documentation. The acceptable summary identifies and recasts the main idea into the student's own words and provides proper attribution to the source itself, an article from New York Times online titled "With Cable TV at M.I.T., Who Needs Napster?"

ORIGINAL

Two students at the Massachusetts Institute of Technology have developed a system for sharing music within their campus community that they say can avoid the copyright battles that have pitted the music industry against many customers. The M.I.T. system, using the analog campus cable system, simply bypasses the Internet and digital distribution, and takes advantage of the relatively less-restrictive licensing that the industry makes available to radio stations and others for the analog transmission. The university, like many educational institutions, already has blanket licenses for the seemingly old-fashioned analog transmission of music from the organizations that represent the performance rights. . . . Although the M.I.T. music could still be recorded by students and shared on the Internet, Professor Abelson said that the situation would be no

> ## Guidelines for Effective Summarizing
>
> 1. Identify the main points as you read the source.
> 2. Put those main points into your own words.
> 3. Condense the original, keeping the summary short.
> 4. Use a table or a list, when appropriate, to summarize the information.
> 5. Be objective rather than interpreting or judging source ideas.
> 6. Integrate the summarized ideas into the flow of your prose.
> 7. Provide proper documentation for the source.

different from recording songs from conventional FM broadcasts. The system provides music quality that listeners say is not quite as good as a CD on a home stereo but is better than FM radio.

POOR SUMMARY [COPIES WORDS AND SENTENCE STRUCTURE DIRECTLY FROM SOURCE AND LEAVES OFF ATTRIBUTION]

NO   Two M.I.T. students have developed a system for sharing music within their campus community to avoid copyright battles. Their system provides music quality that listeners say is not quite as good as a CD but better than FM radio.

GOOD SUMMARY [RECASTS THE MAIN IDEA INTO STUDENT'S OWN WORDS AND PROVIDES SOURCE ATTRIBUTION]

YES   To allow students on the M.I.T. campus to share music with each other without violating copyright laws, two students have developed a system of sharing music by using the campus cable TV network. This ingenious system bypasses the Internet altogether and provides music via cable TV that is better in quality than what can be heard on the radio (Schwartz).

(EXERCISE 11.2)

Using the same article as in Exercise 11.1, choose one brief section or page to summarize. Remember that a summary is a condensed version of the original source. Write up your summary and turn it in to your instructor. Be sure to include a printout or photocopy of the original source, with the relevant sections marked to indicate the key ideas.

11d Quote sources sparingly

Quotations are exact wordings taken from sources. Use direct quotations sparingly in a research paper. A string of quotations can be confusing for readers, especially if each presents information in a different writing style. By paraphrasing and summarizing instead of quoting, you can more smoothly incorporate the ideas from sources into your own writing. However, if an author uses unique language or an interesting image, a brief quotation may be an effective addition to a paper. Generally, you should limit each quotation to a sentence or two so that it does not interrupt the flow of your paper. Enclose it in quotation marks (see 55a) and include documentation (see Chapters 13–15).

1 Using quoted material

When you quote from a source, it is important to be accurate. Unless you download text from the Internet, you are most likely copying from a source into your notes and then into your paper, so it is easy to make a transcription error. Making photocopies of a source can help you to quote exactly because you can recheck the wording from the photocopy.

Every time you copy information from a source, indicate through quotation marks on your note card or in your research notebook that you have taken the exact wording from the original. Figure 11.1 shows a note card with information that a student intended to quote because she felt that the author expressed a key idea in forceful language. This particular quotation came from an article found on the Internet. Note that since Internet sources typically do not provide page numbers, the student could not indicate a specific page on the note card. She also created a corresponding bibliography card for this source (see 8d-1). The number 3.1 in the upper right-hand corner of the note card indicates that this is the first note card from source number 3.

2 Integrating quotations into your paper

When you use a direct quotation, you must integrate it smoothly into the flow of your ideas. You need to use signal phrases to alert your

Quotation on Climate Change   *3.1*

According to researchers at Carnegie Mellon University, "Scientists disagree about whether climate change will be a serious problem in the next 50 to 100 years. The main reason for this disagreement is that nobody knows for sure whether climate changes caused by human actions will be large enough and fast enough to cause serious damage" (U.S. Global Change Research Information Office).

FIGURE 11.1 Note Card with Direct Quotation

reader that a quotation is coming. You also need to attribute the source appropriately (see Chapters 13–15 on documentation formats) and punctuate it correctly (see Chapter 55 on Quotation Marks).

11.6

Examples of integrating quotations into a paper.

When to use direct quotations

In general, use direct quotations sparingly. It is usually preferable for you to paraphrase or summarize source material so that the information is in your own words and in your own writing style (see 11b–11c). Too many direct quotations lead to a very choppy paper because the reader encounters so many writing styles. A short quotation of a sentence or two can be used if the author's wording is so memorable that you simply are unable to paraphrase it. If you decide to use a long quotation of three lines or more in your paper, you are obliged to explain your choice to your readers. In other words, you should introduce the quotation and tell the reader something about it, explaining how it relates to the argument that precedes and follows it. (We discuss this in more depth below.) Particularly in literary analysis papers where your argument is supported by the text you are analyzing and by other literary critics, you may find yourself using several short quotations throughout your paper. For an example of how such quotations are effectively integrated into the flow of your own argument, see Heidi Blankley's analysis of the novel *Regeneration* (17c).

Techniques for incorporating quotations

Observing the five suggestions outlined below for incorporating quotations will help you improve the flow of your paper.

1. *Integrate the quotation into the grammatical flow of your sentences.* The quotation should flow smoothly with the grammatical structure of your own sentence.

(Note) The citation style in the examples below is MLA. The global change example is a quotation from an Internet source and therefore has no page number.

NO   Carnegie Mellon researchers study climate "Scientists disagree about whether climate change will be a serious problem in the next 50 to 100 years" (US Global Change). [Grammar problem— fused sentence]

YES   Researchers at Carnegie Mellon University claim, "Scientists disagree about whether climate change will be a serious problem in the next 50 to 100 years" (US Global Change). [Quotation integrated grammatically]

2. *Use signal phrases.* In the second passage above, the opening clause (*Researchers at Carnegie Mellon University claim*) is a **signal phrase**, that is, a phrase that tells the reader a bit about the source quotation that is to follow. In a signal phrase, you include the author or source organization's name (*researchers at Carnegie Mellon University*) as well as a verb or a form of a verb that tells something about the author's position (*claim*). Some verbs that are commonly used in signal phrases are listed in the box on page 261. You can use a variety of signal phrases to show your own interpretation of the author's point and to provide for stylistic variety. Signal phrases can precede the quotation, interrupt it, or follow it, as in the examples below (the signal phrases are underlined). Signal phrases can also be helpful in showing the reader where source information begins and ends.

SIGNAL PHRASE PRECEDES QUOTATION

Rivers provides an insightful revelation about gender roles: "He distrusts the implication that nurturing, even when done by a man, remains female" (Barker 107).

SIGNAL PHRASE INTERRUPTS QUOTATION

"Stable introverts," another study found, "are the highest academic performers" (Furnham and Medhurst 197).

SIGNAL PHRASE FOLLOWS QUOTATION

"Extroverts prefer locations where socializing opportunities abound," report Campbell and Hawley (141).

Verbs to Use in Signal Phrases for Quotations

acknowledges	confirms	observes
advises	contends	offers
advocates	criticizes	opposes
affirms	declares	recommends
agrees	denies	remarks
alleges	describes	replies
allows	disagrees	reports
answers	discusses	responds
asserts	disputes	reveals
avows	emphasizes	says
believes	expresses	states
charges	interprets	suggests
claims	lists	thinks
concludes	objects	writes
concurs		

If you provide the author's name in the signal phrase, you need only put the page number in parentheses.

NO "During the years with The Nature Conservancy and IUCN, I did some science, some conservation, and a little writing. What I always came back to was the writing—the more heart-filled, the better. In the end, I think I always knew the words would win out" (Pyle 59). [No signal phrase]

YES As Robert Michael Pyle explains, "During the years with The Nature Conservancy and IUCN, I did some science, some conservation, and a little writing. What I always came back to was the writing—the more heart-filled, the better. In the end, I think I always knew the words would win out" (59). [Signal phrase with the verb *explains*]

3. *Provide interpretations or explanations.* Not only do you need to ensure that quotations are integrated smoothly into the flow of your sentences, but you also need to be sure that the ideas found within

the quotations are integrated into your own ideas in the paper. You do so by providing your readers with interpretations or explanations of the quotation and its relevance to your ideas. Too often inexperienced writers simply "dump" quotations into their papers without providing such interpretations, which is invariably ineffective. You cannot assume that a quotation can stand on its own merits. Rather, you are obliged to explain to your readers why you are using a particular quotation. Compare the following examples, with and without introductory explanations.

NO "Everyone in the group contributes to the overall level of emotional intelligence, but the leader holds special sway in this regard. Emotions are contagious, and it's natural for people to pay extra attention to the leader's feelings and behavior" (Goleman, Boyatzis, and McKee 174). [No introductory explanation]

YES Goleman et al. confirm that it is only when groups exhibit the qualities of emotional intelligence that they can be perceived as smarter than individuals. The authors assert, "Everyone in the group contributes to the overall level of emotional intelligence, but the leader holds special sway in this regard. Emotions are contagious, and it's natural for people to pay extra attention to the leader's feelings and behavior" (174). [Includes introductory explanation with signal verbs *confirm* and *assert*]

4. *Indicate omissions or changes to the original quotation.* In order to better integrate a quotation into the flow of your own prose, you may sometimes wish to alter a quotation by omitting a portion of it, altering a verb form or changing punctuation, or adding a clarifying word or phrase.

Using ellipses and brackets

Three spaced periods, called ellipses, are used to indicate any information that has been left out of the original quotation (see Chapter 56). Brackets are used to show any words or phrases within the original that you have changed to conform to the grammar of your own sentence. The example below illustrates both ellipses and brackets.

YES Researchers at Carnegie Mellon University claim, "Scientists disagree about whether climate change will be a serious problem . . . [since] nobody knows for sure whether climate changes caused by human actions will be large enough and fast enough to cause serious damage" (US Global Change). [Shows omissions and changes]

Changing verbs, pronouns, and capital letters

Verbs.   Sometimes it is necessary to change the tense or form of a verb to conform to the grammar of your own prose.

> "One of the worst things," Dr. Minor said, "was the way in which insurance companies insinuate[d] themselves into my dealings with patients" (33). [The original verb in the present tense changed to past tense.]

Prounouns.   For clarity's sake, often a pronoun in the original will be replaced by the noun referent.

> "When [Dr. Minor's] sons said they wanted to be doctors, he insisted that they work awhile as hospital orderlies to see his world from a different perspective" reports a recent *Newsweek* article (32). [The possessive pronoun *his* is changed to *Dr. Minor's* to make the referent clear.]

Capital letters.   You may also need to change capital letters to make the quotation fit grammatically into the flow of your own prose.

> "[D]octors and hospitals," observes a recent *Newsweek* article, "remain prime targets in the battle to reduce medical spending" (32). [In the original, *Doctors* is not capitalized.]

5. *Use indentation to set off a block quotation.* In MLA style, quotations longer than four lines should be set off from the regular text by indenting every line of the quotation ten spaces from the left margin and double-spacing lines throughout. Because the format sets apart the quotation, it is not necessary to use quotation marks. The line spacing and right-hand margin remain the same as for the regular text. A long quotation should also be introduced by a signal phrase. Notice the punctuation at the end of the following block quotation: the period comes before the page number in parentheses rather than at the end as it does for quotations run into the text.

YES   Aronson describes the isolation that is commonly felt by those caring for patients suffering from Alzheimer's disease:

> As the chronic illness develops and the physical and behavior signs of the patient become more pronounced, the caregiver senses his or her isolation even more intensely. Friends and relatives may socialize less frequently. Telephone calls and visits may become few and far between, and the physical and emotional burdens of caring for the patient increase. (167)

The author goes on to describe the other experiences common to caregivers, including frustration, resentment, and trouble with letting go (167–68).

Guidelines for Effective Quoting

1. Use direct quotations sparingly as support for your own ideas.
2. Use primarily short quotations (one or two sentences).
3. Be extremely careful to be accurate when copying a quotation.
4. Attribute quotations to their sources and punctuate them correctly (see 55a).
5. Integrate quotations smoothly into the stylistic flow of the paper.
6. Incorporate quotations in a way that is grammatically correct (see 55e).
7. Provide an explanation to place the quotation in context.
8. Use the author's name or the work's title to introduce the quotation.
9. Use ellipses and brackets when words or phrases are omitted from the quotation (see 56k, 56m).

EXERCISE 11.3

From the article you printed or photocopied in Exercise 11.1, choose a sentence or two in which the author states an important idea in memorable words. Imagine that you will be using the quotation in a research paper. Introduce the quotation by providing a context, and then write the quotation, using correct grammar and punctuation.

FOR COLLABORATION

Exchange rough drafts of your paper with a peer. Use the Guidelines for Effective Quoting above to evaluate your peer's rough draft, looking specifically for how effectively he or she has integrated direct quotations into the flow of the paper.

CHAPTER 12

Writing the Research Paper

FAQs

▶ Is it okay to use "I" in my paper? (12a-3)

▶ How do I arrange all the information? (12b)

▶ How do I write a draft? (12c)

▶ How do I revise? (12d)

▶ Should I use footnotes? (12e-1)

▶ Is it okay to add a photo or graphic? (12e-3)

Now that you have gathered and evaluated your information, you need to step back and assess just where all this research has taken you. Although the writing process that you will follow in writing your research paper is not radically different from the writing process outlined in Part 1 of this handbook, there are some important differences. As mentioned in Chapter 8, the first difference is one of scope; a research paper is longer than most essays. Sometimes students find themselves overwhelmed by the sheer volume of information they have collected. It is indeed an enormous challenge to organize and present research. Another major difference between a research paper and most essays is that you will be using information from sources, in addition to your own ideas, as support for your thesis. The suggestions in this chapter will help you write a successful research paper.

AUDIO
Organizing and presenting research data.

WEBLINK

http://www.wisc.edu/
writing/Handbook/
PlanResearchPaper.html

A good starting point for all researchers with questions

WWW

12.1

A complete guide to writing a research paper.

12a Review your rhetorical stance and thesis

12.2

An online guide to writing research papers.

WEBLINK

http://www.ipl.org/div/aplus/

Internet Public Library's excellent guide to writing research papers

Chapter 3 suggests that you decide on a rhetorical stance, which will help you determine the direction of your research. It would be a good idea to review your rhetorical stance at this time, reassessing your topic, purpose, persona, audience, and hypothesis.

1 Reassessing your purpose, persona, and audience

Remind yourself of your intended purpose for writing the research paper and your persona (see 3b-2, 8a). Ask yourself, "Who is my audience?" You may not be able to determine for certain who your readers will be, but you can assume that they will be intelligent people who have an interest in the topic you are writing about. It is unlikely that they will be experts in the field you are discussing; therefore, you should define terms carefully and avoid using jargon or technical vocabulary.

2 Refining your argument

Your starting questions and working hypothesis helped you to focus your research. Reassess your working hypothesis at this time. Does it still reflect the position you wish to take in your paper? If not, revise the hypothesis. Remember that a hypothesis usually takes a side on a debatable issue.

Testing your hypothesis

Kaycee Sorensen's starting questions about online shopping had to do with its growth, its convenience, and its safety (see 8a for a description of Kaycee's starting process). As she looked over the material gathered in her research, Kaycee was convinced that online shopping was an excellent option for consumers. In other words, she confirmed that her research had supported her working hypothesis.

The number of online shoppers is increasing, which means cybershopping is becoming a convenient, affordable, safe alternative `for consumers.` [Yes, Kaycee determined that this hypothesis was supported by the research.]

Writing a thesis statement

A thesis statement for a research paper is similar to a thesis statement for an essay (see 3e-1 to 3e-3). That is, it states for readers the central idea that the paper will argue. Many times, the working thesis statement is revised during the actual writing process. Kaycee decided to write a thesis that stated her conclusions about online shopping.

`Working thesis: Cybershopping is a safe alternative for consumers.`

Revising the thesis

Most research papers argue a position. However, some research papers are informational; that is, they report on information without taking a position. Your instructor may require that your thesis (and thus your research paper) have an argumentative edge. If so, make sure that you have taken a stand that can be supported through arguments in the paper (see 7a). If your research paper is informational rather than argumentative, your thesis should reflect the fact that you are reporting information rather than taking a stand on an issue. Neither type of research paper is inherently better; the two types are simply different. Your thesis statement should clearly tell readers what direction your paper will take. Readers should not be surprised at the end by a position that was not acknowledged up front in the paper's introduction.

AN ARGUMENTATIVE THESIS

> Whatever the causes, males and females have different perspectives on computers and their uses.

AN INFORMATIONAL THESIS

> This paper will trace the evolution of computers from the first room-sized mainframes to the current hand-held notebooks.

After Kaycee had written a first draft of her paper, she revisited her working thesis statement. Although it stated in brief form her central idea for the paper, it was not specific enough to provide an accurate blueprint of what she had argued in the paper itself. She revised her thesis to be more specific and to reflect her argumentative stance. The revised thesis now states both the central idea and her opinion about it.

Revised thesis: Consumers should shop online because, despite fears of safety and identity theft, its simplicity, the convenience of comparison shopping, and access to a variety of merchandise make online shopping the logical and best choice for consumers.

3 Deciding on a voice and tone

Academic papers should be informative and serious, but they need not be dull or dry. You can still put your own personality into a piece. Although it is generally not appropriate to adopt too informal a tone for an academic research paper, taking yourself out of the piece entirely may leave readers with the impression that the piece is lifeless and uninteresting. However, check with your instructor before using the informal first-person "I" in your research paper. Try to strike a balance in your tone, making it pleasing to readers (see 3b-3).

Before you begin to draft your research paper, answer the following questions about voice. Do I want to sound forceful and authoritative? Do I want to sound reasonable and moderate? Or perhaps passionate and concerned? Notice the voice in the following passage, taken from Kirsten's paper on Net theft (see Chapter 4).

I'm sure all of us once glimpsed a tempting item in a store and, after getting "no" for an answer from Mom or Dad, took matters into our own hands, sneaking the treasure into a hidden pocket. It probably took only a few moments for your parents to notice something was up. I remember well a discussion about why taking the package was wrong. Then my Dad took me back to the store where an apology was made and my Strawberry Hubba Bubba Bubblegum was paid for.

The voice in this passage is light and friendly. Kirsten seems to be speaking directly to her readers. Contrast that voice with Kaycee's.

Transaction security is the first thing to be aware of when shopping on the Internet, and data encryption provides the most secure way to send information from site to site without having anyone in between being able to read it. When an Internet user sends

information, the data is encrypted, or put into code. Anyone who tries
to read the information while it is en route to the site will find it
impossible. Secure Sockets Layer (SSL), the standard for sending
secure data, protects against snooping and possible tampering and then
verifies that the site to which the data is sent is authentic.

In this passage, Kaycee sounds authoritative and knowledgeable. The
much more serious voice is appropriate for a research paper.

12b Plan a structure

Some writers like to work from an organizational plan or outline,
fleshing out the skeleton by incorporating additional information
under each of the major points and subpoints. Others prefer to begin
writing and have the structure evolve more organically. You need not
be overly concerned about formal structure at this point, unless your
instructor stipulates a particular outline format. An outline or plan
should be a guide as you write, not a constraint that confines and limits your thinking. You may need to change your organizational plan
several times as you make new discoveries while writing. Whatever
structure you select must include a format for incorporating opposing viewpoints.

1 Developing an organizational plan or outline

As you write your outline (see 3e-5), remember that you are trying
to make the information or argument accessible to readers as well as
clear and comprehensive. If you used note cards, sort them by heading
and subheading into related ideas and information. If you used a computer research notebook, sort your materials by using the CUT, COPY,
and PASTE features of your word-processing program.

Once you have sorted your source materials, you should be able to
produce an outline or plan from the headings and subheadings in your
notes. For example, after Kaycee decided on the stand she would take
in her paper, as articulated in her thesis, she outlined an organizational
structure in which she systematically answered each of her starting
questions so that her argument would be easy for a reader to follow
and understand. In order to explain cybershopping to her readers,
Kaycee decided on the following plan.

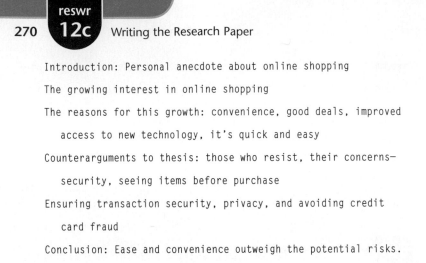

Introduction: Personal anecdote about online shopping

The growing interest in online shopping

The reasons for this growth: convenience, good deals, improved

access to new technology, it's quick and easy

Counterarguments to thesis: those who resist, their concerns—

security, seeing items before purchase

Ensuring transaction security, privacy, and avoiding credit

card fraud

Conclusion: Ease and convenience outweigh the potential risks.

She entered these headings into her electronic notebook, stored in a computer file in her hard drive. (For more information on planning and outlining, see 3e.)

2 Including opposing viewpoints

In an argumentative research paper, it is crucial to present the counterarguments—that is, the arguments on the side opposite the position you are taking. In her paper, it was important for Kaycee to acknowledge that some consumers are reluctant to do their shopping online. In her revised thesis, she acknowledges those concerns ("despite fears of safety and identity theft"). Then, she refutes these concerns on pages 4 and 5 of the research paper by showing that security can be ensured if consumers take reasonable precautions. As she wrote the paper, Kaycee was conscious throughout of possible opposing viewpoints and was careful to acknowledge these concerns and counter them with her own arguments.

12c Write a draft

12.3
How to start
the first draft.

Now you should be ready to begin drafting your research paper. Remind yourself of your general understanding of the topic, of your starting questions and hypothesis, and of the answers to the questions as stated in your thesis. When writing your first draft, use concrete and simple language to explain your research conclusions in your own words. Ideally, you should type your draft on a computer to make revisions easier. Be certain to back up your computer documents and save to a disk frequently so as not to lose any of your hard work.

1 Choosing a drafting strategy

You will need to establish your own strategy for writing a first draft, one that fits your writing style. Here are a few different ways in which writers of research projects proceed.

- Write a draft systematically from a plan, using the building-block technique (see 4b-1).
- Write a draft from piles of notes arranged according to a blueprint from the thesis (see 4b-2).
- Write a sketchy first draft without looking at the notes—just writing down everything you remember from the research; follow up by fleshing out the partial draft with a more complete version while referring to your notes.
- Write a rough first draft and then write a revision outline that suggests ways in which the draft needs to be changed (see 5a-3).
- Write a draft by cutting and pasting information from an electronic research notebook (see 8c).
- Write a draft while viewing electronic note cards in a second window (see 8c-2).

2 Applying the drafting strategy to blend material

As you draft, you blend your own knowledge with material from sources. In writing a first draft, it is best to put down your own understanding of the topic first, rather than relying too heavily on your sources. After you have written your draft, you can go back and add specific sources to support your arguments. Readers want to know what *you* think about the subject. They do not want to read a string of quotations loosely joined by transitions. Studying the topic and reading the source materials should have given you a general understanding of your topic. Writing a working thesis should have provided you with the main point you wish to make. Once you have drafted your paper, important data, facts, illustrations, and supporting evidence gleaned from your sources can be added to your arguments to give them authority and force (see 11b-2, 11c-2, 11d-2).

Kaycee kept all her information in an electronic notebook. After making a backup copy of the notebook document, Kaycee began manipulating information (using CUT, COPY, and PASTE) to put related ideas under the relevant subheadings of her plan. She moved to the end of the document all of the information that did not seem immediately related to her thesis statement. Once the material was in categories, it was easy for Kaycee to see which areas needed additional information. She could then return to her sources or even find new sources if necessary, in order to present a balanced view of the issues. In this way, she wrote the first draft of the research paper, using the building-block technique discussed in 4b-1.

3 Writing a working title

Writing effective titles is discussed in 5b-7; it would be helpful to review that section of the handbook at this time. Writing a title can help you succinctly state the topic your research paper will cover. Try out a few titles before deciding on one. It should be brief yet descriptive.

4 Writing an introduction and conclusion

Composing introductions and conclusions is discussed in 5b-7 and 6h. Because a research paper typically covers more information than an essay, it may take a couple of paragraphs to introduce the topic effectively. Kaycee used two opening paragraphs for her research paper. The first paragraph provides an interesting opening anecdote that leads the reader into the topic of the paper. The second, leading up to her thesis, explains to readers how prevalent online shopping is becoming. Kaycee's conclusion sums up the major points to her argument and restates her stance on the subject.

EXERCISE 12.1

Write an introductory paragraph for a research paper. First, write a straightforward academic paragraph with a serious tone. Then, write a second version of the opening paragraph that is light in tone and perhaps even humorous. You might tell a story or describe a scene.

FOR COLLABORATION

Discuss these two opening paragraphs with your classmates. Which do you like better? Which seems more appropriate for your research paper?

12d Review and revise the draft

A great deal of important work remains to be done on your paper once you complete a rough draft. You must revise the paper to make the most effective possible presentation of the research. Readers expect you to be clear and correct; they should not be distracted by ambiguous source references, confusing language, or incorrect punctuation. It is a good idea to set your draft aside for a day or two, if time allows, so that you can look at it with a fresh eye. It is also a good idea to gather as much feedback as you can from peers. Plan to exchange drafts with a classmate or two for their suggestions (see 5e for more on giving and receiving feedback).

You need to reread your rough draft several times, both on the computer screen and in hard copy (see the Help box on page 102). Each time you read it, pay attention to a different aspect of the paper. The first time, think about the overall structure and style of the paper (see 5b). The second time through, check grammar and punctuation (see 5c–5d). The third time, make sure source materials are incorporated smoothly and accurately into the text (see 11b–11d). Finally, consider formal details such as conventions of documentation and format (see Chapters 13–15). After your paper has been typed and spell checked, proofread it several times to catch and correct all typographical and mechanical errors. For more information on rewriting your draft, refer to Chapter 5.

HELP

How do I automatically number my pages?

1. Almost all word-processing programs will automatically number pages, but because the commands vary, you will have to check the HELP menu or documentation for specifics. Words to look for include *pages, page numbers, headers,* and *footers.*

2. Other commands you should look for include the one that controls the position of the page numbers on the pages (and allows you to include running heads with the page numbers) and the one that suppresses page numbers on particular pages (such as the title page and the Works Cited page).

www

12.4

Step-by-step instructions for automatically numbering pages.

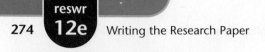

12e Follow formatting conventions

Research paper formatting conventions are customary ways of presenting information that have developed in various disciplines.

The research paper format recommended by the Modern Language Association (MLA) is the same as that outlined for essays in 4e. MLA recommends placing your identifying information in the upper left-hand corner, 1 inch down from the top margin, rather than using a title page. However, check with your instructor about his or her preference for a title page with a research paper. MLA also specifies putting your last name and the page number in the upper

---

Checklist for Revising a Research Paper

1. Does the paper fulfill the promise made by the thesis? (3e-3, 12a)
2. Do the arguments flow smoothly and logically? (12b)
3. Is sufficient attention paid to counterarguments? (12b-2)
4. Does the introduction lead effectively into the paper? (5b-7, 6h)
5. Does the conclusion either summarize or describe implications? (5b-7, 6h)
6. Is the paper focused, adequately developed, and coherent? (5a-2)
7. Are the sources integrated smoothly into the flow of the paper? (11b–11d)
8. Is information in quotes, paraphrases, and summaries accurately related and clearly acknowledged? (Chapter 11)
9. Are the parenthetical citations clear and accurately tied to the works-cited entries? (Chapters 13–15)
10. Are the works-cited entries properly formatted? (Chapters 13–15)
11. Is the format of the piece appropriate for a research paper? (12e)
12. Has the paper been edited and proofread to eliminate errors? (5c–5d)

AUDIO
Revision
checklist.

right-hand corner of each page, ½ inch from the top margin. Everything in your research paper is double-spaced, including the title and the first line of the text. Readers of research papers expect the writer to follow standard conventions, with an organizational pattern that includes an introduction, several body paragraphs, and a conclusion. Notice that Kaycee uses a personal anecdote as a catchy opener, followed by her introduction and thesis statement. She then develops her argument in the body paragraphs, and she ends with a strong conclusion. The final pages of the research paper detail her works cited, using the MLA documentation system.

The documentation conventions common to different disciplines are described in detail in Chapters 13–15. The main systems are the Modern Language Association (MLA) system, typically used in the humanities and fine arts; the American Psychological Association (APA) system, used in the social sciences; the *Chicago Manual of Style* (CMS) system, used in business; and the Council of Biology Editors (CBE) system, most often used in the sciences. We also include examples from the Columbia online style (COS) system. Ask your instructor if there is a particular format you should use. If not, select the format from the discipline most closely related to your research topic.

1 Preparing footnotes, endnotes, and reference lists

Once you have chosen a particular documentation style, follow that style closely for all sources used in your research paper. Depending on the conventions of the particular discipline, your paper may or may not have footnotes or endnotes. All research papers must include a listing of the sources used in the paper. Again, the way this listing is titled and formatted will depend on the particular discipline.

Footnotes and endnotes

Footnotes or endnotes are used most often in the humanities. For information on using them appropriately in MLA format, see 13a-2. In research papers in the sciences, citations generally appear in parentheses within the text. However, there may be times when you need to use explanatory notes, in the form of footnotes or endnotes. Your word-processing program probably includes an automatic FOOTNOTE/ENDNOTE feature (see the Help box on the next page). This feature puts the superscript number in the appropriate location (where the cursor is) and then generates the note, placing it either at the bottom of the page

12.5

Step-by-step instructions for using a computer footnote program.

VIDEO

A demonstration of how to set up a computer footnote or endnote program.

HELP

How do I use a computer footnote program?

1. Place the cursor at the point in the text where you want the number to appear.

2. Find the FOOTNOTE command (typically on the INSERT menu). Select either a footnote or an endnote.

3. Type in the text of the footnote.

4. Close the FOOTNOTE command.

5. The computer will automatically generate the footnote and place it at the bottom of the appropriate page or generate an endnote and place it in a consecutive list at the end of the paper.

NOTE: Most word-processing programs offer considerable control over the appearance of footnotes, but to take advantage of these features, you will need to read the program documentation.

or at the end of the text, whichever you specify. The advantage of using the automatic FOOTNOTE/ENDNOTE feature is that the computer will automatically place the note in the appropriate place as the rest of the text changes during revisions. Check your word-processing program's HELP menu to discover how to activate this feature.

Works Cited or References lists

A Works Cited list or a References list is an alphabetical listing of sources at the end of a paper (see 8d). For information on formatting a Works Cited or References list, see the section in Chapters 13–15 for the appropriate discipline. Your word-processing program may have a feature that will alphabetize references automatically. However, you need to enter the data in a certain fashion in order for the computer to sort appropriately. Once again, check your word-processing program's HELP menu to ascertain whether this feature is available and to learn how to use it (see 8d-1).

2 Understanding formatting conventions

In addition to helping you as a writer, word processing can help you create a text that is professional in appearance. If you are to com-

HELP

How do I use my word-processing program to set up my paper?

1. Locate your word-processing program's command for PAGE SETUP. Usually you can find it in the program's documentation or the online HELP menu.
2. Use PAGE SETUP to set margins, paper size, and page orientation for your paper.
3. Choose margins from PAGE SETUP that are consistent with the formatting style you are using in the paper (MLA, APA, CMS, CBE, or COS); see Chapters 13–15.
4. Use FORMAT > PARAGRAPH to make changes to individual paragraphs.
5. Use other features in the FORMAT menu to adjust fonts, bullets, numbering, columns, tabs, and so on.
6. Use the INSERT menu to insert graphics: pictures, text boxes, diagrams, graphs, charts, or objects such as images.

NOTE: Some word-processing programs let you set the margins and tabs by moving controls on the document's ruler bar. Your program's documentation will also explain how to use this feature.

VIDEO

A demonstration of how to format documents using a word processor.

WWW

12.6

Step-by-step instructions on how to set up an essay on a computer.

---

municate effectively with readers, in the end you must attend to both form and content. However, be sure to make attention to format your last consideration. Too often, writers using word processors spend an excessive amount of time playing with the appearance of the text—varying the fonts, for example—rather than concentrating on content.

Most word-processing programs offer formatting features such as underlining, boldface, and italics, with which you can vary the appearance of the text and highlight important information. (See also 20b.) However, you should check with your instructor about his or her preferences before you spend a lot of time adjusting the format of your paper. Your goal should be to make the paper look professional. An English Gothic typeface with scrolling capital letters is not appropriate for a formal research paper, nor is justifying the text on the right side of the page. It is best to be conservative and justify the text on the left side of the page only. The preferred format for each documentation style is described in Chapters 13–15.

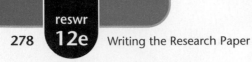
3 Incorporating visuals into your research paper

It is becoming increasingly acceptable for students to incorporate visuals (photos and graphics) into their research papers. However, it would be a good idea for you to check with your instructor before doing so. Listed in the accompanying box are some things

Guidelines for Incorporating Visuals into Your Research Paper

1. *Integrate the visuals into your text carefully.* Visuals complement text but do not substitute for it. Readers will only be irritated if it seems visuals have been inserted as mere decoration.

2. *Explain the visual's significance in words.* If you are using graphs or charts, you need to explain their significance in your text and refer specifically to each one (e.g., "see Table 1").

3. *Use clip art selectively.* Clip art is free artwork that is available in image archives in your word processor and on the Web. Don't include clip art unless you have some specific reason for doing so. It is frequently overused.

4. *Don't mix clip art and photographs.* For visual consistency, it's best to use only one type of graphic medium in a single paper. Also be consistent with any text boxes, lines, and other graphics.

5. *Insert tables and photos.* You can create tables and photos in other programs (such as *PowerPoint* or *Photoshop*) and insert them into your paper at the appropriate location.

6. *Wrap text around the graphic.* For ease of reading, it's often a good idea to place your visual so that the text wraps around it. Your word-processing program will allow you to edit the placement of the graphic in relationship to the text.

7. *Respect copyright protections.* Be sure to secure permission to use any visuals that you have not developed yourself.

to consider to make your visuals as effective as possible. See also Chapter 20 on Design Principles and Graphics.

12f Review an annotated student research paper

The following research paper, written by Kaycee Sorensen, is formatted following the MLA system of documentation. Annotations are included to explain the various conventions. See Chapter 13 for additional information on MLA documentation.

12.7

Examples of student papers on the Web.

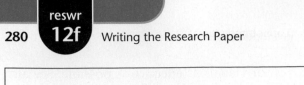
Online Shopping:

Risky (but Better) Business

By

Kaycee Sorensen

Professor Hult

English 2010 H, Section 01

3 May 2003

The *MLA Handbook for Writers of Research Papers*, 6th ed., says that a research paper does not need a title page. However, if your instructor requires a title page, use the format illustrated here. Double-space all material on the title page. Then, on the first page of your paper, put your last name, a space, and the number 1 in the upper right-hand corner (see page 282). The title page is not numbered. If you do not use a title page, follow the first-page format illustrated in Chapter 17.

Title

Student Identification

Course Identification

Sorensen 1

Online Shopping:

Risky (but Better) Business

Recently, I shopped at the Logan Old Navy to find   1
a new pair of jeans, but since I wear an uncommon size,
I could not find exactly what I wanted. The attendant
in the fitting rooms suggested that I visit OldNavy.com
to find what I was looking for. She gave me all the
information I would need to find the jeans and purchase
them online, and when I visited OldNavy.com, I found
the jeans, and they were cheaper than in the store.
Needless to say, I bought more than just the jeans
because of the wonderful prices. This was not my first
experience, but because of the price, the convenience,
and access to more items, I became excited to seek out
new online shopping venues.

I am not alone in my growing interest in online   2
shopping. According to Nielsen/Netratings, 498 million
people worldwide now have access to the Internet from
home, and just as these people are using the Internet
for quick access to information and electronic
communication, millions of them are also turning to the
Internet for shopping purposes (Hupprich and Bumatay).
Consumers should shop online because, despite fears of
safety and identity theft, its simplicity, the
convenience of comparison shopping, and access to a
variety of merchandise make online shopping the logical
and best choice for consumers.

Page Numbering. Kaycee numbered the pages automatically by using the page numbering command. The numbers (arabic) are located ½ inch from the top of the page and flush with the right margin. She included her last name along with the page number as a header. There is a space between the name and the number. The numbering proceeds consecutively throughout, including the Works Cited pages. Any pages that come before the first page of the paper are not numbered in the same sequence. Rather, roman numerals are used for pages that precede the actual text, such as an outline page or an abstract page. The title page is not numbered.

Title. The title of Kaycee's research paper is intriguing, yet simple and direct (see 5b-7). She uses a subtitle to grab our interest. The title is centered 1 inch from the top margin. Notice the spacing between the title and the start of the text (double-spaced).

Introductory Narrative. Kaycee begins with an introduction that includes a personal narrative about online shopping. By using this narrative (story), she immediately grabs the reader's attention (see 5b-7, 6h). She is appealing to her own authority on the topic, thus paying attention to the persona component of her rhetorical stance (see 3b-2). Everything is double-spaced, including the title and the start of the body of the text.

Describing the Controversy. In paragraph 2, Kaycee describes the current controversy over online shopping. Even though it is growing rapidly, consumers still express concerns about such things as safety and identity theft.

Citing an Internet Source. Kaycee uses an Internet source, *Nielsen/ Netratings*, for paragraph 2. Because Internet sources typically do not include page numbers, they are cited in parentheses by the author's names only, in this case Hupprich and Bumatay. Notice how the parenthetical citation is punctuated—the period for the sentence follows the parenthetical citation.

Thesis. At the end of paragraph 2, Kaycee states her thesis (see 7a, 12a-2). In the thesis statement, she takes a clear position on the issue, which she will argue in her paper. The thesis provides direction and structure to the paper that follows.

Sorensen 2

The convenience of online shopping became clear to 3 me not only as a consumer but also as a retailer. During the holidays, I work for Sears in Frisco, Texas. Our store is new and we still only serve the urban areas, so many people travel from rural areas to shop. While working over Christmas I helped one such woman who needed to shop for items for the baby she was expecting. She could not purchase everything she needed in this one trip and did not want to have to make the drive numerous times, so I suggested she go online to see what Sears.com had to offer. After visiting the site she decided to order all of her baby furniture from the comfort of her own home. She informed me that though she was able to buy most of the items she needed online, she would come back to the store to shop for baby clothes, which were not available online.

Rural customers are not the only consumers who 4 benefit from online shopping. More and more shoppers use the Internet to comparison-shop before purchasing items online or in a store, so they save money. There are price-comparison tools on the Internet, and some, such as PriceGrabber.com, find the best price for a particular item and then calculate the tax and shipping costs. This site and others can be used to get price quotes for items varying from airline tickets to cashmere sweaters.

Topic Sentence. The first sentence of paragraph 3 is an example of a topic sentence (see 6a). It tells us what the topic of the paragraph will be—the convenience of online shopping for both consumers and retailers. The paragraph then goes on to develop that topic, using an extended example.

Citing Common Knowledge. In paragraph 4, Kaycee uses information that is considered common knowledge for this topic; that is, anyone who is broadly familiar with the topic would agree on this information. Therefore, it is not necessary to provide any source citation (see 11a-3).

Transitional Sentence. Notice that the first sentences of paragraphs 4 and 5 are examples of transitional sentences (see 5b-2, 6c). Kaycee tells us through the first transitional sentence that it is not only rural customers who can benefit from online shopping. She tells us through the second transitional sentence that consumers, even though they may benefit from online shopping, still may wish to have that personal experience of trying on something before buying it. The use of transitional sentences to link paragraphs is very effective in Kaycee's paper.

Sorensen 3

Many customers may want to try on a cashmere   5
sweater to see how it looks on them before buying it,
even if they have to pay more to do so. For example,
Ahmad Kushairi says, "For me, I would like to browse
the shelves and feel the products before deciding if I
even want to purchase." Online retailers are aware of
this and try to target these consumers by providing new
technologies. For example, My Virtual Model Inc. has
created a tool that allows customers to "try clothes
on" before purchasing them. This technology has
"increased online sales" by leading to 26 percent more
purchases than average and increasing the average order
size by 13 percent. Virtual models are being used by
numerous online retailers, such as Lands' End, Limited
Too, Lane Bryant, and Nutri/System ("Virtual Model").

Retailers also target consumers by offering deals   6
through special online promotions such as credit card
companies offering deals to their cardholders. For
example, American Express, Visa, MasterCard, and
Discover have promotions that include free shipping and
discounts ranging from 5 to 25 percent. To receive
these deals, however, customers must first visit the
credit card site, and they will usually have to use
promotion codes or visit the retailers' sites from a
link on the credit card company's site. The discounts
change frequently and vary among the various credit

Direct Quotation from a Print Source. To give credence to her opening statement in paragraph 5, Kaycee uses a quotation from a print source. Notice how she has used the author's name in a signal phrase. No page number is required because the source is only one page long.

Source Paraphrase. The second half of paragraph 5 paraphrases a print source; that is, the information from the source has been restated in Kaycee's own words and reordered (see 11c). We can tell from the parenthetical citation that no author is listed for this article. Rather, the citation uses the title of the article from the journal *Capital Times*. No page number is needed for a one-page source. Remember that paraphrases tend to be about the length of the original source. They are used when key information needs to be incorporated into the flow of your own wording.

Argument Developed. In paragraph 6, Kaycee further develops her argument by showing how retailers promote online shopping through special offers and deals to credit card holders.

Summary of a Print Source. The second half of paragraph 6 summarizes a print source; that is, the information has been both restated and considerably condensed from the original source. Summaries differ from paraphrases by virtue of their length; summaries are only about one-third as long as the original.

Sorensen 4

card companies. Credit card companies can also offer
promotions for local businesses and attractions, so
consumers can register their e-mail address to learn of
the offers before they are posted on the site (Frey).

In addition to good deals and access to new   7
technology, online shopping offers a place for
consumers to shop quickly and easily online, as well as
quickly and easily offline. One segment of the
population that has benefited the most is teenagers.
Jared Blank, an analyst for Juniper Matrix, points out
that teens today "use the Internet as a shopping
mall--a place to meet friends, play games, and
shop--even without the intent to purchase. Teens spend
almost as much time on <u>Amazon.com</u> as adults, even
though few of those teens can make purchases on the
site" (qtd. in "Nearly One-Third").

Teens are not the only segment of the consumer   8
population who browse for goods online and then choose
to shop in brick-and-mortar stores. According to the
NPD Group, Inc., 92 percent of online consumers use the
Internet to shop and/or purchase online (qtd. in
Pastore). Cyberjournalist Michael Pastore points out
that NPD's data show that even those consumers not
making purchases online are still influenced by what
they see on retailers' Web sites. Eighty-four percent
of occasional buyers, who made at most one online

Development of the Topic. In paragraph 7, Kaycee adds another example of how online shopping can benefit consumers. Notice the use of the transitional expression "In addition" at the beginning of this paragraph.

Introducing a Source Within a Source. In the second half of paragraph 7, Kaycee quotes from a source found within another source. She quotes Jared Blank regarding the behavior of teens as fledgling consumers. However, since Blank's statements are found in a journal article that he did not author, that article's information is included in the parenthetical citation, along with the notation *qtd. in* to let the reader know that Blank is being cited indirectly.

A Paraphrase of an Internet Source Within a Source. Similarly, from reading Pastore's Internet article in the *Cyberatlas*, Kaycee learned about a study from the NPD Group that helped explain some of the complexities of online shopping behavior. She paraphrases the information regarding the study in paragraph 8 and quotes the vice president of online research at NPD indirectly, using the *qtd. in* notation in her parenthetical citation. The designation *qtd. in* is used for indirect paraphrases and summaries as well as indirect quotations.

Sorensen 5

purchase in the past six months, describe their usual
use of the Internet for shopping online and then going
offline to purchase. Pamela Smith, vice president of
NPD Online Research, explains:

> Measuring online sales alone cannot capture
> the full benefit of a retailer having an
> Internet presence. We know that even
> consumers who don't typically purchase online
> are using retailers' web sites to browse and
> decide what to buy. . . . Although it may not
> result in a purchase at that time, it could
> translate directly into an offline sale.
>
> (qtd. in Pastore)

The following chart, which outlines how online shoppers
describe how they typically use the Internet for
shopping, illustrates Smith's point.

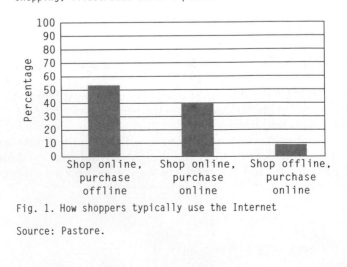

Fig. 1. How shoppers typically use the Internet

Source: Pastore.

Indented Quotation. In MLA style, quotations that are longer than four lines of prose or three lines of poetry are set off from the rest of the text through indentation (see 13a, 20b-3, 55b). The indentation should be ten spaces from the left-hand margin, but the quotation extends to the right margin. Notice that the punctuation of the parenthetical citation for such indented quotations differs from the usual. Usually, the period follows the parentheses of a citation. However, with an indented quotation, the period comes before the citation.

Using Ellipses. Kaycee has used ellipses to show that a portion of the original quotation has been left out of her paper (see 56k). Use ellipses any time you have omitted a section from a quotation.

Citing Statistical Information. Notice how Kaycee has used the chart at the end of paragraph 8 to reinforce her point about the habits of online shoppers. Since Kaycee has created this figure using data from one of her sources, she provides the source information below the figure caption.

Sorensen 6

Since the NPD study was completed, our nation has   9
experienced an economic downturn, but online spending
has increased. A recent study titled "The State of
Retailing Online 5.0" reports that "fully 56 percent of
holiday retailers reported online profits in 2001,
compared to only 43 percent in 2000" (Cox). Profits
from online shopping usually come from holiday
shopping. According to Nielsen/NetRatings, online
shoppers were expected to spend 43 percent more than
the $6.9 billion from the 2000 holiday season. One
hundred six million users were estimated to shop online
for the 2001 holidays, which would be a 27 percent
rise over the 85 million shoppers in 2000. Categories
normally reserved for traditional stores are climbing
in online preference (Chan et al.).

Although online shopping trends and spending are   10
growing, there are still consumers who resist
purchasing products over the Internet. One reason many
people may choose to browse for goods online and then
purchase them offline is their concern about identity
theft. In fact, a report by Taylor Nelson Sofres points
out, "Almost one-third (30 percent) of Internet users
who have not shopped online stated that they didn't
want to give credit card details (up by 5 percent from
2001) and 28 percent cited general security concerns"
(qtd. in Greenspan). In order to confidently shop
online, consumers must be sure that the retail site is

More Statistical Support. Paragraph 9 illustrates an effective use of source statistics to bolster Kaycee's argument. The statistics show that despite the economic downturn, online shopping has increased.

A Source with Multiple Authors. The citation at the end of paragraph 9 indicates a source that has more than four authors (see 13a-2). According to MLA style, a work by four or more authors may be cited using the first author's name plus the designation *et al.* ("and others").

Introducing Counterarguments to the Thesis. In paragraph 10, Kaycee introduces the counterarguments to her thesis, that is, the arguments that might be mounted by the opponents to her position. She acknowledges that some shoppers resist moving online and explains the reasons for their hesitation.

Sorensen 7

safe and secure and that no one can steal personal information from the site. According to the Online Shopping Guide, which is an online shopping directory sponsored by Microsoft Internet, consumers can protect themselves by considering three things: transaction security, privacy, and credit card fraud ("Online-Shopping Safety").

Transaction security is the first thing to be aware of when shopping on the Internet, and data encryption provides the most secure way to send information from site to site without having anyone in between being able to read it. When an Internet user sends information, the data is encrypted, or put into code. Anyone who tries to read the information while it is en route to the site will find it impossible. Secure Sockets Layer (SSL), the standard for sending secure data, protects against snooping and possible tampering and then verifies that the site to which the data is sent is authentic. Netscape Security Center, which is an informational site published on the Internet browser's homepage, explains that shoppers should make sure that their data is always being checked by SSL when sending or receiving confidential information (see Fig. 2). SSL works with certain versions of browsers, such as Netscape, Internet Explorer, and AOL, and can also be verified by simply calling the vendor. Oftentimes, a padlock will appear in the bottom left

11

Refuting the Counterarguments. At the end of paragraph 10, Kaycee asserts that the fears expressed by some consumers can be allayed by following certain precautions, thus refuting the counterarguments.

Topic Sentence. Paragraph 11 begins with a topic sentence, letting the reader know that this paragraph will be about online security.

Development of the Topic. Kaycee develops the topic of online security in paragraph 11. She paraphrases the article "How Encryption Works" from the *Netscape Security Center* Web site in order to explain how consumers can protect themselves.

Sorensen 8

corner to tell you if the site is secure ("How
Encryption Works").

Transaction security can also be ensured by checking   12
the credibility of a source. One way to do this is to
look for the Better Business Bureau Online Reliability
Seal, which guarantees that a retailer has been in
business for at least one year, has become a member of
a local Better Business Bureau (BBB), and has agreed to
arbitration in case of a dispute over sale. The BBB says
that online advertisements or emails with excessive
capital letters, dollar signs ($$$$$) and exclamation
points (!!!!) at every turn, misspellings, and grammatical
errors may indicate a sleazy operation (Better Business).

Fig. 2. Netscape Security Homepage.
Source: "How Encryption Works."

In-Text Citation Without an Author. Notice that the citation at the end of paragraph 11 does not have an author's name. That is because this Internet source does not have any author listed. There is no page number because Internet sources are typically not numbered.

Further Topic Development. A transitional sentence begins paragraph 12, alerting the reader to the fact that this paragraph will describe yet another way consumers can protect themselves against online fraud when shopping via the Internet. Kaycee paraphrases information from the Better Business Bureau's Web site.

Visual. Kaycee includes a screen shot from Netscape's Security Center to illustrate her point about the availability of information regarding security that can be found on the Internet.

Sorensen 9

Privacy is another important consideration for   13
online shopping, and consumers may worry that once
their data gets to the receiver safely, a hacker may
come in and steal uncoded information. Most retailers
move data off their Internet server after receiving it
so it will be inaccessible to hackers. Each company has
a different policy, so it is best to check with
customer support or the help section for specifics.

The Online Shopping Guide also advises that   14
shoppers need to check the policy on credit card fraud
and to be aware of any guarantees that online retailers
make about identity theft ("Online Shopping"). Ellen
Stark reminds us that despite what policies individual
companies have, the Fair Credit Billing Act ensures that
a bank cannot hold a customer liable for more than $50 in
fraudulent charges. So, no matter what concerns consumers
have about a hacker stealing their identity and charging
products to stolen credit card numbers, the federal
government has provided consumers with protection.

Despite concerns about safety and identity theft,   15
more and more people are turning to the Internet to
meet their consumer needs. Retailers are aware of this
trend and are anxious to attract new customers to their
sites, and they are therefore willing to improve site
safety and user-friendly technology to entice shoppers.
While some people choose to shop online because they

Further Topic Development. Paragraph 13 develops another consideration regarding consumer protection. The transitional first sentence of this paragraph uses the word "another" to show us this is an additional aspect of the topic: privacy.

Appeal to Logic. In paragraph 14, Kaycee uses an appeal to logic (see 7f-1) as she builds her case. She cautions readers to be careful to check policies regarding identity theft. She paraphrases information from an expert to support her own assertion.

In-Text Citation of a Print Source. Paragraph 14 shows a citation from a one-page print source that includes the author's name. Notice how the author's name, Ellen Stark, is used in a signal phrase: "Ellen Stark reminds us that. . . ."

Conclusion. In her conclusion, Kaycee summarizes her central arguments (see 5b-7, 6h). This type of summary conclusion is appropriate for her paper.

Sorensen 10

find shopping in brick-and-mortar stores annoying and
time-consuming, others just enjoy the fact that not
only can they shop without leaving their homes but they
can shop without even getting dressed. Others would
rather simply click on a button to order goods than
stand in checkout lines or battle for parking spaces in
a crowded mall lot. Whatever the reason for initially
shopping online, many consumers, like myself, not only
enjoy the benefits of ease and convenience of e-commerce
but also believe that it will only get better.

    Now that you know about online shopping, you are   16
probably wondering where to shop online. These are just
a few links to some of my favorite online shopping
sites. Just remember, just because you shop online does
not mean you buy online. You can shop around and then
visit the store as you normally would; this will save
you a few hours--or days!

    amazon.com

    bn.com

    fossil.com

    landsend.com

    oldnavy.com

    sears.com

    shop.com

    target.com

    wal-mart.com

Action to Be Taken. Following the summary conclusion, Kaycee provides the readers with a few links that she has found useful for online shopping.

Sorensen 11

Works Cited

Better Business Bureau Program. 2002. 22 July 2002
    <www.bbbonline.org>.

Chan, Christine, et al. "Online Spending to Reach $10
    Billion for Holiday Season 2001."
    Nielsen/NetRatings 20 Nov. 2001. 28 July 2002
    <http://www.nielsennetratings.com/pr/
    pr_011022.pdf>.

Cox, Beth. "E-commerce: Color It Green." Cyberatlas
    3 Aug. 2002. 12 Aug. 2002 <http://
    cyberatlas.internet.com/markets/retailing/
    article/0,,6061_1364801,00.html>.

Frey, Christine. "Online Shopper: Advantages of
    Plastic." Los Angeles Times 18 Oct. 2001: T8.

Greenspan, Robyn. "E-shopping Around the World."
    Cyberatlas 5 Aug. 2002. 23 Aug. 2002
    <http://cyberatlas.internet.com/markets/
    retailing/article/0,,6061_1431461,00.html>.

"How Encryption Works." Netscape Security Center.
    5 Aug. 2002 <http://wp.netscape.com/security/
    basics/encryption.html>.

Hupprich, Laura, and Maria Bumatay. "Nielsen/Netratings
    Reports a Record Half Billion People Worldwide Now
    Have Home Internet Access." Nielsen/Netratings 3
    June 2002. 3 Aug. 2002 <http://
    www.nielsen-netratings.com/pr/
    pr_020306_eratings.pdf>.

Works Cited. The Works Cited page is an alphabetical listing of all the sources used in Kaycee's research paper. The title is centered 1 inch from the top margin. The list is double-spaced throughout, including between the title and the text. Notice that the first line of each source is flush left with the margin, but the rest of the information is indented 5 spaces. This practice makes the author's name stand out. The Works Cited pages are numbered consecutively following the research paper text. For more information about the MLA style of documentation, see Chapter 13.

Online Professional Site. The first source is a Web site. Notice the two dates; the first is the date of publication or last update, and the second is the date the source was accessed by Kaycee.

Online Professional Site. The second source is an article found on a Web site. The title of the article is in quotation marks. Since there are more than four authors, the first author is listed by name followed by *et al.* ("and others").

Online Article. The third source is an article from an online publication called the *Cyberatlas.*

Newspaper Article. The fourth source is a print source from a newspaper.

Online Article. The fifth source is another article from the online publication *Cyberatlas.*

Online Article. The sixth source is an online article from a professional Web site.

Online Article. The seventh source is an online article from the same professional Web site as the second source. Each article must be listed separately, even if more than one comes from the same Web site.

Sorensen 12

Kushairi, Ahmad. "The Buying Experience Is Still with
    Offline Shopping." New Strait Times Press 12 Aug.
    2002: 2.

"Nearly One-Third of Teens Make Offline Purchases after
    Window Shopping Online." PR Newswire Association,
    Inc. 18 July 2001: Financial News Section.
    Academic Search Elite. EBSCO. Utah State U Lib.,
    Logan. 20 Aug. 2002 <http://www.epnet.com>.

"Online Shopping Safety and Security." The Shopping
    Guide 8 Aug. 2002. 12 Aug. 2002
    <http://shoppingguide.hypermart.net/safety.html>.

Pastore, Michael. "Web Influences Offline Purchases,
    Especially Among Teens." Cyberatlas 3 Aug. 2002.
    18 Aug. 2002 <http://cyberatlas.internet.com/
    markets/retailing/article/0,,6061_804141,00.html>.

Stark, Ellen. "There's Help on the Way If You Face a
    Credit Card Dispute." Money May 1996: 41.

"Virtual Model Tech Hikes Lands' End Sales." Capital
    Times 27 Sept. 2001: 6E.

Newspaper Article. The eighth source comes from a printed newspaper. Notice that all titles of articles are enclosed in quotation marks and initial capital letters are used for the words in the title.

Article from a Full-Text Database. The ninth source was found by Kaycee via a library subscription database (see 9d-2). Notice that the publication information from the print source (*PR Newswire*) is included first, followed by the information about the database used to locate the source.

Online Newsletter. The tenth source is an article found in an online newsletter.

Online Article. The eleventh source is an article from an online publication.

Magazine Article. The twelfth source is an article from a printed popular magazine.

Newspaper Article. The thirteenth source is an article from a print newspaper.

CHAPTER 13

MLA Documentation Format

FAQs

▶ What is the purpose of documentation in various disciplines?

▶ How can I integrate my sources responsibly? (13a-1)

▶ How do I document MLA sources within the text of my paper? (13a-2)

▶ How do I create a Works Cited list in MLA format? (13a-4)

▶ How do I cite electronic sources in MLA style? (13-b)

You may have noticed that some of the publications you read are careful to provide detailed documentation to show you exactly where the information used in the articles was found, while others are not as thorough. Providing a documentation trail that leads back to the original sources is a feature of scholarly writing that distinguishes it from writing found in the popular press. Scholars and researchers in all disciplines base their own work on the work that others have done in the past. The thread of knowledge can be traced from one scholar to another. In scholarly writing, it is essential to provide readers with evidence of that thread of knowledge, not only so that readers can trace the thread if they so desire but also to let them know that the information is from reliable sources.

Scholars and researchers in various academic disciplines have developed different documentation systems—conventional ways of showing the sources of the scholarship on which their work is built. Although they differ in the details, all these systems have the same purpose: to help readers locate the sources used in the piece of writing.

Thus, the writer needs to alert the reader within the text, by means of an in-text citation, whenever information comes from an outside source. The in-text citation is a kind of shorthand, signaling to readers that source information has been used. The in-text citation provides readers with just enough information to locate the source's complete bibliographical citation, which is generally found at the end of the text in the Works Cited or References list.

This chapter covers the system of documentation commonly employed in the humanities and fine arts, which was developed by the Modern Language Association (MLA). It is detailed in two books: *MLA Handbook for Writers of Research Papers,* 6th ed. (New York: MLA, 2003), by Joseph Gibaldi, is designed for undergraduate students, and *MLA Style Manual and Guide to Scholarly Publishing,* 2nd ed. (New York: MLA, 1998), also by Joseph Gibaldi, is geared to graduate students.

Chapter 14 discusses the system of documentation commonly employed in the social sciences, which was developed by the American Psychological Association (APA). The APA system is set forth in *Publication Manual of the American Psychological Association,* 5th ed. (Washington, DC: APA, 2001).

Section 15a explains the system of documentation commonly used in business and economics as well as in art history, history, philosophy, political science, and communications. It is based on *The Chicago Manual of Style,* 15th ed. (Chicago: University of Chicago Press, 2003).

Section 15b covers the system most widely used in the sciences. It is outlined in a book published by the Council of Biology Editors (CBE): *Scientific Style and Format: The CBE Manual for Authors, Editors, and Publishers,* 6th ed. (New York: Cambridge University Press, 1994).

Section 15c introduces another recently developed system that focuses exclusively on documenting online sources: *The Columbia Guide to Online Style* (1998) by Janice R. Walker and Todd Taylor. COS style can be used for documenting electronic sources in humanities and sciences.

It is not necessary for you to memorize the information found here or in any of the documentation style guides. Rather, refer to these formatting guides as you write your research papers for courses in various disciplines. If you are not sure which system to use, ask your instructor which one he or she prefers. As you document your sources, follow the guidelines for your chosen system closely. Documentation styles, though alike in purpose, vary greatly in their details.

You might wonder why you or anyone else should care whether a period or a comma is used in any given style of documentation. You need to pay attention to these details as a courtesy to your readers, who are expecting you to observe the codified conventions in their field. Observing the conventions expected by your readers is comparable to following the conventions expected at a social gathering. Just as you would be violating social conventions by arriving at a formal dinner party dressed in blue jeans and a T-shirt, you would be violating the conventions of good scholarship by failing to observe standards for documentation.

13a Document using the MLA system

The Modern Language Association (MLA) system of documentation has been adopted by many scholarly writers in the fields of language and literature. The MLA system of documentation consists of in-text citations (found in parentheses) and an alphabetical listing of works cited (found at the end of the paper). For humanities researchers, specific sources and the pages on which information can be found are more important than the date on which the source was published. Thus, in-text citations in the MLA system include the author's last name and the page number of the source information.

WEBLINK

http://www.mla.org
The official Web site of the
MLA, with style guidelines

13.1
Learn more
about MLA
style guidelines.

1 Integrating sources and avoiding plagiarism in the MLA system

In Chapter 11 on Using Sources and Avoiding Plagiarism, we talked in general about the importance of using sources accurately and responsibly in your research papers. To help you do so, the MLA citation format provides for a two-part system of source identification: (1) parenthetical citations within the body of the paper (see 13a-2) and (2) a Works Cited list at the end of the paper (see 13a-4). By using the MLA system, you can integrate your source information appropriately and ethically without inadvertently committing plagiarism.

Plagiarism, a serious academic offense, is often committed by students inadvertently in the following two ways.

1. Failing to acknowledge a summary or paraphrase of a source in the body of the paper through a signal phrase and parenthetical citation.

The MLA Citation System

1. Introduce your source using a signal phrase that names its author: *According* to *Jones*, . . . (see 11d-2; see the box on page 261 for suggested verbs to use in signal phrases).

2. Paraphrase or summarize the information from your source. It's best to use direct quotations sparingly. Rather, recast the source information into your own words. If you do use any words or phrases from the author, be sure to include them in quotation marks (see 11d).

3. At the conclusion of your paraphrase, summary, or quotation, insert in parentheses the page number on which the information was found, followed by a period: *(332)*. (see 13a-2).

4. At the end of your paper, list the source with complete bibliographic information on your Works Cited page (see 13a-4).

2. Using the original authors' words without putting the borrowed words or phrases in quotation marks or including a parenthetical citation.

Acknowledge all sources

A successful research paper will be written as an argument by a writer in his or her own words, expressing the writer's understanding of the answers to specific research questions. In such a paper, sources are used as evidence in support of the writer's own argument. Source support is integrated into the flow of the writer's research paper through the use of paraphrases and summaries in the writer's own words; each source is acknowledged by a parenthetical citation. Failing to acknowledge a source results in plagiarism. In addition to paraphrases and summaries, any other source material must also be acknowledged, such as specific facts, graphics or visuals, cartoons, diagrams, or charts, using the two-part MLA citation system. (See 13a-2 to 13a-4.)

Indicate original source words and phrases with quotation marks

The best research papers use direct quotations sparingly as support for their own ideas and integrate those quotations smoothly. A signal phrase alerts the reader that a direct quotation follows; the quotation marks show exactly which words and phrases are being quoted. Long quotations are formatted using indentation rather than quotation marks (see 55a-2). When students get into trouble by borrowing words and phrases without attribution to a source, it is very often the result of sloppy notetaking. Your notes should accurately record source information in your own words, and you should be able to tell at a glance when looking at your notes which information is from which source. Carelessness at the notetaking stage can result in unintentional plagiarism (see 11a-2).

2 Using the MLA system for in-text citations

In the MLA documentation system, citations within the body of the paper are linked to the Works Cited list at the end. The in-text citations are sometimes called *parenthetical references,* because the documentation is placed within parentheses. Both the author being cited and the page number of the source (when known) are included in the in-text citation in the MLA system. Following are some guidelines for incorporating parenthetical citations in the text of your research paper.

1. Author Named in the Narrative

If a paraphrase or direct quotation is introduced with the name of the author, simply indicate the page number of the source in parentheses at the end of the cited material.

Attempting to define ethnic stereotyping, Gordon Allport states that

"much prejudice is a matter of blind conformity with prevailing

folkways" (12).

No page number is necessary when an entire work is cited. (Note that titles of independently published works are underlined.)

Conrad's book <u>Lord Jim</u> tells the story of an idealistic young Englishman.

The World Wildlife Federation's Web site has links to many helpful

sites about the environment.

2. Author Not Named in the Narrative

If the author's name is not used to introduce the paraphrased or quoted material, place the author's last name along with the specific

(text continues on p. 314)

A Directory to the MLA System

In-Text Citations

Works Cited Entries

Books

(continued)

(continued)

(*continued*)

page number in parentheses at the end of the cited material. Do not separate author and page number with a comma. Note that the parenthetical material precedes the sentence's end punctuation.

When Mitford and Peter Rodd were first engaged, "they even bought

black shirts and went to some Fascist meetings" (Guinness 304).

3. Multiple Sentences Paraphrased

Indicate every instance of borrowed material. If an entire paragraph is taken from a single source, mention the author's name at the beginning of the paragraph and cite the page number where appropriate.

As Endelman shows, the turbulence of the interwar years--

"political agitation, social discrimination, street hooliganism"

(191)--culminated in the formation of the British Union of Fascists.

He states that anti-Semitism "was common enough that few Jews could have avoided it altogether or been unaware of its existence" (194).

4. Work by Two or Three Authors

Include the last names of all the authors (the last two connected by *and*) either in the text or in the parenthetical reference. Because the following references are to entire works, no page numbers are necessary.

Goodsell, Maher, and Tinto write about how the theory of collaborative learning may be applied to the administration of a college or university.

We need to think daily about the implications of our future liberation (Eastman and Hayford).

5. Work by Four or More Authors

In citing a work by four or more authors, either provide the names of all the authors or provide the name of the first author followed by the abbreviation *et al.* ("and others").

In The Development of Writing Abilities, the authors call writing that is close to the self "expressive," writing that gets things done "transactional," and writing that calls attention to itself "poetic" (Britton, Burgess, Martin, McLeod, and Rosen).

or

In The Development of Writing Abilities, the authors present a theory of writing based upon whether a writer assumes a participant or a spectator role (Britton et al.).

6. Work by a Corporate Author

When the author is an organization or corporation, treat the group's name the same way as the name of an individual author. If the name is long, try to incorporate it into the text rather than including it in a parenthetical note.

In the book The Downsizing of America, by the New York Times, a report is quoted as showing "that 131,209 workers had been cast out of their jobs in just the first quarter of 1996" (220).

7. Work in More Than One Volume

If the work consists of more than one volume, provide the volume number, followed by a colon, just before the page number. When referring to an entire volume of a multivolume work, add a comma after the author's name, followed by *vol.* and the volume number.

```
In Ward's introduction to the collected works of Sir John Vanbrugh,

he states that "the Vanbrugh family seems to have been both ancient

and honorable" (1: x).

The collected plays of Vanbrugh show the range of his talent (Ward,

vol. 2).
```

8. Different Works by the Same Author

When the Works Cited list refers to two works by the same author, include in the parenthetical reference the title (which may be abbreviated), as well as the author and the page number of the source. If the author's name is included in the text, cite only the title and page number in parentheses.

```
Her first volume of memoirs, published in 1975, tells the story of

her brother's friend, whom her mother would not allow her to choose

for games at parties (Mitchison, All Change Here 85). In her prewar

novel, Mitchison, who was the housebound wife of an Oxford don,

derives a strange solution to England's economic problems (We Have

Been Warned 441).
```

9. Two or More Authors with the Same Last Name

Include both authors' first and last names in the signal phrase or in parentheses to distinguish two authors who have the same last name.

```
Luci Shaw reveals deep spirituality in her poem titled "Made Flesh"

(31).
```

10. Work Cited Indirectly

If possible, take information directly from the original source. However, sometimes it is necessary to cite someone indirectly—particularly in the case of a published account of someone's spoken words. To indicate an indirect quotation, use the abbreviation *qtd. in* (for "quoted in") before listing the source.

High school teacher Ruth Gerrard finds that "certain Shakespearean characters have definite potential as student role models" (qtd. in Davis and Salomone 24).

11. Two or More Sources within the Same Citation

When referring to two or more sources within the same parenthetical reference, use semicolons to separate the citations. For the sake of readability, however, take care not to list too many sources in a single citation.

The works of several authors in the post-war years tend to focus on racial themes (Mitchison 440; Mosley 198).

If students are allowed to freely exchange ideas about a work of literature, they will come to examine their own sense of the work in light of the opinions of others (Bleich 45; Rosenblatt, Literature as Exploration 110).

12. Anonymous Work

Sources such as magazine articles, Web sites, and reports by commissions may not list an author. Such works are listed by their title on the Works Cited page. For the in-text citation of an anonymous work listed by title, use an abbreviated version of the title, in parentheses, plus the page number when available.

The article points out the miscommunications that can occur between men and women because of differences in communication styles ("It Started" 110).

In many Native American cultures, the feather often symbolizes a prayer ("Feather").

13. Work of Literature

Classic works of literature are often available in different editions. It is therefore helpful to include location information, such as chapter number, section number, act number, and scene number, in the parenthetical reference so that the reader can locate the reference in any edition of the work. Include this location information after a page reference, where appropriate. When citing classic poetry or plays, use the line numbers instead of page numbers. Generally, use arabic numbers rather than roman numerals.

In the novel <u>Lord Jim</u>, Conrad describes the village of Patusan and its inhabitants (242; ch. 24).

In <u>Paradise Lost</u>, Satan's descent to earth is described in graphic detail (Milton 4.9-31).

As Laertes leaves for France, Polonius gives the young man trite and unhelpful advice such as "Beware / Of entrance to a quarrel, but being in, / Bear't that th' opposed may beware of thee" (<u>Hamlet</u> 1.3.65-67).

14. Work in an Anthology

If you are citing a work found in an anthology (collection), use the name of the author of the particular work you are citing, not the editor(s) of the anthology. List the page numbers as they are found in the anthology.

The American Dream crosses many ethnic boundaries, as illustrated by Papaleo (88).

15. Bible

When quoting from the Bible, give the title of the version (e.g., *The Revised Standard Version*), the book of the Bible, and the chapter and verse (separated by a period). If using a signal phrase, spell out the book of the Bible being quoted. In parentheses, abbreviate the book of the Bible if its name is five or more letters (e.g., *Phil.* for *Philippians*).

In his letter to the Philippians, the apostle Paul says, "There must be no room for rivalry and personal vanity among you, but you must humbly reckon others better than yourselves. Look to each other's interest and not merely to your own" (<u>The New English Bible</u>, Phil. 2.3-4).

16. Entire Work or One-Page Article

When citing an entire work or a work that is only one page long, refer to the text in a signal phrase by the author and title without any page numbers.

In his book Losing My Mind: An Intimate Look at Life with Alzheimer's,

Thomas DeBaggio chronicles his battle with Alzheimer's disease.

17. Work with No Page Numbers

A work without page numbers is cited like a one-page work (see item 16). If a work uses paragraph numbers instead of page numbers, use the abbreviation *par* or *pars.*

The reporter from a recent Family Law Conference sponsored by the

American Bar Association, Sarah H. Ramsey, stated, "High-conflict custody

cases are marked by a lack of trust between the parents, a high level of

anger and a willingness to engage in repetitive litigation" (par. 24).

18. Electronic Source

When information is from an electronic medium, usually the entire work is referenced. In such cases, incorporate the reference to the work within the sentence by naming the author of the source (or the title, if no author is listed) just as it is listed on the Works Cited page. No parentheses are needed when an entire work is cited.

One of the features of The Encyclopedia Mythica Web site is its archive

of cultural myths, such as those prevalent in Native American society.

Andy Packer's home page lists a number of links to Star Wars Web sites.

When citing a Web site with secondary pages, list separately each secondary page used in the research paper. Be sure that the Works Cited list includes the correct URL for each secondary page and lists each page independently by its title.

According to Britannica Online, in Native American mythology, a

feather often symbolizes a prayer ("Feather").

Britannica Online shows that mythology has developed in all societies

("Mythology").

When quoting or paraphrasing directly from an electronic source, either give the section title in quotation marks (as in the example above) or cite the paragraph number (with the abbreviation *par.*), if provided, so that a reader will be able to find the section used in the paper. If no numbering is provided, list the source author or title only. Or, you may wish to incorporate the work's author or title into the sentence containing the information.

The writer discusses his reasons for calling Xerox's online site "a great place to visit" (Gomes, par. 5).

The average global air temperature has risen between 0.3 and 0.6 degree Celsius (Hileman).

19. Different Page Numbers in the Same Work

When it is apparent that two citations refer to the same work, there is no need to repeat the author's name. Identifying the appropriate page number will suffice.

In We Have Been Warned, Mitchison's prewar novel, she states that "these commercial ideas have crept into all our morality, art and science" (441). She continues in this vein when she asks, "How could he with that racial inheritance and that education--even if he saw through the education very young?" (444).

20. Long Quotation

When a quotation is lengthy (takes up more than four lines), indent it ten spaces from the left-hand margin (or 1 inch, if you are using a word-processing program). Lines remain double-spaced throughout the indented quotation. Note that the end punctuation is different for indented quotations than for internal citations that are run into the text—the period comes before the parenthetical citation for indented quotations. Also note that no quotation marks are used and generally a colon introduces the quotation.

McMurtry's novel chronicles the growing-up years of a young man in rural Texas. In this passage, we see the alienation that Lonnie feels as his family falls apart around him:

The next day was the last of the rodeo, and I didn't much

care. The whole crazy circle of things got so it tired me

out. When I woke up that morning I could see Jesse down in

the lots, moving around, and I got up to go talk to him. I

had looked for him the night before, after the dance, but

he wasn't around. . . . There was nobody to cook my

breakfast, and I didn't feel like cooking it myself. (112)

3 Formatting bibliographic footnotes according to the MLA system

Generally, footnotes and endnotes are not used in the MLA system of documentation. However, notes may be included to refer the reader to sources that contain information different from the content of the paper. In the text, indicate a note with a superscript number typed immediately after the source that is referred to. Number notes consecutively throughout the text.

Use a note to cite sources that have additional information on topics covered in the paper.

[1]For further information on this point, see Barbera 168, McBrien 56, and Kristeva 29.

[2]For an additional study of Smith's fictional characters, see Barbera's Me Again.

Use a note to cite sources that contain information related to that included in the paper.

[3]Although outside the scope of this paper, major themes in the novel are discussed by Kristeva and Barbera.

Use a note to cite sources containing information that a reader might want to compare with that in the paper.

[4]On this point, see also Rosenblatt's Literature as Exploration, in which she discusses reader response theory.

For the endnote format, start a new page following the end of the text, before the Works Cited list. Type the title *Notes*, centered horizontally 1 inch from the top of the page. Double-space to the first note. Indent the first line five spaces (or ½ inch) from the left margin, and type the note number slightly above the line (or use the superscript format in a word-processing program). Then follow, without any space, to the text of the note. Double-space between and within all notes.

For the footnote format, position the text of the note at the bottom of the page on which the reference occurs. Begin the footnote four lines below the text. Single-space within a footnote, but double-space between footnotes if more than one note appears on a page.

On the Works Cited page, include all the sources mentioned in the notes.

4 Formatting the Works Cited page according to the MLA system

The alphabetical listing of all the sources used in a paper, usually titled Works Cited, comes at the end of the paper. Other names for this listing include References, Literature Cited, Works Consulted, or Bibliography (which may include works not directly cited), and Annotated Bibliography (which includes brief summaries of sources). Check with your instructor to determine which format he or she prefers. The purpose of this listing is to help readers find the information used in the paper, so the entries must be complete and accurate.

List sources alphabetically by the last name of the author, using the letter-by-letter system of alphabetization. When no author is given, alphabetize by the first word of the title (excluding *A, An,* or *The*). Type the first word of each entry at the left margin. Indent subsequent lines of the same entry five spaces (or ½ inch). Double-space the entire reference page, both between and within entries.

When you have more than one work by the same author, arrange the titles alphabetically. Give the author's name for the first entry only. For subsequent works by the same author, substitute three hyphens (followed by a period) for the author's name (see page 326).

Books

A citation for a book has three basic parts.

Author's Name. Book Title. Publication Information.

For books, monographs, and other complete works, include the author's full name as given on the title page—start with the last name first, followed by a comma; then put the first name and middle name or initial, followed by a period. After the author's name, give the complete title of the work as it appears on the title page (underlined), followed by a period. Important words in the title should be capitalized. Include the subtitle, if there is one, separated from the title by a colon. Next, include (if appropriate) the name of the editor, compiler, or translator; the edition of the book; the number of volumes; and the name of the series. Finally, indicate the place of publication, followed by a colon (if several cities are listed, include only the first one); the publisher's name as it appears on the title page, followed by a comma; and the date of publication from the copyright page, followed by a period.

In MLA style, the publication information is abbreviated as much as possible in the bibliographic entry. The city where the book was published is given without a state abbreviation. A country abbreviation may be needed for clarity for some foreign publications (for example, *Ulster, Ire.; Bergen, Norw.*). But if a foreign city is well known (such as London or Paris), a country abbreviation is unnecessary. Abbreviate the publisher's name to one word wherever possible (for example, McGraw-Hill, Inc., to *McGraw*; Houghton Mifflin Co. to *Houghton*). Similarly, abbreviate the names of university and government presses: *Columbia UP* for Columbia University Press; the letters *GPO* for Government Printing Office. (For guidelines on citing electronic sources, see pages 336–350.)

(Note) Unless your instructor directs you differently, show the title of a complete work or a journal in underlined form, even though such titles appear in italics in most printed documents. If the titles you cite were initially in italics (perhaps because you used citations from an electronic file source), remember to run the SEARCH > FIND AND REPLACE routine on your Works Cited document. Set the search to find italic type (it may be under FONT) and replace it with underlined type.

1. Book by One Author

Author's Name	Book Title	Publication Information

Allport, Gordon W. <u>The Nature of Prejudice</u>. Palo Alto: Addison, 1954.

Haire-Sargeant, Lin. <u>H</u>. New York: Pocket, 1992.

Manguel, Alberto. <u>A History of Reading</u>. New York: Viking, 1996.

2. Book by Two or Three Authors

Write multiple authors' names in the order in which they are given on the book's title page. Note that this order may not be alphabetical.

Reverse the name of the first author only, putting the last name first; separate the authors' names with commas.

Goodsell, Anne S., Michelle R. Maher, and Vincent Tinto.

    Collaborative Learning: A Sourcebook for Higher Education.

    University Park: National Center on Postsecondary Teaching,

    Learning, and Assessment, 1992.

Guinness, Jonathan, and Catherine Guinness. The House of Mitford. New

    York: Viking, 1985.

3. Book by More Than Three Authors

For a book with more than three authors, either write out the names of all the authors listed on the book's title page or write only the first author's name, followed by a comma and the Latin phrase *et al.* (for "and others").

Britton, James, Tony Burgess, Nancy Martin, Alex McLeod, and Harold

    Rosen. The Development of Writing Abilities. London: Macmillan,

    1975.

or

Britton, James, et al. The Development of Writing Abilities. London:

    Macmillan, 1975.

4. Organization as Author

When an organization rather than an individual is the author, give the name of the organization as listed on the title page instead of the author, even if the same group also published the book.

Alzheimer's Disease and Related Disorders Association. Understanding

    Alzheimer's Disease. New York: Scribner's, 1988.

5. Book by a Corporate Author

A book by a corporate author is any book whose title page lists as the author a group, rather than individuals. Start with the name of the corporate author, even if it is also the publisher.

Conference on College Composition and Communication. The National

    Language Policy. Urbana: NCTE, 1992.

New York Times, Inc. The Downsizing of America. New York: Random, 1996.

6. Unknown Author

If no author is listed, begin the entry with the title. List the work alphabetically by the first major word in the title.

The American Heritage Dictionary. 4th ed. Boston: Houghton, 2002.

7. Book with an Editor

For books with editors rather than authors, start with the editor or editors, followed by a comma and the abbreviation *ed.* (for "editor") or *eds.* (for "editors").

Barbera, Jack, and William McBrien, eds. Me Again: The Uncollected

   Writings of Stevie Smith. New York: Farrar, 1982.

Cooper, Jane Roberta, ed. Reading Adrienne Rich: Reviews and

   Re-Visions, 1951-1981. Ann Arbor: U of Michigan P, 1984.

Gates, Henry Louis, Jr., and Nellie Y. McKay, eds. The Norton

   Anthology of African American Literature. New York: Norton,

   1997.

8. Chapter or Selection from an Edited Work

An entry for a particular selection begins with the author's name and the title of the chapter or selection. The title is underlined if the work is a book or a play; it is enclosed in quotation marks if the work is a poem, short story, chapter, or essay. Note that the name of the editor or editors follows the book title and is preceded by the abbreviation *Ed.* (for "Edited by"). The inclusive page numbers of the selection follow the publication information.

Bambara, Toni Cade. "Raymond's Run." The Norton Anthology of African

   American Literature. Ed. Henry Louis Gates, Jr., and Nellie Y.

   McKay. New York: Norton, 1997. 2307-13.

Spivak, Gayatri. "Feminism and Deconstruction, Again: Negotiating with

   Unacknowledged Masculinism." Between Feminism and Psychoanalysis.

   Ed. Teresa Brennan. London: Routledge, 1989. 206-23.

9. Book with Author and Editor

When citing the book itself, begin with the author's name, followed by the editor's name, introduced by *Ed.* (for "Edited by") after the title.

L'Engle, Madeleine. <u>O Sapientia</u>. Ed. Luci Shaw. Wheaton: Shaw, 1984.

When citing the editor's contribution to the work, begin with the editor's name followed by a comma and *ed*. Then list the author's name, introduced by *By*, following the title.

Shaw, Luci, ed. <u>O Sapientia</u>. By Madeleine L'Engle. Wheaton: Shaw,

1984.

10. Two or More Items from an Anthology

When citing more than one work from an anthology, list the anthology itself as well.

Madison, D. Soyini, ed. <u>The Woman That I Am: The Literature and</u>

<u>Culture of Contemporary Women of Color</u>. New York: St. Martin's,

1994.

11. Two or More Books by the Same Author

Alphabetize entries by the first word in the title. Include the author's name in the first entry only. In subsequent entries, type three hyphens in place of the author's name, followed by a period.

Rose, Mike. <u>Lives on the Boundary: A Moving Account of the Struggles</u>

<u>and Achievements of America's Educationally Underprepared</u>. New

York: Penguin, 1989.

---. <u>Possible Lives: The Promise of Education in America</u>. Boston:

Houghton, 1995.

12. Article in a Reference Book

An entry for an article in a reference book follows the same pattern as an entry for a work in an anthology. Note, however, that the editor's name and full publication information need not be provided; it is sufficient to provide the edition (if known) and the year of publication. If the article is signed, provide the author's name. (Often the author's name is given in abbreviated form at the end of the article and included in full form elsewhere.)

Robins, Robert Henry. "Language." <u>Encyclopedia Britannica</u>. 1997 ed.

If the article is unsigned, start with the title of the article.

"Lochinvar." <u>Merriam-Webster's Encyclopedia of Literature</u>. 1995 ed.

13. Introduction, Preface, Foreword, or Afterword

Start with the name of the author of the specific part being cited, followed by the name of the part, capitalized but not underlined or enclosed in quotation marks. If the writer of the specific part is the same as the author of the book, give the author's last name, preceded by the word *By*. If the writer of the specific part is different from the author of the book, give the book author's complete name after *By*. Provide complete publication information and inclusive page numbers (even if they are given as roman numerals) of the part being cited.

Tompkins, Jane. Preface. <u>A Life in School: What the Teacher Learned</u>.

By Tompkins. Reading: Addison, 1996. xi-xix.

14. Book in Translation

Begin the entry with the author's name and the title of the book. After the book's title, insert the abbreviation *Trans.* (for "Translated by") and give the translator's name. If the book also has an editor, give the names of the editor and the translator in the order in which they are listed on the title page.

Kristeva, Julia. <u>Powers of Horror: An Essay on Abjection</u>. Trans. Leon

S. Roudiez. New York: Columbia UP, 1982.

15. Second or Subsequent Edition of a Book

If a book is not a first edition, identify the edition in the way that it is identified on the book's title page: by year (*1993 ed.*), by name (*Rev. ed.* for "Revised edition"), or by number (*2nd ed., 3rd ed.*).

White, Edward M. <u>Teaching and Assessing Writing</u>. 2nd ed.

San Francisco: Jossey-Bass, 1994.

16. Work in More Than One Volume

When citing more than one volume of a multivolume work, insert the total number of volumes in the work before the publication material. When citing one volume of a multivolume work, include only the particular volume number before the publication information.

Doyle, Arthur Conan. <u>The Complete Sherlock Holmes</u>. 2 vols. Garden

City: Doubleday, 1930.

Poe, Edgar Allan. <u>The Complete Poems and Stories of Edgar Allan Poe</u>.

Illus. E. McKnight Kauffer. Vol. 2. New York: Knopf, 1982.

17. One Volume of a Multivolume Work

Provide the author and title, followed by the number of the volume you are citing. At the end of the citation, following the date, MLA recommends providing the number of volumes in the complete work.

Poe, Edgar Allan. <u>The Complete Poems and Stories of Edgar Allan Poe</u>.

    Vol. 1. New York: Knopf, 1982. 2 vols.

18. Book in a Series

If the title page indicates that the book is part of a series, insert the series name (do not underline it or enclose it in quotation marks) and the series number, if any, before the publication material.

Berlin, James A. <u>Rhetorics, Poetics, and Cultures</u>. Refiguring College

    English Studies. Urbana: NCTE, 1996.

Jameson, Frederic. Foreword. <u>The Postmodern Condition: A Report on</u>

    <u>Knowledge</u>. By Jean-François Lyotard. Trans. Geoff Bennington and

    Brian Massumi. Theory and History of Lit. 10. Minneapolis: U of

    Minnesota P, 1989. vii-xxi.

19. Republished Book

Insert the original publication date, followed by a period, before the publication material of the work being cited.

Dewey, John. <u>Experience and Education</u>. 1938. New York: Collier, 1963.

20. Government Document

If the author of a government document is unknown, start with the name of the government, followed by the name of the agency that issued the document, abbreviated. The title of the publication, underlined, follows, and the usual publication material completes the entry.

United States. FBI. <u>Uniform Crime Reports for the United States:</u>

    <u>1995</u>. Washington: GPO, 1995.

(*GPO* stands for Government Printing Office.)

21. Published Proceedings of a Conference

Write an entry for proceedings in the same way as for a book. Provide information about the conference after the title of the proceedings.

Kelder, Richard, ed. <u>Interdisciplinary Curricula, General Education,</u> <u>and Liberal Learning</u>. Selected Papers from the Third Annual Conference of the Institute for the Study of Postsecondary Pedagogy, Oct. 1992. New Paltz: SUNY New Paltz, 1993.

22. *Pamphlet or Newsletter*

Cite a pamphlet the same way as a book.

<u>Presbyterian Peacemaking Program</u>. Peacemaking Pamphlets. Louisville: Presbyterian Church USA, 1996.

23. *Title within Another Title*

If there is a title of another book within the title of the book you are citing, do not underline the title within the title.

Steinbeck, John. <u>Journal of a Novel: The</u> East of Eden <u>Letters</u>. New York: Viking, 1969.

24. *Sacred Book*

When citing an individual published edition of a sacred book, begin the entry with the title, including the specific version.

<u>The Torah: The Five Books of Moses</u>. Philadelphia: Jewish Society of America, 1962.

Periodicals

A citation for an article in a periodical follows a format similar to that for a book:

Author's Name. "Title of the Article." Publication Information.

In the publication information, the title of the journal, as it appears on the journal's title page (without introductory articles such as *A* and *The*), is underlined. The volume and issue numbers, if provided, go after the journal title and are followed by the publication date, in parentheses. A colon follows the parentheses. Then, inclusive page numbers are provided for the entire article.

When citing magazines and newspapers, list the day and month (abbreviated except for May, June, and July) of publication, with the day before the month and the month before the year (*19 Dec. 1997*). Provide page numbers for the entire article. Note that if the article is not printed on consecutive pages, you need to provide only the first page number and a plus sign, with no space between them. (For guidelines on citing articles in online periodicals, see page 343.)

25. Article in a Journal Paginated by Volume

Many professional journals are numbered continuously, from the first page of the first issue to the final page of the last issue within a volume. Do not include an issue number when citing this kind of journal.

    Author   Article Title   Journal Title

```
Bloom, Lynn Z. "Why I (Used to) Hate to Give Grades." College

     Composition and Communication 48 (1997): 360-71.
```

                    Volume   Year of   Consecutive
                    number   publication   pages

```
Holbrook, Sue Ellen. "Women's Work: The Feminizing of Composition."

     Rhetoric Review 9 (1991): 201-19.
```

When there are two or more authors, write the authors' names in the order in which they are given on the first page of the article. Note that this order may not be alphabetical. Reverse the name of the first author only (putting the last name first); write the other names in normal order. Write the rest of the entry in the same way that you would an entry for a journal article with one author.

```
Kidda, Michael, Joseph Turner, and Frank E. Parker. "There Is an

     Alternative to Remedial Education." Metropolitan Universities 3

     (1993): 16-25.

Shamoon, Linda K., and Deborah H. Burns. "A Critique of Pure

     Tutoring." Writing Center Journal 15 (1995): 134-51.
```

26. Article in a Journal Paginated by Issue

If each issue of the journal is numbered separately, starting with page 1, include both volume and issue numbers. Put a period after the volume number, and write the issue number after the period—for example, 12.1 signifies volume 12, issue 1.

```
Kogen, Myra. "The Conventions of Expository Writing." Journal of

     Basic Writing 5.1 (1986): 24-37.
```

Mohanty, S. P. "Us and Them: On the Philosophical Bases of Political

Criticism." <u>Yale Journal of Criticism</u> 2.2 (1989): 1-31.

27. Magazine Article

If the article is unsigned, begin with the title. For a weekly or biweekly magazine, provide the day, the month (abbreviated, except for May, June, and July), and the year, followed by a colon and the inclusive page numbers.

"It Started in a Garden." <u>Time</u> 22 Sept. 1952: 110-11.

For a monthly or quarterly magazine, give only the month or quarter and the year before the inclusive page numbers. (If the article is not printed on consecutive pages, give the first page number followed by a plus sign.)

MacDonald, Heather. "Downward Mobility: The Failure of Open

Admissions at City University." <u>City Journal</u> Summer 1994: 10-20.

28. Newspaper Article

Provide the name of the newspaper, but do not use the article (*The, An, A*) that precedes it (*Boston Globe*, not *The Boston Globe*). If it is not included in the newspaper's title, add the city of publication in brackets following the title. Nationally published newspapers, such as *USA Today*, do not need a city of publication in the reference. Next, provide the day, month (abbreviated, except for May, June, and July), and year. (Do not list volume or issue numbers; however, if the edition is given on the newspaper's masthead, do include it, followed by a colon.) Conclude the entry by providing the page numbers, preceded by the section number or letter if each section is separately paginated.

Doherty, William F. "Woodward Jury Seeks Definitions." <u>Boston Globe</u>

29 Oct. 1997: B1+.

Titze, Maria. "Warning: Trust in Courts Needed." <u>Deseret News</u> [Salt

Lake City] 16 Jan. 2001: A1.

"Twenty Percent Biased Against Jews." <u>New York Times</u> 22 Nov. 1992: A1.

29. Editorial

Provide the name of the editorial writer (last name first), if known, and then the title of the editorial (in quotation marks). Next, write the word *Editorial*, but do not underline it or enclose it in quotation marks.

End the entry with the name of the newspaper, magazine, or journal and the standard publication information.

Paglia, Camille. "More Mush from the NEA." Editorial. <u>Wall Street</u>

<u>Journal</u> 24 Oct. 1997: A22.

"Six Who Serve Their Council Districts." Editorial. <u>Boston Globe</u> 31

Oct. 1997: A22.

30. Letter to the Editor

Include the designation *Letter* after the name of the letter writer, but do not underline it or enclose it in quotation marks. End the entry with the name of the newspaper, magazine, or journal and the standard publication information.

Schack, Steven. Letter. <u>New York Times</u> 1 Dec. 1997, late ed.: A20.

31. Review

Start with the name of the reviewer and the title of the review. Then insert *Rev. of* (for "Review of"), but do not underline it or enclose it in quotation marks. Next, provide the title of the piece reviewed, followed by a comma, the word *by*, and the name of the author of the piece being reviewed. If the name of the reviewer is not given, start with the title of the review; if no title is given either, start with *Rev. of*. End the entry with the name of the newspaper, magazine, or journal and the standard publication information.

Ribadeneira, Diego. "The Secret Lives of Seminarians." Rev. of <u>The</u>

<u>New Men: Inside the Vatican's Elite School for American Priests</u>,

by Brian Murphy. <u>Boston Globe</u> 31 Oct. 1997: C6.

32. Abstract from an Abstracts Journal

Begin by providing publication information on the original work. Then provide material on the journal in which you found the abstract: the title (underlined), the volume number, and the year (in parentheses), followed by a colon and the page or item number.

Johnson, Nancy Kay. "Cultural and Psychosocial Determinants of Health

and Illness." Diss. U of Washington, 1980. <u>DAI</u> 40 (1980): 425B.

(*Diss.* means "Dissertation," and *DAI* is the abbreviation for *Dissertation Abstracts International*.)

Juliebo, Moira, et al. "Metacognition of Young Readers in an Early

Intervention Reading Programme." <u>Journal of Research in Reading</u>

21.1 (1998): 24-35. <u>Psychological Abstracts</u> 85.7 (1998): item

22380.

33. Unsigned Article

If an article has no known author, begin with its title, alphabetizing the citation by the first major word of the title on your references list.

"What You Don't Know About Desktops Can Cost You." <u>Consumer Reports</u>

Sept. 2002: 20-22.

Other sources

34. Film or Video Recording

Begin with the film's title (underlined), followed by the director, distributor, and year of release; also provide other pertinent material, such as the names of the performers, writers, and producers, between the title and the name of the distributor.

<u>Indiana Jones and the Temple of Doom</u>. Dir. Steven Spielberg.

Paramount, 1984.

<u>Wayne's World</u>. Dir. Penelope Spheeris. Prod. Lorne Michaels. Perf.

Mike Myers, Dana Carvey, and Rob Lowe. Paramount, 1992.

If citing an individual's work on the film, begin the entry with that person's name and title.

Spielberg, Steven, dir. <u>Indiana Jones and the Temple of Doom</u>.

Paramount, 1984.

35. Television or Radio Program

Provide the title of the episode (enclosed in quotation marks), if known; the title of the program (underlined); the title of the series (not underlined or enclosed in quotation marks), if any; the network; the call numbers and local city, if any; and the date of broadcast.

"Commercializing Christmas." <u>All Things Considered</u>. Natl. Public

Radio. WBUR, Boston. 8 Dec. 1997.

"The Great Apes." <u>National Geographic Special</u>. PBS. WGBH, Boston. 12

July 1984.

36. Sound Recording

For a sound recording that is available commercially, provide the name of the artist, the title of the recording (underlined, unless the piece is identified only by form, number, and key), the manufacturer, and the year of issue. Indicate the medium, if other than a compact disc, before the manufacturer's name.

Ball, Marcia. <u>Blue House</u>. Rounder, 1994.

Ormandy, Eugene, cond. Symphony no. 3 in C minor, op. 78. By Camille

Saint-Saëns. Perf. E. Power Biggs, organ. Philadelphia Orch.

Sony, 1991.

Raitt, Bonnie. "Something to Talk About." <u>Luck of the Draw</u>.

Audiocassette. Capitol, 1991.

37. Performance

An entry for a play, concert, opera, or dance begins with the title (underlined), includes information similar to that given for a film, and ends with the performance site (for example, the theater and city) and the date of the performance.

<u>Blues for an Alabama Sky</u>. By Pearl Cleage. Dir. Kenny Leon. Perf.

Phylicia Rashad, Tyrone Mitchell Henderson, Sean C. Squire,

Deidre N. Henry, and John Henry Redwood. Huntington Theatre,

Boston. 5 Feb. 1997.

<u>Riverdance</u>. Dance Capt. Kevin McCormack. Perf. Colin Dunne, Eileen

Martin, Maria Pagés, and the Riverdance Irish Dance Troupe. Wang

Center, Boston. 18 Jan. 1997.

38. Work of Art

Provide the name of the artist, the title of the work (underlined), the name of the site that houses the work, and the city. If it is available, include the date the work was created immediately after the title. If the work is part of a private collection, provide the collector's name.

Cassatt, Mary. <u>Breakfast in Bed</u>. 1886. Private collection of Dr. and

    Mrs. John J. McDonough, Youngstown, OH.

---. <u>Five O'Clock Tea</u>. Museum of Fine Arts, Boston.

39. Published Interview

Provide the name of the person being interviewed; the title of the interview (enclosed in quotation marks), if any; the title of the source in which the interview is published; and any other pertinent bibliographic material.

Faulkner, William. "The Meaning of 'A Rose for Emily.'" Interview.

    1959. <u>The Story and Its Writer: An Introduction to Short</u>

    <u>Fiction</u>. Ed. Ann Charters. Compact 4th ed. Boston: Bedford-

    St. Martin's, 1995. 772-73.

40. Unpublished Interview

Provide the name of the person being interviewed, the designation *Personal interview* (not underlined or in quotation marks), and the date.

Jensen, Steven. Personal interview. 12 Apr. 1997.

41. Personal Letter to the Author

Bush, George. Letter to the author. 8 Sept. 1995.

42. Dissertation—Published

Cite a published dissertation as a book, but add dissertation information before the publication data. Underline the title of the dissertation, followed by the abbreviation *Diss.* (for "Dissertation"), the name of the degree-granting institution, date, and the publication information.

Deatherage, Cynthia. <u>A Way of Seeing: The Anglo-Saxons and the Primal</u>

    <u>World View</u>. Diss. Purdue U, 1997. Ann Arbor: UMI, 1997. 9821728.

UMI stands for University Microfilms International. (For an example of a dissertation abstract, see item 32.)

43. Dissertation—Unpublished

Cite an unpublished dissertation as follows:

```
Balkema, Sandra. "The Composing Activities of Computer Literate

     Writers." Diss. U of Michigan, 1984.
```

44. Speech or Lecture

Provide the name of the speaker; the title of the presentation (in quotation marks), if known; the meeting and sponsoring organization, if applicable; the place where the speech or lecture was given; and the date.

```
Booth, Wayne. "Ethics and the Teaching of Literature." College Forum.

     NCTE Convention. Cobo Center, Detroit. 21 Nov. 1997.
```

45. Map or Chart

Cite a map or a chart the same way you would cite a book with an unknown author, but add the label *Map* or *Chart* to distinguish it.

```
Wyoming. Map. Chicago: Rand, 1990.
```

46. Cartoon or Comic Strip

```
Schultz, Charles. "Peanuts." Cartoon. Herald Journal [Logan] 15 Aug.

     2002: C6.
```

47. Advertisement

First name the item being advertised; then add the word *Advertisement* and supply the rest of the citation, indicating the source where the ad appeared.

```
Benadryl Severe Allergy and Sinus Headache. Advertisement. Prevention

     Sept. 2002: 55.
```

13b Electronic media in MLA style

13.2
The MLA Web site includes up-to-date information on electronic citation formats.

WEBLINK

http://www.mla.org
MLA's Web site includes information about citing electronic media

Because electronic sources tend to be less permanent and to be subject to fewer standards than printed works, their citations need more information than is required for print sources. Coverage of electronic references in MLA format is given in the *MLA*

Handbook for Writers of Research Papers, 6th ed. (New York: MLA, 2003), by Joseph Gibaldi. The *MLA Handbook* points out that citations for electronic publications may need to include information in addition to the three divisions (author, title, publication data) typically used for print sources (see p. 322) in order to accurately describe the electronic publication itself and how to access it. Thus a citation for an electronic source may have the following five divisions: (1) author's or site creator's name, (2) title of the document, (3) information about a corresponding print publication, (4) information about electronic publication, (5) access information.

Division 5 is especially important in light of the fact that electronic information can be changed quickly, easily, and often. Therefore, the version available to your readers may be different from the one you accessed during your research. MLA recommends listing the last date of posting or updating of the electronic source as well as the date of access (that is, the date you read the source). It would also be wise to print out or save to a disk the electronic source on the day you accessed it so that you have an accurate record. MLA also recommends including the electronic address (URL) within angle brackets to distinguish it from the surrounding punctuation of the citation itself.

Below are tips on citing some of the most commonly used electronic sources for the five divisions outlined. In its guidelines for electronic style, the MLA acknowledges that not all of the information recommended for a citation may be available. Cite whatever information is available. It might be wise to consult your instructor before finalizing your Works Cited list to ensure that you are conforming to his or her requirements for electronic sources.

Item 1: Author's or Site Creator's Name

Begin your citation of electronic sources with the name of an author, listed in the same way as you would for a printed book (p. 322), that is, with the last name first, comma, first name, period.

```
Cohn, Dorritt.
```

Item 2: Title of the Document

List next the full title of the document, enclosed in quotation marks. Exceptions include citations of entire Internet sites or online books (see items 48 and 52). If no author's name is given, begin the entry with the document's title.

```
Cohn, Dorrit. "'First Shock of Complete Perception': The Opening

    Episode of The Golden Bowl, Volume 2."
```

Item 3: Information about the Print Publication

If the document was simultaneously printed as well as posted to the Internet, list the print information next, following the guidelines for print publications. (See Figure 13.1 for an example of an online journal article with corresponding print version.)

```
Cohn, Dorrit. "'First Shock of Complete Perception': The Opening

      Episode of The Golden Bowl, Volume 2." The Henry James Review

      22.1 (2001): 1-9.
```

Item 4: Information about Electronic Publication

Next comes information about the electronic publication, including the title of the site (underlined), the date of electronic publication or the last date the site was updated, and the name of any sponsoring organization. If an editor's name or a version number is provided, include that information as well following the title. Since it is possible for print and electronic versions to vary, it is necessary

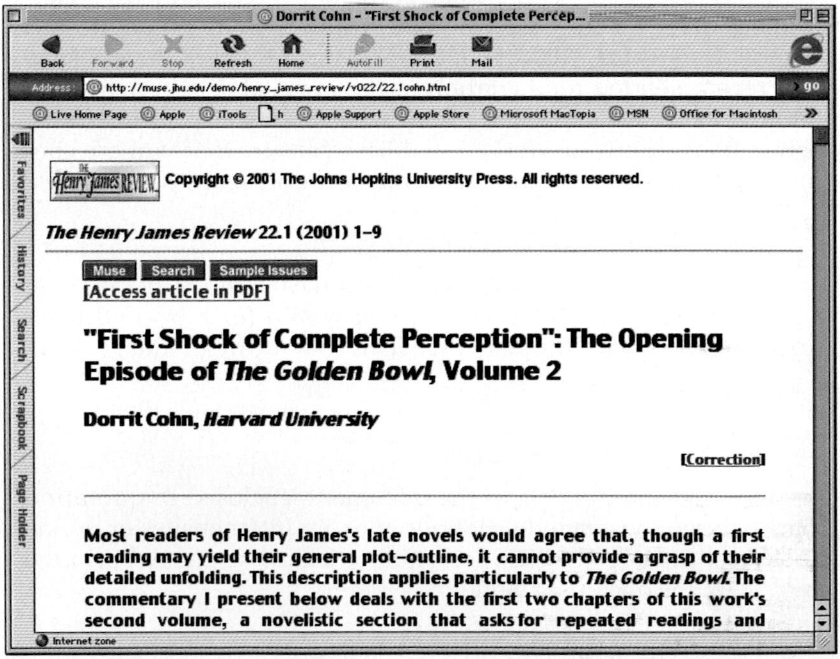

FIGURE 13.1 Online Journal Article with a Corresponding Print Version

to include both types of publication information in your citation. If there is no print version, provide the electronic publication information only.

Cohn, Dorrit. "'First Shock of Complete Perception': The Opening

    Episode of The Golden Bowl, Volume 2." The Henry James Review

    22.1 (2001): 1-9. Project Muse Journals. 2003. Johns Hopkins UP.

Item 5: Access Information

Finally, you want to provide your readers with enough information to be able to locate the source for themselves. The date you last accessed the source comes next in your citation. For works such as the one cited here, you will find three dates (date of print publication, date of electronic publication, date of access). After the date of access comes the Uniform Resource Locator (URL), that is, the address by which the document may be found on the Internet. It is important to be accurate in your listing of the URL. Enclose the URL in angle brackets. If you need to divide a long URL between two lines, make the break after a slash in the address.

Cohn, Dorrit. "'First Shock of Complete Perception': The Opening

    Episode of The Golden Bowl, Volume 2." The Henry James Review

    22.1 (2001): 1-9. Project Muse Journals. 2003. Johns Hopkins UP.

    24 Apr. 2003 <http://muse.jhu.edu./demo/henry_james_review/v002/

    22.1cohn.html>.

You should provide the URL for the exact document you were using. However, in some cases the URL is so long that it is impractical to include the entire address. If that is the case, provide the address of the site's search page, if available. Sometimes, however, a reader proceeds to a certain page via a series of links. In these cases, provide the navigation path. (See Figure 13.2 for an example of an Internet site with both navigation path and search options.) After the URL of the site's homepage, type the word *Path* followed by a colon, and then indicate the links to be followed. Use semicolons as separators between the items in the path.

URL FOR SEARCH PAGE

"Anarchist Archive." Voice of the Shuttle Web Site for Humanities

    Research. Ed. Alan Liu. 2003. University of California, Santa

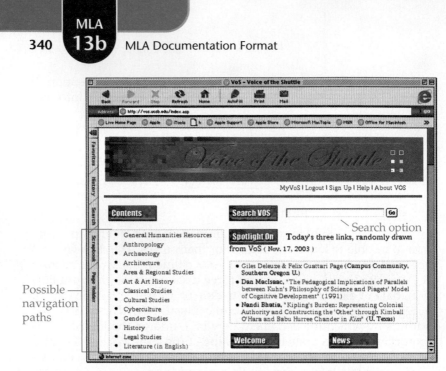

FIGURE 13.2 An Internet Site with Navigation Paths or Search Options

Barbara, English Department. 1 May 2003 <http://vos.ucsb.edu/
search-results.asp>.

URL FOR MAIN PAGE PLUS PATH

"Anarchist Archive." Voice of the Shuttle Web Site for Humanities
Research. Ed. Alan Liu. 2003. University of California, Santa
Barbara, English Department. 1 May 2003 <http://vos.ucsb.edu/
index.asp>. Path: History; Anarchist Archive.

48. Entire Internet Site

13.3
Citing an entire
Web site.

Often it is appropriate to reference an entire Internet Web site,
such as a scholarly project or an information database. Include the
information available at the site, in the following sequence.

1. The title of the site or project (underlined)
2. The creator or editor of the site (if given and relevant)
3. The electronic publication information: version number (if relevant), date of electronic publication or latest update, the name of the sponsoring organization or institution (if provided)
4. The date of access and the URL within angle brackets

The Encyclopedia Mythica. Ed. M. F. Lindemans. 1995-2003. 3 Mar. 2003

    <http://www.pantheon.org/mythica>.

MSN.com. 2003. Microsoft Network. 28 Feb. 2003 <http://www.msn.com>.

The Pew Center on Global Climate Change: Advancing the Debate Through

    Credible Analysis and Cooperative Approaches. 2003. Pew Center

    on Global Climate Change. 15 May 2003 <http://www.pewclimate.org>.

Victoriana Online. Ed. Sylvania Dye. 1996-2002. 12 Jan. 2002 <http://

    www.victorianaonline.com>.

49. Course Home Page

If you wish to cite a course home page, first list the name of the instructor (last name first), then the title of the course (neither underlined nor in quotation marks). Next comes a description, like *Course home page* (neither underlined nor in quotation marks), the dates of the course, the names of the department and institution that offered the course, the date of access, and the URL. Note that *home page* is spelled as two words in MLA style.

13.4
Citing a course home page.

Edwards, Farrell. General Physics. Course home page. Jan. 2003-May

    2003. Physics Department, Utah State U. 6 May 2003 <http://

    www.physics.usu.edu/classes/2210spr03/index.htm>.

50. Home Page for an Academic Department

Begin a citation for a department with its name, then a description such as *Dept. home page* (neither underlined nor in quotation marks), the institution's name, the date it was last updated (if provided), the date of access and URL. (See also item 49.)

Department of English. Dept. home page. Utah State U. 16 June 2003

    <http://websites.usu.edu/english>.

51. Personal Home Page

When citing someone's home page, begin with that person's name, followed by the title of the site or, if none is provided, with the description *Home page* (neither underlined nor in quotation marks). Next provide the date the site was last updated (if provided), the date of access, and the URL. (See also item 49.)

Avila, Alejandro Perez. Home page. 17 Feb. 2003. 1 May 2003 <http://

    www.u.arizona.edu/~aperezav>.

52. *Online Book*

The complete texts of many books are now available online as well as in print. Provide the following items when citing such works.

1. The name of the author (if only an editor, compiler, or translator is mentioned, give that person's name first, followed by *ed., comp.,* or *trans.*)
2. The title of the work, underlined
3. The name of any editor, compiler, or translator (if not given earlier)
4. Publication information from the printed work, if the work has been printed
5. Electronic publication information, such as the title of the Internet site, editor of the site, version number, date of electronic publication, and name of any sponsoring organization
6. The access date and URL in angle brackets

Woolf, Virginia. The Voyage Out. London: Faber, 1914. The EServer.

    Ed. Geoffrey Sauer. 2003. U of Washington. 1 June 2003

    <http://eserver.org/fiction/voyage-out.txt>.

53. *Part of an Online Book*

Sometimes you will be referring to a part of an online book. In such a case, list the title of the part after the author's name. If the part is a work like a poem or an essay, use quotation marks. If the part is a customary section like an introduction or a preface, do not include quotation marks. Be sure to give the complete URL of the specific part of the book if it is different from the entire book's URL.

Pope, Alexander. "Epistle I." Essay on Man. The EServer. Ed. Geoffrey

    Sauer. 2003. U of Washington. 1 June 2003 <http://eserver.org/

    poetry/essay-on-man/epistle-i.txt>.

54. *Online Government Document*

When citing government documents, start first with the information from the printed version and conclude with the electronic citation information.

United States. Dept. of Commerce. US Census Bureau. How the Census

    Bureau Measures Poverty. 24 Sept. 2002. 5 May 2003 <http://

    www.census.gov/hhes/poverty/povdef.html>.

13.5
Citing an online periodical.

55. *Article in an Online Periodical*

Many magazines, newspapers, and scholarly publications are now available in online formats. Generally, citations for online periodicals follow the same sequence as citations for print periodicals. They should include the following:

1. The author's name (if provided)
2. The title of the work, in quotation marks
3. The name of the journal, magazine, or newspaper, underlined
4. The volume and issue number (or other identifying number if provided)
5. The date of publication
6. The range or total number of pages, paragraphs, or sections, if they are numbered
7. The date of access and URL in angle brackets

If you cannot find some of this information, cite what is available.

Sheikh, Nabeela. "True Romance." Jouvert: A Journal of Postcolonial

    Studies 7.1 (2002). North Carolina State University, College of

    Humanities and Social Sciences. 23 Mar. 2003 <http://

    social.chass.ncsu.edu/jouvert/v7is1/sheik.htm>.

This journal is published only online and has no page or paragraph numbers. If page or paragraph numbers were provided, they would be listed after the publication date, for example, (2002): 21-25.

56. *Article in an Online Scholarly Journal via a Journal Database*

In addition to scholarly journals that are published online independently (see item 55), others can be accessed via an online journal database. If the journal is included in a database, include the name of the database (underlined) following the print information for the article; end with the date of access and the relevant URL within the database.

Reinhardt, Leslie Kaye. "British and Indian Identities in a Picture

    by Benjamin West." Eighteenth Century Studies 31.3 (1998).

    Project Muse. 12 July 2003 <http://muse.jhu.edu/journals/

    eighteenth-century_studies>.

57. *Article in an Online Newspaper or on a Newswire*

Dedman, Bill. "Racial Bias Seen in U.S. Housing Loan Program." New

York Times on the Web 13 May 1998. 14 May 2003 <http://

www.nytimes.com/archives>.

58. *Article in an Online Magazine*

Ricks, Delthia. "Sickle Cell: New Hope." Newsday 12 May 1998. 12 May

2003 <http://www.newsday.com/homepage.htm>.

59. *Online Review*

Bast, Joseph L. Rev. of Our Stolen Future, by Theo Colborn et al.

Heartland Institute 18 Apr. 1996: 27 pars. 25 June 2003

<http://www.heartland.org/stolen1.htm>.

60. *Online Abstract*

Reid, Joy. "Responding to ESL Students' Texts." TESOL Quarterly 28

(1994): 273-92. Abstract. 12 July 2002 <http://

vweb.hwwilsonweb.com/cgi-bin/webspirs.cgi>.

61. *Anonymous Article*

"N. Korea May Build New Reactors." MSNBC News Service 16 Feb. 2003.

16 Feb. 2003 <http:www.msnbc.com/news/850567.asp?0s1=31>.

62. *Online Editorial*

"A Nuclear Threat from India." Editorial. New York Times on the Web

13 May 1998. 14 May 2002 <http://www.nytimes.com/archives>.

63. *Online Letter to the Editor*

Lowry, Heath. Letter. Deseret News Online [Salt Lake City] 23 Mar.

1998. 25 Mar. 2003 <http://www.desnews.com/archst.html>.

64. *FTP Site*

Deutsch, Pater. "archie—An Electronic Directory Service for the

Internet." Mar. 1993. 15 Apr. 1995 <ftp://ftp.sura.net/pub/

archie/docs/whatis.archie>.

65. Telnet Site

Gomes, Lee. "Xerox's On-Line Neighborhood: A Great Place to Visit."

    Mercury News 3 May 1992. 5 Dec. 1996 <telnet://

    lambda.parc.xerox.com_8888>.

66. Information Database or Scholarly Project

CNN Interactive. 12 July 2000. Cable News Network. 12 July 2000

    <http://www.cnn.com>.

The Electronic Text Center. Ed. David Seaman. 2002. U of Virginia

    Library. 1 Jan. 2003 <http://etext.lib.virginia.edu>.

13.6
Citing a document from an information database or scholarly project.

67. Document from an Information Database or Scholarly Project

To cite a poem, a short story, an article, or another work within a scholarly project or database, begin with the author's name, if given, followed by the title of the work in quotation marks. If no author's name is given, begin with the title. Continue with relevant information on the project, including the access date and URL. Be sure to give the URL of the specific document rather than the URL of the database itself (if they are different). In the event the specific URL is too long and complicated to include, list the browser path instead. For example, the exact URL for Angelou's poem below is as follows:

<http://etext.lib.virginia.edu/etcbin/

    toccer-new2?id=AngPuls.sgm&images=images/modeng&data=/texts/

    english/modeng/parsed&tag=public&part=all>

The entry with the browser path uses a shortened URL.

Angelou, Maya. "On the Pulse of the Morning." The Electronic Text

    Center. Ed. David Seaman. 2002. U of Virginia Library. 1 Jan.

    2003 <http://etext.lib.virginia.edu>. Path: Collections;

    English; Online holdings; African American; Angelou, Maya.

68. Document or Full-Text Article Found via a Personal Subscription Service

If you are using a personal subscription service, such as AOL, that allows you to locate documents by using keywords, provide the name of the online service (underlined) and the date of access, followed by the keyword.

```
"Dr. Phil's Relationship Rescue." Online with Oprah. 12 July 2000.

    America Online. 15 Aug. 2000. Keyword: Oprah.
```

69. Document or Full-Text Article Found via a Library Subscription Service

13.7

Citing a document from a full-text article found via a library subscription service.

To cite online documents or articles that you derive from a service that your library subscribes to (e.g., *Lexis-Nexis, ProQuest,* or *EBSCOhost*), follow the citation for the source itself with the name of the service (underlined), the site sponsor, the library, and the date of access. If you know the URL of the database service's homepage, provide it in angle brackets at the end of the citation. If the library service provides only a starting page for the article's original printed version rather than numbering the pages, provide the number followed by a hyphen, a space, and a period: *115- .*

```
Bozell III, Brent L. "Fox Hits Bottom--Or Does It?" Human Events 57.4

    (2001): 15-. Academic Search Elite. EBSCO. Utah State U Lib.,

    Logan. 15 Oct. 2002 <http://www.epnet.com>.

King, Marsha. "Companies Here Ponder Scout Ruling." Seattle Times 6

    July 2000: A1. Academic Universe. Lexis-Nexis. Utah State U

    Lib., Logan. 15 Aug. 2000 <http://web.lexis-nexis.com/universe>.
```

70. Nonperiodical Publication on CD-ROM, Magnetic Tape, or Disc

Often, works on CDs, discs, or magnetic tape are published in a single edition, much as books are. To cite such publications, use a format similar to that used to cite print books, with the addition of the publication medium.

```
Corel WordPerfect Suite 8. CD-ROM. Ottawa, CA: Corel, 1998.

DeLorme Mapping. "Paris." Global Explorer. CD-ROM. Freeport: DeLorme

    Mapping, 1993.
```

DeLorme Mapping is the corporate author of this CD-ROM.

```
"Symbolism." The Oxford English Dictionary. 2nd ed. CD-ROM. Oxford:

    Oxford UP, 1992.
```

71. Database Periodically Published on CD-ROM

When citing periodically published reference works, include the information on the printed source as well as the publication medium, the name of the vendor (if relevant), and the electronic publication date.

```
Arms, Valerie M. "A Dyslexic Can Compose on a Computer." Educational

    Technology 24.1 (1984): 39-41. ERIC. CD-ROM. SilverPlatter.

    Sept. 1990.
```

72. Multidisc Publication

To cite a CD-ROM publication on multiple discs, list the number of discs or the specific number of the disc you used.

```
Great Literature Plus. CD-ROM. 4 discs. Parsippany: Bureau of

    Electronic Publishing, 1993.
```

73. Work in More Than One Medium

When a work is published in more than one medium (for example, both as a book and as a CD or both as a CD and as a disc), you may specify all the media or only the medium you used.

```
Hult, Christine A., and Thomas N. Huckin. The New Century Handbook.

    3rd ed. Book, CD-ROM. Boston: Longman, 2005.
```

74. Work in an Indeterminate Electronic Medium

If you cannot tell what medium the source is in (perhaps you accessed the work from a library's Web site and are unsure whether it is on CD-ROM or stored on the library's Internet server), use the designation *Electronic* for the medium.

```
Delk, Cheryl L. Discovering American Culture. Ann Arbor: U of

    Michigan P, 1997. Electronic. Berkeley Public Lib. 20 June 1998.
```

75. Electronic Television or Radio Program

```
Lifson, Edward. "Clinton Meets Kohl." Morning Edition. 13 May 1998.

    Natl. Public Radio. 20 June 1998 <http://www.npr.org/

    programs/morning/archives/1998>.
```

76. Electronic Sound Recording or Sound Clip

Beethoven, Ludwig van. "Symphony no. 5 in C, op. 67." June 1998. New

   City Media Audio Programs. 20 July 1998 <http://newcitymedia.com/

   Radiostar/audio.htm>.

77. Electronic Film or Film Clip

Anderson, Paul Thomas, dir. <u>Boogie Nights</u>. 1997. Trailer. New Line

   Cinema. 13 May 2003 <http://hollywood.com>.

78. Online Work of Art

Van Gogh, Vincent. <u>The Starry Night</u>. 1889. Museum of Mod. Art, New

   York. 20 Mar. 2003 <http://www.moma.org/paintsculpt/index.html>.

79. Online Interview

Gregson-Wagner, Natasha. Interview. <u>Hollywood Online</u>. May 1998. 15

   May 2003 <http://hollywood.com/pressroom/interviews>.

80. Online Map

"Mellow Mountain: Park City, Utah." Map. <u>MapQuest</u>. 17 Feb. 2003

   <http://www.mapquest.com/maps/map.adp?historyid=0>.

81. Online Cartoon

Trudeau, Garry. "Doonesbury." Cartoon. <u>New York Times on the Web</u> 13

   May 1998. 13 May 2002 <http://www.nytimes.com/archives>.

82. Online Advertisement

3D RealAudio. Advertisement. 20 Aug. 1998 <http://www.real.com>.

83. Online Manuscript or Working Paper

Hendrickson, Heather. "Art: Impractical but Essential." Working

   paper, n.d. 28 Aug. 2003 <http://english.usu.edu/W98/204honors/

   index.htm>.

The abbreviation *n.d.* stands for "no date."

84. Email Communication

For email messages that you wish to cite, provide the writer's name (or alias or screen name); the subject or title of the communication, if any (in quotation marks); the designation *E-mail to*; the name of the person to whom the email is addressed; and the date of the message. Note that *e-mail* is spelled with a hyphen in MLA style.

Gardner, Susan. "Help with Citations." E-mail to the author. 20 Mar.

2002.

Gillespie, Paula. "Members of the NWCA Board." E-mail to Michael

Pemberton. 1 Aug. 1997.

85. Online Posting

For a message posted to an email discussion list, in addition to the information provided for an email citation, include the description *Online posting* and the date of the posting. Provide the name of the discussion list, if known. Then give the date of access. Last, provide the URL, if known, or the email address of the list's moderator or supervisor in angle brackets.

Glennon, Sara. "Documenting Sessions." Online posting.

11 Dec. 1996. NWCA Discussion List. 12 Dec. 1997

<wcenter@ttacs6.ttu.edu>.

When possible, cite an archival version of the posting so that readers can more easily find and read the source.

White, Edward. "Texts as Scholarship: Reply to Bob Schwegler." Online

posting. 11 Apr. 1997. WPA Discussion List. 12 Apr. 1997

<http://gcinfo.gc.maricopa.edu/~wpa>.

Citation of a posting to a World Wide Web discussion forum follows the style of an online posting.

Hochman, Will. "Attention Paid This Sunday Morning." Online posting.

5 Apr. 1998. Response to Selfe. 7 May 1998 <http://www.ncte.org/

forums/selfe/#forums>.

Citation of a posting to a Usenet newsgroup also follows the style for an online posting. Be sure to include the name of the newsgroup in angle brackets.

Shaumann, Thomas Michael. "Technical German." Online posting. 5 Aug.

    1994. 7 Sept. 1994 <news:comp.edu.languages.natural>.

86. Online Synchronous Communication

To cite an online synchronous communication (e.g., an online chat or MOO), begin with the name (or alias or screen name) of the speaker, if available and if you are citing only one. Include a description of the event, the date of the event, the forum (for example, the name of the MOO), the access date, and the electronic address.

Pine Guest. Personal interview. 12 Dec. 1994. MediaMOO. 12 Dec. 1994

    <telnet://moo.mediaMOO.com_7777>.

87. Downloaded Computer Software

Fusion. Vers. 2.1. 30 June 2002 <http://www.allaire.com>.

CHAPTER 14

APA Documentation Format

In scholarly writing, it is vital to have a documentation trail that leads back to the original sources. This documentation trail enables readers to retrace the path of your research if they so desire; it also lets readers know that the information in your paper is from reliable sources. Various academic disciplines have developed different documentation systems to demonstrate these research paths. All of the different systems alert the reader to sources that are used, both within the text, by means of an in-text citation, and in the complete bibliographical citation included at the end of the text in a Works Cited or References list.

14a Document using the APA system

The documentation system commonly employed in the social sciences was developed by the American Psychological Association (APA). Detailed documentation guidelines for the APA system are included in the *Publication Manual of the American Psychological*

WEBLINK

http://www.apastyle.org/
faqs.html
A list of frequently asked
questions about APA style

Association, 5th ed. (Washington, DC: APA, 2001). The social sciences use an author/date method of documentation. In-text citations identify the source by the author's name and the date of publication so that the reader knows immediately whether the research cited is current. The date of publication is also emphasized in the References list, which appears at the end of the paper.

1 Integrating sources and avoiding plagiarism in the APA system

In Chapter 11 on Using Sources and Avoiding Plagiarism, we talked in general about the importance of using sources accurately and responsibly in your research papers. To help you do so, the APA

The APA Citation System

1. Introduce your source using a signal phrase that names its author, immediately followed by the date of publication in parentheses: *Jones (1995) states that . . .* (see 11d-2; see the box on page 261 for verbs to use in signal phrases).

2. Paraphrase or summarize the information from your source. It's best to use direct quotations sparingly. Rather, recast the source information into your own words. If you do use any words or phrases from the author, be sure to include them in quotation marks and to provide a *p.* plus a page number in parentheses (see 11d).

3. If you did not name the author in a signal phrase, at the conclusion of your summary insert in parentheses the author's last name, a comma, and the date of publication: *(Jones, 1995).* For a direct quotation or close paraphrase, also provide a *p.* plus a page number: *(Jones, 1995, p. 75)* (see 14b-2).

4. At the end of your paper, list the source with complete bibliographic information on your References page (see 14b-4).

citation format provides for a two-part system of source identification: (1) parenthetical citations within the body of the paper (see 14b-2) and (2) a Reference list at the end of the paper (see 14b-4). By using the APA system, you can integrate your source information appropriately and ethically without inadvertently committing plagiarism.

Plagiarism, a serious academic offense, is often committed by students inadvertently in the following two ways.

1. Failing to acknowledge a summary or paraphrase of a source in the body of the paper through a signal phrase and parenthetical citation.
2. Using the original authors' words without putting the borrowed words or phrases in quotation marks or including a parenthetical citation.

Acknowledge all sources

A successful research paper will be written as an argument by a writer in his or her own words, expressing the writer's understanding of the answers to specific research questions. In such a paper, sources are used as evidence in support of the writer's own argument. Source support is integrated into the flow of the writer's research paper through the use of paraphrases and summaries in the writer's own words; each source is acknowledged by a parenthetical citation. Failing to acknowledge a source results in plagiarism. In addition to paraphrases and summaries, any other source material must be acknowledged, such as specific facts, graphics or visuals, cartoons, diagrams, or charts, using the two-part APA citation system. Note that the APA system stresses the publication date of a source by including that date in the parenthetical citation along with the name of the author. This custom has grown out of a desire in the social sciences to know immediately when reading secondary research that the information found in a particular source is current and up to date (see 14b-2 and 14b-4).

Indicate original source words and phrases with quotation marks

The best research papers use direct quotations sparingly as support for their own ideas and integrate those quotations smoothly. A signal phrase alerts the reader that a direct quotation follows; the quotation marks show exactly which words and phrases are being quoted. Long quotations are formatted using indentation rather than quotation marks (see 55a-2). When students get into trouble by borrowing words and phrases without attribution to a source, it is very often the result of sloppy notetaking. Your notes should accurately record source information in your own words, and you should be able to tell at a glance when looking at your notes which information is from which source and on what page that information is located. Carelessness at the notetaking stage can result in unintentional plagiarism (see 11a-2).

2 Using the APA system for in-text citations

In the APA documentation system, reference citations found in the body of the paper are linked to the References list at the end. Both the author's last name and the year of publication are included in the in-text citation.

1. Author Named in the Narrative

If the author is mentioned in the narrative, provide the year of publication in parentheses just after the name.

```
Hacking (1995) covers much that is on public record about multiple
personality disorder.
```

2. Author Not Named in the Narrative

If the author is not mentioned in the narrative, provide the author's last name and the year of publication in parentheses at an appropriate place. Include a comma between the author's name and the date of publication.

```
In antiquity and through the middle ages, memory was a valued skill
(Hacking, 1995).
```

3. Specific Page or Paragraph Quoted

When quoting or directly paraphrasing the author's words, provide a page number (or a paragraph number if the electronic source includes one). Precede the page reference with the abbreviation *p.* (to cite one page) or *pp.* (to cite more than one page).

```
There may be a causal explanation for multiple personality disorder,
because "multiplicity is strongly associated with early and repeated
child abuse, especially sexual abuse" (Hacking, 1995, p. 73).
```

A Directory to the APA System

(continued)

If the quotation is from an electronic source that does not have numbered pages, provide the author and year only.

Vault Reports makes the following request on its Web site: "If you work (or have worked) for a company we write about, or you have recently gone through a job interview, please fill out our Survey and tell us about your experience" (1998).

4. Work by Two Authors

In citing a work by two authors, provide the last names of both authors. Use the word *and* to separate their names in the narrative, but use an ampersand (&) to separate their names in an in-text parenthetical citation.

As Sullivan and Qualley (1994) point out, many recent publications take the politics of writing instruction as their central concern.

The explanation for recent turmoil in the academy may be found in politics (Sullivan & Qualley, 1994).

5. Work by More Than Two Authors

In the first reference to a work by three, four, or five authors, provide the last names for all authors. In subsequent citations, use the first author's last name and the Latin phrase *et al.* (for "and others"). When a work has six or more authors, include only the name of the first author, followed by *et al.*, in the first and in all following citations.

Writing becomes less egocentric as the child matures (Britton, Burgess, Martin, McLeod, & Rosen, 1975).

According to Britton et al. (1975), mature writers consider their readers more than themselves.

6. Anonymous Work

If no author's name is provided, use either the title or an abbreviated form of the title (usually the first few words) for the in-text citation. Italicize the title of a book, periodical, brochure, or report; use quotation marks around the title of an article or chapter.

Public schools have become overly dependent on the IQ test as an indication of academic potential (*Human Abilities in Cultural Contexts*, 1988).

An individual's success in life depends in large measure on the cultural context in which he or she was raised ("Beyond IQ in Preschool Programs," 1994).

7. Work by a Corporate Author

Generally, provide the full name of a corporate author in in-text parenthetical citations.

Recently published statistics show the gap between the rich and poor to be widening (New York Times, Inc., 1996).

If the name of the corporate author is long (such as United Cerebral Palsy Association) or if its abbreviation is easily recognized (such as APA), use the abbreviation after including both the complete name and the abbreviation in the first text reference.

FIRST TEXT REFERENCE

There is a Web site that explains citing information from the Internet (American Psychological Association [APA], 2001).

SECOND AND SUBSEQUENT TEXT REFERENCES

The documentation system commonly employed in the social sciences is presented in great detail (APA, 2001).

8. Works by Authors with the Same Last Name

When the References list includes two or more primary authors with the same last name, provide those authors' initials in all citations, even if the publication dates are different.

G. A. Fraser (1990) writes about abuse as the cause of multiple personality disorder.

S. Fraser (1987) has written a memoir about incest and its effect on multiplicity.

9. Two or More Sources

To cite several different sources within the same parenthetical citation, list the sources in alphabetical order by the authors' names and use a semicolon to separate the entries.

Several studies (Prinsky & Rosenbaum, 1987; *Record Labeling*, 1985; Thigpen, 1993) show concern about songs with themes of drugs and violence.

10. Personal Communication

Personal correspondence, such as letters, telephone conversations, lecture notes, and email, should be cited only in the text itself. Do not list the communications in the References list because readers cannot access them. Provide the initials and the last name of the correspondent, the designation *personal communication*, and the date.

J. Tompkins suggests that fear and authority prevent true learning in elementary, secondary, college, and university classrooms (personal communication, August 7, 1997).

The misinterpretation of Herrnstein's study is widespread (H. J. Miller, personal communication, April, 1989).

11. Email Communication

Email communication from individuals should be cited as personal communication within the text and is not included on the References list (see item 10). The in-text citation is formatted as follows:

```
L. L. Meeks provided researchers with the pertinent information
regarding teacher training (personal communication, May 2, 2000).
```

12. Web Sites

When referring to an entire Web site (as opposed to a specific document or page on the site) it is sufficient in APA style to give the address of the Web site within the text itself. Such a reference is not included on the References page.

```
Patricia Jarvis's Web site includes a great deal of information about
recent archaeological digs in the Great Basin (http://www.asu.edu/
~students).
```

13. Different Works by the Same Author

To distinguish citations of two or more works by the same author published in the same year, add a lowercase letter after the date of publication in the parenthetical reference: *(1995a), (1995b)*. Assign the lowercase letter after alphabetizing the entries in the References list.

```
The Art of Wondering: A Revisionist Return to the History of Rhetoric
focuses on historical rhetoric in general (Covino, 1988a), while
"Defining Advanced Composition: Contributions from the History of
Rhetoric" concentrates on advanced composition (Covino, 1988b).
```

3 Formatting content notes according to the APA system

The APA discourages use of content notes—they can distract readers from the flow of the text. Content notes should be included only if they enhance or strengthen the discussion. Each note should make a single point. Number notes consecutively throughout the text, using a superscript number. List the notes on a separate Notes page at the end of the text.

4 Formatting the References list according to the APA system

The research paper's References list (the equivalent of the Works Cited listing in MLA style) contains an alphabetical listing of all the works used as sources. The purpose of the References list is to help readers find the materials used in writing the paper, so the entries must be complete and accurate. List sources alphabetically by the last name of the author, using the letter-by-letter system of alphabetization. When no author is given, alphabetize by the first word of the title (excluding *A*, *An*, or *The*). Format the References list in a student paper according to the APA style for a final text: type the first word of each entry at the left margin, and indent subsequent lines of the same entry five spaces (or ½ inch). This is called a *hanging indent* format. Double-space the entire References list, both between and within entries.

Books

A citation for a book has four basic parts:

Author's name. (Publication date). *Book title.* Publication information.

Begin a book citation with the author's last name, followed by a comma and the first and middle initials, when known. Include the year of publication, enclosed in parentheses, next. Underline the title and subtitle of the book. Capitalize the first word of the title, the first word of the subtitle, and any proper nouns. Follow the title with publication information: the city of publication and the publisher, separated by a colon. If more than one location is listed for the publisher, give the site that is listed first on the title page or the site of the publisher's home office. If the city is not known or could be confused with another city, include a state or country abbreviation. Omit the word *Publisher* and abbreviations such as *Inc.* and *Co.* from the publisher's name. Include the complete names of university presses and associations. (For guidelines on citing books in electronic format, see page 370.)

1. Book by One Author

Author   Publication date   Book title

Bolick, C. (1988). *Changing course: Civil rights at the crossroads.*

New Brunswick, NJ: Transaction Books.

    Publication information

Hacking, I. (1995). *Rewriting the soul: Multiple personality and the sciences of memory.* Princeton, NJ: Princeton University Press.

2. Book by Two or More Authors

When a book has two to sit authors, provide all the authors' names (last name first, followed by initials) in the order in which they appear on the title page. Note that this order may not be alphabetical. Connect the final two names with an ampersand (&). Abbreviate the seventh and subsequent authors as *et al.*

Britton, J., Burgess, T., Martin, N., McLeod, A., & Rosen, H. (1975).

    The development of writing abilities. London: Macmillan.

Hindelang, M. J., Hirschi, T., & Weis, J. G. (1981). *Measuring*

    delinquency. Beverly Hills, CA: Sage.

3. Book by a Corporate Author

Begin the entry with the full name of the group; alphabetize the entry by the first important word in the name. Should the same group be listed as author and publisher, include the word *Author* at the end of the entry in place of the publisher's name.

American Psychological Association. (2001). *Publication manual of the*

    American Psychological Association (5th ed.). Washington, DC:

    Author.

National Commission on Excellence in Education. (1984). *A nation at*

    risk: The full account. Cambridge, MA: USA Research.

4. Book with an Editor

For an edited book, provide the editor's name in place of an author's name. Include the abbreviation *Ed.* (for "Editor") or *Eds.* (for "Editors") in parentheses immediately following the editor's name.

Dilts, S. W. (Ed.). (1991). *Peterson's guide to four-year colleges*

    (21st ed.). Princeton, NJ: Peterson's Guides.

5. Chapter or Selection from an Edited Book

To cite a particular chapter or selection in an edited work, start with the author's name, the year of publication, and the title of the selection. Do not italicize the title or enclose it in quotation marks. Next, provide the names of the editors in normal order as they appear on the title page, preceded by the word *In* and followed by the abbreviation *Ed.* or *Eds.* (in parentheses) and a comma. End the entry with the book's title (italicized), the inclusive page numbers for the selection (in parentheses), and the publication information.

Kadushin, A. (1988). Neglect in families. In E. W. Nunnally, C. S.

    Chilman, & F. M. Cox (Eds.), *Mental illness, delinquency,*

    addiction, and neglect (pp. 147-166). Newbury Park, CA: Sage.

6. Two or More Books by the Same Author

When two or more entries have the same author, arrange the entries by the date of publication, with the earliest first. If you have two or more works by the same author published in the same year, alphabetize by title and distinguish the entries by adding a lowercase letter immediately after the year: *(1991a), (1991b).*

Flynn, J. R. (1980). *Race, IQ, and Jensen.* London: Routledge.

Flynn, J. R. (1991). *Asian Americans: Achievement beyond IQ.*

    Hillsdale, NJ: Erlbaum.

7. Article in a Reference Book

If an encyclopedia entry is signed, start with the author's name; if it is unsigned, start with the title of the article. In either case, follow with the publication date. Provide the volume number and page numbers of the article (in parentheses) after the title of the reference book.

Davidoff, L. (1984). Childhood psychosis. In *The encyclopedia of*

    psychology (Vol. 10, pp. 156-157). New York: Wiley.

Schizophrenia. (1983). In *The encyclopedic dictionary of psychology*

    (Vol. 8, pp. 501-502). Cambridge, MA: MIT Press.

8. Book in Translation

Indicate the name of the translator in parentheses immediately after the book's title, with the abbreviation *Trans.*

Freire, P. (1993). *Pedagogy of the oppressed* (New rev. 20th anniv.

    ed., M. B. Ramos, Trans.). New York: Continuum.

9. Subsequent Edition of a Book

If a book is not a first edition, indicate the relevant edition in parentheses immediately following the title of the book. Use abbreviations to specify the type of edition: for example, *2nd ed.* stands for "Second edition" and *Rev. ed.* stands for "Revised edition." (See also item 8.)

Lindeman, E. (1987). *A rhetoric for writing teachers* (2nd ed.). New

York: Oxford University Press.

10. Republished Book

Provide the original date of publication in parentheses at the end of the entry, with the words *Original work published.*

Dewey, J. (1963). *Experience and education.* New York: Collier.

(Original work published 1938)

11. Government Document

Unless an author's name is given, begin an entry for a government document with the name of the agency that issued the publication.

National Center for Educational Statistics. (1996). *The condition of*

education 1996. Washington, DC: U.S. Department of Education,

Office of Educational Research and Improvement.

12. Published Proceedings from a Conference

Van Belle, J. G. (2002). Online interaction: Learning communities in

the virtual classroom. In J. Chambers (Ed.), *Selected Papers*

from the 13th International Conference on College Teaching and

Learning (pp. 187-200). Jacksonville, FL: Community College at

Jacksonville Press.

13. One Volume of a Multivolume Work

Doyle, A. C. (1930). *The complete Sherlock Holmes* (Vol. 2). Garden

City: Doubleday.

Periodicals

A citation of an article in a periodical or a journal follows a format similar to that for a book:

Author's name. (Publication date). Article title. Publication information.

When citing magazines and newpapers, include the month and date of publication. The article title and subtitle appear neither set in quotation marks nor italicized. The publication information begins with the name of the publication as it appears on the publication's title page, with all major words capitalized. Italicize the journal name. Include the volume number (italicized and not preceded by the abbreviation *vol.*) and the issue number (in parentheses and not italicized) for journals not numbered consecutively throughout the volume. End with the inclusive page numbers for the article. (Use the abbreviation *p.* or *pp.* with articles in newspapers but not with articles in journals or magazines.) (For guidelines on citing articles in online periodicals, see pages 370–371.)

14. Article in a Journal Paginated by Volume

Publication
Author   date   Article title   Article subtitle

Popenoe, D. (1993). American family decline, 1960-1990: A review and

    appraisal. *Journal of Marriage and Family, 55,* 527-555.

Publication information

Shotter, J. (1997). The social construction of our inner selves.

    Journal of Constructivist Psychology, 10, 7-24.

15. Article in a Journal Paginated by Issue

If each issue of a journal begins with page 1, provide the issue number (in parentheses and not italicized) immediately following the volume number.

Alma, C. (1994). A strategy for the acquisition of problem-solving

    expertise in humans: The category-as-analogy approach.

    Inquiry, 14(2), 17-28.

16. Article in a Monthly Magazine

Include the month, not abbreviated, in the publication date.

Katz, L. G. (1994, November). Perspectives on the quality of early

    childhood programs. *Phi Delta Kappan, 76,* 200-205.

17. Article in a Weekly Magazine

Provide the year, month, and day of publication.

Ives, D. (1994, August 14). Endpaper: The theory of anything. *The New*

    York Times Magazine, 58.

If the article has no known author, start the entry with the title of the article, and alphabetize by the first important word in the title (usually the word that follows the introductory article).

The blood business. (1972, September 7). *Time*, 47-48.

In the References list, this entry would appear in the B's.

18. Newspaper Article

Provide the complete name of the newspaper (including any introductory articles) after the title of the article. List all discontinuous page numbers, preceded by *p.* or *pp.*

Fritz, M. (1992, November 7). Hard-liners to boycott German anti-

racism rally. *The Dallas Morning News*, pp. 1, 25.

Twenty percent biased against Jews. (1992, November 22). *The New York*

Times, p. A1.

19. Editorial

Add the word *Editorial*, in brackets, after the title of the editorial.

Paglia, C. (1997, October 24). More mush from the NEA [Editorial].

The Wall Street Journal, p. A22.

Six who serve their council districts [Editorial]. (1997, October

31). *The Boston Globe*, p. A22.

20. Letter to the Editor

Add the designation *Letter to the editor,* in brackets, after the title of the letter or after the date if there is no title.

Schack, S. (1997, December 1). [Letter to the editor]. *The New York*

Times, p. A20.

21. Review

Provide the name of the reviewer, the date of publication (in parentheses), and the title of the review, if given. Then, in brackets, write the designation *Review of* and the title of the piece that was reviewed.

Ribadeneira, D. (1997, October 31). The secret lives of seminarians

[Review of the book *The new men: Inside the Vatican's elite*

school for American priests]. *The Boston Globe*, p. C6.

22. *Unsigned Article*

Quacks in European solidarity (2002, August). *The Economist*, 50.

23. *More Than One Work by the Same Author in the Same Year*

List the works alphabetically by title and use the lowercase letters *a, b, c,* and so on after the dates to distinguish the works.

Hayles, N. K. (1996a). Inside the teaching machine: Actual feminism

and (virtual) pedagogy. *The Electronic Journal for Computer*

Writing, Rhetoric and Literature, 2. Retrieved Nov. 15, 1996,

from http://www.cwrl.utexas.edu/cwrl

Hayles, N. K. (1996b). Self/Subject. In P. Vandenberg & P. Heilker

(Eds.), *Keywords in composition* (pp. 217-220). Portsmouth, NH:

Heinemann/Boynton-Cook.

Other sources

24. *Film or Video Recording*

Begin with the names of those responsible for the film and, in parentheses, their titles, such as *Producer* and *Director*. Give the title (italicized), and then designate the medium in brackets. Provide the country of origin and the name of the studio.

Michaels, L. (Producer), & Spheeris, P. (Director). (1992). *Wayne's*

world [Motion picture]. United States. Paramount Pictures.

25. *Television or Radio Program*

Identify those who created the program, and give their titles—for example, *Producer, Director,* and *Anchor*. Give the date the program was broadcast. Provide the program's title (underlined), as well as the city and the station where the program aired.

Miller, R. (Producer). (1982, May 21). *Problems of freedom*. New York:

NBC-TV.

26. *Technical Report*

Write an entry for a technical report in a format similar to that for a book. If an individual author is named, provide that information; place any other identifying information (such as a report number) after the title of the report.

Vaughn Hansen Associates, in association with CH2M Hill and Water

Research Laboratory, Utah State University. (1995).

Identification and assessment of certain water management

options for the Wasatch Front: Prepared for Utah State Division

of Water Resources. Salt Lake City, UT: Author.

27. Published Interview

For a published interview, start with the name of the interviewer and the date. In brackets, give the name (and title, if necessary) of the person interviewed. End with the publication information, including the page number(s), in parentheses, after the title of the work in which the interview is published.

Davidson, P. (1992). [Interview with Donald Hall]. In P. Davidson,

The fading smile (p. 25). New York: Knopf.

28. Unpublished Interview

Follow the format for a published interview.

Hult, C. (1997, March). [Interview with Dr. Stanford Cazier, past

President, Utah State University].

29. Unpublished Dissertation

Provide the author's name, the date, and then the title of the dissertation, italicized and followed by a period. Add the phrase *Unpublished doctoral dissertation,* a comma, and the name of the degree-granting institution.

Johnson, N. K. (1980). *Cultural and psychological determinants of*

health and illness. Unpublished doctoral dissertation,

University of Washington.

30. Speech or Lecture

For an oral presentation, provide the name of the presenter, the year and month of the presentation, and the title of the presentation (italicized). Then give any useful location information.

Meeks, L. (1997, March). *Feminism and the WPA.* Paper presented at the

Conference on College Composition and Communication, Phoenix, AZ.

31. Paper Presented at a Conference

Provide information about the location of the meeting as well as the month in which the meeting was held.

Klaus, C. (1996, March). *Teachers and writers.* Paper presented at the

meeting of the Conference on College Composition and

Communication, Milwaukee, WI.

14b Electronic media in APA style

The electronic documentation formats found in the *Publication Manual of the American Psychological Association*, 5th ed., recommend a retrieval statement. When citing electronic media, use the standard APA format to identify authorship, date of origin (if known), and title, much as for print material; the Web information is then placed in a retrieval statement at the end of the reference. If you are referencing an electronic version that duplicates exactly a print source, simply use the basic journal reference format for print sources. Indicate the electronic version by including the terms [*Electronic Version*] in brackets immediately following the citation.

32. Online Professional or Personal Site

To comply with APA style, present information in the following general sequence when citing documents found on a Web site:

1. The author's or editor's last name and initial(s).
2. The creation date of the work, in parentheses; use *n.d.* (no date) if the electronic publication date is not available.
3. The title of the complete work in italics.
4. The relevant subpage or program (if the document is contained within a large, complex site).
5. The designation *Retrieved* followed by the access date (in order of month, day, year) *from http://URL*. Break URL lines only after a slash or before a period; do not follow the URL with a period.

Jarvis, P. (n.d.). *My Homepage.* Retrieved December 3, 2003, from

http://www.mtu.edu/~students

McCarthy, B. (1997). *Reflections on the Past--Antiques.* Retrieved

January 20. 1998, from the Resources for Victorian Living Web

site: http://www.victoriana.com

33. *Online Book*

Provide any data on the print publication before giving details
on where the electronic version can be located.

Aristotle, (1954). *Rhetoric* (W. R. Roberts, Trans.). Retrieved April

8, 2003, from Carnegie Mellon University, *The English Server* Web

site: http://www.rpi.edu/~honeyl/Rhetoric/index.html

34. *Article in an Online Work*

Generally, citations for articles in online works follow the same
sequence as citations for their print counterparts, followed by the
retrieval statement.

Britt, R. (1995). The heat is on: Scientists agree on human

contribution to global warming. *Ion Science.* Retrieved November

13, 2002, from http://www.injersey.com/Media/IonSci/features/

gwarm

Women in American History. (1998). In *Encyclopaedia Britannica.*

Retrieved May 25, 2003, from http://www.women.eb.com

35. *Article in an Online Newspaper or on a Newswire*

Schmitt, E. (1998, February 4). Cohen promises "significant" military

campaign against Iraq if diplomacy fails. *The New York Times on*

the Web. Retrieved from http://www.nytimes/com/archives

There is no need to repeat the date of retrieval if it is the same as the
publication date.

Wright, R. (1998, February 4). U.S. wins support but no mandate

against Iraq. *The Los Angeles Times,* p. A1. Retrieved January

25, 2003, from http://www.latimes.com/home/archives

36. Article in an Online Magazine

Thakker, S. (1998, May). Avoiding automobile theft. *Ontario Police Crime Prevention Magazine.* Retrieved May 26, 2003, from http://www.opcpm.com/inside/avoidingautomobile.html

37. Online Review

Spiers, S. (1998). [Review of the report "Blood poisoning" by *Prevention/NBCToday*]. *OBGYN.net.* Retrieved August 3, 2003, from http://www.obgyn.net/women/articles

38. Online Abstract

Reid, J. (1983). Computer-assisted text-analysis for ESL students. *Calico Journal, 1*(3), 40-42. Abstract retrieved August 2, 2003, from DIALOG database. (ERIC Item: EJ29870)

39. Online Editorial

Spilner, M. (1998, May). Walking club welcome [Editorial]. *Prevention.* Retrieved June 20, 2003, from http:// www.prevention.com/ walking.welcome.html

40. Online Letter to the Editor

Rivel, D. (1998, May 6). Art in the schools [Letter to the editor]. *The New York Times on the Web.* Retrieved May 6, 2003, from http://www.nytimes.com/yr/mo/day/letters

41. Article in an Online Scholarly Journal

Britt, R. (1995). The heat is on: Scientists agree on human contribution to global warming. *Ion Science.* Retrieved November 13, 1996, from http://www.injersey.com/Media/IonSci/features/ gwarm

42. Document or Full-Text Article Found via a Reference Database

To cite a full-text article you derive from a service that your library subscribes to (e.g., *Lexis-Nexis, EBSCOhost,* or *ProQuest*), follow the citation for the source itself (the same as for its print counterpart) with the name of the service (italicized) and the library. Provide the date of access and the URL of the service's homepage in a retrieval statement.

King, M. (2000, July 6). Companies here ponder scout ruling. *Seattle*

Times, A1. *Lexis-Nexis*. Utah State U. Library, Logan. Retrieved

August 15, 2000, from http://web.lexis-nexis.com/universe

43. Nonperiodical Publication on CD-ROM, Magnetic Tape, or Diskette

To cite works distributed on CDs, diskettes, or magnetic tape, give the authors, publication date, title, and publication information in standard APA format. After the title, identify the type of electronic medium in brackets—for example, [*CD-ROM*].

ClearVue, Inc. (1995). *The history of European Literature* [CD-ROM].

Chicago: Author.

44. Online Work of Art

Seurat, G. (1884). *A Sunday Afternoon on the Island of La Grande*

Jatte. Art Institute of Chicago. Retrieved August 3, 2003, from

http://www.artic.edu/aic/collections

45. Online Interview

Jorgenson, L. (1998, May 26). For a change, Jazz feel bullish

[Interview with Jeff Hornacek]. *Deseret News*, 15 paragraphs.

Retrieved May 27, 2003, from http://desnews.com/playoffs

46. Online Posting

Although unretrievable communication such as email is not included in an APA References list, more public or retrievable Internet postings from newsgroups or listservs may be included.

Heilke, J. (1996, May 3). Webfolios. *Alliance for Computers and Writing Discussion List.* Retrieved December 21, 2003, from http://www.ttu.edu/lists/acw-1/9605/0040.html

47. Online Synchronous Communication

WorldMOO Computer Club. (1998, February 3). Monthly meeting. Retrieved February 3, 2003 from telnet:world.sensemedia.net1234

CHAPTER 15

CMS, CBE, and COS Documentation Formats

FAQs

▶ What are the CMS, CBE, and COS systems of documentation? (15a–15c)

▶ How do I avoid plagiarizing? (15a-1, 15b-1)

▶ How do I let a reader know that I'm using a source within my paper? (15a-2, 15b-2, 15c-1)

▶ How do I use footnotes in CMS style? (15a-3)

▶ What does a reference list look like in CMS, CBE, or COS format? (15a-4, 15b-3,15c-2, 15c-3)

▶ How do I document electronic sources when using CMS, CBE, or COS formats? (pages 382, 391)

All of the disciplines have in common a need to provide readers with a documentation trail that they can use to retrace the research path. Even though the details of documentation format might vary somewhat by discipline, the guiding principles are the same: (1) show the reader within the text itself, by using in-text citations or note numbers, that you are using source information; and (2) provide your readers with complete bibliographical information so that they can find the source should they wish to do so.

15a Document using the Chicago Manual of Style (CMS) system

The documentation system used most commonly in business, communications, economics, and the humanities and fine arts (other than languages and literature) is outlined in *The Chicago Manual of Style*, 15th ed. (Chicago: The University of Chicago Press, 2003). This two-part system uses footnotes or endnotes and a bibliography to provide publication information about sources quoted, paraphrased, summarized, or otherwise referred to in the text of a paper. Footnotes appear at the bottom of the page; endnotes appear on a separate page at the end of the paper. The Bibliography, like the Works Cited list in the MLA documentation style, is an alphabetical list of all works cited in the paper.

WEBLINK

http://www.press
.uchicago.edu/Misc/
Chicago/cmosfaq.html
Answers to frequently
asked questions about
Chicago style

WWW

15.1

FAQs about
CMS
documentation.

1 Integrating sources and avoiding plagiarism in the CMS system

In Chapter 11 on Using Sources and Avoiding Plagiarism, we talked in general about the importance of using sources accurately and responsibly in your research papers. To help you do so, the CMS citation format provides for a two-part system of source identification: (1) footnote superscript numbers and footnotes within the body of the paper (see 15a-2 and 15a-3) and (2) a Bibliography at the end of the paper (see 15a-4). By using the CMS system, you can integrate your source information appropriately and ethically without inadvertently committing plagiarism.

Plagiarism, a serious academic offense, is often committed by students inadvertently in the following two ways:

1. Failing to acknowledge a summary or paraphrase of a source in the body of the paper through a signal phrase and footnote number.

2. Using the original authors' words without putting the borrowed words or phrases in quotation marks or including a footnote number.

The CMS Citation System

1. Introduce your source using a signal phrase that names its author, with a superscript footnote number following the source information: *Jones states that . . .* ¹ (see 11d-2; see the box on page 261 for verbs to use in signal phrases).

2. Paraphrase or summarize the information from your source. It's best to use direct quotations sparingly. Rather, recast the source information into your own words. If you do use any words or phrases from the author, be sure to include them in quotation marks (see 11d).

3. Format your footnotes (which are listed on the page on which the source was cited) or endnotes (which are typed in a consecutive list at the end of the paper before the bibliography) according to the CMS style (see 15a-2 and 15a-3).

4. At the end of your paper, list the source with complete bibliographic information on your Bibliography page (see 15a-4).

Acknowledge all sources

A successful research paper will be written as an argument by a writer in his or her own words, expressing the writer's understanding of the answers to specific research questions. In such a paper, sources are used as evidence in support of the writer's own argument. Source support is integrated into the flow of the writer's research paper through the use of paraphrases and summaries in the writer's own words; each source is acknowledged by a parenthetical citation. Failing to acknowledge a source results in plagiarism. In addition to paraphrases and summaries, any other source material must also be acknowledged, such as specific facts, graphics or visuals, cartoons, diagrams, or charts, using the CMS footnote citation system (see 11a-3).

Indicate original source words and phrases with quotation marks

The best research papers use direct quotations sparingly as support for their own ideas and integrate those quotations smoothly. A signal phrase alerts the reader that a direct quotation follows; the quotation marks show exactly which words and phrases are being quoted. Long quotations are formatted using indentation rather than quotation marks (see 55a-2). When students get into trouble by borrowing words and phrases without attribution to a source, it is very often the result of sloppy notetaking. Your notes should accurately record source information in your own words, and you should be able to tell at a glance when looking at your notes which information is from which source and on what page that information is located. Carelessness at the notetaking stage can result in unintentional plagiarism (see 11a-2).

2   Using the CMS system for in-text citations

In the text, indicate a note with a superscript number typed immediately after the information that is being referenced. Number notes consecutively throughout the text.

In A History of Reading, Alberto Manguel asserts that "we, today's readers, have yet to learn what reading is."[1] As a result, one of his conclusions is that while readers have incredible powers, not all of them are enlightening.[2]

3   Formatting notes according to the CMS system

For footnotes, position the text of the note at the bottom of the page on which the reference occurs. Separate the footnotes from the text by skipping four lines from the last line of text. Single-space within a note, but double-space between notes if more than one note appears on a page.

For endnotes, type all of the notes at the end of the paper, in a section titled *Notes*. The title, centered but not in quotation marks, should appear at the top of the first page of the notes. List the notes in consecutive order, as they occur in the text. Double-space the entire endnote section—between and within entries.

The other details of formatting are the same for both footnotes and endnotes. Indent the first line of each note using the paragraph indent. Use a number that is the same size as and is aligned in the same way as the note text (do not use a superscript); follow the number with a period and a space. Begin with the author's name (first name first), followed by a comma. Then provide the title of the book (italicized) or article (enclosed in quotation marks). Finally, provide the publication information. For books, include (in parentheses) the

A Directory to the CMS System

place of publication, followed by a colon; the publisher, followed by a comma; and the date of publication. Conclude with the page number of the source, preceded by a comma. For articles, include the title of the periodical (underlined or italicized), followed by the volume or issue number. Then add the date of publication (in parentheses), followed by a colon and the page number.

1. Alberto Manguel, *A History of Reading* (New York: Viking, 1996), 23.

2. Steven Brachlow, "John Robinson and the Lure of Separatism in Pre-Revolutionary England," *Church History* 50 (1983): 288-301.

In subsequent references to the same source, it is acceptable to use only the author's last name and a page number.

3. Manguel, 289.

Where there are two or more works by the same author, include a shortened version of each work's title.

4. Merton, *Mystics*, 68.

5. Merton, *Buddhism*, 18.

Books

1. Book by One Author

6. Iris Murdoch, *The Sovereignty of Good* (New York: Schocken Books, 1971), 32-33.

2. Book by Two or Three Authors

List the authors' names in the same order as on the title page of the book.

7. John Sabini and Maury Silver, *Moralities of Everyday Life* (New York: Oxford University Press, 1982), 91.

8. Anne S. Goodsell, Michelle R. Maher, and Vincent Tinto, *Collaborative Learning: A Sourcebook for Higher Education* (University Park, Pa.: National Center on Postsecondary Teaching, Learning, and Assessment, 1992), 78.

3. Book by More Than Three Authors

Use the abbreviation *et al.* after the first author's name; list all authors in the accompanying bibliography.

9. James Britton et al., *The Development of Writing Abilities* (London: Macmillan, 1975), 43.

4. Book by a Corporate Author

10. American Association of Colleges and Universities, *American Pluralism and the College Curriculum: Higher Education in a Diverse Democracy* (Washington, D.C.: American Association of Higher Education, 1995), 27.

5. Book with an Editor

11. Jane Roberta Cooper, ed., *Reading Adrienne Rich: Review and Re-Visions, 1951-1981* (Ann Arbor: University of Michigan Press, 1984), 51.

12. Robert F. Goodman and Aaron Ben-Ze'ev, eds., *Good Gossip* (Lawrence: Kansas University Press, 1994), 13.

6. Book with an Editor and an Author

13. Albert Schweitzer, *Albert Schweitzer: An Anthology*, ed. Charles R. Joy (New York: Harper & Row, 1947), 107.

7. Chapter or Selection from an Edited Work

14. Gabriele Taylor, "Gossip as Moral Talk," in *Good Gossip*, ed. Robert F. Goodman and Aaron Ben-Ze'ev (Lawrence: Kansas University Press, 1994), 35-37.

15. Langston Hughes, "Harlem," in *The Norton Anthology of African American Literature*, ed. Henry Louis Gates, Jr., and Nellie Y. McKay (New York: Norton, 1997), 1267.

8. Article in a Reference Book

The publication information (city of publication, publisher, publication year) is usually omitted from citations of well-known reference books. Include the abbreviation *s. v.* (*sub verbo,* or "under the word") before the article title, rather than page numbers.

16. Frank E. Reynolds, *World Book Encyclopedia*, 1983 ed., s. v. "Buddhism."

17. *Encyclopedia Americana*, 1976 ed., s. v. "Buddhism."

9. Introduction, Preface, Foreword, or Afterword

18. Jane Tompkins, preface to *A Life in School: What the Teacher Learned* (Reading, Mass.: Addison-Wesley, 1996), xix.

10. Work in More Than One Volume

19. Arthur Conan Doyle, *The Complete Sherlock Holmes*, vol. 2 (Garden City, N.Y.: Doubleday, 1930), 728.

11. Government Document

20. United States Federal Bureau of Investigation, *Uniform Crime Reports for the United States: 1995* (Washington, D.C.: GPO, 1995), 48.

Periodicals

12. Article in a Journal Paginated by Volume

21. Mike Rose, "The Language of Exclusion: Writing Instruction at the University," *College English* 47 (1985): 343.

13. Article in a Journal Paginated by Issue

22. Joy S. Ritchie, "Confronting the 'Essential' Problem: Reconnecting Feminist Theory and Pedagogy," *Journal of Advanced Composition* 10, no. 2 (1989): 160.

14. Article in a Monthly Magazine

23. Douglas H. Lamb and Glen D. Reeder, "Reliving Golden Days," *Psychology Today*, June 1986, 22.

15. Article in a Weekly Magazine

24. Steven Levy, "Blaming the Web," *Newsweek*, 7 April 1997, 46-47.

16. Newspaper Article

25. P. Ray Baker, "The Diagonal Walk," *Ann Arbor News*, 16 June 1928, sec. A, p. 2.

17. Abstract from an Abstracts Journal

26. Nancy K. Johnson, "Cultural and Psychological Determinants of Health and Illness" (Ph.D. diss., University of Washington, 1980), abstract in *Dissertation Abstracts International* 40 (1980): 425B.

Other sources

18. Speech or Lecture

27. Wayne Booth, "Ethics and the Teaching of Literature" (paper presented to the College Forum at the 87th Annual Convention of the National Council of Teachers of English, Detroit, Mich., 21 November 1997).

19. Personal Letter to the Author

28. George Bush, letter to author, 8 September 1995.

Electronic media in CMS style

The *Chicago Manual of Style* (15th edition, 2003) covers formats for electronic media thoroughly, integrating its coverage of electronic documentation formats with coverage of print citations. In general, electronic sources are cited much as print sources are cited. The URL is listed at the end of the citation and is not placed in angle brackets. CMS points out that dates of access are of limited usefulness because of the changeable nature of electronic sources and suggests using the date of access only in fields in which the information is particularly time-sensitive, such as medicine or law. If an access date is needed, place it in parentheses following the URL, as in this example from an online law journal.

29. Ruthe Catolico Ashley, "Creating the Ideal Lawyer," *New Lawyer*, April 3, 2003, http://www.abanet.org/genpractice/newlawyer/april03/ideal.html (accessed July 20, 2003).

20. Online Professional or Personal Site

30. Academic Info, "Humanities," 1998-2000, http://www.academicinfo.net/index.html.

31. Michelle Traylor, "Michelle Traylor Data Services," 1989-1998, http://www.mtdsnet.com.

32. John C. Herz, "Surfing on the Internet: A Nethead's Adventures Online," *Urban Desires* 1.3, March/April 1995, http://www.desires.com.

21. Online Posting

Archived source addresses are given separately from any other addresses in citing listserv messages. The date of posting is the only date given.

33. James Heilke, email to Alliance for Computers and Writing mailing list, May 3, 1996, http://www.ttu.edu/lists/acw-l/9605.

22. Computer Software

To cite computer software, start with the title and then include the edition or version, if any. Next, give the name and location of the organization or person with rights to the software.

34. A.D.A.M.: Animated Dissection of Anatomy for Medicine, Benjamin Cummings/Addison-Wesley and A.D.A.M. Software, Inc., Reading, Mass.

23. Online Book

35. Vernon Lee, *Gospels of Anarchy and Other Contemporary Studies* (London: I. Fisher Unwin, 1908), http://www.indiana.edu/~letrs/vwwp/lee/gospels.html.

24. Article in an Online Professional Journal

36. Felix Ayala-Fierro et al., "*In Vitro* Tissue Specificity for Arsine and Arsenite Toxicity in the Rat," *Toxicological Sciences* 52 (1999): 122-129, http://toxsci.oupjournals.org/.

25. Article in an Online Magazine

37. David Glenn, "Sherry B. Ortner Shifts Her Attention from the Sherpas of Nepal to Her Newark Classmates," *The Chronicle of Higher Education*, August 8, 2003, http://chronicle.com.

26. Article in an Online Newspaper

38. Heather May and Christopher Smart, "Plaza Legal Battle Revived," *The Salt Lake Tribune*, August 7, 2003, http://www.sltrib.com/ 2003/Aug/t08072003.asp.

27. DVDs and Videocassettes

39. "Let's Get Together," *The Parent Trap*, DVD, directed by David Swift, II (1961; Burbank, Calif.: Walt Disney Home Video, 2002).

4 Formatting Bibliography entries according to the CMS system

The style for Bibliography entries is generally the same as that for Works Cited entries in MLA style. Follow the formatting conventions outlined in 13a-4 when creating a Bibliography page.

15b Document using the CBE system

15.2
An overview of CBE documentation style.

WEBLINK

http://www.
councilscienceeditors.org
Web site for the CSE

Although source citations in the sciences are generally similar to those recommended by the APA, there is no uniform system of citation in the sciences. Various disciplines follow either the style of a particular journal or that of a style guide, such as the guide produced by the Council of Biology Editors: *Scientific Style and Format: The CBE Manual for Authors, Editors, and Publishers,* 6th ed. (New York: Cambridge University Press, 1994).

The Council of Biology Editors (CBE) became the Council of Science Editors (CSE) on January 1, 2000. The new name, which was voted on by the membership during 1999, more accurately reflects its expanding membership. Until it is revised and updated by the CSE, CBE style will remain the preferred system for science citations.

1 Integrating sources and avoiding plagiarism in the CBE system

In Chapter 11 on Using Sources and Avoiding Plagiarism, we talked in general about the importance of using sources accurately and responsibly in your research papers. The CBE citation format provides for a two-part system of source identification: (1) parenthetical citations or citation numbers within the body of the paper (see 15b-2) and (2) a References list that is either alphabetical or numerical at the end of the paper (see 15b-3). By using the CBE system, you can integrate your source information appropriately and ethically without inadvertently committing plagiarism. Since the CBE citation system closely resembles the APA system, for more on integrating sources and avoiding plagiarism, see 14b.

2   Using the CBE system for in-text citations

The CBE system of documentation offers two alternative formats for in-text citations: the name-year (or author-year) system and the number (or citation sequence) system.

Name-year system

An outline of the CBE's name-year system for in-text citation can be found at *<http://www.wisc.edu/writing/Handbook/DocCBE.html>*.

WWW

15.3
A guide to the CBE's name-year systems for in-text citations.

1. Author Named in the Narrative

If the author's name is used to introduce the source material, include only the publication date in the citation.

According to Allen (1997), frequency of interactions and context of occurrence were unknown.

2. Author Not Named in the Narrative

If the author is not mentioned in the narrative, the source material is followed, in parentheses, by the last name of the author and the publication date of the source (no comma).

Frequency of interactions and context of occurrence were unknown (Allen 1997).

3. Specific Page or Paragraph Quoted

If the source material is paraphrased or directly quoted, include the page numbers after the source material, in parentheses and preceded by *p* or *pp* (no period).

Allen (1997) reported "only one encounter that described defensive behavior by a fox toward a coyote" (p 125).

A Directory to the CBE System

(continued)

4. Work by Two Authors

If the work has two authors, join their last names with *and*.

Categories of behavior included traveling, resting, hunting small
mammals, and feeding on a carcass (Bekoff and Wells 1981).

5. Work by Three or More Authors

To cite a work with three or more authors, give the first author's
name, followed by *and others* and the publication year.

Social status was categorized as alpha, beta, or young (Rabbet and
others 1967).

6. Different Works by the Same Author

To differentiate between two or more works published by the same
author in the same year, add a lowercase letter following the year.

Sargeant and Allen (1989a, 1989b) noted only a single encounter of
defensive behavior by a fox toward a coyote.

7. Work Cited Indirectly

When information comes from work cited in another work, the in-
text citation should mention both works.

Deterrence was recorded when coyotes caused foxes to avoid the area
(Mech 1970, cited in Bekoff and Wells 1981).

8. Two or More Sources within the Same Citation

When two or more sources are cited, arrange the sources in
chronological sequence from earliest publication to latest. Sources
published in the same year should be arranged alphabetically.

```
Separate hierarchies of dominance for males and females were observed

within each resident pack (Rabbet and others 1967; Schenkel 1967;

Mech 1970).
```

Number system

In the number or citation sequence system, numbers are assigned to the various sources, according to the sequence in which the sources are initially cited in the text. Then the sources are listed by number on the References page. Set citation numbers within the text as superscripts.

```
Temperature plays a major role in the rate of gastric juice secretion.[3]
```

Multiple sources are cited together.

```
Recent studies[3,5,8-10] show that antibodies may also bind to microbes

and prevent their attachment to epithelial surfaces.
```

3 Formatting the References list for the number system in CBE style

Like the MLA's Works Cited page, the CBE's references list contains all the sources cited in the paper. The title of this page may be References or Cited References. Since the purpose of this list is to help readers find the materials used in writing the paper, information must be complete and accurate.

The format of the References list will depend on whether the name-year system or the number system is used. The primary difference is the placement of the date in the citation. In the name-year system, the date is placed immediately following the author's name. In the number system, it is placed at the end of the citation. We will consider here the References list for the number system. For an example of a student paper using the name-year system, see 18c. (Note that initial numerals accompany citations in the list *only* when the number system is used. The citations appear in alphabetical order when the name-year system is used.)

Double-space the entire References list, both between and within entries. Type the citation number, followed by a period, flush left on the margin. Leave two word spaces to the first letter of the entry. Align any turn lines on the first letter of the entry. List the citations in order of appearance in the text.

List authors with last names first, followed by initials. Capitalize only the first word of a title and any proper nouns. Do not enclose titles of articles in quotation marks, and do not underline titles of books. Abbreviate names of journals, where possible. Include the year of publication. Cite volume and page numbers when appropriate.

Books

1. Book by One Author

1. Kruuk H. The spotted hyena: a study of predation and social behavior. Chicago: Univ Chicago Pr; 1972.

2. Abercrombie MLJ. The anatomy of judgment. Harmondsworth (Eng.): Penguin; 1969.

2. Book by Two or More Authors

3. Hersch RH, Paolitto DP, Reimer J. Promoting moral growth. New York: Longman; 1979.

3. Book by a Corporate Author

4. Carnegie Council on Policy Studies in Higher Education. Fair practices in higher education: rights and responsibilities of students and their colleges in a period of intensified competition for enrollment. San Francisco: Jossey-Bass; 1979.

4. Book with Two or More Editors

5. Buchanan RE, Gibbons NE, editors. Bergey's manual of determinative bacteriology. 8th ed. Baltimore: Williams & Wilkins; 1974.

5. Chapter or Selection from an Edited Work

6. Kleiman DG, Brady CA. Coyote behavior in the context of recent canid research: problems and perspectives. In: Bekoff M, editor. Coyotes: biology, behavior, and management. New York: Academic Pr; 1978. p 163-88.

6. Government Document

7. Mech D. The wolves of Isle Royale. National Parks fauna series. Available from: United States GPO, Washington; 1966.

Periodicals

7. Journal Article by One Author

8. Schenkel R. Expression studies of wolves. Behavior 1947;1:81-129.

8. Journal Article by Two or More Authors

9. Sargeant AB, Allen SH. Observed interactions between coyotes and red foxes. J Mamm 1989;70:631-3.

9. Article with No Identified Author

10. [Anonymous]. Frustrated hamsters run on their wheels. Nat Sci 1981;91:407.

10. Newspaper Article

11. Blackman J. Aldermen grill Peoples officials on heating costs. Chicago Tribune 2001 Jan 16; Sect 1A:2(col 3).

11. Magazine Article

12. Aveni AF. Emissaries to the stars: the astronomers of ancient Maya. Mercury 1995 May:15-8.

Other sources

12. Unpublished Interview

13. Quarnberg T. [Interview with Dr. Andy Anderson, Professor of Biology, Utah State University, 1988 Apr 15].

13. Dissertation

14. Gese EM. Foraging ecology of coyotes in Yellowstone National Park [dissertation]. Madison (WI): University of Wisconsin; 1995. 124 p.

14. Unpublished Manuscript

15. Pegg J, Russo C, Valent J. College cheating survey at Drexel University. [Unpublished manuscript, 1986].

15. Personal Letter

16. Fife A. [Letter to President Calvin Coolidge, 1930]. Located at: Archives and Special Collections, Utah State University, Logan, UT.

Electronic media in CBE style

Internet formats are covered briefly in *Scientific Style and Format: The CBE Manual for Authors, Editors, and Publishers,* 6th ed. The Vancouver style for electronic citations, a set of conventions observed by the American Medical Association, the American College of Physicians, and the World Association of Medical Editors, expands basic CBE citation conventions to encompass electronic journals and print-based Internet sources (<*http://www.nlm.nih.gov/pubs/formats/internet.pdf*>).

16. Online Professional or Personal Site

17. Gelt J. Home use of greywater: rainwater conserves water--and money [Internet]. 1993 [cited 2003 Nov 8]. Available from: http://www.ag.arizona.edu/AZWATER/arroyo/071.rain.html

17. Online Book

18. Bunyan J. The pilgrim's progress from this world to that which is to come [book on the Internet]. London: Kent; 1678 [cited 2001 Jan 16]. Available from: http://www.bibliomania.com/0/0/frameset.html

18. Article in an Online Journal

19. Lechner DE, Bradbury SF, Bradley LA. Detecting sincerity of effort: a summary of methods and approaches. Phys Ther J [serial on the Internet] 1998 Aug [cited 2003 Sept 15]. Available from: URL: http://www.apta.org/pt_journal/Aug98/Toc.htm

19. Article in an Online Newspaper

20. Roan, S. Folic acid may mask vitamin deficiency [Internet]. Salt
    Lake Tribune; 2003 Aug 7 [cited 2003 Aug 8]. Available from:
    http://www.sltrib.com/2003/aug/08072003/thursday/81868.asp

20. Email Message

21. Shaver, A. Regarding toxicity screen [email on the Internet].
    Message to: Jack Schmidt. 2003 Feb 5, 4:30 pm. Accessed 2003
    Feb 6.

21. Electronic Posting to a Listserv

22. Kasianowicz, J. Careers in biochem. In: MEDLINE-L [posting on the
    Internet]. Washington: Bureau of Weights and Measures; 2003
    Mar 2. Accessed 2003 Apr 23.

15c   Document using the COS system

Columbia Online style (COS) was developed to fill a gap
between the need to cite rapidly changing online sources and the
citation styles of professional organizations such as the MLA or APA,
which tended to favor print sources. Today, most professional organizations have begun to include online sources as a part of their citation
styles. However, some instructors prefer to use this COS system for
documenting all online sources. The COS system can be adapted for
either humanities or science research papers. We provide a brief
overview of the COS system below. For a more complete reference,
see Janice R. Walker and Todd Taylor, *The Columbia Guide to Online
Style* (New York: Columbia UP, 1998).

1 **Using the COS system for in-text citations in the
humanities and sciences**

15.4

An overview
of the COS
documentation
system.

The *humanities* system of in-text citations typically requires the
author's last name plus a page number. Since most online sources do

not include page numbers, simply cite by the author's last name—or cite the title of the work, in quotation marks, if no author's name is available—in parentheses.

As more programs become Web-based, "it may seem natural for

prospective distance-education students to look for information about

courses and programs online" (Carr).

A recent study suggests that spermicide use may increase the risk for

contracting AIDS ("Spermicide").

For *science* in-text citations, provide the year of publication or last update following the author's last name, separated by a comma. Of course, some Web sources will not have any dates at all. In that case, include the date you accessed the source instead.

Undergraduates studying introductory psychology perform better in

distance-education courses but are less happy with them (Carr, 2000).

Distance education is neither better nor worse than traditional

classroom education, says the NEA on its Web site (15 July 2000).

2 Formatting the Works Cited page for the humanities in the COS system

At the end of your paper, you will provide an alphabetical listing for all the sources you used in the paper, usually called Works Cited. The purpose of this list is to help readers find the materials you used when writing your paper. Like the citations in other systems, COS citations include important information about the source, such as the author, title, and publication data. Because COS is for online sources, it also includes information about the date of publication or posting, the electronic address (URL), and the date of access.

Stout, David. "Israeli Decision on Radar Sale Made Public at Peace

Talks." The New York Times on the Web 15 July 2000.

http://www.nytimes.com (15 July 2000).

3 Formatting the References list for the sciences in the COS system

The References list for the sciences includes all of the information that is provided for the humanities, but COS style formats it differently to match science citations for print sources.

```
Arango, T. (2000, January). UBS to purchase Paine Webber. Deseret

    News Online. http://www.desnews.com (2 Jan. 2000).
```

CHAPTER **16**

Disciplinary Discourse

FAQs

▶ Do disciplines ask different questions? (16a-1)

▶ How do I provide evidence in different disciplines? (16a-2)

▶ What is "genre knowledge"? (16b)

▶ Is there a difference in writing formats and styles by discipline? (16b-1 to 16b-3)

▶ How do I learn all the new words in my major? (16b-4)

As a college student, regardless of your major, you are probably taking courses in the sciences, such as geology or chemistry; the social sciences, such as sociology or political science; and the humanities, such as philosophy or English literature. You may also be taking "applied" courses in home economics, agriculture, engineering, or business. Each of these academic disciplines seeks understanding and knowledge in traditional ways; each shares basic research processes. Exploring the important relationships among disciplines will help you interpret and use the methods and established ways of proceeding employed by researchers (see 16a).

Furthermore, the research that you conduct in any discipline needs to be communicated to others—primarily through writing (papers and articles) although sometimes through speech as well (conference presentations and lectures). Writing that is clear, cogent, and logically developed is key to communicating information regardless of the discipline. We have discovered in the written communication field that students do not learn to write simply by taking one writing class. Rather, they need continual practice with writing in order to improve, including writing in various disciplines as they become familiar with the research and writing practices common to those fields of study.

Even though the basic principles of researching and writing in the disciplines share many common elements, the types of questions

asked and evidence used, the customary ways in which the information is reported, the language and writing style preferred, and the genre conventions—that is, the **disciplinary discourse**—often will vary by the field of study. Researching and writing, however, are vitally important in all disciplines. This chapter provides a broad overview of disciplinary research and writing. Chapters 17–19 contain more specific information about researching and writing in the humanities, natural sciences, and social sciences.

16a Disciplinary research

What is research in the disciplines? Broadly defined, all research is systematic inquiry designed to further our knowledge and understanding of a subject. Using this definition, nearly everything you do in college is research. You seek to discover information about people, objects, and nature; to revise your findings in light of new information that comes to your attention; and to interpret your experience and communicate that interpretation to others. This is how learning proceeds both for each of us as individuals and for human beings together as we search for knowledge and understanding of our world.

16.1

A physician uses the research process.

1 Questions asked in the disciplines

People are interpretive animals. In our interaction with the world, we seek to represent internally to ourselves what we have experienced externally. We generally assume that the universe is an orderly, reasonable, meaningful place, and that if we but look, we will be able to discern that order. When we are confronted with a problematical experience, we seek a reasonable explanation for it; that is, we "research" the subject to discover its meaning.

The cartoon in Figure 16.1 shows a person confronted with a problematical experience. As he relaxes under a tree, he is rudely

FIGURE 16.1 Reprinted by permission of Johnny Hart and Creators Syndicate, Inc.

awakened from his reverie. In searching his internal representation of the world, the character finds an explanation for what happened. The humor of the cartoon is the result of its parody of Archimedes, who shouted "Eureka!" when he discovered a new principle of physics, and Newton, who deduced the principle of gravity from a falling apple. We recognize the circular reasoning the character has used in solving the problem. Because we are familiar with the orderly procedures people use to solve problems—procedures that this character has not used—we understand that his response is ludicrous.

This same issue concerning the falling apple could be researched by a scientist, perhaps a physicist, who might ask the following questions: Why does the apple fall? How fast does it fall? How long will it take to reach the ground? Such questions involve broad issues about the nature of the physical universe and the "laws" that govern it. The physicist observes natural phenomena and then develops a systematic body of principles to account for or predict other similar events in the universe. For example, physicists have deduced the following principle: "Any object at a distance from the earth will be acted on by gravity, which is the force of mutual attraction among all bodies, proportional to the product of the masses of the bodies divided by the square of the distance between them."

A social scientist, perhaps an economist, researching the same issue might focus on the need for a reliable food source in a society, asking such questions as these: How do people meet their basic need for food? What laws of supply and demand operate on the production and distribution of food? An economist also seeks to define the broad issues of how people in society structure their economic relationships. The economist develops a systematic body of ideas to be used in accounting for other similar economic systems or events. Responding to this issue, the economist might make the following statement: "The increasingly prevalent view by consumers that food is a public good and that all citizens should be assured of an adequate and nutritious food supply, in addition to the fear of prolonged food shortages, has led to a growing demand for change in the agricultural economic policy of this nation."

A humanist—perhaps a historian—researching this issue would attempt to explain and explore the human experience of the character in the cartoon by asking other questions: What is the significance of the event to this character and to others of his historical period? How does this event relate to other similar events? The historian would account for, reconstruct, and narrate all the events related to this character's so-called discovery that apples cure hunger, relating the discovery to other more general cultural events. Then the historian might postulate the following explanation: "The invention of agriculture was a significant historical event, often called the Neolithic Revolution. Occurring between 8000 and 3000 B.C., the Neolithic Revolution involved a change from a hunter-gatherer society in which humans obtained wild foods to an agricultural society in which humans prepared the soil and sowed seeds for harvesting."

It is clear that researchers in different disciplines ask different questions about the same subject. What distinguishes them is the perspective that the researcher in each field takes.

2 Evidence used in the disciplines

In addition to asking different questions, researchers in the disciplines have customary ways in which they "prove" their hypotheses or provide reasons for their point of view. What constitutes an acceptable reason or appropriate evidence may vary by discipline. For example, evidence to a historian may be a diary or a memoir written during a specific historical period; evidence to a psychologist may be a case study of an individual suffering from a particular mental illness. Anyone who is learning about a specific discipline will also be learning how to argue a case and present evidence in that discipline. Evidence can vary from quantitative (using statistical and numerical data) to qualitative (using observations and interviews). Data can be presented in the form of visuals such as tables, graphics, and charts, or it can be described in narratives (stories). Information can be gathered either through primary sources (firsthand data collection) or through secondary sources (reading and reporting on the work of others). Chapters 17–19 discuss these different uses of evidence in the disciplines in more detail.

16b Disciplinary discourse

In addition to variations in questions and evidence, disciplines can vary in the ways they present information, sometimes called disciplinary **genres.** Genres are the typical forms that writing and speech can take in various contexts. One of the tasks of students in college is to discover the genre conventions common to the discipline in which they are studying. Authors Huckin and Berkenkotter call this skill "genre knowledge" in their 1995 book *Genre Knowledge in Disciplinary Communication: Cognition/Culture/Power.* They state:

16.2
Examples of disciplinary discourse.

> [Academic] knowledge production is carried out and codified largely through generic forms of writing: lab reports, working papers, reviews, grant proposals, technical reports, conference papers, journal articles, monographs, and so on. Genres are the media through which scholars and scientists communicate with their peers. Genres are intimately linked to a discipline's methodology, and they package information in ways that conform to a discipline's norms, values, and ideology. Understanding the genres of written communication in one's field is, therefore, essential to professional success. (Huckin and Berkenkotter 1)

Your task as an apprentice in a particular discipline is to uncover the discipline's genres and practice them in your own writing.

1 Format

A discipline's genres will incorporate specific formats in which to organize its writing. The *lab report,* for example, is a genre of scientific writing. A typical lab report will contain the same conventional features and formats for many scientific disciplines. For an example of an informal lab report, see page 7 in Chapter 1. Another genre of both natural and social science writing is the informal research report. For examples, see pages 436 and 459. Notice the use of headings and subheadings in both of these genres.

The use of visuals is especially important in fields within the sciences and social sciences. Often data is presented in the form of visuals—tables, graphs, and charts (see 20c). Such visuals can be very effective, particularly in presenting a great deal of data in a compact form (see Figure 16.2).

Because of the ease with which documents can now be desktop published, writers in all disciplines have at their fingertips access to

Table 1

Test Conditions for Specificity of Enzymes

Treatment	Sugar or Control (4 ml)	Enzyme or Control (2 ml)	Yeast (10 ml)
	HYPOTHESIS		
1	Lactose	β-galactosidase	Yeast
2	Melibiose	β-galactosidase	Yeast
3	Lactose	α-galactosidase	Yeast
4	Melibiose	α-galactosidase	Yeast
	ASSUMPTIONS		
5	H_2O	α-galactosidase	Yeast
6	Melibiose	H_2O	Yeast
7	Lactose	H_2O	Yeast
8	H_2O	H_2O	Yeast
9	Glucose	H_2O	Yeast

FIGURE 16.2 Table from a Biology Lab Report

many more visuals than ever before—clip art, photographs, cartoons, drawings, maps, and so on. These visuals should be used judiciously and strategically so that your reader is not overwhelmed with too many competing graphics (see 20d).

Readers of disciplinary genres expect to find certain organizational patterns, certain types of connections between ideas, and a logical sequence. It is your job as an apprentice in a discipline to find out what genre conventions to follow. Don't hesitate to ask your instructors for suitable models of what they consider excellent disciplinary writing.

2 Style

Another distinguishing feature of disciplinary writing is style—that is, the customary sentence patterns chosen by writers in that discipline. Features of style that can differ by disciplines include *tone* (How objective is the writing? How formal is the tone?), *rhetorical stance* (Do the writers try to achieve distance from their audience? Or do they try to identify with their audience?), and *sentence style* (How long are the sentences and paragraphs in this discipline? Are the verbs active or passive? Are headings and subheadings used? What citation style is used to document sources?).

3 Documentation

A third distinguishing feature of disciplinary genres is revealed by their documentation conventions. Even though the general principles of documentation are the same (that is, your goal is to provide your reader with an indication of what sources you used and how to find them), formatting conventions differ by discipline. Documentation in the humanities emphasizes the importance of being able to locate a particular quotation on the page on which it was found; hence, internal citations in MLA style use the author's last name and a page number. In contrast, documentation formats in the natural and social sciences emphasize the importance of a source's currency and timeliness; hence, internal citations in APA style use the date of publication as well as the author's last name and the page number. Documentation styles in various disciplines are discussed in Chapters 13–15.

4 Vocabulary

The vocabulary customarily used in a discipline is an important part of its discourse. One of your primary jobs as you study a discipline will be to learn its specialized vocabulary. Not only will you need to recognize the specialized and technical words when you read them, but you will also need to employ these words appropriately in your writing. It may be helpful to keep your own dictionary of specialized terms as you are studying a particular field. The following three chapters in Part 3 provide more information about writing in the humanities, natural sciences, and social sciences.

(EXERCISE 16.1)

Browse through some of the journals that are used frequently in your field of study. Do you notice any common elements in format, style, or language? Do some journals follow a distinctive style that differs from others in the field? What would you say are the common elements that define the writing genre for your discipline?

Strategies for Learning New Vocabularies

- *Begin a learning log or journal.* In either a handwritten journal or a computer file, list new vocabulary words that you encounter in class and in your reading. Be sure to record an example of each word as it is used in a sentence.

- *Take notes.* When in lectures, take careful notes, including any new vocabulary used by your instructor. Review your notes after class and highlight or underline the new words. Look up in the dictionary any words that you don't recognize and write down their definitions in your learning log.

- *Use flash cards.* Create your own vocabulary flash cards, using 3 × 5 index cards. Practice defining the words on the cards with a classmate.

- *Join online discussions.* Online listservs and discussion forums provide a way to "lurk" in your discipline (see 24b-1). Read some of the prior posts and note the vocabulary being used. Are there words that recur over and over? Are there new terms? Again, record any new words in your learning log.

- *Keep at it.* Be persistent about noting and practicing your new vocabulary. You will not be able to learn it all at once.

FOR COLLABORATION

Bring a photocopy of a journal article from your field to class to share with a small group of your peers. Discuss with them what you see as the genre that is exhibited in the article. Compare with each other to decide whether the fields represented have different discourse conventions regarding format, style, and language.

CHAPTER 17

Writing in the Humanities

FAQs

▶ What are the humanities, and why do people study them?

▶ I have to write a paper about a poem we read in class. Where should I start? (17b)

▶ How is a literary analysis paper formatted? (17c)

▶ How can I find information in the library or on the Internet for a humanities research paper? (17d)

The humanities are disciplines that attempt to explore and explain the human experience. They include classical and modern languages and literature, history, and philosophy. Scholars and students in the humanities are interested in exploring difficult questions about humankind. Humanists deal in significance, insight, imagination, and the meaning of human experience. They write to express their understanding of some aspect of the world. John Steinbeck's *The Grapes of Wrath* focuses on a family of farmers forced to migrate to California during the Great Depression. In general, humanists inquire into consciousness, values, ideas, and ideals as they seek to describe how experience shapes understanding of the human condition.

VIDEO

Disciplines within the humanities share similar types of inquiry and analysis.

17a | Know the different types of writing in the humanities

AUDIO

Chapter overview.

In history, philosophy, and literature, written texts are extremely important. Historians document and analyze past events, usually

17.1

The inquiry process in the humanities.

focusing on a particular group of people, country, or period. Philosophers examine human ideas, constructing logical systems to explain our thoughts and interactions and our relationships with each other and the rest of nature. Literary authors attempt to capture in writing their own experiences or, through their imaginations, the experiences of other people in other settings. Through stories, they convey their understanding of the world.

Written texts in the humanities fall into three broad categories: (1) creative writing, such as fiction, poetry, and drama; (2) interpretive and analytical writing, such as literary and art criticism; and (3) theoretical writing, such as historical, philosophical, and social theories of literature and art.

1 Creative writing

Human beings have always been storytellers. The impulse to create works of literature, whether in the form of oral folk narratives or formal written sonnets, is as old as humankind. Creative writing, or literature, provides readers with an aesthetic experience. Readers expect a literary work to mean something to them—to show them new ways of looking at themselves and the world.

The major **literary genres,** or types of literature, are poetry, fiction, and drama. Biography and autobiography are also sometimes considered literary genres.

2 Interpretive and analytical writing

17.2

Primary research in the humanities.

Readers of literary works ask interpretive or analytical questions: What sort of work is it? Does it have a message? How powerful or meaningful is the message? Critical writing in the humanities is usually either interpretive, analytical, or some combination of the two. **Interpretive writing** discusses the author's intended meaning or the impact of the work on an audience. For example, an interpretive writer might try to explain a novelist's attitude toward the heroine of her or his book or weigh the aesthetic impact of a dance. Interpretive writers support their claims by using evidence from the work itself. A book report that summarizes the plot and discusses the significance of a work is an example of interpretive writing. **Analytical writing** takes interpretation one step further, examining the whole of the work in relationship to its component parts. For example, an analytical writer might try to understand how the plot of a play is reinforced by its setting or how a ballet's musical score contributes to its theme. A critical essay that argues for a particular position with respect to a literary work is an example of analytical writing.

When you read a piece of literature or view a work of art, you are not a neutral observer; you allow the work to speak to you on many levels. As you absorb its meaning, you question and probe. Assignments that call for interpretation and analysis require you to set down in words the results of this questioning and probing process.

3   Theoretical writing

The third type of humanistic writing is **theoretical writing.** Theorists look beyond individual works of literature and art to see how they exemplify broader social and historical trends. For example, a theorist might use the characters in a Dickens novel to speculate about shifts in class structure in nineteenth-century England. Or he or she might look at the use of perspective in a medieval fresco to theorize about the origins of Renaissance painting. Theorists provide links among art, literature, and other disciplines such as history, sociology, and psychology. Their writing involves interpretation and analysis, but their goal is to *synthesize*—to present interpretations in a larger context. Many of the articles published in professional humanities journals exemplify theoretical writing.

AUDIO
Critical reading and writing in literature.

17b   Write interpretively or analytically about literature

Much of the writing you will do in college literature courses is interpretive or analytical. Instructors generally expect you to make a claim about a literary work and then support that claim through reasoned arguments and evidence from the work itself (see Chapter 7). Your goal in writing interpretively or analytically is to shed light

WEBLINK

http://www.crayne.com/howcrit.html
"How to Critique Fiction"—an excellent introduction to literary analysis

www
17.3
A guide to literary analysis.

on an aspect of the work that the reader might not otherwise see.

1   Reading literature critically

Begin by reading the work critically (see 2b). Using the following critical reading process when you read a piece of literature will start you on the way to writing an interpretive or analytical essay.

First, read the work straight through, with an eye toward understanding the text and noting its impressions on you as a reader. Does the work make you feel happy or angry? Is there a character, event, or scene that is particularly moving or striking? Does anything in the text confuse or puzzle you? Keep a journal (either on a computer or in a notebook) in which you jot down impressions as you read.

Once you have finished reading the work, skim it in its entirety to highlight important passages, such as scenes that are pivotal to the plot, revealing character descriptions, and vivid descriptive passages. Then try writing a brief plot outline for the work to be sure that you have a clear sense of the chronology. You might also list key characters and their relationships to each other.

Finally, review your marginal notes, outline, and lists to determine what aspects of the work interested you most. Try freewriting at your computer or in your journal for ten minutes (see 3c-2), recalling your overall impressions and any important points you may have overlooked earlier.

2   Determining purpose, audience, and persona

Once you have completed your critical reading, establish a rhetorical stance for your paper (see 3b-2). In determining your rhetorical stance, you will make decisions about your purpose for writing, your persona, and your intended audience. If you are writing to complete an assignment, begin by carefully studying the assignment itself.

To decide on your purpose for writing, look for key terms in the assignment, such as *analyze* or *discuss.* Both of these terms imply an interpretive or analytical purpose for writing (see 27a-3). Your instructor may have specified some aspect of the work that you should write about, or he or she may have left the topic open-ended. In most cases, your instructor will expect you to write a piece with an argumentative edge that makes a point about the work and supports that point with examples and illustrations from the text. Examples of some typical assignments follow.

Writing Assignments Calling for Interpretation

- Discuss the key ideas or themes that the author of the poem "One Art" is trying to convey. Connect the poem to your own experiences of loss.

- Explain how the setting of *Regeneration* affects its major themes.

Writing Assignments Calling for Character Analysis

- Analyze the relationship between Cathy and Adam Trask in *East of Eden*.
- Explore the character of Lady Macbeth in the play *Macbeth*.

General Assignments That Allow the Writer to Decide the Purpose

- Discuss in depth some aspect of one of the novels we read this term.
- Explain how one of the authors we read this term uses imagery.

Next, think about your persona for the paper. How do you wish to come across as a writer? Will you be objective and fair or heated and passionate? Your persona is revealed in the paper through the words and sentence structures you choose (see 32g, 32h).

Finally, ask yourself who the audience for the paper will be. Most often the audience, in addition to your instructor, will be intelligent readers who are interested in literature but who may not be acquainted with the particular text you are writing about. Your paper should provide your readers with background information about the text so that they will be able to follow your argument.

3 Developing a claim and writing a thesis

How you interpret or analyze a work of literature will depend on what you have read, your interests, your prior knowledge, the information presented in class, and your general understanding of the work in question. If you have a choice, write about something that interests or intrigues you about the work. You will need to come up with your own critical interpretation or analysis of the work and then write a thesis statement that articulates your claim (see 3e-1 to 3e-3).

Literary works are typically analyzed with respect to some major aspect such as characters or plot. Following are various questions you can use in arriving at a thesis related to one of the major aspects of literary works. The list does not cover every possible topic, but it should help you get started.

Characters (major actors)

- How convincing are the characters?

- Does a particular character's behavior seem consistent throughout the work?
- Does the author reveal the narrator's thoughts?

Plot (what happens)

- How effective is the plot?
- Does it hold your interest and build to an effective climax?
- Does the plot line seem well connected or is it disjointed and hard to follow? What difference might this make to an interpretation of the work?

Theme (major idea or main message)

- What is the overall theme or point that the work is trying to make?
- Is the point one that you agree with?
- Does the author convince you that the point is well taken?
- Is the theme used consistently throughout the work or are there contradictions?

Structure (organization)

- What is the structure, or overall design, of the text itself?
- Does it skip around chronologically or geographically?
- Does one chapter lead logically to the next?
- What is the author trying to accomplish with the particular structure he or she chose?

Setting (where and when the events take place)

- How has the author used setting?
- Are descriptions of people and places particularly vivid?
- Did you feel as though you were in the place being described?
- How well did the author recreate a sense of place?

Point of View (perspective of whoever presents the ideas)

- What is the point of view adopted by the writer?
- Who is the narrator?
- Did the narrator influence the way you reacted to the work?
- Does the point of view remain consistent?

Rhythm (meter or beat) and Rhyme (correspondence in the sounds of words)

- Are there striking rhythmic patterns or rhyme schemes?
- What is the impact of the work's language?

Imagery (visual impressions created) and Figures of Speech (metaphors and similes)

- Did the author use imagery and figures of speech effectively?
- Is a particular image repeated throughout the work?

Symbolism (use of familiar ideas to represent something else) and Archetypes (traditional models after which others are patterned)

- How have symbols and archetypes been used in the work?
- Does the author repeat a certain key symbol? To what purpose?
- Is there a mythical archetype at work? How effective is it?

Style (writer's choice of words or sentence structures)

- Does the writer characteristically choose certain words or sentence structures?
- Does the language tend to be simple and direct or ornate and formal?

Tone and Voice (persona of the author as reflected through word choice and style)

- What tone or voice has the writer adopted?
- Is the tone appropriate to the theme? To the characters?
- How does the writer's tone affect you as a reader?

4 Using the appropriate person and tense

In writing interpretively about literature, it is generally appropriate to use the first person (*I, we, our*) to express your own point of view: "*I* was greatly moved by the character's predicament." However, in academic papers, the third person (*he, she, it, they*) is typically used to discuss information found in sources.

Also, in writing about a work of literature, the commonly accepted practice is to use the present tense (sometimes called the *literary present*) when describing events that happened in the work: "Adam Trask *learns* about his wife's true character slowly." Similarly, use the present tense when discussing what an author has done in a specific literary work: "Steinbeck *uses* Cathy and Adam Trask to illustrate his point about the pure evil that *exists* in human nature."

5 Writing your literature paper

WEBLINK

http://subject.lib.umn
.edu/hum/writinglit.html
*Writing About Literature:
A Guide to Research,* from
the University of Minnesota
libraries

Once you have articulated a thesis, you can proceed to write your paper, following the advice in Part 1 of this handbook. In particular, you may wish to review the stages of the writing process (see 3a). If your assignment specifies that you support your thesis through research, follow the advice in Part 2 of this handbook on researching your topic. In particular, review Chapter 8 on the research project.

AUDIO

Introduction to
student papers.

17c Review some model student papers

Let us now look at how two students approached the task of writing about literature, one to produce a literary interpretation and the other to produce a literary analysis.

1 An example of literary interpretation

www

17.4

Another model
student paper.

In a first-year course on understanding literature, students were asked to interpret the poem "One Art" and discuss the impact of its major theme—loss. Wayne Proffitt began his task by rereading the poem, circling and annotating words relating to its major theme (see Figure 17.1). He then listed those items he had highlighted in outline form. For his rhetorical stance, he decided on an interpretive purpose, an objective persona, and a novice audience. Next, Wayne wrote his working thesis, which articulated the claim he would make in his paper: "Bishop wrote a poem specifically about loss and accepting it." This thesis makes an interpretive claim about the meaning of the poem. Wayne then went on to write the paper, using the poem itself as his source as he explained and justified his claim.

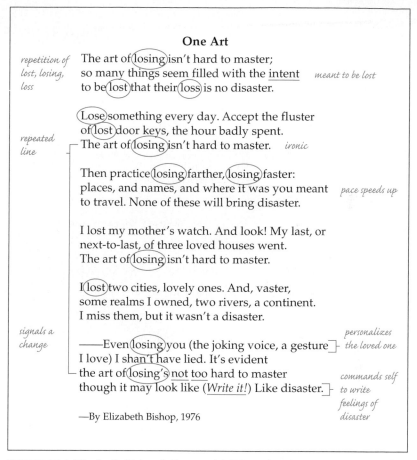

One Art

repetition of
lost, losing,
loss

The art of losing isn't hard to master;
so many things seem filled with the intent   *meant to be lost*
to be lost that their loss is no disaster.

Lose something every day. Accept the fluster
of lost door keys, the hour badly spent.

repeated
line

The art of losing isn't hard to master.   *ironic*

Then practice losing farther, losing faster:
places, and names, and where it was you meant   *pace speeds up*
to travel. None of these will bring disaster.

I lost my mother's watch. And look! My last, or
next-to-last, of three loved houses went.
The art of losing isn't hard to master.

I lost two cities, lovely ones. And, vaster,
some realms I owned, two rivers, a continent.
I miss them, but it wasn't a disaster.

signals a
change

personalizes
——Even losing you (the joking voice, a gesture   *the loved one*
I love) I shan't have lied. It's evident
the art of losing's not too hard to master   *commands self*
though it may look like (*Write it!*) Like disaster.   *to write*
feelings of
disaster

—By Elizabeth Bishop, 1976

FIGURE 17.1 Elizabeth Bishop's Poem with Wayne's Interpretive Annotations

No title page. For a model with
a title page, see Chapter 12.

| Last name
and page
number in
upper right-
hand corner

Student and
course
number

Wayne Proffitt

Professor Miller

English 1116-03

Double-
spaced

15 May 2004

Emotional Distance and Loss in a Poem

by Elizabeth Bishop

Internet
source

Thesis

Elizabeth Bishop (1911-1979) has only recently
been recognized as one of the greatest poets of the
twentieth century (Burt). Bishop wrote a poem
specifically about loss and accepting it. She offers
her knowledge with humor and a casual air in "One
Art." It seems that this poem may be autobiographical,
as it describes not only things that people in general
tend to lose but also specific items that the poet
herself has lost during her lifetime. The reader is
led through a list of lost objects that the speaker

Words of the
author in
quotation
marks

claims were meant to be lost. "So many things seem
filled with the intent" that when they finally do get
lost it "is no disaster." The reader is advised--in a
casual way--to get used to losing things and to
practice getting better at letting go. The ironic
encouragement of "the art of losing isn't hard to
master" helps make clear the speaker's real emotions
and attitudes toward losing.

Interpreta-
tion of the
change in
voice

The humorous and casual voice of the speaker
becomes quite forced toward the end of the poem,

Proffitt 2

however, and readers suspect that the loss of her loved one was not really one that could be shrugged off. It is almost as if the speaker is trying to gear herself up for the final loss by convincing herself that there is nothing she cannot handle losing. With this armor in place, she attempts to deal with the grief of losing one well loved, but finds that in the end she cannot hold her nonchalance and indifference steadily enough. At this point, perhaps both the speaker and the reader suddenly feel the art of losing for what it really is--an inevitable task--and

Interpretation of the meaning of loss in the poem

that it can truly be "disaster" for the one who has lost. The remembered "joking voice, a gesture I love" bring a real beloved person into the poem and emphasize the enormity of the loss. The speaker has difficulty completing the closing sentence and must goad herself to "write it" and be done.

Emotional impact of the poem

The ability to create such distance between the speaker and the object being discussed increases the impact of the submerged emotion when it is finally allowed to surface. The very distance of this poem's opening stanzas is one of the reasons that the emotional loss at the end of the poem contains so much power. Personal suffering and loss is not openly exposed in this poem, and because of this, careful reading is necessary to see past the

Proffitt 3

distance crafted into the poem. The effort of seeing
more than is directly stated contributes to the
reader's eventual understanding and even sharing of
the sense of loss.

Proffitt 4

Works Cited

Print source

Bishop, Elizabeth. "One Art." <u>The Complete Poems
1927-1979 by Elizabeth Bishop</u>. New York:
Farrar, 1983. 215.

Internet
source

Burt, Steve. "Elizabeth Bishop's 'One Art': A
Review." <u>The Harvard Advocate</u> 1998. 20 Apr.
1998 <http://hcs.harvard.edu/~advocate/
main.html>.

2 An example of literary analysis in MLA format

For a sophomore-level course on the British novel, students were asked to analyze a significant theme in one of the novels they read for the course. Heidi Blankley decided to write about the novel *Regeneration*. She was fascinated by the theme of gender stereotypes, which had been discussed in class and also in a conversation she had with her professor during office hours. She found the theme compelling, especially in light of her own interest in the changing roles of men and women in contemporary society. Her essay illustrates literary analysis—an analytical argument about a work of literature.

> ### WEBLINK
> http://start.at/
> literarycriticism
> An extensive collection of links to literary criticism sites on the Internet

17.5
How to search literary criticism sites on the Internet.

In her first two sentences, she articulates her critical stance. Notice how she begins with a quotation stating the general topic of the book (the treatment of shell-shock victims after World War I), followed by her own claim that the book is even more profoundly about the theme of gender stereotypes. This claim, or thesis, provides the reader with a clear understanding of the analysis Heidi plans to make in her paper. As the writer, she must prove to her readers, using examples from the text, that the novel *does* explore the theme of gender stereotyping.

The paper exemplifies the MLA documentation and formatting conventions (see Chapter 13). The list of works cited shows that Heidi read secondary sources about the novel and used information from her class, from a journal article, from a book, and from the Internet as support for her essay.

Writer's last
name and
page number
appear on
every page

Student,
professor,
and course
identifica-
tion

Heidi Blankley

Professor Kristine Miller

British Novel

2 April 2000

Internet
source

In MLA
style, source
citations
typically
include the
author and
the page
number,
with no
comma

Thesis

Ending the Violence

Pat Barker, a contemporary British author and
winner of the prestigious Booker Prize, writes
novels about England during the war years
(Middlemiss). In <u>Regeneration</u>, Pat Barker "examines
the treatment of shell-shock victims at Edinburgh's
Craiglockhart hospital during World War I"
(Perry 44). Although Barker's novel is mainly about
the acculturation of shell-shock victims from World
War I, it is more concerned with the larger issue
that lurks behind the battle scenes: gender
stereotypes. Barker suggests that the violence
created by adhering to the masculine stereotype--
that men are brave warriors and not nurturers--is
not merely a social problem, but a mythical,
psychological obstacle, the effects of which are
seeping into all facets of life. If humans are ever
to recover from the violence, Barker thinks we must
analyze the root of the violence and come to terms
with our destructive behavior toward the
environment, other species, and one another.

Blankley 2

First example of coming to terms with violence

In chapter 4, a relatively bizarre scene occurs which forces the patient, David Burns, to realize he can exert influence on the violence surrounding him. Burns boards a bus that takes him away from the hospital at Craiglockhart into the countryside. There he comes into contact with a tree that reeks of death, "The tree he stood under was laden with animals. Bore them like fruit" (Barker 38). Burns's first impulse is to give in to fear and run from the grotesque tree, but Barker has a different plan in mind for Burns. Instead, Burns faces his fear head-on and unties the animals:

Long quotation from the novel is indented

10 spaces → When all the corpses were on the ground, he arranged them in a circle round the tree and sat down within it, his back against the trunk. He felt the roughness of the bark against his knobby spine. He pressed his hands between his knees and looked around the circle of his companions. Now they could dissolve into the earth as they were meant to

Punctuation precedes the citation for indented quotations only

do. (Barker 39)

This scene is so strange and so grotesque that it forces the reader to question Barker's motives for including it. The scene Burns stumbled upon becomes a reflection of the war; the animals

Blankley 3

represent the hundreds of decaying soldiers. The
inhumane hanging of the animals suggests that the
soldiers are dying for an inhumane and unnatural
purpose. Just as this scene is unnatural in its
placement of the animals, so are the massive murders
involved with the war (Miller).

Furthermore, the circle Burns makes with the
decaying animals resembles the cyclical pattern of
history; humanity has spawned war after war,
apparently without learning anything from its own
violence. As the creator of the circle and also the
one who sits within it, Burns recognizes that he is
both a physical perpetrator of violence and a
psychological victim of it. He copes with this
paradoxical situation simply by revising gender
stereotypes. As he steps into the circle and returns
the animals to the earth, he takes on the qualities
of a nurturer, a role contradictory to the masculine
stereotype. However, although Burns might wish to
remove himself from the situation, from his
contributions to the war and violence in general, he
is still a part of it, the "white root" of it
(Barker 39).

What Barker is trying to accomplish with this
scene is to show that no matter what gender, we are
a part of the recurring historical pattern of

The example
is related to
the theme
of gender
stereotypes

Critical
analysis of
the scene
described

Blankley 4

violence, whether it is toward humans or other creatures. The only way to get out of the circle, as Burns does later in his dream about the scene he had witnessed, is to see ourselves inside the circle: "He folded his arms across his face and . . . began drifting off to sleep. He was back in the wood, outside the circle now, but able to see himself inside it" (Barker 40).

Another character, Rivers, also displays his sensitivity to the destruction around him. Rivers, modeled after a real-life doctor, is shown by Barker to be a humane and sensitive man (Perry 44). In chapter 13, a bumblebee is trapped inside a room where Craiglockhart officials are holding a meeting. Rivers is unable to concentrate on the meeting and keeps scanning the windows, trying to find the bee because "the noise was unreasonably disturbing" (Barker 132). When he finally finds the insect, he "fetch[es] a file from the desk and, using it as a barrier, guide[s] the insect into the open air" (Barker 132). When he turns back into the room, he finds "everybody, Burns included, staring at him in some surprise" (Barker 132-33); judging from this reaction, we can assume that Rivers's response to the bee is an abnormal one. Perhaps the others in the room were unaware of the bee's presence,

Second example of coming to terms with violence

Brackets show letters changed from the original to fit the sentence

Blankley 5

or if they were aware, maybe they would have acted like "bloodthirsty little horrors" (Barker 172), smacking the bee with the file instead of rescuing it.

The second example is related to the theme of gender stereotypes

Through his action, Rivers transcends the masculine stereotype, which is why his action is met by surprise from the other men. The release of the bee might simply be symbolic of Rivers's escape from Craiglockhart--for at the end of this chapter, he takes some time off for sick leave. But this connection seems too obvious. Barker is once more forcing the reader to question gender stereotypes. By releasing the bee instead of smashing it, Rivers becomes Barker's ideal human. He is a man with the capacity to nurture not only other men but nature as well. In this instance, he represents the balance, a human being acting on natural instinct to save another creature, without questioning his own motives.

The myth of regeneration is related to the theme of violence

Throughout her novel, Barker plays with the myth of regeneration. Typically (in American mythology), the myth of regeneration involves a male character who seeks to escape the bonds of his old life. To do so, he retires from civilization into the purity of wilderness and, after a while, is reborn a newer, wiser man who is more in tune with himself and his surroundings. Although the wilderness in <u>Regeneration</u> is civilized, Burns and Rivers try to use the wilderness in the same way. Burns returns to his native home in Suffolk hoping to recuperate from the psychological trauma he experienced in the war. Burns invites Rivers to join him there, hoping Suffolk will have the same invigorating effect on Rivers.

The theme of violence is analyzed

Barker's idea of regeneration appears to apply to violence in general, to the war, and to gender roles. Early in the novel, Rivers has an insightful revelation about gender roles:

Ellipses indicate omissions

> He distrusted the implication that nurturing, even when done by a man, remains female, as if the ability were in some way borrowed, or even stolen from women--. . . . If that were true, then there was really very little hope. (Barker 107)

The two themes of violence and gender stereotypes are connected

If women are the only ones who can be considered nurturers, if men are permanently locked into the role of brave warriors, and if neither females nor males have the capacity to extend the boundaries of these roles, then there is little hope that the psychological trauma of war can be overcome. There is also little hope that the cycle of violence will

Blankley 7

ever cease, because the masculine gender stereotype depends on war and violence for the man to prove himself as a brave warrior, while the female stereotype depends on wounded soldiers to nurture. The result of clinging to these stereotypes is a perpetual cycle of violence that extends past the war and into the physical qualities of the environment. If the stereotypes are left unquestioned, the cycle of violence will continue, and neither men nor women will be able to recover from the violence.

The use of metaphor is analyzed

However, in chapter 15, Barker illustrates a remedy for the destructive cycle of violence with a brilliant metaphor:

> Rivers knew only too well how often the early stages of change or cure may mimic deterioration. Cut a chrysalis open, and you will find a rotting caterpillar. What you will never find is that mythical creature, half caterpillar, half butterfly, a fit emblem of the human soul, . . . No, the process of transformation consists almost entirely of decay. (Barker 184)

Barker reveals that the only way to abolish war and all the violent behavior equivalent to war is to internalize those traits which are perceived as

Blankley 8

inherently masculine and inherently feminine--to
view the soul as a combination of butterfly and
caterpillar, enclosed in the delicate chrysalis of
the earth. War is a transition period, a devastating
event which can lead to the positive transformation
of social roles, if we let it.

Introduces the quotation with the author's name in a signal phrase

In her article on women's fiction, Pykett
suggests that "Pat Barker, like a number of other
recent women writers, does not interrogate or
deconstruct history . . . but rather she seeks to
recover and reclaim the past on behalf of those who
have been silenced and marginalized by history"

Conclusion returns to thesis idea

(75). In this novel, the shell-shock victims are
those who have historically been silenced. Barker
gives them a voice in <u>Regeneration</u>. Through them,
she suggests that it is possible to heal society if
we cease adhering to the stereotypical male and
female gender roles. What we need in order to solve
the trauma of war and to prevent future violence are
not heroes or warriors, but a reconsideration of
gender, a restructuring of the rules so that men may
reveal their "feminine" sensitivity without being
typecast as effeminate, homosexual, or motherly.

Blankley 9

Works Cited

MLA citation style

Novel
|
Barker, Pat. <u>Regeneration</u>. New York: Plume, 1993.

Internet
source
Middlemiss, Perry. Homepage. 1 Jan. 1997. 15 May

|
2000 <http://ncc1701.apana.org.au/~/arrikin/

lit/prizes/booker.html>.

Class notes
and
interview
Miller, Kristine. Class notes and personal

|
interview. 10 May 2000.

Nonfiction
book
Perry, Donna. <u>Backtalk: Women Writers Speak Out</u>. New

Book title is
underlined

|
Brunswick, NJ: Rutgers UP, 1993.

Journal
Pykett, Lyn. "The Century's Daughters: Recent

Second line
is indented

Initial
capitals are
used in
article titles,
which are
also put in
quotation
marks
Women's Fiction and History." <u>Critical</u>

<u>Quarterly</u> 29.3 (1987): 71-77.

Journal
name is
underlined

17d Look to the Internet and the library for resources

Scholars in the humanities are beginning to use technology in their research and their writing. Students of the humanities, too, should familiarize themselves with available resources, particularly those in library databases and the Internet. (Chapter 9 discusses the types of library and Internet resources and how to locate and evaluate them.) Take a look at some of the Internet sources in the following list, such as the *Project Gutenberg* Web site, which contains numerous full texts of important works of literature, or the *Ancient World* Web site, which has links to sites on classical languages and literature. There are also numerous discussion groups, bulletin boards, and newsgroups related to the humanities. You can find these discussion sites through an Internet search (see Chapter 24 for information on using computer networks).

17.6
Major web links for the humanities.

Resources for the Humanities

Art and Architecture

Dictionaries

Dictionary of Contemporary American Artists. 5th ed. Cumming, P. New York: St. Martin's, 1988. Concise information on living American artists.

Dictionary of Architecture. Meikleham, R. New York: Gordon, 1980. 3 vols. General information.

Indexes and Abstracts

Art Abstracts

Art Index

Web Sites

The Center for Creative Photography <http://dizzy.library.arizona.edu/branches/ccp>

The Parthenet <http://www.mtholyoke.edu/~klconner/parthenet.html>

World Wide Arts Resources <http://www.world-arts resources.com>

English Literature and Language

Dictionaries and Encyclopedias

Dictionary of Literature in the English Language. Meyers, R. New York: Pergamon, 1978. 2 vols. Useful background information on classic English literary works.

Princeton Encyclopedia of Poetry and Poetics. 3rd ed. Preminger, A., and T. V. Brogan, eds. Princeton: Princeton UP, 1993. Concise information on poetry and poetics through time; covers history, theory, technique, and criticism of poetry.

Indexes and Abstracts

MLA International Bibliography

Wilson Biographies (full text)

Literary Index

Web Sites

English Server—Iowa State University <http://www.eserver.org>

Literary Resources on the Net <http://andromeda.rutgers.edu/ ~jlynch/Lit>

Project Bartleby <http://www.bartleby.com>

Project Gutenberg <http://www.gutenberg.net/index.shtml>

Voice of the Shuttle: English Literature <http://vos.ucsb.edu>

History and Classics

Dictionaries and Encyclopedias

Encyclopedic Dictionary of American History. 4th ed. Faragher, J. M., ed. Guilford: Dushkin, 1991. Complete background information on American history.

Encyclopedia of American History. 7th ed. Morris, R. B., and Morris, J. B., eds. New York: Harper, 1996. Valuable overview of American history; contains brief biographies of famous Americans.

Encyclopedia of World History: Ancient, Medieval, and Modern. Langer, W. L., ed. Boston: Market House, 1999. Major world events from earliest times to the 1990s. (The *New Illustrated Encyclopedia of World History* is essentially the same work with illustrations.)

Indexes and Abstracts

Historical Abstracts
America: History and Life

Web Sites

Nineteenth Century Scientific American <http://
  www.history.rochester.edu/Scientific_American>
Ancient World Web <http://www.julen.net/ancient>
Perseus Project <http://www.perseus.tufts.edu>

Music

Dictionaries

Dictionary of Composers and Their Music. Gilder, E. New York:
  Random, 1993. Useful background information.
The New Grove Dictionary of Music and Musicians. Sadie, S., ed.
  London: Groves Dictionaries, 1998. 20 vols. Information on
  musical topics from ancient to modern times.

Indexes and Abstracts

International Index to Music Periodicals
RILM Abstracts of Music Literature
Music Index

Web Sites

Music Education Links <http://www.music.indiana.edu/
  music_resources/mused.html>
Music Link: Music on the Internet <http://www.lib.utk.edu/
  ~music>

Philosophy

Encyclopedias

Encyclopedia of Philosophy. Edwards, P., ed. New York: Macmillan,
  1973. 4 vols. Complete reference work on both Eastern and
  Western philosophical thought.
Encyclopedia of Bioethics. 2nd ed. Reich, W. T., ed. New York:
  Macmillan, 1995. Information on philosophy and religion.

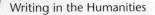

Index

Philosopher's Index

Web Sites

The American Philosophical Association <http://
www.apa.udel.edu/apa/index.html>
Handilinks to Philosophy <http://www.handilinks.com>

Religion

Dictionaries and Encyclopedias

Dictionary of Comparative Religions. Brandon, S. G., ed. New York:
Scribner's, 1978. Information on world religions.
Encyclopedia of Religion. Eliade, M., ed. New York: Macmillan,
1993. 14 vols. Concise articles on world religions.

Indexes and Abstracts

Religion One Index
Religious and Theological Abstracts

Web Site

Comparative Religion <http://www.academicinfo.net/
religindex.html>

Theater and Film

Indexes and Abstracts

New York Times Theater Reviews
Play Index
Film Literature Index
International Index to Film Periodicals

Web Site

The Theatre Links Page <http://www.theatre-link.com>

(EXERCISE 17.1)

Investigate the Internet resources available for one of the disciplines
within the humanities. Search by topic for a newsgroup or a bulletin
board (see 24b-2).

FOR COLLABORATION

Bring to class a printout of a Web site that you found in your disciplinary Internet search. Share the information with a small group of your peers. What kinds of resources are available for the disciplines within the humanities?

CHAPTER 18

Writing in the Natural Sciences

FAQs

▶ What kinds of writing assignments can I expect in science courses? (18a)

▶ What makes scientific writing different from other kinds of writing? (18b)

▶ Should I use headings in a scientific report? (18c)

▶ How can I find information in the library or on the Internet for a science research paper? (18d)

AUDIO
Chapter overview.

WWW

18.1

Closeup view of the NAS home page.

The natural sciences hold an authoritative position in society and thus are a dominant force in our lives. Using a widely accepted methodology, scientists formulate and test theories about the natural and physical world, and their findings are used to solve problems in medicine, industry, and agriculture. Typically, the natural sciences are classified into two categories: pure and applied. The pure sciences include the life sciences (such as biology and botany), the physical sciences (such as mathematics, physics, and chemistry), and the earth sciences (such as geology and geography). The applied sciences include the medical sciences (such as forensics, pathology, surgery, and ophthalmology), engineering (mechanical, environmental, aerospace, civil, and electrical), and computer science.

> **WEBLINK**
>
> http://www.nas.edu
> Homepage of the National Academy of Sciences

18a Know the different types of writing in the natural sciences

18.2
The inquiry process in science and technology.

To solve problems in a systematic way, scientists use the scientific method. Writing plays a critical role in each step of the scientific method. The first step is to express the problem in writing, clearly and objectively, in the form of a statement, usually called a *problem statement*. The second step is to gather all relevant information needed to solve the problem, including information found in library sources such as books and journals. The third step is to analyze that information and formulate a hypothesis. A *hypothesis* is a statement that predicts what the scientist expects to find by conducting controlled experiments related to the problem under investigation. The fourth step is to design and conduct controlled experiments to test the hypothesis. The scientist must keep a detailed record of each experiment and its outcome. The fifth step is to analyze these records to determine how well they support the hypothesis or predicted results. Finally, the sixth step is to restate the hypothesis as a conclusion that explains how the experimental data supported, refuted, or modified the initial hypothesis. Whether you are writing up your own work in the form of a research report or summarizing and evaluating other people's work in the form of a review of literature, you need to be familiar with the scientific method.

1 Research report

AUDIO
The difference between primary research reports and reviews of literature.

The majority of scientific writing is in the form of research reports, which are found in all branches of the sciences and technology. Research reports are based on primary research conducted by scientists. The motivation for much primary research in the natural sciences is an event or experience that challenges existing ideas and promotes inquiry. In general, the aim is to improve the congruency between theories and concepts about the world and actual experiences or experimental results.

It is through primary research that great breakthroughs in the advancement of knowledge occur, and it is through research reports that these developments are announced to the scientific community. One famous example of primary research is the studies conducted by the English biologist Sir Alexander Fleming. When he noticed that one of his cultures of *Staphylococcus* bacteria had been contaminated by a microorganism from the air outside, Fleming examined the contaminated plate in detail and noticed a surprising phenomenon: where the colonies of bacteria had been attacked by microscopic fungi, a large region had become transparent. Fleming hypothesized that the effect could be due to an antibacterial substance secreted by the foreign microorganism and then spread into the culture. Fortunately, Fleming proceeded to research the phenomenon at length, and the secretion turned out to be a variety of the fungus *Penicillium,* from which the antibiotic penicillin is now made.

Whether a research report announces the discovery of penicillin or the results of a student lab experiment, the basic outline is the same, as it parallels the steps in the scientific method. The standard format used to report scientific findings is as follows:

- *Abstract,* which summarizes the report in one compact paragraph
- *Introduction,* which states the problem, background information, and the hypothesis
- *Literature review,* which summarizes related research
- *Research methods,* which outlines the processes used in the experiments
- *Research results,* which describes the outcomes and findings of the experiments
- *Discussion and conclusion,* which relates the research back to the problem and hypothesis and speculates on the implications of the research
- *Endmatter,* which may include notes, references, and appendixes

VIDEO
Key elements
of a scientific
report.

Individual scientists use many variations on this standard format, depending on the audience they are addressing. Less formal reports may not include an abstract or a literature review, for example. An abbreviated version of the research report may serve as a laboratory report or a progress report.

2 Review of literature

WWW

18.3
Writing
exercises for
students in
science and
engineering.

WEBLINK

http://filebox.vt.edu/eng/mech/writing

An excellent writing workbook for students of science and engineering

The second major category of scientific writing is the review of literature. In this type of writing, based on secondary research, the writer discusses literature found in the library rather than his or her own original research. Only by analyzing and synthesizing the findings of other scientists, reported in journal articles and other relevant sources, can students, scholars, and researchers keep up on developments in their field.

A literature review may be a brief summary of the literature on a specific topic; it may be a lengthy critical review of a single work or an extended critical review of several works on the same topic. A literature review may even take the form of annotations—critical or explanatory notes added to another text.

18b   Write objectively about science

Because it is used to inform audiences about scientific findings and data, scientific writing needs to be objective, exact, and complete. In most cases, it describes scientific problems and their solutions.

As a student, when you are writing about the natural sciences, generally you are responding to an assignment. The assignment may specify whether you are to write a research report or a review of literature. If it does not, you are probably better off reviewing the literature on a particular topic, unless you are already involved in a scientific experiment. If the assignment calls for primary research, you will probably need your instructor's help in designing an appropriate method for collecting data. (For information on how to report your research, see 18a-1.)

18.4
Primary research in the natural sciences.

If your instructor has not assigned a particular topic, you can turn to the media—television, radio, magazines, and the Internet—for ideas. Look for controversies or new discoveries in the natural sciences and begin to ask questions about them. For example, a television documentary on some of the newest findings about the planet Mars might lead you to wonder if there really is evidence of life on Mars. What exactly did the scientists working on the Pathfinder mission discover?

1   Determining purpose and audience

Once you have a topic, you can establish a rhetorical stance (see 3b-2). To decide on your purpose for writing, begin by carefully studying the assignment itself. Look for key terms, such as *analyze* or *discuss*. Both of these terms imply an interpretive or critical purpose for writing. Your instructor will expect you to write a piece that makes a point, supported by secondary sources.

Next, ask yourself who your audience will be. Usually you can assume that you are writing for intelligent readers who are interested in the subject but may not know many details about the topic. You should provide enough background information so that such readers will be able to follow your argument. (Because of the focus on objectivity, the writer's persona is less of an issue in scientific writing.)

2 Writing a thesis

To write a thesis, you need to refine your topic. For example, if you decided to write about life on Mars, you could use print sources and the Internet to find out more about the Pathfinder mission and then write an informative thesis describing what you found out. If your instructor wanted your report to have an argumentative edge, your thesis could argue for or against the claim that life exists on Mars (see 3e-1 to 3e-3).

3 Completing the research and writing your paper

In any writing assignment, regardless of the discipline for which you are writing, you should follow the writing process described in Part 1 of this handbook. Refer to Chapters 3–5 for advice on prewriting, drafting, revising, and editing. If your paper consists of or includes a literature review, refer to Part 2 of this handbook for information on library research. See the list of reference materials commonly used in the sciences, including Internet resources (18d).

4 Using visuals

In the natural sciences, visuals such as graphs, charts, and diagrams are often used to convey information and statistical data in a compact format. As an apprentice science writer, you will need to learn the customary ways in which statistical data are presented in your field. Notice how the table included by the engineering students in their report on domestic water supply (page 445) manages to capture in a succinct and readable fashion the weighted selection criteria for water supply alternatives. Refer to 20c for more information about using graphics and visuals in your writing.

18c An example of a research report in CBE format

In a sophomore-level engineering course, the students worked with their peers on a primary research project. Following is a report produced by one group of four students. Notice how the students' report begins with a cover memorandum, which includes an executive summary outlining the study and its recommendations. Then, in the body of the report, the students describe their own research, which was designed to determine the method that would best solve the water shortages anticipated in a neighboring community.

The report illustrates an adapted scientific report format. It begins with a cover memo to introduce the problem and proposed solutions. The cover memo also serves as an abstract. Next comes a title page. The sections have headings that parallel the research itself. However, not all of the sections typically found in a research report are included. The students did not include a formal literature review, choosing instead to integrate references within the body of the report. They followed the CBE citation style (see 15b), electing to use the name-year system rather than the number system. Notice that the sections of the report are numbered; this practice is common in scientific and engineering reports, as it helps readers find relevant information quickly and easily.

18.5
Additional
model student
papers in the
sciences.

AUDIO
Reports in the
natural sciences.

Cover memo

TO: Brent Adams, CEE Professor

FROM: Group 4: David Hunter, Carl Jones, Lee Duong,
Rhonda Peterson

SUBJECT: RECOMMENDATION FOR CHOOSING AN ALTERNATIVE
WATER SOURCE/SYSTEM

REF.: Your letter of request, September 10, 2003

DATE: January 5, 2004

DIST.: Sonia Manuel-Dupont, Project Supervisor

Smithfield City will not have an adequate supply of
culinary water in the future. Their current supply
is adequate for only another 5 years (Gass 1996). We
were asked by you to research and derive a solution
for this problem. After discussing as a group the
various alternatives that could be implemented, we
decided on four alternatives that would be the most
effective. Each of us in the group researched
articles and conducted personal interviews to
determine the most appropriate solution. From our
findings we have gathered that the most effective
alternative is installing a new well that will have
enough supply to meet future demand.

Executive
summary
used in place
of abstract

Executive Summary

The population of Smithfield City is growing
rapidly. The current water supply for Smithfield is
not adequate to meet the needs of the city over the

next 25 years. We need to find a source to provide
an additional 70 million gallons of water per month
to Smithfield City in order to have an adequate
water supply for the next 25 years. We have
researched the problem in scientific journals and
books and have spoken with the Smithfield City
Engineer and also others who deal directly with
water supply.

Our purpose of communication is to inform you
of our 4 researched alternatives: (1) development of
a new well, (2) no action, (3) installation of a
dual system, and (4) water reuse. Only the
development of a new well will supply enough water
for Smithfield City over the next 25 years.
Development of a new well was ranked best on cost,
feasibility, and adequacy, and average on
maintenance and impact on the environment.
Therefore, we recommend the development of a new
well to provide the necessary water for Smithfield
City.

Title page

Recommendation for Installing
a Well for Smithfield City

To:

Brent Adams

CEE 361 Professor

From:

Group 4

Dist:

Dr. Sonia Manuel-Dupont

Project Supervisor

January 5, 2004

Sections numbered per CBE and CMS multiple-numeration system

1.0 Introduction and Problem Statement

The City of Smithfield currently receives most of its culinary water from springs in Smithfield Canyon. There are 8 springs near the top of the canyon and 3 springs located further down the canyon. These springs produce an estimated flow rate that varies seasonally from 1800 gallons per minute in the spring to 1100 gallons per minute in the winter (Gass 1996). In addition to the springs, Smithfield has a secondary water supply provided by a 12 inch diameter, 40-foot-deep well located at Forrester Acres, west of the city. Water is pumped from this well during 3 or 4 months out of the year, only as a secondary water source to provide for residential summer irrigation. This well was recently modified to be able to supply up to 1500 gallons per minute but rarely runs at such capacity (Forsgren 1995). With full use of the springs and supplementation from the well, a minimum of 77 million gallons of water per month can be supplied to Smithfield at all times.

The current water supply is enough to sustain the residents of Smithfield. However, the population of Smithfield City is growing rapidly; therefore, additional water must be found to supply the future

Introduction

Problem statement

Page number centered at the bottom of each page

residents of Smithfield. The population, as of now, is about 6800 people (Gass 1996). The average water use per service is 36,862 gallons per month. Our predictions show that 14,346 people will be living in Smithfield City by the year 2021 and the amount of water they use will average approximately 144.52 million gallons per month, assuming the amount of water use per service remains constant. Appendix B contains the equation used to predict the population growth and a yearly prediction of population for the next 25 years. Appendix C contains information on the current and projected water use.

The difference between the minimum current water supply for Smithfield (77 million gallons per month) and the predicted water use in 25 years (144.52 million gallons per month) is 67.52 million gallons per month. We used 70 million gallons per month as the amount of water that Smithfield needs to meet the water demand in the year 2021.

2.0 Four Proposed Alternative Solutions

Given the problem of finding an additional water supply, we researched Smithfield's current population and water supply to make predictions for the next 25 years. We also researched 4 different

First-level
heads
centered

Literature
review
included in
discussion of
proposed
solutions

alternatives to find out what would be the best
option to meet the expected demand. The alternatives
considered were (1) drill a new well, (2) take no
action, (3) implement a dual water irrigation
system, and (4) recycle graywater.

2.1 Drill a New Well

The 1st alternative is to drill a new well for
culinary water. This new well will be located on
the north end of the Smithfield City golf course.
There is a large protected aquifer in that area
(Gass 1996). The well will be about 400 feet deep,
and it will use a 16-inch-diameter pipe. After the
water leaves the well, it will pass through a
chlorine gas chlorinator. The chlorine mixes with
the water to disinfect it. Time is required for the
chlorine to treat the water, so the water will enter
an 18-inch pipe to slow down the velocity of the
water. The water will then travel 2500 feet to
connect with the existing water lines (Gass 1996).
The system will be run automatically. Monitors in
the storage tank and water lines will inform a
computer when the storage supply is low. The
computer will then activate the well to supplement
the water demand. When the storage water is
sufficiently recharged, the computer will shut down

3

Second-level heads flush left and underlined

Sources cited by author name and year, with no comma

the well, thus conserving energy and the water in the aquifer.

2.2 Take No Action

The 2nd alternative is that of no action. This means that Smithfield's water system would remain the same and run at present capacity.

2.3 Implement a Dual Water Irrigation System

The 3rd alternative that was considered is the implementation of a dual water irrigation system. A dual water system consists of 2 parts: (1) a culinary distribution system to provide potable water for residential use and (2) a distribution system to provide untreated, "raw" water for irrigation purposes (Vaughn 1995). Approximately 65 percent of the households in Smithfield are currently using some type of dual water irrigation system. Almost all of those using the current dual system are supplied water by Smithfield Irrigation Company (Gass 1996). Implementation of a dual system would consist of routing canals and irrigation lines to those residences that are not using dual water and also to any new homes in the city. Under this alternative, irrigation would be provided separately for everyone, and the strain on the culinary supply would be reduced.

2.4 Recycle Graywater

The 4th alternative that was considered is recycling graywater. Recycling graywater is a relatively inexpensive and effective way to reuse waste water. Greywater is defined as "untreated household wastewater which has not come into contact with toilet waste. Greywater includes used water from bathtubs, showers, bathroom wash basins, and water from clothes washing machines and laundry tubs. It shall not include wastewater from kitchen sinks or dishwashers" (Pope 1995, p 2). A schematic of graywater reuse for a typical residential home is listed in Appendix D, Figure D-1. After clear water has been used in a home, it becomes graywater. The water then goes through a settling and filtration process; it then can be reused in some areas of the home. Graywater is most suitably reused for subsurface irrigation such as that of nonedible landscape plants. This cuts down on the amount of culinary water used for lawn irrigation. All of the information (including values) given under this alternative is given under the assumption that, as with the dual system, only 35 percent of the present homes in Smithfield City would be affected by a graywater system. A graywater system will be useless

Direct quotation requires page number

5

to the people who receive irrigation water separately from their culinary supply. We assumed that the number of connections that currently use water from the canal irrigation system will remain relatively constant through the next 25 years.

3.0 Research Methods

3.1 Five Evaluative Criteria

Each of the alternatives we have described has been examined with respect to 5 criteria. The criteria we have selected, in order of significance, are (1) cost of implementation, (2) feasibility, (3) adequacy of supply, (4) maintenance required, and (5) impact on the environment. Table 1 shows the alternatives and the criteria. The alternatives are ranked on a scale from 0 to 2, 0 being the least favorable and 2 being the most favorable. The rankings are multiplied by a weighting factor of 1, 2, or 3, depending on the importance of the criterion involved. A description of our criteria is as follows:

1. Cost--The complete cost of installation and implementation of the alternative

2. Feasibility--The ease of implementation and whether it is allowable

6

3. Adequacy--Whether or not it will supply a
   sufficient amount of water
4. Maintenance--The person-hours and cost for
   upkeep
5. Impact on the Environment--How the alternative
   affects land usage and habitat

Table used to
report data

Table 1. Weighted Selection Criteria for Water
Supply Alternatives

			Alternatives		
Multiplier	Criterion	Well	No Action	Dual Water	Reuse
3	Cost	2	2	1	0
2	Feasibility	2	2	1	0
2	Adequacy	2	0	0	0
2	Maintenance	1	1	2	1
1	Environment	1	2	1	2
	TOTALS	17	14	10	4

Based on our findings and the rankings provided
by Table 1, our recommendation to Smithfield City is
to construct a new well to provide water for its
domestic supply.

In sections 3.2–3.5, students analyze the four alternatives in detail,
in light of their criteria.

7

4.0 Results and Discussion

With the increasing population, Smithfield City has concerns over water demand. Our research shows that with the increasing population, Smithfield will need to provide more water for its citizens. We developed alternatives to help Smithfield meet demands.

Statement of suggested solution to the problem

Given the 4 alternatives--groundwater well, no action, dual water system, and water reuse--we believe constructing a groundwater well is the best choice for the City of Smithfield. For a reasonable price, an efficient well can be built to meet the predicted needs of Smithfield with low maintenance and minimal impact to the environment. The well could carry Smithfield into the next century and beyond.

8

Appendix A

References

Burgess M, Distributor, Fairbanks Morse Pump Corp. 1996 Dec 3. [Personal communication].

Carter R. 1994. Trickle-down economy. Sierra 79: 18-19.——Page nos.   Title   Journal   Volume

[DWR] Division of Water Resources. 1992. State water plan--Bear River Basin executive summary [online]. Available from: www.nr.state.ut.us/WTRRESC/WTRRESC.htm. Accessed 1996 Nov 8.

[Forsgren] Forsgren Association, Inc. 1995. Computer simulation and master plan for domestic water system: prepared for the Smithfield City Corporation. Salt Lake City: Forsgren Assoc., Inc.

Gass J, Smithfield City Engineer. 1996 Nov 8. [Personal communication].

Gelt J. 1993. Home use of greywater: rainwater conserves water--and may save money [online]. Available from: www.ag.arizona.edu/AZWATER/arroyo/071.rain.html. Accessed 1996 Nov 8.

[IAPMO] International Association of Plumbing and Mechanical Officials. 1996. Uniform plumbing code. Los Angeles: Plumbing Assoc.

9

Pope T. 1995. Greywater, a recyclable resource
    [online]. Available from: www.waterstore.com/
    article1.html. Accessed 1996 Nov 8.

[Roscoe] Roscoe Moss Co. 1995. The engineers' manual
    for water well design. Los Angeles: Roscoe
    Moss Co.

Rowland P. Assistant City Engineer. 1996 Nov 17.
    [Personal communication].

[Vaughn] Vaughn Hansen Associates, in association
    with CH2M Hill and Water Research Laboratory,
    State University. 1995. Identification and
    assessment of certain water management options
    for the Wasatch Front: prepared for the State
    Division of Water Resources.

Wilding D, Water Department Head. 1996 Dec 2.
    [Personal communication].

In addition to Appendix A (References), students included the following appendixes:

Appendix B: Population Projections
Appendix C: Projection of Water Flow Rates
Appendix D: Schematic of Graywater Reuse System
Appendix E: Individual Cost of Water Well Construction
Appendix F: Discussion of Cost of Implementation of a
            Dual System
Appendix G: Calculations for Percentage of Water Use

18d Look to the Internet and the library for resources

Scientists were quick to see that technology could help them with their research and their writing. As a student of the natural sciences, you too should familiarize yourself with the available resources, particularly those in library databases and on the Internet. (Chapter 9 discusses the types of library databases and Internet resources and how to use them.) An extended listing of useful Internet sites for the natural sciences follows. Take a look, for example, at the *Discovery Channel* site, which has many links to general science information on the Internet. There are also numerous discussion groups, bulletin boards, and newsgroups related to the natural sciences. You can find these discussion sites through an Internet search (see Chapter 24 for information on using computer networks).

> **WEBLINK**
>
> http://fauxpress.com/kimball/w/logo.htm
> "Exercises in Science: A Writing Course"—a superb writing-for-the-sciences page, focusing on ESL

www

18.6

A closeup view of the writing-for-the-sciences Web site.

Resources for the Sciences and Technology

Biology and Animal Science

Dictionaries and Encyclopedias

Dictionary of Biology. 4th ed. Martin, E., ed. New York: Oxford UP, 2000.

The Encyclopedia of Bioethics. 2nd ed. Reich, W., ed. New York: Macmillan, 1995.

Indexes and Abstracts

Biological and Agricultural Index
Biological Abstracts

Web Sites

Biozone <http://www.biozone.co.nz/links.html>
American Society of Animal Science <http://www.asas.org>

Botany and Plant Genetics

Indexes and Abstracts

Botanical Abstracts
Genetics Abstracts
Plant Breeding Abstracts

Web Sites

Genetics <http://www.biology.arizona.edu/mendelian_genetics/mendelian_genetics.html>

Bio Online <http://bio.com/resedu>

Chemistry

Dictionaries, Encyclopedias, and Handbooks

Dictionary of Chemistry. Daintith, J., ed. New York: Oxford UP, 1996.

Handbook of Chemistry and Physics. 69th ed. Weast, R. C., ed. Cleveland: Chemical, 1990. Facts and data on chemistry and physics.

Indexes and Abstracts

Chemical Abstracts

Analytical Abstracts

Web Sites

American Chemical Society <http://www.chemistry.org>

The Learning Matters of Chemistry <http://www.knowledgebydesign.com>

Computers

Dictionaries and Encyclopedias

Dictionary of Computing. 4th ed. Illingworth, V., ed. New York: Oxford UP, 1997.

Encyclopedia of Computer Science. 4th ed. Ralston, A., ed. New York: Groves, 2000. Concise information in the fields of computer science and engineering.

Encyclopedia of Computer Science and Technology. Belzer, J., ed. New York: Dekker, 1997. 37 vols. Short articles on subjects in computer science.

Indexes and Abstracts

Computer Abstracts

Computer and Control Abstracts

Computing Reviews

Web Sites

Electronic Frontier Foundation <http://www.eff.org>

Internet Society <http://www.isoc.org>

Engineering

Encyclopedias

McGraw-Hill Encyclopedia of Engineering. 2nd ed. New York: McGraw, 1993. Short articles on all fields of engineering.

Indexes

Engineering Index (Eicomendex)
Electrical and Electronics Abstracts

Web Sites

Cornell's Engineering Library <http://www.englib.cornell.edu>
ICARIS for Civil Engineering <http://itc.fgg.uni-lj.si/ICARIS>

Environment and Ecology

Encyclopedias

McGraw-Hill Encyclopedia of Environmental Science. 3rd ed. Parker, S. P., ed. New York: McGraw, 1993. Information on the earth's resources and how they have been used.

Indexes

Environment Index
Environment Abstracts

Web Sites

ATSDR Science Corner (Agency for Toxic Substances and Disease Registry) <http://www.atsdr.cdc.gov/cx.html>
International Institute for Sustainable Development <http://iisd1.iisd.ca>

Geography and Geology

Dictionaries

Dictionary of Geology and Geophysics. Lapidus, D. F., ed. New York: Facts on File, 1988. Definitions of many terms in the context of modern geological theories.
Dictionary of Earth Science. New York: McGraw-Hill, 1996.

Indexes

Bibliography and Index of Geology
Geographical Abstracts

Web Sites

American Geological Institute <http://www.agiweb.org>
Geological Surveys and Natural Resources <http://www.lib.berkeley.edu/EART/surveys.html>

Health Sciences

Handbooks

Medical and Health Information Directory. 8th ed. Detroit: Gale, 1999. 3 vols. Comprehensive guidebook.

Physician's Handbook. 22nd ed. Krupp, M. A., et al., eds. E. Norwalk: Appleton and Lange, 2000. Useful, quick reference book for all medical questions.

Indexes

Cumulated Index Medicus
Medline Clinical Collection

Web Sites

National Institutes of Health <http://www.nih.gov>
World Health Organization <http://www.who.int/en>

Mathematics and Statistics

Dictionaries and Encyclopedias

Dictionary of Mathematics. Lincolnwood: NTC, 1996.
CRC Concise Encyclopedia of Mathematics. Weisstein, E. W., ed. Boca Raton: C-R-C, 1999. Short articles on all areas of mathematics.

Indexes

MathSci
American Statistics Index

Web Sites

American Mathematical Society <http://www.ams.org>
Math Archives <http://archives.math.utk.edu>
National Council of Teachers of Mathematics <http://www.nctm.org>

Physics and Astronomy

Dictionaries and Encyclopedias

Dictionary of Physics. New York: McGraw, 1996. Comprehensive dictionary of terms.

The Encyclopedia of Physics. Lerner, R. G., and Trigg, G. L., eds. Reading: Addison, 1990. Background information on major principles and problems in physics.

Indexes

Physics Abstracts
SPIN

Web Sites

American Institute of Physics <http://www.aip.org>
American Physical Society <http://www.aps.org>

Wildlife and Fisheries

Indexes

Wildlife Worldwide
Fish and Fisheries Worldwide

Web Sites

National Audubon Society <http://www.audubon.org>
National Fish and Wildlife Foundation <http://www.nfwf.org>
U.S. Fish and Wildlife Service <http://www.fws.gov>

(EXERCISE 18.1)

Investigate the Internet resources available for one of the disciplines within the natural sciences. Search by topic for a newsgroup or a bulletin board (see 24b-2).

(FOR COLLABORATION)

Bring to class a printout of a Web site that you found in your disciplinary Internet search. Share the information with a small group of your peers. What kinds of resources are available for the disciplines within the natural sciences?

CHAPTER 19

Writing in the Social Sciences

FAQs

▶ What makes writing in the social sciences different from writing in other sciences? (19a)

▶ What kinds of writing assignments can I expect in social science courses? (19a)

▶ How should I use the scientific method in a social science report? (19a-1)

▶ How can I find information in the library or on the Internet for a social science research paper? (19d)

The social sciences—psychology, anthropology, political science, sociology, and education—have as their overall goal the systematic study of human behavior and human societies. The social sciences are comparatively young disciplines; most came into their own in the early part of the twentieth century. To establish their credibility as academic disciplines, they adopted methods used in the natural sciences. Today, many social scientists use the scientific method to study people: they develop hypotheses and then design and conduct controlled experiments or observations to test those hypotheses (see 18a).

WWW

19.1

A closeup view of the IPL's guide to writing research papers.

WEBLINK

http://www.ipl.org/div/aplus/

The Internet Public Library's excellent guide to writing research papers

19a Know the different types of writing in the social sciences

AUDIO
Chapter overview.

The goal of any science is the systematic, objective study of phenomena. Thus, social scientists study the only objectively observable aspect of people—behavior. They cannot observe human emotions and consciousness directly, but they can observe the behaviors that result from feelings and thoughts in human consciousness. Social scientists write to convey research findings discovered by observing human behavior. Writing in the social sciences often begins with the careful recording of field or observation notes. From these notes, the social scientist formulates a hypothesis, and then he or she seeks to test that hypothesis through further systematic experiments or observations. Notes from these experiments are then analyzed and compared to the hypothesis. Finally, the social scientist writes a conclusion explaining how the experimental and observational data supported, refuted, or modified the initial hypothesis. The entire process is typically recounted in a research report. Then that research report and others are typically summarized and evaluated by other social scientists in a review of literature.

www
19.2
The inquiry process in the social sciences.

1 Research or case study report

The majority of social science writing, like natural science writing, is in the form of research reports and case study reports. Research reports are based on primary research conducted by social scientists using interviews, surveys, questionnaires, and the like.

Because much of what social scientists study has not been examined before, they often collect and analyze their own data, announcing their results in research reports. One well-known example is Stanley Milgram's book-length research report *Obedience to Authority: An Experimental View* (New York: Harper, 1974). Milgram, a Yale psychologist, sought to determine to what extent ordinary individuals would obey the orders of an authority figure. Through his experiment, he hoped to probe the psychological processes that allowed the Germans to carry out mass human extermination during World War II. The research process Milgram used closely followed that of other scientific researchers. He began with a question: How could Hitler have succeeded in marshaling so much support from those who were called on to carry out his inhuman orders? After much preparation, Milgram designed and conducted an experiment to test his hypothesis. Using simulated shock experiments, which he admitted were controversial, Milgram showed that an alarming proportion of adults (65 percent of those tested) were willing to inflict severe and, as far as they knew, permanent damage on strangers simply because they were instructed to do so by an authority figure—in this case the experimenter. From the results of these tests, Milgram concluded that, indeed, many people will follow immoral orders, particularly when acting out of a sense of duty and obligation to someone in command.

Whether it summarizes years of laboratory experiments on human motivation or presents the results of a survey conducted in class, a research report in the social sciences typically follows the same pattern as a research report in the natural sciences. (The structure of a typical research report is detailed in 18a-1.) Many research reports begin with a brief review of the literature, to set the current study in context.

2   Review of literature

The second major category of social science writing is the review of literature. In this type of writing, based on secondary research, the writer discusses literature found in the library rather than his or her own original research. Primary researchers, students, and scholars all must keep up with current research in their fields. Researchers need to know what other researchers have found so that they can replicate the experiments, either to confirm or to disprove the hypotheses. Students and scholars should be aware of controversies in their fields so that they can present balanced reports and make observations and contributions of their own. Scholars in a field often publish reviews of literature, in which they analyze, critique, and discuss journal articles. These literature reviews, or summaries, can take a variety of forms—the same forms found in the natural sciences. (For a description of the forms of literature reviews, see 18a-2.)

19b   Write persuasively about social science

Most writing in the social sciences is argumentative in nature. You need to take a stand or make a claim about a particular issue and then argue for that position. You can support your argument with primary research and/or secondary sources.

19.3

Primary research in the social sciences.

As a student, when you write about the social sciences generally you are responding to an assignment. If the assignment calls for primary research, you will probably need your instructor's help in designing an appropriate method for collecting data. (For information on how to report primary research, see 18a-1.)

If your instructor has not assigned a particular topic, you can turn to the media—television, radio, magazines, and the Internet—for ideas. Look for controversies about human behavior and begin to ask questions about them. For example, a magazine article on the influence parents have on their children's use of alcohol or drugs might lead you to wonder if there really is a connection between parenting and drug use. If so, who researched the connection and what exactly did they discover?

1 Determining audience and purpose

Once you have a topic, you can establish a rhetorical stance (see 3b-2). To decide on your purpose for writing, begin by carefully studying the assignment itself. Look for key terms, such as *analyze* or *discuss*. Both of these terms imply an interpretive or critical purpose for writing. Your instructor will expect you to write a piece that makes a point, supported by secondary sources.

Next, ask yourself who your audience will be. Usually you can assume that you are writing for intelligent readers who are interested in the subject but may not know much about the topic. You should provide enough background information so that such readers will be able to follow your argument. Because social science writing attempts to be objective, the writer's persona is less of an issue than in other forms of writing. You should attempt to sound reasonable and informed on your topic.

2 Writing a thesis

The thesis of a social science paper will generally relate to a claim about a particular kind of observed behavior. With regard to children and drugs, for example, you might claim (based on a literature review and/or observational or survey data) that, indeed, parents are the most important determining factor in whether their children ever experiment with alcohol and drugs (see 3e-1 to 3e-3).

3 Completing the research and writing your paper

In any writing assignment, regardless of the discipline for which you are writing, you should follow the writing process described in

Part 1 of this handbook. Refer to Chapters 3–5 for advice on prewriting, drafting, revising, and editing. The writing habits that you have developed in English courses will serve you well in social science courses; try keeping a journal, outlining the information you are reading, exploring through brainstorming or clustering, or working collaboratively with peers (see Chapter 3). If your paper consists of or includes a literature review, refer to Part 2 of this handbook for information on library research. See the list of reference materials commonly used in the social sciences (18d).

19c Review a sample research report in APA format

AUDIO

The model student paper in the social sciences.

19.4

Supplementary sample student papers.

In a first-year liberal arts and sciences course, students worked with partners on a primary research project that included a brief review of literature. In the following paper, notice how the student authors begin with an overview of the current research on the study habits of introverts and extroverts. Then, they report the results of their own research, which tested the findings in the literature review against the experiences of their fellow students. Brandy and Sarah used a typical research report format for their paper, following the conventions of the American Psychological Association (APA) (see Chapter 14).

Title page

Shortened title appears with Introverts and Extroverts   1
page number on every page

Running Head: INTROVERTS AND EXTROVERTS

If the paper is being submitted for publication,
include the shortened title to be used as a header
on every page of the printed version

Title   An Investigation of the Study Habits of

Introverts and Extroverts

Student and   Group: True Colors
course
identification   Brandy Black

Sarah Summers

Liberal Arts and Sciences 124

Professor Long

October 30, 2000

SOC
19c   Writing in the Social Sciences

An abstract is a brief (no more than 120 words) summary of the paper, often included in social science papers

Abstract

This research report reviews the literature on student study habits and presents information from our research about ways in which students on our campus study. We reviewed several articles on study habits in journals such as *Psychological Reports*, *Personality and Individual Differences*, and *The Journal of Research in Personality*. We also investigated the study habits of two student personality types on our campus: introverts and extroverts. Our research included a four-page survey about academic success and study habits (which we asked 15 students to answer) and a six-day study log to chart the length of study time, duration of breaks, and type of studying. This report shows that our own research, for the most part, replicated the findings of many of the national studies.

Title

An Investigation of the Study Habits of

Introverts and Extroverts

Double-
spaced text

Research about personality types and their

study habits has become increasingly important. In

particular, psychologists have studied how to

recognize personality types of students and how to

teach different kinds of students. Because of this

national interest, we decided to investigate the

Hypothesis

study habits of two personality types, introverts

and extroverts. We began this study with two general

assumptions. First, we thought that introverts would

be less socially active in their study habits, spend

more time studying, and have a higher degree of

academic success. Second, we thought that extroverts

would study in groups, study less, and have slightly

lower grades. In order to investigate our

Background
information

assumptions, we read several articles in journals

such as *Psychological Reports, Personality and

Individual Differences,* and *The Journal of Research

in Personality.*

We constructed a four-page survey about

academic success and study habits which we asked 15

students to answer. In addition, we also created a

six-day study log to chart the length of study time,

duration of breaks, and type of studying done by the

Introverts and Extroverts   4

students. The purpose of this research report is to review the literature and to present information

Thesis — from our own research. This report shows that our own research, for the most part, replicated the findings of many of the national studies.

Information in this paper will be presented in two sections. First, findings from the larger, national studies will be summarized. Then, findings from our study will follow.

Literature Review

First-level heading is centered

According to national studies, there are three major trends used in tracing the academic life of extroverts and introverts. The first trend is the

Others' research is reviewed and summarized

academic success of the student, classified into self-rated academic success and actual degree of success. The second trend is preferred study locations and situations. The third trend is the number of study breaks taken by extroverts and introverts, measured by frequency and duration.

Third-level heading is set flush on left margin and italicized → *Academic Success*

Several studies chart the success of extroverted and introverted students. These have

In APA style, source citations include last name and date, with a comma

divided academic success into two categories: self-rated academic success (Irfani, 1978) and the actual degree of success (Furnham & Medhurst, 1995; Olympia

Introverts and Extroverts   5

et al., 1994). One study showed that more extroverts
rated themselves as academically successful than
introverts (Irfani, 1978). So, according to this
study, "the possibility [that] a student will rate
himself academically successful is likely to be
greater when the student is extroverted rather than
introverted" (Irfani, 1978, p. 505).

Brackets show wording change

In contrast, another national study found that
"stable introverts [are] the highest academic
performers" (Furnham & Medhurst, 1995, p. 197). This
study charted the actual degree of academic success
and concluded that "introverts predominate among
outstanding students" (p. 207). It was also noted
that although introverts are frequently among the
top students, the GPA of introverts and extroverts
differs only slightly.

Direct quotations require a page number in the citation

Preferred Study Locations and Situations

Several studies addressed preferred study
locations and discussed whether students favored
working in groups or alone. One report concluded
that introverts choose to study where the number of
people and amount of stimulation is minimized
(Campbell & Hawley, 1982, p. 141). Group study is
usually minimal because introverts study better when
they are not being distracted. Introverts tend to

The relevant literature under each topic is reviewed

Introverts and Extroverts   6

select study environments that have few or no
people, such as their bedroom. When they study in
libraries, they prefer locations that allow them to
be alone.

When we look at preferred study environments
and study groups for extroverts, the results are
nearly the opposite. Campbell and Hawley (1982)
found that "extroverts . . . prefer locations where
socializing opportunities abound and the level of
external stimulation is high" (p. 141). Extroverts
typically spend more time studying in groups and
choose "busier" locations to study in, such as
student centers and dining halls. Campbell and
Hawley stated that "the typical extrovert is
sociable, . . . needs to have people to talk to, and
does not like reading or studying by himself"
(p.139). If extroverts do study at the library, they
"occupy library study locations which maximize
external stimulation" (Campbell, 1983, p. 308).
These reports suggest that introverts and extroverts
differ in regard to study location and studying in
groups.

Number of Study Breaks

Campbell and Hawley (1982) discovered that
there were differences in the frequency of breaks

and the reason for taking these breaks between
introverts and extroverts. Introverts prefer study
locations without a lot of external stimuli so they
are not distracted or influenced to take breaks.
Consequently, they study for longer periods of time
before they take a break. On the other hand, because
extroverts are sociable and prefer to study in areas
where there is a great deal of external stimulation,
they are more easily distracted, leading to a higher
frequency of breaks.

The hypothesis to be tested is stated

According to the national research reports, we
expected to find differences in the study habits of
introverts and extroverts in our own research, as
follows: extroverts should rate themselves higher
than introverts for academic success; the average
GPA should be fairly similar between the two groups;
introverts should prefer to study alone in quiet
places while extroverts should prefer groups in
busier places; and introverts should take fewer
study breaks.

The primary research study is described and the results discussed

Methods: The State University Study

To determine how state university students
would compare to reports found in our literature
review, we administered a four-page questionnaire to
15 students. We also asked the students to keep a

six-day study log. The methodology used to create
this questionnaire follows.

Developing the Research Questions

We designed a questionnaire to learn about the
academic life of introverts and extroverts. The main
areas we wanted this questionnaire to address were:

1. How do students view themselves? As introverts
   or extroverts? As successful academically?

2. Do introverts or extroverts do better in
   school?

3. Do introverts and extroverts study differently?

After writing these research questions, we were able
to design the actual questionnaire. We randomly
selected 15 students in the library who agreed to
answer the questionnaire. The students were given a
brief personality survey to determine whether they
were introverted or extroverted. The subjects were
divided into two groups: 8 introverts and 7
extroverts. Thirteen of the students also agreed to
keep a six-day study log.

Results and Discussion

Demographic Information

The following demographic information was
obtained in order to categorize our subjects.
Students were asked to check off their age from a

Introverts and Extroverts   9

range of ages 18 through 26. From Table 1 it can be

seen that the majority of the students that we

surveyed fell in the 18-20 range.

Table 1

Age of Subjects

Table is
used to
report data

Age	<18	18-20	21-23	24-26
Introvert	0	63%	25%	12%
Extrovert	0	71%	29%	0%

Students analyzed other demographics as well—years in school,
gender, marital status, number of roommates, and number of children. Then, they analyzed the academic success, time management
skills, study habits, and preferred study situations and locations of
their subjects by using the questionnaire and study log data.

Results of
the study
are compared
to the
hypothesis

Conclusions

In comparing the national studies with our

state university study, we made several observations

about the three major trends we had intended to

address. Our first trend dealt with academic

success. Both studies agreed that the GPA is

only slightly different between introverts and

extroverts. In the national studies, more extroverts

rated themselves as academically successful. In

contrast, our study showed more introverts rated

themselves as academically successful.

In one area,
results run
counter to
hypothesis

The second trend dealt with the preferred study

locations and situations of introverts and

Introverts and Extroverts   10

extroverts. The national studies concluded that
introverts liked quiet environments; however, our
study showed that the majority of introverts
preferred to listen to music while studying. Both
the national studies and our study concluded that
introverts like to be alone while studying and that
extroverts prefer group study. Our final trend dealt
with the frequency of study breaks. Our study showed
that introverts took fewer study breaks than
extroverts, which agreed with the national studies.

APA citation
style

Initials

Date

Journal
name, in
capital and
lowercase
letters, is
italicized

Volume
number is
italicized

Only first
word and
proper
nouns are
capitalized
in article or
book title

Page
numbers

No quotation
marks
around title

References

Campbell, J. B. (1983). Differential relationships
of extroversion, impassivity, and sociability
to study habits. *Journal of Research in
Personality, 17,* 308-313.

Campbell, J. B., & Hawley, C. W. (1982). Study
habits and Eysenck's theory of extroversion-
introversion. *Journal of Research in
Personality, 16,* 139-146.

Furnham, A., & Medhurst, S. (1995). Personality
correlates of academic seminar behavior: A
study of four instruments. *Personality and
Individual Differences, 19,* 197-208.

Irfani, S. (1978). Extroversion-introversion and
self-rated academic success. *Psychological
Reports, 43,* 505-510.

Olympia, D. E., Sheridan, S. M., Jenson, W. R., &
Andrews, D. (1994). Using student-managed
interventions to increase homework completion
and accuracy. *Journal of Applied Behavior
Analysis, 27,* 88-99. Retrieved September 25,
1998, from the World Wide Web:
http://www.envmed.rochester.edu/www.rap/
behavior/jaba.htm

Following the References was
Appendix A, which included
Tables 2–7.

19d Look to the Internet and the library for resources

Social scientists were among the first to realize that technology could help them with their research and writing. As a student of the social sciences, you too should familiarize yourself with the available resources, particularly those in library databases and on the Internet. (Chapter 9 discusses types of library and Internet resources and how to use them.) An extended listing of useful Internet sites for the social sciences follows. Take a look, for example, at the *Social Research* site, which has many links to general social science information on the Internet. There are also numerous discussion groups, bulletin boards, and newsgroups related to the social sciences. You can find these discussion sites through an Internet search (see Chapter 24 for information on using computer networks).

WEBLINK

http://www.clas.ufl.edu/users/gthursby/socsci/subjects.htm

The WWW Virtual Library guide to social science links

WWW

19.5

Major web links for the social sciences.

Resources for the social sciences

AUDIO

An overview of resources in the social sciences.

Anthropology

Dictionaries

Dictionary of Anthropology. Barfield, T. London: Blackwell, 1997. Information on anthropological topics.

Indexes and Abstracts

Abstracts in Anthropology

Anthropological Index Online

WWW

19.6

Discipline links for the social sciences.

Web Sites

American Anthropology Association <http://www.aaa.net.org>

Anthropology Institute—University of Oxford <http://www.rsl.ox.ac.uk/isca/index.html>

Business and Economics

Dictionaries

American Dictionary of Economics. D. Auld and G. Bannock. New York. Facts on File, 1983. Short, factual information on economics.

Dictionary of Business. 3rd ed. P. H. Collins. Middlesex, England: Peter Collins, 2000. Defines key terms and explains major economic theories.

Indexes

ABI-INFORM

Public Affairs Information Services

Web Sites

Library of Congress Business Resource References <http:// lcweb.loc.gov/rr/business/>

Ethnic Studies

Indexes

Black Index: Afro-Americans in Selected Periodicals

Index to Periodical Articles by and about Negroes

Bibliography of Asian Studies

Web Sites

University of Texas Internet Resources for African American Studies <http://www.utexas.edu/subject/african/afweb.html>

University of Georgia Institute for African American Studies <http:// www.uga.edu/~iaas>

Asian Studies Resources <http://www.ibiblio.org/ucis/Asian .html>

University of Texas Asian Studies Network Information Center <http:// asnic.utexas.edu/asnic/index.html>

Education

Dictionaries and Encyclopedias

Dictionary of Education. Goodman, F., ed. Phoenix: Oryx, 2000. Concise definitions of terminology in education.

Encyclopedia of Educational Research. 7th ed. Alkin, M., ed. New York: Macmillan, 2001. Excellent summaries of research in education.

International Encyclopedia of Education. Husen, T., and Postlethwaite, T. N., eds. New York: Pergamon, 1994. Background information on topics related to education beyond high school.

Indexes

ERIC on Disc
Resources in Education

Web Sites

Educator's Reference Desk <http://www.eduref.org>
Department of Education <http://www.ed.gov>

Journalism and Communication

Abstracts

Journalism Abstracts

Web Sites

CNN <http://www.cnn.com>
The New York Times on the Web <http://www.nytimes. com>
USA Today <http://www.usatoday.com>
Wall Street Journal <http://www.wsj.com>

Political Science

Almanacs, Dictionaries, and Encyclopedias

Congressional Quarterly Almanac. Washington: Cong. Quar., annual (1945-present). Summary of the activities of Congress, including voting records and major legislation.

Dictionary of Political Thought. Scrutin, R., ed. New York: Hill & Wang, 1984.

Encyclopedia of Policy Studies. Nagel, S., ed. Public Administration and Public Policy Services. New York: Dekker, 1994. Information about public policy issues.

Indexes and Abstracts

Public Affairs Information Service Bulletin
International Political Science Abstracts

Web Sites

Political Science Resources on the Web <http://www.lib.umich .edu/govdocs/polisci.html>

Psychology

Dictionaries and Encyclopedias

Dictionary of Psychology. 2nd ed. Chaplin, J. New York: Dell, 1985. Concise definitions of psychological terms.

Encyclopedia of Psychology. 3rd ed. Corsini, R., ed. New York: Wiley, 1996. An overview of important terms and concepts in psychology.

International Encyclopedia of Psychiatry, Psychology, Psychoanalysis, and Neurology. Wolman, B. B., ed. New York: Van Nostrand, 1997. 12 vols. Concise information on psychology and related fields.

Indexes and Abstracts

Psychological Abstracts

PsycLit

Web Sites

A Guide to Psychology Resources <http://www.guidetopsychology.com>

American Psychological Association <http://www.apa.org>

Sociology and Social Work

Encyclopedias

Encyclopedia of Sociology. Borgata, E. F., and Borgata, M. L., eds. New York: Macmillan, 1999. Terms, concepts, major ideas, major theorists in sociology.

Encyclopedia of Social Work. 19th expanded ed. Edwards, R.L., ed. New York: Natl. Assn. of Social Workers, 1995. General information on a variety of topics related to social work; includes both articles and biographies.

Indexes and Abstracts

Sociological Abstracts

Social Work Research and Abstracts

Web Sites

American Sociological Association <http://asanet.org>

Bureau of Justice Statistics <http://www.ojp.usdoj.gov/bjs>

Bureau of Labor Statistics <http://stats.bls.gov>

Statistical Abstract of the United States <http://www.census.gov/statab/www>

EXERCISE 19.1

Investigate the Internet resources available for one of the disciplines within the social sciences. Search by topic for a newsgroup or a bulletin board (see 24b-2).

FOR COLLABORATION

Bring to class a printout of a Web site that you found in your disciplinary Internet search. Share the information with a small group of your peers. What kinds of resources are available for the disciplines within the social sciences?

CHAPTER **20**

Design Principles and Graphics

FAQs

▶ How should I format a paper? (20b)
▶ What is the best font to use? (20b-7)
▶ How can I best use graphics? (20c)
▶ When is one type of graphic better than another? (20d)

In today's consumer-oriented, message-dense society, people are inundated with advertisements, solicitations, entertainment, news reports, and all other manner of electronic and print documents. In this environment, people tend to read selectively, focusing only on documents that are interesting, inviting, and clear.

AUDIO
Chapter overview.

This is where *document design* comes in. By using headings, itemized lists, graphics, white space, effective layouts, and special typefaces, you can increase the chances that people will read your writing. These design elements can also help you emphasize the most important parts of your writing.

WEBLINK

http://www.informit.com/ articles/article.asp?p=176460

Tips on using MS Word for document design

The key to good document design is to keep your reading experience in mind as you compose. In other words, as in every other aspect of writing, always try to put yourself in the reader's shoes. In particular, ask yourself these questions.

Design Principles and Graphics   **475**

- Who will be reading this document?
- If these readers only skim the document, what parts do I want them to focus on?
- How can I get them to focus on these parts?
- How can I make these parts especially clear?

Underlying these questions is an important guideline: *Do not use design elements just for decoration. Use design elements to enhance your readers' understanding of the document.*

20a Follow the three basic design principles

Adhering to the three basic principles of graphic design will make your documents more meaningful and more readable. These principles, which we will refer to as "the three C's," are clustering, contrasting, and connecting.

1 Clustering: grouping closely related items

Ideas or concepts that are closely related in meaning or communicative value should be clustered together visually. Consider the title page from a student paper shown in Figure 20.1 at the upper left. The layout is neat and centered, but there appear to be five separate pieces of information, none of them having anything to do with any of the others.

Logically, the title and subtitle go together, as do the title of the course and the name of the instructor. Grouping them, as shown in the revised version in the lower right, produces a better layout, because the reader can now see at a glance that there are three main pieces of information instead of five. In addition, the writer's name (Devon Johnson) stands out more.

An example of clustering is found at the beginning of this chapter, where the FAQs are grouped together in a box. These questions have a similar origin and a similar purpose, so it makes sense to present them together.

2 Contrasting: highlighting differences

A second way of using design to make documents more meaningful and readable is to create visual contrasts that mirror important differences in content. For example, the heading for this section is set in

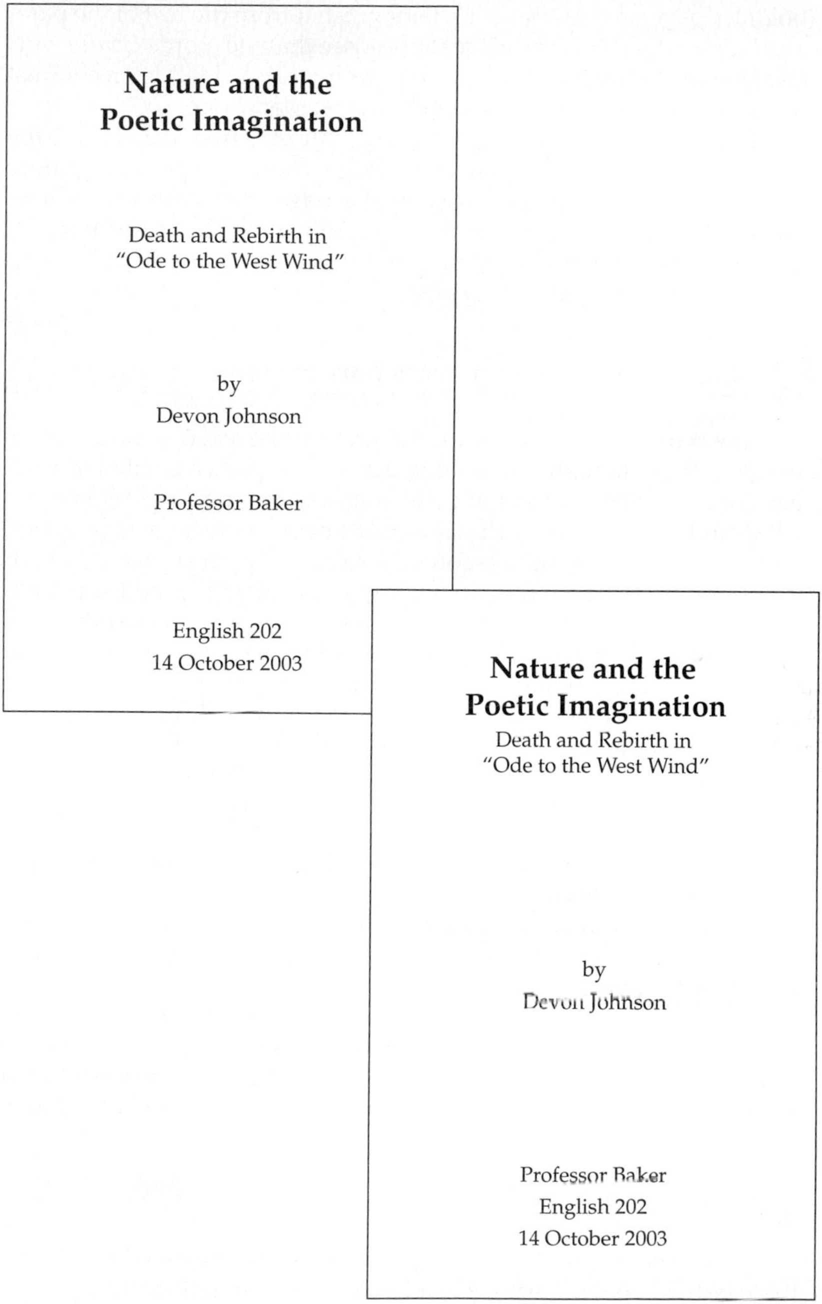

Nature and the Poetic Imagination

Death and Rebirth in
"Ode to the West Wind"

by
Devon Johnson

Professor Baker

English 202
14 October 2003

Nature and the Poetic Imagination
Death and Rebirth in
"Ode to the West Wind"

by
Devon Johnson

Professor Baker
English 202
14 October 2003

FIGURE 20.1 Different ways to group related items

boldface over a red line so as to distinguish it from the rest of the paragraph. This makes it easy for readers to see that the words *Contrasting: highlighting differences* represent an introductory guideline (in contrast to the rest of the paragraph, which is an explanation).

Contrast can also be seen in Devon Johnson's title page, where the main title is set off by virtue of its larger, bolder type. Being more important than the other items on the page, the main title is *foregrounded*, that is, given more visual prominence. The other items on the page, being relatively less important, are given less visual prominence, or *backgrounded*.

3 Connecting: relating every part to some other part

20.1

A business card illustrating the three C's.

The third way of employing design to make text more coherent is to repeat important graphical or typographical elements—that is, visually connect different parts of a document so that no single element is left stranded. These connections should not be made haphazardly but, rather, in a way that underscores connections in meaning, value, or purpose. In this handbook, for example, the headings and subheadings are set off in different colors, to make it easier for readers to skim through the chapters and see how sections are related. Notice the colons in the three subheadings in this section; by reinforcing the grammatical parallelism (see Chapter 42) of these subheadings, the colons emphasize the fact that these three guidelines relate to a single concept.

(EXERCISE 20.1)

Design your own business card or greeting card, adhering to the principles in this section. Feel free to use the document design program on your computer, if it has one.

(FOR COLLABORATION)

Bring examples of advertisements from the Internet, newspapers, or magazines, and discuss with your group the effectiveness of each example. Try to bring both good and bad examples from each genre.

20b Use formatting tools

Formatting is another powerful way of using visual representation to make a document easier to read and more emphatic in its message. Formatting can be done for decorative reasons only, but it is more effective if it also helps readers understand the text. Today's word-processing programs provide all the formatting tools you are likely to need, from boldface type to hanging indents. Familiarize yourself with the common formatting tools, discussed in this section.

AUDIO
Avoiding the overuse of formatting tools.

1 Headings

Headings (and subheadings and titles) are useful for several reasons. They draw attention, they mark off parts of a text, and they give the reader a quick sense of what those parts are about. Headings are especially beneficial for readers who only skim a text instead of reading it closely. Such readers are common in business and the professions (see Chapter 25). College instructors, who are expected to read all student papers thoroughly, may not have the same need or appreciation for headings. (To be on the safe side, ask your instructors whether they want headings.)

VIDEO
Designing academic papers.

Headings should always be informative; that is, they should give the reader an idea of what the paper, section, or illustration is about. If this chapter had been labeled simply "Chapter 20," you would have had no clue as to what it covered. Yet a long descriptive label can be distracting. We suggest that you strive for informative headings that are no longer than four or five words.

Headings are also useful during the writing process, to help you keep track of your overall writing plan. If you write an outline before composing, you can often convert the main points of the outline into headings and subheadings for your paper, especially if you are using a word processor (see 3f, 4a). Always check to make sure that your headings promote the kind of connectedness discussed in 20a. Do they form a list? If so, are they in grammatically parallel form (see Chapter 42)? If one heading is less important than another, is this relationship clear? Are numbers and letters used accurately and consistently?

Writers generally use from one to four levels of headings, depending on how complex the document is. In this chapter, we have used three levels.

1. The chapter heading, or title (Chapter 20: Design Principles and Graphics)
2. Section headings (for example, 20b: Use formatting tools)
3. Subsection headings (for example, 20b-2: Itemized lists)

To create a consistent and distinctive formatting scheme, we have used typography (see 20b-7), color, numbering, white space, and parallelism. Using the same format for all of the headings at a particular level helps readers to see how the chapter is constructed and, thus, to get a better grasp of the subject itself.

The following example from a technical report on handicapped access to campus buildings uses three levels.

RESULTS

First level: Large, bold font; all caps; centered

Student Center

Second level: Stands alone; flush left or centered; bold font or underlined

Main Entrance.

Third level: Flush left, runs in to text; smaller font than second-level heading; bold, italics, or underlined

Headings that are part of a list are often numbered, lettered, or bulleted. For example, different sections of a document might be numbered 1, 2, 3, . . . (or A, B, C, . . .) to help orient readers as they work through the text. Numbering and lettering is especially helpful in online documents.

2   Itemized lists

One of the most effective ways of organizing and drawing attention to details in a text is to put them in an *itemized list*. Itemized lists are a powerful form of visual clustering, as they show how several things form a closely related set. There are two main types of list formats. A *numbered list* or *lettered list* has ordered numbers or letters, suggesting either a ranking of the items or a stepwise procedure, as in the Help box. The main headings in each chapter of this book (including this one) constitute a numbered list, in most cases reflecting our ranking of the sections. A *bulleted list,* which uses bullets (•), diamonds (◆), dashes (—), or some other symbol, is useful for an unordered set of items, such as the list of questions in the third paragraph of this chapter.

Since itemized lists attract a lot of attention, be careful not to overuse them. If you have too many lists too close together, their effectiveness will be lost. Try to have no more than one itemized list per man-

How do I create an itemized list?

1. Introduce the list with a title or brief sentence describing the topic covered.

2. Set off each item with a number, letter, bullet, dash, asterisk, or other marker, and align the markers. Most word-processing programs will automatically do this formatting for you—check the user's manual or online HELP to make sure you are taking full advantage of the LIST feature.

3. Put all of the items in the same grammatical form (see Chapter 42). You will have to do this yourself, as no computer can do it for you.

uscript page or computer screen. Remember: Use lists only when you want to draw special attention to a set of items.

3 Indentation and spacing

In academic papers, the first line of each paragraph is customarily indented five spaces or ½ inch. This indentation provides contrast with the other lines, indicating that a new idea or point is about to be introduced (see Chapter 6). With a word-processing program, you can set this indentation automatically, using either the ruler or the PARAGRAPH feature on the FORMAT menu. Quotations that are longer than four lines of prose or three lines of poetry are set off as a block, with each line indented ten spaces (see Chapter 55). In bibliographies, résumés, bulleted lists, and certain other types of writing, you may want to use *hanging indents,* where the first line begins at the left margin and following lines are indented. Hanging indents can usually be set on the PARAGRAPH menu.

Normally, your instructor will want you to use double spacing throughout your paper (except perhaps in footnotes). You should leave a space after all end punctuation, such as periods, question marks, and exclamation points, and after commas, semicolons, colons, and each dot in ellipses. (See the sample student papers in 5f, 12f, 17d, and Chapters 17–19.)

4 Margins

For academic papers, the standard margin is 1 inch all around, to give the instructor space in which to write comments. These are also the default margins used by most word-processing programs. Such margins leave a line length of about 6 inches, or sixty to seventy characters. Longer lines will make your writing less readable. Word processors are normally set to *left justify* your text—that is, start lines at the left margin and leave the right margin ragged, thus avoiding the need to hyphenate at the end of a line (see Chapter 59). Academic papers are usually written with left justification.

If you prefer the formal look of a commercial publication, you can *block justify* your text, starting lines at the left and ending them evenly at the right; just click the appropriate icon in the toolbar. Block justification sometimes looks more elegant (especially in documents with columns, such as newspapers or brochures), but bear in mind that it can leave unsightly gaps in lines unless you use appropriate hyphenation. A word processor can resolve this problem by automatically hyphenating lines, but the result may be another problem—too many hyphens. You will have to use your best judgment in such cases, either making manual adjustments in hyphenation or reverting to a ragged right margin. (See 59e for further discussion.)

5 Frames and boxes

20.2

More on frames and boxes.

An effective way to highlight a paragraph, graphic, or other part of a document is by putting a rectangular frame or box around it. Frames and boxes are especially useful for summarizing main points or procedural steps, because they simultaneously cluster these points or steps and set them off, through contrast, from the rest of the text. Frames and boxes are commonly found in textbooks, handbooks, user manuals, and other instructional documents (including this one). They are rarely found in academic writing and can be tricky to position, so you should use them only with caution. (You may want to check with your instructor to see whether he or she finds them acceptable.)

A **box** (or *text box*) is a rectangular container for a text or graphic. In many word processors, you can also use boxes to put imported graphics behind text, as "watermarks" for special effects.

This is a text box.

HELP

How do I create a frame?

1. Create a TEXT BOX (INSERT menu) and fill it with text.
2. Select the text box.
3. On the FORMAT menu, click TEXT BOX; then click TEXT BOX tab.
4. Click CONVERT TO FRAME.
5. Click OK. You now have a frame.
6. Drag the frame to the desired location.
7. On the FORMAT menu, click FRAME to resize, reposition, or text-wrap your frame.

NOTE: This procedure is for *MS Word 2000*. Other word-processing programs may have a different procedure. Consult your HELP menu.

A **frame** is more dynamic and flexible than a box, as most word processors will automatically adjust a frame to fit on the page and will allow text to flow around it. You can anchor a frame to a paragraph, thereby ensuring that if you move the paragraph, the framed object will move with it. Its placement still requires care, however. Be aware that when frames and boxes are converted to another medium, they may not appear in the same form as in your application. If you plan to transfer your document to a Web site, frames are usually the better way to go.

> This is a frame. Notice how you can wrap the outside text around it.

Aligning text within boxes and frames can sometimes be tricky. If you are new at it, avoid complications by using simple spacing, tab commands, and hanging indents.

6 Columns

Putting text into columns is a useful way of clustering information in documents such as brochures, newsletters, résumés, and Web pages. (See Chapter 21 for a sample brochure and newsletter and Chapter 25 for a sample résumé.)

There are basically two kinds of columns: newspaper and tabular. In *newspaper columns*, the text starts on the left, flows down the first column, and then continues at the top of the next column to the right. In other words, the text is continuous. Newspaper columns are created with the COLUMNS feature on the FORMAT menu. Most word-processing programs will create this kind of column when the COLUMNS setting is chosen.

Tabular columns consist of independent texts side by side. They are useful if you want to have text in one column and numerical data in another, as in a table, or different kinds of corresponding entries, as in a résumé. Tabular columns are created by using the TABLE feature on a word processor.

Whenever you set up columns, either newspaper or tabular, be sure to leave a reasonable amount of space between the columns. If the space is too narrow or too wide, you can adjust it in either the COLUMNS menu or the TABLE menu.

7 Typography

Since readers will be focusing their eyes on your words, the typographical appearance of your text will have an effect on them. *Typography* refers to all the features associated with individual letters, numbers, and other symbols: font type, font style, font size, color, and case.

Font type refers to the distinctive design of the typeface; some of the most common font types are `Courier`, Times New Roman, Garamond, and Helvetica. Font types typically occur in families, so you have several variants to choose from. For example, the Helvetica family includes standard Helvetica, **Helvetica Black,** Helvetica Narrow, and **Helvetica Rounded Bold.** Font types that have little extra lines (*serifs*) at the ends of the letter strokes are called *serif fonts*. The font used for the main text of this book (Palatino) is a serif type. *Sans serif* (literally, "without serif") *fonts* lack such extra lines. The font used for the FAQs at the start of each chapter in this book (Stone Sans) is a sans serif type.

This sentence is written in a serif font.

This sentence is written in a sans serif font.

Because the extra lines help the eye move from letter to letter, serif fonts are often considered better for extended prose. Sans serif fonts have a more contemporary look and are often preferred for short texts such as advertisements, signs, and instructions. Avoid more creative fonts such as Dolores, Western, and *Brush Script* in academic writing.

Font style (or *font weight*) refers to the particular variant of a single typeface: regular, *italic*, **bold**, or ***bold italic***. Italic, bold, and bold italic type can all be used for emphasis, but they have other uses as well. Italic type, for example, is commonly used for book titles (see 57e) and for words that are set off as vocabulary items (see examples in Chapter 43). Bold type is often used for introducing new terms, as in this handbook, and for headings. It is important to be consistent in your use of these font styles so as to avoid confusing the reader. Also, overuse of italic and bold type for emphasis, like use of all capital letters in email, will give readers the impression that you are shouting at them.

Font sizes range from 4 to 144 points, although most word-processing programs offer sizes from about 6 to 72 points. The standard size range for academic papers is 10 to 12 points, with section headings often set in 14-point type and the title of the paper in 20- or even 24-point type.

This is 20-point Times New Roman.

This is 14-point Times New Roman.

This is 12-point Times New Roman.

This is 10-point Times New Roman.

More specialized bulletins or reports may use a wider range of heading sizes and styles to distinguish sections and subsections.

One other typographical variable is *case*. Academic writers normally use the standard combination of lowercase (small) and uppercase (capital) letters, except for acronyms and other abbreviations (see Chapter 57). In rare cases, all uppercase letters may be used for emphasis or for special categories of headings.

8 Color

Color is another option that has become available with the widespread use of computers. Use color for clarity, emphasis, and aesthetic appeal— and use it systematically. Specifically, you can use color to

- Draw *attention* to an item in your document.
- Show *connections* between different items in your document.

- Create *contrast* between items.
- Invoke certain emotional *associations*.
- Give your document a *polished look*.

As has been done with the headings and subheadings in this book, try to establish a color theme that promotes connections within your document. To draw maximal attention, put one color against a very different background color, as in these examples.

High Contrast/Emphasis	Low Contrast/Emphasis

Bright colors typically have more eye appeal than dull colors. Note also that certain colors often carry certain associations for people. For example, red is a color we often associate with warnings, as in roadside stop signs and a police car's flashing lights. Green, on the other hand, is a color we generally associate with safety and nature, among other things. You can take advantage of such associations by using color accordingly. Bear in mind, however, that color associations can differ from one culture to another. In Western culture, for example, black is associated with death, while in some Eastern cultures, white is.

20.3

Examples of
the use of
color in design.

Like bold and italic type, use color sparingly. If your final product is hard copy, do not forget that only color printers and color copiers will be able to produce and reproduce, respectively, the colors you have chosen.

Figures 20.2 and 20.3 present two versions of the same flyer that differ greatly in terms of their design quality. The flyer in Figure 20.2 has numerous design flaws.

1. It doesn't create visual *connectedness* between key terms such as *Salt Lake Peer Court* and *volunteers*. The connections it does create, for example, between *students* and *offenders*, are misleading.

2. The *contrasts* it creates give prominence to the wrong words, such as the name of the courthouse and the email address (respondents are more likely to phone than email). More important items (such as the word *volunteers*) are de-emphasized.

3. It doesn't *cluster* information as well as it should. For example, the footnoted information should be located near the title, to explain what the Salt Lake Peer Court does.

SALT LAKE PEER COURT*

Is seeking volunteers (for the 2001/02 school
year).

Work directly with **students** as they adjudicate,
mediate, and mentor youth **offenders**.

Volunteers are needed (for Thurs. evenings from 6-8
PM) at the *MATHESON COURTHOUSE, 450 SOUTH STATE
STREET*.

Please contact: **Iris Salazar** in the Bennion Center
@581-4811
e-mail Little Rainbo@yahoo.com
Kathleen Zeitlin or Lenna Penisi 322-1815

*(An alternative to juvenile court for youth offenders)

FIGURE 20.2 A poorly designed flyer

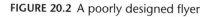

4. It has *inconsistent typography*. It switches from one font to another
   for no apparent reason, has too many parentheses, and uses the
   @ sign inappropriately with a telephone number.
5. It uses *color* inappropriately, evoking wrong associations (for
   example, red in the title) and not making relevant *connections* (for
   example, linking *students* and *offenders*). Color seems to have only
   a decorative purpose here.
6. The page as a whole is *not visually balanced*. The scales in the upper
   right-hand corner seem to be no more than a decorative touch.

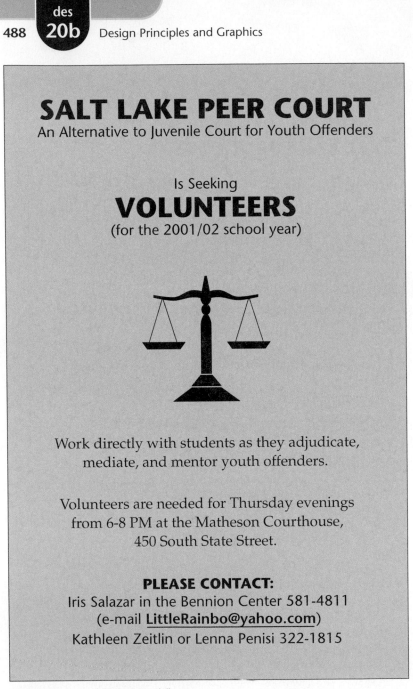

FIGURE 20.3 A well-designed flyer

The revised version in Figure 20.3 is better in a number of ways.

1. Through the use of blue lettering and all uppercase type, visual *connectedness* is created between the key terms *Salt Lake Peer Court*, *volunteers*, and *Please contact*. This flyer is seeking *volunteers* for the *Salt Lake Peer Court*, so those two terms are the ones that deserve highlighting.

2. The bright blue *contrasts* nicely with the tan background and the black lettering of other words, giving visual emphasis to these key terms.

3. The flyer *clusters* information appropriately, for example by putting "An Alternative to Juvenile Court for Youth Offenders" right below the title, where it serves to explain what the Salt Lake Peer Court is.

4. The *typography* is consistent and not distracting. The sans serif font gives the flyer a contemporary look that should appeal to students, and the use of all uppercase letters gives emphasis to selected items.

5. *Color* is used functionally rather than just decoratively. The words and phrases that are set off in blue are key terms in this document and should catch the reader's eye. The tan background is designed to lend warmth to a subject that can be quite grim.

6. The document is *balanced* by having all elements, including the graphic, centered on the page. White space is used in a way that creates nice "breathing spaces."

7. The graphic, enlarged and centered, serves as a *focal point* instead of just marginal decoration. By drawing attention, it visually supports the theme of the flyer.

9 Page numbering

Number the pages in a multipage document. This helps you keep track of the pages as you scroll through the document and as you staple the pages together after printing. Page numbering also makes it easier for an instructor to refer to a particular page in end comments. Consult your word processor's documentation on how to operate the PAGE NUMBERING feature, as well as how to adjust numbering if you create section breaks in your document. Headers and footers can be used to put other types of information—such as your name, a file name, the date and time, or even a company logo—at the top or bottom of the page along with the page number.

10 Document review

Before you print out a document, review it to be sure that the page numbers and headers or footers are set up as you want them to be. Reviewing the document is particularly important if you change from one printer to another, as you may need to adjust the formatting of the document to accommodate the fonts, spacing, and different graphics of the new printer.

The best way to review a document on a computer is by selecting either PAGE LAYOUT (VIEW menu) or PRINT PREVIEW (FILE menu) and then scrolling through to simulate a reader leafing through the document. A two-page view is especially useful with newsletters and brochures.

In reviewing a document, check for the following features.

- *Widowed or orphaned lines.* Single lines left stranded at the top or bottom of a page are known as widowed and orphaned lines, respectively. Particularly irritating to readers are orphaned headings. Although you should still inspect your document, you can avoid having to make a lot of manual adjustments by using the automatic features found in many word-processing programs.

- *Interrupted lists.* Like widowed or orphaned lines, short lists that start on one page and end on another have an adverse effect on readability. You will have to visually check all short lists for this problem, as the computer will not do it for you.

- *Misplaced graphics or boxes.* Graphics and boxes should appear on the same page as their text reference, and generally they should be centered on the page. Your word-processing program will prevent such elements from being placed on a different page from their reference, provided you anchor the graphic or box properly to the reference. Otherwise, you will have to make manual adjustments. Centering a graphic is best done by positioning it at the left margin, highlighting it, and then clicking on the CENTER button in the toolbar. Alternatively, you can either position the graphic manually using the ruler or use the PAGE SETUP menu to input the numbers for the placement desired.

- *Errors in page or section numbering.* Numbering errors are likely to annoy and even confuse readers. You can avoid page numbering errors by having the word-processing program do the page numbering automatically. Using outlining and templates consistently through the development of your paper will prevent section numbering problems as well. Still, you should visually survey your paper to make sure all sections are properly numbered.

- *White space.* Unused space is important because it makes different elements of a text (such as graphics, lists, and titles) stand out. By surveying your document in the PAGE LAYOUT or PRINT PREVIEW mode, you can decide whether specific elements are getting proper emphasis. White space is also important simply for aesthetic reasons. As readers leaf through your document, they should find its look appealing—neither too crowded nor too empty. Many readers will appreciate the "breathing space" afforded by white space.

EXERCISE 20.2

Find a poorly formatted page from a user manual, junk mail, or the Internet. Referring to the principles discussed in this section, write a critique of the page; then, reformat the document.

FOR COLLABORATION

Share your critiques and reformatted documents with your group. Choose one document to reformat together, using the group's best suggestions for redesign.

20c Use graphics

Graphics include tables, line graphs, bar graphs, pie charts, clip art, photographs, cartoons, drawings, maps, and other forms of visual art. Each type of graphic has its own special uses and features. In our increasingly visually oriented culture, graphics add a lot of power to a document. This power, however, should be used judiciously to emphasize or clarify an important point. Using too many graphics dilutes their effectiveness.

AUDIO
Choosing the most appropriate graphic.

1 Tables

Tables are the best type of graphic for presenting a lot of data in compressed form. Although tables are not as visual as other types of graphics in that they require readers to compare numbers rather than look at direct visual representations, they provide a convenient way to organize data, and they do draw readers' attention. Table 20.1 on page 492 illustrates how information-rich a table can be.

TABLE 20.1 Annual World Carbon Dioxide Emissions (million metric tons carbon equivalent)

	1990	1999	2010	2020
Industrialized Countries	2,849	3,129	3,692	4,169
Eastern Europe, Former Soviet Union	1,337	810	978	1,139
Developing Countries	1,641	2,158	3,241	4,542
Asia	1,053	1,361	2,139	3,017
Middle East	231	330	439	566
Africa	179	218	287	365
Central and South America	178	249	377	595
Total World	5,827	6,097	7,910	9,850

Sources: 1990 and 1999, Energy Information Administration (EIA), *International Energy Annual 1999*, DOE/EIA-0219(99). Washington: GPO, Feb. 2001. Projections, EIA, *World Energy Projection System*. Washington: GPO, 2002.

Notice how Table 20.1 adheres to the four guidelines for using graphics.

1. It immediately follows the text to which it relates.
2. It is introduced by the phrase "Table 20.1 illustrates. . . ."

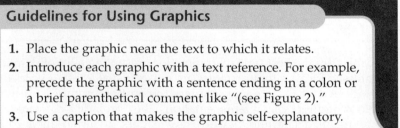

Guidelines for Using Graphics

1. Place the graphic near the text to which it relates.
2. Introduce each graphic with a text reference. For example, precede the graphic with a sentence ending in a colon or a brief parenthetical comment like "(see Figure 2)."
3. Use a caption that makes the graphic self-explanatory.
4. Keep the graphic as simple and uncluttered as possible.

3. The caption, "Annual World Carbon Dioxide Emissions (million metric tons carbon equivalent)," makes the table self-explanatory.

4. The table is simple and uncluttered.

Notice, in particular, how the designer has "factored out" the units of measurement (million metric tons carbon equivalent), putting them in the caption instead of alongside each entry.

Current word-processing programs offer a variety of table formats to choose from. Just click on TABLE and explore the options it gives you.

Once you have the data laid out in a table, you can convert to other formats (such as line graphs and bar graphs) by selecting certain cells to import into whatever graphics program you have on your computer.

2 Line graphs

Line graphs generally do not contain as much data as tables do. But they can make data more understandable and are especially effective for showing changes over time. Figure 20.4 is a line graph representing the top three rows of data in Table 20.1. The line graph visually depicts the change in world CO_2 emissions from 1990 to 2020. It allows the viewer to notice the divergence between with the former

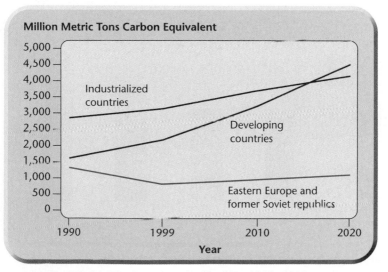

FIGURE 20.4 World CO_2 Emissions by Region, 1990–2020

Soviet republics and the rest of the world. The graph is uncluttered and properly labeled.

As shown in Figure 20.4, you can highlight the line on your line graph by using color or a heavy line. If your graph has more than one line, be sure to distinguish the various lines clearly (for example, by having one solid, another dotted, and a third dashed). Do not use more than three lines in a graph, as too many lines will produce a cluttered effect.

3 Bar graphs

Bar graphs emphasize discrete points rather than continuity, but they can also show changes over time, sometimes more dramatically than line graphs. For example, the sheer weight of the bars in Figure 20.5 emphasizes, more than the line graph, the increase in global CO_2 emissions that we will likely experience in the next two decades.

Like the line graph, this bar graph is simple and uncluttered. The caption makes it self-explanatory, and the units of measurement are mentioned only once.

When is a line graph better than a bar graph? Because they do not emphasize discrete points, line graphs are better for showing continuous variation over time. Thus, if many points in time can be plotted

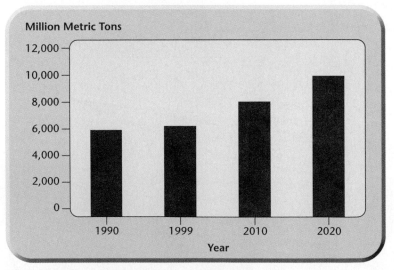

FIGURE 20.5 Global CO_2 Emissions, 1990–2020

(for example, forty-eight months instead of four years), a line graph may be preferable. Also, line graphs are better for tracking several variables at once. If you wanted to compare the CO_2 emissions of, say, four developing regions, a line graph with four lines running approximately in parallel would be more manageable and more comprehensible than a bar graph with sixteen different bars.

WEBLINK

http://writing.colostate.edu/references/index.cfm?guides_active=graphics

An excellent guide to using illustrations, graphics, tables, and figures in document design

4 Pie charts

Pie charts are effective in showing how a fixed quantity of something is divided into fractions. The "pie" as a whole should represent 100 percent. Figure 20.6 shows the projected CO_2 emissions data for a single year (2020) for all developing countries.

This pie chart depicts the massive atmospheric pollution we can expect from Asia in coming decades. It is especially vivid with the Asia "slice" placed in the foreground. If Asia were more in the background, its dominating effect would be somewhat less emphasized. It is relatively simple, in part because it contains no units of measurement. Since pie charts depict ratios rather than absolute quantities,

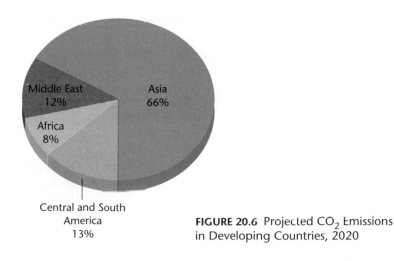

FIGURE 20.6 Projected CO_2 Emissions in Developing Countries, 2020

TABLE 20.2 Effects of the Bush Tax Cut, 2004–2010*

Income Level	2004	2006	2008	2010
Lowest 20%	1.7	1.4	1.4	1.2
Second 20%	7.7	6.8	7.0	6.2
Third 20%	11.5	10.0	10.3	9.6
Fourth 20%	18.1	16.3	15.6	13.2
Highest 20%	61.0	65.4	65.7	69.8

*Projected percentage reduction in federal income taxes.
Source: Children's Defense Fund and Citizens for Tax Justice
<http://www.ctj.org./html/gwb0602.htm>.

units of measurement are unnecessary. (Some word-processing programs offer the option of including percentages in a pie chart.)

(EXERCISE 20.3)

Use information from Table 20.2, above, to create (a) a line graph, (b) a bar graph, and (c) a pie graph. In each case, write a caption that describes what the graph illustrates.

5 Clip art

Clip art, or ready-made images, can add a decorative touch to a document. A well-chosen image can enhance the appeal of a newsletter, brochure, business card, or advertisement. Do not get carried away, though; too much of a good thing may only distract or annoy readers. Be especially cautious about using clip art in academic papers. Professionals in most academic fields take their work seriously and may not appreciate decorative artwork.

You can find a gallery of computer clip art in *MS Works, Corel/WordPerfect Office,* and other programs such as *Windows 2000.* Clip art is also available commercially on disk, as well as in traditional print form (for example, *Clip Books*) from companies such as Dynamic Graphics. Whatever the source, be sure to determine whether the owner has authorized republication of the art and whether there are restrictions on its use.

The major drawback of purchasing commercial clip art is the cost. In general, good-quality reproducible clip art—in print or digital form—is expensive. If you have to choose between poor-quality clip art and no clip art at all, choose none; poor-quality clip art will make your documents look amateurish. Here are some principles to keep in mind when using clip art.

- *Select art by its theme.* Sticking to one theme or one type of art in a document will help unify the document—that is, give it more connectedness.

- *Reconfigure any clip art you use.* Change the size, shape, crop, background, and other features of the art as necessary to adapt it to your document.

- *Use a contrasting color.* If available, a contrasting color will make the clip art stand out from the rest of the document.

6 Diagrams, maps, and cartoons

You may find that you want to use other types of art besides clip art in your documents. The advent of graphical scanners and Internet downloading has made it easy to incorporate various published images such as cartoons, diagrams, and maps into documents. But remember that you cannot republish (on a Web site, for example)

HELP

How do I use a scanner?

If you have access to a scanner, follow this process to insert cartoons, diagrams, photographs, or other hard-copy images in a document.

1. Start with a good original and center it on the scanner plate.
2. Go to CONTROL PANEL and click on SCANNERS.
3. Follow the menu options.

Once you have saved the image, you can edit it (or, better, a copy) using the image editor residing on your computer. From the START menu, click on PROGRAMS and then the image editor (for example, *Microsoft Picture It!* or *Adobe Photoshop*). From there, follow the menu options to get special effects (see 20c-7).

VIDEO
Working with illustrations on a word processor.

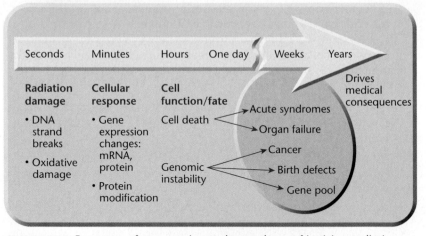

FIGURE 20.7 Response of an organism to heavy doses of ionizing radiation
Source: Science & Technology Review, Jul./Aug. 2003, Lawrence Livermore
National Laboratory.

copyrighted materials created by someone else without that person's
permission.

Diagrams are used especially often in scientific, technical, and
business documents, as they put complex concepts into a quickly
comprehensible visual form. Figure 20.7 shows the short- and long-
term effects of ionizing radiation (which comes from medical procedures, electronic consumer products, nuclear waste, rocks, and other
natural and artificial sources) on the human body. This single diagram captures in visual form a large amount of interrelated information. Though complicated, the information is surely easier to digest
than it would be if it were written out in paragraph form. (Also see
the diagram in Cecelia Chung's newsletter about global warming in
Chapter 21.)

Similar benefits can be obtained with cartoons, maps, drawings,
and other visual images. Be sure to give them a proper label, as illustrated in Figure 20.7.

7   Photographs

20.4

Techniques and
ethics of digital
manipulation.

Photographs add realism to a piece of writing, giving it a "here
and now" feeling. And with the widespread availability of scanners
and digital cameras, photographs are easy to use. To be most effective, photographs often need to be digitally edited. Popular photo
editors on today's market include *Adobe Photoshop, Microsoft Picture*

FIGURE 20.8 Original photo

FIGURE 20.9 Edited version

It!, *Paint Shop Pro, iPhoto,* and many others. You will likely find several to choose from in your college computer lab, and many good shareware programs are available for your home computer.

All photo editors have the same basic capabilities, giving you the ability to rotate, crop, resize, touch up, and apply other special effects to pictures. However, each program has its own way of doing so. The best approach is to spend some time playing with your photo editor, exploring its menu options, and generally getting to know how it works.

Figures 20.8 and 20.9 show how editing can improve a photograph. The original photo of a raft going through a rapid in the Grand Canyon is off-center, out of focus, and too dark. By cropping, resizing, and sharpening it, and by increasing the contrast and brightness, the photographer created a much more engaging and dynamic image.

(EXERCISE 20.4)

Find an old photo that needs editing. Scan it into your computer. Then use a photo editor to make it better. Review 20c-6 and 20c-7 if you need help.

(FOR COLLABORATION)

In a small group, share and discuss the graphics you have created. Do the captions provide accurate and appropriate descriptions of your graphics?

20d Respect different norms and preferences

Headings, lists, and graphics are more common in some fields and genres than in others. For example, a business professor may expect your reports to have frequent headings and subheadings, lists, and graphics, while an English professor may expect your literary essays to have only a title. Be sensitive to these differences, and respect the norms of the field. If your field of study does not typically employ certain document design features, you may be able to achieve the same effects in other ways. In literary essays, for example, you can emphasize main points by putting well-crafted topic sentences at the beginnings of paragraphs and by using parallelism, contrast, and the other techniques discussed in Chapter 43.

Designing Print Documents

FAQs

▶ How do I design and produce a brochure? (21a)

▶ How can using a brochure or newsletter template help me? (21a-1)

▶ How do I decide what to include in my newsletter? (21b-1)

▶ How can I use white space and color effectively? (21a-2, 21b-2)

Desktop publishing refers to the process of producing printed documents on a personal computer. Although special publishing programs such as *QuarkXpress* and *Pagemaker* offer many more design options, word-processing programs can produce a variety of exciting designs. **Templates,** which are preformatted files available in word-processing programs, allow you to desktop publish a first project with ease. **Wizards** may also be available to guide you through the process of formatting your document. Refer to Chapter 20 on Design Principles and Graphics as you work on your desktop publishing projects. If you cannot find a template that suits your needs, search for a printed model to follow. You can find brochures suitable for use as models in libraries, doctors' offices, and local promotional outlets such as the Chamber of Commerce.

AUDIO

Chapter overview.

WEBLINK

http://desktoppublishing
.com/open.html

An awesome collection of desktop publishing resources, collected in one place for one-stop shopping

www

21.1

A closeup view of desktop publishing pages.

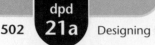

21a Produce a simple brochure

A brochure is a particular type of document with the following characteristics.

21.2

Examples of brochures.

- An informative or persuasive purpose
- An uncommitted audience
- Text and/or graphics focused on a single objective
- A direct or indirect persuasive style
- Limited space
- Layout designed for quick and easy readability
- A physical design that typically uses a single sheet of folded paper

—Jeri Cassity, *Brochure Writing*

1 Making decisions about content

The content decisions you make when you produce a brochure should be based on a rhetorical analysis (see 3b-2). Notice that the list of brochure characteristics addresses not only topic but also purpose,

HELP

21.3

Step-by-step instructions for using templates.

How do I use a document template?

1. Write the text of your document and save it.
2. Select the desired template (for example, brochure, newsletter, memo, or report) and style.
3. Follow the instructions within the template to begin formatting your document; for example, select the number of columns or select a border.
4. Insert your document into the template, using the INSERT command. Your document will be "poured" into the columns of the template.
5. Revise your document, observing the design principles described in this chapter and in Chapter 20.
6. In most programs, the template itself may also be altered to fit your needs and saved for future use.

NOTE: These steps apply to *Word for Windows* and *WordPerfect*. For other word-processing programs, check your documentation.

persona, and audience. A brochure is focused on a specific topic, and its purpose is clearly persuasive. Designed to reflect a knowledgeable and convincing persona, it is targeted toward readers who have not yet committed to a point of view on the topic and might be swayed by the brochure's message.

In this section, we will follow a student as she produces a simple brochure. Felicia Alvarez set out to write a brochure that would help to advertise the school in which she worked part-time. The topic of the brochure was the school and its philosophy; the purpose was to inform the parents of prospective students about the school; the persona was that of an informed insider who knew much about the school and its philosophy; the readers were parents of prospective students.

Since Felicia was new to brochure writing, she turned to her word-processing program for help. She discovered that she could access a brochure template through the FILE menu. When she opened the template, she discovered that it provided a preset format that she could adapt to her own needs.

AUDIO
Using
templates.

2 Making decisions about layout and design

Chapter 20 discusses three basic design principles, called the three C's: clustering, contrasting, and connecting. When you design a brochure, you must attend to all of these principles, paying particular attention to the following considerations.

- *An enticing cover.* The first thing a brochure needs to do is entice someone to read it. Use a combination of lively copy and strategically placed graphical images to draw readers' interest. To spark interest, Felicia decided to use a photograph of children from the school on the cover panel.

> **WEBLINK**
>
> http://www.graphic-design.com/
>
> The Design and Publishing Center home page, featuring an impressive collection of desktop publishing resources

WWW

21.4
Suggestions for
using the
Design and
Publishing
Center pages.

- *A cohesive story.* Once you have enticed readers to open the brochure, lead them through the text in a logical way. The text should tell a story; that is, each panel should relate to the previous one and to those that follow. The template helped Felicia construct a logical story line for her brochure.

- *Coherent graphics.* In a brochure, graphics often play as important a role as copy in telling the story. Like the copy, the graphics should be logical and consistent. Several design features were incorporated into the brochure template Felicia used, including font styles and sizes, shaded boxes, icons, and line breaks. Such features help provide visual coherence throughout a brochure. Felicia added a photograph to draw readers in and color to provide additional coherence throughout the brochure.

- *Adequate white space.* Because the space available in a brochure is extremely limited, you should include only essential information. You can always provide readers with a method for obtaining more information, as Felicia did by including a phone number. Leave plenty of white space to maintain readability. Small chunks of text broken up by white space and informative headings, plus simple and direct language, help make a brochure readable. Aim for a 3:2 ratio between text and white space—that is, three parts of text for every two parts of white space. If the text seems dense, try reducing the font size and adding space between paragraphs. But be sure that you do not make the type too small to be read easily.

3 Refining the brochure

Once you have prepared the first draft of your brochure with all of the text you intend to include, print it out and evaluate it, keeping in mind the three C's of design. When Felicia printed her draft, she discovered that it did not make good use of the clustering principle—everything was too spread out, and the photograph was too small. She revised by clustering related text together and by enlarging the photograph. She liked the contrast provided by the color in the headings and decided to repeat that design element in the shaded boxes. Then, Felicia looked for coherence or connectedness in her brochure. Did all of the elements connect to each other? After experimenting with various combinations of justifications (right, left, block), she decided that left justification would best show how each of the panels was connected to the others. So she changed the justification on the title, which the word-processing program had centered. She checked to make sure that all the text fonts were compatible, with the exception of titles (for contrast). She added a caption to the picture in all capital letters. Finally, she opened the brochure in the two-page view window to verify that the alignment was consistent throughout. The finished brochure appears in Figure 21.1 on pages 506–507.

(**EXERCISE 21.1**)

Write a brochure to announce a party or to advertise a business or an event. First, decide who your readers will be and what information

The Brochure Writing Process

1. Deciding on the content and writing the text:
   a. Conduct a rhetorical analysis.
   b. Choose a template.
   c. Write and insert the text.
2. Deciding on the layout and design:
   a. Design an enticing cover.
   b. Tell a cohesive story.
   c. Add coherent graphics.
   d. Include adequate white space.
3. Refining the brochure:
   a. Check for clustering.
   b. Check for contrast.
   c. Check for connectedness.

you will want to include. Then, select a brochure template from your word-processing program. See the Help box on page 502 for instructions. Enter text for the cover and for the other panels. If you want to write the text in your word-processing program first, the Help box explains how to transfer the contents of the document to your template.

FOR COLLABORATION

When you have completed the brochure, print it out, and ask a few friends or classmates to respond to these questions:

1. What clues does the cover provide about the brochure's contents, and what emotional effects does it create?
2. What story does the brochure tell?
3. How well do the graphics help to convey the story?
4. Is the brochure easy to read? Why or why not?

Revise your brochure based on the feedback you gather.

EXERCISE 21.2

Find a brochure on your campus, in a library, doctor's office, or at a local promotional outlet such as the Chamber of Commerce. Write a one-page critique of the brochure, commenting on how well it meets the brochure writing criteria as outlined in this section.

Content tells a consistent story

Good use of **clustering** related ideas within subheadings

OUR SCHOOL'S PHILOSOPHY

We, the teachers and staff at Nohua School of Natural Learning, are united in these goals and objectives:

1. We affirm the unique nature and abilities of each child.

2. We accept and meet each child where s/he is in every area of development.

3. We instill excitement and enthusiasm for learning in every child.

4. We communicate with each child at all times.

5. We match each child's needs and abilities to learning materials.

6. We enrich perspective on life through a wide range of cultural, educational, and social activities.

7. We assist each child to develop responsible attitudes toward self, others, and the environment.

8. We support and nurture parental involvement in their child's education.

9. We affirm that self-expression is essential to personality growth and self-esteem.

10. We support expressive art, music, speech, etc., as it reveals the essence of each child.

EDUCATION THROUGH DISCOVERY

In a picture perfect setting on the edge of the Ali Wai Canal, Nohua School's award-winning buildings are set in a native Hawaiian park. The comprehensively designed classrooms offer an abundance of learning materials which evoke movement, manipulation, and thoughtful activity from our children. Visitors will observe our children teaching themselves, as they enjoy our profoundly simple and effective self-teaching materials. Each teacher observes children and matches tasks to growing skills, becoming a catalyst between the child and a beautifully enriched environment.

All of our Teachers are Board-Certified!!

OUR TEACHERS

Our teachers bring diverse backgrounds and teaching styles to the classroom. We demonstrate our philosophy of acceptance, encouragement, and a holistic approach to education by allowing our teachers independence in their implementation of the school's curriculum with their students.

Our professional teachers are Board-certified with A.A. or B.A. degrees. We work in partnership with parents to meet your child's physical, emotional, and intellectual development needs.

THE HARMONY OF GROWING

We welcome your child into an especially friendly group of supportive adults. We respect the individuality and developmental differences of each child. Our time together

brings a bonding between child and adult, enhancing the magical, formative learning years.

PARENTAL INVOLVEMENT

Our parents are encouraged to become involved in their child's school and education by learning about the Natural Learning philosophy and curriculum. We recognize that you are the first and most important teacher of your child. Through education, communication, and understanding, we promise to do everything we can to enhance the experience of sharing your child's care with us.

APPLICATION PROCEDURES

Contact the school office to receive an application form or to schedule a school tour.

Telephone: (123) 456-7890

Deadline for applications for 2002-03 academic year is March 31, 2002. A $50 non-refundable fee is due with the form. You will be notified in late April if your child is accepted.

FEES YOU CAN AFFORD

Tuition is $5,000 per academic year. Fees are $350 per year for materials and field trips.

We will work with you to ensure your ability to pay the tuition and fees at Nohua School. We will also help you to secure a need-based scholarship, if appropriate.

Call (123) 456-7890

Panel 1   Panel 2   Panel 3

Good use of white space

Good **contrast** between headings and text font sizes

FIGURE 21.1 Felicia's Brochure

21b   Produce a simple newsletter

WWW

21.5

Contrasting examples of newsletters.

Newsletters are extremely versatile print publications that deliver timely information to a target audience with similar interests, such as business customers or employees of an organization. Many newsletters use an 8½" x 11" page size and are four pages long. They are frequently printed front and back on 11" x 17" paper and folded; they sometimes include an additional one-page, two-sided insert, for a total of six pages. The design and production decisions you must make for a newsletter are similar to those for a brochure. However, in a newsletter you have more space to work with.

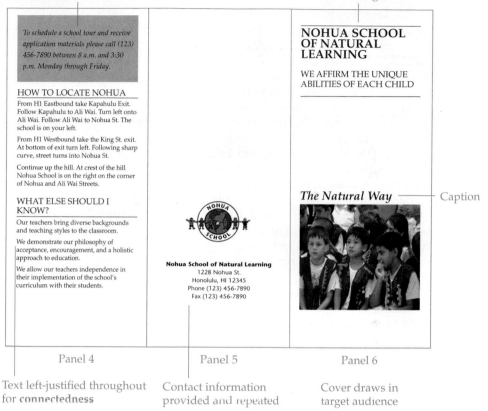

Rose color used for **connecting** and in **contrast** to black and white

Title and subtitle **clustered** together

To schedule a school tour and receive application materials please call (123) 456-7890 between 8 a.m. and 3:30 p.m. Monday through Friday.

HOW TO LOCATE NOHUA

From H1 Eastbound take Kapahulu Exit. Follow Kapahulu to Ali Wai. Turn left onto Ali Wai. Follow Ali Wai to Nohua St. The school is on your left.

From H1 Westbound take the King St. exit. At bottom of exit turn left. Following sharp curve, street turns into Nohua St.

Continue up the hill. At crest of the hill Nohua School is on the right on the corner of Nohua and Ali Wai Streets.

WHAT ELSE SHOULD I KNOW?

Our teachers bring diverse backgrounds and teaching styles to the classroom.

We demonstrate our philosophy of acceptance, encouragement, and a holistic approach to education.

We allow our teachers independence in their implementation of the school's curriculum with their students.

Nohua School of Natural Learning
1228 Nohua St.
Honolulu, HI 12345
Phone (123) 456-7890
Fax (123) 456-7890

NOHUA SCHOOL OF NATURAL LEARNING

WE AFFIRM THE UNIQUE ABILITIES OF EACH CHILD

The Natural Way — Caption

Panel 4

Panel 5

Panel 6

Text left-justified throughout for **connectedness**

Contact information provided and repeated

Cover draws in target audience

FIGURE 21.1 (cont.)

1 Making decisions about content

As always, you first need to consider your rhetorical stance, looking at the topic in terms of purpose, persona, and audience (see 3b-2). Articles or stories should both enlighten and entertain the newsletter's audience; they should be informative rather than overtly persuasive. Since readers already have some stake in the organization, business, product, or service that sponsors the newsletter, you can assume they will be interested in the subject matter. But you still want to make your writing lively and engaging. If the newsletter will be published at regular intervals, plan ahead to stay on top of new developments in the field, to ensure that you have timely information for each issue.

2 Making decisions about layout and design

Be sensitive to the needs of busy, selective newsletter readers by including a table of contents on the first page and providing headings, subheadings, lists, and graphics to help readers find information quickly and easily. Observing the three C's—clustering, contrasting, and connecting—is particularly important in newsletter design. Available design elements include different type fonts, pull-out quotations that are set off from the regular text and printed in larger type, special initials, rules (lines), boxes, color, and graphics.

Newsletters are typically printed in columns, with a masthead, or banner, at the top of the first page, followed by text arranged in either two or three columns per page. Think of white space as an element of contrast—it does not emphasize itself but rather draws attention to something else. It also provides a place for readers to pause. Do not "trap" white space in the fold area of a two-page spread; the only white space down the center of the spread should be the space between the text columns. Instead, use white space creatively to draw the reader's eye toward important information. This will help to give the spread coherence.

Graphical elements such as color, pictures, and text art are used in a newsletter for emphasis. Generally, the banner will be the first graphic a reader will see in a newsletter. Other graphics should coordinate with the banner, in accordance with the design principle of connectedness. Pick up and repeat colors or visual elements from the banner, for example, elsewhere in the newsletter. (For some ideas on using text art, see 20c.) Graphics can occupy one, two, or three columns in a newsletter. Of course, the larger the graphic, the stronger the emphasis. You might consider using a small graphic in the lower right-hand corner of the first page, to balance the banner at the top of the page.

Titles and headings in newsletters are very important, because they indicate important topics and grab readers' attention. Take care to write titles and headings that are both descriptive and interesting. To set off titles or headings and subheadings in a newsletter, use a larger type font and/or color. Such graphic cues will help readers locate the major sections of your newsletter.

3 Refining the newsletter

Most word processors have newsletter templates. Cecelia Chung decided to publish her research paper in newsletter format. In the FILE menu on her word-processing program, she found a newsletter template. The template first asked her to select a title, subtitle, volume number, issue number, and date. It next asked her to decide on the number of columns she wished to use and whether she wanted those columns divided by a rule (vertical line). The program then created a template for the first page of the newsletter.

The template left space for a table of contents, which would be generated automatically as Cecelia supplied the copy for headings and subheadings. Once she had the various elements in place, Cecelia inserted her research paper file into the template by choosing INSERT. The template arranged the text automatically into columns. Cecelia then began the job of formatting the newsletter to make it reader-friendly and visually appealing. She chose a blue border for subsequent pages, to match the gold and blue banner. In the lower right-hand corner of the first page, she inserted a graphic to balance the banner. She opted for block justification and consequently centered the image of the sun on the fourth page. She used the same font throughout; only the banner was set in a different font. The larger font size and added line spaces set off the headings and the white space around the sun image draws the reader's eye out toward the text itself.

The finished newsletter appears in Figure 21.2 on pages 510–513. Note that unlike many newsletters, this example does not contain independent "stories" but rather is a published research paper. Most newsletters will consist of several stories rather than one continuous argument.

The Newsletter Writing Process

1. Deciding on the content and writing the text:
   a. Conduct a rhetorical analysis.
   b. Choose a template.
   c. Write and insert the text.

2. Deciding on the layout and design:
   a. Choose a banner.
   b. Select a color scheme.
   c. Include white space.
   d. Place graphics.
   e. Select fonts for the text, and add headings and a table of contents.

3. Refining the newsletter:
   a. Check for clustering.
   b. Check for contrast.
   c. Check for connectedness.

Global Climate Change

Cecelia Chung — Banner November 14, 1998

Global Warming: What, How, Why Care?
— Larger bold font for headings

Global Warming: Is It Really Happening?

Global warming, at least as measured by climate experts, *is* really happening. Over the last 100 years, it has been estimated that the average global air temperature has risen between 0.3 and 0.6 degree Celsius (I Iileman). Though there is debate over other aspects of global warming, scientists generally agree that global temperatures have risen.

However, a big source of disagreement is whether this is a normal or an abnormal warming. Too little is known about long-term global temperature cycles, some say, to determine if this is abnormal. Reliable weather data, it is true, have only been kept for the last century or so (Montague 1). As a result, some question whether there is significant cause for alarm about global warming as a real problem. While I agree that some caution is warranted when predicting the final outcome of this warming trend, I feel that to disregard the problem altogether is extremely short-sighted, because the effects of even a temporary, normal warming trend are potentially devastating for earth and its inhabitants. Most people would agree. It is in our best interests to know as much as possible about global warming, its causes and potential effects. Before we discuss the true nature of the controversy, let's look at how global warming works.

Table of contents

What Is Global Warming and How Does It Work?

Global warming is an increase in average air temperature on earth's surface, as measured from many points across the globe. Global warming, in its simplest form, is a product of two factors: so-called greenhouse gases and radiation from our local star, the Sun. The idea is that sunlight enters earth's atmosphere, hits molecules of atmospheric gas on earth's surface, and is converted to other forms of energy such as heat. Sometimes this energy is prevented from escaping back into space by a "blanket" of gases such as carbon dioxide, and a net gain of heat occurs (Britt). Without

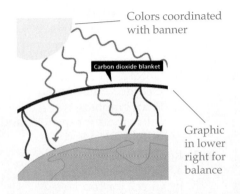

Colors coordinated with banner

Carbon dioxide blanket

Graphic in lower right for balance

FIGURE 21.2 Cecelia's Newsletter

these gases, our planet would be about 60 degrees Fahrenheit colder than it is today (Montague 1), too cold for many terrestrial life forms that now thrive here. But there is concern that too much heat buildup caused by unnatural levels of so-called greenhouse gases will be dangerous for our planet.

White space

Why Are Global Temperatures Increasing?

Now that scientists have established that global warming is taking place, the next question is *why*? Is this, as before stated, a normal trend for our planet? Or is this something that is occurring because of human interference with earth's natural systems?

Most likely, our planet does experience warming and cooling cycles, and it is possible that the current warming trend is one of them. However, the normal warming trend may be compounded by human practices that increase atmospheric levels of the four principal greenhouse gases: carbon dioxide, methane, nitrous oxide, and chlorofluorocarbons (CFC's) (Montague 1). Many of our activities could potentially lead to a buildup of these gases and a resulting increase in global temperatures.

Carbon dioxide makes up the majority of the atmospheric gases. Therefore its emission is of the most concern. The greatest source of increase in atmospheric carbon dioxide is suspected to be the burning of fossil fuels such as coal and oil. Since the beginning of the Industrial Age, burning of fossil fuels has increased dramatically, resulting in an increase of atmospheric carbon dioxide of almost 55% (Montague 1). According to current theory, this is a major cause of the current warming trend, and the whole effect of this has yet to be seen.

What Are Possible Effects of Global Warming?

Already, increased temperatures have had many effects, including weather pattern changes, increased rates of glacial melting, subsequent sea-level increases, and air and sea-surface temperature increases, sometimes with resulting shifts in plant and animal species.

Models predict that, if current theories hold true, temperatures will rise between 1 and 3.5 degrees Celsius by 2100 (Hileman). Temperature increases are expected to be highest over land, changing climates and affecting habitat suitability for terrestrial species, which may be forced to migrate or go extinct. These temperature increases are also expected to result in a sea-level rise of 15 to 95 cm (Hileman) due to increased glacial melting. This would result in flooding in low-lying coastal regions. Changes in ocean circulation will result in warmer local sea temperatures, causing unforeseeable effects for species in these areas.

The biggest immediate effect of global warming is changes in weather, especially greater variability in temperatures and precipitation. Extreme seasonal temperatures can contribute to formation of hurricanes and tornados. Hurricanes are encouraged by high air temperatures, which lead to increased water temperatures over the oceans. A current increase in US tornados within the last four decades is thought to be associated with temperature increases, as well.

What Will Happen to Life on Earth?

Will global warming lead to mass extinctions, or will species migrate to the cooler poles and adapt to life there? Both are likely, but extinctions are inevitable if, as predicted, global temperature increases continue far into the future.

But even without these continued increases, minor temperature changes can have huge effects on habitats, simultaneously affecting populations of many species. For instance, a long-term study of coastal waters off

FIGURE 21.2 (cont.)

3 Global Climate Change

White space around graphic draws eye outward to the text

Matching colors

November 14, 1998

southern California, conducted by John Mc-Gowan and Dean Roemmich of the Scripps Institute of Oceanography, has shown a 2–3 degrees Fahrenheit temperature increase in the sea-surface temperature in the last fifty years (Svitil 36). This has led to density changes in the surface waters, which have had broad implications for the suitability of the habitat for the species living there.

Changes in habitat naturally lead to changes in energy resources as species unable to cope with change die out or disperse to other areas. As one population shrinks, other dependent species populations are stressed for food resources, in turn stressing the populations dependent upon them. In the study previously mentioned, changes in density stratification of the water altered the amount of chemical nutrients carried up from the bacterial beds in the depths of the ocean. As nutrient levels declined near the surface, plants dependent upon these nutrients suffered declines in population, which in turn reduced populations of plant-dependent phytoplankton. The population-reducing effects moved up the food chain reducing populations, from phytoplankton to zooplankton to fish to seabirds (Svitil 36). Clearly, even minor temperature changes have the capacity to significantly alter population numbers, and, as the scale of climate lation increases, extinctions are inevitable.

Alternatively, some say that extinctions due to climate change will be limited because populations will migrate to cooler climates, avoiding the effects of climate change. To a point, I agree. However, rates at which warming will continue are unknown, and successful migrations are dependent upon populations being able to move faster than the rate of change. If warming is gradual, some species may be able to outpace the change (Krebs 115).

However, some predictions state that temperatures will rise exponentially as compounding factors come into play. According to Krebs, as temperatures rise, rates of successful migration will be affected by individual mobility (locomotion), energy resource mobility, reproductive rate, habitat dispersal, and geography. Since a population can only migrate as quickly as its slowest-moving resource, and only to places with suitable habitat unblocked by barriers beyond their capacity to overcome (such as deserts, mountains, oceans), many species will be unable to migrate quickly enough to keep up with rates of climate change (115).

For example, historical models have shown that the geographic range of American beech has moved just 0.2 km per year since the last Ice Age. However, to keep pace with current predictions of climate change, beech will have to move 7–9 km per year to the north (Krebs 113). Thus, the beech is destined to extinction unless we intervene. I predict that many species, both plant and animal, will be unable to move quickly enough to keep up with change and well become extinct.

What does this mean for human life on earth? The answer to this question is unknown. If this warming trend continues to escalate, then it is possible that even humanity as we know it will eventually reach its capacity for adaptation and become extinct, perhaps replaced by another, revolutionarily advanced species. If the trend does not continue but the earth begins to cool, then the effects for human populations will be less drastic. Regardless of the duration of this warming trend, humans cannot fail to feel the effects of a warming trend, as we already are to some degree. Oceans are rising and may eventually encroach upon beaches and seaside homes. Ocean microorganisms are shift-

FIGURE 21.2 (cont.)

4 Global Climate Change   November 14, 1998

ing in abundances and will affect conditions in many economies. It is impossible for humanity to escape entirely unaffected by even a minor warming trend.

What Can Be Done about Global Warming?

Already, many groups and individuals are concerned and taking action about global warming and the problems it may bring. The cooperative effort of local, national, and international entities is necessary, because the potential effects of global warming are so huge. Global warming will affect not only individuals but businesses and governments as well.

Businesses dependent upon world conditions are especially concerned about global warming, for economical if not environmental reasons. Two of these are the global insurance and banking industries. These industries are working with the United Nations to reduce environmentally damaging activities. This is largely because, says UN Environment Program director Hans Alder, "They know that a few major disasters caused by extreme climate events . . . could literally bankrupt the industry in the next decade" (Hertsgaard C1).

Why Care?

Global warming is, after all, a global problem. The effects of global warming, destructive and severe, will be felt increasingly by everyone. Scientists agree that it is happening, so we should all support efforts to research and combat its causes. The changes global warming will eventually cause are unknown in their severity and scope but already we can feel some of them. Let's take action to prevent further escalation of global warming.

Works Cited

Britt, Robert. "The Heat Is On: Scientists Agree on Human Contribution to Global Warming." *Ion Science* 1995. 13 Nov. 1998 <http://www.injersey.com/Media/IonSci/features/gwarm/gwarm.html>.

Hertsgaard, Mark. "Who's Afraid of Global Warming?" *Washington Post* 21 Jan. 1996: C1. 13 Nov. 1998 <http://www.ji.org/jinews/newsline/afraid2.htm>.

Hileman, Bette. "Climate Observations Substantiate Global Warming Models." *Chemical and Engineering News* 27 Nov. 1995. 13 Nov. 1998 <http://jcbmac.chem.brown.edu/baird/Chem221/global/pg1.html>.

Krebs, Charles J. *Ecology: The Experimental Analysis of Distribution and Abundance*. 4th ed. New York: Harper, 1994.

Montague, Peter. "Global Warming—Part 1: How Global Warming Is Sneaking Up on Us." *Rachel's Hazardous Waste News* 26 Aug. 1992: 1. 22 Nov. 1998 <http://www.envirolink.org/pubs/rachel/rhwn300.htm>.

Svitil, Kathy A. "Collapse of a Food Chain." *Discover* July 1995: 36–37.

Graphics Sources

Carbon dioxide blanket. 13 Nov. 1998 <http://www.injersey.com/Media/IonSci/features/gwarm/gwarm.html>.

Friendly sun. 13 Nov. 1998 <cuisun9.unige.ch/eao/www/gif/New_Sun.color.gif>.

FIGURE 21.2 (cont.)

EXERCISE 21.3

Analyze the design of Cecelia's newsletter with respect to the three C's. Write your evaluation of Cecelia's application of each design principle. Or, evaluate a newsletter that you have seen on your campus or at work.

EXERCISE 21.4

Design your own newsletter, using a template found on your word-processing program. Or, design a class newsletter as a collaborative project.

FOR COLLABORATION

Once you have written a draft of your newsletter, exchange it with a classmate for peer review.

CHAPTER 22

Designing Web Documents

FAQs

▶ What does it mean to "design" a Web site? (22a, 22b-5)

▶ What is hypertext? (22a-2)

▶ How can I get my Web files to appear on the Internet? (22b-1)

▶ What is a storyboard? (22b-3)

▶ How can I help readers navigate through my Web site? (22b-4)

As you begin to think about designing Web documents, it is important to remember that writing for the Web is not all that different from writing for other purposes. The basic rhetorical principles outlined in Part 1 of this handbook still apply. Web authors need to consider their rhetorical stance carefully (purpose, persona, and audience) and let it dictate the content and structure of their Web sites. However, Web documents differ from print documents in two important ways: they tend to be more visual (that is, they include more graphics and photographs), and they are hypertextual and weblike in structure (that is, they have electronic links).

WEBLINK

http://www.w3.org/Provider/Style/

A hypertextually organized manual on Web design from the creator of the WWW, Tim Berners Lee

22.1

A hypertextual manual on Web design from the W3C.

You may not associate design with writing. Perhaps you think of design in terms of designing graphics or designing page layouts (discussed in Chapters 20–21). But designing is something that happens during any writing process. We will use the term *design* to refer broadly to the ongoing planning involved in developing and writing for a complicated project such as a Web site. We discuss the broad design issues in this chapter. Chapter 23 provides more specific guidance on constructing Web pages.

22a Generate a basic design for the Web

AUDIO

Web design begins with preplanning.

A third grader in Huntsville, Alabama, and a research scientist in Osaka, Japan, have equal access to a worldwide audience on the Web. And, like anyone else who authors a Web site, both proceed through a design planning process in which they generate ideas and then plan, draft, revise, and publish the Web site. When a Web page is well designed, the author's message is successfully conveyed to readers, and the look and content of the page match the author's purposes. Thus, effectively designed Web sites make good use of both graphics and hypertext.

1 Using visuals effectively

In print media, the printed words convey most of the text's meaning. But even printed texts contain other meaningful visual cues in addition to the words themselves—for example, by indenting five spaces at the beginning of a paragraph, using italics for titles of books, and using boldface for chapter titles. When Web authors consider document design, formatting, and graphics, they make deci-

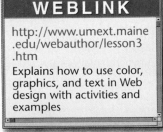

WEBLINK

http://www.umext.maine.edu/webauthor/lesson3.htm

Explains how to use color, graphics, and text in Web design with activities and examples

www

22.2

Writing for the Web, and how readers read on the Web.

sions similar to those made by writers of print documents. However, the role of visual features in conveying meaning is greater in Web documents than in print documents. Web authors typically use images instead of words to show readers how to find information and to help them understand concepts. They employ visual tools such as color, background images, typographical distinctions, spacing, graphics and icons, lists, and tables and frames (see Figure 22.1). Increasingly, Web sites are becoming **multimedia**; they use sound and even movement (sometimes called **hypermedia**) to convey their messages to readers. However, Web designers still need to pay close attention to the size of multimedia and graphics files so that readers who access the Web via modems do not have to wait endlessly for files to download (see 23b-5).

Black graphic on light background   Colorful image   Table used to position elements on the page   Site table of elements with links to secondary pages on the Web site

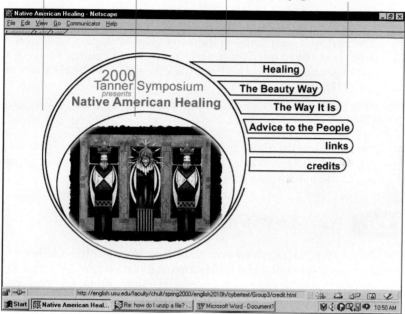

FIGURE 22.1 A Student Web Page Illustrating Design Features

2   Using hypertext effectively

Effective writers accommodate the busy, selective reader through the use of headings, itemized lists, and graphics (see Chapter 20). Hypertext goes a logical step beyond print by allowing busy readers to choose among short chunks of text on specific topics, deciding what to read and what to ignore. **Hypertext** is text that is broken down into discrete pieces, which are then connected through electronic links. The first page of a Web site appears to be a flat, one-dimensional document, but it is not. It is hypertext, linked to other pages that will appear onscreen at the click of the mouse. These links are embedded in "hot" words, phrases, and graphics, which lead the reader to related texts within the same Web site (relative links), graphics and other media (hypermedia), and other related Web sites (remote links). One of the greatest challenges in writing hypertext is to make it easy for readers to navigate through the links. Careful design is the key to constructing a successful Web site.

(EXERCISE 22.1)

Find two Web sites that you think are visually appealing. Describe what makes them interesting. How has each site's author used color, graphics, and other media? Bookmark the sites (see the Help box on page 211).

(FOR COLLABORATION)

Print copies of the Home pages for your classmates, or post them to your class's common directory. Discuss the sites and your evaluation of them, with your classmates.

22b Plan your Web document

As you think about how you want your Web site to look, keep in mind the basic strengths and limitations of this medium. Although the Web allows you to be extremely creative in using graphics, photos, colors, and even video and sound, the Web authoring language HTML (HyperText Markup Language) is not as versatile as many desktop publishing programs. For example, constructing columns for a Web page is more complex than producing a newsletter in columns using a word-processing program. In addition, the number of fonts available may be limited.

---

1 Learning about design technology

You do not compose a Web site directly on the World Wide Web. Instead, you create the text and graphics as files on your computer's hard drive or on disk. When the files are complete and stored in appropriate folders and directories, you transfer them from your computer or the lab's server to your college's Internet server or to an Internet service provider **(ISP)**.

WWW

22.3

Organizing
your Web files.

Naming and storing your Web files

Naming Conventions.   When you begin any Web project, it is important to get organized from the start. Since servers may be picky about what file names they will accept, you need to decide on a simple yet understandable system for naming the files that will make up your

Web project. For example, use only lowercase letters in Web file names and do not use any spaces or characters such as periods since those can also cause problems for servers. Web file names should be kept short and must end in either *.htm* or *.html*. At one time, these extensions distinguished Mac from PC Web files, but they have since become interchangeable. Graphics files will end in either *.gif* or *.jpg* since these are the image formats recognized by Web browsers.

Creating a directory for your project. It is a good idea to create a project directory or folder on your computer's hard drive or disk in which to store all documents and graphics related to a particular Web project. As you construct your Web site, you will probably create a number of separate documents and graphics files that will later be connected to each other with hypertext links. If you keep them all in the same location on your disk or hard drive, you will find it easier to organize your Web site. Furthermore, you will be able to transfer all of the related files to your Internet server at once if they all reside in the same folder. Be certain to make backup copies of everything you are using for your Web site, and remember to save frequently as you work on the project.

Understanding how Web files are stored. Before you begin your Web project, it is also important to understand how Web files are stored on your college's or service provider's computer system. If your college provides Internet access for students and faculty, it will have dedicated storage space on a large computer that is used as the campus Internet server. To use your college server, you will need to secure an account, which will include a user name and password unique to you.

Publishing your Web pages with a browser. The major Internet browsers, *Netscape* and *Explorer,* both provide you with a method to publish your Web pages, once you have set up an account on a server. For example, on *Netscape Composer,* click the PUBLISH icon to send your Web page to the campus server. It will ask you for information such as the server address, as well as your user name and password. *Composer* will send all the files associated with your Web page, including image files, if you so desire. If you decide to make a change to a file, simply send it again and it will replace the old file on the server. (See Figure 22.2 on page 520.)

Publishing your Web pages with FTP. Another way to publish your Web pages is by using file transfer protocol (**FTP**). There are several versions of ftp software, but the most commonly used is *Windows*

Publish icon

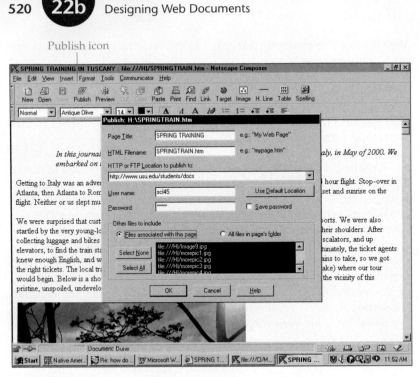

FIGURE 22.2 Publishing a Web Page with *Netscape Composer*

FTP (WS_FTP). When you open the ftp software, it asks you to supply the information about the destination server and the location on that server for your files. You will need to find out from your lab supervisor or instructor the correct information to provide so that your files will be transferred to the proper location on the destination server. In Figure 22.3, notice that there are basically two windows; the one on the left shows the drives, directories, and files on your local computer system (that is, the computer and network you are currently using); the one on the right shows those on the destination computer system (that is, the host server, called here the "remote system"). The arrows in between the two windows are used to transfer the files back and forth between the two computer systems.

Publishing your Web pages with an ISP. Finally, in addition to publishing your Web pages on your campus server, it is also possible to publish them on other Internet service providers (ISPs), such as AOL or Microsoft Network or on "free" sites offered by companies on the Web such as GeoCities at <*http://geocities.com*> or Angel Fire at

Transfer buttons to send files
from one server to another

Directory to which you
wish to transfer files on
the destination server

Subdirectories

Disk drives and files
on your local computer

Web file

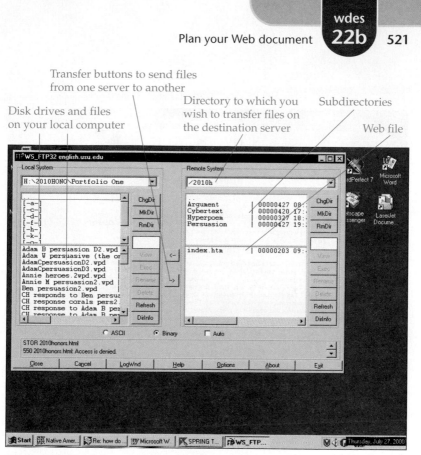

FIGURE 22.3 Publishing a Web Page with *Windows FTP*

<*http://angelfire.com*>. The downside of these free sites is that advertising banners will automatically be included along with your Web pages.

Basic design elements

As you think about your Web site, you will need to consider whether or not to use some basic design elements to structure the Web pages, such as tables, frames, style sheets, and JavaScript. Depending on your site's purpose and the needs of your audience, you can select among these design options. We will provide a brief explanation below, but you will need to research them further if you wish to try them yourself (see also 23b-8).

AUDIO

Organize
content with
basic design
elements.

Using tables. Web page authors use tables to control page layout so that text and graphics appear on the page where they'd like them to

Column 1
of table

Column 2
of table

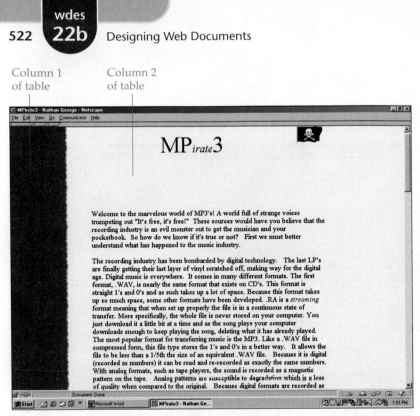

FIGURE 22.4 Using Tables to Organize Content on a Student's Web Page

appear. When using tables, you can decide on the number of columns and rows that will be used on each page and what data will "fill" cells formed by the intersection of those columns and rows. If you select a zero width as the table border, the table itself will not appear on the page. Instead, the table will provide you with "cells" in which you can insert appropriate data. (See Figure 22.4.)

WWW

22.4
Using tables and frames to design Web pages.

Using frames. **Frames** are used like tables to organize the text and graphics on a Web site. They differ from tables, though, in their ability to show in the browser window multiple files displayed in different portions of the frame. The frame itself consistently appears on the page, but different Web pages may be displayed within the frame windows. (See Figure 22.5.)

Using style sheets. Style sheets provide another sophisticated way to format your Web pages. Style sheets for the Web work in much the same way as style sheets for word-processing programs.

Table of contents with
relative links to   Linked secondary page
secondary pages   Scroll bar   will appear in this window

```
Annie's Argument - Netscape                                    _ [8] [X]
File  Edit  View  Go  Communicator  Help
```

Who's Controlling Your Children?

Home Page

The Problem

*Parental
Responsiblities*

Censorware

Survey

Conclusion

Credits

The Internet, a wonderful invention that brings knowledge and information
straight to our homes in a matter of seconds. Messages can be sent and
received instantaneously across the world, and at no charge. Our world has
been dramatically impacted and changed, doors have been opened for people
of all races and classes. But, are these doors always good? Is the
information, which is instantly transmitted to your home, what you would
classify as appropriate? Do the strangers your children communicate with
hold the same moral values and principles established in your home? How
then, can concerned parents protect their children from becoming victims of
this Internet abuse? Parents need to talk with and offer advice to their
children on Internet safety. There are also many programs available that
provide censorship of Internet sites. Which is the best solution for you?

```
Document: Done
Start   Annie's Argu.   Re: how do I un...  Microsoft Word ...  SPRING TRAIN..           12:34 PM
```

FIGURE 22.5 Using Frames to Organize Content on a Student's Web Page

They allow you to set default elements such as fonts and colors that
will then be applied uniformly to your document. For example, if
you wanted all of your first-level headings to be black on a red background, you could define the header 1 style to associate the colors,
fonts, and typestyle that you'd like them to appear in throughout
your Web document.

Using JavaScript. **JavaScript** is a programming language that
allows for miniature programs to be embedded into Web pages as
applets. These applets can perform functions within a larger Web
page, generating information that would otherwise have been sent
over the Internet. (See Figure 22.6 on page 524.) Java Script is a complicated language to learn and beyond the scope of this book.
However, if you would like to learn more on your own, you can go to
the Sun Microsystems Web site at <*http://www.javasoft.com*>.

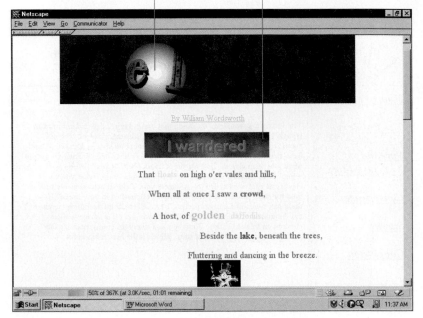

JavaScript Applet: Spotlight ball roves across the title.

JavaScript Applet: Scrolling text that prints the first line of the poem, "I wandered lonely as a cloud."

FIGURE 22.6 JavaScript Applets on a Student's Web Page

2 Deciding on a rhetorical stance

The kinds of writing decisions you must make in determining a rhetorical stance for your Web site are similar to those you confront in writing a paper (see 3b-2). If you are creating a Web site as a class assignment, analyze the requirements of the assignment. Think about what knowledge and information you will need in order to write a successful Web site. If you are to choose your own topic, think through what topics might be appropriate (see 8a).

Purpose

You should have a clear purpose in mind before you start. What specific goals do you want to accomplish with your Web site?

- Do you want to share your own creative work—such as poetry, fiction, music, or art—with others?

- Do you want to educate your audience about a topic that concerns you, such as the plight of the African elephant or the health dangers of nuclear waste?
- Do you want to provide a service to readers, such as a link to materials about a particular topic?

The Web has thousands of sites that focus on specific topics, such as individual authors, musicians, health and environmental concerns, and political causes.

Persona

If you look at various Web sites, you will notice that they convey distinctive impressions. Some are whimsical and humorous, while others are professional and serious. As you consider your own Web site, think about how you want to portray yourself.

- What kind of background would be most suitable for the site?
- What colors would be appropriate?
- Which images would enhance the site?
- What text would reflect best on you as an author?

Audience

Most readers want a balance between graphics and text. And they like a hypertext structure that allows them to choose their own path through the site. They appreciate helpful elements such as navigational buttons, which guide them through the site (see 21b-4). Plus, an appealing site will go a long way toward holding your readers' attention. In thinking about your audience, consider the following questions.

VIDEO
About balancing Web design and content.

- Is the text so dense that it is difficult to read onscreen?
- Will the text be interesting to readers?
- Are there too many graphics?
- Does the site allow readers to skim and read selectively?
- Are there enough navigational tools? (see 21b-4, 21b–5)
- Will the page hold readers' attention?

3 Storyboarding your Web presentation

Storyboarding—that is, making a drawing of a work's component parts— is a technique developed by journalists and graphic artists to plan newspapers, magazines, TV commercials, movies, and other

Planning a Web Site

Purpose

The general purpose of my Web site is

The specific objectives of my Web site are

1.
2.
3.

Persona

The persona I want my Web site to reflect is

The specific ways in which I will reveal my persona are

1.
2.
3.

Audience

The readers I want to address in my Web site are

The specific ways in which I will help my readers are

1.
2.
3.

media that mix text with graphics. One way to storyboard a Web site is to outline the text and sketch the graphics for each page on a 3" x 5" index card. Pin the cards to a bulletin board, and then move them around until you have a unified story. You can show the links between the cards by stretching a piece of string from one card to another. You also can storyboard by doing small, "thumbnail" page plans on a sheet of paper. Figure 22.7 illustrates two types of organizational structures used for Web sites: linear and hierarchical. In a simple Web site with a straightforward story, the pages can be linked in a linear sequence, with one leading to the next in a straight line. The pages of a more com-

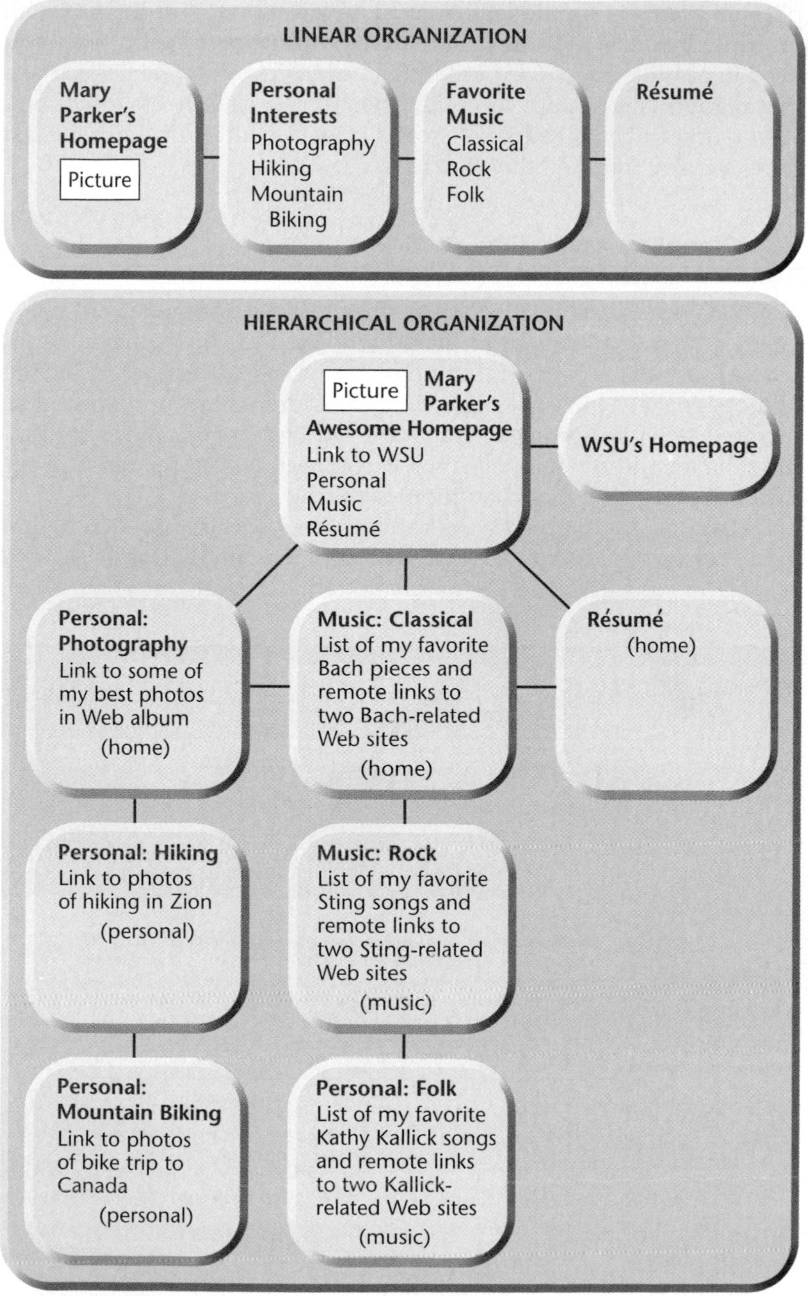

LINEAR ORGANIZATION

Mary Parker's Homepage
Picture

Personal Interests
Photography
Hiking
Mountain Biking

Favorite Music
Classical
Rock
Folk

Résumé

HIERARCHICAL ORGANIZATION

Picture **Mary Parker's Awesome Homepage**
Link to WSU
Personal
Music
Résumé

WSU's Homepage

Personal: Photography
Link to some of my best photos in Web album
(home)

Music: Classical
List of my favorite Bach pieces and remote links to two Bach-related Web sites
(home)

Résumé
(home)

Personal: Hiking
Link to photos of hiking in Zion
(personal)

Music: Rock
List of my favorite Sting songs and remote links to two Sting-related Web sites
(music)

Personal: Mountain Biking
Link to photos of bike trip to Canada
(personal)

Personal: Folk
List of my favorite Kathy Kallick songs and remote links to two Kallick-related Web sites
(music)

FIGURE 22.7 Two Storyboards for a Web Site

plicated Web site should be linked in a hierarchical structure or with multiple linkages that provide readers with numerous options. You need to provide enough information about yourself on each Web page that readers can contact you with questions or comments. Including your name and email address should be sufficient, along with the last date that you updated the page (see 23b-7).

4 Planning navigation

AUDIO

Navigational links connect content on the Web.

As Figure 22.1 shows, a Web site begins with a homepage (the first page), which also serves as an introduction to the site. It often includes several secondary pages (**relative links**), which are accessed from the homepage. Each page (designated by a different file name) should be no more than two or three screens long. For high-impact pages, try limiting the length to what will fit on one screen so that readers can see the entire page at a glance without scrolling.

Links are highlighted words and phrases within a document that allow readers to get from one page to another. **Navigational buttons** are graphical icons, such as arrows, symbols, buttons, or pictures,

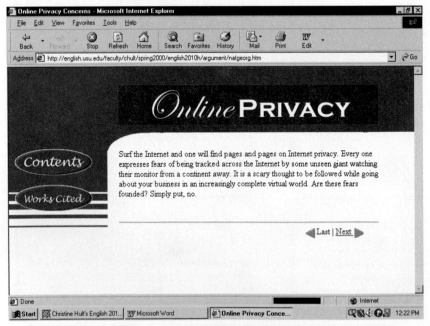

FIGURE 22.8 One Page of a Student Collaborative Web Site with Navigational Buttons

that will take readers in a particular direction or to a particular location. You may need to include text in addition to the graphic, as on the "Contents" and "Works Cited" buttons in Figure 22.8, if the purpose of the graphic is not readily apparent. Navigational buttons may be included at the top, bottom, or one side of each page within a multi-page Web site.

5 Applying the basic design principles to a Web site

Given the vast quantity of information on the World Wide Web, accommodating the busy, selective reader is imperative. The homepage is the first page readers will see when they access your site, so it should introduce your site concisely, providing an overview of the content and organization of the site. Do not waste readers' time with decorative design elements; rather, include elements that will enhance readers' understanding of your message. Observing the basic design principles (see Chapter 20) exemplified by the three C's—clustering, contrasting, and connecting—may be even more critical to Web design than to print design (see Figure 22.9 on page 530). Note that some Web sites offer the reader a choice between two versions: one that is intensively graphical and one that is text-based. This option allows readers to read the page even if they do not have a graphics-capable browser. You may want to consider text alternatives for your readers (see 23b-5).

> ## WEBLINK
> http://www.its2.uidaho
> .edu/design/index.htm
> A site for exploring many aspects of Web site production, including great advice on effective Web site design and graphics

22.5
Examples of effective Web design.

AUDIO
Apply design principles for print to the Web.

Clustering: grouping closely related items

When designing Web pages, position chunks of information that are related in meaning close to one another. Emphasize clusters of information by placing white space around them. Group important elements at the top left and lower right of the screen, as readers of the English language are trained to move their eyes from left to right. Use numbered and bulleted lists to show relationships among items in a group.

Contrasting: highlighting differences

Use contrasting fonts or font sizes to highlight basic elements. For example, you might use the largest HTML headings (H1) for titles and

Connectedness: Navigational links are provided in the canoe graphic at the top; that graphic appears at the top of every page at the site. At the bottom (off this view) are buttons to Home, Links, and Credits, also in green.

Contrasting: Boldfaced type, colored fonts, and black text on light background increase readability. Font sizes show headings and set them apart.

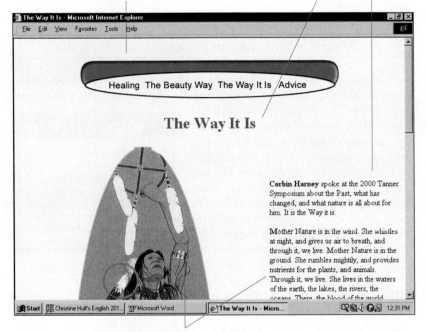

Clustering: Related items are grouped—text on right, graphic on the left. Navigation icons are at the top of the screen.

FIGURE 22.9 The 3 C's of Design as Used by a Group of First-Year Students

smaller HTML headings (H3) for any subtitles (see 23b-2). Use colors or patterns to contrast other elements on the page.

Connecting: relating every part to some other part

Adhering to the principle of connectedness is especially important for Web authors. Since readers can access the pages within a site in any sequence, use a design template (see 21a, 21b-3) and a consistent graphic, title, or logo to foster visual connectedness. Furthermore, because readers can easily become lost when reading hypertext, it is

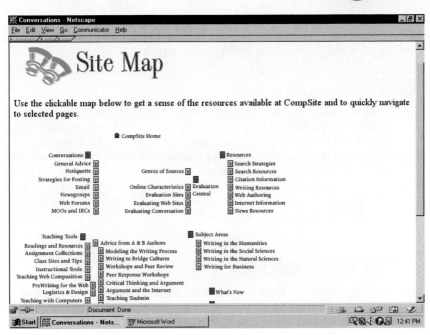

FIGURE 22.10 A Site Map

important to include navigational aids to connect all pieces of the Web site. One way to do so is to provide a "home" link on every secondary page that takes readers back to the homepage. You might also supply a site map, showing how all of the pieces are connected (see Figure 22.10).

Some Dos and Don'ts of Web Design

Do organize your information before designing your site.

Do aim for pages that are no more than two or three screens long.

Do accommodate text-only browsers.

Do use a template and repeat visual elements.

Do use other Web pages to learn new code (see 23b).

Don't include unnecessary design elements.

Don't use graphics files of over 30 K (kilobytes).

Don't use copyrighted text or graphics without permission and acknowledgment.

It is a good idea to provide readers with alternative routes through the site's pages so that they are not forced along a single path. Busy, selective readers will appreciate the optional routes.

(EXERCISE 22.2)

> Begin planning and designing a Web site. Set goals for your Web site by filling in the blanks in the box on Planning a Web Site on page 526. Then storyboard your Web site on 3" x 5" cards or by making a sketch in a notebook. Pay careful attention to planning the navigation through the various linked pages within your site. What pages need to be linked to each other? Draw arrows on your storyboard to indicate links. To ensure that readers are not left stranded on a page, plan to provide icons or buttons that lead them home or on to the next page.

(FOR COLLABORATION)

> Exchange drafts of your Web sites with a classmate for peer review. Comment specifically on the features of the Web site that are visual and hypertextual.

(EXERCISE 22.3)

> Visit the *Voice of the Shuttle* "Laws of Cool" page at *<http://vos.ucsb.edu/ shuttle/cool.html>*. Find a site that you think illustrates effective Web design. List the reasons why you find the design compelling, referring to the criteria outlined in this chapter. Share your sites and your evaluation with the class.

CHAPTER 23

Writing Web Pages

FAQs

▶ How do I save a word-processing document into HTML? (23a)

▶ What is HTML code? (23b-2)

▶ How do I add a link to another site? (23b-3)

▶ Where can I find images to use? (23b-4)

▶ How should I refine my Web site? (23c)

In Chapter 22, we explored some of the important issues that you need to consider when planning and designing any Web document. In this chapter, we turn our attention to the actual writing of Web pages. Just as the more general writing process covered in Part 1 of this handbook is a recursive process, so is writing for the Web. You will necessarily find yourself returning to many of the planning issues covered in the previous chapter even as you are in the midst of writing your Web pages. The designing does not stop when the actual writing begins. In this chapter we will only be able to address some of the most basic issues of writing for the Web—how to use hypertext markup language (HTML) to construct simple Web documents and how to add links that attach graphical images and other documents to pages in a hypertextual "web."

VIDEO
Understanding
Web
compositions.

The homepage of your Web site is the first page that readers will come to when they locate your Web site by using its uniform resource locator (URL). From the homepage, you can provide **relative links** to secondary pages that you have written. You also can include on your pages **remote links** to other Web sites located elsewhere on the Internet.

23.1

Resources for
Web authoring.

AUDIO

Composing
content for
your Web
pages.

AUDIO

Formatting
content for
your Web
pages.

23a Methods used to construct Web pages

Once you have an overall plan for your Web site (see Chapter 22), you can begin to compose your Web pages. The text of a Web site—what it "says" to the reader—is as important as how it looks; Web pages communicate through both text and graphics. There are several methods for composing Web pages—or you may use a combination of methods.

1. *Use an HTML editor or composer, software that is designed to help with writing Web pages.* Some commonly used commercial HTML editors include *Macromedia Dreamweaver, Adobe PageMill, Microsoft Front Page,* or *Claris Home Page.* There are also HTML editors available in free versions that can be downloaded from the Internet (e.g., *HomeSite*). To find free HTML editors, you can type "HTML editor" as a search term in a search tool (see 9c-1). The most popular Internet browsers, *Netscape* and *Explorer,* also include their own HTML editor/composers, along with much useful advice and tutorials on writing Web pages. *Netscape,* for example, provides software called *Composer* that allows you to construct Web pages. Newer versions of *Explorer* allow you to move from writing Web pages in *Microsoft Word* to viewing those pages via *Explorer.* We will discuss this process in more detail in 23b-1.

2. *Use a translator program that changes a word-processing or database file into a Web file.* Newer versions of *Microsoft Word, WordPerfect, Excel,* and *PowerPoint,* for example, all include a SAVE AS HTML command, typically found in the FILE > SAVE AS menu. You may wish to elect this option when you have already written an extensive text in a word-processing program that you wish to convert into a Web file. Another plus of the translation method is that you can take full advantage of all the features found in a word-processing program (such as a spell checker, grammar checker, or thesaurus), which may not be available to you in an HTML editor or composer. (See also the Help box on page 535.)

3. *Use a text editing or word-processing program (e.g.,* Windows NotePad *or Microsoft Word) and enter the HTML code by hand.* When authors first began writing in HTML for the Web, this is the method they used—that is, they typed in all of the HTML codes that the browser would need to interpret and display the Web pages. This is the most difficult and time-consuming method for composing Web pages. However, despite the help of the sophisticated editors and composers available today, sometimes it is still necessary to insert HTML codes by

HELP

How do I save a word-processing document into HTML?

1. If your word-processing program allows you to save a document as HTML, just use its SAVE AS feature and specify HTML.
2. If your word-processing program will not save a file as HTML, then you must follow these steps.
   a. Highlight the text you want to convert to HTML, and COPY it.
   b. Open your HTML editor, and PASTE the copied text into it.
   c. Use the HTML editor's features to format the text for the Web.

WWW

23.2

Steps for converting a document into HTML.

hand in order to achieve exactly the result you desire. It is important to understand enough HTML coding to be able to revise and rewrite the code that underlies any of your Web pages.

To illustrate writing for the Web, we will use Cecelia Chung's research paper. Cecelia first wrote her research paper using a word-processing program. After she completed the paper, she decided to desktop publish it as a newsletter, shown in Chapter 21. Then, her instructor provided her with the opportunity to publish her research paper on the World Wide Web. To do so, she first saved the paper as an HTML document, causing her word-processing program to automatically convert the text into an HTML document by adding important codes. This HTML document would form the basis for Cecelia's Web site (see composing Web pages 23a-2).

23b HTML editors and HTML codes

Hypertext markup language (HTML) is not really a language but rather a system for embedding codes into text. These codes tell a Web browser how to display the text in the browser window. To introduce yourself to HTML, surf the Web until you find a site that you think is lively and

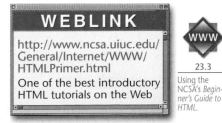

WEBLINK

http://www.ncsa.uiuc.edu/General/Internet/WWW/HTMLPrimer.html

One of the best introductory HTML tutorials on the Web

WWW

23.3

Using the NCSA's *Beginner's Guide* to HTML.

HELP

How do I view the source code of a Web page?

23.4

Steps for viewing the source code of a Web page.

1. On many browsers, you can view the HTML source code of a document by selecting the appropriate menu item. Often, the command VIEW or VIEW PAGE SOURCE will bring the source code onto the screen. (See Figure 23.1 for an example of HTML source code.)

2. If you cannot find a VIEW command, you can save the document to a file and then view the source code in a text editor (such as *Windows NotePad*) or word-processing program.
   a. On the FILE menu of your browser, select the SAVE or SAVE AS command to save the document to a file. (Remembering where you saved the file will be helpful when you want to view it.)
   b. Start your text editor or word-processing program.
   c. Open the file and display the code.

well designed. Then view the source code by following the instructions in the Help box. In writing the code for your own pages, you can analyze the code from other Web sites and use it as a model, as long as your pages are for educational and not commercial purposes. However, if you rely heavily on another Web page's design, be sure to credit the original site.

EXERCISE 23.1

Following the steps outlined in the Help box, look at the source code of a simple Web site. Notice how the author has coded various items on the page, including the graphics, the background, and the links. Save and print the source code.

FOR COLLABORATION

▌ Bring a copy of the source code to class to share with your classmates.

AUDIO

Using *Netscape Composer* and *Microsoft Word* to write Web pages.

1 **Using *Microsoft Word* or *Netscape Composer* to compose a Web page**

As noted above, there are three methods for generating HTML files: (1) using an HTML editor or composer, (2) using a translator pro-

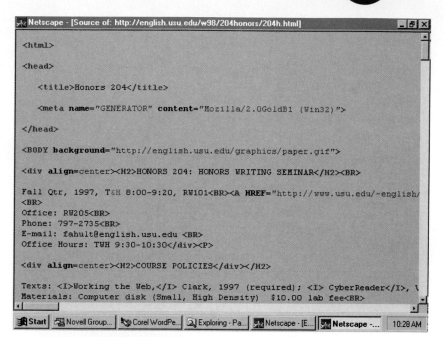

FIGURE 23.1 View of Source Code

gram to save a word-processed document as an HTML file, or (3) embedding the HTML code by hand. Most Web authors begin with either 1 or 2 but also find that they need to embed some codes by hand, which means you will still need to know enough HTML coding to be able to make adjustments and refinements to your HTML files. We discuss the most commonly used HTML codes in 23b-2. In this section, we will discuss the first method—using an HTML editor or composer. As examples, we will use two common HTML editors—*Microsoft Word/Explorer* and *Netscape Composer*. For method 2, see the Help box on page 535.

Using *Microsoft Word* and *Internet Explorer* to create Web pages

The newest Microsoft products let you construct Web files directly in *Word* and then preview them on *Internet Explorer*. To do so, you need to be sure that the *Word* Web templates have been loaded onto your computer. These templates provide you with the HTML editor necessary to begin writing Web pages. To find the Web templates, go to the FILE menu and click on NEW. One of the types of templates available to you should be WEB PAGES. You will see several options (depending on your version of *Word*), including a BLANK WEB PAGE, a WEB PAGE WIZARD, and several preset Web page formats.

23.5
Building Web pages with *Word* and *Explorer*.

- If you click on BLANK WEB PAGE, *Word* will construct a Web page for you that includes the basic underlying codes necessary to begin any Web document. *Word* uses a WYSIWYG ("What You See Is What You Get") editor, so you will not see the underlying HTML codes unless you go to the VIEW menu and view the HTML source.
- If you click on WEB PAGE WIZARD, *Word* will walk you through the creation of a simple Web page using Web templates.
- If you click on one of the preset formats, *Word* will create a blank Web page using that format, for example, a left-aligned column.

(EXERCISE 23.2)

If you have access to *Microsoft Word*, open the WEB PAGE tab and try out a few of the options for creating a simple Web page. At first, try a simple layout with a basic style. Notice how the *Word* template constructs a page for you (see Figure 23.2). Save that file on your hard drive or disk. Try a different template, perhaps a more difficult one this time with two or three columns. *Word* will make the columns by using the TABLE feature of HTML, which is discussed in 23b-8. Try using the Web toolbar to make changes to your Web page.

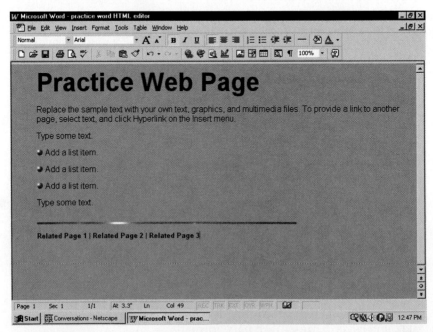

FIGURE 23.2 Practice Web Page Using *Word* Web Template

Once you have created a Web page in *Word,* you can open that page in the *Explorer* browser to preview how it would actually look on the Internet. You must save the page first before previewing it; then, select WEB PAGE PREVIEW from the FILE menu or click on the WEB PAGE PREVIEW icon on the Web toolbar. *Word* will open the page in your default browser. You can alternate between working on your Web page in *Word* and previewing it using the Web browser. You can also open any Web page that you have saved as a file directly in a Web browser. To do so, choose OPEN PAGE from the FILE menu of either *Explorer* or *Netscape.* A window will open that allows you to browse your disk drives and select the HTML file that you wish the browser to open. Once you have selected the appropriate file, the browser will display it in the window (see Figure 23.3).

Using *Netscape Composer* to create Web pages

The *Netscape* Internet browser comes with an HTML editor called *Netscape Composer.* Launch the *Netscape* browser by choosing NEW and BLANK PAGE from the FILE menu. This will put you in the *Composer* window. You should name and save the file by using the SAVE option from the file menu or clicking the DISK icon. Notice the toolbar at the top of

23.6
Building Web pages with *Netscape Composer.*

Netscape

File Edit View Go Communicator Help

Back Forward Reload Home Search Netscape Print Security Shop Stop

GLOBAL WARMING

| Cecelia Chung | November 14, 1998 |

Global warming, at least as measured by climate experts, *is* really happening. Over the last 100 years, it has been estimated that the average global air temperature has risen between 0.3 and 0.6 degree Celsius (Hileman). Though there is debate over other aspects of global warming, scientists generally agree that global temperatures have risen.

However, a big source of disagreement is whether this is a normal or an abnormal warming. Too little is known about long-term global temperature cycles, some say, to determine if this is abnormal. Reliable weather data, it is true, have only been kept for the last century or so (Montague 1). As a result, some question whether there is significant cause for alarm about global warming as a real problem. While I agree that some caution is warranted when predicting the final outcome of this warming trend, I feel that to disregard the problem altogether is extremely short-sighted, because the effects of even a temporary, normal warming trend are potentially devastating for earth and her inhabitants. Most people would agree: it is in our best interests to know as much as possible about global warming, its causes and potential effects. Before we can discuss the true nature of the controversy, let's look at how global warming works.

Document: Done

Page 2   Sec 1   2/2   At 3.8"   Ln 16   Col 1   REC TRK EXT OVR WPH

Start   Microsoft Word ...   Chapter 7 from ...   Netscape   English Departm...   10:25 AM

FIGURE 23.3 View of Cecelia's Web Page in Browser Window

the screen. You will use the tools on the toolbar to embed HTML code into your document (see Figure 23.4). However, the number of codes available from the toolbar is quite limited. To embed other HTML tags, choose HTML TAG from the INSERT menu. We will discuss the most commonly used tags in 23b-2. To find out what each of the tools on the toolbar is for, move your mouse over the icon without clicking and read the description provided. If you wish to preview your Web page, you can click on the PREVIEW icon or select BROWSE PAGE from the FILE menu. *Netscape* opens your page in a second window so that you can easily switch back and forth between the browser view and the *Composer* view as you work on your page. Remember to save and reload your page so that you will see the newest version in your browser window.

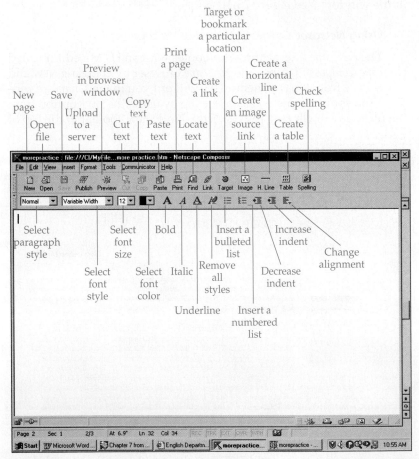

FIGURE 23.4 *Netscape Composer*—Blank Page

<hr>

(EXERCISE 23.3)

If you have access to *Netscape Composer,* begin a blank page by select-ing NEW and BLANK PAGE from the FILE menu. Try out a few of the options for creating a simple Web page using the *Composer* toolbar. Save the practice file on your hard drive or disk. Try using one of *Netscape's* Web templates, available by choosing NEW and PAGE FROM TEMPLATE from the FILE menu. Or, you can try using the WEB WIZARD to create a page, also available under the FILE > NEW menu.

Editing the HTML source code in *Word* and *Composer*

Oftentimes you will find it necessary to edit the HTML source code that the HTML editor has embedded into your Web page. To do so, you first need to use the EDIT SOURCE option of your Web page. In *Word,* choose HTML SOURCE from the Web page VIEW menu. You may be prompted to save your file, if you have not already done so. *Word* will provide you with a view of your HTML source code that you may edit. You can delete codes, insert codes, change existing codes, add text, and so on. When you are finished editing, click on EXIT HTML SOURCE or close the source code window. You will once again be prompted to save your editing changes or refresh your screen upon returning to the Web document.

In *Composer,* you can also edit your source code as long as you select an external editor in which to do so. There are two ways to view the source code in *Composer*: one from the VIEW menu and one from the EDIT menu. When you click on PAGE SOURCE from the VIEW menu, you will be able to see the source code, but not edit it. However, when you click on HTML SOURCE from the EDIT menu, you will be prompted to select an HTML editor. You can choose a shareware HTML editor, such as *HomeSite,* that you have downloaded from the Internet. Or, you can simply choose a text editing or word-processing program, such as *Windows NotePad* or *Microsoft Word.* If you change your mind about the editing program you wish to use, you can select PREFERENCES from the EDIT menu to change your *Composer* preferences.

2 Using basic HTML codes

As mentioned in the previous section, there will be times when you will want to edit the HTML codes in your Web page file by hand. To do so, you need a working knowledge of HTML. Most HTML

AUDIO
The basic prin-ciples of HTML.

codes, called **tags**, come in pairs: the first tag turns on the feature and the second turns it off. The second tag includes a slash, which the browser reads as signaling the end of that feature. All tags must be enclosed in angle brackets like this:

```
<B>Bold this sentence</B>
```

The pairs of HTML tags that surround the text they affect are called **containers**. Any text between the containers will be affected by the code. It does not matter whether the tag is in lowercase or uppercase letters.

Tags fall into two basic categories: **document tags**, which tell the browser how to handle major elements of the document such as the head and the body, and **appearance tags**, which tell the browser how to handle the appearance of the text. Some tags can take **attributes**, that is, codes that provide additional formatting information. For example, a header tag might include an alignment attribute, telling the browser how to place the header on the page.

```
<H1 ALIGN="center">My Title</H1>
```

Document tags

The major document tags are HTML, head, title, and body. Your first task in composing a Web page is to enter the basic codes for these major document components. If you saved your word-processed document as an HTML file, or if you are using an HTML editor, these document tags will be entered for you.

1. *Creating the head and title.* All HTML documents begin with the tag <HTML> and end with the tag </HTML>. Within these containers, the information is divided into two major categories: head and body. Within the head of the document is included any descriptive information about the HTML document, such as date of origin, author of the page, version number, and so on. See, for example, the information included within the <HEAD> containers on the blank Web page in *Microsoft Word* (Figure 23.5). Also included within the head is a document title, which may be different from the document's file name. It is important that you supply an accurate and descriptive title within the title containers because the title will help others to find your page when using search tools or bookmarks to navigate the Web. If you are working with a *Word* Web template or in *Netscape Composer*, you will only see the document tags when you view the HTML source code. Try opening a new Web page in *Word* or *Composer*. You will see a blank page with a toolbar at the top. Click the VIEW HTML SOURCE menu. You will now see the underlying document tags, as illustrated in Figure 23.5. To revise your title in *Composer*, select PAGE COLORS AND PROPERTIES from the FORMAT menu. In *Word*, select PROPERTIES from the FILE menu.

2. *Creating the body.* The body tag surrounds the rest of the Web file (after the head). The body tag can have a number of attributes that will specify how the body is to be interpreted by the browser. Such body attributes might include a background color or graphic, text color, or link color. In Figure 23.5, notice that the body tag includes both a text color (TEXT="#000000") and a background color (BGCOLOR= "#ffffff") attribute. Other attributes that might have been provided include the color of the links (LINK="green") or the color of visited links (VLINK="red"). To identify a color, your HTML editor will

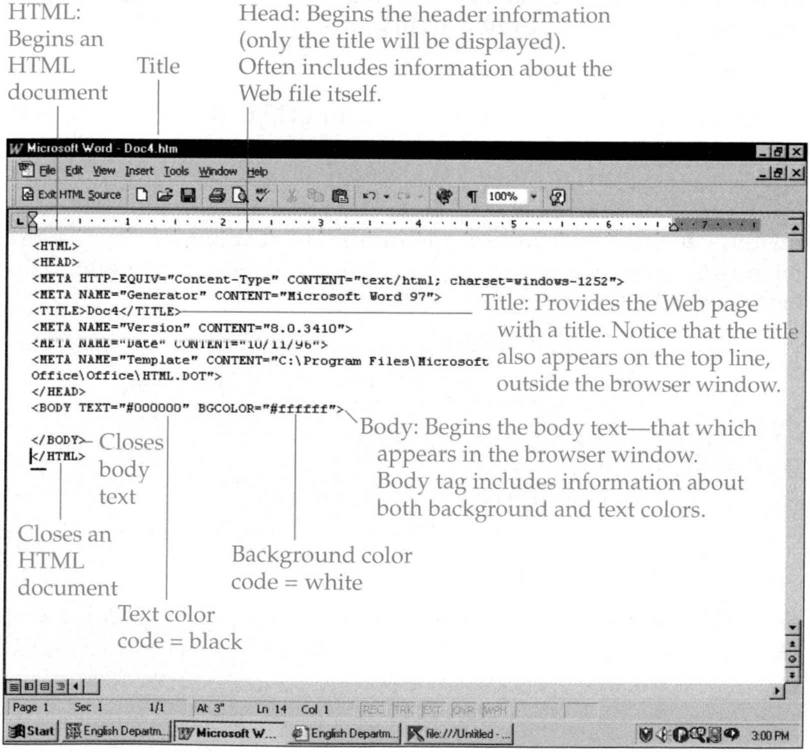

FIGURE 23.5 View of HTML Document Tags for a Blank Web Page in *Microsoft Word*

insert either a color code number or a color name. Either can be interpreted by the browser. In *Word*, you change the background color by selecting BACKGROUND from the FORMAT menu. In *Composer*, select PAGE COLORS AND PROPERTIES, also from the FORMAT menu. The code for the pale yellow color Cecelia selected for her onscreen background is

```
<BODY BGCOLOR="FFFFCO">
```

It is also possible to specify a graphics file as a background instead of a color. Using a background can greatly enhance the look of a page, provided it is light enough that the text shows through clearly. If Cecelia had wanted to include the graphics file name "sunpic.gif" as a background instead of a color, the body tag attributes would have read as follows:

```
<BODY BACKGROUND="sunpic.gif">
```

3. *Creating a document comment.* Another frequently used but optional document tag is the comment tag, which always begins with an exclamation point and double hyphens.

```
<!--Remember to add the link here-->
```

If you wish to insert a comment into your HTML document that will not show up as text, you can use the comment tag. As long as the appropriate code is included, the comments will not show up in the browser window. You may use comments to remind yourself of information you need to include or to provide instructions for future work on the document. Comment tags can be included anywhere within the body of the Web file.

Here is what Cecelia's HTML source looked like after she added text and more instructional tags for interpreting that text.

```
<html>
<head>
<title>Global Warming</title>
</head>
<BODY BGCOLOR="#FFFFCO" TEXT="#000000">
<H2>Cecelia's Global Warming Newsletter</H2>
<B>Global Warming: What, How, Why Care?</B>
<p>
Global warming, at least as measured by climate experts, is really
happening. Over the last 100 years, it has been estimated that the
average global air temperature has risen between 0.3 and 0.6 degree
```

```
Celsius (Hileman). Though there is debate over other aspects of
global warming, scientists generally agree that global temperatures
have risen.
<!--Remember to add the link here-->
</body>
</html>
```

As you can see in Figure 23.6, the view from the browser window looks quite different from the HTML source view. By moving back and forth between the two windows, you will be able to see how the tags you have inserted into the document are being read by the browser. In this way, you can make corrections as you work.

Appearance tags

HTML documents do not include embedded codes for typographical distinctions such as boldface, underlining, and highlighting in the same way that word-processing programs do. To create these typographical distinctions, you must use formatting, or appearance, tags. In the code that produced Figure 23.6, the <H2> and </H2>

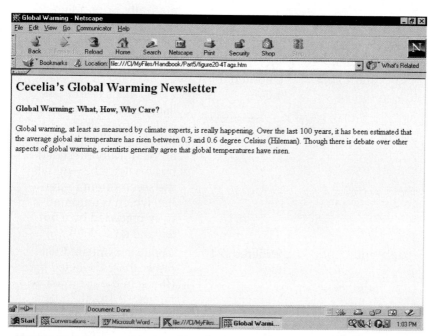

FIGURE 23.6 Browser Window After Document Tags Were Added

Major HTML Appearance Tags

<p>	Paragraph tag	Skip a line to start a new paragraph.
 	Line break tag	Start a new line (without leaving a blank line).
<hr>	Horizontal rule tag	Insert a long line stretching across the display window.
<H> and </H>	Heading tags	Put the information in a larger font and set it apart as a heading or subheading. (Headings can be numbered from <H1>, the largest heading, to <H5>, the smallest heading. The browser automatically skips a line following any heading.)
<blockquote> and </blockquote>	Block quote tags	Set the information apart as an indented quotation.
<ul> and </ul>	Unordered list tags	Create a list of bulleted items. (Each item in the list must also be tagged. <L1> signals the first item in the list, which is automatically preceded by a bullet; <L2> signals the second item in the list, which is automatically preceded by a bullet; and so on.)
<ol> and </ol>	Ordered list tags	Create a numbered list rather than a bulleted list. (Items in the list must be tagged <L1>, <L2>, and so on, the same as for an unordered list.)

(continued)

Major HTML Appearance Tags *(continued)*

<em> and </em>	Emphasis tags	Emphasize a word or phrase with italics or some other typographical distinction specified under STYLE.
<strong> and </strong>	Stronger emphasis tags	Strongly emphasize a word or phrase, usually through boldface.
<cite> and </cite>	Citation tags	Format the bracketed text as a citation line, usually in a different font.
<B> and </B>	Boldface tags	**Boldface the bracketed text.**
<I> and </I>	Italics tags	*Italicize the bracketed text.*
<U> and </U>	Underline tags	<u>Underline the bracketed text.</u>
<tt> and </tt>	Typewriter text tags	`Show the bracketed text in a monotype font, as a typewriter would.`

NOTE: The style for the <em>, <strong>, and <cite> tags can be adjusted by using the browser's STYLE feature in the OPTION menu. Be sure to insert a container tag with a slash where you want the feature turned off.

appearance tags tell the browser to create a standard heading that is large and bold, and the <B> and </B> appearance tags tell the browser to boldface the words contained between the tags.

An appearance tag must also be inserted to begin a new line. The <br> tag instructs the browser to break, or begin a new line. Because the HTML system of coding assumes blocks of texts, blank lines (rather than indents) are typically used to distinguish one paragraph from the next. The <p> tag instructs the browser to insert a blank line to designate a new paragraph. Most HTML editors allow you to insert the major appearance tags (which tell the browser how to format text) with a click of your mouse.

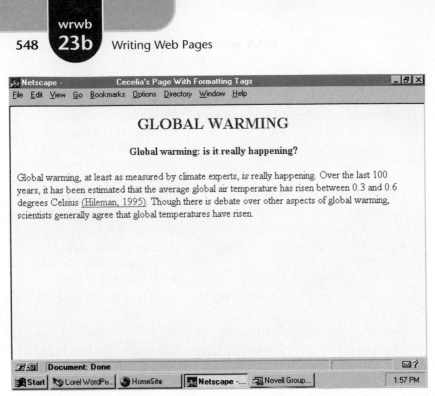

FIGURE 23.7 Browser Window After Appearance Tags Were Added

Here is Cecelia's HTML source code after she added more appearance tags; the view from the browser window is shown in Figure 23.7.

```
<html>
<head>
<title>Cecelia's Page with Formatting Tags</title>
</head>
<BODY BGCOLOR="#FFFFC0" TEXT="#830071">
<center><H2>GLOBAL WARMING</H2>
</center>
<center><H4>Global warming: is it really happening?</H4>
</center>
<p>
Global warming, at least as measured by climate experts, <I>is</I>
really happening. Over the last 100 years, it has been estimated that
the average global air temperature has risen between 0.3 and 0.6
degree Celsius <A HREF="http://jcbmac.chem.brown.edu/baird/chem22I/
global/pg1.html">(Hileman, 1995)</A>.
```

```
<!--This is an example of a link, discussed in 23b-3, Creating Links-->
Though there is debate over other aspects of global warming,
scientists generally agree that global temperatures have risen.
</body>
</html>
```

EXERCISE 23.4

Open your HTML editor's EDIT SOURCE window and type in the basic codes Cecelia used to create her homepage. Then change the text information to create a homepage of your own. Try out a number of the appearance tags listed in the Major HTML Appearance Tags box on (page 546–547). View your homepage in the browser window.

3 Creating links

To provide readers with links to other documents on the World Wide Web, to other locations within the same document, or to related documents within the same Web site, you create a link. Your HTML editor will assist you in creating the link when you select the LINK icon from the toolbar. However, links can be tricky; they take a certain amount of practice and experimentation. If you know the underlying HTML code for various links, you will be able to troubleshoot by editing the HTML source code as needed.

23.7
Details on how to create links on the Web.

Basic hyperlinks

Hyperlinks are coded with tags that refer to a specific Web site's URL. The basic format of a hyperlink is as follows:

```
<A HREF="http://www.webaddress.com">highlighted text</A>
```
Anchor   Reference   URL   Hot text   Anchor
tag   tag   tag

The <A tag indicates the start of a hyperlink. HREF, which stands for Hypertext REFerence, refers to the address of the Web page with which you want to establish a link. In actual code, you would supply the Web address (URL) inside the quotation marks. The highlighted text becomes the **hot text,** linked to the referenced address. When the user clicks on the highlighted text, the browser will retrieve the document indicated in the hypertext reference. The </A> tag at the end closes the hyperlink.

In Figure 23.7, a hyperlink connects Cecelia's homepage to the URL of her Web reference source, Hileman. When a reader points to the highlighted word using a mouse, a small hand appears, indicating a link, and the URL for the link appears in the lower left-hand portion of the browser's screen. When the reader clicks on the highlighted word, the browser links to the URL indicated.

Link to a specific location on the same Web page

You can provide a link to a destination (a word, phrase, or paragraph) on the same Web page, allowing the reader to jump quickly from one part of the document to another. To jump within a single Web page, insert the name of a location that you have bookmarked or targeted, instead of the URL, inside the quotation marks.

```
                                Anchor  Reference  Name of the bookmark
                                tag       tag         or target
You may wish to read my résumé in the <A HREF="#Résumé">resume</A>
section found later in this document.          Hot link  Anchor tag
```

To show the browser where the linked text begins, you also need to name a destination tag (also called a bookmark or a target in some HTML editors). The destination tag indicates the point to which the browser should jump.

```
<A NAME="Résumé"></A>
Anchor  Name  Bookmark  Anchor
tag     tag   or target tag
```

Link to another Web page on the same Web site

Often Web sites are made up of a series of documents that are linked to each other. When the documents all reside at the same location (in the same directory or folder) within the Web server, the links are called relative links or **anchors** and you do not need to include the entire URL. Simply supply the appropriate file name inside the quotation marks and then, in your highlighted text, describe the page you want linked.

```
<A HREF="ceceliap2.html">next page</A>
Anchor  Reference  File name  Hot text  Anchor
tag     tag                             tag
```

Figure 23.8 shows relative links to subsequent pages of Cecelia's Web site.

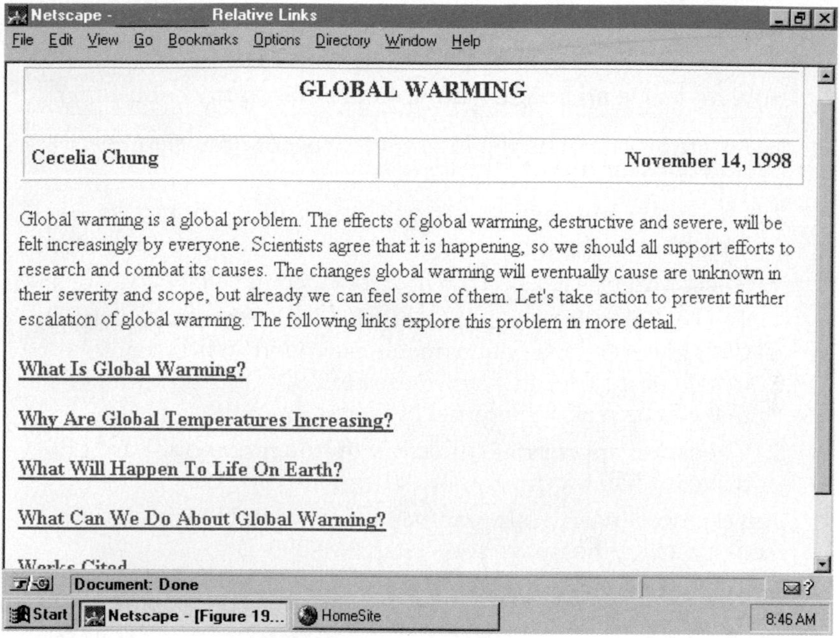

FIGURE 23.8 Relative Links

4 Locating images

Many wonderful images can be found on the Web. However, you need to be aware that all graphics, by virtue of their publication on the Web, are automatically copyrighted by the author. To use another person's graphics from a Web site, you must secure that person's permission. If an email address is included at a site, you can email the person and ask his or her permission to replicate the graphic on your site. Or, you may find a statement on the page permitting certain limited, non-commercial uses of the graphics. Remember: Using someone else's graphic on your own site without prior permission is a form of plagiarism (see 11a-3).

Many sites on the Web were created specifically to make images available for use by others. A search engine will help you locate these images. For example, the *Google.com* and *AltaVista* search tools include image directories. Or, you can search by name for the image you are looking for. For example, if you are looking for a picture of a tiger, you can instruct the search engine to search for "tiger image." For more information on graphics, go to the *PageWorks* homepage at

HELP

How do I save an image from the Internet to my computer?

1. Locate an image on the Internet that is not protected by copyright.
2. Click your mouse button (for PC users, the right mouse button) over the image.
3. Select SAVE IMAGE AS on the menu that comes up.
4. The original file name will be displayed in the dialog box. Give the graphic a new name, if desired. (It will already be in a *gif* or *jpg* format, since these are the graphical formats that can be read by Internet browsers.)
5. Choose an appropriate directory or folder on your hard drive or disk for the graphics file.

You can now insert your graphics file into an HTML document by using the image source tag (see 23b-5).

NOTE: Some operating systems and browsers will not provide a menu in response to a mouse click.

WWW

23.8

Steps for saving an image from the Internet.

<*http://www.snowcrest.net/kitty/hpages*>, which discusses fair use of graphics and has links to numerous image directories on the Web. Other useful sites include the *Clip Art Connection* at <*http://www.clipartconnection.com/index.html*> and *Barry's Clip Art Home Page* at <*http://www.barrysclipart.com*>. In addition to clip art, these sites include numerous backgrounds and animated graphics.

WWW

23.9

Instructions for adding images to a Web page.

5 Using visuals

To include visuals in a Web document, you need to insert a code called an **image source tag** in the body of the page telling the browser where to locate the image. Your HTML editor will assist you in creating the image source tag when you click the IMAGE or INSERT PICTURE icon on the Web toolbar. Image source tags allow you to incorporate into your document many kinds of graphical images, such as photographs, clip art, drawings, icons, charts and graphs, and animations. The basic format for the image source tag is as follows:

```
<IMG SRC="gwarmpic.gif">
```
Image source tag   File name

Include the name of the image file you wish to use within the quotation marks. The graphical image itself is not located within the HTML document; rather, it is linked to the document. The image source code tells the browser to retrieve the appropriate graphics file. You must indicate the exact directory path in your image source tag so that the browser can locate the image's source.

AUDIO
Troubleshooting when graphics do not open.

Here is Cecelia's code with the image source tags added; the view from the browser window is shown in Figure 23.9.

```
<html>

<head>

<title>Example of image source</title>

</head>

<--!What follows is a table definition, creating the table used for
the banner. See 23b-8-->

<table border cellpadding=5 width="100%">

<tr>

<td colspan="2" align="center" valign="top" width="54%">
```

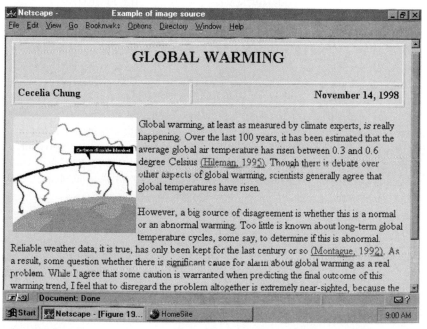

FIGURE 23.9 Browser Window After Image Source Tags Were Added

```
<BODY BGCOLOR="#FFFFC0" TEXT="#830071">
<H2>GLOBAL WARMING</H2></td></tr>
<tr>
<td valign="top"><B>Cecelia Chung</B></td>
<td align="right" valign="top" width="54%">
<B>November 14, 1998</B></td>
</tr>
</table>
<p><IMG SRC="gwarmpic.gif" width="190" height="175" align="left">
Global warming, at least as measured by climate experts, <em>is</em>
really happening. Over the last 100 years, it has been estimated that
the average global air temperature has risen between 0.3 and 0.6
degree Celsius <A HREF="http://jcbmac.chem.brown.edu/baird/chem22I/
global/pg1.html">(Hileman, 1995)</A>. Though there is debate over
other aspects of global warming, scientists generally agree that
global temperatures have risen.
<p>
However, a big source of disagreement is whether this is a normal or
an abnormal warming. Too little is known about long-term global
temperature cycles, some say, to determine if this is abnormal.
Reliable weather data, it is true, have only been kept for the last
century or so <A HREF="http://www.envirolink.org/pubs/rachel/
rhwn300.htm">(Montague, 1992)</A>. As a result, some question whether
there is significant cause for alarm about global warming as a real
problem. While I agree that some caution is warranted when predicting
the final outcome of this warming trend, I feel that to disregard the
problem altogether is extremely short-sighted, because the effects of
even a temporary, normal warming trend are potentially devastating
for earth and its inhabitants. Most people would agree. It is in our
best interests to know as much as possible about global warming, its
causes and potential effects. Before we discuss the true nature of
the controversy, let's look at how global warming works.
</body>
</html>
```

Providing text alternatives to images

It is a courtesy to use the ALT tag as an attribute along with image source tags so that all users will receive a text explanation for what appears in a graphics box. Having an ALT tag is important for users who have turned off graphics to increase the speed of their browsers as well as for visually impaired users who have special browsers that "read" to them the information that appears on screen. To allow all visitors to your site to see descriptive text of an image, add the following ALT tag within the image source tag itself.

```
<IMG SRC="sunpic.gif" ALT="Sun Graphic">
```
Image source   File name   ALT tag   Alternative text
tag   description

Aligning images and text

When you insert an image into a document, the written text that follows the image tag will normally be aligned with the bottom of the graphic. If you want the text to appear somewhere else, you need to include the appropriate instructions in your image source tag.

```
<IMG SRC="sunpic.gif" ALIGN="left" ALT="Sun Graphic">
```
Image source tag   File name   Graphic alignment   Alternative description
                                                       for text browsers

The ALIGN="left" code tells the browser to put the graphic to the left of the text. The text will wrap around the graphic. Other possible alignments include "right," which puts the graphic to the right of the text, and "center," which centers the graphic. If you do not want the words to wrap around the graphic, use the <BR CLEAR="left"> or the <BR CLEAR="right"> code. If you just want the text to drop down below the graphic before it resumes, include the break tag <br> as the next command following the image source tag. An HTML editor can make this alignment process easier. In *Word* or *Composer* you can simply click and drag the image to the appropriate location.

Sizing your images

Notice that the image source code that produced Figure 23.9 includes a size command (width="190" height="175"). This code tells the browser how many pixels wide and high the picture should be when displayed on the screen. To avoid distorting the image, it is better to size the graphic before you save it rather than using the size codes in your image source tag. However, size code can be used to make minor adjustments to the width and height of the image after it has been saved as a file.

23.10

Steps for altering images with *Photoshop*.

HELP

How do I revise a graphical image?

1. Launch your graphics program, such as *Photoshop*, and open the graphics file you wish to revise.

2. Find the menu item that allows you to resize images. You may be able to use either pixels or inches to adjust width and height.

3. Change any other aspects of the graphic that need revising, such as shading, contrast, and sharpness.

4. Check the size of the graphics file to make sure that you have not made the file too large to load easily on the Web (30–50 K is a reasonable size; navigation graphics should be less than 10 K).

5. Resave the graphic. Be sure it is still in a *gif* or *jpg* format, since these are the graphical formats that can be read by Internet browsers. To be the most efficient, save multicolored graphics as *jpg* files and graphics with few colors as *gifs*.

NOTE: To keep graphics files reasonably sized, choose only the resolution needed for screen displays. Computer screens display an average resolution of 96 dpi (dots per inch) so your graphics should be saved at a dpi of 96 or less.

6 Scanning pictures and photographs

You may wish to scan your own photographs or graphics and save them as graphics files. To use a scanner, you will need basic instructions from your lab supervisor or instructor. Remember that graphics files should not exceed 30–50 K (kilobytes). For advice on how to revise your graphic appropriately, see the Help box.

7 Inserting your address

You should include your name, address, and the date of posting on any Web site you author (preferably at the bottom of every page). To do so, enclose your name, the dates on which the site was posted or last updated, your email address, plus any copyright or acknowledgment information within a pair of address tags, <address> and </address>. In order to link your email address, use the following code, entering the appropriate information within the address containers.

Address tag
|
```
<address> Cecelia Chung<br>
```

```
Established: 14 November 1998, Last Updated: 25 January 1999<br>
```

Anchor tag   Reference tag   Mail tag and address   Hot text   Close anchor tag
| |
```
<A HREF=mailto:cecelia@cc.usu.edu>cecelia@cc.usu.edu</A>
```

```
</address>
```
|
Address tag

This coding follows the typical pattern of links: the first part after HREF tells the browser what email address should be linked, and the second part indicates the text to be highlighted on the page. When readers click on the highlighted text, they will be provided with an email screen that includes space to type an email message.

8 Using tables and frames

To place information appropriately on a page, you can use a table, which divides the page both vertically and horizontally into cells. The individual cells can vary in size, have borders of various types (either visible or invisible), and contain text or graphics. Tables allow Web authors to display information in vertical columns, for example. Look at the code used to produce the banner in Figure 23.9. Notice that the table code begins with the table command, including the border definition (5 pixels wide). Each new table row is indicated with the <tr> command; each table cell is defined with the table definition <td> command. Remember to close the code with the slash command (</td> or </tr>) once each cell is completed. Most HTML editors will help you create a table. Or, you can create a table in your word-processing program; then the table will be converted into HTML code automatically when you save the document as an HTML file. This is how Cecelia created the table for her banner.

Another way Web authors divide information is by using frames to put the information into different windows on the page. It is beyond the scope of this handbook to describe writing in frames. However, most HTML editors provide such instruction, as do guidebooks on HTML authoring.

9 Using other media

In addition to using visual images to enhance your Web documents, you can also use other types of media, such as audio and video, to complement your discussion. However, it is important to remember that you should use only media elements that are integral to the meaning of your Web pages. Most Web users have experienced Web pages in which the multimedia applications overwhelm and obscure the message of the site: audio clips that automatically begin when you enter the page, visuals that take forever to load, and so on. When used inappropriately, multimedia components can distract or irritate your readers.

If audio or video media seem appropriate to your Web document, then be sure that you integrate such elements smoothly into the flow of your writing and explain them to your readers. For example, a student writing a Web document about singer Jimmy Buffet naturally wanted to incorporate into the site audio clips of some of Buffet's songs. The student found audio clips readily available on the Internet. He placed links to the sound files into his document at the appropriate places, along with icons that indicated the nature and size of each audio clip. By clicking on the audio link icon, the reader would be connected to the Buffet site to hear the song. If you want to use sounds that are not readily available as freeware on the Internet, you can record your own sounds with the appropriate microphone and software, save the recordings as audio files, and add links to them in your Web document.

Whenever you add multimedia elements to your pages, be certain that you consider the "load time" of the clip. Video and audio files tend to be quite large—and hence take a long time to load into a browser. Waiting endlessly for a video clip to load can be extremely irritating to a reader. It is best to give readers a choice as to whether to load a file or not. Indicate somewhere the size of the file so that readers can anticipate how long it will take to load. To shorten load time, you can use excerpts of files or still shots from videos instead of the entire files. It just makes good rhetorical sense to consider your readers when incorporating multimedia elements into your Web documents. Also, be sure to secure permission before incorporating any copyrighted media into your web site.

10 Creating a template

Once you have created your homepage, you may want to design or customize your own template. It is easier for readers if all the pages at your site have the same look. The template should include elements such as background information, fonts, colors, headers, navigational buttons, author information, and your email address, if it will appear on all secondary pages at your site as well as your homepage. Save the template as a separate document, and title it template.htm. Then, each time you begin a new page for your site, you can open the template and use the SAVE AS option to save it under that page's designated file name.

Here is a sample template.

```
<html>
<head>
<title>Your site's name</title>
</head>
<BODY BGCOLOR="red">
<H2>The page's title as a number 2 heading</H2>
<!--Place the page's text here, including all relative and remote
links.-->
<p>
<A HREF="http:URL of your homepage">Home</A>
<!--This link will return to homepage-->
<Address>
Created by (Your Name)<br>
Established: (date), Last Updated: (date)<br>
<AHREF=mailto:yourlogin@yourschool.edu>yourlogin@yourschool.edu</A>
</address>
<!--This links to your email address-->
</body>
</html>
```

EXERCISE 23.5

Using your homepage as a starting point, create a template. The template should include all features that will be consistent throughout your Web site. Delete the text of the homepage, leaving only the necessary codes. Your template should look something like the sample template in this section. Save the template as a document in an appropriate directory or folder.

AUDIO

Revise areas of your site that need improvement.

23c Evaluate and refine your Web site

WWW

23.11

Evaluating Web sites.

Once you have created your homepage and secondary pages, review them carefully to ensure that the text is correct, the links are accurate, the graphics are well located, and the overall look of the

www

23.12

An HTML
resource page
that can be
used to refine
your site.

WEBLINK

http://lcweb.loc.gov/
iug/html/
The Library of Congress
HTML resource page

site is pleasing. Refine your Web site, using the HTML editor of your choice. Preview your pages in the browser window from time to time to see how the site is shaping up. It would be a good idea to review the design principles in Chapter 22 at this time.

1 Checking the text

Web texts should be written in simple, direct sentences that speak to all visitors to the site. Typically, you will want to use the second person "you" when addressing your readers. Since many readers may enter your site via secondary pages rather than the homepage, make certain that the text on each page is explanatory enough to stand on its own.

Be sure that the text of your page is absolutely correct—there should be no spelling or punctuation errors. Some HTML editors do not have spell checkers, so you should carefully spell check the text through your word-processing program prior to saving it as an HTML file. Proofreading is more difficult onscreen than on paper, so you might want to print out a copy of your Web site for proofreading. (See also the editing and proofreading advice in Chapter 5.) When you post your work to the Web, it will be published in a forum that can be read by anyone anyplace in the world. You want your site to reflect well on you and to highlight your abilities as a writer. In addition to being correct, information must be properly attributed; be certain that you give credit for anything that you have taken from other sources—whether the material is graphics or text, and whether the sources are on the Internet or in print.

2 Checking the relative links

The relative links—to other Web pages on the same site and to other destinations on the same Web page—should all work in the browser window. If they do not, go back to the HTML editing window and check your codes. Internet browsers are extremely literal— if a period or a quotation mark is missing in the code, the link will not work.

3 Checking the remote links

The remote links—to Web sites other than your own—should all be checked with the Internet browser. Open each page in the browser to ensure that all of the links connect to the correct location on the Web. If they do not, you need to go back to the HTML editing window to check your codes. The URL for the link must be typed *exactly* as it is listed at the site or the link will not work. When you link to another person's Web site, as a courtesy, you should notify that person by email of your intention. Also be certain that you have given clear attribution to all information used from a remote site so as not to give a false impression that someone else's work is your own.

4 Checking the graphics

When you open your document in the Internet browser, the graphics that you have included should all appear. To check, open your Web pages in both major browsers, *Explorer* and *Netscape*, since browsers can differ as to how they display the pages and the graphics. If something is wrong, the browser will display an icon instead of the graphic. When an icon appears, first check the code for image source tags. Each graphics file name needs to be listed in the image source tag in exactly the same way as it is in your folder. Second, check the location of your graphics file. Either the graphics file must be in the same folder on your disk or hard drive as the HTML document file or you must provide the exact path, including all subfolders. If the graphics file is in a different folder (perhaps an image folder), the browser will not be able to locate it without such a path. When you uncover a problem, the easiest thing to do—rather than changing the path in all your image source links—is to move or copy the graphic into the appropriate folder.

5 Checking the overall look

As a final check, once again open your Web site in your Internet browser (using the OPEN FILE IN BROWSER option from the FILE menu). Try to read the site as an objective reader might. Does the rhetorical stance you wish to portray (persona, purpose, audience) come across? Ask a friend, a classmate, or your instructor to view your site and give you feedback. Did he or she have any trouble with navigation? What impression did your site leave?

23d Transfer your site to an Internet server

Prior to sending the Web files to your Internet server, be certain that your site is exactly as you want it to be. Once the files are on the server, they will stay there until you send them again. You cannot edit your Web site from the server. Rather, you have to edit the files in the HTML editor and transfer them again, overwriting the original files. Use PUBLISH or FTP (file transfer protocol) to send your Web files to the Internet server. (See also 22b-1.)

EXERCISE 23.6

Check your Web documents carefully. Open the documents in your Internet browser and use the suggestions in 23c to evaluate and refine your Web site. Finally, PUBLISH or FTP all of the files in your Web site directory, including the graphics files and secondary page files, over to your Internet server.

FOR COLLABORATION

Once it has been posted to the Web, arrange for another student in your class to review your Web site. Student reviewers should use the suggestions outlined in 23c for evaluating and refining a Web site. Exchange emails with your peers in which you outline your revision suggestions.

CHAPTER **24**

Email and Electronic Communications

FAQs

▶ How do I become a member of an email community or study group? (24a)

▶ How formal should my email messages be? (24a-4)

▶ What is netiquette? (24a-4)

▶ How can I participate in real-time discussions online? (24c)

▶ How can I make use of Web course tools? (24d)

▶ How can I write collaboratively online? (24e)

The Internet—or the Net, as it is affectionately called—is a system of interconnected computer networks. It allows users to communicate with each other through a variety of forums.

AUDIO

Chapter overview.

- Personal email
- Electronic mailing lists
- Bulletin boards and newsgroups
- Instant messaging and chat rooms
- Collaborative writing online

The most common ways of logging on to the Internet are through a direct link and through a telephone or cable link. To connect to a network through a telephone line, many people use a modem. To use a modem, you first need an Internet service provider (ISP) that will supply you with a connection to the Internet. Many such providers exist;

investigate several to find the provider that works best for you. Often, colleges and universities provide the academic community with direct Internet access from campus labs, faculty offices, classrooms, and dorm rooms. At some schools, students are given an electronic mailing address during orientation when they first arrive on campus.

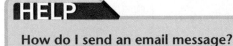

24a Build community through electronic mail

24.1

Using email to build community.

AUDIO

Use email for peer review.

Using electronic mail, you can communicate with others around the world, much faster than through traditional "snail mail." Because it is fast, easy, and relatively inexpensive, email is enormously popular.

There may be several options available to you for accessing your email. Through its email program (called a **mail client**), your college may provide you with access to an email account on its Internet server. Or, you may use your Web browser's email program to read your mail. You may have access to a local mail client that resides on your own computer, such as *Eudora, Microsoft Outlook,* or *Outlook Express.* Finally, there are free email services available on the Internet, such as *Hotmail* or *Netscape Mail.*

24.2

Step-by-step instructions for sending email.

HELP

How do I send an email message?

1. Open the email program (mail client) that you wish to use. Some common ones are *Eudora, GroupWise, Outlook,* and *Netscape Communicator.*

2. Select NEW MESSAGE, and type the recipient's address in the "to" or "send" slot. (To reply to a message, click on the REPLY option rather than NEW MESSAGE. Your mail client will supply the address automatically.)

3. Type the subject on the "subject" line (for example, "Your question about our paper" or "Responding to Sara's point").

4. Type the full address of any other recipients on the "cc" line.

5. Type your email message, and then send it.

NOTE: If the program notifies you that the message has been returned, check the address in one of the directories listed in 24a-3.

1   Collaborative work or study groups

Email is a great way to maintain contact with classmates in a work or study group. Email **addresses** have two parts: the user name and the domain name. These parts are separated by the @ sign, as in <mparker@cc.mtu.edu>. Collect your classmates' email addresses just as you would their phone numbers. Store these addresses in the address book on your mail client so that you do not have to retype them each time you want to send a message. Most mail clients allow you to store multiple addresses in an address book under one heading, such as "study group." Each time you select the group name, all of the addresses will appear in the "to" slot of your SEND MAIL dialogue box.

VIDEO
Participating
in electronic
conversations.

(**FOR COLLABORATION**)

Using your mail client, set up a study group with a group address that includes the addresses of all members of the group. Mail a few test messages to each other, and use the REPLY TO ALL function to reply to everyone in the group. Discuss the ways in which this email study group could help you with your class work.

2   How to use electronic mail

There are many different email programs available today, many of which are free. In this section of the chapter, we will provide a general description of how email programs typically work. However, please note that the email program you are using may differ somewhat from those discussed and illustrated here. It would be a good idea for you to find out what email program your campus typically uses and to learn about it on your own.

Writing and sending email messages

The email program you are using will allow you to write and send email messages to specific recipients. You will need to type an exact email address on the "send to" line—even one incorrect letter will result in an unsuccessful delivery. There will also be a "subject" line on which you should give a brief description of the email's content. If you are sending copies of the message to other email recipients, include their email addresses on any "cc" or "copy to" line(s). Most email programs will also allow you to "attach" a document file from your word-processing program to your email message (see 23a-6). When you have

ecomm

all the destination addresses, subject, and attachments completed, then you can compose your email message. Typically, it is acceptable to write in an informal, conversational style when composing email. However, there are exceptions, such as when you are using email to send a cover letter to a prospective employer. Be sensitive to the need for adjusting the formality of your email to your intended audience. See Figure 24.1 below for an illustration of an email message that is ready to be sent.

Responding to email messages

When you respond to an email that you have received, you can use the REPLY TO or RESPOND option, rather than creating a new email message. The recipient's email address will be automatically configured for you by the email program. Double-check to be certain that the person or persons you wish to reply to are indicated correctly in the address line. Some email programs allow you to reply to everyone who received a message (including all those to whom copies were sent) by selecting REPLY ALL. Also, check to be certain that the subject line is still appropriate and change it if necessary.

Email programs typically give you the option of including the original message in your reply—an option that can be changed via the

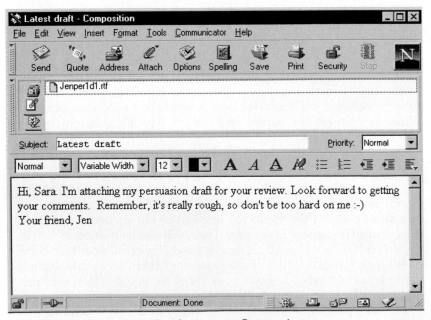

FIGURE 24.1 Sending Email with *Netscape Communicator*

email program's settings. If the original message is included in your reply, you may wish to incorporate your responses directly into the text of the previous message. If you do, be certain that your text is delineated from the original text in some fashion. Many email programs will use a line or dash in the margin to show what text is quoted from the original. You may also wish to set your text apart using a different font style, such as italic or bold. However, remember that not all email programs will support different font styles so your recipients may not see the highlighting that you intended. See Figure 24.2 for an illustration of an email reply message.

In addition to replying to email messages, it is also possible to forward a message that you received to someone else. To do so, you select the FORWARD option on your email client. However, you will want to be selective about forwarding email. As noted in the netiquette discussion below, it is usually not wise to forward an email message unless you have a compelling reason to do so and unless you have the permission of the original message's author.

3 Email addresses

To find the address of a student on your own campus, go to your college's homepage on the Web and look for an email directory of stu-

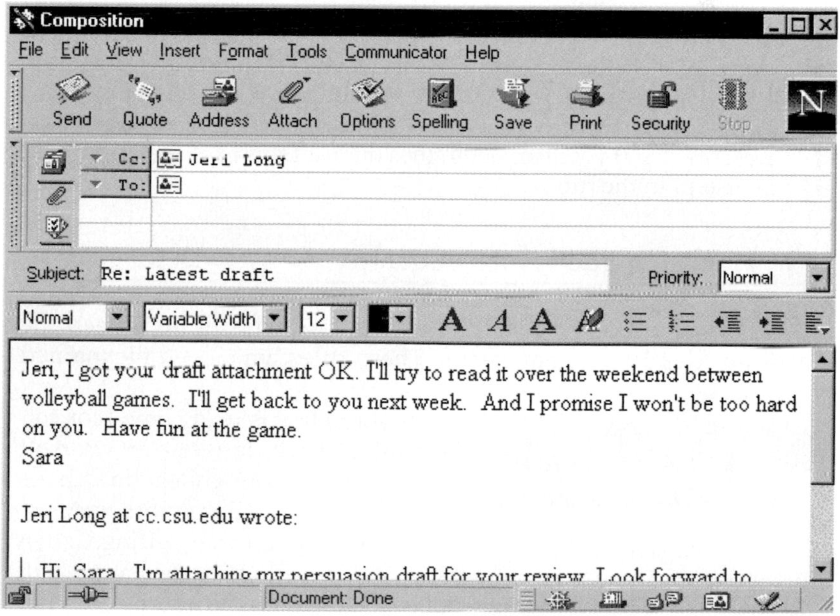

FIGURE 24.2 Replying to Email with *Netscape Communicator*

dents. To search for the address of someone on another campus, go to one of the Web search tools and type in the name of the college as the search term. For example, if you wanted to contact a friend at Washington University, you would type "Washington University" as the search term. Once you found and opened the university's homepage, you could look for your friend's address in the student email directory. Note, however, that not all schools allow outside access to their student directories.

Here are some other Internet sites that offer help in locating email addresses.

Bigfoot	<http://www.bigfoot.com>
WhoWhere Lycos	<http://www.whowhere.lycos.com>
Yahoo People Search	<http://people.yahoo.com>
Internet Address Finder	<http://www.iaf.net>
Usenet Addresses Database	<http://usenet-addresses.mit.edu>
World Email Directory	<http://www.worldemail.com>

Such email directories are not always comprehensive. If you cannot find someone's email address by using directories, contact that person directly via regular mail or telephone and ask for his or her email address.

(EXERCISE 24.1)

Look in several email directories for the email address of a friend or acquaintance in another state. Discuss your results with classmates. How successful were you? What problems, if any, did you have? Brainstorm about other similar searches you might want to conduct. Describe what you learned, in the course of this exercise, that might be useful in the future.

---

4 **Practicing good email etiquette**

Internet users have developed a set of rules to help keep the medium friendly and courteous. These rules have been nicknamed **netiquette.**

24.3

Some guidelines for electronic etiquette.

WEBLINK

http://www.albion.com/ netiquette/

A great netiquette homepage

If your class is using email for collaborative work, familiarize yourself with any rules your college may have about email use. Behaviors that are not acceptable in other settings, such as verbal or sexual harassment, will not be tolerated on the Internet. It is not

Netiquette

- Always type a subject heading for your email that describes the message's content. Use the REPLY function to maintain continuity on a topic.

- Use an appropriate salutation. For informal messages, you can just begin with the person's name. For business messages, use the standard business salutation and form of address (for example, "Dear Ms. Smith:").

- Keep messages brief and to the point.

- End messages with your name and email address. Keep this information in your AUTOTEXT file or store it as a macro or the equivalent in your word-processing program. Alternatively, if your email program allows you to create and store a signature file, you can insert it at the end of your message with a click of the mouse. (Note: Some mail clients automatically attach the **signature file**, once it has been established.)

- Do not forward a message you received unless you have a compelling reason to do so. When people send you an email message, they are communicating with *you*, not with some undetermined person to whom you might forward the message. If you decide to forward a message, check to see if personal messages copied within the current message need to be deleted.

- Do not quote from an email message unless the writer has given you explicit permission to do so.

- Be careful about punctuation and spelling—but also be tolerant of others' errors. Email is often less formal than many other types of writing, and many people neglect to proofread their messages because of the conversational nature of the medium. However, try not to make these mistakes yourself as they can reflect negatively on your professionalism.

- Avoid using all capital letters in email messages; it is the electronic equivalent of shouting. Do not overuse punctuation—especially exclamation points. Do not use all lowercase, either.

- Carefully consider the potential effect of your message before you send it. If there is any chance that the message could be misinterpreted by the reader, take time to revise it.

AUDIO
The importance of netiquette.

appropriate to use your classmates' email addresses for chain letters, advertising, or other similar purposes. Nor is it appropriate to use those addresses to ask someone out on a date. Also, avoid "flaming"—writing angry or abusive messages. If you are flamed, do not reply in kind. Either ignore the message or respond calmly.

You should also be aware that the informal messages that you are accustomed to writing among family and friends may not be appropriate for email you are writing in school or at work. Often writers fall into the habit of writing the same way for all audiences rather than adjusting the tone and style of their email communications based on the rhetorical context—the audience and purpose for the message. In general, you should use a more formal tone, greeting, and closing in messages to someone you don't know well or to an authority at school (such as your instructor) or a superior at work (such as your supervisor). Except for the most informal situations (when writing to your friends or family), you should always use the conventions of Standard Edited English, even in your email messages. Take care to use your spell checker, for example, and to proofread carefully so that your writing is clear and error-free before you send it off. Taking care at this stage can help you avoid embarrassment later.

5 Email shortcuts

Because email is conversational, users have evolved a kind of shorthand to get their meanings across. You may encounter some of the following acronyms.

BTW	by the way
FWIW	for what it's worth
FYI	for your information
IMHO	in my humble opinion
TIA	thanks in advance
TTFN	ta ta for now
TTYL	talk to you later

Some Common Emoticons

:-)	smile	;-)	wink	:-(	chagrin
:-o	shock	:-/	sarcasm	>:D	demonic laugh

Email diacritics are the asterisks, emoticons, and other characters or punctuation used to add emphasis or other flavoring to email messages. Creativity is the rule here, so we will only mention some common practices. However, take care not to overuse email diacritics or the content of your message may become lost. Please note that email shortcuts are not appropriate for professional email such as a memo or report.

In lieu of underlining or italicizing, putting asterisks before and after a word or phrase is the most common way to indicate emphatic or contrastive intonation.

```
That exam was *way too hard*, if you ask me!
```

(Notice that the final asterisk precedes the comma.) To increase the force of the emphasis, you can put asterisks around *each* of the words in the phrase.

```
That exam was *way* *too* *hard*, if you ask me!
```

You can also surround the words you want to emphasize with other unusual characters, as in "#way too hard#" or "_way_too_hard_." Some people use UPPERCASE LETTERING for emphasis, but many people consider uppercase lettering to be too much like shouting.

Emoticons are those combinations of standard keyboard characters that look like faces when they are turned sideways. They are appropriate only in informal messages to friends and not in professional or work correspondence. Some word-processing programs will automatically convert :-) to ☺ and :-(to ☻. Check your FORMAT menu.

As always, be conscious of your audience when using acronyms and emoticons. Include them only when the situation is appropriately informal.

6 File attachments

Many email systems allow you to attach files or documents to your messages. Check your mailing system for an ATTACHMENT option. Using attachments is a convenient way to send your work to a classmate for peer review. One of the advantages of using attachments over the COPY and PASTE method of incorporating text into an email message is that much of your word-processing format can be preserved. Instructors may ask that assignments be turned in as attachments so that they can see the exact formatting of your bibliography, for example, or the way in which you have formatted subheadings in your paper.

When you select the ATTACH feature, you will be prompted to browse for and select the file you wish to attach. Be sure the file name

24.4
Tips for
using file
attachments.

shows up on the attachment line or that there is some other icon to indicate you have successfully attached the file. When the recipient receives your email message and attachment he or she will then be able to download and save the attachment to his or her own computer drive or disk. The document can then be opened in a word-processing program for reading, comment, and response.

If you and your correspondent use two different word-processing programs (e.g., *Microsoft Word* and *WordPerfect*), you can check to be certain that each program will be able to open the other's documents. One way to solve the compatibility problem is to save your document in a generic word-processing format before attaching and sending them. Such formats include rich text format with the file extension *.rtf* and generic text format with the file extension *.txt*. To save your document in another format, use the SAVE AS feature of your word-processing program and select the appropriate file format from the SAVE AS TYPE dialogue box.

Some experimenting may be needed before you can send attachments successfully. But it is worth the effort to investigate this feature because of the ease with which you can then share your writing (see 4c).

> **FOR COLLABORATION**
>
> Using the ATTACHMENT feature of your email program, send a classmate a paper you are currently working on. In the email message itself, specify the kind of advice you would find helpful. Discuss in person the success you had sending the attachment. Describe how you could use attachments to help you write and revise your papers.

24b Build community through online networks

In addition to using electronic mail to communicate with others, there are many other Internet resources that promote the building of online communities. We will discuss several of these resources in this section of the chapter, including electronic mailing lists, bulletin boards, newsgroups, and threaded discussion forums; real-time writing chat rooms; Web class tools; and other specialized Internet applications.

Many students are already familiar with some of these online communication tools, which they use to keep in touch with each other or participate in online forums based on specific hobbies or interests. When you are using these online tools to collaborate with your peers on schoolwork, it may be tempting to slip into your famil-

HELP

How do I find a mailing list about a particular topic?

1. To check via the Web, go to one of the following addresses: <http://tile.net/lists> or <http://www.liszt.com>.
2. To check via email:
   a. Address a message to *listserv@listserv.net*, leaving the subject line blank. (When using listserv software, you do not need a subject.)
   b. As your message, type "list global" or "list global/[your subject]." For example, if you were interested in lists having to do with the subject of writing, you would type "list global/writing." The listserv will respond with a listing via email.
3. When you identify a list you would like to join, follow the instructions in the Help box on page 574.

www

24.5

Step-by-step instructions for finding a mailing list.

iar behaviors of socializing on the Internet. However, it is important to stay focused on the work at hand. Don't get distracted into using the class forums to discuss your college football team or an upcoming fraternity party.

1   Electronic mailing lists

Mailing lists, which are special-interest email lists, distribute messages simultaneously to their many participants, or subscribers. There are thousands of mailing lists on the Internet. Mailing lists are begun by people with a common interest, who want a forum in which to talk to each other. Lists can facilitate committee meetings, fan club meetings, scholarly discussions, and even class discussions and research projects. For example, first-year writing students might want to find a mailing list that will help them better understand a research paper topic. (See the Help box above for details on finding relevant mailing lists.)

One subscriber or group "hosts" the list, providing the software necessary to start and maintain it. The most commonly used software is called list-

WEBLINK

http://www.lsoft.com/
Use "Catalist Search," a search engine for listserv lists worldwide

www

24.6

How to find listservs.

24.7

Step-by-step instructions for subscribing to a mailing list.

serv. **Listserv** software facilitates group discussions and stores and indexes those discussions for later access by participants. When listserv is working well, you will not notice its operation.

Many lists allow anyone who wishes to subscribe to do so. Other lists are selective about their participants and limit the number who can join. In either case, you must subscribe to the list in order to join the discussion or access its archives. (See the Help box for instructions on subscribing to a mailing list.)

Some lists are **moderated**; that is, an individual designated as the list's **moderator** evaluates the appropriateness of messages before they are sent out to everyone on the list. Other lists are unmoderated; that is, anyone can send any message to the others on the list. You should realize that mailing lists sometimes entail a considerable investment of time. Once you subscribe, all of the group's messages will appear in your electronic mailbox. If the group is large and active, your mailbox will quickly fill up with messages. For this reason, you should be selective about the number of mailing lists you subscribe to. When you first join a list, it is a good idea to spend a few days just reading the messages of others—an activity called **lurking.** In this way, you will get a sense of the discussions and the subscribers.

Mailing lists can help you become informed about topics currently under discussion in a particular field as you prepare for a research paper project. For example, joining a mailing list of psychologists would provide you with information on the hot topics in psychology. You can also use mailing lists to do preliminary background research on a topic. However, take care not to request information that you could easily find in books or journals, as this will certainly annoy the other subscribers. (See 24a-4 for more on netiquette, and see 24a-5 for information on email formatting.)

If you use information from a mailing list in a research paper, the posting must be cited either in the text itself or in your list of works cited (see Chapters 13–15). Do not quote anyone's mailing list posting without his or her permission. Here is an example of a listserv posting, reprinted with permission of Barrett M. Briggs.

```
From: IN%"WPA-L@ASUVM.INRE.ASU.EDU" "Writing Program Administration"
1-DEC-1997 09:20:43.95
To: IN%"WPA-L@ASUVM.INRE.ASU.EDU"
Subj: Resuscitating Trigger
Date: Mon, 01 Dec 1997 09:08:27-0700
From: BMB <bmbriggs@CCIT.ARIZONA.EDU>
Howdy,

In what sense, sphere or context are students required to take first
year composition? Don't we all (fairly often) elect to put ourselves
into situations where, once there, we are required to behave in
certain ways? Also, I suggest to my students, vigorously and often,
that no class is more important than one such as first year
composition (fyc) that helps them understand how to manipulate,
consciously, the world for their benefit, and how people will try to
manipulate them ("manipulate" in the neutral sense, that is, meaning:
"to manage and handle skillfully"). Even if "required" meant
something akin to being arbitrarily forced, I'd say fyc should be
required, if only to give students a dawning sense of the value and
power of language consciously manipulated and consciously
interpreted.
Barrett M. Briggs
Tucson
```

EXERCISE 24.2

Following the directions found in the Help boxes in this section, find and join a mailing list on a topic that interests you. Read the conversation for a few days—that is, lurk on the list without posting any messages yourself. What is the thrust of the discussion? Does it surround a controversy? Write a brief summary of the discussion to share with your classmates.

2 Bulletin boards, newsgroups, and threaded discussion forums

24.8

More information and links to bulletin boards, newsgroups, and discussion forums.

Like mailing lists, bulletin boards provide a forum for discussion. However, instead of sending email messages to subscribers, **bulletin boards** post messages electronically for anyone to access and read. There is no need to subscribe individually to a bulletin board.

A **newsgroup** is a type of bulletin board consisting of a collection of email messages tied to a specific topic. **Usenet** has the most extensive array of public newsgroups. In order for you to access Usenet newsgroups from campus labs, your college must subscribe to them. Newsgroups are organized by topic under several umbrella categories, indicated by a prefix.

Umbrella category	Topics covered	Example
talk	discussion of issues	talk.politics.gun
alt	alternative topics	alt.smokers
comp	computer topics	comp.sys.mac
rec	recreational topics	rec.sport.golf
soc	social topics	soc.culture.Kurdish

One way to access newsgroups is through an Internet browser. You may need to configure the Internet browser to allow you to read the newsgroups. Once your system is appropriately configured, you might choose NETSCAPE NEWS from the WINDOW menu, for example, to get a listing of the newsgroups to which your college subscribes. There are literally thousands of Usenet newsgroups to choose from. For a directory of Usenet newsgroups, see *Liszt* (the mailing list directory) at

24.9

Email discussion resources.

WEBLINK

http://www.usenet.about.com/cs/usenetresources/ Usnet information and resources

<http://www.liszt.com>. Like mailing lists, newsgroups can be especially useful as you begin to think about topics for essays and research papers. To search Usenet groups by subject, you can use a search tool such as *Lycos* at *<http://www.lycos.com>* or *Deja News* at *<http://www.dejanews.com>*. Figure 24.3 shows a sample *Deja News* screen.

AUDIO

More on "threads."

Threaded discussion forums are another tool, in addition to listservs and email groups, that may be used by writing classes to conduct class discussions online. These discussion forums are called "threaded" because the posts or messages on the same topic form a dis-

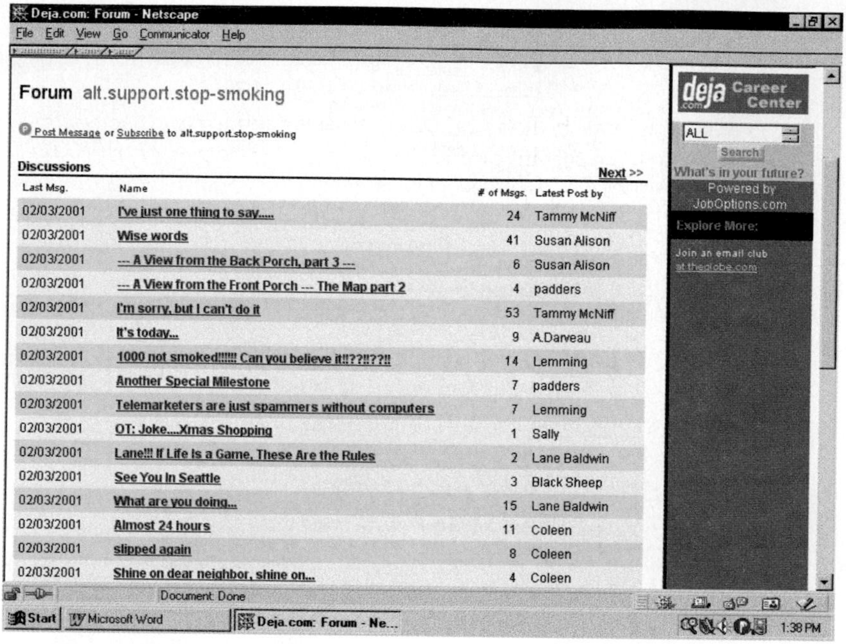

FIGURE 24.3 *Deja News* Screen

cussion "thread." You may begin a new thread by posting a message yourself or you may join an ongoing thread by replying to another message in that thread. Figure 24.4 illustrates an online threaded discussion forum. Notice how the threads of posts and replies are also visually marked by indented margins. Often these discussion forums are a feature of an online Web classroom such as *WebCT* or *BlackBoard*. Web classrooms are discussed in 24d.

EXERCISE 24.3

If your college subscribes to Usenet newsgroups, choose one on a topic that interests you and read a few of the postings. What is being discussed? Who are the participants in the newsgroup? Print out a few postings to discuss with your classmates, and then brainstorm as to how you might use bulletin boards in a research project (see Chapter 10).

```
Christine Hult's English 307 Section 01 - Netscape                          _ □ X
File  Edit  View  Go  Communicator  Help
```

Group 4: Kuhio **Park Terrace** **Discussion on** **Gender from** **CyberReader**	■ ICS 101 Mandatory Brian Kajiyama (9/12/00 2:36:20 PM) (2)
	  ■ ※ **Seems workable** Christine Hult (9/12/00 3:42:43 PM) (3)
	• Persuasion Topic... Kelly Mao (9/12/00 2:09:06 PM) (12)
	  ○ RE: Persuasion Topic... Georganne Nordstrom (9/12/00 2:16:09 PM) (4)
	  ○ ※ **Maybe a bit broader?** Christine Hult (9/12/00 3:43:55 PM) (4)
	  ○ RE: Persuasion Topic... Amy Hu (9/13/00 6:28:09 PM) (1)
	• 2000Election Ellisa Vendiola (9/12/00 2:12:02 PM) (15)
	  ○ RE: 2000Election Charles Bohannan (9/12/00 2:17:57 PM) (4)
	  ○ RE: 2000Election Richard Schnittger (9/12/00 2:19:22 PM) (3)
	  ○ Voting Brian Kajiyama (9/12/00 2:50:05 PM) (3)
	  ○ ※ **Are there two sides?** Christine Hult (9/12/00 3:45:53 PM) (3)
	  ○ RE: 2000Election Amy Hu (9/13/00 6:18:50 PM) (0)
	• Assignment #2-Persuasion Courtney Kunimura (9/12/00 2:12:57 PM) (16)
	  ○ RE: Assignment #2-Persuasion Kelly Mao (9/12/00 2:15:28 PM) (7)
	  ○ RE: Assignment #2-Persuasion Richard Schnittger (9/12/00 2:16:32 PM) (7)
	  ○ RE: Assignment #2-Persuasion Meridith Morisaki (9/12/00 2:19:26 PM) (3)
	  ○ ※ **This has possibilities** Christine Hult (9/12/00 3:46:37 PM) (2)
	    ■ RE: This has possibilities Jason Laricchia (9/14/00 4:26:45 AM) (2)
	• Persuasion Topic Kimberly Koide (9/12/00 2:18:25 PM) (10)
	  ○ RE: Persuasion Topic Richard Schnittger (9/12/00 2:21:18 PM) (3)
	  ○ ※ **Good questions** Christine Hult (9/12/00 3:47:27 PM) (2)
	• my topic is... Nina Murakami (9/12/00 2:19:26 PM) (7)
	  ○ ※ **Yes, good idea.** Christine Hult (9/12/00 3:48:32 PM) (5)
	• Mainstreaming Brian Kajiyama (9/12/00 2:25:11 PM) (7)
	  ○ ※ Interesting & workable Christine Hult (9/12/00 3:49:29 PM) (4)
	    ■ RE: Interesting & workable Georganne Nordstrom (9/13/00 1:09:15 AM) (3)
	  ○ Target and purpose Brian Kajiyama (9/14/00 1:22:15 AM) (1)

```
 ⬛ =🔅=          Document: Done                              🔆 ⬛ ⬛ ⬛ ⬛
 🏁 Start  📝 Microsoft Word    🌐 Christine Hult's Englis...        ◑👁✊◐◙  1:51 PM
```

FIGURE 24.4 Threaded Discussion Forum from *SyllaBase* Web Classroom

24c Build community through instant communication

The communication tools discussed thus far (email, mailing lists, bulletin boards, and newsgroups) are lacking in one respect: they do not allow for conversations in real time (also called **asynchronous communication**). With mailing lists and newsgroups, users post their messages, and others access those messages at their convenience. However, Internet users sometimes like to exchange messages more rapidly, as if they were conversing face to face. Such instant exchanges, called **synchronous communications,** include Internet relay chat (IRC), MUDs and MOOs, and instant messaging.

1 Internet relay chat (IRC)

To provide a more conversational forum, a variety of real-time Internet tools have been developed. One such tool is Internet relay chat (IRC). To use IRC, you need to know the Internet address and port number of an IRC server. Once connected to IRC or a similar chat program, each participant opens a "chat" window on his or her computer. An IRC directory can be found at <*http://www.liszt.com*>.

Anyone who has his or her chat window open can read what the participants in the same chat room are saying. The words that are typed scroll

WEBLINK

http://www.du.org/cybercomp.html

Associated with *Diversity U*, a site on composition in cyberspace, with a focus on MOOs and MUDs

WWW

24.10
More on the "Composition in Cyberspace" homepage.

onto the screen for others to read and respond to. In this way, Internet users can chat with each other. The only delay is the time it takes for a message to travel through phone or cable lines to the participants' computers. However, depending on how many participants are in a given chat room, the delay can be considerable—and can result in a strange conversation in which participants have to wait several seconds or even minutes between replies. Figure 24.5 shows a sample Internet chat window.

FIGURE 24.5 Internet Chat Window from *SyllaBase* Web Classroom

2 Instant messaging

24.11

More on instant
messaging.

Another feature of email communication called **instant messaging** allows you to create a circle of online friends, classmates, or colleagues. The instant messaging service will notify you whenever someone on your group list is also online so that you can begin a chat session with that person via the network, should you desire to do so. You can exchange instant messages with several people in the same conversation window. The automatic typing indicator lets you know when a member of your messaging circle is typing a response. If you are working on a collaborative project, it might be worthwhile for everyone in the group to set up instant messaging accounts on the same service.

3 MUDs and MOOs

Another type of real-time writing tool used on the Internet is provided by MUDs and MOOs. Both a **MUD** (multi-user dimension) and a **MOO** (MUD, object oriented) define a space on the Internet where users can interact with each other simultaneously (hence the name *Multi-User Dimension*). Those who wish to participate in a MUD or a MOO need to establish a remote connection between their own computer and the computer that controls the MUD's or MOO's Internet space. Such a connection can be established by using *Telnet* or other Internet software that provides an interface, such as *Pueblo*. You need to know the Internet address and port number of the MUD/MOO server. Instructions for connecting to a MUD or a MOO vary considerably from site to site. You can use an Internet search tool to find out more about the MUDs and MOOs that are currently available.

MUDs and MOOs were originally developed to allow users in different locations to play computer games with each other. Increasingly, these forums are being used for educational and business purposes. For example, some colleges, such as Kapi'olani Community College in Hawaii, have created MOO spaces in which students can meet to access class assignments or discuss course readings (see Figure 24.6).

(E X E R C I S E   2 4 . 4)

Access the Diversity University MOO at its Web site at <*http://www .du.org/cybercomp.html*>. Log on to the site as a guest. Move around in the site's various rooms and read the conversations you find there. What are the students and instructors talking about? Join in the discussion, if you would like.

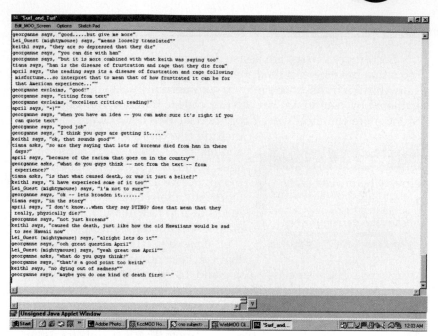

FIGURE 24.6 Kapi'olani Community College MOO

FOR COLLABORATION

Discuss your experience using a MOO with classmates. How might this medium be used to enhance class discussions or peer reviews?

24d Use classroom Web tools

Many courses now make use of the Internet as a means of communication, and we have described some of the individual communication tools that you may encounter in your writing courses (e.g., email listservs, discussion forums, or chat rooms). However, in addition to separate tools, your teacher may make use of a Web classroom site where several tools are bundled into one Web location. Such a Web site often provides course information, such as the course syllabus (outline of the course and its policies), assignments, and class schedule, in addition to communication tools such as discussion forums and chat rooms. The classroom tools are made available to members of the class from any computer that is connected to the Internet to be used at their own convenience.

24.12
A tour of a Web classroom.

ecomm

1 Web courseware packages

Sometimes classes are assisted by an entire fleet of Web course tools that have been pulled together to help your class to function smoothly. Such collections may be commercially packaged or may be gathered by your instructor or your college into one Web site. Some of the more commonly used commercial Web courseware packages include *BlackBoard, WebCT, TopClass*, and *eCollege*. To use one of these packages, your college needs to subscribe to the service for a fee. In fact, in some distance education courses, the class never meets face to face at all, but rather the class is conducted entirely through a Web classroom. It is very important that you become familiar with any Web course tools that your class is using and that you visit the class Web site frequently for updates and bulletins. Teachers will use their online classrooms for different purposes, so you should take the initiative to find out exactly what is included in your class's online Web site and how to use each of the available course tools. This is doubly important in a distance education course, since all of the instructions for participating in the course will be found at the class Web site.

www

24.13

More on how to surf the Net.

WEBLINK

http://learnthenet.com/
english/section/www.html

A site that helps newcomers
learn about using the Net

AUDIO

How the Web
is used in
college
classrooms.

2 Getting started

To begin using a Web classroom, you will first need to know the URL at which your class's Web site can be found. For example, the URL for Web classes in the English department at Utah State University is *<http://syllabase.rp1750.usu.edu/SyllaBase>*. At the opening page for your class's Web site, you will typically be asked to type in a **login name** and password that has been assigned to you by your teacher. Keep careful track of your username and password since it is your key to entering the Web classroom. One of the biggest problems that students often have is finding themselves "locked out" of the classroom because they forgot their passwords!

When you are actually admitted to the online classroom, there will probably be an opening screen with a menu of options (see Figure 24.7). There may be a "getting started" or introductory screen that will help you to become oriented to the tools that are available to you. There may also be course information provided by your instructor that helps you to understand the course policies and expectations.

FIGURE 24.7 *WebCT* Welcome Screen

Take the time to become familiar with the classroom and its tools. This is just as important to your success in the course as attending the face-to-face class sessions and paying attention to the instructor. We will discuss below some of the tools that you are likely to find in your Web classroom.

3 Course information

Web classrooms may include a course calendar (see Figure 24.8), a bulletin board for important messages from the instructor, a syllabus with a course outline and course information such as meeting times, instructor's office hours, descriptions of assignments, and so on. Read all of this information carefully. When instructors make use of online classrooms, they generally do not also provide you with printed "hard" copies of course information but rather rely on you to garner the relevant information directly from the Internet. You can, of course, always print or download this information for your own use, if you wish.

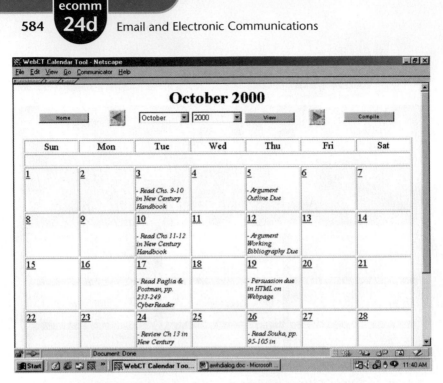

FIGURE 24.8 *WebCT* Class Calendar

4 Course communication tools

Your Web classroom will also provide a number of tools that you will use to communicate with your teacher and others in your class. These may include discussion forums, class email or listservs, chat rooms, homework managers, and file-sharing spaces. Again, take the time to become familiar with any of the communication tools that your class will be using. We discussed email, discussion forums, and chat rooms in 24b-1 to 24b-3. The comparable course tools in your Web classroom will function in a similar fashion to those already described (see Figure 24.9 for an illustration of a post on a discussion forum). The only difference will be that the tools are gathered into one location on the Web, that of your particular Web classroom.

Other course tools not previously described may include a homework manager and a file-sharing space. Both of these tools allow you to share your written work, either with the instructor alone (as in the case of the homework manager), or with everyone in the class (as with the file-sharing space).

Reply   Quote   Save

[Prev Thread][Next Thread][Prev in Thread][Next in Thread]
Article No. 1: posted by **Christine Hult** on Wed, Oct. 25, 2000, 15:02
Subject: Portfolio review

```
Dear Class,

I've finished your first portfolio reviews and I'm very
happy with your work so far.  Please remember that your
argument first draft is due on the Homework Manager on
October 31.

Dr. Hult
```

[Prev Thread][Next Thread][Prev in Thread][Next in Thread]

FIGURE 24.9 *New Century Handbook WebCT* Discussion Post

Homework Manager

With a homework manager, the instructor posts the assignment and when you are ready to turn it in, you browse for your file and then "upload" it to the Web server. Your instructor in turn downloads your work, corrects it or comments on it electronically, and then uploads it once again to the class Web site. In this fashion, work can easily be submitted, graded, and returned without ever being printed out in a hard copy. Homework managers can also keep track of your grades and let you know how you are doing in the class.

File-sharing space

With a file-sharing space, you can post a document to the Web for others in the class to download and read. File sharing works particularly well for peer reviewing and commenting on one another's files. In Figure 24.10 you will see an illustration of a file-sharing space in which students may upload their work to the class Web site. To open one of the files, the student will click on the file name and a dialogue box will appear. By clicking on SAVE LINK AS the student can save the file to his or her own disk drive and then subsequently open it in a word-processing program for commenting. Using the DOCU-MENT COMMENT feature of the word-processing program (see the Help box on page 105), the student can insert document comments

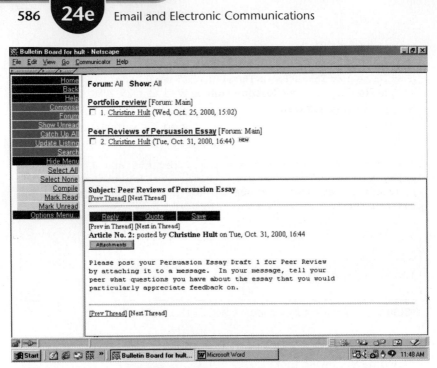

FIGURE 24.10 *WebCT* File Sharing Using Bulletin Board

as part of a peer review session. Once the document has been commented on, it is then uploaded once again to the file-sharing space so that the original author of the document can read the comments. You will need to check with your instructor to learn exactly how the file-sharing system works for your particular Web classroom.

24e Collaborative writing online

Many students are finding that the Internet can facilitate collaborative writing projects. You may be assigned a group project to research a particular service agency in your area and create a Web site for it. Or, you may be asked to collaborate on a newsletter that describes an entity such as your campus writing center that students could benefit from knowing about. Using the community-building Internet tools discussed in this chapter can help your group work efficiently without the need for frequent in-person meetings. Your group can form an email listserv and an instant messaging circle to keep in contact. You can send each other drafts of work in progress via email attachments, and you can use document comments to provide electronic feedbeck to your peers on their drafts. For more information about collaborating via network, see 4c-3.

Increasingly, Internet users are taking advantage of specific software designed to help writers work collaboratively via networks. Using collaborative writing software such as Microsoft's *NetMeeting*, several writers can work simultaneously on the same document. For example, suppose a writer wants advice from an editor on a chapter of her book. Both the author and the editor can open up the chapter in a collaborative writing program and discuss changes that might be made. When a change is made on the document, it shows up on both screens at the same time. Each person's cursor becomes a unique symbol so that it is clear who is doing what with the text. The editor need not even possess the particular software in which the chapter was written; the collaborative writing software will display pages from any other application. Although few colleges are currently using this software, it is gaining acceptance in the workplace.

FOR COLLABORATION

If collaborative writing software is available to you, try revising a paper together with a friend. Discuss the experience with your classmates.

CHAPTER 25

Business Correspondence and Reports

AUDIO
Chapter overview.

25.1
Samples and guidelines for professional writing.

Writing at work differs significantly from writing in school. Rather than analyzing or reflecting on some intellectual topic, workplace writing typically addresses a *practical problem* and proposes some *action* to solve that problem. Instead of writing for a single reader (the instructor) who is obligated to read and evaluate your entire written document, you often must write for multiple readers who are under no such obligation. These readers may choose to only glance at your writing, rather than read it thoroughly. Thus, when writing letters, memos, reports, proposals, and other forms of business correspondence, you should convey your message clearly and concisely.

> **WEBLINK**
>
> http://owl.english
> .purdue.edu/handouts/
> pw/index.html
> A collection of useful handouts from Purdue's OWL

Writing at work also tends to be more collaborative than writing in school. Two or more people may coauthor a report or proposal or even a letter, and others may be asked to read it over and insert changes or corrections. "Boilerplate" from other writers' reports might also be incorporated, perhaps without attribution. This kind of collaboration is commonplace and acceptable in the business world, quite different from writing in school.

Today the most common form of written correspondence in the business world, as in many other environments, is email (see Chapter 24). Because email is so easy and convenient to use, many writers do not give it the care and attention they should. But readers of business email are no different from readers of letters, reports, résumés, and memos, working under time pressure to solve practical problems. When you write business email, apply the same rhetorical considerations to it that you would to other forms of business correspondence.

25a Write concise and professional business letters

People write business letters for a variety of purposes: to make an inquiry or a request, to complain, to apply for a job, to issue an announcement, to sell something, to respond to a previous letter. Letters are typically addressed to a specific person, but they may be circulated to other readers as well. Thus, you should anticipate the possibility that people other than the addressee (an assistant, for example) might read it. Be clear and concise (see Chapter 40), and try to strike a friendly, courteous, and professional tone (see 45c).

Rhetorical considerations

The best way to structure a letter depends on how you think the reader will react to its message. If your reader is likely to respond favorably or neutrally, take the *direct approach* by getting to the point quickly and providing necessary explanations and details later. On the other hand, if your reader is likely to respond to your message unfavorably or skeptically, take a more *indirect approach*, in which you begin with background information or some other form of "bad news buffer" before getting to the main point.

Try to give your letter as positive a tone as possible. Emphasize good news by putting it in positions of prominence (such as at the beginning and end of paragraphs). Try to word your sentences in ways that accentuate the positive. If possible, avoid words with negative connotations such as *regretfully, unfortunately, refuse, will not,* or *failure.* Of course, this should not be overdone; in business writing, clarity is more important than comfort.

Format

The traditional business letter is printed on white or light-colored 8½" x 11" stationery, with every line starting at the left margin (this is known as the *full block format*). If you do not have letterhead stationery, put your return address at the top of the page, on the left with the date. Then type the name and address of the recipient. Be sure to spell the recipient's name correctly. If you are not sure how to spell it, call his or her office and ask someone there. For the salutation, use *Dear Mr. ___* or *Dear Ms. ___* or an appropriate title. If the addressee's first name is gender-neutral, omit *Mr.* or *Ms.* and use the full name: *Dear Dana White.* Avoid using either a first name (unless you know the recipient personally) or a generic term such as *Dear Sir.* If you do not know the recipient's name, use an institutional title or position: *Dear Sales Manager* or *Dear Service Department.* The body of the letter should be divided into block paragraphs, though you may want to use an indented list to draw the reader's attention to special information. Use a conventional close such as *Sincerely, Sincerely yours,* or *Yours truly.* After leaving enough space for your signature, type your name and any other pertinent information, such as your email address, your phone number, and the word *enclosure* if any items are enclosed. The letter should be centered on the page, with at least 1-inch margins all around. A sample business letter in the traditional format appears in Figure 25.1.

Business letters sent by email (see Chapter 24) should satisfy the same general requirements as other business letters: a clear purpose, sufficient background information, correct grammar and spelling, a friendly yet professional tone. But email business letters are usually less formal than traditional ones and have a different format. Since email

Guidelines for Email Letters

1. Use the subject line to orient the reader.
2. Provide any necessary background information in the first sentence or two; if appropriate, reference previous correspondence.
3. Quickly establish your purpose.
4. Focus on the main point.
5. Use simple sentences and short paragraphs.
6. Use personal pronouns and active verbs.
7. Keep it short.
8. Consider letting your letter sit for a while before sending it because once sent, it can't be retrieved.
9. Remember that no email message is strictly confidential.

VIDEO

Levels of formality in email messages.

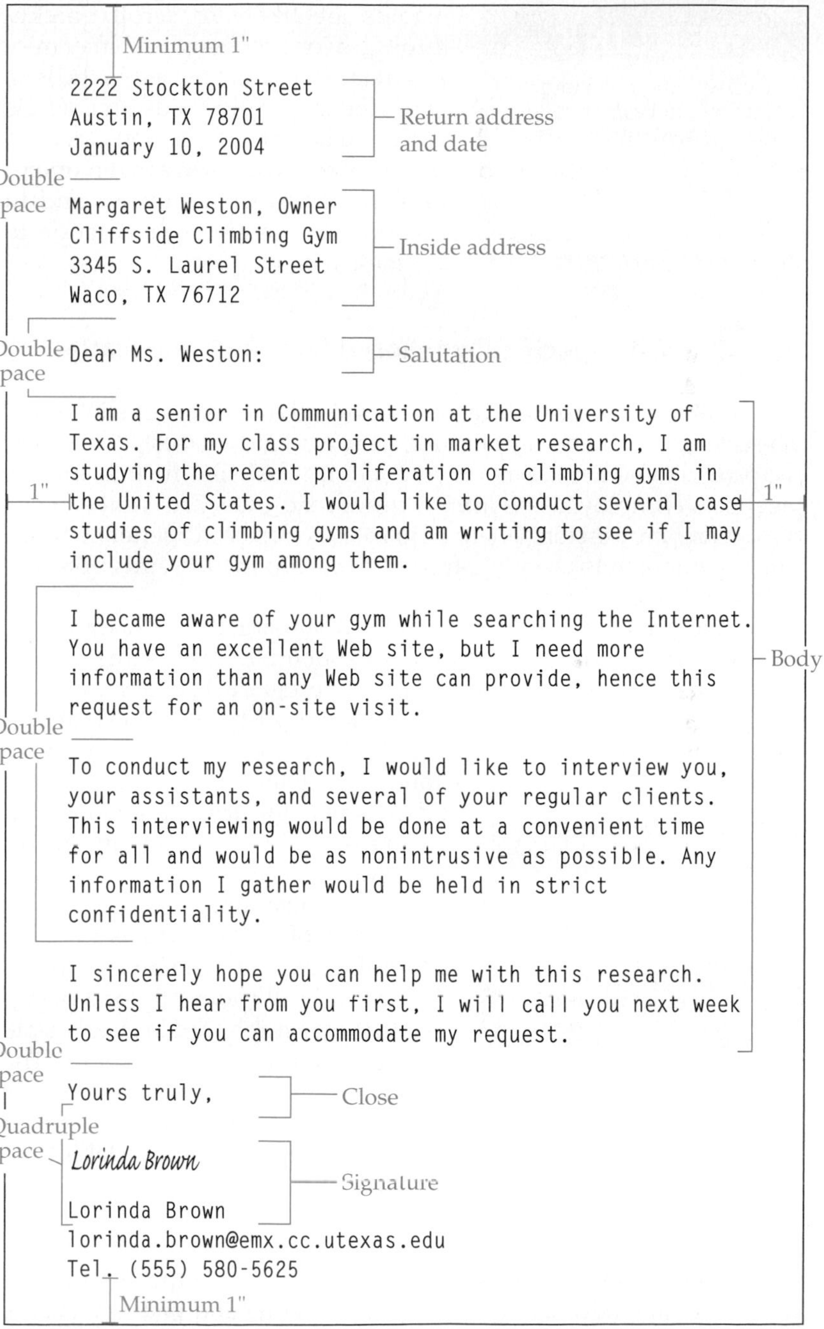

Minimum 1"

2222 Stockton Street
Austin, TX 78701 ⎤ — Return address
January 10, 2004 ⎦   and date

Double ——
space Margaret Weston, Owner
⎡Cliffside Climbing Gym
3345 S. Laurel Street ⎬ — Inside address
Waco, TX 76712

Double ⎡Dear Ms. Weston: ⎤ — Salutation
space

I am a senior in Communication at the University of
Texas. For my class project in market research, I am
studying the recent proliferation of climbing gyms in
1" ─the United States. I would like to conduct several case ─1"
studies of climbing gyms and am writing to see if I may
include your gym among them.

I became aware of your gym while searching the Internet.
You have an excellent Web site, but I need more
information than any Web site can provide, hence this ⎬ — Body
request for an on-site visit.
Double
space
To conduct my research, I would like to interview you,
your assistants, and several of your regular clients.
This interviewing would be done at a convenient time
for all and would be as nonintrusive as possible. Any
information I gather would be held in strict
confidentiality.

I sincerely hope you can help me with this research.
Unless I hear from you first, I will call you next week
to see if you can accommodate my request.
Double
space
Yours truly, ⎤ — Close
Quadruple
space ⎨ *Lorinda Brown*
⎬ — Signature
Lorinda Brown
lorinda.brown@emx.cc.utexas.edu
Tel. (555) 580-5625
Minimum 1"

FIGURE 25.1 Sample Business Letter

WEBLINK

http://writing.colostate
.edu/references/
documents/bletter/index
.cfm

A great guide to writing
business letters

readers are likely to scroll quickly
through a long message and may miss
key items if they are buried in the text,
email letters should focus on a single
topic and be short enough, if possible,
to fit on one screen. Always remember
to observe proper netiquette and to
consider your audience's reaction to
the message.

25b Write specifically tailored letters of application

Knowing how to write a good application letter is crucial to the
job-seeking process. An application letter is a kind of sales pitch, where
the product you are selling is yourself. It is usually the first thing a
prospective employer sees from you, and, of course, you want to make
a good first impression. There is no room for error in a letter of application—no room for beating around the bush, shyness, misrepresen-
tations, or misspellings.

Usually, a letter of application is accompanied by a résumé and
includes some of the same information. But unlike the résumé, the letter should be tailored to one specific job or program. Whereas a résumé
contains a full summary of your past accomplishments, the letter includes only those accomplishments that are relevant to the job or program you are applying for. The tone of the letter should be polite, confident, and enthusiastic, but not pushy.
Where possible, it should emphasize
how your skills would benefit this particular organization.

WEBLINK

http://www.io.com/
~hcexres/tcm1603/
acchtml/lettov.html

All about business corre-
spondence and résumés

A letter of application has the same
general format as a business letter. It
should be brief (normally one page).
The first paragraph should clearly state
what position you are applying for. The
next paragraph or two should describe your primary credentials for
the position. The closing paragraph should express your desire for an
interview and give the reader information about your availability. A
sample letter of application is shown in Figure 25.2.

AUDIO
Proofread job
letters and
résumés.

The envelope

The envelope for a business letter should have the addressee's
name, title, and address in the lower right center and your own name
and address in the upper left corner, as shown on page 594.

2222 Stockton Street
Austin, TX 78701
February 4, 2004

Mr. Jeffrey Lee
Director of Marketing Training
Future Consumer, Inc.
4444 North Sycamore Avenue
Los Angeles, CA 90009-4444

Dear Mr. Lee:

I am writing to apply for acceptance into your marketing training
program. I am especially impressed with the program's emphasis
on market research, product planning, and catalog sales. As a
marketing major at the University of Texas, I believe I am ready
to undertake this challenge and would welcome the opportunity
to prove myself.

Marketing has been a major focus of my college and work
experience. My studies have provided a strong foundation in
communication and business. I have also had experience in
product testing and merchandising through my jobs in market
research and retailing and have been on the "receiving end" of
customer indecision and anxiety. My ability to handle difficult
customers earned me a promotion from direct sales to sales
management.

My résumé is attached. I will be graduating in early June and
would be available for training immediately thereafter. I look
forward to hearing from you.

Sincerely yours,

Lorinda Brown

Lorinda Brown
lorinda.brown@emx.cc.utexas.edu
Tel. (555) 580-5625

enclosure

FIGURE 25.2 Sample Letter of Application

LORINDA BROWN
2222 STOCKTON ST
AUSTIN TX 78701

MR JEFFREY LEE
DIRECTOR OF MARKETING TRAINING
FUTURE CONSUMER INC
4444 N SYCAMORE AVE
LOS ANGELES CA 90009-4444

For better machine readability, the United States Postal Service recommends using all capital letters and no punctuation (use spacing instead). Use standard compass point abbreviations (N = north, SE = southeast, and so on). Use street and state abbreviations as recommended by the US Postal Service at *<http://www.framed.usps.com/ncsc/lookups/usps_abbreviations.htm>*. Using the correct zip code is important as well. A convenient zip code lookup service is available at *<http://www.usps.com/zip4/>*.

For international addresses, use the address provided by your addressee but print the full English name of the country in capital letters at the bottom. For example, instead of *Italia*, write *ITALY*.

25c Write densely but appropriately packed résumés

A **résumé** is a concise summary of an individual's accomplishments, skills, experience, and personal interests. It is more complete and inclusive than a letter of application; the same résumé can be sent to more than one potential employer, whereas each letter of application should be different.

(ESL Note) In some countries, a résumé may include an individual's age, marital status, religious affiliation, and other highly personal information. In the United States, such information cannot legally be considered in hiring and so should not be included.

A résumé should be densely packed with appropriate information. You should neither pad a résumé with irrelevant information nor include any information that is not true. Most résumés use five standard categories of information: (1) Position Desired or Objective, (2) Education, (3) Experience or Employment, (4) Related Activities, and (5) References, in that order. If you think your experience or employment history is more impressive than your educational achievements, you may want to reverse the position of those two categories. The entries within any one category are normally listed in reverse chronological order (that is, the most recent achievement is listed first). For most students and other workers just starting out, a résumé should be no longer than a single full page.

An alternative to the standard résumé just described is the **functional résumé,** in which certain skills are emphasized through categories such as Computer Skills, Management Skills, and Language Skills or Ability to Solve Problems, Ability to Motivate Others, and Ability to Maintain Diverse Interests. If you do not have a long employment history but have been doing volunteer work or internships or want to emphasize your coursework, the functional résumé may be a better format for you to use. Keep in mind, though, that the functional résumé is somewhat unconventional; some employers may not care for it.

25.2
Formatting a functional résumé.

Today, résumés may be submitted and inspected in a variety of ways.

1. A traditional hard-copy résumé, sent by post or fax or delivered by hand, may be reviewed personally by one or more people at the receiving company.

2. A hard-copy résumé, sent by post or fax or delivered by hand, may be scanned into the receiving company's computer for review onscreen.

3. An electronic résumé, sent by email, may be reviewed as is by one or more people at the receiving company.

4. An electronic résumé, sent by email, may be converted by the receiving company into its own database format for review on screen.

5. An electronic résumé, posted to a Web site, may be available for prospective employers to locate through a keyword search.

Also, it is becoming increasingly common for companies to have job applicants log on to their Web site and fill out electronic application forms, or **e-forms,** the information from which is then added to the company's résumé databank.

Given all this variety, you may want to prepare several versions of your résumé. In the next few pages, we will show you how. Many Internet sites can help you, too (see the Help box on page 601).

1 Formatting a traditional résumé

A traditional hard-copy résumé should be designed to be pleasing to the eye. It should be centered on the page, and it should approximately fill the page. A skimpy résumé suggests that you have not accomplished much, while an overcrowded one puts too much pressure on the reader to absorb all the information provided. Use suitable margins (about 1 inch all around), and use white space to set off the major categories and groupings. Use boldface type for your name and for major headings and subheadings. (See Chapter 20 for a more complete discussion of document design principles.) Use verb phrases instead of full sentences to describe your various activities and achievements; consistent use of such phrases will produce an elegant parallelism (see Chapter 42). Using active-voice verbs will give you a dynamic image (see 32g). Always use white or light-colored paper. Avoid printing in color, as it will not reproduce well on black-and-white copiers. A sample traditional résumé is shown in Figure 25.3. Note that the applicant added a category for Awards.

2 Formatting a scannable résumé

Many companies are now using computer technology to quickly scan large numbers of hard-copy résumés and insert the results into a databank. Later, a keyword search can be used to select only those applicants whose self-descriptors fit a certain profile. If you are applying to technologically oriented organizations, you should format your résumé to take advantage of this technology. Some significant differences exist between the traditional résumé and the scannable résumé.

Since computer scanning of résumés is based mainly on keyword searches and keywords usually are nouns or noun phrases, use a noun-heavy style instead of the verb-heavy style favored in traditional résumés. Rather than verb phrases such as "Performed maintenance on . . . ," try noun phrases such as "Maintenance mechanic for . . . ." *Maintenance mechanic* is more likely to be a key phrase than *performed maintenance* is. Do not shy away from using technical jargon. Many computer programs use technical jargon as a way of sorting out candidates. Since some computer programs process only the first 50 or 75 words of a résumé, it is a good idea to list your keyword self-descriptors in a separate section at the beginning of your résumé.

Computer scanners are not entirely reliable when it comes to distinguishing letters and other marks on paper. So, in putting together

Lorinda Brown
2222 Stockton Street
Austin, TX 78701
(555) 580-5625

OBJECTIVE

Marketing/management trainee in the retail industry. Am willing to relocate if necessary.

EDUCATION

Bachelor of Science, University of Texas at Austin, June 2004 (present GPA: 3.4)

Major: Communication. Minor: Marketing. Completed 25 credit hours in marketing and management.

BUSINESS EXPERIENCE

Retail sales, Stevens Brown Sports, Austin, since September 2003. Started with floor sales; promoted to assistant manager of weekend operations. Designed the company's Web site, which features links to local bike trails, golf courses, and other sites of recreational interest. Drew up new marketing plan that increased sales by 15%.

Intern, Frito-Lay, Inc., Austin, June–August 2003. Completed 10-week marketing internship, which included product testing and merchandising. Handled accounts during 6 weeks' absence of local representative.

Server, Tony Roma's Restaurant, Austin, September 2002–May 2003. Responsible for five-table section. Used sales and public relations techniques in a high-volume environment.

OTHER EXPERIENCE

Vice-President, University of Texas Black Student Association, September 2003 to present. Represented the Association at the 2004 Southwest meeting.

Counselor-Tutor, Upward Bound, Austin, January–May 2002.

AWARDS

Employee of the Month, Stevens Brown, November 2003.

REFERENCES

Available on request from the University of Texas Placement and Career Information Center, 350 SSB, Austin, TX 78704. Tel. (555) 581-6186.

FIGURE 25.3 Sample Traditional Résumé

Using Keywords

Instead of	Write
performed maintenance	maintenance mechanic
designed a Web site	Web site designer
tested products	product tester
worked in a laboratory	laboratory technician
developed software	software developer
wrote grant proposals	grant proposal writer

a scannable résumé, do everything you can to make things easy for the scanner.

1. Use white or light-colored, standard-size (8½" x 11") paper.
2. Use a clean original, not a photocopy.
3. Use laser or inkjet printing, not dot matrix.
4. Use a standard typeface, such as Palatino, Futura, Optima, or Helvetica.
5. Use 10- to 14-point font sizes.
6. Do not use italics, underlining, or fancy type styles.
7. Do not use lines, graphics, boxes, or color.
8. Keep normal spacing between letters; do not use kerning.
9. Start every line from the left margin; do not use columns.
10. Do not fold or staple the résumé.

A scannable version of Lorinda Brown's résumé is shown in Figure 25.4.

3 Formatting an electronic résumé

It is becoming increasingly common for companies to solicit résumés via email or the Internet. In such cases, you should format your résumé so that it conforms to the company's specifications.

Email résumés

Given the variety of word-processing programs, text editors, and email programs available, if you plan to send your résumé by email to

Lorinda Brown

2222 Stockton Street
Austin, TX 78701
(555) 580-5625

KEY WORDS: Marketing/management trainee, retail
sales, Web site designer, communication major, management
experience, marketing planner, recreation industry, product
testing, merchandising.

OBJECTIVE: Marketing/management trainee in the retail
industry. Willing to relocate.

**EDUCATION: Bachelor of Science, University of Texas at
Austin,** June 2004 (present GPA: 3.4). Major: Communication.
Minor: Marketing. Completed 25 credit hours in marketing and
management.

**BUSINESS EXPERIENCE: Retail sales, Stevens Brown
Sports,** Austin, since September 2003. Assistant manager, Web
site designer, marketing planner. Management of weekend
operations after promotion from floor sales. Web site design
features links to local bike trails, golf courses, and other sites
of recreational interest. New marketing plan has increased
sales by 15%.

Intern, Frito-Lay, Inc., Austin, June–August 2003. Marketing
internship, 10 weeks, which included product testing and
merchandising. Did accounting during 6 weeks' absence of
local representative.

Server, Tony Roma's Restaurant, Austin, September 2002–May
2003. Responsible for five-table section. Used sales and public
relations techniques in a high-volume environment.

OTHER EXPERIENCE: Vice-President, University of Texas
Black Student Association, September 2003 to present.
Representative for the Association at the 2004 Southwest meeting.
Counselor-Tutor, Upward Bound, Austin, January–May 2002.

AWARDS: Employee of the Month, Stevens Brown, November
2003.

REFERENCES: Available on request from the University
of Texas Placement and Career Information Center, 350 SSB,
Austin, TX 78704. Tel. (555) 581-6186.

FIGURE 25.4 Sample Scannable Résumé

several different companies you should put it into as simple and universal a format as possible. This means (1) using a simplified layout with a prominent keywords section, like that of the scannable résumé, and (2) putting the résumé in ASCII, text only, or simple text format. Most companies prefer that you embed the résumé in the email message itself, after the cover letter, rather than as an attached file. You would be wise to first send a test copy to a friend who has a different system than you do. If the look of the résumé is of great importance to you, you might try using RTF (rich text format) and sending your résumé as an attachment to your email message (24a-6).

Homepage résumés

Although designing your own homepage résumé can be fun, it is generally not the most effective way to go about searching for a job. Most potential employers will not go to the trouble of logging on to your Web site. You would make better use of your time logging on to *their* Web sites and submitting your résumé according to *their* specifications.

If, however, you are determined to have your own homepage résumé, we suggest that you follow these guidelines.

1. Make sure that you are familiar with the principles of good Web page design (see Chapter 22).
2. Put your keyword self-descriptors up front, as in a scannable résumé.
3. Use keywords in your page's title and URL. Companies' search engines will not recognize your name, but they will recognize certain keywords.
4. For personal safety, do not include your home address or phone number. Give only an email address.
5. Consider creating an additional page containing an ASCII version of your résumé, with all HTML tags removed, in case employers want to copy it into their database.
6. Surf the Web and look at some other homepage résumés. If you look at enough of them, you will get a sense of what works and what does not.

(**EXERCISE 25.1**)

On the Internet, on a campus bulletin board, or in your local newspaper, find an advertisement for a job that you would want, and write a letter of application for the job.

Where can I get online information about writing and posting a résumé?

Try these Web sites.

- *Rebecca Smith's eRésumés and Resources*
  http://www.eresumes.com
- *Proven Resumes.com Career Center*
  http://www.provenresumes.com
- *Resumania On-Line*
  http://www.umn.edu/ohr/ecep/resume/
- *JobStar Resume Guide*
  http://www.jobsmart.org/tools/resume/
- *Guaranteed Résumés Career Library*
  http://www.gresumes.com/library.htm

VIDEO

Tips for formatting electronic résumés.

FOR COLLABORATION

Prepare a scannable résumé and share it with your group. Exchange ideas on how to improve the formatting of your résumé, as well as what additional or alternative keywords you may want to include.

25d Write clearly organized reports

A report, as the name implies, is a document that describes the results of an activity. If you do experiments in a chemistry lab, you will be expected to write them up in a lab report. If you research a topic for your composition class in the library, you may be asked to write a library report. Company employees who go on a business trip are usually asked to submit a trip report. Scientists and engineers conducting research projects are expected to submit ongoing progress reports and then, at the end, a final report. There are many other kinds of reports as well, including feasibility reports, environmental impact statements, and activity reports. A report can be as short as one or two pages or as long as a thousand pages. Short reports (for example, lab reports and trip reports) usually have a small, local readership; longer reports are often circulated to a variety of readers both inside and outside the organization in which they are written.

1 Making decisions about content, layout, and design

Designing reports is generally easier than designing brochures or newsletters, because most instructors and businesses have specific formats or conventions that they expect you to follow. For example, the report in 18c follows a format commonly used in engineering courses. It is important to find out what format your instructor expects you to use for a report.

2 Dividing the report into four basic parts

There are four basic parts to a report: a header, an introduction, a body, and a conclusion. Reports may have additional components as well, such as a title page, an abstract, attachments, a table of contents, and a cover letter or memo. If you do not have a specified format to follow, many word processors provide document templates that can help get you started.

Header. The first part of a report is called the header. It provides basic information about the document, such as for whom it is intended, who wrote it, when it was written, and what it is about. If you are writing a report in memo form, the header should contain four standard lines: TO, FROM, SUBJECT (or RE), and DATE. Fill in each of these lines with the appropriate information. In a more formal report, you may want to use a title page instead of a header (see 25d-3).

Headers can include other information, such as a distribution list (recipients other than the person named on the TO line may be listed under DIST or CC), a list of enclosures or attachments (indicated by ENCL or ATTACHMENT), and a reference to previous correspondence (indicated by REF). (In their header in 18c, the engineering students used TO, FROM, SUBJECT, REF., DATE, and DIST.)

Introduction. The introduction serves the vitally important purpose of orienting and informing busy readers. Like brochures and newsletters, reports are often distributed to a variety of readers both inside and outside the organization from which they originate. Many of these readers may be unfamiliar with the report's subject matter. Furthermore, unlike college instructors, who are obligated to read entire student papers, readers in the "real world" often skim reports. In your introduction, you should tell readers quickly (1) what problem you are addressing, (2) how you have addressed it, and (3) what your findings and recommendations are. Begin with a brief problem statement, usually only one paragraph long, and then follow it with a separate summary, also only one paragraph long. (The engineering students in 18c stated the problem and their recommended solutions in a two-paragraph executive summary that preceded the report itself.)

Body. The main part of the report should contain your claim(s), present your evidence, lay out your reasoning, acknowledge counterarguments, and cite references—in short, provide a good, solid argument (see Chapter 7). If the problem statement on the first page of your report needs elaboration, elaborate at the beginning of the body. Visual aids, including typographical distinctions, itemized lists, graphs, and tables (see Chapter 20), should be used throughout to distinguish and clarify important information. If your report is two or more pages, divide the body into sections, using informative headings such as Introduction, Method, Results, and Discussion. (The engineering students in 18c used the following headings for the body of their report: Introduction and Problem Statement, Four Proposed Alternative Solutions, Research Methods, and Results and Discussion.)

Conclusion. Conclude the report with a summary of your main points, a recommendation, a proposal for action, and/or an expression of appreciation. You can repeat information from the summary section of the introduction for emphasis. (The engineering students in 18c did this in the conclusion of their report.)

AUDIO

Repeat key information.

3 Adding optional parts

Title page. Formal reports of more than five pages often have a title page instead of a header. The title page should include the name of the person or group to whom the report is addressed, the names of any other recipients, the names of the writers, the date, the subject (that is, the title), and references to any funding sources.

Abstract. An *abstract* is a concise synopsis (100–150 words) of the report that (1) introduces the topic, (2) briefly describes the method of investigation, (3) details the main findings, and (4) states the general conclusions and implications of these findings. If your report is published, the abstract may be separated from the report and entered into a computerized database; therefore, it should be comprehensible on its own.

WWW

25.3

A sample abstract.

Attachments.   Many reports are based on detailed information—lengthy calculations, drawings, published articles, and other secondary matter—that not every reader will need or want to see. Rather than including such materials in the report, append them either as a formal appendix or as attachments. If you have multiple attachments, include a separate table of contents prior to the attachments. (In addition to listing their references in Appendix A, the engineering students in 18c presented much of their supporting data in Appendixes B through G.)

Table of contents.   A table of contents helps readers get a sense of the overall structure of the report and allows busy readers to skip directly to those parts that interest them. If your report is fairly long and complex, with a title page, abstract, and attachments, you should include a table of contents just after the abstract.

Cover letter or memo.   A cover letter (also called a letter of transmittal) or a memo often accompanies a long report sent to specific readers. This letter gives the writer an opportunity to (1) introduce the report to readers who are not expecting it and (2) draw readers' attention to specific parts of the report. Writers often send different cover letters to different readers. (The engineering students in 18c included a memo to introduce their report to readers.)

4 Formatting for the selective reader

Some readers will want to read the entire report, while others will want to read only parts of it. Thus, it is important that reports—especially long reports—be formatted to accommodate selective reading behavior.

> (EXERCISE 25.2)
>
> Write a two-page report evaluating the engineering students' report in 18c for ease of skimming. Use the guidelines given in How to Make It Easy for Readers to Skim a Report on page 605.

25e Write focused memos

One of the most important types of documents in business and professional contexts is the memorandum, or memo. People write memos for a variety of purposes: to inform, to summarize, to recom-

How to Make It Easy for Readers to Skim a Report

1. Use an informative *title*.
2. Provide a short *abstract*.
3. At the very beginning, define the *problem* the report is addressing.
4. Provide an *executive summary* on the first page of the report.
5. Provide good *visual aids* to accompany appropriate text (see Chapter 20).
6. Divide the report into logical sections, with informative *section headings*.
7. Provide informative *subheadings* as well.
8. Begin each paragraph with a good *topic sentence* (see 6a).
9. Give *typographical prominence* to key points (without overdoing it).
10. Relegate supporting information (such as calculations and reference materials) to *appendixes,* making sure to reference such information in the body of the report.
11. For a long report, include a *table of contents*.

mend, to make a request. Memos are usually quite short, informal in tone, and focused on a single topic. Unlike reports (see 25d), memos are typically written to only a local audience, such as supervisors, colleagues, or employees internal to a company or department.

Structurally, a memo has the same four basic parts as a report: a header, an introduction, a body, and a conclusion (see 18c and 19c for example reports; see 25d for an explanation of these parts). In addition, like a report, a memo may have attachments. But all of these components are typically much shorter in a memo than in a report, and the document as a whole seldom exceeds two pages. The opening component is usually compressed into a background description or problem statement of only two or three sentences; depending on how the message is likely to be received (either favorably or unfavorably), it should take either a direct or indirect approach as in business letters (see 25a). There is typically no summary in the opening component unless the memo is two pages or longer. The body may range in length from a few

	To:	Prof. Gilbert
Header containing basic information	From:	Mona Kitab and Fernando Marquez
	Date:	June 4, 2004
	Subject:	Proposal for a service-learning project

Introduction, describing the problem and proposed solution

After telephoning five agencies, we have decided that the project we would most like to work on is an information brochure for the city's homeless shelter. Although about 150 homeless people use the shelter on a regular basis, the shelter is badly underfunded and needs more volunteers to help out. Miriam Hatcher, the shelter director, told us she thought that more university students would volunteer to help if they only knew more about it. She said that a well-written brochure answering students' questions about the shelter might be the answer, because it could be easily distributed all around campus.

We plan to create a six-panel, folded brochure that will answer the following questions:

Body of memo giving details

- What is the homeless shelter?
- How many people does it serve, and in what way?
- Why does it need volunteer help? Why doesn't the government pay for it?
- If I volunteered, what would I be doing? How much time would it take?
- How do I sign up?

According to Ms. Hatcher, these are the questions that students are most likely to ask. The brochure will be well written, nicely illustrated, and elegantly formatted.

Conclusion, summarizing the main point of the memo

We are enthusiastic about this project, as it seems to address an important need in our community, and we hope that it meets your approval. We look forward to getting your feedback on this.

FIGURE 25.5 Sample Memo

HELP

How do I use a memo template?

1. On the FILE menu, select NEW.
2. When a screen pops up, select the desired option (for example, MEMO).
3. Select the desired style (for example, PROFESSIONAL MEMO).
4. Fill in the blanks or type over the text that is already there.
5. To customize the memo, follow the onscreen instructions.

sentences to eight to ten paragraphs. The conclusion may be only a sentence or two.

With most word-processing programs, you can create a document template (a preset form). If your department or company has a standard format for memos, you can create a template that conforms to this standard.

The sample memo in Figure 25.5 was written by two students to their writing instructor. The instructor, Professor Gilbert, had asked all the students in the class to form two-person teams, call local nonprofit agencies to find a suitable service-learning project, and then submit to her a one-page memo describing their proposed project.

FOR COLLABORATION

With one or more members of your group, write a short memo to your instructor on a topic of your own choosing. For example, you might request special help on an upcoming writing project, pose some questions about English grammar, or describe a new Web site you recently discovered. If your computer has a document template program, use it to write your memo.

CHAPTER 26

Oral Presentations Using *PowerPoint* and Other Tools

FAQs

▶ How can I organize my oral presentation? (26a)

▶ What kinds of visual aids are best for an oral presentation? (26b)

▶ How can I get over my nervousness? (26d)

▶ What makes a good *PowerPoint* slide? (26f)

VIDEO

A student's tips for oral presentations.

In many occupations, the ability to communicate orally is just as important as the ability to write well. Simple conversations, interviews, phone calls, meetings—these are all staple forms of communication in the workplace. And so are oral presentations. This chapter offers advice on how to give good presentations.

26a Prepare thoroughly

WWW

26.1

Web resources for preparing oral presentations.

The basic principle to keep in mind in preparing any kind of oral presentation is this: *All listeners have a limited attention span.* Thus, you cannot expect them to follow closely everything you say. Their attention will probably wander from time to time, even if your presentation is only ten minutes long. So, if you want to make sure your listeners will come away from your talk with your main points clear in their minds, you must organize your presentation in such a way that these main points stand out. Here is how to do it.

1. *Analyze your audience and limit your topic accordingly.* What do your listeners already know about the topic? What do they need or want to know about it? If you tell them what they already know, they'll be bored. If you give them too much new information too fast, they may not be able to keep up.

2. *Determine your primary purpose.* Is there some main point or idea you want to get across? If so, use it as the cornerstone on which to build your presentation.

3. *Select effective supporting information.* What kind of evidence will best support your main point? What kind of information will appeal to your listeners? These things will constitute the heart of your presentation, so put some thought into it.

4. *Choose an appropriate pattern of organization.* Do your subject matter and purpose lend themselves to a certain pattern of organization such as problem and solution, narrative, or classification? (See Chapter 6.) If so, building your presentation around such a pattern will help you organize and present the talk and make it easier for your listeners to follow.

5. *Prepare an outline.* Keep it brief: main points and main supporting points only. Arrange these points according to the pattern of development you chose in step 4.

6. *Select appropriate visual aids.* (See 26b.)

7. *Prepare a suitable introduction.* A good introduction should set up the topic so that your audience will be interested in what you have to say. You must convince your listeners that it's an important subject, worthy of their attention. Are you addressing some problem? Make sure you define it so that your listeners know exactly what it is and can appreciate your proposed solution. Are you taking sides on an issue and arguing for your point of view? If so, make sure your listeners know exactly what the issue is.

8. *Prepare a closing summary.* Listeners are typically very attentive at the beginning of a presentation, less attentive as it wears on, and then suddenly more attentive again as it comes to an end. In other words, they perk up at the end, hoping to catch a summarizing comment or recommendation. You can take advantage of this fact by reemphasizing your main points at the end.

(EXERCISE 26.1)

Prepare a brief (5–10 minute) oral presentation using the guidelines in 26a.

26b Select visual aids carefully

Visual aids are of great help in giving an oral presentation. First, they serve as "cue cards" reminding you of all your important points and allowing you to stay on track without reading from a manuscript or from notes. Second, visual aids have tremendous power as attention-getters. Studies have shown that people remember the visual parts of speeches far better than they do the verbal parts. Finally, visual aids can help clarify your message. Pick your visual aids carefully. Here are the basic options.

- *PowerPoint* projection
- Overhead transparencies
- Chalkboard
- Flip charts or posters
- Handouts
- Three-dimensional objects

Each of these technologies has its own strengths and weaknesses and should be evaluated with the following questions in mind: Is it easy to prepare? Can it be altered easily during the presentation? Will it allow you to control the audience's attention—or will it distract attention from what you're saying? Will it let you present at an appropriate speed? How much information can it convey? How large an audience can you use it with? How reliable is it—does it depend on electronic equipment? Can the audience keep it for future reference? How well does it work as a "cue card"? Using these criteria, Table 26.1 compares the six types of visual aids listed above.

As can be seen, *PowerPoint* is probably the best overall visual aid for an oral presentation. It has more strengths and fewer weaknesses than any of the others. But each of the others has its own good uses for particular situations and should not be overlooked. (See 26e–26f for more information on using *PowerPoint* and overhead transparencies.)

(EXERCISE 26.2)

Decide what kinds of visual aids would be most appropriate for the oral presentation you prepared in Exercise 26.1. Be prepared to justify your choices.

	Power-Point	Overheads	Chalkboard	Flip Charts or Posters	Handouts	3-D Objects
Ease of preparation	Excellent	Good	Excellent	Fair	Good	Good
Ease of alteration	Fair	Good	Excellent	Fair	Poor	Poor
Audience control	Excellent	Excellent	Excellent	Excellent	Poor	Varies
Speed	Excellent	Good	Poor	Good	Excellent	Excellent
Amount of information	Good	Good	Fair	Good	Excellent	Fair
Audience size	Excellent	Excellent	Fair	Fair	Excellent	Fair
Reliability	Fair	Good	Excellent	Excellent	Excellent	Excellent
Future reference	Good	Poor	Poor	Poor	Excellent	Poor
Cueing	Excellent	Excellent	Poor	Excellent	Excellent	Good

TABLE 26.1 Types of Visual Aids Evaluated for Use with Oral Presentations

26c Practice, practice, practice

Nothing is more helpful to the success of an oral presentation than practice. Not even the best of speakers can give a totally effective presentation without first practicing it. Practice allows you to spot the flaws in a presentation and correct them. It enables you to work on making smooth transitions instead of awkward stops and starts. And practice gives you an idea of how long your presentation will take, allowing you to make adjustments so that you can deliver it at a comfortable tempo. All these benefits promote greater self-confidence, which will give you a more emphatic, convincing, and effective style of delivery.

The best way to practice a talk is by rounding up a few friends and trying it out on them. Ask them to hear you all the way through, taking notes but not interrupting you. Then ask them for an honest critique. In the absence of friends, you can use a video recorder or audiotape recorder and then critique yourself during playback. Here are some specific things to work on while practicing an oral presentation.

1. *Devise ways of reiterating your important points without being too repetitive.* Since your important points should all contribute to a single cumulative effect, it's a good idea to reiterate these points occasionally as you go along—especially in summary form at the end of your talk. However, exact repetition of a point can become annoyingly monotonous the third or fourth time around, so try to vary your wording.

2. *Create smooth transitions between sections.* Take note of places where the flow of your presentation seems to break down and see if you can insert a phrase or two to act as a bridge. If you can't, there may be a fundamental flaw in the overall structure of your presentation; in that case, try to reorganize it.

3. *Familiarize yourself with the equipment you'll be using.* It's embarrassing—and annoying to the audience—to waste precious time fumbling with a computer, slide projector, or other equipment. Check out any equipment beforehand and become familiar with it, and have a backup plan in case something goes wrong.

4. *Prepare yourself for questions.* Listeners may raise questions at any point in your presentation, and it is vitally important that you answer them satisfactorily. If you don't, your most precious asset as a speaker—your credibility—may be jeopardized. So be sure you know your topic *well*. One way to prepare yourself is to have some friends listen to you and deliberately throw tough questions at you; if they succeed in stumping you, do some more research.

5. *Develop your own speaking style.* Practice presenting as if you were telling friends a story. Be natural and expressive. Use animated gestures and vary your intonation and rate of speech. In short, let your enthusiasm show! At the same time, try to get rid of any distracting habits you might have, such as leaning against something, pacing back and forth, or fiddling with a pencil.

6. *If you will read from a manuscript, work on a lively, expressive intonation.* There is a strong tendency when reading aloud to adopt a monotonous style of delivery that is boring for an audience. As you read aloud, practice varying your intonation as you would if you were talking spontaneously. Mark up the manuscript, underlining words that warrant special intonation and places where you may want to pause. Give special emphasis to contrasting terms.

(**EXERCISE 26.3**)

> For practice, find a text of about 200 words that you could imagine reading aloud to someone. Print it out double-spaced. Read it aloud, trying to make it as natural and expressive as you can. Then go back and mark up the text, noting places where you want to use special intonation. Then read it aloud again.

26d Speak with enthusiasm and focus

As the time draws near for delivering your oral presentation, you will experience what all speakers do—nervousness. One key to an effective delivery is to convert your nervousness into the kind of energy that injects liveliness, enthusiasm, and animation into your speech.

How can you control your nervousness? First of all, make sure you're properly prepared for your talk. This means getting your visual aids and notes organized and making sure you're properly dressed and groomed. Your personal appearance is one of the most powerful "visual aids" you have. Looking your best will boost your confidence.

Second, as you are about to start your presentation, look for an opportunity to say something off-the-cuff. For example, you could acknowledge the occasion or share a spontaneous bit of humor. Don't feel you have to tell a prepared joke or story.

Finally, as you are actually giving your presentation, *concentrate your full attention on what you want to say.* Stick to your outline, and make sure you cover all your main supporting points. Convince your listeners that the topic is important, and be enthusiastic about it. Show each of your visual aids long enough for the audience to understand and appreciate it, and then move on to the next one. Keep up the pace—don't dally.

Encourage questions from the audience, but don't let questions disrupt your presentation. Above all, do not show any antagonism toward a questioner. It will make your entire audience feel uncomfortable, and they may hold it against you even if the questioner is unfair or unpleasant.

(**FOR COLLABORATION**)

> With several friends or classmates as your audience, deliver the oral presentation that you prepared in Exercises 26.1–26.2. Be sure to follow the suggestions outlined in 26d. Afterward, ask your audience for constructive criticism.

26e Design overhead transparencies

Overhead transparencies provide good visual support for an oral presentation. They are relatively easy to prepare, and they can be written on (with a transparency marker) during the presentation itself. You can use them as cues to keep your thoughts on track without reading from a manuscript. At the same time, they allow you to control the attention of the audience while easily moving from one transparency to the next.

It's important to give your audience time to digest the information on your transparencies. Usually, that means putting relatively little information on each one so that you can keep moving along. Figures 26.1 and 26.2 show how a student converted index card notes to an overhead transparency for a class presentation on service learning.

This student wisely used only some of her index card notes for the overhead transparency. Putting too much information on any one transparency may confuse an audience; distract attention from you, the speaker; and slow down your presentation. It's better to split up the information and put it on two or more transparencies. Notice also the neat design of this transparency. It has a clear, thematic title, and its main points are cleanly set off as a bulleted list. It also has ample white space.

> 20% of the students on this campus (= 1,500 students) are involved in community service projects. We can do even better.
>
> Have served 72 nonprofit agencies in past year. Examples: YWCA, Family Literacy Center, Save Water Coalition, Peace Now.
>
> Designed Web sites, wrote brochures, measured lead paint on old buildings, planted trees, distributed leaflets, helped elderly, etc.
>
> Students usually work in teams, but there are also many individual volunteers.

FIGURE 26.1 Notes on an Index Card

> **Student Involvement in Community Service**
>
> - 1,500 students on this campus participate, equal to 20 percent of the student population
> - 31 courses have service learning projects
> - The Bennion Center sponsors outreach programs
> - Many more possibilities exist

FIGURE 26.2 Overhead Transparency Using Same Notes

26f Use *PowerPoint* effectively

Use of presentation software such as *PowerPoint* is becoming more common because this medium offers almost all the benefits of overhead transparencies as well as some special advantages. *Power-Point* projects color better than overhead transparencies; it can include animation, video, and sound; it is easily managed with a notebook computer and a projector; and it can be converted into HTML and put on a Web site for later reference. The software comes with a wizard and templates that make it easy and fun to create slides and put together a presentation. Although the standard *PowerPoint* templates are business oriented, some of them can be adapted to academic presentations as well.

VIDEO
Designing a
PowerPoint
presentation.

Like overhead transparencies, *PowerPoint* slides should be neatly formatted, easily readable, and uncluttered. For presentation in a darkened room, the slides should have a light background; for a well-lit room, they should have a darker background. Wherever possible, the slides should have some visual imagery, not just words; these images should be relevant to the theme of the slide or presentation, not used just for decoration.

Figures 26.3 and 26.4 illustrate before and after versions of a *PowerPoint* slide created from the index card notes in Figure 26.1.

Although they have obvious attractions, *PowerPoint* presentations also have several pitfalls that you should be aware of. First, avoid the temptation to let the slides do the talking for you. Your

Before

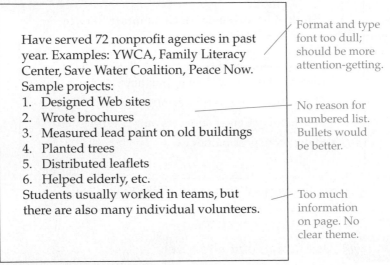

Have served 72 nonprofit agencies in past year. Examples: YWCA, Family Literacy Center, Save Water Coalition, Peace Now. Sample projects:
1. Designed Web sites
2. Wrote brochures
3. Measured lead paint on old buildings
4. Planted trees
5. Distributed leaflets
6. Helped elderly, etc.
Students usually worked in teams, but there are also many individual volunteers.

Format and type font too dull; should be more attention-getting.

No reason for numbered list. Bullets would be better.

Too much information on page. No clear theme.

FIGURE 26.3 Poor *PowerPoint* Slide.

After

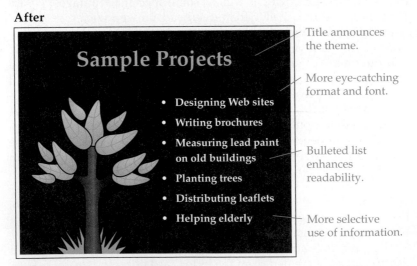

Title announces the theme.

More eye-catching format and font.

Bulleted list enhances readability.

More selective use of information.

FIGURE 26.4 Good *PowerPoint* Slide.

audience will be there to hear what *you* have to say, and they should focus more on you and your message than on your slides. The slides should be used only as *support* for your talk. Prepare your talk first; add the slides later. Second, do not make your presentation fancier than is useful. *PowerPoint* technology offers special effects such as streaming text, fade-ins and fade-outs, but they are easily overdone and can become irritating to your audience. Third, try not to have your *PowerPoint* presentation be just a series of note cards transposed to the screen. Look for opportunities to make it truly visual, using appropriate photos, sketches, maps, and so on (not just clip art) to support your words. Finally, be aware that a *PowerPoint* presentation tends to be a one-way form of communication, with the audience cast in a passive role. This is especially true of presentations that are little more than slide shows going rapidly through one slide after another. Slow your pace a bit, and try to give the audience opportunities to intervene with questions or comments.

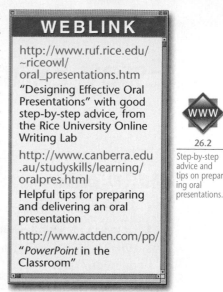

WEBLINK

http://www.ruf.rice.edu/~riceowl/oral_presentations.htm
"Designing Effective Oral Presentations" with good step-by-step advice, from the Rice University Online Writing Lab

http://www.canberra.edu.au/studyskills/learning/oralpres.html
Helpful tips for preparing and delivering an oral presentation

http://www.actden.com/pp/
"*PowerPoint* in the Classroom"

26.2
Step-by-step advice and tips on preparing oral presentations.

(**EXERCISE 26.4**)

Using the presentation you prepared for Exercise 26.1, decide what points could be usefully illustrated with *PowerPoint* slides. Then find a computer with a *PowerPoint* program and create those slides.

(**FOR COLLABORATION**)

Following the guidelines in 26f, deliver the presentation you designed for Exercise 26.4 to a small group of friends or fellow students. Afterward, ask them for feedback.

CHAPTER 27

Essay Exams

FAQs

▸ What are some things I can do to prepare for an exam? (27a)

▸ How can I tell what exam questions are really asking? (27a-3)

▸ What steps should I follow writing a response to an exam question? (27b)

▸ How can I avoid mistakes in my written exam? (27b-4)

VIDEO
Tips for taking essay exams.

In college and on the job, much of the writing you do will be "on demand"—that is, you will have a limited time in which to complete it. In college, such writing often takes the form of a timed essay exam or an in-class writing assignment. This chapter discusses some ways you can prepare for this type of writing.

AUDIO
Writing under time constraints for essay exams.

27a Prepare for an essay exam

You can use a number of strategies to prepare for on-demand writing in general and essay exams in particular. These strategies include keeping up on your reading and notetaking, studying and reviewing your notes, and analyzing the exam question.

1 Keeping up with your reading and notetaking

Many instructors judge your success in a course by how well you are able to analyze and apply course material in a timed essay exam. In order to do a good job on such exams, you must be well prepared. Few essay exams are open-book, so you must learn the material well

618   Essay Exams

How do I use a keyword search to find important information in lecture notes?

If you keep your lecture notes in an electronic notebook, you can search for key information by doing the following:

1. Use your word-processing program's WORD COUNT feature to find out how many times a particular keyword appears in your notes.
2. Use your word-processing program's SEARCH function to search for each occurrence of the keyword.
3. Highlight the word by using italics or a contrasting color.
4. For review purposes, make a hard copy of pages that contain the keywords.

27.1

A step-by-step demonstration of keyword searches of lecture notes.

enough to be able to remember and write about it without access to your notes or textbooks.

You can prepare by keeping up with course assignments and discussions on a daily basis throughout the term. Attend every class and read your textbooks carefully, looking for key

WEBLINK

http://www.english.uiuc .edu/cws/wworkshop/

Tips on writing essay exams

27.2

Access essay exam advice online.

ideas and arguments. Pay close attention to chapter summaries, subheadings, and key terminology. Write the key ideas and terms down in a notebook for later review. When your instructor lectures, do not write down everything he or she says; rather, listen for and record main points and ideas that show relationships.

2 Studying and reviewing your notes

As the exam date approaches, you will want to study more systematically. Ask the instructor if he or she is willing to provide models of previous exam questions or some general guidelines about the kinds of questions that might be included on the exam. Organize a study group to discuss and review the course materials. If possible, the study group should meet regularly during the term, either in person or through an email discussion group (see 24b-1). Practice responding to

course readings by taking a stance opposite that of the authors or by questioning the authors' position. Review your class notes, paying particular attention to your lists of key ideas and terms. For each key idea, develop a practice thesis statement that you could explore and support in an essay.

Avoid the last-minute cram session. Cramming for several hours prior to the exam will not give you enough depth of knowledge to succeed on an essay exam. And if you stay up all night before an exam studying, you will be in no condition to take it the next day. Instead, pace your studying over several days and try to get a good night's sleep so that you will be fresh for the exam itself.

3   Analyzing the exam question

When you receive the exam question, the first step is to analyze it carefully. The question itself will guide the organization of your response. An essay question will ask you to focus on a specific issue, and you should address it rather than cataloging everything you learned from the course. Try to minimize your anxiety by taking a deep breath and focusing your thinking on the structure of your response. If the exam contains more than one question, determine how much time you have to devote to each question, so that you do not run out of time before you complete your writing. Table 27.1 shows appropriate responses to some of the organizational cue words that typically appear in essay questions.

How do I write an essay exam in a computer lab?

If your instructor allows you to write your timed response to an essay exam in a computer classroom or lab, do the following:

1. Briefly attend to the stages of the writing process, as described in 27b.

2. Budget your time carefully. Check your watch or the clock periodically.

3. Save your work frequently—to your disk or hard drive— so that you do not inadvertently lose your essay because of a computer glitch or power failure.

4. Run the spell checker before turning in your exam.

27.3

Step-by-step instructions for writing an essay exam in a computer lab.

Example question	Cue word	Organizational scheme of response
Analyze Shakespeare's use of dreams in *Macbeth*.	**Analyze:** Divide something into parts and discuss the parts in relationship to the whole.	1. State your thesis. 2. Discuss the play's major themes. 3. Identify places where dreams occur, and explain each instance in relation to the play's major themes. 4. State your conclusion.
Argue either for or against caps on political spending in presidential campaigns.	**Argue:** Take a position or stand and support it with reasoned arguments and evidence.	1. Choose a side—either for or against such caps—and state that position in a thesis sentence. 2. List each point that supports your side, with evidence. 3. Conclude by restating your side.
Classify street people into types based on their sociological characteristics.	**Classify:** Divide some larger whole into groups on the basis of shared traits.	1. State your thesis, pointing out the number of types of street people. 2. Identify one type and describe its characteristics. 3. Continue identifying types and describing their characteristics. 4. State your conclusion.
Describe the mechanism of the transmission of the disease typhus.	**Describe:** Systematically explain something's features, sometimes visually or sequentially.	1. State your thesis—that typhus is transmitted by parasites. 2. Describe the disease carrier—lice. 3. Explain how lice spread typhus. 4. State your conclusion.
Discuss the structure of US society in terms of its economic relationships.	**Discuss:** Consider as many important elements related to an issue as you can.	1. State your thesis, outlining what you take to be the important relationships. 2. Consider as many key elements of US society and economics as you can, such as monetary policy, agricultural policy, and political policy. 3. Conclude by restating your thesis.

AUDIO
Cue words can guide your essay responses.

TABLE 27.1   Cue Words in Essay Exam Questions   *(continued)*

Example question	Cue word	Organizational scheme of response
Evaluate the effectiveness of the performance of Handel's *Water Music* by the San Francisco Symphony.	**Evaluate:** Give your opinion about something's value and provide the reasons on which your judgment is based.	1. State your opinion about the effectiveness of the performance in the form of a thesis. 2. Briefly summarize the performance. 3. List the reasons on which your opinion is based, with supporting evidence from the performance itself. 4. Conclude by restating your opinion.
Explain why an object thrown up into the air falls to the ground.	**Explain:** Tell about something complex in a way that makes it clear.	1. State the physical principle in the form of a thesis. 2. Tell about the nature of gravity that causes the object to fall. 3. Tell about the physical principles that determine how objects are affected by gravity, including the scientific formula for gravitational pull. 4. State your conclusion.
Illustrate the importance of color in Duchamp's *Nude Descending a Staircase.*	**Illustrate:** Provide examples and detail about something.	1. State in your thesis why color is important in the painting. 2. Provide an example relating to color. 3. Provide additional examples relating to color. 4. State your conclusion.
Summarize the major advantages of mainstreaming handicapped children in school.	**Summarize:** Repeat the main points in abbreviated form.	1. State your thesis. 2. List the advantages, one after another, along with reasons that support each point. 3. State your conclusion.

TABLE 27.1   *(continued)*

(EXERCISE 27.1)

Reread Chapter 2 of this handbook, and follow the suggestions outlined in 2b-2 and 2b-3 on taking and reviewing notes. Formulate a set of essay exam questions based on what you take to be the key ideas in Chapter 2.

Bring the essay exam questions that you generated in Exercise 27.1 to class. Discuss your exam questions with a group of your peers. How effective are the questions? What makes them effective or not effective?

27b Attend to the writing process

When you write an essay exam, you should briefly attend to each stage of the writing process (see also 3a).

1 Preparing an outline

When taking an essay exam, you will not have much time for prewriting, but you should take a few minutes to jot down in an informal outline (see 3e-5) some of the key concepts you want to cover in your answer. Begin your response with a thesis statement and a short introductory paragraph that captures the main thrust of your response. Then, in subsequent paragraphs, you can elaborate with examples and details until you run out of time. As you outline, try to cover the most important points first, leaving the less important ones for last. If you have less than an hour to respond to the question, do not spend more than about five minutes planning and outlining your response.

2 Drafting your response

Try to remain focused as you draft your response. Your instructor will have many essays to read and will not want to plow through a lot of extraneous information. If you know a great deal about the question, resist the temptation to write down everything. Rather, stick to your thesis, and plan your writing so that your response is coherent and organized. The easier it is for the instructor to follow your line of argument, the better.

3 Analyzing and evaluating your response

As you draft your response, allow time to ensure that you have satisfied the demands of the assignment. When you read over your essay, you may find that you have overlooked the second part of a two-part

question, for example, or that you have concentrated on defining terms when the question asked you to analyze information. Do not panic. If possible, write a new final paragraph that addresses the issues you missed. If you do not have time for that, write your instructor a brief message explaining where you went wrong and outlining how you would correct your essay if you had the time. Many instructors will give at least partial credit for such a response.

Also, look carefully at your thesis statement. Does it accurately reflect the direction of your essay? If not, then revise it. Check your organization. Does your essay read smoothly and flow logically? If not, then perhaps you can insert transitional words or phrases that will help your instructor follow your argument. Have you included enough examples to support your thesis? If you need more, write a new paragraph and use an arrow to indicate where it should be inserted. Finally, does your conclusion provide a clear understanding of the main point of your essay? If not, then add a sentence or two to sum up your argument.

4 Proofreading and editing your response

Your instructor will not expect your writing to be grammatically and structurally perfect in a timed writing situation. However, he or

---

Checklist for Writing Successful Essay Exam Responses

- Have I shown my understanding of the question by including a thesis statement at the beginning of my response?
- Have I organized my response so as to present my ideas in a logical progression that supports my thesis?
- Have I used the specific details, facts, or analyses called for in the question?
- Have I shown my own independent thoughts and insights in my response?
- Have I concluded with a brief sentence that sums up the gist of my response?
- Have I evaluated and edited my response as time allowed?

she will expect your exam response to be readable and clear. If possible, write your response in pencil so that you can easily erase and correct errors. Take a few minutes to proofread and also to check your penmanship. If your response is unreadable, your instructor cannot evaluate it fairly.

27c Review sample student responses to an essay exam question

www

27.4

Sample student responses to essay questions.

To help you write better exam responses, we include here two student responses to the following exam question, which appeared on the midterm for a course in twentieth-century British literature.

AUDIO

ESL students and essay exams.

> Below you will find a quotation from a novel we read this term. Spend 15 minutes writing a short essay that performs a close reading of the passage. Pick out specific details from the quotation that illustrate some of the central themes or ideas of the novel. Your response should demonstrate both an ability to read closely and a general understanding of the novel.
>
> From Henry James's *The Turn of the Screw:* "I remember feeling with Miles in especial as if he had had, as it were, nothing to call even an infinitesimal history. We expect of a small child scant enough 'antecedents', but there was in this beautiful little boy something extraordinarily sensitive, yet extraordinarily happy, that, more than in any creature of his age I have seen, struck me as beginning anew each day. . . . I could reconstitute nothing at all, and he was therefore an angel."

The instructor considered the first response to be a good response and the second one to be a poor response.

GOOD STUDENT RESPONSE

This quotation expresses the governess's naivete regarding the innocence of the children she is looking after. She assumes that just because they are children, they have had little experience and are, thus, pure "angels." Her perception of this, however, is erroneous and detrimental to Miles. Assuming that he is pure, she takes all measures to protect him from any horrors that may have happened in the past, not realizing that the past is part of Miles's history. His past takes the form of ghosts which haunt the governess, although they do not seem to frighten the children. In fact, the children are drawn to the ghosts and want the governess to go away. Her lack of experience and her innocence are actually greater than the children's, who no longer have parents and have experienced the death of two servants. Her inability to see this truth ends up killing Miles. Caught between the image of the governess and Peter Quint, Miles finally has to make evident to her what is so obvious to everyone else--Peter Quint exists, the past is a part of his present. Not willing to let Miles exist outside of her perceptions, the governess ironically reassures him, "I caught you." She strips him of his history, his identity, and he dies a young boy "dispossessed."

POOR STUDENT RESPONSE

The governess here is expressing how she feels about the child Miles vs. the Miles she knew once upon a time. The use of the run-on sentence is a radical change from the accepted format of the past. The form represents thought put on paper and not interpreted through writing. The effect that the child had on her doesn't seem realistic. It seems more mystic and of fantasy.

The instructor wanted the exam responses to demonstrate both an ability to read closely and a general understanding of the novel. In the first response, the student shows a clear understanding of the major themes of the novel, using specific details from the quotation to illustrate that understanding and connect the passage to the larger themes of innocence and history. In contrast, the second response does not draw any specific connections between the quotation and the major issues or themes of the novel. It appears from the second response that this student did not really understand the novel. Furthermore, the second response does not answer the question posed. As reading these responses makes clear, you must understand both the subject and the examination question in order to answer well.

27.5
Suggestions for writing essay exams.

WEBLINK
http://web.uvic.ca/wguide/
Pages/ExamEssays.html
More on essay exams

EXERCISE 27.2

Using the Checklist for Writing Successful Essay Exam Responses on page 624, analyze the two student essay exam responses. In each of the responses, which of the guidelines were observed? Which were not? How could each response have been improved?

CHAPTER 28

Writing Portfolios

FAQs

▶ What is a portfolio and why do I need one? (28a)

▶ How do I develop a writing portfolio? (28b)

▶ How do I prepare the final portfolio? (28c)

▶ What does a reflective cover letter look like? (28d)

Many courses, majors, and even entire college programs are now requiring students to submit portfolios as a part of their college work. Teachers report that students frequently misunderstand the purposes and audiences for these portfolios. This chapter provides an overview of portfolios and the expectations that frequently lie behind this assignment.

28a Learn about types of portfolios

The three common types of portfolios you may encounter in your college career vary in rhetorical stance (see also 3b-2). You will need to work with your instructor to determine the type of portfolio you are going to compile, along with its purpose and audience. Similarly, you will need to consider carefully your own persona—that is, how you want to present yourself through the content and organization of your portfolio.

1 Types of portfolios

Perhaps the most common type is the individual course portfolio that reflects your work for a particular term in a specific course. Many disciplines use portfolios for assessment purposes, as a way

28.1
Examples
of course
portfolios.

for students to display the work they have accomplished that term. Some of the disciplines that typically use portfolios include written composition, art, photography, and education. As you can imagine, the items included in portfolios for different disciplines vary widely. In art and photography, for example, portfolios include primarily visual materials. In composition and education, portfolios consist largely of written documents in a variety of formats. An education portfolio, for example, typically includes lesson plans, whereas a composition portfolio typically includes essays and research papers.

A second common type is the program assessment portfolio (see Figure 28.1). This type is used by a program to assess the progress of students. It is usually administered on a large scale—perhaps to all sophomores as a measure of their writing competency following the completion of the general education requirements. Be sure to find out exactly what is expected in the program assessment portfolio. Typically, a program will draw up specific guidelines as to content and purpose. You would be well advised to follow such guidelines explicitly.

A third commonly used type is the student career portfolio (see Figure 28.2). Such a portfolio is used to track your progress through a

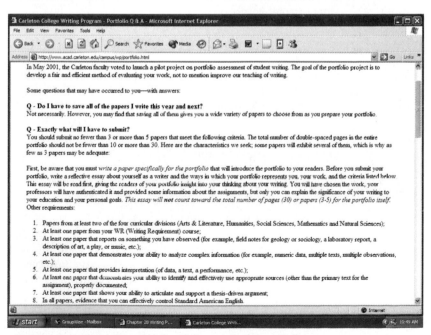

FIGURE 28.1 Guidelines for Portfolios at Carleton College

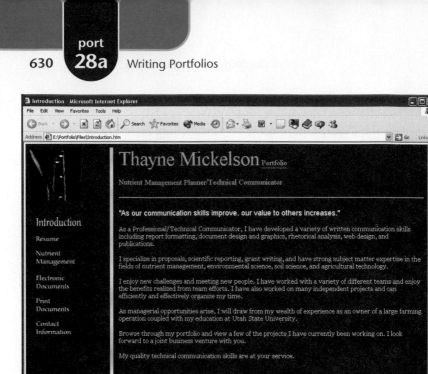

FIGURE 28.2 Student Career Portfolio

major course of study. The main purpose of such portfolios is to high-light the personal growth you have experienced over the length of your education. For example, an English major specializing in professional communication might compile such a portfolio as evidence of his or her job skills and potential as an employee. Often students find career portfolios useful when they go into the job market after graduation.

2 Goals or purposes of portfolios

To many students the primary goal of a portfolio is to get a good grade in a course. However, as you work to reach that specific goal, you'll find that you have achieved other goals as well. For example, an important goal for any portfolio is to reflect the knowledge you have gained from a course or program of study. In content courses such as the humanities and social sciences—for example, music, history or so-ciology—it is important that your portfolio accurately reflect your un-derstanding of the major concepts covered. If the portfolio is being used to assess a program, it is also important that your portfolio show you have mastered the core concepts and skills of the program.

Other goals of portfolios include reflecting an improvement in your writing skills and reflecting an effective presentation format and style. For composition and other writing-intensive courses such as the social sciences, portfolio readers will expect your portfolio to show your growth as a writer. Including early drafts of pieces is one way of reflecting growth. Including a reflective cover letter is another. Your portfolio will need to show that you have mastered the conventions of Standard Edited English—that is, your writing should be correct and error-free. Similarly, portfolio readers will expect you to present your work effectively—that is, the portfolio should be organized, neat, and complete. How you present the portfolio will also send a message to your readers about your professionalism.

3 Audiences for portfolios

Your course's instructor is typically the primary audience for your portfolio. However, there may be other equally important secondary audiences. For example, other faculty evaluators and administrators may read the portfolio if it is used for program assessment. Peers may review your portfolio and provide advice, particularly if your instructor uses peer review as a feature of the course. Future employers may also read your portfolio. Many fields use portfolios as a measure of someone's work. When your portfolio is the result of work from a major capstone course, it can be particularly valuable when you are looking for employment.

4 Your persona

Because you are the primary author of the portfolio, you are ultimately responsible for its success. How you put together your portfolio will communicate your persona to your readers, whether you want it to or not. They will judge you as a "slacker" or a hard worker depending on how you present yourself through your portfolio. If you are diligent about meeting deadlines, revising and editing, visiting the writing center, and asking questions of your instructor when you are confused, you have every reason to believe your portfolio will be successful.

(EXERCISE 28.1)

Review the guidelines for portfolio assessment of writing from Carleton College shown in Figure 28.1. What is the purpose of the assessment? What do the students actually have to do to fulfill the requirement? Are these tasks suitable to the purpose?

Discuss the Carleton guidelines with a small group of your peers. What does your group think the purpose is for this assessment? Do you find the guidelines explicit enough for students to be successful?

28b Develop a writing portfolio

The type of writing portfolio you are developing, in addition to your audience, purpose, and persona, will help determine the materials to be included. Make sure that you understand completely the assignment itself: Do you have options for the number and types of assignments you will include in the portfolio? Should you include rough drafts as well as polished pieces? Are there additional required elements, such as a reflective cover letter? What should be included in the reflective cover letter? What should the portfolio convey about

Possible Types of Writing to Include in Your Portfolio

- Personal essay
- Creative writing (creative nonfiction, poem, short story)
- Academic essay
- Short, informal report
- Long researched report
- Researched argument with sources
- Report of primary research
- Proposal
- Position paper
- *PowerPoint* presentation
- Web hypertext or Web site
- Newsletter or brochure
- Business writing (résumé, business or application letter, memo)
- Essay exam
- Lab report
- Group or team collaborative writing project

your overall learning? Be sure to ask your instructor if the answers to these questions are not clear in the assignment.

1 Good writing habits

Portfolios should begin taking shape the minute you receive your first assignment for a course. Don't think of the portfolio as a "final exam" and put it off until the end. Rather, see the portfolio as a term-long preparation that will reflect the entire range of your work. Don't procrastinate—rather, work steadily toward your goal of a finished portfolio. The guidelines provided by this handbook can help you in your writing (Part 1) and research (Part 2) for individual pieces in your portfolio. The latter parts of the handbook can help you with revising and editing your writing.

2 Selecting materials to include

Once again, knowing the purpose for the portfolio will be crucial to selecting the appropriate materials. Many times portfolios fail not because the individual pieces within them are poor but rather because the wrong pieces have been selected or the portfolio itself is incomplete and disorganized. Whatever the type of portfolio, find out from your instructor whether or not prewriting, research notes, rough drafts, outlines, and so on should be included. If the instructor allows choice and wants you to include process writing, don't take that as a blanket invitation to include everything. Be selective so as not to overwhelm your readers. Select finished writing that is clear, coherent, and appropriate for its audience; that has a strong thesis; and that is organized, thoughtfully developed, and correct.

3 Reflecting on the process

A common feature of many portfolio assignments is the reflective statement or cover letter. Students are frequently confused about what to include in such a statement. Because you are the writer, editor, and compiler of the portfolio, the reflective statement should be written in your own unique voice and should reflect your personality. In general, it is your opportunity to explain why you chose each piece and what, from your perspective, makes it stand out. The more specific your statement is about the changes you made in your writing and the learning that occurred along the way, the better. Focus on how you developed as a writer and/or how your knowledge and skills have improved. Give specific examples from your writing to illustrate each point—such as specific revisions that were done on individual pieces and overall features of your writing that have improved. Finally, comment generally about the experience of the course and the entire portfolio process. How has your writing improved? How have your critical thinking and analytical skills improved? What, specifically, have you learned?

4 Organizing the final portfolio

Before you compile the final portfolio, look once again at the assignment sheet. Is there a required format? Some portfolios need to be submitted in folders with dividers, for example. Is there a specific order of contents? Find out if the reflective statement should come first as a cover letter and/or if brief reflective statements need to be included before each piece in the portfolio. Check to see how each piece should be labeled, and find out if you need a table of contents. Ask to see successful model portfolios that you can emulate. Following your instructor's guidelines explicitly will surely help you succeed.

28c Prepare the final portfolio

Now you have come to the final stages of your portfolio project. You have selected and organized the pieces to include; you have written your reflective statement(s) and decided how to best order the contents; you have rechecked your instructor's guidelines and consulted models. Your portfolio will most likely be submitted in one of the two following ways: physically or electronically.

1 Physical submission

Your instructor or program may require you to submit an actual portfolio folder. In some cases, it will be supplied to you; in others, you will be expected to supply your own appropriate folder (a manila folder, a large envelope, a paper folder with pockets, a hardbound or spiral folder). Do not substitute one folder for another—rather, follow the guidelines explicitly. Your instructor has reasons for requiring the physical presentation a certain way. Check again to see in which order the materials should be placed—for example, table of contents followed by reflective cover letter. Use dividers, introductory statements, clear titles, and so on to help your readers navigate through your portfolio. Be consistent in the use of fonts and colors. Do not become overly elaborate and ornate—that will only distract your reader from the content. Remember, appearance and neatness count.

2 Electronic submission

Many courses and programs in the new century make use of the latest technologies to submit and store portfolios electronically. Electronic portfolios provide a number of advantages: they allow for multimedia presentations, multiple paths for readers to navigate, and relatively unlimited storage and retrieval capabilities. Once again, it will be important for you to find out the exact specifications for electronic submission of your portfolio. Will it be on a disk, via email attachment, on a CD, or on a Web site? Electronic portfolios sometimes do not include rough drafts since these may not have been stored along the way. You should discover early on whether or not you need to save copies of early drafts to be included in your electronic portfolio. Of course, an electronic portfolio has the added benefit of demonstrating your knowledge and expertise in electronic media. A word of caution: Be sure to always back up your work electronically by saving it on a disk or a network prior to submission. Allow yourself extra time for those inevitable last-minute electronic glitches.

WEBLINK

http://www.kzoo.edu/pfolio/

The Kalamazoo College Web site includes a database of schools that require portfolios, plus sample portfolios online

28.2
Examples of electronic portfolios.

28d A sample reflective cover letter

The reflective cover letter shown in Figure 28.3 was written by a student in a first-year composition course. The student discusses the changes made to each paper in the portfolio and reflects on the concepts learned in the course.

EXERCISE 28.2

Analyze the reflective cover letter shown in Figure 28.3. What did this student learn in the composition course? Are these important lessons? Did the student learn anything about global revision or just about details of grammar?

FOR COLLABORATION

Discuss your analysis of the reflective cover letter in Figure 28.3 with a small group of your peers. Do you agree as to its effectiveness?

Student Reflective Statement

Throughout the course of my first year in college, I think my writing has improved substantially. I have always enjoyed writing, and I usually use proper grammar, mechanics, punctuation, etc. However, this year I have learned to write more effectively using sophisticated sentences and active voice, yet also being concise in my thoughts and ideas. I have also learned many argumentative strategies that are resourceful when trying to persuade audiences. I noticed an improvement in each of my writings as the semester passed, learning to write more professionally and still appeal to the reader.

My first paper, a reflective argument about LBL, had very few mechanical errors. Only a small number of structural changes were required, so I had to revise it once more and make the necessary adjustments. Mainly, I needed to tighten some of my ideas and state my point in a more succinct manner. For example, I used prepositional phrases and some other words that were superfluous and had to be condensed. I also got rid of a nominalization by changing the noun formation back into a verb.

My second paper was a research report in which I stated and analyzed the results of a survey I conducted. Like my first paper, this one didn't have

FIGURE 28.3 Student Reflective Cover Letter

many grammatical errors, but it did have a few organizational problems. To correct these, I moved a couple of sentences around so that each sentence of every paragraph was related to the topic sentence of that paragraph. As always, there were some words that I changed and omitted in order to make sentences sound better and more suitable.

My last paper, a rhetorical analysis detailing the effects of alcohol in inner cities, had some minor errors that needed to be corrected. I had to clarify a few points and rearrange a sentence so that I could be understood better. Mainly, I changed several "be" verbs to action verbs and eliminated as many passive sentences as possible. This helped to make the paper more interesting and concise.

I have noticed several improvements in my writings as I progressed throughout the semester. I have tried to write using as many active verbs as possible and do away with needless words and phrases. To make my writings sound more professional, I have also tried to cut down on short, choppy sentences and write more elaborate, sophisticated sentences. However, I still attempt to organize my ideas so that they are condensed and logical to the reader. I learned to use the three persuasive strategies: logos, ethos, and pathos. These are very important when trying to convince and influence others, and I

FIGURE 28.3 Student Reflective Cover Letter *(continued)*

will always try to use them when they are needed. I now know that writing can be a very effective means of communication, and when done correctly, it can be even better than speaking. If I continue to work on these areas of my writing, especially sentence structure and organization, I think I can become a good, maybe even great, writer as I continue on in college and the rest of my life.

FIGURE 28.3 Student Reflective Cover Letter *(continued)*

CHAPTER **29**

Word-Processing Tools for Improving Sentences

FAQs

▶ Should I change everything my grammar checker points out in my writing? (29a-1)
▶ Are there Internet sites that can help me with my writing?
▶ What kind of revision programs are there? (29b)

Parts 6–12 of this handbook will help you improve your grammar and writing style so that you will be able to express your thoughts more precisely and make your writing more readable and interesting.

Among the conveniences of using a computer for writing is the ready access to editing and formatting tools, which are found in any standard word-processing program. But these tools must be used with care. This chapter discusses such word-processing tools as grammar checkers and revision programs. (Other tools, including thesauruses and spell checkers, are discussed in Chapters 48 and 49.)

29a Use a grammar checker with caution

A typical **grammar checker** will scan your document and apply whatever rules it has been programmed to observe. Since the rules reflected in the programs are taken from traditional grammar and style books, computerized grammar checkers are similar in the kinds of

VIDEO
Options for using style/ grammar checkers.

things they flag, such as long sentences, archaic words, sexist expressions, double negatives, sentence fragments, and passive verbs.

You may be able to get a full listing of the rules observed by your grammar checker, along with an explanation of each, by clicking on the customization feature. You can then select which rules you want to apply to your writing. Some word processors allow you to choose a particular set of rules appropriate to a particular style—formal or informal, for example.

WEBLINK

http://seattlepi.nwsource.com/
business/217802_grammar28
.asp?searchpagefrom=
1&searchdiff=0

A skeptical professor's take
on grammar checkers

(Note) For extra speed when using a grammar checker, turn off the spell checker.

1 Understanding the limitations of grammar checkers

Grammar checkers can be useful in pointing out potential trouble spots, but they have serious shortcomings. First, *they overlook many potential problems.* Of all the stylistic and grammatical problems illustrated in the examples in Part 7 of this book, for example, our grammar checker could identify only a third. It was unable to identify any of the pronoun reference problems in Chapter 37, or any of the modifier problems in Chapter 38, or any of the consistency problems in Chapter 39.

29.1

Misdiagnoses
by grammar
checkers.

Second, *grammar checkers flag many things that are not problematic.* In some cases, the computer misreads the sentence. In other cases, it applies a rule too simplistically. For example, if your grammar checker flags a passive-voice verb, you may decide that you should change it to active voice. But using the passive voice is not always wrong; indeed, sometimes it is the best choice (see 40d). Many stylistic choices depend on things that a computer cannot assess—such as purpose, tone, coherence, ambiguity, pronoun reference, consistency, emphasis, and variety. When we ran our grammar checker on this paragraph, we received eight suggestions, none of which were constructive and all of which we chose to ignore.

AUDIO

Use style and
grammar
checkers with
caution.

(E X E R C I S E 2 9 . 1)

Select a professionally written paragraph from an Internet site, copy it, and save it as a document. Then run your grammar checker on it. Look at each "error" that the computer identifies, and make a guess as to why the writer might have chosen to write the offending item that way.

Typical Rules Found in Grammar Checkers

Cross-references to sections in this book appear in parentheses.

1. Make clear comparisons. (31f, 40i)
2. Prefer active voice to passive voice. (32g, 40d)
3. Make subjects and verbs agree in number. (33a)
4. Avoid long noun strings. (34b)
5. Use comparative and superlative forms correctly. (34e)
6. Avoid multiple negatives. (40j)
7. Avoid sentence fragments. (35)
8. Avoid sentences beginning with *and, but,* or *plus.* (35a-2)
9. Use *who, which,* and *that* correctly. (37b)
10. Avoid misplaced modifiers. (38)
11. Avoid excessively long sentences. (40a)
12. Avoid wordiness. (40e)
13. Avoid long strings of prepositional phrases. (40f)
14. Avoid common word confusions. (45a)
15. Avoid informal expressions in formal writing. (45c-1)
16. Avoid jargon. (45d)
17. Avoid overused phrases and clichés. (45g-3)
18. Avoid sexist expressions. (46c)
19. Use homophones correctly. (49b)
20. Avoid common apostrophe errors. (54d)
21. Avoid capitalization errors. (57)
22. Avoid hyphenation errors in compound words. (59a–59b)
23. Make nouns and their quantifiers agree in number. (60f)
24. Do not use more than one modal auxiliary verb at a time. (32c, 61h)

2 Making appropriate use of a grammar checker

To make appropriate use of a grammar checker, you should first customize the checker to your needs. Here's how: (1) Open the TOOLS menu, click on OPTIONS, and then SPELLING & GRAMMAR. (2) Look for the WRITING STYLE menu and select the desired style—for most college writing it would be FORMAL. (3) Click on SETTINGS and select all of the grammar options. (You can always deselect some of these later.)

Next, pull up a piece of writing you want to check. It should be a next-to-final draft that needs only polishing, not an early draft that may still need extensive rethinking or restructuring. Then run the grammar checker on it.

For each item the grammar checker flags, consider the recommended alternative. If you don't understand why a certain alternative is recommended, consult the HELP menu or HELP wizard. You should also consult the relevant section in this handbook (see the Typical Rules on page 641), which should have more detailed information and advice on what to do. Using all of this information, make your own decision about whether to change the item or leave it as is. Remember: A computerized grammar checker is often wrong; it does not consider your rhetorical stance (see 3b-2); and its suggestions are only suggestions.

Here is an example:

After revising a paper about the state legislature's failure to honor Martin Luther King, Jr.'s birthday, Eva ran it through her grammar checker. The opening sentences appeared like this:

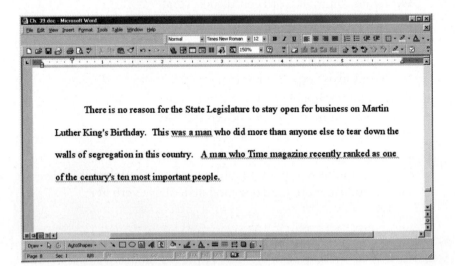

The grammar checker said that the expression *was a man who* was "wordy" and suggested *man* as a substitute. So Eva tried the substitution: *This man did more than anyone else to tear down the walls of segregation in this country.* This version was certainly more concise than the original, and it did not change the basic meaning of the sentence. However, Eva felt it somehow "didn't have as much emphasis" and lost the parallelism she wanted with the beginning of the next sentence (*a man who . . . A man who . . .*). She decided that her original version was better, and so she left it unchanged.

In the next sentence, the grammar checker had this comment: "Fragment (consider revising)." However, it did not say how it should be revised. Eva could not see an immediate solution to the problem, so she turned to Chapter 35, Sentence Fragments. There, she noted that a clause starting with *who* was a subordinate clause (35a-3), not a main clause; this made her realize that what she had punctuated as a sentence did not have a complete predicate (35a-1). Using the Checklist for Fixing Fragments, item 1 on page 719, she realized that simply changing the punctuation would correct the problem: "This is a man who did more than anyone else to tear down the walls of segregation in this country, a man who *Time* magazine recently ranked as one of the century's ten most important people."

Eva's use of the grammar checker was effective because she used her own judgment in deciding whether to follow its suggestions. Rather than looking at each sentence in isolation (as a grammar checker does), she considered the composition as a whole, including her rhetorical stance toward the topic.

EXERCISE 29.2

Run your grammar checker on a paragraph of your own writing. Analyze each "error" the computer identifies, referring to the corresponding section in this book (see the Typical Rules on page 641). Make whatever changes you think appropriate.

29.2
Readability scores.

29b Use sentence revision applications

Today's word-processing programs offer a number of special functions that can be used in revising sentences or paragraphs. One such application is a *change-tracking program*, which allows you to insert changes in a draft and then compare what the draft looks like with and without the changes. There is usually a variety of options with such a program. For example, the revisions can appear on the screen (during or after editing) and/or on the printed document; the

VIDEO
Tracking changes in documents.

changes can be marked by underlining, boldface, or italics in the left or right margin; and the deletions can be marked by different-colored strikethroughs. With some programs you can compare Before and After versions side by side.

Here is an example of change-tracking from the continuation of Eva's paper on Martin Luther King, Jr.:

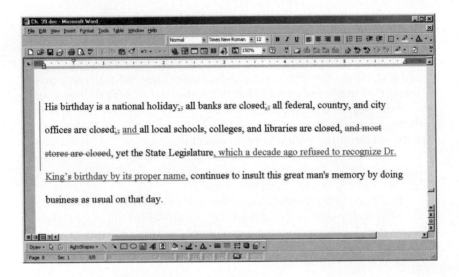

Eva converted several commas to semicolons, deleted a clause, and inserted a conjunction and a clause. She can now examine these changes and decide whether she wants to keep them. If not, the change-tracking program allows her to revert to the previous draft.

Another good tool for sentence and paragraph revision is a *Comment* (or *Annotation*) program. This type of application allows your instructor, a peer, or you to select a portion of text and leave an annotation or comment about it. The text being commented on is either highlighted in a different color or marked by a vertical line in the left margin. Clicking on a comment reference mark brings the comment up on the screen; when the document is printed, however, the comment is kept hidden (unless you choose to have it printed). With some programs, comments can be audiotaped and played back.

Following is an example of a comment made by one of Eva's reviewers (identified as "sum1"). The phrase being commented on is highlighted in yellow; the comment itself is presented in a separate window at the bottom of the screen. Notice how "sum1" is identified both in the text and in the Comments window.

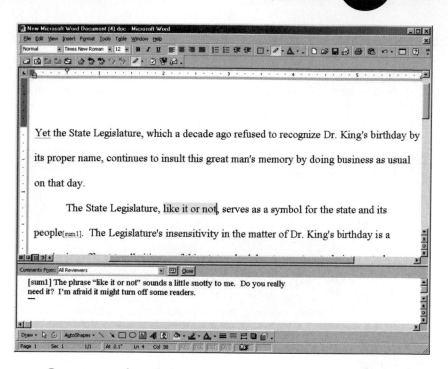

Comment tools and change-tracking tools are suitable for use by multiple reviewers (see 4c). Each reviewer can use a specific color to highlight his or her comments or revisions, and each comment reference mark includes the reviewer's initials. *Version control* is enhanced by the use of different versions (each with a truncated set of comments and stored as a separate file) accessed via the FILE menu.

FOR COLLABORATION

Exchange drafts of your latest composition with one of your classmates. Then each of you use a Comment program to provide feedback to the other person. Using this feedback, revise the draft. Then send it back to your classmate to see whether the revisions are satisfactory.

29c Use other applications

In addition to grammar checkers and revision programs, most word-processing applications offer a number of other functions that can be helpful to a writer. For example, there are *window display options*, including split-screen windows that allow you to modify one

WEBLINK

http://webster.commnet.edu/grammar/index.htm

A fabulous guide to grammar and writing

section of a document while keeping another in view. A number of word-processing programs let you keep two or more files open simultaneously, thereby allowing you to modify one document while viewing or copying material from another document.

Help Boxes in Parts 6–12

- How do I use a grammar checker? (Chapter 30)
- How do I customize a grammar checker to search for pronoun case problems? (Chapter 31)
- How do I locate sentence fragments? (Chapter 35)
- How do I identify comma splices and run-on sentences? (Chapter 36)
- How do I identify possible pronoun reference problems? (Chapter 37)
- How do I guard against using excessively long sentences? (Chapter 40)
- How do I find places where I should be using parallelism? (Chapter 42)
- How can I speed up spell checking? (Chapter 49)
- How do I identify punctuation errors in my writing? (Chapter 51)
- How can I spot places where I need a semicolon with a conjunctive adverb? (Chapter 52)
- How do I find out whether I have a "parenthesis habit"? (Chapter 56)
- How do I check my placement of adverbs? (Chapter 62)

Other useful word-processing programs discussed elsewhere in this book include the following:

- Discovery or invention programs (see Chapter 3)
- Outlining programs (see Help boxes on pages 64, 118, and 167)
- Bibliography programs (see Help box on page 186)
- Graphics programs (see 20c)
- Thesaurus programs (see 48a)

You also may want to take advantage of **bookmarks,** or place-ment markers, that allow you to flag key passages in the document to which you may want to return as you revise. Once you give the key location a tag name, it appears in a menu of bookmark items from which you may choose when selecting key passages for com-parison or revision.

One of the most common word-processing applications is the SEARCH, or FIND, *feature* (often located in the EDIT menu). This feature can help you locate any word or word configuration in a text. Most applications allow you to specify the context in which you want to find a specific word or letter combination. For example, if you want to track each instance of *the* in your text (but not *them, theater,* or *there*), you might simply type SPACE-*t-h-e*-SPACE in the SEARCH box. To replace all instances of a certain form, just use the SEARCH and REPLACE features. For instance, if you have made a mistake repeat-edly throughout a paper—for example, writing *it's* when you meant *its*— just enter *it's* in the SEARCH box and *its* in the REPLACE box and then run the program; the problem will be taken care of in a flash. Of course, if you correctly used the contraction *it's* anywhere to stand for *it is,* it too will be replaced by *its,* creating an error. In general, it is a good idea to learn what you can about the SEARCH function on your computer. The Help boxes in Parts 6–12 include many suggestions for using this function to locate key items likely to need revision.

(EXERCISE 29.3)

Using a sample of your own writing, follow the procedures in *three* of the Help boxes listed on page 646.

CHAPTER 30

Sentence Structure

FAQs

▶ What is an adverb? (30a-5)
▶ What is the difference between a participle and a gerund? (30a-9)
▶ What is a sentence subject? (30b-1)
▶ What is a predicate? (30b-2)

AUDIO
Chapter
overview.

Because grammar checkers have many shortcomings, you cannot rely on them to fix grammatical errors in your writing. Instead, you need to know the basic elements of sentence structure and do much editing on your own. This chapter will give you the necessary knowledge.

30a Learn to identify parts of speech

In writing a sentence, you put words together in certain combinations. These combinations depend, in part, on the different kinds of words, or **parts of speech,** you use: nouns, pronouns, adjectives, verbs, adverbs, prepositions, conjunctions, and interjections.

1 Nouns

A **noun** (n) is the name of a person, place, thing, quality, idea, or action. Some examples of nouns are

Picasso	Mexico	printer
honesty	democracy	juice

How do I use a grammar checker?

1. Start the checker. (It may be on the TOOLS menu.)
2. Position your cursor on the IGNORE (or SKIP) command, and be prepared to click on it often.
3. Consider each suggestion the checker makes, but do not automatically follow its advice. In most cases, you will decide to click IGNORE.
4. If you are not sure whether to accept the checker's suggestion, use the EXPLANATION feature (if there is one).
5. If you are still in doubt, read the relevant discussions in this handbook (see 29a or the index). Use the book's advice to help you decide whether to revise.

Common nouns refer to general persons, places, things, concepts, or qualities.

> man   city   mouse   philosophy   generosity

Proper nouns, which are almost always capitalized, name particular persons, places, institutions, organizations, months, and days.

> Tom Cruise   Salt Lake City   the World Court
> Duke University   Buddhism   Monday

Concrete nouns specifically refer to things that can be sensed through sight, hearing, touch, taste, and smell.

> bookshelf   fork   billboard   hamburger

Abstract nouns refer to ideas, emotions, qualities, or other intangible concepts.

> beauty   sadness   truth   love

Count nouns name things that can be counted and thus can have a plural form.

> lake(s)   violin(s)   baseball(s)   goose (geese)

Noncount nouns, or **mass nouns,** name things that typically are not counted in English and thus cannot be made plural.

> water   snow   hatred   health   news

Some nouns can serve as either count or noncount nouns, depending on their meaning. For example, *experience* can be used as a count noun (*I've had many interesting experiences*) or as a noncount noun (*Experience is the best teacher*). (See 60a for further discussion.)

Collective nouns name groups; they are plural in sense but singular in form.

    committee   team   class   crowd

2 Pronouns

Pronouns (pron), such as *she, they,* and *it,* are words that substitute for nouns and usually refer to a noun, which is called the **antecedent** of the pronoun. The noun antecedent usually precedes the pronoun in a sentence:

    Lucinda said *she* was not feeling well.

Sometimes the noun antecedent follows the pronoun:

    Saying *she* was not feeling well, *Lucinda* left the room.

Pronouns can be singular or plural, and their case can vary depending on how they are used in a sentence. The change from *he* to *him* or *his* reflects pronoun use according to case—subjective, objective, or possessive. (See Chapter 31 for a discussion of pronoun case and Chapter 33 for a discussion of pronoun-antecedent agreement.)

3 Adjectives

An **adjective** (adj) is a word that modifies a noun or pronoun by qualifying or describing it. In English, the adjective usually precedes the noun it modifies (an *old* tree, the *other* day), but in literary usage an adjective occasionally follows the noun (a woman *scorned*). In sentences such as "The program was *challenging*," the adjective falls on the other side of a verb linking it to the noun it modifies. An adjective used in this way is called a **predicate adjective.**

Many adjectives have comparative and superlative forms created by the addition of *-er* and *-est* (*small, smaller, smallest*). (See Chapter 34.) Many other adjectives have the same form as the present or past participle of a verb (a *roaring* lion, a *deserted* island).

(ESL Note) If you use two or more adjectives before a noun, you often must put them in a certain order (see 62a).

Types of Pronouns and Their Roles

Type	Role
Personal pronouns Singular: *I, you, he, she, it; me, you, him, her, it; mine, yours, his, hers, its* Plural: *we, you, they; us, you, them; ours, yours, theirs*	Refer to specific persons or things and serve to distinguish the speaker or writer (first person), the person or thing spoken to (second person), and the person or thing spoken about (third person): "Michael gave *me* his book and *I* gave *him mine.*"
Demonstrative pronouns *this, that, these, those*	Point to their antecedent nouns: "*That* was an interesting idea!"
Indefinite pronouns *all, any, anybody, anyone, anything, both, everybody, everyone, everything, few, many, one, no one, nothing, somebody, someone, something, several, some*	Refer to nonspecific persons or things and do not require an antecedent: "*Nothing* could be done."
Relative pronouns *that, what, which, who, whom, whose, whoever, whichever, whatever*	Introduce dependent clauses: "She is the teacher *who* runs marathons."
Interrogative pronouns *who, whom, which, what, whose*	Introduce questions: "*Whose* bike is this?"
Reflexive and **intensive pronouns** (consist of a personal pronoun plus *-self* or *-selves*) Singular: *myself, yourself, himself, herself, itself* Plural: *ourselves, yourselves, themselves*	A reflexive pronoun refers back to the subject to show that the subject itself is the object of an action: "She saw *herself* in the mirror." An intensive pronoun is used for emphasis: "They did it *themselves.*"

(continued)

Types of Pronouns and Their Roles *(continued)*

Type	Role
Reciprocal pronouns *one another, each other*	Refer to the separate parts of a plural antecedent: "They gave presents to *each other*."
Expletive pronouns *there, it*	Serve as introductory, "empty" words occupying the position of grammatical subject: "*There* are many kinds of hummingbirds."

Some of the pronouns discussed in 30a-2 can also function as **possessive adjectives** (*our* school), **demonstrative adjectives** (*this* page), **interrogative adjectives** (*Which* button do I push?), and **indefinite adjectives** (*some* money). These, along with **articles** (*the, a, an*), comprise the category of **determiners.** Determiners serve to introduce nouns and noun phrases:

> *the* kitchen

> *my* DVD player

> *some* interesting news

Unlike most adjectives, however, they do not occur as predicate adjectives, do not have comparative or superlative forms, and do not occur in combination. (For further discussion, see Chapter 60.)

See Chapter 34 for a more detailed discussion of adjectives.

4 Verbs

A **verb** (v) is a key word that expresses an action (*swim, read*) or a state of being (*is, seemed*). Main verbs are often accompanied by **auxiliary verbs** (also called **helping verbs**), which include forms of the verbs *be, have,* and *do,* and/or by **modal verbs,** such as *may, might, can, could, will, would, shall, should,* and *must.* Auxiliary and modal verbs are special verb forms that express questions, future tenses, past tenses, and various degrees of doubt about or qualification of the main verb's action. (See Chapter 32 for more on verbs.)

Transitive verbs (VT) transfer action from an agent (usually the subject of the sentence) to an object or recipient (usually the direct object of the sentence): "Michael *fumbled* the ball." Some common transitive verbs are *carry, reject, show, build,* and *destroy* (see 30b-2, 30b-3). **Intransitive verbs** (VI) may express action, but they do not transfer it to an object or recipient: "The bridge *collapsed*." Some common intransitive verbs are *sleep, fall, die, erupt,* and *disappear.* Many verbs can be used either intransitively or transitively: "Frank *eats* often, but he does not *eat* red meat." **Linking verbs** (LV) such as *be, seem,* and *appear* connect the subject of a sentence to a subject complement (typically an adjective), as in "Mary *is* Irish" or "Your friend *seems* bored." Some linking verbs express the result of an action: "The apples *turned* sour," "Her predictions *came* true."

The five major forms a verb takes are usually referred to as its **principal parts.** They are the **base form** (or **infinitive form**), **present tense** (third-person singular), **past tense, past participle,** and **present participle.**

Base form	Present tense	Past tense	Past participle	Present participle
(to) erase	erases	erased	(have) erased	(am) erasing
(to) run	runs	ran	(have) run	(am) running

These different forms of a verb serve different functions. For **regular verbs,** the past tense and the past participle are formed by adding *-d* or *-ed* to the base form (*erased*). For **irregular verbs,** the past tense and past participle are formed differently (*ran/run*). (See 32b for more on irregular verb forms.)

Verbs also have an **active form,** called the **active voice** ("He *committed* the crime"), as well as a **passive form,** called the **passive voice,** consisting of a form of the verb *be* and a past participle ("The crime *was committed* by him"). In addition, verbs may take on alternative forms to reflect different **moods.** Normally they are in the **indicative mood,** used to make assertions, state opinions, and ask questions. But they can take past-tense forms to express unreal conditions or wishes, in the **subjunctive mood:** "I wish I *were* in Hawaii." They can appear in the base form, usually with no apparent subject, to issue a command, in the **imperative mood:** "Don't *do* that again!" or, occasionally, "Don't you *do* that again!" Finally, verb forms become verbals when they change their function and are used as nouns, adverbs, or adjectives (see 30a-9).

See Chapters 32 and 61 for a more complete discussion of verbs.

5 Adverbs

An **adverb** (adv) modifies a verb, an adjective, another adverb, or an entire clause or sentence. Adverbs usually answer one of the following questions: when? where? how? how often? to what extent?

The mayor lives *alone* in a downtown apartment.   [*Alone* modifies the verb *lives*.]

She has a *very* busy schedule.   [*Very* modifies the adjective *busy*.]

She *almost* never takes a vacation.   [*Almost* modifies the adverb *never*.]

Apparently, she doesn't seem to need one.   [*Apparently* modifies the entire sentence.]

Many adverbs (*quickly, hopefully*) are formed by adding *-ly* to an adjective, but many others (*very, not, always, tomorrow, inside, therefore*) are not.

(ESL Note) Adverbs must be positioned properly within a sentence (see 62d).

Conjunctive adverbs, such as *however, thus,* and *consequently,* modify an entire sentence or clause while linking it to the preceding sentence or clause. (See Chapter 41.)

Today's weather will be beautiful. *However*, we expect rain tomorrow.

See Chapter 34 for a more detailed discussion of adverbs.

6 Prepositions

A **preposition** (prep) is a word such as *in, on, of, for,* or *by* that comes before a noun or pronoun and its modifiers to form a **prepositional phrase.** Some examples of prepositional phrases are *in the water, off the deep end,* and *toward them.* The noun or pronoun in such phrases (*water, end, them*) is called the **object of the preposition.** Here are some of the most common prepositions used in English:

30.1

English on
"Who Wants
to Be a
Millionaire?"

about	beneath	into	through
above	beside	like	to
across	between	near	toward
after	by	of	under
along	despite	off	underneath
among	down	on	unlike
around	during	onto	until
at	except	out	up
before	for	outside	upon
behind	from	over	with
below	in	past	without

Prepositions also occur in multiword combinations: *according to, along with, because of, in case of, in spite of, on account of,* and *with respect to.*

Prepositions can be linked to certain verbs to form **phrasal verbs,** such as *do without, put up with,* and *look over.* In phrasal verbs, the preposition is called a **particle.** Compare the following sentences:

> She *came across* a dead animal.   [*Came across* is a phrasal verb meaning "discovered."]

> She *came* across the bridge.   [*Came* is a simple verb; *across* is part of the adverbial phrase *across the bridge.*]

(**ESL Note**) Phrasal verbs are common in idiomatic English. (See Chapters 61 and 63.)

7 Conjunctions

A **conjunction** (conj) joins two sentences, clauses, phrases, or words. The relationship between the two parts may be an equal, or coordinate, one; it may be an unequal, or subordinate, one.

Coordinating conjunctions (*and, but, or, nor, yet, so, for*) connect sentences, clauses, phrases, or words that are parallel in meaning and grammatical structure. **Correlative conjunctions** (*both/and, neither/nor, either/or, not/but, whether/or, not only/but also*) are pairs of conjunctions that give extra emphasis to the two parts of a coordinated construction (see 42c). **Subordinating conjunctions** introduce dependent clauses and connect them to main clauses. Some common subordinating conjunctions are *although, because, if, since, unless,* and *while.*

See Chapter 41 for further discussion of conjunctions.

8 Interjections

An **interjection** is a short utterance such as *Wow!, Ouch!, well,* or *oh* that usually expresses an emotional response. Interjections often stand alone and are often punctuated with an exclamation mark.

> *Wow!* What a show!

> *Oh,* I thought it was just so-so.

30.2
Examples of commonly used interjections.

9 Verbals

In additional to the traditional parts of speech, there are also **verbals.** A verbal is a verb form that functions in a sentence as a noun, an adverb, or an adjective. There are three types of verbals: participles, gerunds, and infinitives.

Participles are words such as *sweeping* and *swept,* the present and past participles of a verb (*sweep*) that function as adjectives and can modify nouns or pronouns.

AUDIO

Comparing
gerunds and
participles.

> Beware of *sweeping* generalizations.

> *Swept* floors make a house seem more livable.

Gerunds are verb forms that end in *-ing* and function as nouns.

> *Sweeping* the floors is something I do not enjoy.

An **infinitive** is the base form of a verb preceded by *to* (*to read, to fly, to ponder*). Infinitives can function as nouns, adjectives, or adverbs.

NOUN   *To quit* would be a mistake.

ADJECTIVE   Her desire *to quit* is understandable.

ADVERB   He is eager *to quit.*

30b Learn to identify basic sentence patterns

Sentences are the basic units for expressing assertions, questions, commands, wishes, and exclamations. All grammatically complete sentences have a subject and a predicate. In a sentence fragment, one of these elements may be missing. (See Chapter 35 for more on fragments.)

1 Sentence subjects

The **subject** (sub) of a sentence is a noun, a pronoun, or a noun phrase (a noun plus its modifiers) that identifies what the sentence is about. Usually it directly precedes the main verb.

> *You* probably have a pointing device (or PD) connected to your computer.

> *Many PDs* have a ball that rolls against wheels.

> *The rubber ball found inside most PDs* oxidizes over time and begins to slip.

> *The preference settings for double-click speed and for the ratio of hand or finger travel to pointer travel* are set in the OPTIONS menu.

The **simple subject** is always a noun or pronoun. In the example sentences, the simple subjects are *you*, *PDs*, *ball*, and *settings*. The **complete subject** is the simple subject plus all its modifiers; the complete subjects are italicized in the example sentences. Some sentences have a **compound subject** including two or more simple subjects.

Tips and techniques can be found in the HELP menu.

In imperative sentences, which express a command or a request, the subject is understood to be *you*, even though it is not usually stated.

> [*You*] Use macros to automate repetitive tasks.

> **WEBLINK**
>
> http://owl.english.purdue.edu/handouts/grammar/index.html
> Comprehensive coverage of parts of speech and sentence construction

The subject of a sentence always agrees in number and person with the main verb. For example, a third-person singular subject such as *he* needs a third-person singular verb such as *runs*.

Subject-verb agreement is discussed further in Chapter 33.

EXERCISE 30.1

Put brackets around the complete subject in each of the following sentences. The first one has been done for you.

1. After its Industrial Revolution, [England] led the world as the most advanced nation in mechanization and mass production.
2. The Arts and Crafts Movement in Victorian England started as a mild rebellion by a group of artists, designers, and architects.
3. These artisans were concerned about the poor standard of design in English building and furnishings.
4. One of the most influential leaders of the Arts and Crafts Movement was William Morris (1834–1896).
5. Unable to find the fabrics he wanted for his home, Morris set up his own textile design firm in London in 1861.
6. Each year, the students at MIT compete to execute ever more creative pranks.
7. One year, they managed to park a car on top of a building.
8. In the winter, people need to be alert for signs that their heating systems are malfunctioning and emitting carbon monoxide gas.
9. The light breeze was welcome on that hot summer afternoon.
10. Most of us look forward to the hamburgers and potato salad served at summer cookouts.

EXER

Select the complete subject.

2 Predicates

The **predicate** is the part of a sentence that contains the verb and makes a statement about the subject. The **simple predicate** is the verb plus any auxiliary (helping) verbs.

The World Wide Web *offers* information, graphics, music, movies, and much more.

With a Web browser, you *can locate* information efficiently.

The **complete predicate** consists of the simple predicate plus any objects, complements, or adverbial modifiers.

The World Wide Web *offers information, graphics, music, movies, and much more.*

A **compound predicate** has two or more verbs that have the same subject.

A Web page *informs and entertains.*

A **direct object** (DO) is a noun, a pronoun, or a noun phrase that completes the action of a transitive verb (see 30a-4)—one that is capable of transmitting action. In this sentence, *information* is the direct object of the verb *locate:*

Sub   V   DO

You can locate *information.*

An **indirect object** (IO) is a noun, a pronoun, or a noun phrase that is affected indirectly by the action of a verb. It usually refers to the recipient or beneficiary of the action described by the verb and the direct object. The verbs *give, buy, bring, teach, tell,* and *offer* commonly take indirect objects.

Sub   V IO DO

The teacher told *us* a story.

Most indirect objects can be presented instead as the object of the preposition *to* or *for.*

The teacher told *us* a story.

OR

The teacher told a story *to us.*

I bought *my mother* a plant.

OR

I bought a plant *for my mother.*

An **object complement** (OC) is a noun, a noun phrase, an adjective, or an adjective phrase (an adjective plus its modifiers) that elaborates on or describes the direct object.

<pre>
    Sub   V   DO   OC
  ┌────────┐
  The news made us depressed.
</pre>

Sub   V   DO   OC

They appointed Laurie *head of the task force.*

A **subject complement** (SC) is a noun, a noun phrase, an adjective, or an adjective phrase that follows a linking verb (such as *is, was,* or *seems*) and elaborates on the subject.

Sub LV   SC
She was *happy.*

Sub LV   SC

Laurie is *the new head of the task force.*

---

3   Basic sentence patterns

The complete predicate is usually structured according to one of six basic sentence patterns:

Pattern 1: A sentence may have an intransitive verb and no object.

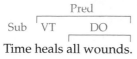

Time flies.

Pattern 2: A sentence may have a transitive verb with a direct object.

<pre>
              Pred
        ┌───────────────┐
  Sub VT   DO
Time heals all wounds.
</pre>

Pattern 3: A sentence may have a transitive verb with a direct object and an indirect object.

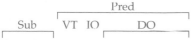

Free time gave us an opportunity.

Pattern 4: A sentence may have a transitive verb with a direct object and an object complement.

$$\text{Pred}$$

Sub · VT DO OC

Time pressures made us tense.

Pattern 5: A sentence may use a **linking verb,** which connects the subject to a subject complement, indicating a condition, quality, or state of being.

Pred

Sub LV SC

Time is precious.

Pattern 6: A sentence may start with an auxiliary verb such as *is, do,* or *can* to form a question or exclamation.

Aux Sub V

Does time fly?

EXERCISE 30.2

Insert a slash (/) between the subject and the predicate in each sentence.

1. I enrolled at Albany State in 1972.
2. My major interests were music and biology.
3. I was a soloist with the choir.
4. We sang three types of music.
5. The choir specialized in spirituals.
6. They had major injections of European musical harmony and composition.
7. Gospel music comprised a major part of black church music at the time.
8. Black choral singing was full, powerful, and richly ornate.
9. The hymns were offset by upbeat call-and-response songs.
10. People in church sang and prayed until they shouted.

EXER

Identify the subject and predicate in each sentence.

AUDIO

Expand sentences for greater variety.

30c **Learn to expand sentences**

The six basic sentence patterns can be expanded with **modifiers,** which are words, phrases, or clauses used to modify the subject or predicate.

1 Modifying with single words

Any simple sentence part can be modified, qualified, or described by appropriate single words. Verbs, adverbs, and adjectives can be modified by adverbs, and nouns can be modified by adjectives.

Sub   V   Adv
Time flies *quickly.*

Adj   Sub   V   Adv   Adv
Spare time flies *very quickly.*

Adjectives usually are placed before the noun or pronoun they modify (*terrible* burden). Adverbs are placed near the verb, adjective, or other adverb they modify. Adverbs that modify an entire sentence can be placed at the beginning, the middle, or the end of a sentence.

> **WEBLINK**
>
> http://www.uottawa.ca/ academic/arts/writcent/ hypergrammar/ bldsent.html
>
> All about sentence structure and options—even includes review exercises

30.3
An online guide to building sentences.

Frantically, Martha crammed for the exam.

Martha *frantically* crammed for the exam.

Martha crammed for the exam *frantically.*

See Chapters 34 and 62 for more on placing adjectives and adverbs.

2 Modifying with phrases

Sentence parts can also be modified by phrases. A **phrase** is a group of words consisting of (1) a noun and its related words or (2) a verbal and its related words. Phrases add detail to any of the subjects, verbs, objects, or complements used in the six basic sentence patterns.

Adding Prepositional Phrases

A preposition and its object (a noun or a pronoun) form a **prepositional phrase:** *in the dark, on time, outside Dallas.* Prepositional phrases can be used to modify nouns, verbs, or adjectives.

Sub   Prep phr   V   Prep phr
The TV *in the corner* does not work *without an antenna.*

Sub   V   Adj   Prep phr
Juan was jealous *beyond reason.*

Adding Verbal Phrases

A **verbal** is a verb form that functions as a noun, an adverb, or an adjective (see 30a-9). The three kinds of verbals—infinitives, gerunds, and participles—can be combined with other words to form infinitive phrases, gerund phrases, and participial phrases.

An **infinitive phrase** consists of the *to* form of a verb plus modifiers, objects, and/or complements. Such a phrase can function as a noun, an adjective, or an adverb.

> He wanted *to plant the garden.* [The infinitive phrase functions as a noun and is the object of *wanted.*]

> Free time gave us an opportunity *to reflect.* [The infinitive phrase functions as an adjective modifying *opportunity.*]

> The company was eager *to expand its operations.* [The infinitive phrase functions as an adverb modifying *eager.*]

A **gerund phrase** consists of the *-ing* form of a verb plus modifiers, objects, and/or complements. Gerund phrases function as nouns and thus can be used as sentence subjects, objects, or complements.

> ┌────── Sub ──────┐
> *Lifting boxes all day* made Stan tired.

>   DO
> Rebecca hates *cooking.*

>   ┌──── SC ────┐
> Her favorite activity is *watching old movies.*

(**ESL Note**) Some English verbs can take only one kind of verbal as a complement—an infinitive ("I want *to go*") or a gerund ("I enjoy *biking*"); other verbs can take either ("Rebecca hates *cooking*" or "Rebecca hates to *cook*"). For further discussion, see Chapter 61.

A **participial phrase** consists of a present participle (the *-ing* form of a verb) or a past participle (the *-ed* or *-en* form of a verb) plus modifiers, objects, and/or complements. Participial phrases function as adjectives, modifying subjects and objects of sentences.

> *Having decided to quit his job,* Roberto began looking for another one. [The participial phrase modifies the sentence subject, *Roberto.*]

> I caught someone *trying to break into my car.* [The participial phrase modifies the object *someone.*]

As these examples illustrate, participial phrases should be placed next to the words they modify. Failure to do so may produce dangling modifiers or other modification problems. (See Chapter 38.)

Adding Appositive Phrases

An **appositive phrase** is a noun phrase that describes or defines another noun. Appositive phrases directly follow or precede the nouns they modify and are usually set off by commas.

> *One of the world's most famous celebrities,* Muhammad Ali draws crowds wherever he goes.

> The Ford Mustang, *a car originally designed by Lee Iacocca,* has been an enduring icon of the US automotive industry.

Adding Absolute Phrases

An **absolute phrase** consists of a subject and an adjective phrase (most commonly a participial phrase). Unlike other kinds of phrases, which modify single words, absolute phrases are used to modify entire clauses or sentences.

Abs phr
Sub   Part phr
His curiosity satisfied, Marco decided to move on to other topics.

Abs phr
Sub   Adj phr
Her face white as a sheet, Sue put down the phone and slowly stood up.

Maria could not wait to start writing another book,

Abs phr
Sub   Part phr
her first book having been well received by critics.

(**EXERCISE 30.3**)

Download several paragraphs from an Internet site or photocopy a newspaper or magazine article. In the text, find (1) three prepositional phrases, (2) two gerund phrases, (3) two participial phrases, and (4) an appositive phrase or an absolute phrase.

(FOR COLLABORATION)

In your group, share the phrases you have identified and explain how you came to your conclusions.

3 Modifying with clauses

A **clause** is a group of words that has a subject and a predicate. If a clause can stand alone as a sentence, it is an **independent clause** (or **main clause**); if it cannot, it is a **dependent clause** (or **subordinate clause**). There are three major types of dependent clauses: adjective, adverb, and noun.

Adjective clauses (also called **relative clauses**) modify nouns and pronouns. An adjective clause usually begins with a relative pronoun (*which, that, who, whose, whom*) or a subordinating conjunction (*where, when, why*) and immediately follows the noun or pronoun it modifies.

The student *who is best prepared* is most likely to succeed.

The place *where I work best* is in my basement.

If the relative pronoun is the direct or indirect object in the adjective clause, it can be omitted.

The person [*whom*] *I gave the money to* has disappeared.

Chapter 37 discusses the correct use of relative pronouns; Chapter 41 describes how to use adjective clauses to subordinate ideas.

Adverb clauses modify verbs, adjectives, clauses, or other adverbs, answering questions such as the following: when? where? why? how? An adverb clause begins with a subordinating conjunction (*if, although, because, whenever, while*).

If you cannot find the topic you want, double-click on the HELP button.

Although I have been late for work three times in the past two weeks, my boss has not said anything to me.   [The adverb clause modifies the entire main clause.]

Noun clauses function in a sentence the way simple nouns do—as subjects, objects, complements, or appositives (see 31c). Noun clauses typically begin with a *wh-* element such as *whoever, which,* or *whether;* with *that;* with *to* or *for;* or with a gerund (marked by *-ing*).

Sub

Whoever leaked the news should be punished.

DO

We told her *that she was wrong.*

SC

The plan is *to march on City Hall.*

App

His one hobby, *collecting old bottles,* takes up much of his time.

EXERCISE 30.4

Combine each of the following pairs of sentences to form a single sentence. In so doing, turn one of the sentences into a dependent clause attached to the main clause.

1. Some people live in a cold climate. They should anticipate car battery problems.
2. Your car will not start. You reach for some jumper cables.
3. You attach the cables to your battery. You should consider the possibility of explosion or injury.
4. Hydrogen gas in the battery case combines with air. It becomes a very explosive material.
5. There is a risk that an explosion will hurt your eyes. You should carry a pair of safety goggles with your cables.
6. Some drivers do not know how to use battery cables. They should not try to do it on their own.
7. You want to attempt a jump start. It is a good idea to read the owner's manual.
8. Car computers can lose memory when batteries fail. You will have to reset some things.
9. Prevent battery drain. Be certain to shut the car doors tightly.
10. It is easy to forget your headlights are on when you leave your car. Be sure to double-check.

EXER
Working with subordinate clauses.

30d Learn how to classify sentences

Good writers vary the types of sentences they use in order to make their writing more interesting. The two main categories of sentence types are functional and structural.

1   Functional classifications

Sentences can be categorized functionally, or rhetorically, according to their role. A **declarative sentence,** for example, makes a direct assertion about something.

Our political system is heavily influenced by corporate interests.

An **interrogative sentence** asks a question and ends with a question mark.

Have you ever traveled overseas?

An **imperative sentence** makes a request, gives a command, or offers advice. Although it is always addressed to *you*, the pronoun is usually omitted.

Use the TOOLBAR buttons to align or indent text.

Please send me a short reply.

An **exclamatory sentence** expresses strong emotion and ends with an exclamation point. Sometimes an exclamatory sentence is written in a form that is not a complete sentence.

We're finally connected!

What a show [it was]!   [Although not part of the sentence, *it was* is understood.]

2   Structural classifications

Sentences can also be categorized structurally according to their overall grammatical construction. A **simple sentence** has a single independent clause and no dependent clauses. Though a simple sentence has only one clause, it may have many phrases and thus be quite long.

I walk.

The high plateau of western Bolivia, called the *altiplano,* is one of the world's highest elevation populated regions, with several towns at over 12,000 feet above sea level.

A **compound sentence** has two or more independent clauses and no dependent clauses. A compound sentence is created when two or more independent clauses are connected with a comma and a coordinating conjunction (*and, or, but, nor, for, so, yet*), with a semicolon and a conjunctive adverb (*therefore, however, otherwise, indeed*), with a semicolon alone, or with a correlative conjunction (*either/or, neither/nor, both/and, not only/but also*).

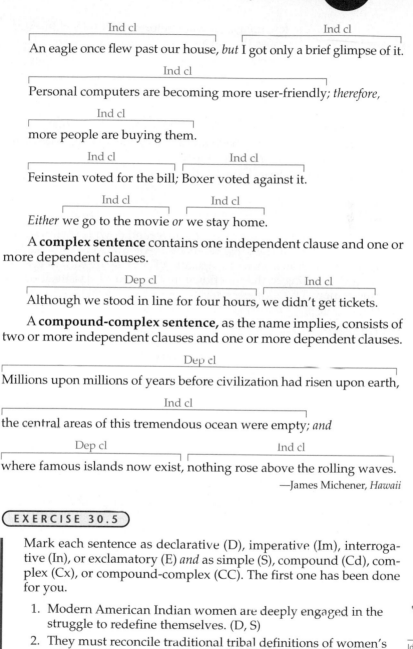

Ind cl | Ind cl

An eagle once flew past our house, *but* I got only a brief glimpse of it.

Ind cl

Personal computers are becoming more user-friendly; *therefore,*

Ind cl

more people are buying them.

Ind cl | Ind cl

Feinstein voted for the bill; Boxer voted against it.

Ind cl | Ind cl

Either we go to the movie *or* we stay home.

A **complex sentence** contains one independent clause and one or more dependent clauses.

Dep cl | Ind cl

Although we stood in line for four hours, we didn't get tickets.

A **compound-complex sentence,** as the name implies, consists of two or more independent clauses and one or more dependent clauses.

Dep cl

Millions upon millions of years before civilization had risen upon earth,

Ind cl

the central areas of this tremendous ocean were empty; *and*

Dep cl | Ind cl

where famous islands now exist, nothing rose above the rolling waves.

—James Michener, *Hawaii*

(EXERCISE 30.5)

Mark each sentence as declarative (D), imperative (Im), interrogative (In), or exclamatory (E) *and* as simple (S), compound (Cd), complex (Cx), or compound-complex (CC). The first one has been done for you.

1. Modern American Indian women are deeply engaged in the struggle to redefine themselves. (D, S)
2. They must reconcile traditional tribal definitions of women's roles with industrial society's definitions of these roles.
3. How does society define the role a woman should play?
4. If women are told they are powerless, they will believe it!

EXER
Identifying
sentence types.

5. In the West, few images of women form part of the cultural mythos, and those that do are usually sexually charged.
6. The Native American tribes see women variously, but they do not question the power of femininity, which has always been a strong force.
7. Go cook the food.
8. Would you be friends with someone you couldn't trust?
9. The Indian women I have known have shown a wide range of personal styles and demeanors.
10. We must celebrate cultural differences!

EXERCISE 30.6

Log on to an Internet site of your choice, and download into a file a block of text of at least five sentences. (Alternatively, photocopy a block of text from a book or magazine.) Then classify each of the sentences according to the functional and structural classifications in this section.

FOR COLLABORATION

Share your classifications, and the reasons for your decisions, with your group.

Pronoun Case

Case refers to the form a pronoun takes to indicate its grammatical relation to other words in a sentence. For example, the difference between *he, him,* and *his* is a matter of case: *he* is the **subjective case,** indicating its use as a grammatical subject, whereas *him* is the **objective case,** indicating its use as a grammatical object, and *his* is the **possessive case,** indicating its use as a grammatical possessive.

AUDIO
Chapter overview.

	Subjective	Objective	Possessive
First-person singular	I	me	my, mine
Second person singular	you	you	your, yours
Third-person singular	he, she, it	him, her, it	his, her, hers, its
First-person plural	we	us	our, ours
Second-person plural	you	you	your, yours
Third-person plural	they	them	their, theirs
Relative and interrogative	who, whoever	whom, whomever	whose

VIDEO
Learining what pronouns to use.

WWW
31.1
A brief history of English pronouns.

Writers and speakers familiar with English seldom have a problem using the correct case when a single pronoun occupies the position of subject, object, or possessive in a sentence.

SUBJECT   *She* hoped that *they* would do well.   [Subjects in both clauses.]

OBJECT   The crew helped *her.*   [Direct object]
            Sarah gave *him* timely help.   [Indirect object]

OBJECT OF A PREPOSITION	Help came for *them* immediately, thanks to *her*.
POSSESSIVE	Two of *my* friends have recently quit *their* jobs.

In some special situations, however, choosing the correct pronoun form can be confusing.

31a Use the subjective case when a pronoun functions as a sentence subject, clause subject, or subject complement

The subjective case (*I, you, he, she, it, we, they, who, whoever*) is required for all pronouns used as subjects, including pronouns that are paired with a noun to form a compound subject or to rename the noun (see 31c).

> *She* and Octavio are good friends.   [Sentence subject]

> It seems that only Harrison and *I* were not invited.   [Clause subject]

A common problem with the subjective case pronouns occurs in a distinctive kind of subject-complement construction (see 30b-2). The verb *be* is used to set up an "equation" between a noun subject or a pronoun subject such as *it, that, this* and a personal pronoun such as *he, she, it,* or *they*.

> Who deserves to get the award? It is ~~them~~ *they*, the actors.
>
> "Hello, is Carol there?" "Yes, this is ~~her~~ *she*."
>
> Will the lead actor be ~~him~~ *he* or ~~me~~ *I*?

In casual conversation, many people would say "It is them" or "this is her" or "him or me." But standard English grammar requires the subjective forms, as is clear from these related versions of the examples: "*They* deserve to get the reward" or "*She* is here" or "Will *he* or will *I* be the lead actor?" (See 45c for a discussion of levels of formality.)

31b Use the objective case when a pronoun functions as an object

The objective case (*me, you, him, her, it, us, them, whom, whomever*) is required for all pronouns used as objects, indirect objects, and objects of prepositions, including any pronoun paired with a noun or another pronoun to form a compound object. (See 31c for more on compound objects and 30b-2 for more on objects.)

> Deborah called *us* as soon as she heard the good news. [Pronoun as direct object]

> The boss invited Janice and *him* to lunch. [Pronoun as indirect object]

> Just between *you* and *me*, don't you think Marty's been a little out of line lately? [Pronoun as object of a preposition]

31c Test for pronoun case in compound constructions by using the pronoun alone

Most problems with pronoun case arise in compound constructions, when a pronoun is paired with a noun:

> The instructor gave Natasha and [*me, I*] an extra project to do.

In such sentences, the case of the pronoun—subjective or objective—depends on its function in the sentence. If you are unsure about which case to use, the best way to find out is to try the sentence without the noun:

WEBLINK

http://www.uottawa.ca/academic/arts/writcent/hypergrammar/pronouns.html

All about pronouns and their proper uses

> The instructor gave [*me, I*] an extra project to do.

Seeing it in this form makes it easier to decide what the correct form is:

> The instructor gave Natasha and *me* an extra project to do.

A special type of pronoun-noun pairing, called an **appositive,** occurs when a pronoun is conjoined with a noun.

> *We Americans* tend to be patriotic.

> Sometimes people from other countries complain about *us Americans*.

> The sorority members chose to send *one person—me*—to the national convention.

Again, if you are unsure about which case to use in such situations, just omit the noun and see which pronoun form is correct.

> *We* tend to be patriotic.

> Sometimes people from other countries complain about *us*.

> The sorority members chose to send *me* to the national convention.

HELP

How do I customize a grammar checker to search for pronoun case problems?

1. Open the grammar checker.
2. Click on the OPTIONS feature.
3. Instead of one of the standard rule sets (such as FORMAL or CASUAL), select a CUSTOM file.
4. Open the customization feature.
5. Deselect all the grammar features except the one for pronoun case problems, which should be called something like PRONOUN ERRORS.
6. Run the program on your document. *Remember:* It may not catch all your errors!

NOTE: You can use the customization feature for many similar purposes. For example, if you want to check for run-on sentences (Chapter 36), turn off PRONOUN ERRORS and select CLAUSE ERRORS instead.

(E X E R C I S E   3 1 . 1)

Circle the correct pronoun in each of the following sentences.

1. Are you going to invite her and [I, me] to your party?
2. It is unfair to make Paul and [I, me] do all the extra work by ourselves.
3. The coach asked Chris and [I, me] to design a new team logo.
4. Neither Paco nor [she, her] wants to go to Alaska to study.
5. It is unfair to stereotype [we, us] Asians as people who do nothing but study all the time.
6. She is not willing to give up her ticket, and neither are Luis and [he, him].
7. [We, us] New Yorkers love the city life.
8. The neighborhood council has asked [we, us] club members to keep the sidewalk clean.
9. Tokashi and [I, me] do not always see eye to eye, but we are generally good friends.
10. She read the manuscript to Eiko and [I, me].

EXER

Identify correct pronoun case.

31d Choose the form for an interrogative or relative pronoun based on how it functions in its clause

The *wh-* pronouns *who, whom, whoever, whomever,* and *whose* are used in questions and relative clauses (see 30c-3). In questions, they are called **interrogative pronouns;** in clauses, they are called **relative pronouns.**

Who reserved this book?   [Interrogative pronoun]

I'd like to find the person *who* reserved this book.   [Relative pronoun]

When you ask a question and reverse normal sentence word order, choosing the correct interrogative pronoun is often puzzling:

[*Who, Whom*] are you going to invite to the wedding?

AUDIO
That versus *who.*

In conversational English, most speakers would use *Who* in this sentence. But, according to the rules of English grammar, the correct form is *Whom.* To understand why, rearrange the question into a statement, using a personal pronoun: "You are going to invite [*he, him*] to the wedding." After rewording, you will have no trouble recognizing the correct personal pronoun—in this case, *him.* The rewording clearly points to the objective case and the choice of the objective form *whom.*

As a writer, you must decide whether the *wh-* pronoun functions as a subject or an object in the clause in which it is used. Because independent and dependent clauses are often tightly

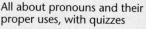

WEBLINK

http://webster.commnet
.edu/grammar/pronouns1
.htm

All about pronouns and their proper uses, with quizzes

www
31.2
A complete guide to pronouns online.

linked, the choice can be unclear. If you are uncertain about which form to use, try this test: (1) isolate and, if necessary, transpose the clause in which the *wh-* pronoun occurs, (2) substitute different personal pronouns (such as *she, her, he,* or *him*) for the *wh-* pronoun and see which case sounds best, and then (3) select the corresponding *wh-* pronoun. For example, consider this sentence:

One fellow playwright [*who, whom*] Shakespeare admired was Marlowe.

1. The *wh-* pronoun occurs in the relative clause *wh___ Shakespeare admired;* transposed, the clause becomes *Shakespeare admired wh___.*
2. Of the different personal pronouns substituted in the *wh___* slot, the one that sounds best is *him: Shakespeare admired him.*
3. The *wh-* pronoun that corresponds in case to *him* is *whom.* So the grammatically correct form of the sentence is

One fellow playwright *whom* Shakespeare admired was Marlowe.

The same process can be used for the pronouns *whoever* and *whomever:*

The place is open to [*whoever, whomever*] wants to go there.

1. The *wh-* pronoun occurs in the relative clause *wh___ wants to go there.*

2. Of the different personal pronouns substituted in the *wh___* slot, the ones that sound best are *she* and *he: She (or he) wants to go there.*

3. The *wh-* pronoun that corresponds in case to *she* or *he* is *whoever.* So the grammatically correct form of the sentence is

The place is open to *whoever* wants to go there.

EXERCISE 31.2

Select the correct form of the pronoun in each sentence.

1. How can someone [who, whom] makes the minimum wage invest in the stock market?
2. My financial adviser, [who, whom] most of the business community trusts, has recently moved to New York.
3. [Who, Whom] does she wish to contact at the law firm?
4. She made it perfectly clear that [whoever, whomever] wants to come is welcome.
5. Judge Reynolds is a man in [who, whom] the community has placed great trust.
6. Barbara Ehrenreich is someone [who, whom] I have long admired.
7. He addressed his remarks to [whoever, whomever] would listen.
8. Fortune sometimes comes to those [who, whom] seek it.
9. Richard, [who, whom] updated his investment portfolio last week, decided against purchasing the no-load mutual fund.
10. We will support [whoever, whomever] the people elect.

31e Distinguish between possessive adjectives and possessive pronouns

Possessive adjectives (*my, your, her, his, its, our, their*) precede and modify a noun:

This is *my* car.

Possessive pronouns (*mine, yours, hers, his, its, ours, theirs*) replace a noun and stand alone:

> This car is *mine*.

> *Mine* is the one in back.

Note that the possessive forms ending in *-s* (*yours, hers, ours, its, theirs*) do not take an apostrophe (see 54a-1).

Gerunds require an attributive possessive pronoun:

> *His* wanting to do extra work was what impressed me.

In this sentence, *wanting to do extra work* is a gerund phrase. Since gerunds act as nouns, the possessive pronoun modifying this phrase should be an adjectival one (*his*). Be sure not to make the mistake of using the objective case pronoun (*him*) in this kind of construction.

> ~~Him~~ wanting to do extra work was what impressed me.
>   ^His^

31f **Choose the case for a pronoun in a comparison based on how it would function in its own clause**

What is the meaning of this sentence?

> Mark likes school more than me.

Technically, it means that Mark has a greater liking for school than he does for the speaker of the sentence. It does not mean that Mark has a greater liking for school than the speaker does. The latter meaning is correctly expressed with this construction:

> Mark likes school more than I.

Many writers fail to make this distinction, thereby potentially confusing their readers.

How can you avoid this problem? You can avoid it by recognizing that the second part of the comparison (the part after *than*) is an incomplete clause. The complete versions of the two sentences make the distinction clear:

> Mark likes school more than [he likes] me.

> Mark likes school more than I [like school].

A similar procedure can be used with *as . . . as* constructions:

WEBLINK

http://owl.english.purdue
.edu/handouts/grammar/
g_proncase.html

A discussion of pronoun case problems in compound structures, comparisons, and formal vs. semiformal writing

President Bush's wife is as much a Republican as *he*.

He is the correct pronoun here (not *him*) because the complete sentence actually is

President Bush's wife is as much a Republican as *he is a Republican*.

The writer has simply dropped *is a Republican* from the end of the sentence. Alternatively, you can write

President Bush's wife is as much a Republican as *he is*.

EXERCISE 31.3

Circle the correct pronoun in each sentence.

1. My brother is as conservative as [me, I].
2. The recruiter rated Susan higher than [me, I].
3. Trang claims that she enjoys the opera as much as [him, he].
4. Mark went to Paris this summer and liked it as much as [we, us].
5. Without even realizing it, Pia hurt Kelly's feelings today as much as she hurt [my, mine] last week.
6. Ronaldo does not play volleyball as well as [her, she].
7. I think it was Martin who said that Stacy is taller than [him, he].
8. Are you going to talk to [he, him] about the controversy created by the proposal?
9. He is as much to blame for the tension in the office as [her, she].
10. Ahmad felt that Jerry was better suited for the position than [me, I].

EXER

Choosing correct pronouns.

FOR COLLABORATION

Discuss your conclusions for the above exercise, and the reasons for your decisions, with your group.

CHAPTER 32

Verbs

FAQs

▶ What is wrong with the sentence "He believed that his thesis is credible"? (32e-2)

▶ How can I decide when to use *sit* or *set*? (32f)

▶ When I make an "if" statement, where should I put the *would*? (32h-1)

Using verbs correctly can help make writing lively and precise. This chapter explains some of the major aspects of verb usage: form, tense, voice, and mood. (Two other aspects, gender and number, are discussed in 33a and 33b.)

AUDIO
Chapter
overview.

32a Learn the regular verb forms

All verbs in English, except *be*, have five possible forms or **principal parts.**

Base form	Present tense (third-person singular)	Past tense	Past participle	Present participle
jump	jumps	jumped	jumped	jumping
erase	erases	erased	erased	erasing
add	adds	added	added	adding
veto	vetoes	vetoed	vetoed	vetoing

Most English verbs are **regular verbs.** That is, starting with the base form, their forms follow the pattern of the preceding examples: adding -*s* (or -*es*) to the base form to make the third-person singular present tense, adding -*d* (or -*ed*) to make the past tense and past participle, and adding *-ing* to the base form (and sometimes dropping the final *e*) to make the present participle.

The **base form,** or **simple form,** of a verb is the form listed in a dictionary. It is the form normally used with subjects that are plural nouns or the pronouns *I, you, we,* or *they* to make statements in the present tense.

Hummingbirds *migrate* south in winter.

I *walk* two miles every day.

When the subject of a sentence is a singular noun or a third-person singular pronoun (*he, she* or *it*), the **present tense** of the verb has an *-s* added to it.

She *visits* New York every month.

My neighbor *walks* laps around our block.

Sometimes a slight change is required in the spelling of the base form (*fly/flies, veto/vetoes*).

The **past tense** of a verb is used to describe action that occurred in the past. For a regular verb, add *-d* or *-ed* to the base form to get the past tense:

Fox TV *televised* Super Bowl XXXVIII.

We *wanted* to see the game.

The **past participle** of a regular verb is similar in form to the past tense. The past participle can be used (1) with *has* or *have* in the present perfect tense, (2) with *had* in the past perfect tense, (3) with some form of *be* to create a passive-voice construction, and (4) by itself, as an adjective, to modify a noun.

We *have petitioned* the school board for a new crosswalk. [Present perfect]

Before last night's meeting, we *had talked* about going directly to the mayor.   [Past perfect]

Last year, two students *were injured* trying to cross this street. [Passive voice]

The parents of the *injured* students are supporting our cause. [Adjective]

The **present participle** is created by adding *-ing* to the base form of a verb. It is used (1) with some form of *be* to indicate ongoing action (the progressive tense), (2) as a gerund, and (3) as an adjective.

Joaquin *is working* on a new project.   [Progressive tense]

He enjoys *working.*   [Gerund]

This is a *working* draft of my paper.   [Adjective]

(E X E R C I S E 3 2 . 1)

What are the principal parts of the following regular verbs?

1. print
2. drown
3. compile
4. drag

32b Learn common irregular verb forms

An **irregular verb** is one whose past tense and past participle do not follow the standard pattern of being created by adding *-d* or *-ed* to the base form. Instead, these forms often have different internal vowels than in the base form (base form: *find*; past tense: *found*; past participle: *found*). Other variations are possible as well; for example, the past tense and past participle may be the same as the base form (*set/set/set*) or may be radically different (*go/went/gone*). (Note: *Be* and *have* also have irregular present-tense forms.)

VIDEO

Using irregular verbs.

Base form	Past tense	Past participle
beat	beat	beaten
become	became	become
begin	began	begun
bite	bit	bit, bitten
blow	blew	blown
break	broke	broken
bring	brought	brought
build	built	built
burn	burned, burnt	burned, burnt
buy	bought	bought
catch	caught	caught
choose	chose	chosen
come	came	come
cost	cost	cost
cut	cut	cut
dig	dug	dug
dive	dove, dived	dived
do	did	done
draw	drew	drawn

Base form	Past tense	Past participle
drink	drank	drunk
drive	drove	driven
eat	ate	eaten
fall	fell	fallen
feel	felt	felt
fight	fought	fought
find	found	found
fly	flew	flown
forget	forgot	forgotten, forgot
freeze	froze	frozen
get	got	gotten, got
give	gave	given
go	went	gone
grow	grew	grown
hang	hung	hung
have	had	had
hear	heard	heard
hide	hid	hidden
hit	hit	hit
keep	kept	kept
know	knew	known
lay	laid	laid
lead	led	led
leave	left	left
lend	lent	lent
lie	lay	lain
lose	lost	lost
make	made	made
mean	meant	meant
pay	paid	paid
prove	proved	proved, proven
read	read	read
ride	rode	ridden
run	ran	run
say	said	said
see	saw	seen
send	sent	sent
set	set	set
shake	shook	shaken
shoot	shot	shot
show	showed	shown, showed
shrink	shrank	shrunk

Base form	Past tense	Past participle
sing	sang	sung
sink	sank	sunk
sit	sat	sat
sleep	slept	slept
speak	spoke	spoken
steal	stole	stolen
stick	stuck	stuck
strike	struck	struck, stricken
swear	swore	sworn
swim	swam	swum
swing	swung	swung
take	took	taken
teach	taught	taught
tear	tore	torn
think	thought	thought
throw	threw	thrown
wake	woke, waked	woken, waked
wear	wore	worn
win	won	won
write	wrote	written

As you can see, many of the most common verbs in the English language are irregular. Therefore, it is important that you learn their forms.

The two most common verbs in English, *be* and *have,* are also two of the most irregular. The third person singular present tense of *have* is not *haves* but *has.* See the Forms of *be* chart on the next page for a complete outline of the forms of this irregular verb.

(**EXERCISE 32.2**)

What are the principal parts of each of the following irregular verbs? (To figure out the past tense form, use the verb in a sentence with *yesterday.* To figure out the participle, use the verb in a sentence with *have.*)

1. arise
2. dream
3. ring
4. stand
5. sweep

Forms of *be*

Present Tense

	Singular	*Plural*
First person	I *am*	we *are*
Second person	you *are*	you *are*
Third person	he/she/it *is*	they *are*
	Michael *is*	people *are*

Past Tense

	Singular	*Plural*
First person	I *was*	we *were*
Second person	you *were*	you *were*
Third person	he/she/it *was*	they *were*
	Michael *was*	people *were*

32c Know how to use auxiliary verbs

An **auxiliary verb** (or **helping verb**) is one that is used with a main verb to indicate tense (see 32d), mood (see 32h), or voice (see 32g). The most common auxiliary verbs are *be, have,* and *do.* Some form of one of these helping verbs is frequently used with a base form, present participle, or past participle of a main verb to create a more complex **verb phrase.**

> She *is finishing* her paper.   [Progressive tense, indicating ongoing action]

> The college *has adopted* a new honor code.   [Present perfect tense, indicating past action with ongoing effects]

> We *do need* to get going.   [Emphasis]

> My roommate *has been asked* to run for the student senate.   [Passive voice, present perfect tense]

> *Does* he *know* what's involved?   [Question]

Other important helping verbs are the **modal auxiliary verbs** (*may/might, can/could, will/would, shall/should, must, ought to,* and *have to*). These verbs communicate degrees of probability, necessity, or obligation. A modal auxiliary verb is used only with the base form of another verb:

> The concert *might be* sold out.

> We *should get* tickets before it is too late.

Most of the modal auxiliaries do not have a third-person present *-s* form or a participle form; *have to* is the only exception.

> Sandra *has to* write a paper.

> Yesterday she *had to* spend all afternoon in science lab.

> Earlier she *had had to* prepare for a math test.

Modal auxiliaries can be used with forms of *be, have,* or *do,* but not with other modal auxiliaries. For example, "We might could do that" is ungrammatical in standard English. You can often create a standard English version of such a double-modal expression by substituting a synonymous verb phrase for one of the modal auxiliaries:

> NONSTANDARD   We might *could* do that.

> REVISED   We might *be able to* do that.

In some cases, you can simply eliminate one of the modal auxiliaries:

> NONSTANDARD   Sally *should ought to* cancel her appointment.

> REVISED   Sally *should* cancel her appointment.

> OR

> Sally *ought to* cancel her appointment.

(**EXERCISE 32.3**)

In the following sentences, underline the verb phrases, circle the modal auxiliary verbs, and correct any double modals.

1. Joey is working on his chemistry assignment tonight.
2. Li-Ping wanted Michael to have lunch with her, but he told her that he might ought to work.
3. Angelica must should go with us to see the soccer match.
4. I heard that the company has adopted a new policy with regard to employee absences.
5. Does she know that he might not come to the play with us?
6. Fernando is staying home tonight.
7. He must not leave the house while he is recovering from knee surgery.

EXER
Identify different verbs.

8. School uniforms should ought to be the standard in the public schools.

9. Ikuto may be walking over to our house right now.

10. My neighbor has been accused of stealing company office supplies.

32d Learn the verb tenses

Verb tense expresses the time of the action or the state of being indicated by a verb. English has three basic tenses: past, present, and future. Each tense can also take on a **verbal aspect,** indicating duration or completion of the verb's action or state of being. The three verbal aspects in English are progressive, perfect, and perfect progressive. With all possible combinations of tenses and aspects, English has twelve verb tenses.

SIMPLE PRESENT TENSE	we wonder
PRESENT PROGRESSIVE TENSE	we are wondering
PRESENT PERFECT TENSE	we have wondered
PRESENT PERFECT PROGRESSIVE TENSE	we have been wondering
SIMPLE PAST TENSE	we wondered
PAST PROGRESSIVE TENSE	we were wondering
PAST PERFECT TENSE	we had wondered
PAST PERFECT PROGRESSIVE TENSE	we had been wondering
FUTURE TENSE	we will wonder
FUTURE PROGRESSIVE TENSE	we will be wondering
FUTURE PERFECT TENSE	we will have wondered
FUTURE PERFECT PROGRESSIVE TENSE	we will have been wondering

1 Present tenses

The **simple present tense** is used to express a general truth, to make an observation, or to describe a habitual activity.

A rolling stone *gathers* no moss.

Oates's stories *depress* me.

My father *mows* the lawn every week.

With an appropriate time expression, the simple present can be used to refer to a scheduled future event.

The show *begins* in five minutes.

The simple present is used in stage directions and in critical discussions of literary works.

Max suddenly *appears* at the door.

In *The Tempest,* all the action *occurs* in one place during one day.

The simple present also is used to express a scientific fact or law.

Water *boils* at 100° Celsius.

Gravity *causes* objects to fall.

The **present progressive tense** is formed with the auxiliary verb *am, are,* or *is* and the present participle (*-ing* form) of a main verb. The present progressive is used to indicate action occurring at the present time.

Jennifer *is preparing* for the MCAT exam.

With an appropriate time expression, the present progressive can be used to announce future events.

A new supermarket *is opening* next week.

(ESL Note) Certain verbs, called **stative verbs,** do not have any progressive tenses. These verbs include *know, believe, need, consist,* and *exist.* Thus, it is incorrect to say "I am needing a new computer" (see 61f).

The **present perfect tense** is formed with the auxiliary verb *have* or *has* and the past participle of a main verb. The present perfect is used to indicate action that began in the past and either is continuing or has continuing effects in the present.

Many people *have expressed* alarm about environmental degradation.

(ESL Note) The present perfect tense and the simple past tense cannot be used interchangeably. The present perfect implies *duration* of past action; the simple past tense expresses *completed* past action. The sentence "She was at the university since 1996" is incorrect, because the *since* phrase refers to a continuous time period. The grammatically correct version of this sentence is "She *has been* at the university since 1996."

The **present perfect progressive tense** is formed by combining *have been* or *has been* with the present participle of a main verb. The present perfect progressive is used similarly to the present perfect but emphasizes the ongoing nature of the activity.

> Eric *has been studying* German for two years.

This sentence means that Eric is still studying German, whereas the sentence "Eric *has studied* German for two years" could mean that he is not currently studying it (although he might again study it someday).

2 Past tenses

The **simple past tense** is used to describe actions or conditions that occurred or applied entirely in the past.

> Jonas Salk *invented* the polio vaccine.

> In 1950, the United States *consisted* of only forty-eight states.

The **past progressive tense** is formed by combining the auxiliary verb *was* or *were* with the present participle of a main verb. The past progressive describes action continuing over a period of time in the past. It is often used to set the stage for another action of shorter duration.

> He *was cleaning* the living room when the phone rang.

The **past perfect tense** is created by combining the auxiliary verb *had* with the past participle of a main verb. The past perfect is used to describe a past action that preceded another past action.

> Amanda *had thought* of volunteering for the job, but then she got sick.

The **past perfect progressive tense** functions like the past perfect tense but puts more emphasis on the continuing or repetitive nature of the past action. The past perfect progressive is formed by combining *had been* with the present participle of a main verb.

> Amanda *had been thinking* of volunteering for the job, but then she got sick.

(EXERCISE 32.4)

EXER
Verb tense
errors.

Correct the verb tense errors in the following sentences.

1. Eli Whitney has invented the cotton gin in 1793.
2. She divulged the secret, even though she promised not to.
3. It was five years since I last saw Aihua.
4. Three years ago, I had visited China.

5. The United States first was consisting of thirteen colonies.

6. Joseph Conrad was writing *The Heart of Darkness* in English, his third language.

7. She waited for the phone to ring when her brother came into the bedroom.

8. Miguel did well in the course until last week, when he unexpectedly received a D on an important quiz.

9. Tim has learned the results of his preliminary examinations two weeks after he took them.

10. He was my best friend, even though he had been two years older.

3 Future tenses

The **simple future tense,** as its name implies, expresses actions or conditions that will occur in the future. The simple future consists of the modal auxiliary verb *will* and the base form of a main verb.

Ames *will be* a half hour late.

(For *shall*, see the Glossary of Usage, page G-17.)

(ESL Note) In casual English, future conditions are often expressed using the modal auxiliary *is going to* instead of *will*, as in "Ames *is going to* be a half hour late." It is best to avoid this usage in formal English.

The **future progressive tense** is formed by combining *will be* with the present participle of a main verb. The future progressive expresses action that will be continuing or repeated in the future.

Right now my son is working, but next year he *will be going* to college.

The **future perfect tense** consists of *will have* and the past participle of a main verb. The future perfect is used to describe an action that will occur in the future but before some specified time.

By the end of this year, gun-related violence *will have taken* the lives of more than 2,000 American teenagers.

The **future perfect progressive tense** is similar to the future perfect but emphasizes the continuous or repetitive nature of the action. The future perfect progressive consists of *will have been* plus the present participle of a main verb.

By tomorrow morning, I *will have been working* on this paper for eighteen hours.

32e Observe sequence of tenses

Good writing presents a coherent framework of time. Since time is indicated in part by verb tense, it is important to select verb tenses carefully and logically. The relationship between two or more verbs in the same sentence or in adjacent sentences is called the **sequence of tenses.**

1 Sequence of verb tenses in compound or adjacent sentences

Two or more independent clauses about closely related events or situations may be connected by a coordinating conjunction (*and, or, but*) to form a compound sentence. Alternatively, two related independent clauses may be presented as consecutive sentences. Typically, the main verbs in each clause or sentence have the same tense.

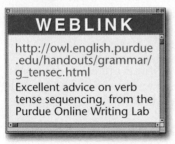

WEBLINK

http://owl.english.purdue
.edu/handouts/grammar/
g_tensec.html

Excellent advice on verb
tense sequencing, from the
Purdue Online Writing Lab

Joe *wants* to go to the game, but Lori *does* not.

He *likes* baseball. She *dislikes* the game.

Sometimes, however, one event or action may logically precede or follow the other, requiring different verb tenses to indicate which of the two came first.

Joe *could* not *go* to the game, because he *had* not *done* his homework.

2 Sequence of verb tenses in complex sentences

A complex sentence has one independent clause and one or more dependent clauses (see 30d-2). Each clause has its own main verb. The appropriate tense for each main verb depends on the context and the intended meaning. If the actions expressed by these verbs occur at approximately the same time, the verbs should be in the same tense.

When the conductor *gives* the signal, the musicians *start* playing.

Before you *sit* down, *adjust* the height of your chair.

When you need to make it clear that one past action or event preceded another, use the past perfect or past perfect progressive tense in one clause and the simple past tense in the other clause.

Although Amanda *had thought* of volunteering for the job, she *was* now no longer interested.

When you need to show that a past action or event preceded a present or future one, use the present perfect or present perfect progressive tense to express the past action or event.

Since the Pope *has been* to Mexico already, he probably *will* not *go* again.

---

3 Sequence of verb tenses with infinitives

There are two kinds of infinitives: the **present infinitive** (*to* plus the base form of a verb) and the **perfect infinitive** (*to have* plus the past participle of a verb) (see 30a-9). Use the present infinitive for an action that occurs at the same time as or later than the action expressed by the main verb.

Samantha *wants* me *to pick up* the car.

Use the perfect infinitive for an action that occurs prior to the action expressed by the main verb.

Samantha *wants* me *to have picked up* the car.

Guidelines for Choosing the Correct Sequence of Tenses in a Complex Sentence

1. Consider the two adjacent clauses: Does the action in clause A occur at approximately the same time as the action in clause B? If so, use the same verb tense in both clauses.

2. If the action in clause A *precedes* the action in clause B, follow these guidelines:
   a. If clause B is in the *present* tense, put clause A in the *past* or *present perfect*.
   b. If clause B is in the *past* tense, put clause A in the *past perfect*.
   c. If clause B is in the *future* tense, put clause A in the *present* or *present perfect*.

AUDIO

Choosing correct sequences of tenses in sentences and paragraphs.

4 Sequence of verb tenses with participles

The **present participle** (the *-ing* form of a verb) can be used to represent an action that occurs at the same time as that expressed by the main verb.

Walking into the house, Jim sensed that something was wrong.

The **past participle** is used to indicate that an action occurs before or during the action expressed by the main verb.

Stung by criticism of his latest film, Costner is working hard on a new one.

The **present perfect participle** (*having* plus the past participle) expresses an action occurring prior to the action of the main verb.

Having signed a contract, Deanna was afraid she had to go through with the deal.

EXERCISE 32.5

Correct any sequence-of-tense errors in the following sentences.

1. As soon as she entered the room, several people rush over to say hello.
2. He was disappointed when some of his sources are found to be fraudulent.
3. He believed that his thesis is credible.
4. We insisted on using pesticides, even though this is not proven to be the best solution to an insect problem.
5. Her eyesight has begun to fail, and she turned to the radio for information.
6. Who expected that old car to lasted all these years?
7. His roommate has expected him to have done the laundry by Friday.
8. Entering the workplace, they have understood the safety concerns of the employees.
9. Having fired the employees who reported the safety problem, the manager had faced a lawsuit.
10. Concerned that the number of beds in the emergency shelter would be inadequate, the city council votes to open another shelter during the winter.

EXER

Choose correct
tense sequence.

32f   Use transitive and intransitive verbs correctly

A **transitive verb** is a verb that takes a direct object (see 30a-4). In other words, a transitive verb transfers an action from a subject to an object. The sentence "A virus damaged my hard drive" has a transitive verb (*damaged*) that transfers the action to the direct object (*hard drive*). Some typical transitive verbs are *see, hear, consult, kick, recognize,* and *mix.* Transitive verbs are usually marked in dictionaries with the abbreviation *vt* or *tr.*

An **intransitive verb** is one that does not take a direct object. Some typical intransitive verbs are *sleep, relax, die, go, fall, come,* and *walk.* Intransitive verbs are usually identified in dictionaries by the abbreviation *vi* or *intr.*

Many English verbs can be used either transitively or intransitively. For example, the verb *jump* is transitive in the sentence "Mike jumped the fence" but intransitive in the sentence "Mike jumped for joy." Some other common "two-way" verbs are *run, dream, write, eat, grow,* and *develop.*

Many speakers of English confuse *sit* and *set, lie* and *lay,* and *rise* and *raise.* The two verbs in each of these pairs sound somewhat alike and have related meanings, but they differ as to whether they can take an object (see 30b-3). The first member of each pair is intransitive and cannot take an object; the second member is transitive and does take an object.

INTRANSITIVE	Jorge *will sit* over there. [The verb has no object.]
TRANSITIVE	Jorge *will set* the *flowers* over there. [The verb has an object, *flowers.*]
INTRANSITIVE	I think I *will lie* down. [The verb has no object.]
TRANSITIVE	We *will lay* the *groundwork* for the project. [The verb has an object, *groundwork.*]
INTRANSITIVE	The sun *rises* in the east. [The verb has no object.]
TRANSITIVE	The senator always *raises* a lot of *money* for his re-election campaigns. [The verb has an object, *money.*]

EXERCISE 32.6

Select the correct verb in each of the following sentences. (You may want to consult the list of irregular verbs in 32b.)

1. We should all (sit, set) our watches for daylight saving time.

EXER

Choosing
correct verbs.

2. The winner usually (raises, rises) the trophy over his head.

3. Russ was so tired he (lay, laid) down for a quick nap.

4. If the dictator tries to stay in power, the people may (raise up, rise up) and overthrow him.

5. Please (set, sit) down and make yourself comfortable.

6. The young mother wanted to (lay, lie) her baby on the counter to change its diaper.

7. A member of the audience (rose, raised) from his seat.

8. The jury (sat, set) still for more than three hours.

9. The parents (laid, lay) a wreath on their son's grave.

10. Congress is talking about (rising, raising) the minimum wage.

32g Favor active over passive voice

Voice is the characteristic of a verb that indicates whether the subject of a sentence is acting or being acted upon. In the **active voice,** the subject of the sentence performs an action on a direct object (see 30b). In the **passive voice,** the subject of the sentence is acted upon. Only transitive verbs can be cast in active and passive voice (see 32f).

VIDEO

Using the
passive voice.

                  Subject/Actor   DO

ACTIVE   My friend Julie *handcrafted* this pin.   [The subject acts upon an object.]

                  Subject   Actor

PASSIVE   This pin *was handcrafted* by my friend Julie.   [The subject is acted upon by the object following the verb.]

The passive voice consists of an appropriate form of the auxiliary verb *be* and the past participle of a main verb (see 32a). A passive-voice sentence may refer to the performer of the action in a *by* phrase following the verb. In practice, though, such a *by* phrase is often omitted, which has the effect of concealing or de-emphasizing the performer of the action.

PASSIVE   This pin *was handcrafted.*   [The phrase *by my friend Julie* is omitted.]

In general, good writers favor the active voice over the passive voice. The active voice is more concise and more direct—and thus more vigorous—than the passive. In some cases, however, the passive voice works better than the active voice. For example, when identifying the performer of an action is unimportant or difficult, using the passive voice allows you to write a grammatical sentence without mentioning the actor (see 40d).

Bacterial infections are usually treated with antibiotics.

(**Grammar Checker Alert**) If the grammar checker you use is preprogrammed to eliminate the passive voice, it will highlight most of the passive verbs in your writing and make a comment such as "This main clause may contain a verb in the passive voice." If you decide to change some of the passive verbs to the active voice, you can do so by simply making the actor (whether stated or concealed) the subject of the sentence and changing the predicate. Note, however, that some passive-voice sentences are perfectly fine and should be left unchanged (see 40d).

WEBLINK

http://cctc2.commnet
.edu/grammar/verbs.htm

A superb resource on verbs, including quizzes and lots of cool graphics

www

32.1

A fun online review of verbs and verbals.

(**EXERCISE 32.7**)

Some of the following sentences are in the passive voice; others are in the active voice. For practice, change all passive-voice sentences to active-voice sentences (which may require inventing an actor) and all actives to passives (which may involve omitting the actor). (Note: Some sentences have intransitive verbs, which cannot be changed.)

1. We can recycle most ordinary materials.
2. Twelve protesters were arrested by the police.
3. Cartilage serves as padding material in joints.
4. It keeps bones from grinding on bones.
5. You can use toolbar buttons instead of menu or keyboard commands.
6. A group of marine scientists and conservationists in 2000 voted Palau, Micronesia's coral reef, one of the seven underwater wonders of the world.
7. *A Tale of Two Cities* by Charles Dickens should be reread by everyone who thinks reading it in high school was enough.
8. In the summer of 1996, scientific evidence pointing to the possible existence of life beyond Earth was announced by NASA.
9. The purported evidence was found in a 4.5-pound meteorite that landed in Antarctica 13,000 years ago.
10. Did someone switch off the copier?

EXER

Changing between active and passive voice.

32h Make sure verbs are in the proper mood

The **mood** of a verb indicates the type of statement being made by the sentence—an assertion, a question, a command, a wish, or a hypothetical condition. English verbs have three moods: indicative, imperative, and subjunctive.

The **indicative mood** is used to make assertions, state opinions, and ask questions (see 30a-4). It is the most commonly used mood in English.

Washington *was* the first president of the United States.   [Assertion]

Citizens *should take* more interest in local government.   [Opinion]

Do you *want* to vote?   [Question]

The **imperative mood** is used to express commands and give instructions. Commands are always addressed to a second person, although the explicit *you* is normally omitted. Instructions are often cast in the imperative mood (see 30b-1).

Insert Setup Disk 1 in the floppy disk drive. Then *run* the program.

32.2

Examples of
formulaic
uses of the
subjunctive.

The **subjunctive mood** is used for hypothetical conditions, polite requests, wishes, and other uncertain statements. A verb in the subjunctive mood often appears in dependent clauses beginning with *if* or *that*. The present subjunctive is the same as the base form of the verb. The past subjunctive is identical to the past tense of the verb. The only exception is *were*, which is used for all subjunctive uses of *be* except after verbs of requesting, requiring, or recommending, where *be* is used.

I wish I *were* an A student!

The defense attorney requested that her client *be* given probation.

The past perfect subjunctive has the same form as the ordinary past perfect.

1 Hypothetical *if* constructions

When an *if* clause expresses a contrary-to-fact or unreal condition, the verb of the clause should be in the past subjunctive or past perfect subjunctive mood. The main clause verb should include the modal auxiliary *would, could,* or *might.*

If I *were* you, I *would* make up my Incompletes as soon as possible.
[Expresses a hypothetical future condition.]

If John *had been* there, he *might* have been able to help.   [Expresses a hypothetical past condition.]

Do not use *would, could,* or *might* in a hypothetical *if* clause. In contrary-to-fact sentences, modal auxiliaries such as *would* and *could* belong in the main clause, not in the conditional (subordinate) clause. Use the subjunctive in the conditional clause.

SUBJUNCTIVE FORM REVISED

If we ~~would live~~ *lived* closer to San Francisco, we would go there more

often.

2 Dependent clauses expressing a wish

In a dependent clause following the verb *wish,* use the past subjunctive for present contrary-to-fact conditions and the past perfect subjunctive for past contrary-to-fact conditions.

AUDIO

Correct use of the subjunctive.

I wish [that] he *were* here.

I wish [that] he *had stayed.*

3 Dependent clauses expressing a request, suggestion, or demand

Verbs such as *require, demand, suggest,* and *insist* are usually followed by a dependent clause beginning with *that.* The verb in the *that* clause should be in the subjunctive mood. (Note: Sometimes *that* is omitted.)

The police require that all pets *be* kept on a leash.

They suggested that he *go* to the emergency room.

EXERCISE 32.8

Correct any errors in mood in the following sentences.

EXER

Choosing proper verb mood.

1. If I was rich, I would go on a world tour.
2. If Denju would get a job, he could move out of his parents' house.
3. If she would have been more careful, the accident might never have occurred.

4. I might believe you if you would have been more honest with me in the past.
5. Rahim knew that if he was to eat less, he would lose weight.
6. I wish that Shu-Chuan was still my roommate.
7. Nedra might be able to leave town for the weekend if she would finish her history research paper before Friday night.
8. Was he to actually consider Joanne's stock-option offer, he might take more interest in the future of the company.
9. If Josh was any better a dancer, he could probably be in an MTV video.
10. If he could have gone to the store, I am sure he would have remembered to buy the strawberries.

FOR COLLABORATION

Select one exercise in this chapter to share with your group. (You may want to discuss an exercise that was particularly difficult for you.)

CHAPTER 33

Agreement

FAQs

▶ Which is correct: "Athletics *are* . . ." or "Athletics *is* . . ."? (33a)

▶ Should I say "The jury took *its* time" or "The jury took *their* time"? (33b)

▶ How can I avoid using *he, him,* or *his* to refer to people in general? (33b)

Agreement refers to two related facts about standard English. First, subjects and verbs should agree in number and person (33a). "He go to work at nine o'clock" is ungrammatical because the subject *he* is third-person singular and the verb *go* is not; the third-person singular form of *go* is *goes*. Second, pronouns should agree in number and gender with their antecedents. "An athlete should always do his best" is unacceptable to many people because the use of *his* implies that all athletes are male.

AUDIO

Chapter overview.

(**Grammar Checker Alert**) Your grammar checker should identify most errors of subject-verb number agreement. However, it will probably *not* be able to identify errors of pronoun-antecedent agreement.

33a Make verbs agree in number and person with their grammatical subjects

Here are some guidelines on subject-verb agreement.

VIDEO

How to
recognize
subject-verb
problems

1 Plural subjects require plural verbs; singular subjects require singular verbs

A **subject** is a noun, pronoun, or noun phrase that identifies what the sentence is about (see 30b-1). Plural subjects usually have a distinctive -s or -es ending (*friends, trees, boxes*), while singular subjects do not (*friend, tree, box*). Verbs, on the other hand, are alike for both plural and singular—with the exception of the third-person singular present-tense verb, which is typically marked with an -s or -es ending. (The verb *be* is also exceptional; see the box on page 682.)

FIRST-PERSON SINGULAR	I *go* to work.
SECOND-PERSON SINGULAR	You *go* to work.
THIRD-PERSON SINGULAR	He or she *goes* to work.
FIRST-PERSON PLURAL	We *go* to work.
SECOND-PERSON PLURAL	You *go* to work.
THIRD-PERSON PLURAL	They *go* to work.

Be sure to use a third-person singular verb form with a subject that is third-person singular.

rides
Megan ~~ride~~ the bus every day.

Be sure *not* to use a third-person singular verb form with a subject that is *not* third-person singular.

ride
We ~~rides~~ the bus every day.

2 With a modified subject, be sure to make the verb agree with the simple subject (see 30b-1)

Meg's <u>circle</u> of friends <u>gives</u> her a lot of support.   [*Circle* is the simple subject of the phrase *Meg's circle of friends*.]

When a singular subject is followed by a phrase beginning with *as well as, along with, in addition to,* or *together with*, the verb should be in the singular.

<u>Meg</u>, as well as her friends, usually <u>votes</u> for the more liberal candidate.

If this seems awkward to you, you can restructure the sentence to create a compound subject (which takes a plural verb):

Meg and her friends usually <u>vote</u> for the more liberal candidate.

3 Compound subjects usually require plural verbs

Compound subjects refer to two or more people, places, or things and are formed with the conjunction *and*. In most cases, compound subjects have a plural sense and thus require plural verbs.

<u>Geography and history</u> <u>are</u> my favorite subjects.

In some cases, a compound subject has a singular sense and requires a singular verb.

<u>Law and order</u> <u>is</u> a desirable feature for all modern societies.

<u>Rock and roll</u> <u>has remained</u> popular for decades.

WEBLINK

http://cctc2.commnet.edu/grammar/sv_agr.htm

A great guide to subject-verb agreement, complete with quizzes and exercises

4 With a disjunctive subject, the verb should agree in number with the part of the subject closest to it

A **disjunctive subject** consists of two nouns or pronouns joined by *or* or *nor*. The verb in a sentence with such a subject agrees with the second part of the subject.

Either my sister or my <u>parents</u> <u>are</u> coming.

Neither my parents nor my <u>sister</u> <u>is</u> coming.

If the singular verb sounds awkward to you with such a mixed subject, you can switch the two parts of the subject and use the plural form of the verb:

Neither my sister nor my <u>parents</u> <u>are</u> coming.

5 Indefinite pronouns with a singular sense take singular verbs; those with a plural sense take plural verbs

Indefinite pronouns include *anybody, everyone, nothing, each,* and *much.* Unlike regular pronouns, they do not necessarily refer to any particular person or thing. Most indefinite pronouns are grammatically singular. Therefore, when used as subjects, they should have singular verbs.

No one <u>is</u> here.

Something <u>needs</u> to be done about this.

<u>Each</u> of the candidates <u>is</u> giving a short speech.

A few indefinite pronouns, including *both* and *others*, are plural and therefore require plural verbs. Other indefinite pronouns, such as *some*, *all*, *any*, *more*, and *none*, can be used with either singular or plural verb forms, depending on what they refer to.

<u>All</u> of the committee members <u>were</u> at the meeting.

<u>All</u> of their attention <u>was</u> directed at the speaker.

In the first example sentence, *all* is plural because it refers to the plural noun *members*; *all of the committee members* could be replaced by the pronoun *they*. In the second example sentence, *all* is singular because it refers to the singular noun *attention*; *all of their attention* could be replaced by *it*.

6 Collective nouns typically take singular verbs

Collective nouns are words such as *team, faculty, jury,* and *committee,* which can have either a singular or a plural sense depending on whether they refer to the group or to the individuals within the group (see 30a-1). These nouns usually take singular verbs.

The <u>team</u> <u>is doing</u> better than expected.

The <u>band</u> <u>seems</u> to be road-weary.

When the noun refers to individuals within the group, use a plural verb:

The <u>faculty</u> <u>are divided</u> in their opinion of the new president.

To emphasize the plural sense of collective nouns, simply insert an appropriate plural noun.

The <u>band members</u> <u>seem</u> to be road-weary.

OR

The <u>members</u> of the band <u>seem</u> to be road-weary.

7 Nouns that are plural in form but singular in sense require singular verbs

Words such as *mathematics, athletics, politics, economics, physics,* and *news* look like plural nouns because of the -s ending. However, these nouns are usually singular in meaning and thus require singular verbs.

> <u>Economics</u> <u>is</u> my favorite subject.

> The <u>news</u> from Lake Wobegon always <u>interests</u> me.

Likewise, titles of creative works and names of companies that look plural in form but actually refer to a singular entity take a singular verb.

> *The Brothers Karamazov* <u>was</u> probably Dostoevsky's best novel.

> *Allyn & Bacon* <u>publishes</u> college textbooks.

In some cases, however, a word may take either a singular or a plural verb depending on whether it refers to an entire field (singular) or to a set of activities or properties (plural).

> The <u>physics</u> of fiber-optic technology <u>are</u> pretty complicated.
> [Here, *physics* refers to properties.]

> At our school, <u>physics</u> <u>is</u> required for all college-bound seniors.
> [Here, *physics* refers to a field of study.]

8 A linking verb always agrees with its subject

Sometimes you may find yourself faced with a sentence of the form "X is Y," in which the subject X is singular and the subject complement Y is plural, or vice versa. In such cases, the linking verb should agree in number with the subject, not with the subject complement (see 30b-3).

> Her main <u>interest</u> <u>is</u> boys.

> <u>Boys</u> <u>are</u> her main interest.

9 In a sentence beginning with the expletive *there* or *here* and some form of the verb *be*, the verb should agree with its true subject

The true (grammatical) subject of such a sentence is usually the noun that immediately follows the *be* verb form.

> There <u>are</u> some <u>people</u> at the door.

> Here <u>is</u> the <u>address</u> you were looking for.

(**ESL Note**) Many languages besides English have expletive constructions (for example, *hay* in Spanish, *il y a* in French, *es gibt* in

German), but number agreement between the verb and the noun following the verb generally is not required.

(EXERCISE 33.1)

WWW

33.1
Presidential
subject-verb
agreement
errors.

In each of the following sentences, select the correct verb form and draw an arrow to its grammatical subject. The first one has been done for you.

1. The clocks in this building [run, runs] slow.
2. Basketball and football [is, are] Lucy's favorite sports.
3. Either my brother or my cousins [is, are] coming to babysit the children.
4. Neither my sisters nor Todd [is, are] interested in going to college.
5. Each of the Spanish club members [is, are] going to bring an authentic Hispanic dish to share.
6. All of the Norwegians studying in the United States [celebrates, celebrate] Norwegian Independence Day on May 17.
7. All of her love [was, were] manifest in the poem she wrote him.
8. The faculty of the English department [decides, decide] how many fellowships are granted each year.
9. Many Americans believe that White House politics [is, are] corrupt.
10. There [is, are] several different dresses you can try on that are in your size.

EXER

Identify correct
verb forms.

33b Make pronouns agree in number and gender with their antecedents

VIDEO

Recognizing
pronoun-
reference
problems.

A **pronoun** substitutes for a noun (or noun equivalent), which is called the **antecedent** of the pronoun (see 30a-2). Pronouns and their antecedents must agree in number and gender.

Antecedent   Pronoun
  Bad luck can happen to anyone, and *it* can happen at any time.

In this sentence, *bad luck* and *it* are both singular; therefore, they agree in **number.** They also agree in **gender** because *bad luck* is neuter (neither masculine nor feminine) and *it* can serve as a pronoun for neuter antecedents.

Be especially careful about agreement when the pronoun is far away from its antecedent:

Each of the graduating football players was asked to say a few words about what ~~they~~ ᵗʰᵉʸ thought was the highlight of the season.

Here are some rules on pronoun-antecedent agreement.

1 A compound antecedent usually is plural and thus requires a plural pronoun

A **compound antecedent** is a noun phrase containing two or more terms joined by *and*.

Mr. and Mrs. Kwan are here for *their* appointment.

2 With disjunctive antecedents, the pronoun should agree in number with the nearest part

A **disjunctive antecedent** is a noun phrase consisting of two or more terms joined by *or* or *nor*. When a disjunctive antecedent contains both a singular and a plural part, this rule works well if the singular noun precedes the plural one.

> Either Tamara Wilson or *the Changs* will bring *their* barbeque set to the next picnic.

> Neither the President nor *the Democrats* will give *their* support to this bill.

WEBLINK

http://cctc2.commnet.edu/grammar/pronouns.htm
A fun guide to pronoun agreement, with quizzes and exercises

WWW

33.2
A Web site on pronouns.

If the plural noun precedes the singular one, however, following the rule usually leads to an awkward-sounding sentence:

> Neither the Democrats nor *the President* will give *his* support to this bill.

In such cases, it is best to reword the sentence so as to either get rid of the pronoun or put the singular noun before the plural one.

3 As an antecedent, a collective noun can be either singular or plural, depending on its sense

Both of these sentences are correct:

The jury took only two hours to reach *its* verdict.
The jury took only two hours to reach *their* verdict.

The first sentence emphasizes the singularity of the jury as a body, while the second puts more emphasis on the jury as a group of individuals.

4 Pronouns must agree with antecedents that are indefinite pronouns

Some indefinite pronouns (such as *everything, anything,* and *each*) are singular. When such a pronoun serves as the antecedent for another pronoun, that pronoun should also be singular.

> *Everything* was in *its* place.

> *Each* of the women had *her* reasons for opposing the plan.

Some indefinite pronouns (*some, all, more*) can have either a singular or a plural sense. When one of these indefinite pronouns is used as the antecedent for another pronoun, the other pronoun can be either singular or plural, depending on the sense of the sentence.

> *Some* of the *news* was as bad as we thought *it* would be.

> *Some* of the team's *players* have lost *their* motivation.

Still other indefinite pronouns (*everyone, everybody, nobody*) have a plural, collective sense, which is often reflected in plural pronouns referring back to them.

> *Everyone* hoped *they* would get a raise.

> *Everybody* applauded me, and I was glad *they* did.

Note, however, that such pronouns are treated as grammatically singular when it comes to subject-verb agreement.

> *Everyone hopes* they will get a raise.

> *Nobody wants* other people to think badly of them.

This confusion over number agreement can sometimes be resolved by using the singular *he or she,* which conforms with the verb.

> *Everyone hopes* that *he or she* will get a raise.

Sometimes, however, such a maneuver only leads to awkwardness.

> *Nobody wants* other people to think badly of *him or her.*

In such cases, it is often best to explore alternative wordings.

> *Nobody wants* to be thought badly of by other people.

5 Sexist use of pronouns should be avoided

Which one of the following sentences is correct?

A doctor should listen carefully to his patients.

A doctor should listen carefully to her patients.

In the past, the first sentence was the accepted way to make this general statement about the behavior of doctors. Since *his* (*he, him*) was used as the all-purpose, or generic, pronoun, readers understood the sentence as referring to doctors in general, both male and female. Today, however, the gender bias of such constructions is no longer acceptable to many writers and readers. Singling out one gender at the expense of the other is unfair, inaccurate, and unnecessary. Thus, both sentences are incorrect. There are better ways to make generic statements.

WEBLINK

http://www.wisc.edu/ writetest/Handbook/ SubjectVerb.html

Hypertext discussion of a variety of agreement issues, including subject-verb and pronoun-antecedent agreement

The three most effective techniques for avoiding sexist pronoun usage are (1) making the pronoun and its antecedent plural, (2) rewording the sentence, and (3) using an occasional disjunctive pronoun such as *he or she.*

> *Doctors* should listen carefully to *their* patients.   [Plural]

> An important part of medical practice is listening carefully to patients.   [Rewording]

> *A doctor* should listen carefully to *his or her* patients.   [Disjunctive pronoun]

As you can see, these three revisions of the unacceptable sentence have subtle differences in tone and meaning. One version might work best in a certain context; another might be best in a different context. Knowing this, good writers do not rely exclusively on any single technique for avoiding sexism but instead use whichever they deem most appropriate in the given situation. (See also 46c.)

In conversation, many people use the third-person plural pronoun (*they*) to refer back to a singular antecedent, as in this sentence:

> If *a doctor* is conscientious, *they* will listen carefully to *their* patients.

In formal writing, such usage is incorrect. You can correct the error by making all the referents plural, as shown below:

> If *doctors* are conscientious, *they* will listen carefully to *their* patients.

(**E X E R C I S E   3 3 . 2**)

Select the correct pronoun in each of the following sentences, and draw an arrow to its antecedent.

EXER

Identify pronouns and antecedents.

1. Earthquakes most often occur near a fault line, and [it, they] are usually impossible to predict.
2. Tony and Michiyo are here to pick up [his, their] final research projects.
3. Some of the coaches have lost [its, their] faith in the team.
4. Drinking and driving can cause fatal automobile accidents, but [it, they] can easily be prevented.
5. Everything in the office was in [its, their] proper place.
6. The members of the committee took three hours to make [its, their] decision.
7. Choong was required to take physics during his undergraduate course of study, and he was sure that [it, they] would be a very difficult subject.
8. The NBA imposes fines on [its, their] athletes if they break the rules.
9. Neither the former owners nor the current owner could find [his, their] signature on any of the documents.
10. A lawyer should always treat [his or her, his/her] clients with respect.

Adjectives and Adverbs

Using adjectives and adverbs allows writers to add details to their work, making it more precise and colorful. But adjectives and adverbs have their proper uses, and it is important not to confuse them or use them incorrectly.

AUDIO

Chapter overview.

34a Use adjectives to modify nouns

An **adjective** is a word that modifies a noun (see 30a-3). Typically, adjectives answer one of the following questions: which? what kind? how many? Sometimes an adjective is placed next to the noun it modifies, either directly before the noun (an *ancient* building, the *first* page) or directly after (a dream *forsaken,* his curiosity *satisfied*). Other times an adjective is separated from the noun it modifies, as in the sentence "The movie was *exciting.*" In these cases, a linking verb (such as *is, was,* or *seemed*) connects the noun and its modifier.

Some adjectives have "pure" forms; others are derived from nouns or verbs by adding a suffix. Examples of pure adjectives include *small, hot, blue, quick, correct, ambiguous, ornery,* and *sharp.* Examples of derived adjectives are *beautiful, annoying, suitable, restless, foolish, supportive,* and *perilous.*

Base form	Suffix	Adjective
harm	-ful	harmful
interest	-ing	interesting
desire	-able	desirable
biology	-ical	biological
worth	-while	worthwhile
fool	-proof	foolproof
sweat	-y	sweaty

Many adjectives have the same form as the present and past participles of verbs (a *roaring* lion, a *deserted* island). There also are many pronoun-like adjectives: **possessive adjectives** (*her* guitar), **demonstrative adjectives** (*that* tree), **interrogative adjectives** (*Which* way do I go?), and **indefinite adjectives** (*some* ideas).

34b Avoid overuse of nouns as modifiers

A noun can modify another noun and thus function as an adjective. Some examples are *park* bench, *soda* pop, *letter* opener, *telephone* book, *fender* bender, *tape* player, and *movie* theater. Indeed, this **noun compounding** is such a common occurrence in English that some noun-noun combinations eventually become single words (*windshield, placekicker, flowerpot, dishrag, sideshow, screwdriver*). And it is not uncommon to find three nouns in a row, with the first two serving as adjectival modifiers of the third (*soda pop dispenser, brass letter opener, tape player cabinet, movie theater lobby*). In principle, there is no limit to the number of nouns that can be stacked up as adjectives before another noun. (Here is an example from a cookbook: *rose-hip jam dessert ideas.* Can you figure out what it means?)

WEBLINK

http://webster.commnet
.edu/grammar/adjectives
.htm
A basic discussion of
adjectives

Noun compounding can help you save a few words—*windshield* is more concise than *shield against the wind*—but it can be confusing for readers, especially if you use more than three nouns in a row. To avoid long noun strings such as *the picnic table cross brace*, use a prepositional phrase: *the cross brace under the picnic table.* Such phrasing may take a few more words, but the meaning will be clearer.

(**Grammar Checker Alert**) Grammar checkers typically flag any string of four or more nouns. But they often have trouble distinguishing nouns from other parts of speech. For example, our grammar checker flagged *picnic table leg brace* but missed *picnic table cross brace*; apparently, it thought *cross* was a verb!

34c Use adverbs to modify verbs, adjectives, other adverbs, and clauses

An **adverb** is a word that modifies a verb, an adjective, another adverb, or a clause (see 30a-5). Adverbs modify verbs by answering one of the following questions: when? how? how often? where?

Bob *quickly* raised his hand.

Linda *often* goes to the gym to work out.

In the following examples, the adverb modifies a clause, an adjective, or another adverb.

Luckily, I was able to find a backup disk.   [Modifies the entire clause]

They made a *very* bad mistake.   [Modifies the adjective *bad*]

The car was turned *almost* upside down.   [Modifies the adverb *upside down*]

34d Be aware of some commonly confused adjectives and adverbs

VIDEO

Recognizing adjectives and adverbs.

The pairs of words *good/well* and *bad/badly* are misused by many writers who fail to recognize that *good* and *bad* are adjectives while *well* and *badly* are adverbs. The sentence "Fielder runs *good* for a man his size" is ungrammatical. The correct version is

> **WEBLINK**
>
> http://webster.commnet
> .edu/grammar/adverbs
> .htm
> A basic discussion of adverbs

www

34.1

A comprehensive guide to adverbs.

Fielder runs *well* for a man his size.
[The adverb *well* modifies the verb *runs.*]

The adjective *good* is appropriate when the word being modified is a noun.

He has a *good,* long stride.   [The adjective *good* modifies the noun *stride.*]

When the main verb expresses a feeling or a perception (such verbs include *look, appear, feel, seem, taste,* and *smell*), the correct modifier is an adjective complement.

I feel *bad* about what I did.   [Not *badly; bad* modifies *I*]

AUDIO

Well as an adjective or adverb.

This gazpacho tastes *good*.   [Not *well; good* modifies *gazpacho*]

You look *wonderful*.   [Not *wonderfully; wonderful* modifies *You*]

EXERCISE 34.1

Circle the correct adjective or adverb in each sentence.

1. Although David played [good, well] for the audition, he did not get the job.
2. Many students study long hours, sleep [bad, badly], and have trouble concentrating in class.
3. Mariko looked [good, well] in her new school uniform.
4. The senator felt [bad, badly] about his involvement in the scandal.
5. It seems like a [good, well] idea to refrigerate the leftovers.
6. Whenever I do too much heavy lifting, I ache [bad, badly] the next day.
7. After the sultry heat of the afternoon sun, it feels [good, well] to sleep in the shade.
8. After Tom eats garlic, his breath smells [bad, badly].
9. The athlete swam [good, well] in spite of her injured knee.
10. Teresa got off to a [bad, badly] start in the fourth race.

34e Use comparative and superlative forms of adjectives and adverbs correctly

Most adjectives and many adverbs can be used to make comparisons.

Ted works *hard*. He is *determined* to get ahead.

Ted works *harder* than I do. He is *more determined* than I am.   [Comparative forms]

Ted works the *hardest* of anybody I know. He is the *most determined* person I have ever met.   [Superlative forms]

Adjectives of one or two syllables usually add -er and -est in their comparative and superlative forms. For adjectives with more than two syllables, the comparative and superlative forms typically consist of the positive base form with *more* and *most*.

Positive	Comparative	Superlative
smart	smarter	smartest
tasty	tastier	tastiest
beautiful	more beautiful	most beautiful
interesting	more interesting	most interesting

A few common adjectives have irregular comparative and superlative forms:

good	better	best
bad	worse	worst
far	farther/further	farthest/furthest

Many adverbs have regular comparative and superlative forms, including the following:

early	earlier	earliest
fast	faster	fastest
hard	harder	hardest
late	later	latest
long	longer	longest
near	nearer	nearest
quickly	more quickly	most quickly
carefully	more carefully	most carefully
elegantly	more elegantly	most elegantly

Several other adverbs have irregular forms:

badly	worse	worst
far	farther/further	farthest/furthest
little	less	least
much	more	most
well	better	best

1 Avoid redundancy of comparative or superlative forms

Using both *more* (or *less*) and a comparative form of an adjective or adverb (with the *-er* ending) is incorrect:

Ted works ~~more~~ harder than I do.

Likewise, using both *most* (or *least*) and a superlative form of an adjective or adverb (with the *-est* ending) is incorrect:

Ted is the ~~most~~ hardest working person I know.

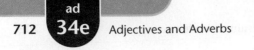
2 When making comparisons, be accurate, complete, and logical

When comparing two items, use the comparative form. When comparing three or more items, use the superlative form.

Of the two candidates, I like Johnson *better.*

Of the three candidates, I like Johnson *best.*

3 Use *fewer* and *less* correctly

Use *few, fewer,* or *fewest* with count nouns (such as *books, calories, flowers,* and *dollars*). Use *little, less,* or *least* with noncount nouns (such as *water, understanding,* and *progress*).

The team has *fewer* fans that it used to have.

The new package contains *less* rice.

4 Make sure the terms of a comparison are complete

Do not write a sentence such as "This headache remedy works better." Many readers will wonder, "Better than what?" Including a *than* phrase as part of the comparison makes it clear:

> **WEBLINK**
>
> http://cctc2.commnet.edu/
> grammar/adverbs.htm
> An excellent review of
> adverbs, with exercises

This headache remedy works better *than any other.*

Occasionally, the context allows you to omit the *than* phrase. For example, if you have been discussing the movies *Star Wars* and *The Empire Strikes Back,* you could say, "I think *Star Wars* is better."

5 Do not qualify inherently absolute terms

Certain adjectives, by definition, express an absolute condition or quality and thus logically cannot have different degrees. Words such as *unique, dead, pregnant, final,* and *incomparable* belong in this category. It makes no sense to say that something or someone is *more unique* or *less dead.*

Michael Jordan is the most ~~unique~~ basketball player in the world.

ad

(**Grammar Checker Alert**) Your grammar checker will probably flag redundant comparative and superlative forms such as *more better* and *most hardest*, as well as illogical colloquialisms such as *most unique*. It should also catch misuses of *fewer, fewest, less,* and *least.* However, it will probably not detect a more subtle error such as *Of the two candidates, I like Johnson best.*

(**EXERCISE 34.2**)

Correct the errors of comparative or superlative form in the following sentences.

1. Chris is the most smartest friend I have.
2. I went to the grocery checkout line marked "Twelve Items or Less."
3. The morning paper will give us a more newer update on the situation in the Middle East.
4. The most far that AAA recommends driving in a single day is 200 miles.
5. My grandmother's chocolate cheesecake is my most favorite dessert.
6. The store manager told the cashiers that they had to dress less casual for work.
7. A 1990 study by the Federal Reserve Board showed that African Americans and Latinos were 60 percent more likelier than European Americans to be rejected for home mortgages.
8. There are experts who believe that in some more early societies women and men may have been social equals.
9. These societies had lesser gender discrimination than does the contemporary world.
10. Forced to choose among several appealing options on the menu, I opted for the one that intrigued me more.

EXER

Choosing
comparative or
superlative
forms.

(**FOR COLLABORATION**)

Discuss the results of the exercise above in your group. Share with your group which kinds of errors are most difficult for you to identify.

CHAPTER 35

Sentence Fragments

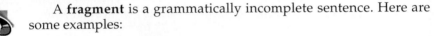

AUDIO

Chapter
overview.

A **fragment** is a grammatically incomplete sentence. Here are some examples:

The one in the corner.

Runs like the wind.

Because we had no choice.

Whichever film you prefer.

In ordinary conversation, people say things like the above. But these are not complete sentences, and formal English requires that complete sentences be used to convey meaning. Complete sentences (1) have a complete predicate, (2) have a grammatical subject, and (3) do not begin with a subordinating conjunction or relative pronoun unless they are connected to a main clause (see 30c-3). In the four examples of fragments, the first has no predicate, the second has no subject, the third begins with an unattached subordinating conjunction (*Because*), and the fourth begins with an unattached relative pronoun (*Whichever*).

Sometimes writers produce fragments because they write an idea the way they would talk about it. But formal writing and casual speech are two different things. In casual speech, conversational interactions usually fill in the meaning of brief phrases. Therefore, people do not always need to follow all the rules of standard English grammar—and often do not. When you are writing a college paper or some other piece that requires a formal style, employing the casual speech you use when talking with friends will leave your meaning vague and unclear.

More often, writers produce fragments through mispunctuation. This chapter provides many examples of how to correct sentence fragments with proper punctuation. (You may want to consult Part 10, Punctuation, while reading this chapter, especially 50a, 51a, 51e, 52a, 53b, 56a, and 56d.)

35a Make sentences grammatically complete

(Grammar Checker Alert) If you have a good grammar checker in your computer, it should identify most of the sentence fragments in your writing. But it will not be able to tell you how to fix them. When we ran a grammar check on this chapter, our word processor flagged only three of the fragments listed at the beginning. For the first two, it said only "This does not seem to be a complete sentence"; for the third, it said, "This sentence does not seem to contain a main clause." So, even with a good grammar checker, you will need to solve these problems on your own.

1 Does the sentence have a complete predicate?

In standard formal English, all sentences must have a complete predicate—that is, a main verb plus any necessary helping verbs and complements. The main verb must be a *finite* (full) verb, not an infinitive (*to* form) or a participle (*-ing* form).

The second part of the following example has been incorrectly set off as a separate sentence; it does not have a finite verb and so cannot be a full sentence:

> Seven is a very symbolic number in Judeo-Christian culture. *Appearing often in the Bible and other sacred texts.*

Simply replacing the period with a comma will correct the problem:

> Seven is a very symbolic number in Judeo-Christian culture, appearing often in the Bible and other sacred texts.

2 Does the sentence have a subject?

In standard English, all sentences (except commands) must have a grammatical subject (see 30b).

Sometimes, a fragment can be corrected by simply inserting an appropriate subject and making other related changes:

> Most of today's sitcoms are not about families in suburbia. ~~But~~
> *Rather, they are*
> ~~rather~~ *about young adults in the big city.*

Sometimes, simply changing the punctuation and making the fragment part of the previous sentence will correct the error:

> Most of today's sitcoms are not about families in suburbia ~~But~~ *but*
>
> *rather about young adults in the big city.*

By removing the period after *suburbia*, you allow *most of today's sitcoms* to serve as the subject for the rest of the sentence, thereby eliminating the fragment.

(Grammar Checker Alert) Your grammar checker will probably flag any sentence beginning with *and*, *but*, or other coordinating conjunction and suggest that you replace it with a conjunctive adverb such as *in addition* or *however*. This is not an ironclad rule, however. If what follows the *and* or *but* is a grammatically complete sentence, and if you want to set it off for emphasis, using *and* or *but* at the beginning is acceptable, even to most expert writers.

3 Are the subordinating phrases or clauses connected to a main clause?

Check to be sure that word clusters beginning with a subordinating conjunction (such as *because, although,* or *if*) or a relative pronoun (such as *which, who,* or *that*) are connected or subordinated to a main subject and predicate (see 35b).

Common Subordinating Conjunctions

after	before	though	whenever
although	even if	unless	wherever
as	if	until	whether
because	since	when	while

35b   Connect dependent clauses

Dependent clauses have a subject and a predicate but are linked to a main clause with a subordinating conjunction (such as *because, although,* or *if*) or a relative pronoun (such as *which, who,* or *that*). Because dependent clauses depend on their connection to a main clause for their meaning, they cannot stand alone. Therefore, if you begin a clause with a subordinating conjunction or relative pronoun and then end it with a period or semicolon before connecting it to a main clause, you have produced a fragment, not a sentence. In the following sentence, changing the period to a comma allows the *Before* clause to serve as a dependent clause:

FRAGMENT   *Before you delve into critically analyzing the characters.*
            You should first discuss the opening sequence.

REVISED   *Before you delve into critically analyzing the characters,*
            you should first discuss the opening sequence.

Likewise, relative clauses also need to be connected to a main clause. In the following sentence, the solution is simply to eliminate the period, joining the two clauses:

What seems annoying to me, ~~May~~ *may* not bother you at all.

35c   Connect phrases

AUDIO

How poor
punctuation
causes
fragments.

Phrases are similar to clauses except that they lack full verbs (see 30c-2). Phrases can be used as modifiers, subjects, objects, or complements—but never as sentences. Make sure that all of your phrases are connected to main clauses.

HELP

How do I locate sentence fragments?

1. Open the SEARCH function of your word-processing program.
2. Launch a search to locate each period in your document.
3. Look carefully at the group of words preceding each period located. Determine whether each group is indeed a complete sentence, using the questions raised in 35a.

FRAGMENT *To prevent powerful foreign corporations from gaining too much influence.* Some African governments insisted on owning 51 percent of key national industries.

35.1

A guide to revising fragments, plus exercises.

WEBLINK

http://owl.english.purdue
.edu/handouts/grammar/
g_frag.html
A basic discussion of fragments, with exercises

REVISED *To prevent powerful foreign corporations from gaining too much influence,* some African governments insisted on owning 51 percent of key national industries. [Putting a comma after *influence* connects the modifying phrase (*To . . . influence*) to the main clause.]

FRAGMENT Many nations began to process their own food, minerals, and other raw materials. *Using foreign aid and investments to back their efforts.*

REVISED Many nations began to process their own food, minerals, and other raw materials, *using foreign aid and investments to back their efforts.*

EXERCISE 35.1

Correct the fragments in the following sentences.

1. John Lennon was killed in 1980, By a deranged young man.
2. Were it not for the dynamics of racism in US society. Chuck Berry probably would have been crowned king of rock and roll.
3. It was the phenomenal success of "Rapper's Delight." That first alerted the mainstream media to the existence of hip hop.
4. Barry Bonds hit seventy-three home runs in one year. Setting a new record.
5. Mauritania is an Islamic country. Which is located in northwest Africa.
6. Lamarck thought that acquired traits could be passed on to one's offspring. His ideas being challenged much later by Charles Darwin.
7. Having thought about our situation. I have decided I should take a second job.

Checklist for Fixing Fragments

1. Can I connect the fragment to an independent clause by changing the punctuation?

FRAGMENT   Some African nations emphasized the growing of export crops. *Which provided badly needed capital for development.*

REVISED   Some African nations emphasized the growing of export crops, which provided badly needed capital for development.   [Inserting a comma after *crops* connects the relative clause (*which . . . development*) to the main clause.]

FRAGMENT   Agricultural development was hampered by natural disasters. *Such as locust plagues and cattle diseases.*

REVISED   Agricultural development was hampered by natural disasters such as locust plagues and cattle diseases.   [The phrase beginning with *such* has been attached to the main clause.]

2. Can I turn the fragment into an independent sentence?

FRAGMENT   Some of the problems facing African nations can be traced to colonialism. *Some European nations doing little to prepare their colonies for independence.*

REVISED   Some of the problems facing African nations can be traced to colonialism. Some European nations did little to prepare their colonies for independence.   [Changing the verb of the fragment into a full verb turns the fragment into an independent sentence.]

8. This is a good economic arrangement. For working and taking care of the children.

9. Two years after his disastrous invasion of Russia in 1812. Napoleon was exiled to the island of Elba.

10. He regained power the following year. But was defeated at Waterloo.

35d Use sentence fragments only for special effect

35.2

Using fragments
for special
effect.

Occasionally sentence fragments can be used for special effect, to add emphasis or to make writing sound conversational. Here is an example from the writing of Molly Ivins:

WEBLINK

http://webster.commnet
.edu/grammar/fragments
.htm

A full review of sentence
fragments, with exercises

Shrub's proposal to cut property taxes, on which our public schools depend, by $1 billion merely shifts the tax burden even more dramatically to the folks with the least money. *Nice work, Shrub.*

—Molly Ivins, "Truly Happy News"

In this editorial column, Ivins is criticizing a state politician. After giving her interpretation of the politician's proposal in the first sentence, she uses a common conversational expression, in the form of a fragment, to make a sarcastic comment.

Be cautious about using fragments in any kind of formal writing you do. Since they are rarely found in such writing, readers might see them only as grammatical mistakes, not as "special effects."

EXER

Identify the
fragments and
full sentences.

EXERCISE 35.2

Fragments are commonly seen in advertisements. Find a magazine ad or Internet ad containing at least three sentence fragments.

1. Underline all the fragments in the ad.
2. Rewrite the ad, turning the fragments into complete sentences.

FOR COLLABORATION

In your group, explain why you think the writers of the ad chose to include the fragments.

CHAPTER 36

Comma Splices and Run-on Sentences

FAQs

▸ What is a "comma splice"?

▸ How do I know when I have written a run-on sentence?

▸ How do I correct a comma splice or run-on sentence?
(36a–36d)

Joining two independent clauses with a comma creates a **comma splice:**

> The best keyboard for one-handed users is the Dvorak keyboard, it has a more convenient layout than the standard Qwerty keyboard.

AUDIO
Chapter overview.

Although comma splices are acceptable in casual English, they are generally not acceptable in formal written English. (Exceptions are allowed with short, closely related, parallel sentences such as *Sometimes you win, sometimes you lose.*)

Putting two independent clauses together without a conjunction or any punctuation creates a **run-on sentence** (or *fused sentence*):

> Dvorak keyboards put the most frequently typed characters within easy reach they are often used in speed-typing competitions.

WEBLINK

http://cctc2.commnet.edu/grammar/runons.htm
All you need to know about comma splices and run-on sentences, with exercises

WWW
36.1
Guidelines for revising run-on sentences.

(**Grammar Checker Alert**) When looking for comma splices and run-on sentences with a grammar checker, remember that grammar checkers are

HELP

How do I identify comma splices and run-on sentences?

1. Open your grammar checker.
2. Click on the OPTIONS feature.
3. Select a CUSTOM file.
4. Open the customization feature.
5. Deselect all the grammar features except the one called something like CLAUSE ERRORS or COMMA SPLICE OR FUSED SENTENCE.
6. For extra speed, turn off the spell checker.
7. Run the program on your document.

WWW

36.2

Sample misdiagnoses from a grammar checker.

not always reliable. You should look carefully at each case the checker identifies to see whether it is really a comma splice or a run-on sentence.

Run-on sentences are incorrect in standard English and are often confusing to readers. There are four main ways to correct comma splices and run-on sentences:

- Turn one clause into a subordinate clause.
- Add a comma and a coordinating conjunction.
- Separate the clauses with a semicolon.
- Separate the clauses with a period.

36a Turn one clause into a subordinate clause

Often the best way to correct a comma splice or run-on sentence is to convert one of the two clauses into a subordinate clause. This can be done by using either a subordinating conjunction (such as *while, although, because,* or *if*) or a relative pronoun (such as *which, that,* or *who*).

The best keyboard for one-handed users is the Dvorak keyboard, ~~it~~ *which* has a more convenient layout than the standard Qwerty keyboard.

Because ‸Dvorak keyboards put the most frequently typed characters within easy reach, they are often used in speed-typing competitions.

Sometimes this technique may require switching the two clauses around:

> *Because* it has a more convenient layout than the standard Qwerty keyboard, the best keyboard for one-handed users is the Dvorak keyboard.

36b Separate clauses with a comma and a coordinating conjunction

If the two parts of a comma splice or run-on sentence are of equal importance, you can put a comma and a coordinating conjunction (such as *and, or, but, nor,* or *yet*) between them:

> An eagle once flew past our house, but I got only a brief glimpse of it.

Simply inserting a comma in a run-on sentence is not enough, for that only produces another error (a comma splice); you must also insert a conjunction.

36c Separate independent clauses with a semicolon

VIDEO

Recognizing comma splices.

If the two parts of a comma splice or run-on sentence are of equal importance, you can insert a semicolon between them:

> Desktop computers usually have bigger screens than laptops do; laptops are easier to carry around.

If you use a conjunctive adverb such as *however, therefore,* or *for example,* place the semicolon before it:

> Laptops are coming down in price; *therefore,* more people are buying them.

36d Separate independent clauses with a period

Often the easiest way to correct a comma splice or run-on sentence is by inserting a period between the two independent clauses:

> The best keyboard for one-handed users is the Dvorak keyboard. It has a more convenient layout than the standard Qwerty keyboard.

> Dvorak keyboards put the most frequently typed characters within easy reach. They are often used in speed-typing competitions.

WEBLINK

http://www.wisc.edu/
writetest/Handbook/
CommonErrors.html
An essential checklist that covers all sorts of common writing problems, including comma splices

Although adding a period is the easiest way to correct these errors, it is not usually the best way. Inserting a period between the two clauses turns them into two separate sentences, thereby making it more difficult for the reader to see the relationship between them. As a general rule, try to use one of the other three methods before settling on this one.

EXERCISE 36.1

Correct the following comma splices and run-on sentences.

1. Ritchie Valens was the first Chicano rock and roll star, he recorded a string of hits before his fatal plane crash in February 1959.

2. In order to access the Internet via modem you must install the Dial-Up Networking option click here to start.

3. I started reading Russian literature when I was young, though I did not know that it was Russian, in fact I was not even aware that I lived in a country with any distinct existence of its own.

4. We always ate dinner at eight o'clock we spent the whole day anticipating the time we could talk and eat together as a family.

5. Mine is a Spanish-speaking household we use Spanish exclusively.

6. The side pockets of her jacket were always bulging they were filled with rocks, candy, chewing gum, and other trinkets only a child could appreciate.

7. Some people seem to be able to eat everything they want they do not gain weight.

8. The VCR was not a popular piece of equipment with movie moguls, the studios quickly adapted.

9. Some magazines survive without advertising, they are supported by readers who pay for subscriptions.

10. A multimillion-dollar diet industry has developed, they sell liquid diets, freeze-dried foods, artificial sweeteners, and diet books by the hundreds.

CHAPTER 37

Pronoun Reference

FAQs

▶ Can my computer help me spot pronoun problems? (37a-3)
▶ Is there anything wrong with beginning a sentence with *this*? (37b)
▶ When should I use *that* and when should I use *which*? (37d)

Using pronouns in place of nouns often makes writing more concise and readable. But pronouns can be confusing to readers if they are not used correctly.

AUDIO
Chapter overview.

37a　Refer to a specific noun antecedent

Pronouns (such as *she, it,* and *that*) work best when they refer back to a particular noun, called the **antecedent.**

The conductor announced to the orchestra members that *she* was resigning.

Only one of the new hockey players knew what *his* position would be.

WWW

37.1
Pronoun agreement and reference.

VIDEO
Recognizing pronoun-reference problems.

1　Avoiding use of generalized *they* or *you*

In casual speech, people often use pronouns in vague ways, without explicit antecedents ("*They* say that television is dulling our brains"). In formal writing, however, such vagueness can sabotage meaning and must be avoided.

VAGUE *THEY* REVISED

Some people
~~They~~ say that television is dulling our brains.

Similarly, avoid using the pronoun *you* unless you are addressing the reader directly.

VAGUE *YOU* REVISED

One never knows
~~You never know~~ when calamity will strike.

2 Avoiding use of implied antecedents

Pronouns should refer back to specific antecedents, not implied ones.

IMPLIED REFERENCE REVISED

the notes
Notetaking is very helpful in doing research, especially if ~~they~~ are

well organized.

3 Clarifying references with more than one possible antecedent

Writers sometimes get into trouble by using a pronoun that could refer to more than one noun.

VAGUE REFERENCE

Hannibal's troops used elephants to carry their equipment across the Alps, but many of *them* died in the harsh winter weather.

In this sentence, the pronoun *them* could refer to either Hannibal's troops or their elephants, since both are plural. In such cases, you should either replace the pronoun with its specific antecedent or re-word the sentence to eliminate the vagueness.

VAGUE REFERENCE REVISED

Hannibal's troops used elephants to carry their equipment across
the elephants
the Alps, but many of ~~them~~ died in the harsh winter weather.
[Specifies the antecedent]

OR

> # HELP
>
> ## How do I identify possible pronoun reference problems?
>
> 1. Open the SEARCH feature of your word-processing program.
> 2. Enter *it* in the SEARCH field.
> 3. Run the search.
> 4. Whenever the program highlights an *it*, use the guidelines in this chapter to determine whether you have used the word correctly.
> 5. Do a similar search for *this, that,* and *which.*

army

Hannibal's ~~troops~~ used elephants to carry their equipment across the Alps, but many of them died in the harsh winter weather.
[Replaces one of the plural antecedents with a singular one, eliminating the vagueness]

37b Avoid vague use of *this, that, which,* and *it*

The pronouns *this, that, which,* and *it* may be used with care to refer broadly to an entire statement:

> According to the linguistic school currently on top, human beings are all born with a genetic endowment for recognizing and formulating language. *This* must mean that we possess genes for all kinds of information, with strands of special, peculiarly human DNA for the discernment of meaning in syntax.
>
> —Lewis Thomas, *Lives of a Cell*

In this excerpt, the word *this* leading off the second sentence refers clearly to the main clause of the first sentence ("human beings . . . language").

In many cases, though, using pronouns for broad reference may confuse the reader. What does *it* refer to in the following paragraph?

> Watching Monday Night Football on ABC has become a ritual for countless American sports lovers. *It* is symbolic of contemporary American life.

It could refer to (1) Monday Night Football, (2) watching Monday Night Football, or (3) watching Monday Night Football has become

AUDIO
Using *this* without ambiguity.

a ritual for countless American sports lovers. One way to resolve this ambiguity is to replace the pronoun with a full noun phrase:

VAGUE REFERENCE REVISED

Watching Monday Night Football on ABC has become a ritual for countless American sports lovers. *Monday Night Football* ~~It~~ is symbolic of contemporary American life.

37c Avoid mixed uses of *it*

The word *it* can function either as a pronoun or as an expletive. Do not use the word both ways in the same sentence (see 37b):

The manual
~~In the manual it~~ says that it is important to turn off all other applications before installing a new program.

37d Be consistent with use of *that, which,* and *who*

The relative pronoun *that* is used only with essential (restrictive) relative clauses—clauses that are essential to identify the nouns they modify:

37.2

An online guide to pronoun reference.

WEBLINK

http://www.uottawa.ca/
academic/arts/writcent/
hypergrammar/pronref
.html

All you need to know about pronoun reference issues

ESSENTIAL CLAUSE

First prize went to the long-haired collie *that came all the way from Hartford.* [There were other long-haired collies in the competition.]

Although many people prefer using *which* only for nonessential relative clauses, the relative pronoun *which* can be used either with essential relative clauses or with nonessential (nonrestrictive) relative clauses—clauses that merely add extra information (see 51e, 51j):

NONESSENTIAL CLAUSE

First prize went to the long-haired collie, *which came all the way from Hartford.* [It was the only long-haired collie in the competition.]

37.3

More essential and nonessential clauses.

ESSENTIAL CLAUSE

First prize went to the long-haired collie *which came all the way from Hartford.* [There were other long-haired collies in the competition.]

(**Grammar Checker Alert**) The grammar checker on your computer will probably suggest that you use *that* for essential clauses, but this is not a strict rule. Many expert writers use either *that* or *which* for essential relative clauses, depending on how formal they want to sound. (*Which* is slightly more formal than *that*.)

It is conventional to use the personal relative pronouns *who*, *whose*, and *whom*, rather than *which*, when referring to people.

PERSONAL REFERENCE REVISED

This is the ambulance driver ~~which~~ rescued me.
^{who}

(**Note**) In reference to objects and nonspecific or unnamed animals, it is conventional to use *that*, *which*, and *whose*, not *who*.

(**EXERCISE 37.1**)

Correct the pronoun errors in the following sentences.

1. *Sesame Street* is a valuable children's program. Not only is one able to learn from a show like this, one also is able to fall in love with your favorite character who has the ability to become your friend and teacher.
2. Then there is the Disney book club, that provides short-story versions of the animated films.
3. The most popular sitcoms today are set in big cities and do not have anything to do with family, which is a change from the sitcoms of old.

EXER
Correct pro-
noun errors.

4. We do not tear your clothing with machinery. We do it carefully by hand.
5. Every student must bring their books to class tomorrow and be prepared to discuss Chapter 6. It is important for you to do this.
6. Only one of the members of the House of Representatives decided that they would vote against the proposed bill.
7. They say that drinking and driving kills more people each year than cancer. They should not drink and drive.
8. Filling out college applications and worrying about SAT scores are annual rituals for many high school seniors. It is a part of the admissions process.
9. In the annual report it says it has been a disappointing year for the company.
10. The dog which chases my cat lives in the house across the street.

CHAPTER 38

Misplaced and Dangling Modifiers

FAQs

▶ What is a modifier?
▶ How can I tell when I have misused a modifier?
  (38b–38d)
▶ What is a "split infinitive"? (38d-2)
▶ What is a "dangling modifier"? (38e)

AUDIO

Chapter
overview.

Modifiers are words, phrases, or clauses that qualify other words, phrases, or clauses. Used properly, modifiers can make writing richer and more precise.

(**Grammar Checker Alert**) With the exception of split infinitives (see 38d-2), grammar checkers typically cannot identify misplaced or dangling modifiers.

VIDEO

How to repair
misplaced
modifiers.

38a   Position modifiers close to the words they modify

For maximum clarity, modifiers should be placed as close as possible to (ideally, right next to) the words they modify.

Unlike George,
 ˌKramer does not need the approval of anyone,ˣ~~unlike George.~~

frequently
Businessesˌpublish the URLs for their Web sites ~~frequently~~ in

advertisements.

Take special care with modifiers such as *only, just, even, not,* and *almost,* which are often used imprecisely in ordinary speech. In formal writing, they should generally be positioned directly before the word or phrase they modify.

The yucca plant ~~only~~ grows well ^only^ in full sunlight.

England ~~did not win~~ ^won^ the battle ^not^ because of superior firepower but because of better tactics.

38b Avoid ambiguity

A modifier that is not carefully positioned may present the reader with two or more possible interpretations.

Bound, gagged, and trussed up nude in a denim bag with plugs in her ears and tape over her eyes, Cleveland teacher Brenda P. Noonan told yesterday how she was kidnapped and taken to Florida without knowing where she was going or why.

—Quoted in Richard Lederer, *Anguished English*

WEBLINK

http://www.uottawa.ca/academic/arts/writcent/hypergrammar/msplmod.html

How not to use misplaced and dangling modifiers in your writing

38.1
A guide to avoiding misplaced modifiers.

It must have been quite a trick to describe these things while being bound and gagged! This sentence recounts three main actions (telling, being kidnapped, and being taken to Florida); the writer should have positioned the modifiers closer to the third action:

Cleveland teacher Brenda P. Noonan told yesterday how she was kidnapped and taken to Florida bound, gagged, and trussed up nude in a denim bag with plugs in her ears and tape over her eyes, without knowing where she was going or why.

Adverbs such as *happily, quickly,* and *easily* are often ambiguous if they are positioned between two verb phrases.

Most people who responded to the ad *quickly* decided not to look at the car.

In this sentence, does *quickly* modify *responded* or *decided*? The ambiguity can be resolved by repositioning the modifier:

Most people who *quickly* responded to the ad decided not to look at the car.

OR

Most people who responded to the ad decided *quickly* not to look at the car.

Shifting the position of certain limiting adverbs can alter the meaning or emphasis in a sentence (see 38a). The following sentences differ in meaning because of the different locations of *only*:

Only Martha crammed for the exam.   [Other students did not cram.]

Martha *only* crammed for the exam.   [She did not prepare in any other way.]

Martha crammed for the exam *only*.   [She did not cram for quizzes and other assignments.]

38c   Try to put lengthy modifiers at the beginning or end

WWW

38.2

Examples of
embedded
transitional
words.

When a lengthy modifier is placed in the middle of a sentence, it tends to disrupt the basic structure (subject–verb–complement) of the sentence. By moving such modifiers to the beginning or end of the sentence, you preserve the basic structure and make the sentence more readable.

MODIFIER IN THE MIDDLE OF THE SENTENCE

A television network usually, after it airs a documentary, makes the film available to groups for a nominal rental fee.

REVISED

After it airs a documentary, a television network usually makes the film available to groups for a nominal rental fee.

38d   Avoid disruptive modifiers

English sentences are made up of subgroupings of words, such as the verb and its object or the word *to* and the rest of the infinitive construction. When modifiers are inserted into these subgroupings, there is a risk of interrupting and obscuring the vital connections between key words.

1   Modifiers between the verb and its object

Readers like to be able to move easily through the main predicate of a sentence, going from verb to object without interruption. For this reason, it is best to avoid inserting any interrupting modifiers between the verb and its object.

The magician ^*quickly* shuffled ~~quickly~~ the cards.

Sometimes, in following this advice, you may also be heeding the guideline that recommends moving a lengthy modifier to the beginning or end of the sentence (see 38c).

^*After reading the news report, several* ^Several customers decided, ~~after reading the news reports,~~ to boycott the store.

2   Split infinitives

A **split infinitive** occurs when the two parts of a *to*-infinitive construction (*to escape*) are separated, as in "He hoped *to* easily *escape*." Traditionalists claim that split infinitives are ungrammatical, but this belief is based on an eighteenth-century confusion between Latin and English. In any case, most readers have no trouble with such sentences; indeed, *Star Trek* fans have long enjoyed the split infinitive in their motto, "Star Trekkers hope *to boldly, loyally, and optimistically go* where none have gone before." (See 44d for further discussion.)

As a general guideline, though, it is best to avoid any long or complex "splits" in a *to* infinitive. "He hoped to easily escape" would be acceptable to most readers, but "He hoped to without detection escape" would not.

(Grammar Checker Alert) Many grammar checkers allow a range of choices regarding split infinitives. The checker for *Microsoft Word 6.0*, for example, offers five different warning options on split infinitives to suit readers and situations: no warning (allowing any split to go unnoticed); warning against splits of any length; or warning against splits of one, two, or three words between *to* and the base form. Look at the options on your checker to see what choices are available for different writing occasions.

38e Avoid dangling modifiers

A mistake that plagues many writers is the use of the **dangling modifier,** a verbal phrase that does not have a clear referent.

> Breaking in through the window of the girls' dormitory, the dean of men surprised ten members of the football team.
>
> —Quoted in Richard Lederer, *Anguished English*

Did the dean break into the girls' dormitory? To prevent this misinterpretation, the writer should have put the real culprits in the subject position of the main clause.

> Breaking in through the window of the girls' dormitory, *ten members of the football team* were surprised by the dean of men.

AUDIO

Placing modifiers next to what they modify.

It will not do simply to mention the missing agent somewhere in the main clause; in this case, the referent must be in the subject position so that it is next to the modifier.

www

38.3

Examples of misplaced and dangling modifiers.

WEBLINK

http://cctc2.commnet.edu/
grammar/modifiers.htm

Another site on using modifiers correctly

Plunging 1,000 feet into the gorge, we saw Yosemite Falls.

—Quoted in Richard Lederer,
Anguished English

(But it was only a hurried glimpse, as we soon smashed into the ground!) Of course, the reader can figure out that it was Yosemite Falls that was plunging, not the writer. But why force the reader to make this kind of mental correction? A better version puts the modifier next to what it modifies:

> We saw Yosemite Falls plunging 1,000 feet into the gorge.

EXERCISE 38.1

Correct the modifier errors in the following sentences.

1. Politicians who run for office frequently need to raise a lot of money.
2. Two cars were reported stolen by the Groveton police yesterday.
3. To get the job, his résumé had to be completely revised.
4. Please take time to look over the brochure that is enclosed with your family.
5. Before installing a new program, all other applications should be turned off.
6. Having missed class four times in three weeks, Professor Kateb decided that Melissa should be penalized.

EXER

Correct misplaced and dangling modifiers.

7. Yoko Ono will talk about her husband, John Lennon, who was killed in an interview with Barbara Walters.

8. The patient was referred to a psychiatrist with a severe emotional problem.

9. A former scout leader will plead guilty to two counts of sexually assaulting two boys in a New Hampshire court.

10. The judge sentenced the killer to die in the electric chair for the second time.

(Sentences 2, 4, 7, 8, 9, and 10 are courtesy of Richard Lederer, *Anguished English*.)

FOR COLLABORATION

Find some examples of dangling modifiers on the Internet, and share them with your group.

CHAPTER 39

Faulty Shifts

FAQs

▶ What does it mean to say that writing is "inconsistent"?
(39a–39c)

▶ What is a "mixed construction," and how can I avoid it? (39d)

AUDIO

Chapter
overview.

Readers expect a certain consistency in what they read. They expect writers to use a consistent tone, time frame, and point of view. Writers should try to satisfy this expectation by avoiding unnecessary shifts.

39a Avoid unnecessary shifts in person and number

Person, which indicates to whom a discourse refers, is denoted mainly by pronouns. The first-person pronouns *I, me, we,* and *us* refer to the writer or speaker. The second-person pronoun *you* refers to the reader or listener. The third-person pronouns *he, him, she, her, they,* and *them* refer to people being written or spoken about. Use care when making shifts in person.

You should start writing a paper well before the deadline; other-
you
wise, ~~one~~ may end up doing it at the last minute, with no chance to
revise it.

We were hoping to get tickets to the Smashing Pumpkins' concert.
we
But the line was so long ~~you~~ had no chance.

Number refers to whether a noun, pronoun, or verb is singular or plural. If you use two or more words to refer to the same thing, make sure that they are consistently singular or consistently plural (see Chapter 33).

Anyone who weaves in and out of traffic is endangering ~~their~~ *his or her* fellow drivers.

OR

~~Anyone~~ *People* who weaves✔ in and out of traffic ~~is~~ *are* endangering their fellow drivers.

39b Avoid unnecessary shifts in verb tense, mood, subject, and voice

Verb tense indicates the time frame of an action (see 32e). Readers will be confused by arbitrary shifts in time frame. Unless you are describing a situation where there is a natural or logical difference in time frames, it is best to use the same verb tense throughout.

In 1995, the median pay for full-time female workers in the United States was $22,497, while the median pay for males was $31,496. In other words, women ~~make~~ *made* seventy-one cents to a man's dollar.

> **WEBLINK**
>
> http://owl.english.purdue.edu/handouts/grammar/g_tensec.html
> How to avoid inappropriate shifts of verb tense

39.1
A guide for controlling shifts in verb tense.

Accounts of literary narratives are usually written consistently in the present tense:

Huxley's *Brave New World* depicts a nightmare utopia in which there ~~was~~ *is* no passion, no frustration, and no deviation from normalcy.

There are three **moods** in English: indicative, imperative, and subjunctive. The **indicative mood** is used for facts and assertions, the **imperative mood** for commands, and the **subjunctive mood** for conditions that are contrary to fact (see 32h). If you mix moods in the same sentence, you may confuse your readers:

INCONSISTENT MOOD

If China were a democracy, it will have elections at periodic intervals.

Is China a democracy? Does it have regular elections? Or is the writer just posing a hypothetical idea? The mixing of subjunctive mood (in the first clause) and indicative mood (in the second clause) makes it impossible to know. Either of the following revisions would clarify the meaning:

REVISED

> If China *is* a democracy, it *will have* elections at periodic intervals.
> [Both verbs are in the indicative, suggesting a factual assertion.]

> If China *were* a democracy, it *would have* elections at periodic intervals. [Both verbs are in the subjunctive, indicating a contrary-to-fact condition.]

The grammatical **subject** of a sentence serves as a focal point for the reader (see 30b-1). It usually indicates what the sentence is about and who is performing the verb's action. By repeating the same subject from one sentence to the next, the writer helps readers maintain focus on it. Conversely, by shifting from one subject to another in sentence after sentence, the writer may disorient readers.

INCONSISTENT SUBJECT

> When people try to move an accident victim, they should use proper lifting techniques. The legs should be used, not the back. The body should be bent at the knees and hips, and all twisting should be avoided.

Notice how the grammatical subjects change from one clause to another:

> people
> they
> the legs
> the body
> all twisting

A better version would retain the focus on *people* by keeping it in the subject position:

REVISED

> When *people* try to move an accident victim, *they* should use proper lifting techniques. *They* should use their legs, not their backs. *They* should bend their bodies at the knees and hips and avoid all twisting.

Maintaining a consistent subject usually helps maintain a consistent **voice** as well. Voice is a feature of the verb that indicates whether the subject of a sentence is acting or being acted upon (see 32g). In the "Inconsistent Subject" example on page 738, the first sentence is in active voice and the next two are in passive voice. The Revised version consistently uses the active voice throughout.

39c Avoid shifts in tone

Tone refers to the writer's attitude toward the subject matter or the audience (see 45c). It can be formal or informal, ironic or direct, friendly or hostile, and so on. Since readers need to get a clear sense of what the writer's attitude is, a writer should strive to maintain a consistent authorial tone.

INCONSISTENT TONE

> The world of folklore and fairy tales is one that attracts adults and children alike. As adults, we look back fondly on childhood cartoons and still get a kick out of 'em.

Because most of this passage is written in a fairly formal tone, the colloquial "still get a kick out of 'em" is jarring. The following revision has a more consistent tone:

REVISED

> The world of folklore and fairy tales is one that attracts adults and children alike. As adults, we look back fondly on childhood cartoons and find them as enjoyable as ever.

39.2
Examples of
shifts used for
effect.

(EXERCISE 39.1)

Correct the shifts in the following sentences.

1. One should do some type of physical activity at least three times a week for thirty minutes. Regular exercise is good for your heart and lungs.
2. We wanted to go to the U2 concert. However, the tickets sold out before I even got there, and there was no chance that you could buy them from scalpers for less than $100.
3. Someone who does not love themselves can never hope to love anyone else.
4. We hike up in the mountains every Saturday morning. We love the feeling of sheer exhilaration. We were happy to be tired.
5. Elizabeth Bishop's *A First Death in Nova Scotia* discusses death from the point of view of a child. It painted a picture of a young girl's emotional reaction to the death of her cousin.

EXER
Correct faulty
shifts.

6. If she were rich, she will buy all her clothes at Nordstrom and Lord & Taylor.

7. If you want to learn to speed-read, you have to first learn to concentrate. We need to focus on the words on the page. It is important not to let the attention wander. The eyes should always catch the center of each page.

8. If our goal is educational and economic equity and parity, then we need affirmative action to catch up. We are behind as a result of discrimination and denial of opportunity, and that is totally not fair.

9. Married couples make a deep commitment to one another and to society; in exchange, society extends certain benefits to them, which really helps them out with money and other stuff.

10. There can be no excuse for what you did. The act is shameful, and one should not be forgiven for it.

39d Avoid mixed constructions

Mixed constructions are those that result when a writer starts a sentence in a certain way but then changes track and finishes it differently. The two parts of the sentence end up being incompatible—and confusing to the reader.

WEBLINK

http://cctc2.commnet.edu/
grammar/confusion
.htm#mixed_constructions
Upbeat advice on maintaining consistency—even includes a quiz

MIXED   In the world created by movies and television makes fiction seem like reality.

Where is the grammatical subject in this sentence? The writer began with a prepositional phrase but then apparently got sidetracked and failed to create a complete main clause. One way of revising this sentence would be to turn the prepositional phrase into a noun phrase, which could then serve as the grammatical subject.

REVISED   The world created by movies and television makes fiction seem like reality.

Another option would be to set off the prepositional phrase with a comma and then reconstruct the rest of the sentence to form a main clause.

REVISED   In the world created by movies and television, fiction seems like reality.

Subordinating adverbs such as *although, since, because,* and *if* are used only in subordinate clauses. Thus, if you start a sentence with such an adverb, you must finish the subordinate clause and then construct a main clause.

MIXED   Since the campus parking situation makes you want to take the bus.

REVISED   Since the campus parking situation is so bad, you will want to take the bus.

Alternatively, you can omit the subordinating adverb and reconstruct the entire sentence.

REVISED   The campus parking situation makes you want to take the bus.

39e Create consistency between subjects and predicates

Subjects and predicates should always harmonize, both logically and grammatically. When they do not, the result is **faulty predication.**

FAULTY   Writer's block is when you cannot get started writing.

In this sentence, a noun (*writer's block*) is compared to an adverb of time (*when*). This is ungrammatical and illogical. In a sentence of the form *A is B,* the *A* and *B* terms must be of the same grammatical type (see 30b).

         N   N
REVISED   *Writer's block* is *a condition* in which you cannot get started writing.

Make sure the predicate fits logically with the subject.

AUDIO

Mixing spoken and written English.

FAULTY   Shaw's *Pygmalion* wins out over the snobbish aristocrat, Henry Higgins.

Pygmalion is the name of a play, so it cannot "win out" over one of its characters.

REVISED   In Shaw's *Pygmalion,* the lowborn Eliza Doolittle wins out over the snobbish aristocrat, Henry Higgins.

39f Avoid unmarked shifts between direct and indirect discourse

Direct discourse is language that is taken word for word from another source and thus is enclosed in quotation marks. **Indirect dis-**

course is language that is paraphrased and therefore is *not* enclosed in quotation marks. If you shift from one mode to the other, you may have to alter not only punctuation but also pronouns and verb tenses so as not to confuse your readers.

CONFUSING	Agassiz, the legendary Swiss scientist and teacher, once said I cannot afford to waste my time making money. [Without quotation marks, this statement seems to refer to two different people: Agassiz and the writer.]
REVISED	Agassiz, the legendary Swiss scientist and teacher, once said, "I cannot afford to waste my time making money." [By signaling direct discourse, the quotation marks make it clear that Agassiz is talking only about himself.]
REVISED	Agassiz, the legendary Swiss scientist and teacher, once said that he could not afford to waste his time making money. [Without quotation marks but with the pronoun *he* and consistent past-tense verbs, the statement clearly refers only to Agassiz. This is an example of indirect discourse.]

(E X E R C I S E   3 9 . 2)

EXER

Correct mixed constructions and faulty predications.

Correct the mixed constructions and faulty predications in the following sentences.

1. By using the terms *alligator* and *crocodile* to refer to the same reptile misleads many people.
2. A foot is when you can measure 12 inches.
3. The job of all UPS drivers delivered packages from its city of origin to their final destinations.
4. She asked did you like the concert?
5. One reason the Slavic Festival was so popular was because they had a band play polka music.
6. To creative writers, such as Lita, romanticized her adventures.
7. The reason why strawberries are picked while slightly green is because if left to ripen they rot before they are picked.
8. When the homecoming parade included William Smith and Ted Jackson became school heroes.
9. In processing caramel at high heat softens their centers.
10. The Great Salt Lake is a lake that is easy to swim in where there is a high salt content to make the water more buoyant.

CHAPTER 40

Clarity and Conciseness

FAQs

▶ What is a passive sentence? (40d)

▶ How can I tighten up my writing so that it is not so wordy? (40e)

▶ How can I be sure that readers will understand my meaning? (40g–40j)

Readers today are often under time pressure and are not willing to spend valuable minutes trying to decode a piece of writing. Writers must accommodate their readers by making their writing as clear and concise as possible.

AUDIO
Chapter overview.

40a   Avoid excessively long sentences

Sentences that are more than about twenty-five words long can sometimes be difficult for a reader, especially if the sentences are complicated.

VIDEO
Revising for clarity.

> Despite their significance in contemporary society, social movements seldom solve social problems, because in order to mobilize resources a movement must appeal to a broad constituency, which means that the group must focus on large-scale issues which are deeply embedded in society.

This sentence is forty-two words long. The following three shorter sentences say the same thing and are much easier for the reader to understand:

HELP

How do I guard against using excessively long sentences?

1. Open your grammar checker.
2. Select the CUSTOMIZE SETTINGS feature. (It may be under OPTIONS.)
3. If there is a sentence length entry, use it to set a maximum word limit of twenty-five words.
4. Thereafter, whenever you write, use your grammar checker to flag all sentences longer than twenty-five words.
5. Check each sentence. If a sentence is overly long and complicated, use the other guidelines in this chapter to simplify it, or divide the sentence into two or more shorter ones.

Despite their significance in contemporary society, social movements seldom solve social problems. To mobilize resources, a movement must appeal to a broad constituency. This means that the group must focus on large-scale issues which are deeply embedded in society.

40b Avoid unnecessary repetition and redundancy

A certain amount of repetition is necessary, both for emphasis and to maintain focus. Repetition is especially useful for linking one sentence to another (see 6c). However, unnecessary repetition will only clutter your writing and irritate readers.

Life offers many lessons ˄about life.

People seem to learn things best when they ~~learn~~ *experience* them firsthand.

If you repeat nouns too often, you will end up with a dull, heavy writing style. The best way to avoid repetition of nouns is to use pronouns (see 30a-2). Pronouns can establish and maintain coherence in paragraphs just as repeated nouns do, but with a lighter touch.

Redundancy is the use of words that could be left out without changing the meaning of the sentence. Saying that something is *blue in color* is redundant, because readers already know that blue *is* a color. Some other redundant phrases are *repeat again, combine together,* *end result, true fact,* and *basic essentials.* Such phrases should always be pruned.

I was caught ~~unexpectedly~~ off guard by the boss's telling me I had

~~successfully~~ made the grade in my new job.

40.1
Examples
of wordy
sentences.

40c Use expletives only where appropriate

An **expletive** is an "empty" phrase, such as *there* or *it,* that occupies the subject position in a sentence but is not its grammatical subject. Expletives have useful functions. The construction *there is (are, was, were)* typically introduces a new topic for discussion, whereas *it is (was)* typically creates special emphasis. Because expletives can be overused, look for opportunities to convert expletive constructions into more direct expressions.

My computer has many new features.
~~There are many new features that can be found in my computer.~~

                      should
~~It is recommended that~~ all candidates be on time for their interviews.

40d Use passive voice only where appropriate

In passive-voice constructions, the subject position is occupied not by the agent of the verb's action but by the recipient (see 32g). Since passive-voice constructions tend to be wordier and less direct than active-voice constructions, try to write most of your sentences in the active voice.

PASSIVE   Flexible songs, containing a variety of motifs arranged to its liking, are sung by the robin.

ACTIVE   The robin sings flexible songs, containing a variety of motifs arranged to its liking.

WEBLINK

http://webster.commnet
.edu/grammar/concise.htm
A helpful guide to concise
writing

40.2
A guide to
writing concise
sentences.

The passive version of this sentence is wordy and confusing, whereas the active version is direct and clear.

Passive sentences are appropriate when the recipient of the verb action is the topic of discussion or when the agent can be omitted without loss of clarity.

Over the past ten years, more than three million white-collar jobs have been eliminated in the United States.

AUDIO

Considerations for choosing active or passive voice.

Using the active voice would force the writer to mention the agent of this job elimination (presumably management), taking the focus of the sentence off the loss of jobs.

Over the past ten years, management has eliminated more than three million white-collar jobs in the United States.

40e Eliminate wordy phrases

Many commonly used phrases are unnecessarily long. If you can replace them with no loss of meaning, you should do so.

~~In a very real sense,~~ *T*rickle-down economics ~~exhibits a tendency~~ *tends* to

trickle up, benefiting mainly the wealthy.

Wordy phrases	Concise phrases
as a matter of fact	in fact
at the present time	today, presently
at this point in time	now
due to the fact that	because
in spite of the fact that	although, even though
in the event that	if
in the final analysis	finally, ultimately
until such time as	until

(Grammar Checker Alert) Although a typical grammar checker will identify many wordy phrases, it will also miss quite a few. Therefore, you need to be vigilant and double-check your writing. For example, our grammar checker flagged *as a matter of fact* and *due to the fact that* but not *in the final analysis* or *in the event that*.

(E X E R C I S E 4 0 . 1)

Revise the following sentences to make them as clear and concise as possible.

1. Millions of people witnessed the first lunar landing on the moon.
2. She did the daily paperwork every day.
3. I experienced a frightening experience when my teenage daughter took me out for a drive.

4. The quarterback who had been injured early in the season and had undergone extensive knee surgery to repair the damage had been conscientious about his rehabilitation exercises and was therefore feeling ready to play again only four months after the surgery.

5. The lack of a warm pair of mittens and a hat on that very cold morning led to the trumpeter's inability to play well during the halftime show at the Thanksgiving game.

6. Several unusual songs were sung by the Girl Scouts during their annual awards ceremony.

7. The Boy Scout Eagle rank was achieved by a boy who works with my son during the summer.

8. Hundreds of items were marked down by the store management for the annual August clearance sale.

9. There are many people in this society who do not have enough leisure time.

10. It is often that students find their work piling up at finals time.

40f Avoid a noun-heavy style

A noun-heavy style is a writing style characterized by many more nouns than verbs. It tends to make excessive use of the verb *be* (*am, are, is, was, were*) and have strings of prepositional phrases. A noun-heavy style results partly from the use of **nominalizations**—that is, nouns derived from verbs. For example, *determination* is a nominalization derived from the verb *determine.* Other examples include *remove/removal, insist/insistence, develop/development,* and *jog/jogging.* Although nominalizations can be useful for certain purposes, using too many of them will make your style ponderous and dull. Turning some of your nominalizations into verbs will give your writing a more active, concise flair.

WEBLINK

http://www.wisc.edu/writetest/Handbook/ClearConciseSentences.html

A resource for writing clear and concise sentences

NOUN-HEAVY   The preference of most writers is for an understanding of their composing as a species of fine frenzy.

MORE VERBAL   Most writers prefer having it understood that they compose in a fine frenzy.

NOUN-HEAVY   Thomas Jefferson was not a believer in the divinity of Jesus Christ and indeed was the author of a version of the Four Gospels that included the removal of all references to "miraculous" events.

MORE VERBAL   Thomas Jefferson did not believe in the divinity of Jesus Christ and indeed wrote a version of the Four Gospels from which he removed all references to "miraculous" events.

Noun-heavy writing also is created through the use of phrasal expressions such as *perform an examination* instead of simple verbs such as *examine*.

Before ~~making the purchase of~~ *purchasing* a used car, one should always ~~perform an examination on~~ *examine* it.

(**Grammar Checker Alert**) Although most grammar checkers are supposed to flag a noun-heavy style, especially long strings of prepositional phrases, they seldom do. For example, when we ran a grammar check on the three noun-heavy sentences given above, it failed to detect anything wrong.

A somewhat more reliable indicator of a noun-heavy style can be found in readability statistics (see TOOLS > OPTIONS > SPELLING & GRAMMAR). For example, the three noun-heavy sentences given above were rated at the twelfth-grade reading level, while the revised versions of these same sentences were rated two grades easier. Of course, readability statistics are only a superficial indicator; to make specific improvements in your style, apply the advice found in this chapter.

(**EXERCISE 40.2**)

The following phrasal expressions are characteristic of a wordy, noun-heavy style. Convert them into simpler verb forms. (The first one has already been done.)

1. create an improvement in   *improve*
2. give a summary of
3. put emphasis on
4. perform an operation on
5. do an analysis of
6. make an estimate of
7. come to the realization that

8. provide an explanation for   _____
9. have a lot of sympathy for   _____
10. conduct an inspection of   _____

(**EXERCISE 40.3**)

Revise the following sentences to make them less noun-heavy.

1. The scientist came to the conclusion that she had made an important discovery.
2. The United Nations wanted to conduct an inspection of the country's weapons storage facilities.
3. The committee reached a decision to hire the man it had interviewed.
4. The stance of the institution in regard to the question of affirmative action was unclear.
5. The group held the belief that disaster was coming at the close of the century.
6. The opinion of my mechanic is that there is nothing wrong with the transmission of my car.
7. Their press release gave an explanation for the behavior of the demonstrators.
8. The education reform law passed by the legislature demands that schools make improvements in their ways of teaching.
9. The composition of a piece of music is a requirement of the music theory course.
10. The man was justifiably proud of the achievement of his goal.

40g Choose words that express your meaning precisely

Good writing conveys its meaning efficiently, with precision. Such precision is achieved largely through the careful selection of words. Minimize your use of vague nouns such as *area, aspect, factor, kind, nature, situation, sort, thing,* and *type,* as well as your use of vague adjectives such as *bad, good, interesting, nice,* and *weird* and vague adverbs such as *basically, completely, definitely, really,* and *very.*

Democracy
A democratic type of government basically requires a pretty *an*
informed citizenry.

Word use is discussed in more detail in Part 9.

40h Use *that* to clarify sentence structure

Clear sentence structure helps the reader see how the pieces of a sentence fit together. In sentences with a main clause–*that* clause structure, it usually helps to include the *that*.

> It is important *that* we understand the instructions before we proceed.

Sometimes, failure to include *that* can cause the reader to misinterpret the sentence initially.

> Some people are claiming their rights have been violated by the government.

By beginning with a string of words that looks like a sentence in itself ("Some people are claiming their rights . . ."), the writer of this sentence risks misleading the reader. Inserting *that* after *claiming* helps to clarify the sentence structure.

> Some people are claiming *that* their rights have been violated by the government.

40i Make comparisons complete and clear

Comparative constructions inherently involve two terms: "*A* is _____er than *B*." In casual conversation, speakers sometimes omit the *B* term on the assumption that listeners can easily figure out what it is. In writing, however, you should make both terms of the comparison explicit.

INCOMPLETE   Talk radio has become a popular form of entertainment because it gets people more involved.   [More involved than what?]

COMPLETE   Talk radio has become a popular form of entertainment because it gets people more involved than most other media do.

Comparative constructions are sometimes open to two possible interpretations. In such cases, add a few words to help the reader know which interpretation is meant.

AMBIGUOUS   Abstract expressionism was more influenced by cubism than surrealism.

CLEAR   Abstract expressionism was more influenced by cubism than surrealism *was*.

AUDIO
The best way
to identify writ-
ing problems.

CLEAR   Abstract expressionism was more influenced by
             cubism than *by* surrealism.

(See 34e on comparative and superlative forms.)

(Grammar Checker Alert) Although grammar checkers may spot certain kinds of problematic comparative constructions (such as the
ambiguous "We need more thorough employees"), they miss many
others. For example, our grammar checker did not flag either the
"Incomplete" sentence or the "Ambiguous" sentence on page 750.

40j Avoid multiple negation

A single negative word, such as *no, not, never, nobody, unhappy,* or
unpleasant, can change the entire meaning of a sentence. If you put two
or more negative words in the same sentence, you may change the
meaning in multiple ways and confuse the reader.

CONFUSING   Not many of the assignments were left unfinished,
             but none of the students did all of them.

By rewriting the first part of the sentence in positive rather than negative terms, you can make its meaning much clearer:

CLEAR   Most of the assignments were finished, but none of
             the students did all of them.

(ESL Note) In many other languages, multiple negation is correct
and clear. In Spanish, for example, "don't say anything to anybody"
is rendered as *no le digas nada a nadie* (literally, "don't say nothing to
nobody").

(FOR COLLABORATION)

Make the following sentences as concise as you can without changing the meaning. Then compare your answers with those of two
other students and see whose version uses the fewest number of
words.

1. I think that people learn the most from personal experience
   and hard work, not from memorizing dates or facts, and that
   hard times or failure is a success if you learn something from it
   and improve.
2. In our natural childbirth class, I planned a calm and relaxing
   natural childbirth plan for my own pregnancy.

EXER

Practice
sentence
clarity and
conciseness.

3. This book contains a significant amount of information on art in history because without a knowledge of art history, one may find it difficult to discern the principles of art which are clearly crucial to an understanding of the aspects of art today.

4. I have come to conclude that to serve the purpose of conveying the overall benefit of chemical weapons incineration, the report should maintain an argumentative tone while clarifying the success of chemical weapons incineration and the safety standards followed by those who carry it out, and through this, to contradict any negative views.

5. Although she was in a family way, she continued in the fulfillment of her familial and employment responsibilities.

6. In recent months, research has come to light that bright red, green, yellow, and other colored fruits and vegetables may be instrumental in preventing lung cancer.

7. The weather, which was hostile, and the native inhabitants, the Indians, led to the death of most of the expedition members, who died.

8. The grassy area, which contains grass and trees, will be turned into a parking lot, so that students can park their cars there.

9. During that time period, many people who were car buyers preferred cars that were large in size and bright in color but not of a cheap quality.

10. Truly, for all intents and purposes, the industrial productivity in America generally depends on various and certain factors which are really usually more psychological in kind than of any true given technological aspect.

CHAPTER 41

Coordination and Subordination

FAQs

▶ What is the best way to avoid "choppy" writing? (41a)

▶ How can I emphasize some ideas and de-emphasize others? (41c)

In any piece of writing, readers will instinctively look for the most important points. By emphasizing these points and de-emphasizing others, writers make their main points easier to locate in the text and thereby make their writing more readable.

AUDIO
Chapter overview.

Two important ways to create emphasis are through coordination and subordination of sentence elements. Remember, *form should reflect content*. If two related ideas are equally important, *coordinate* them by putting them on the same grammatical level. If they are not equally important, put the less important idea in a grammatically *subordinate* form. (For other ways to create emphasis, see Chapter 43.)

41a **Look for a way to combine closely related sentences**

Writing that contains one short sentence after another not only is unpleasantly choppy but also fails to emphasize some sentences more than others.

TOO CHOPPY

I was born and raised in a small midwestern town. It was easy to make friends. I got to know a lot of people. I was able to achieve almost all of my goals. I could do almost anything I wanted to. School and sports were a challenge. But I could always make my way to where I wanted to be.

This paragraph is so choppy that it is hard to get a sense of what the writer's main point is. You can solve this problem by noticing that several pairs of sentences are closely related and combining these sentences.

REVISED VERSION

I was born and raised in a small midwestern town. It was easy to make friends, *and so* I got to know a lot of people. *Since* I could do almost anything I wanted to, I was able to achieve almost all of my goals. School and sports were a challenge, *but* I could always make my way to where I wanted to be.

41.1

Advice on combining sentences.

WEBLINK

http://leo.stcloudstate.edu/
style/sentencev.html

How to combine sentences using coordination or subordination

Instead of seven sentences, there are now four sentences, each conveying a single idea. This reorganization helps readers get a sense of the writer's main point—that growing up in a small town made it easy for him to be popular and successful.

The revised paragraph has three instances of sentence combining. In two of these cases, the sentences seemed to be of equal value and so *coordination* was used.

It was easy to make friends, *and so* I got to know a lot of people.

School and sports were a challenge, *but* I could always make my way to where I wanted to be.

In the third case, one sentence seemed to be more important than the other, so *subordination* was used.

Since I could do almost anything I wanted to, I was able to achieve almost all of my goals.

AUDIO

More on combining sentences.

Whenever you have written two closely related sentences, you should consider combining them into one, with either a conjunction, an adverb, or punctuation.

41b Coordinate related sentences of equal value

Coordination is the pairing of sentences or sentence elements by putting them in the same grammatical form and linking them via a

Common Conjunctive Adverbs

also	hence	likewise	otherwise
consequently	however	meanwhile	similarly
finally	indeed	moreover	therefore
furthermore	instead	nevertheless	thus

coordinating conjunction, conjunctive adverb, or semicolon. The coordinating conjunctions include *and, but, or, nor, for, so,* and *yet* (see 30a-7).

USE OF A COORDINATING CONJUNCTION

> A high-fiber diet appears to lower the risk of certain cancers, *so* the National Cancer Institute recommends consuming 25–35 grams of fiber a day.

Conjunctive adverbs provide another way of giving equal emphasis to two conjoined sentences (see 30a-5). The conjunctive adverbs include *however, consequently, therefore,* and *otherwise.* They are often preceded by a semicolon.

USE OF A CONJUNCTIVE ADVERB

> The 1928 Pact of Paris offended nobody, since it included no compulsory machinery of enforcement; *hence,* the European nations rushed to sign it.

A coordinate relationship also can be created between two sentences simply by using a semicolon.

USE OF A SEMICOLON

> People are affected by social forces sometimes far removed from their immediate perceptions; they perceive only a relatively small portion of the influences that play upon them.

For further discussion of semicolon use, see Chapter 52.

41c Subordinate less important ideas

To combine two closely related but unequal ideas, use **subordination;** put the more important idea in a main clause and the lesser one in a subordinate clause. Subordinate clauses are typically set off by subordinating conjunctions (such as *although, because, if, since, though,* *unless, until,* and *while*) or by relative pronouns (such as *that, which, who, whom,* and *whose*). (See 30c-3.)

Consider these two sentences:

We know that advertisers are "out to get us."

We do not make much of an attempt to refute advertising messages.

These two statements are closely related, so they could be combined. Since the author's point is that people allow themselves to be seduced by advertising, the second statement is more important (that is, more topic-oriented) than the first. Therefore, the second statement should become the main clause and the first statement should become the subordinate clause.

USE OF A SUBORDINATING CONJUNCTION

Even though we know that advertisers are "out to get us," we do not make much of an attempt to refute their messages.

Here is another example of how a subordinating conjunction can be used to set off a subordinate clause:

Using hands-on experience is one of the best ways of learning. It helps the student learn on a more interactive level.

USE OF A SUBORDINATING CONJUNCTION

Using hands-on experience is one of the best ways of learning, *as* it helps the student learn on a more interactive level.

When one sentence adds information to the entire preceding sentence, it is often possible to convert the second sentence to a relative clause.

The Great Lakes cool the hot winds of summer and warm the cold winds of winter. This gives the state of Michigan a milder climate than some of the other north central states.

USE OF A RELATIVE CLAUSE

The Great Lakes cool the hot winds of summer and warm the cold winds of winter, *which gives* the state of Michigan a milder climate than some of the other north central states.

Relative clauses can sometimes be shortened by getting rid of the relative pronoun.

The Great Lakes cool the hot winds of summer and warm the cold winds of winter, *giving* the state of Michigan a milder climate than some of the other north central states.

When two sentences modify the same noun, you can sometimes embed one into the other as an appositive (see 30c-2).

Julia Cameron was a British photographer. She is considered one of the most important portraitists of the nineteenth century.

USE OF AN APPOSITIVE

Julia Cameron, *a British photographer,* is considered one of the most important portraitists of the nineteenth century.

EXERCISE 41.1

Each of the following items contains two or more sentences that can be combined into one. Use coordination or subordination, as appropriate, to do the combining. (You may rearrange the order of the information any way you like.)

1. In a Molière comedy, the central character is a type, only slightly individualized.
   Tartuffe, for example, is a great artistic creation.
   He is not a living human being.
2. In his youth, Watergate burglar G. Gordon Liddy listened to Hitler's speeches in German on the radio.
   Liddy knew only a few German phrases.
   Liddy often found these speeches very persuasive.
3. In 1848, the Treaty of Guadalupe Hidalgo was signed.
   This treaty ended the Mexican War.
   About half the territory of Mexico was incorporated into the United States.
4. With the land came its inhabitants.
   Many of these inhabitants were Mexican citizens of Spanish or Spanish-Indian descent.
   The majority were Indians.
5. Under the terms of the treaty, former Mexican citizens were granted US citizenship.
   The Indians were treated in the traditional American fashion.
   The subsequent history of the Mexican-American has been one of dispossession and discrimination.
6. There are many ways to form opinions about current events.
   First, you have to gather information.
   You can gather information from a variety of sources, such as newspapers, magazines, and television.

EXER

Practice combining sentences.

7. When you write a paper, the statements should be your own.
   You should never claim a statement as your own if it is not.
   That is called plagiarism.

8. You can help shape your audience.
   You can send your writing to a particular person or persons.
   You can also send your writing to a publication chosen for its readership.

9. Spoken conversation is different from written conversation.
   In spoken conversation, you have limited control over whom you will talk with.
   In written conversation, you have many more options and wider-ranging possibilities in determining the conversation's participants.

10. Margaret Mead was an anthropologist.
    She communicated with many different groups of people, from Samoan tribe people to international political leaders.
    Her writing reflects her unique sense of audience.

(FOR COLLABORATION)

Bring a sample piece of writing to your group; exchange your writing samples, and identify any areas of "choppy" writing that could be improved.

CHAPTER 42

Parallelism

FAQs

▶ What does it mean to make sentences "parallel"?

▶ If I want to set two or more sentences up in parallel, how can I make sure that they match each other? (42a)

▶ How do parallel sentence elements work to make comparisons? (42d)

▶ Why is a set of parallel elements sometimes considered "incomplete"? (42e)

When two or more sentence elements represent comparable ideas, putting them in the same grammatical form helps the reader to see the relationship between them. This stylistic device is called **parallelism.** When Benjamin Franklin wrote "A penny saved is a penny earned," he was using parallelism. The adjective *saved* parallels in content and form the adjective *earned*. If he had written "A penny saved is a penny that someone has earned," his sentence would have been out of balance (and would not have been so memorable!).

Parallelism can not only make writing more elegant; it can also direct the reader's attention to important structural relationships among ideas within sentences. Putting two elements in parallel form makes it easy for the reader to compare them.

AUDIO
Chapter overview.

VIDEO
Achieving parallelism.

42a Put parallel content in parallel form

Words and phrases that are linked by the coordinating conjunctions *and, but, or,* or *nor* often are parallel in content. In such cases, they also should be parallel in form.

cease and *desist*   [Both verbs]

hook, line, and *sinker*   [All nouns]

of the people, by the people, [and] *for the people*   [All prepositional phrases]

Sometimes parallel structures are quite complicated, as in this famous sentence from Abraham Lincoln's Gettysburg Address, contrasting politicians' speeches with soldiers' bravery:

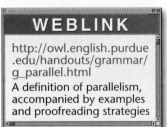

To make sure that you use parallelism appropriately, follow this three-step procedure:

1. Whenever you write a sentence that has words or phrases joined by *and, but, or,* or *nor,* ask yourself whether there is comparable content somewhere on each side of the conjunction. If so, identify exactly what that comparable content is. In the Gettysburg Address, for example, "what we say here" is compared with "what they did here."

WEBLINK

http://owl.english.purdue
.edu/handouts/grammar/
g_parallel.html

A definition of parallelism, accompanied by examples and proofreading strategies

2. Check to see whether the comparable parts are in the same grammatical form. The two parts cited from the Gettysburg Address are both relative clauses, beginning with the same relative pronoun (*what*), followed by a personal pronoun (*we/they*), a verb (*say/did*), and the same adverb (*here*).

3. If the comparable parts are not in the same grammatical form—but should be—use the elements in one part of the sentence as a model and put the elements in the other parts in the same grammatical form.

                              long remember
The world will little note *nor* ~~remember forever~~ . . .

All of this may seem quite complicated, but it is worth learning because parallelism is one of the most powerful tools a writer has for presenting ideas clearly and memorably.

In the following sentence, the conjunction *and* alerts the reader to the possibility that there is comparable content in the two parts of the sentence. The writer seems to be saying that creativity has two identifying characteristics of a similar kind, and the sentence seems to have this kind of structure: Creativity = $X + Y$.

FAULTY   Creativity is being able to identify a situation or problem and the knowledge of how to solve it.

Are *X* and *Y* in the same grammatical form? No: "being able to identify a situation or problem" is a gerund (*-ing*) phrase, whereas "the knowledge of how to solve it" is a noun phrase.

To fix this problem, use the first part of the sentence as a model for the second part. The first part is a gerund phrase, so you can create parallelism by turning the second part into a gerund phrase as well: "knowing how to solve it."

REVISED   Creativity is *being* able to identify a situation or problem and *knowing* how to solve it.

Consider these additional examples of similar sentence elements that can be confusing if their elements are not made parallel:

FAULTY   An expert is someone who knows more and more about increasingly little.

REVISED   An expert is someone who knows *more and more* about *less and less.*

FAULTY   The young talk about what they are doing; old people reminisce about the past; fools only tell what their plans are.

REVISED   The young talk about what they are doing; the old about what they have done; fools about what they plan to do.   [Old French proverb]

(**EXERCISE 42.1**)

Correct the faulty parallelism in the following sentences.

1. Her interests include skiing, running, and bike rides.
2. We must either turn left on Martin Luther King Drive or take a right turn on Main Street.
3. Nothing in the world can take the place of persistence: talent will not, genius will not, being educated won't.
4. My present occupation is repairing appliances, VCRs, and refinishing floors.
5. Mark Twain claimed that a friend is one who will side with you when you are wrong, since when you are right anyone is willing to be on your side.
6. Prejudice is the real robber, and vice murders us.

HELP

How do I find places where I should be using parallelism?

1. Open the SEARCH (or FIND) feature of your word-processing program.
2. Enter the word *and* in the search field, and run the program.
3. Whenever the program highlights an *and*, examine the phrases linked by it to see whether they represent comparable or equivalent content. If they do, they should be in parallel form.
4. Follow the same procedure with *but, or*, and *nor*.

7. What we call the beginning is often the end, and what we referred to as an ending was a place to begin.
8. Destiny is not a matter of chance. It is a matter to be chosen. It is not a thing to be waited for. It is a thing you should try to be achieving.
9. Ask not what your country can do for you; ask what can be done by you for your country.
10. The television commercial is not at all about the character of the products to be consumed. It is about the product consumers' character.

(EXERCISE 42.2)

Select a sample of your own writing. Following the instructions in the preceding Help box, identify all phrases that should be parallel. Where necessary, make appropriate corrections.

42b Make all items in a list or series parallel

Whenever you present any kind of listing in formal or academic writing, whether it is a formatted list such as an outline or just a series of items in a sentence, all of the items should be in the same grammatical form. They are, in effect, being lined up for comparison on an "apples with apples" basis, and readers expect each item to be in similar form. For example, the headings in this chapter constitute a formatted list, with each item set off with a number. Notice how each heading is in the form of an imperative verb phrase ("Put parallel content in . . . ," "Make all items in . . . ," "Use parallelism with . . . "). This parallel structure helps the reader approach each guideline for writing in a similar way; phrasing that goes off in different directions is likely to distract the reader.

NONPARALLEL SERIES REVISED

The last decades of the nineteenth century through the early decades of our present century marked a period when Americans confronted rapid industrialization, a communications revolution, and ~~big business was growing.~~ *the growth of big business.* [A third noun phrase is put into the series to replace the distracting clause.]

All addictions are characterized by compulsion, loss of control, ~~there are~~ negative consequences, and ~~people deny they're addicted.~~ *denial.* [Turning the last two items into noun phrases makes it clear that the sentence contains a series of four items.]

42c Use parallelism with correlative conjunctions

Whenever you use correlative conjunctions such as *both/and, either/or, neither/nor,* or *not only/but,* you are lining up two sentence elements for comparison (see 30a-7). Thus, those elements require parallel grammatical form.

AUDIO

The beauty of correlative constructions.

Either *we go full speed ahead* or *we stop right here.*

In lining up the sentence elements, make sure you place the two conjunctions exactly where they belong, so that the elements after each conjunction are grammatically parallel to each other.

INCORRECT	Solar energy is both used to heat homes and to run small appliances.
REVISED	Solar energy is used *both* to heat homes *and* to run small appliances.
INCORRECT	These three books by Morrison have not only received critical acclaim but also have been widely read.
REVISED	These three books by Morrison *not only* have received critical acclaim *but also* have been widely read.

42d Use parallelism for comparisons or contrasts

A comparison or contrast involves two statements or terms that are seen as somehow equivalent; indeed, it is this equivalence that allows them to be compared. These two statements or terms therefore should be parallel. Abraham Lincoln's use of parallelism in the Gettysburg Address excerpt is a good example. Another good example of contrasting parallelism can be found in Neil Armstrong's famous utterance upon first stepping on the moon: "That's one small step for man, one giant leap for mankind."

42e Make parallel constructions complete and clear

In addition to similar grammatical form, parallelism generally involves one or more words that appear in both parts of the construction. In the Gettysburg Address example, the words *what* and *here* are found in both parts of the sentence; *world* is referred to again with the pronoun *it*. Usually only a few matching words are needed. As writers create parallel sentences, they sometimes forget to pull all the grammatical elements together to make the comparison complete. Some-

42.1
This guide to parallelism includes two quizzes.

> **WEBLINK**
>
> http://webster.commnet.edu/ grammar/parallelism.htm
> Full coverage of parallelism, with good examples and quizzes

times an extra word or two is all that is needed to complete the parallelism and clarify the connection for the reader.

INCOMPLETE PARALLELISM REVISED

It seems apparent to even the casual observer that all people crave some form of recognition,$_\wedge$*that* no one lives in total isolation, and$_\wedge$*that* any

healthy society will find some way to meet this human imperative. [Inserting *that* makes it clearer that there are three things "that seem apparent."]

In other cases, a rearrangement of words or phrases is called for.

MISLEADING   Speculation leads to learning, in the same way that science is supported by theory.

AUDIO
Make parallel elements stand out.

In this sentence, the conceptual analogy between the first part of the sentence and the second part is not clear. Rearranging the words of the mixed comparison solves the problem.

CLEARER   Speculation leads to learning, just as theory leads to
science.   [The revision puts the second part of the sentence into the active voice, matching the first part and
enabling the reader to line up *speculation* and *theory* on the
one hand and *learning* and *science* on the other.]

42f Use parallelism to enhance coherence

As mentioned in Chapter 6, parallelism promotes coherence within
paragraphs (see 6e). If two related sentences are equivalent in function
and content, show their relatedness by putting both in the same grammatical form. In the following example from a psychology text, two
similar *if* constructions are used to create parallel explanations.

> The distinction between formative and summative assessment
> is based on how the results are used. The same assessment proce-
> dure can be used for either purpose. *If the goal is to obtain information
> about student learning for planning purposes, the assessment is formative.
> If the purpose is to determine final achievement (and help determine a
> course grade), the assessment is summative.*
>
> —Anita E. Woolfolk, *Educational Psychology*

42.2
More on
parallelism and
coherence.

Checking for Parallelism with Grouped Elements

1. How many of your sentences have words or phrases
   joined by *and, but, or,* or *nor*? (You can use the SEARCH,
   or FIND, feature to identify them. See the Help box on
   page 762.) *Example:* "She liked apples, but pears were
   what she always preferred."
2. Do your sentences have equivalent content linked by
   these conjunctions—elements that might be compared or
   contrasted? If so, identify exactly what those equivalent
   elements are. *Example:* ". . . liked apples" and "pears . . .
   preferred."
3. Are these comparable sentence elements in the same
   grammatical form? If not, use the elements in one part of
   the sentence as a model, and arrange the other parts in the
   same grammatical form, so that all parts are consistent.
   Example: "She liked apples but always preferred pears."

EXERCISE 42.3

Correct the faulty parallelism in the following sentences.

1. We live in a time when people seem afraid to be themselves, when a hard, shiny exterior is preferred to the genuineness of deeply felt emotion.

2. Most people prefer to watch others exercise rather than participate because exercise is so difficult and it is so easy to lie on a couch.

3. The responsibilities of a stagehand include keeping track of props, changing scenery, and they sometimes help out with special effects.

4. Two complaints being investigated by the task force were lack of promotions for women and writing company memos that were not gender inclusive.

5. Just a generation ago, people would not have dreamed of eating strawberries in September, nor would corn have been available in May.

6. Objectivity is assumed to be fundamental to news reporting, but public relations and advertising personnel are not assumed to be objective.

7. The history of television is a history of technology and policy, economics and sociology, and entertainment and news are part of it, too.

8. Watching an animal in its natural habitat is the most authentic form of animal-viewing experience, followed by a circus or zoo, showing one televised in its natural habitat, and seeing one featured on a late-night talk show.

9. Good therapists will assess a client's general problem fairly early, and provisional goals will be set for the client.

10. Minor hassles—losing your keys, the grocery bag rips on the way to the door, you slipped and fell in front of everyone in a new class, finding that you went through the whole afternoon with a big chunk of spinach stuck in your front teeth—may seem unimportant, but the cumulative effect of these minor hassles may be stressful enough to be harmful.

FOR COLLABORATION

Proverbs often use parallelism. Working together with a friend or classmate, complete each of the following proverbs by putting the words in parentheses into a form that parallels the first part of the sentence. The first one is already done for you.

1. A wise man knows his own ignorance; (fool, thinks, knows, everything). <u>Answer:</u> A wise man knows his own ignorance; a fool thinks he knows everything.

2. Love is a furnace, but (not cook, the stew).

3. If a man steals gold, he is put in prison; (if, land, made, king).

4. You can hardly make a friend in a year, but (easily offend, an hour).

5. Perspective continues to be our greatest shortage, just as (our ironies, most abundant product).

6. We promise according to our hopes, and (perform, fears).

7. She who leaves nothing to chance will do few things ill, but (she, very few things).

8. Fear less, hope more (eat, chew; whine, breathe; talk, say; hate, love); and all good things are yours.

9. The harder the conflict, (glorious, triumph). What we obtain too cheap, (esteem, lightly).

10. Live your own life, for (you, die, death).

EXER

Practice choosing parallel structure.

CHAPTER 43

Emphasis

FAQs

▶ How can I make my main ideas stand out more? (43a–43c)
▶ Why should I avoid using underlined words or fancy typography to create emphasis? (43e)

AUDIO
Chapter overview.

VIDEO
A student's perspective on her writing.

In any writing, some ideas are more important than others. It is helpful to readers if those ideas stand out. This is where emphasis comes in. Emphasis can be created in various ways. Emphatic writing is clear and concise (see Chapter 40), employs coordination and subordination (see Chapter 41), and uses parallelism (see Chapter 42). This chapter discusses some other ways of creating emphasis.

43a Create emphasis through end-weight

All other things being equal, the most emphatic part of a sentence is its ending. This explains the power of Franklin Roosevelt's famous line "The only thing we have to fear is fear itself." If you read that sentence aloud, you can hear your voice rising naturally at the end before abruptly falling. This natural intonation pattern underlies **end-weight.** Using end-weight means putting a key word or phrase where intonation naturally gives it emphasis—at the end of the sentence. If FDR had said "Fear itself is the only thing we have to fear," he would have missed out on a good opportunity to use this principle.

As you edit your writing, look for opportunities to give end-weight to key concepts. In this example, note how the writer made the phrase *better and wiser* more prominent by shifting it toward the end of the sentence:

768 Emphasis

FIRST DRAFT   We all muddle through life, falling along the way. But we will become better and wiser people if we pick ourselves up and keep moving on.

REVISION   We all muddle through life, falling along the way. But if we pick ourselves up and keep moving on, we will become better and wiser for it.

AUDIO

Making a sentence memorable.

EXERCISE 43.1

The following are email tag lines, rewritten in a form less elegant than their original form. Using the end-weight principle, try to restore them to their original form. (Suggestion: First identify a key concept, then try to move the phrase related to that concept to the end of the sentence.)

WWW

43.1

More examples of end-weight.

1. Television is very educational: I go to the library and read a book the minute someone turns it on.
2. Recycled electrons were used to print this message.
3. The tree of liberty grows only when the blood of tyrants waters it.
4. Where ignorance is bliss, to be wise is folly.
5. The heart has its reasons which are not known by reason.
6. You risk even more if you do not risk anything is the trouble.
7. Life is nothing if it is not a daring adventure.
8. Time is the stuff life is made of. Do not squander time if you love life.
9. To gain your heart's desire and to lose it are the two tragedies in life.
10. Courage is the mastery of fear. It is not the absence of it.

43b Create emphasis through selective repetition

Another powerful way of emphasizing important ideas is through repetition—especially when combined with some form of grammatical parallelism. Notice how Studs Terkel uses the repetition of the simple pronoun *my* to emphasize the personal significance of his work:

A further personal note. I find some delight in *my* job as a radio broadcaster. I'm able to set *my* own pace, *my* own standards, and determine for myself the substance of each program. Some days are more sunny than others, some hours less astonishing than I'd hoped for; *my* occasional slovenliness infuriates me . . . but it is, for better or worse, in *my* hands.

—Studs Terkel, *Working*

Repetition is effective only if used judiciously. Overdoing repetition will make your writing boring and wordy (see 40b).

43c Create emphasis through contrast

You can create emphasis through attention-getting contrasts. One approach is to set up opposing words or phrases within a sentence. As with repetition, this technique benefits from the use of parallelism (see 42d).

AUDIO
Contrast and end-weight.

WWW
43.2
Contrast and correlative conjunctions.

The democratic faith is based not as much upon the assumption of leadership by the few as upon the wisdom and conscience of the many.

—Norman Cousins, *Human Options*

In this sentence, the author uses the contrast between *few* and *many* to emphasize the broad-based nature of democratic governance. Note the parallelism between *leadership by the few* and *wisdom and conscience of the many*. If the author had written "The democratic faith is based mainly upon the wisdom and conscience of many people," the statement would have been less emphatic.

Another way of creating emphasis through contrast is by using transitional expressions such as *however, though, while, yet*, or *but* (see 6c-1) to "trump" one idea with another. In this example from a discussion of investigative journalism, note how the writer uses *though* and *while* to emphasize her main point:

While most newspapers carry on a continuous series of investigations of local and often national or international issues, these investigations are limited in their scope. In particular, local journalistic investigations tend to be focused on the illegal, unethical, or personally extravagant activities of public officials or the harmful actions of private individuals or business firms acting against the public interest. *Though* there is often great value to these investigations in keeping both public officials and private interests from plundering the commonweal, they too infrequently address questions like the efficacy or wisdom of the public proposals and plans.

—Phyllis Kaniss, *Making Local News*

43d Create emphasis through careful word choice

You can often produce emphatic writing simply by using vivid, powerful words (see Chapter 45). Even a single carefully chosen word can have a powerful effect. Note the effect Angela Napper achieves by using the words *rages* and *take a stand* in the opening paragraph of her essay on Cybercensorship (see Chapter 7):

With more and more regulations being formed about what citizens

are allowed to view on the Internet, concerns as to the constitutional

rights of these citizens are being raised. At public libraries, at

colleges and universities, and at businesses the debate *rages* as to

how much privacy users should have, and whether censorship of certain

materials is needed to protect the public welfare. More and more it is

becoming clear that citizens need to *take a stand* to protect their

right to privacy and freedom of speech . . . [italics added]

Angela could have chosen a milder expression such as *there is a debate* and *act,* but neither of these have had the power of *the debate rages* and *take a stand.* These more emphatic expressions draw the reader's attention and encourage him or her to take action.

Even simple adverbs can make a difference in how emphatic a statement is. Which of the following sentences seems more emphatic to you?

Robert's GPA is 3.79.

Robert's GPA is *just under* 3.8.

Robert's GPA is *nearly* 3.8.

All three sentences say essentially the same thing, but the second and especially the third subtly imply that Robert's GPA is very high. For readers who already know about GPAs, the extra wording simply adds emphasis.

In using emphatic vocabulary, be sure to be accurate. If you use powerful words just for shock effect without regard for accuracy, you will be accused of *hyperbole* (exaggeration for effect) and will lose your credibility (see 7f-2). To find appropriate powerful replacements for dull expressions, consult your online thesaurus and dictionary (see Chapter 48).

(FOR COLLABORATION)

Pair off with another student and exchange compositions that you have each written. Try to find at least three sentences in your partner's composition that lack emphasis. Following the guidelines in this chapter, revise these sentences.

43e Create emphasis through punctuation or typography

With all the style options available in today's word-processing programs, it is tempting to create emphasis simply through punctuation, formatting, or typography. You can use <u>underlining</u>, **boldface,** *italics,* ALL CAPS, or a special font to draw attention to certain words or phrases. You can use exclamation points (see 50g) and dashes (see 56e). (Note that quotation marks are *not* used for emphasis.) You can use white space, bulleted lists, boxes, and other formatting devices (see 20b). In email, you can even use emoticons, such as :-) to represent ☺ (see 24a-5).

WEBLINK

http://owl.english.purdue
.edu/handouts/general/
gl_emphasis.html

Five techniques for adding
emphasis to your prose

www

43.3

More about the
Web site.

These are all effective techniques, but only if they are used sparingly. Readers quickly become irritated if these kinds of visual devices are used excessively. In general, the more formal the writing, the less you should use such devices. Learn to rely instead on end-weight, parallelism, selective repetition, contrast, and other sentence-construction techniques to add emphasis to your writing.

(EXERCISE 43.2)

Restructure the following sentences so that emphasis is created not by punctuation and typography but by sentence structure.

1. Gravity is the <u>law</u> (and it is also a good idea).
2. Truth can set you free, and it is the only thing that can.
3. A hero is braver than an ordinary man by only five minutes!

4. It was <u>Polish</u> that was Joseph Conrad's first language not English, and most people do not understand that.

5. It would be a LIE if I said that I did not want to see you again.

6. George is looking for a woman who is athletic, romantic, and adventurous and who looks like a super model :-)

7. Capital punishment is one of the most controversial issues discussed in the United States today. The reason why it is such a controversial issue is that it raises many questions—political questions and moral questions. It is an *immensely* difficult issue to deal with!

8. It was **Emily** Brontë who wrote *Wuthering Heights*, not her sister Charlotte.

9. The <u>family</u> cannot be replaced when it comes to keeping children away from drugs. Schools, religious institutions, the police—they all can help.

10. <u>Either</u> passage A or reading passage B, *not both*, should be chosen to be summarized!

EXER

Name the technique used to create emphasis.

CHAPTER 44

Variety

FAQs

▶ How can I jazz up my writing style? (44a–44c)

▶ How much variety should I aim for in my writing? Are there some situations that call for more variety than others? (44d)

AUDIO

Chapter overview.

VIDEO

A demonstration of how to achieve variety.

Good writers always try to make their writing interesting, not only in content but also in style. This is where variety comes in. By varying your style, you change the rhythm of your writing and keep your readers interested. If you write the same kind of sentence over and over again, you are likely to put your readers to sleep.

44a Vary sentence length

One of the easiest and most effective ways to alter the rhythm of your writing is to vary the length of your sentences. Readers usually process one sentence at a time. If sentences are all of similar length, the result will be a monotonous tempo that will bore readers. A mixture of sentences—long, short, and something in between—is much more interesting. You do not have to change length with every sentence, but you certainly should do so from time to time. Note how Barbara Kingsolver does it in the opening paragraph of *The Bean Trees*:

> I have been afraid of putting air in a tire ever since I saw a tractor tire blow up and throw Newt Hardbine's father over the top of the Standard Oil sign. I'm not lying. He got stuck up there. About nineteen people congregated during the time it took for Norman Strick

to walk up to the Courthouse and blow the whistle for the volunteer fire department. They eventually did come with the ladder and haul him down, and he wasn't dead but lost his hearing and in many other ways was never the same afterward. They said he overfilled the tire.

—Barbara Kingsolver, *The Bean Trees*

There are six sentences in this paragraph, varying in number of words as follows: 32-3-5-27-29-6. Not only is this kind of variety pleasing for variety's sake; it also allows the author to emphasize the three short sentences and spin out details in the three long sentences.

Of course, creative writers like Barbara Kingsolver are supposed to do whatever they can to make their writing interesting. But does this principle apply to the kind of ordinary, everyday writing the rest of us do? Yes, it does. Varying the length of your sentences will make your writing more interesting—more readable—no matter what kind of writing it is. Believe it or not, even textbooks can benefit from varied sentence length. Here is an example from the opening paragraph of *Fundamentals of Anatomy and Physiology:*

> The world around us contains a staggering number of living organisms with very different appearances and lifestyles. Despite the diversity of sizes and habits, all living things perform the same basic functions. They respond to changes in their immediate environment. You move your hand away from a hot stove, dogs bark at approaching strangers, fish are scared by loud noises, and tiny amoebas glide toward potential prey. Living things also show adaptability, and their internal operations and responses to stimulation can vary from moment to moment.

—Frederic Martini, *Fundamentals of Anatomy and Physiology*

The sentences in this passage vary in length as follows: 17-15-8-27-19. There is not as much sentence-length variation as in the Kingsolver piece, but it adds to the writing style nonetheless. Notice in particular how the short third sentence makes the main point, while the long fourth sentence provides supporting details. As well as being pleasing to the ear, varying sentence length also helps the reader distinguish between main points and details.

EXERCISE 44.1

Examine a sample of your own writing. Do your sentences vary in length? (Use your word count program to check.) If not, try to revise them so that they do.

44b Vary sentence structure

Another way to alter the rhythm and cadence of your writing is by varying the structure of your sentences. Based on clause structure (see 30c-3), sentences can be divided into four basic types (see 30d-2):

A **simple sentence** contains one independent clause and no other clauses.

A **compound sentence** contains two independent clauses.

A **complex sentence** contains one independent clause and one or more subordinate clauses.

A **compound-complex sentence** contains two independent clauses and at least one subordinate clause.

All four sentence types are found in the following paragraph.

Complex	One of the great paradoxes in history is that the truest expression of Christianity is to be found not in the West but in the East. In India countless millions of people are living
Complex	out the ideas of Christ, though they do not call themselves Christians and are unfamiliar with Christian theology. They
Simple	are the poor, the meek, the merciful, and the pure in heart.
Compound	They regard life as sacred and they will not harm it in any of
Simple	its forms. They practice renunciation. They believe in non-violence and they worship the memory of a human being
Compound-Complex	who perhaps has come closer to enacting Christianity than anyone in modern history. Interestingly enough, Gandhi's
Simple	struggle was directed against a Western Christian nation.

—Norman Cousins, *Human Options*

Notice how pleasing this paragraph is to the ear. By using a variety of sentence structures, Cousins changes the tempo of the writing, avoiding monotony. Notice, too, how the changes in tempo lead to sentences of different length, ranging from three to twenty-six words. Thus, the two strategies—varying sentence length and varying sentence structure—work together.

44c Avoid excessive repetition

Repetition always draws attention. If you use it deliberately to create parallelism (see Chapter 42) or emphasis (see 43b), that is fine. But if you use it for no particular reason, you will only draw attention to your repetitiveness—not a good way to liven up your style! This

var

problem of excessive repetition can occur in a number of ways. Following are some typical sources of excessive repetition:

44.1

A guide to sentence variety.

> **WEBLINK**
>
> http://owl.english
> .purdue.edu/handouts/
> general/gl_sentvar.html
> How to create variety by
> combining, restructuring,
> or varying the length of
> sentences

1. Continual use of sentences of the same length.
2. Continual use of the same sentence type.
3. Overuse of a special grammatical form (for example, passive voice, *there is,* or *it is*).
4. Continual use of the same grammatical subject.
5. Frequent use of the same kind of sentence opener (for example, a subordinate clause, transitional phrase, or adverbial phrase).
6. Frequent use of the same word.

Here is how to avoid these problems: After you have written a draft or two and are ready to edit for style, read the text aloud. Listen especially for rhythm and cadence—the tempo of the writing. Do you notice a consistent tempo from one sentence to the next, creating a sing-song rhythm? If so, revise your writing, using one or more of the Strategies for Increasing Sentence Variety on page 779.

Let us try this procedure on the following short essay:

ORIGINAL

Out of all the experiences I've had throughout my life, I've learned the most through real-life experiences. Working with people, how a hospital system works, and the value of health are a few of the skills I've gained through volunteer work at Rosewood Hospital.

First, working with people has been one of the greatest joys I've had the opportunity to learn. For example, in the hospital there are many patients who need special attention. I am often asked to get them supplies, help them with reading, or just be there for someone to talk to. Through volunteering to help with patients, I've learned how to work easily with others.

Next, gaining knowledge about how the hospital system works is something else I've learned. Watching nurses care for patients and

running errands for them to other areas of the hospital has given me
this knowledge. Observing the hospital system has also helped me
realize that I want to study for a health career in the future.

Finally, the principle of the value of health is the skill I
hold most valuable. Taking care of sick patients has made me realize
how valuable health is. For instance, ...

If you read this essay aloud, you will notice that it suffers from a
monotonous rhythm, which almost lulls you to sleep. This is because
the sentences are similar in length, type, and structure. Except for the
second one, the sentences vary in length from only thirteen to twenty-
one words. Most are complex sentences, and many start with a gerund
phrase (*First, working with people; Next, gaining knowledge about*). It
seems that the writer is trying overly hard to categorize the different
things she has done and learned.

The following revision incorporates many changes that contribute
to sentence variety.

REVISED

Of all the experiences I've had throughout my life, I've learned
the most through real-life ones. By doing volunteer work at Rosewood
Hospital, for example, I've learned how to work with people, how a
hospital system operates, and how important health is.

Learning how to work with people has been a particular joy. Many
patients need special attention, and I am often asked to get them
supplies, help them with reading, or just be there for someone to
talk to. In this way, I've learned how to interact easily with
others.

Something else I've learned is how the hospital system works. By
watching nurses care for patients and running errands for them to
other areas of the hospital, I've learned enough about the hospital
system to know that I want to begin studying for a future career in
healthcare.

var

```
Finally, and most importantly, taking care of sick patients has
made me realize how valuable health is. For instance. . . . .
```

What changes have been made? First, deleting unnecessary verbiage has reduced the total number of words by 19 percent (from 196 to 159). Second, sentence combining has created eight sentences from the original eleven. The result is sentences of varying length—some as short as ten words, others as long as thirty-eight. Third, the types of sentences vary more; now only half the sentences are complex. Furthermore, putting the writer (*I*) more frequently into the grammatical subject position has broken up the heavy pattern of starting sentences with a gerund phrase.

(Caution) In making stylistic changes, be careful not to violate any of the guidelines discussed in Chapters 35 through 43. For example, do not create an excessively long sentence (see 40a); if you decide to move a modifier, do not misplace it (see Chapter 38).

(E X E R C I S E   4 4 . 2)

Test a sample of your own writing for sentence variety. Read it aloud, then revise it as necessary, following the Strategies for Increasing Sentence Variety.

EXER

A self-test on variety.

Strategies for Increasing Sentence Variety

1. Revise for clarity and conciseness (see Chapter 40).
2. If sentences sound short and choppy, try forming an occasional long sentence by combining two shorter ones.
3. If sentences are so long that you have to take a deep breath after each one, create some shorter sentences by dividing a few of the long ones.
4. Move some transitional expressions; they do not always have to be at the beginning of the sentence.
5. Move some modifiers. They often can either precede or follow what they are modifying.
6. Restructure some sentences.
7. Eliminate excessive repetition of words and phrases.

(**FOR COLLABORATION**)

Exchange samples with a friend or member of your group. Offer suggestions for revision by increasing sentence variety.

44d Respect different standards and purposes

In seeking to make your writing more varied and interesting, be sensitive to the kind of writing you are doing and who your audience is. In technical and business writing (see Chapter 25), for example, stylistic variety is not valued as highly as it is in, say, literary or magazine writing (see Chapter 17). Your biology or accounting instructor will probably be less concerned about variety than will your English or history instructor. In this respect, different academic fields are likely to value different styles. The guidelines offered in this chapter will be especially useful in those classes where the instructor puts a premium on stylistic variety.

WEBLINK

http://webster.commnet.edu/ grammar/sentences.htm

Dazzling advice for spicing up your writing, with great examples and a quiz

In nonacademic situations, such as when writing email to friends, you will probably want to use sentence variety for the same reason—to spice up your writing and make it more interesting. But in this case, you can do it in different ways—with sentence fragments, quick shifts of topic, jokes, or digressions (see 24a). In this type of writing, you can punctuate your sentences any way you like—even with emoticons.

44.2

The flexibility of "rules" about style.

Another issue of concern is correctness, especially when you are writing in formal (Standard Edited) English. Dictionaries, grammar books, and handbooks have long included guidelines about what constitutes correct usage and what does not. In general, it is best to observe such guidelines, especially when they are based on the actual practices of our best writers. On the other hand, there are certain other "rules" that are passed along by word of mouth yet have no linguistic or communicative logic to them, such as "Never split an infinitive" (see 38d-2), "Do not end a sentence with a preposition," and "Do not use *hopefully* to mean *I hope*." Expert writers routinely disregard such "rules," and therefore, so should you.

CHAPTER **45**

Choosing the Right Words

FAQs

▸ What is the difference between "denotation" and "connotation"? (45a–45b)

▸ Is there anything I can do to make my writing more colorful? Should I try using figures of speech? (45g-1–45g-2)

▸ What are "clichés"? What is wrong with using them? (45g-3)

Since meaning is conveyed through words, a writer's choice of words, or **diction,** is crucial. Choose your words carefully, and you will make your writing clearer and more interesting; choose your words carelessly, and you may leave your readers frustrated.

AUDIO

Chapter overview.

45a Choose the right denotation

The **denotation** of a word is its basic dictionary meaning. The verbs *walk, stroll, hobble, saunter, promenade, hike, march,* and *tramp* all have the same basic meaning, or denotation—"to move by alternately putting one foot in front of the other, always having at least one foot on the ground." Unlike these words, the verbs *run, walk,* and *crawl* differ in denotation:

Immediately after the accident, Julie *ran* to the nearest house.

Immediately after the accident, Julie *walked* to the nearest house.

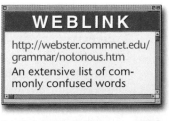

WEBLINK

http://webster.commnet.edu/ grammar/notorious.htm

An extensive list of commonly confused words

Choose the right denotation **781**

Immediately after the accident, Julie *crawled* to the nearest house.

Your first obligation in choosing words is to select ones that accurately denote whatever idea you are trying to convey. If Julie *crawled* to the nearest house, it would be a misrepresentation to say that she either *walked* or *ran.*

By choosing among the various words denoting an event, activity, idea, or object, you can make your focus general or specific, abstract or concrete.

1 General statements versus specific details

As noted in Chapter 6, all good writing involves a mixture of general statements and specific details. General statements establish main points, while specific details make these points precise, vivid, and memorable. Good writers thus continually make choices among words whose denotations range from general to specific. For example, instead of deciding whether Julie *ran, walked,* or *crawled,* the writer could have chosen to use a verb with a more general meaning, such as *go:*

Immediately after the accident, Julie *went* to the nearest house.

This would be an accurate statement regardless of whether Julie crawled, walked, or ran. But it would lack the specificity of the three earlier versions and could mislead the reader, since the manner in which Julie moved tells us something about the seriousness of the accident.

Always look for ways to add specific details to your generalizations. As you do, take care to choose the words that most accurately depict those details.

(EXERCISE 45.1)

Rearrange the words in each of the following sets in order of increasing specificity. The first one has been done for you.

1. vegetation, tree, small tree, small fir tree, small subalpine fir tree
2. pollution, smog, air pollution, dense urban smog, urban smog
3. decoration, plants, ferns, potted plants, interior decoration
4. log cabin, dwelling, old log cabin, building, cabin
5. animal, cow, organism, grazing animal, Guernsey cow
6. wood, building material, hardwood, oak, material
7. casserole, food, shrimp creole, main dish, rice casserole

8. sport, tennis, recreational activity, racquet sport, mixed-doubles tennis

9. garment, men's suit, clothing, tuxedo, suit

10. ceremony, baptism, religious ceremony, baptism by immersion, ritual

2 Abstract versus concrete nouns

Abstract nouns are those that have broad, often vague denotations, such as *power, romance,* and *democracy.* Such words refer to concepts rather than to tangible objects. **Concrete nouns** refer to things that are available to the senses—things that we can see, touch, hear, smell, or taste. For example, *raccoon, Statue of Liberty,* and *radishes* all bring to mind tangible, concrete objects. As with general statements and specific details, you should aim for a mixture of the abstract and the concrete. Abstractions state ideas, while concrete expressions make those ideas more vivid and real.

In the following example, Norman Cousins defines and describes an abstract concept (despair) by means of a series of vivid concrete images: *calling out to one another, frozen faces, clouds racing across the sky.* He even talks about the "breaking up" of words!

> Human despair or default can reach a point where even the most stirring visions lose their regenerating and radiating powers. It will be reached only when human beings are no longer capable of calling out to one another, when words in their poetry break up before their eyes, when their faces become frozen toward their young, and when they fail to make pictures out of clouds racing across the sky.
>
> —Norman Cousins, *Human Options*

3 Commonly confused word pairs

Certain words are commonly confused with certain other words. For example, *imply* is often misused for *infer,* and vice versa. *Imply* means "suggest without stating outright," while *infer* means "derive a conclusion from what is not explicitly stated." *Imply* is something that writers and speakers do; *infer* is something that readers and listeners do. Thus:

When he spoke to the employees, Mr. Adams ~~inferred~~ *implied* that they

would get a raise.

Some employees ~~implied~~ *inferred* from his comments that it would be a big raise.

In other words, *imply* and *infer* have different denotations, and as a careful user of English you should observe this difference.

Other word pairs that are often confused include *install/instill, emigrate/immigrate, adapt/adopt, specially/especially, respectfully/respectively, raise/rise, lay/lie,* and *sit/set.* If you are uncertain about any of these, consult the Usage Glossary at the end of this book.

(**Grammar Checker Alert**) Grammar checkers flag only those words that are in their list of "commonly confused words"—typically a restricted list. For example, *Microsoft Word 2000* has eighty-six entries in its list, most of which are confused only in spelling (see 49b), not pronunciation, such as *yolk/yoke, urn/earn,* and *no/know.* It does not include any of the words mentioned above, which are often confused in both spelling *and* pronunciation. Thus, do not rely on your grammar checker to identify commonly confused words for you. You'll have to do much of the work yourself.

45b Choose the right connotation

Connotations are the extra nuances of meaning that distinguish otherwise synonymous words. *Walk, stroll, hobble, saunter, promenade, hike, march,* and *tramp* all are considered synonyms, yet each brings to mind a somewhat different image. Make sure that you are aware of a word's connotations before you use the word; otherwise, the message you convey to your readers may be very different from the one you intended, as in this excerpt from an annual Christmas letter to family and friends.

WEBLINK

http://www.uottawa.ca/
academic/arts/writcent/
hypergrammar/diction
.html

A hyperlinked discussion of denotation, connotation, catch phrases, and clichés

45.1

Some basics about diction.

MISLEADING   It was another interesting year on the social scene. People say we have the most *contrived* parties in town.

The writer meant to say that their parties reflect ingenuity and cleverness. But *contrived* connotes a phoniness and artificiality that the author did not mean to convey.

The synonyms in each of the following sets can be used to describe people. But some of the terms have more favorable connotations than others. Rearrange each set to order the terms from most favorable to least favorable. If you are unsure of the synonyms' connotations, choose the most common term in the group and look it up in a dictionary. You may find usage notes there to help you.

1. apt, intelligent, clever, bright, smart, shrewd
2. gaunt, skinny, slender, thin, slim, lanky
3. aggressive, domineering, dynamic, assertive, pushy, forceful
4. funny, silly, humorous, comical, amusing, ridiculous
5. poor, insolvent, destitute, broke, penniless, indigent
6. clique, circle, clan, faction, gang
7. solitary, independent, self-reliant, separate, autonomous
8. immature, childlike, innocent, green, callow
9. animalistic, bestial, wild, untamed, unbroken
10. unkempt, sloppy, disheveled, messy, untidy

45c Find the right level of formality

Sometime in the course of growing up, children learn that they should speak more formally, or "correctly," to adults than to their peers. In other words, they learn to shift **registers,** or levels of formality. People continue to adjust registers naturally, if imperfectly, throughout their lives, in part through their selection of words. Words vary in their level of formality, from very formal to colloquial. Always listen to what you are writing, to make sure that you consistently use words in the appropriate register.

1 Formal, academic vocabulary

Virtually all writing you do for school and college assignments (except for special cases such as creative writing or personal narratives) should be in a fairly formal register, as is this handbook. Formal, academic vocabulary consists largely of words derived from Latin and Greek—words like *inevitable, hypothesis, perception, theory,* and *superfluous*—which is why you are tested on such words when you take the SAT or ACT exam. The formal register excludes contractions (such as *can't, they'll,* and *you're*) and colloquialisms (such as *uptight, get movin',* and *dig up*).

Try to learn as many Greco-Latinate words as you can (see Chapter 47). And once you have learned them well, feel free to use them wherever they seem appropriate. *Appropriate* is the key word here; simply using as many "big words" as possible will not impress anyone. If you overdo it, you will likely misuse some of the words; in any case, your writing will sound stuffy and pretentious.

2 Informal vocabulary

Informal words are those you might use in ordinary, everyday contexts such as talking with friends and sending email messages. The informal register consists mainly of words derived from the Germanic roots of English—words such as *keep, laugh, throw, kitchen,* and *hassle.* Such words tend to be shorter than their Latinate equivalents, but they are often used with prepositions to form longer **idiomatic expressions.** For example, the formal Latinate words *inspect* and *examine* have as their equivalent the informal idiomatic phrase *take a close look at.* The informal register also contains many **contractions,** such as *can't, she's,* and *they'll.*

(**ESL Note**) The difficulties of idiomatic phrases for non-English speakers are discussed in Chapter 63 (63c).

Although informal vocabulary is sometimes acceptable in formal writing, you should generally try to use the more formal equivalents where possible.

Informal	*Formal*	*Informal*	*Formal*
friendly	amicable	do again	repeat
worn out	exhausted	go faster	accelerate
hard-working	industrious	take apart	dismantle
funny	amusing	get hold of	seize

(**Grammar Checker Alert**) Your grammar checker will probably identify some common colloquialisms, such as *real, awfully, kind of,* and *plenty,* but it will generally not draw your attention to informal expressions such as those listed above. You will need to monitor your own word usage.

(**EXERCISE 45.3**)

Give a formal equivalent for each of the following informal terms.

1. cheap

2. put up with
3. take into account
4. under the weather
5. a lot of clapping
6. kind of like
7. put down
8. get something straight
9. take grief from
10. a bunch of

EXERCISE 45.4

Translate each of the following sentences into a more formal register.

1. If you turn up any glitches in the program, let me know.
2. Ahab was so hung up on tracking down the white whale, he went out of his mind.
3. When the savings and loans started going belly up in the 1980s, many small investors found themselves up a river without a paddle.
4. Right now, good jobs are hard to come by.
5. Too often the blame for all the ills of welfare is put on the backs of social workers.
6. The guy next door got taken by a con artist selling vinyl siding.
7. My kid brother fixes cars at the garage downtown.
8. The food at the new restaurant is cheap but good.
9. Customers shouldn't have to put up with crappy service.
10. Government waste makes me sick.

45d   Avoid jargon, slang, or dialect

There are many versions of English, only one of which—Standard Edited English—is represented in this book. Standard Edited English is the version most widely used in academic and professional contexts and most widely understood around the world. Other versions, including jargon, slang, and dialect, are valuable in their own right. However, they are less widely understood, and thus you should refrain from using them except with audiences composed of "insiders" or members of special interest groups.

VIDEO

Exploring appropriate language.

Jargon is any technical language used by professionals, sports enthusiasts, hobbyists, or other special interest groups. By naming objects and concepts that are unique to a group's special interests, jargon facilitates communication among members of the group. (Imagine computer engineers trying to get by without terms like *buffer, cache, serial port, CPU,* and *configuration.*) But it has the opposite effect when used with outsiders. Unless you are addressing an audience of fellow insiders, avoid using jargon.

Used by teenagers and other subcultures, **slang** is a deliberately colorful form of speech whose appeal depends on novelty and freshness. For this reason, slang terms tend to be short-lived, quickly giving way to newer, fresher replacements. At the time this book was written, student slang included terms such as *deebo, diss, phat, chill,* and *stoked,* and hacker slang included *obviosity, fritterware, hackification, frob,* and *cruft* (all of which are now probably outdated). Like jargon, slang is understood and appreciated only by insiders. If you are trying to reach a broad audience, avoid using it.

(**Grammar Checker Alert**) Your grammar checker will probably not be able to help you identify much jargon or slang. Word analysis is done by accessing the dictionary on your computer, and such dictionaries often do not include jargon or slang terms. Thus, if you use a slang word such as *tweak* or *bro',* your grammar checker will flag the word but say only, "Not in dictionary." If the word happens to have an ordinary nonjargon, nonslang meaning, such as *cache* or *buffer,* the grammar checker will find it in the dictionary and not flag the word at all.

(**ESL Note**) A good Web site for learning American slang and idiomatic expressions is *Weekly Words* at *<www.students.uiuc.edu>.*

45.2

A brief linguistic discussion of Ebonics.

AUDIO

Using jargon, slang, and dialect appropriately.

A **dialect** is the type of speech used by a specific social, ethnic, or regional group. Dialects typically have a distinctive accent, many unique words and expressions, and even some grammatical patterns that differ from those of Standard Edited English. For example, in some dialects you might hear a sentence like "She be working hard" or "They might could of done it." While perfectly logical and correct within that dialect, such sentences are likely to confuse outsiders— that is, people who do not speak that dialect. Thus, if you are addressing a broad audience, avoid using dialect in your writing.

(**EXERCISE 45.5**)

Log on to a chat group, newsgroup, or other Internet site where slang, jargon, or dialect is being used. Print out several sentences, and translate them into Standard Edited English.

Share both the initial sentences and your "translated" versions with your group.

45e Avoid pretentiousness

College students are continually exposed to the discourse of academics—professors, scholars, textbook writers—who have spent most of their adult lives developing a large vocabulary and an embellished style of writing. If you find yourself tempted to imitate this style of discourse, do so with great caution. You are at risk of sounding pretentious.

VIDEO
Avoiding pretentiousness in academic writing.

PRETENTIOUS   By virtue of their immersion in a heterogeneity of subcultures, the majority of individuals have internalized an extensive repository of collective aphorisms about a multitude of quotidian concerns.

The following rewritten version says essentially the same thing but in clearer, simpler language:

45.3
Prize-winning examples of pretentious writing.

BETTER   Because of their participation in a variety of subcultures, most people know a large number of common sayings about many everyday issues.

Two of the most common causes of pretentiousness are:

1. *Using literary language in nonliterary writing.* When you are reading a great work of literature such as *Moby Dick,* you may become enthralled with words such as *doleful, naught,* and *convivial.* But such words have very restricted conditions of usage; indeed, that is one reason why poets and other creative writers like to use them. Unless you know exactly how these words should be used, do not use them—you will only sound foolish.

2. *Using big words just because they are big.* Academic vocabulary has many long, Latinate-sounding words such as *recalcitrant, egalitarian,* and *indissoluble.* Be sure you know exactly what these words mean and how to use them, however, or you will likely misuse them.

EXERCISE 45.6

Common sayings and proverbs usually use simple words so that children can easily learn them. Notice how silly they sound when reworded below with pretentious vocabulary. Restore these sentences to their normal form.

1. In locales displaying visible fumes, one can expect to find combustion.
2. A dyad of uppermost anatomical extremities outperforms a single such entity.
3. Genetically similar members of the aviary realm manifest a pronounced desire to congregate.
4. The greater the number of alterations in whatever is perceived to have a separate existence, the greater the amount of equivalency in those entities.
5. The fruit of any of the various trees of the genus *Quercus,* after moving under the influence of gravity, does not come to rest at any considerable distance from the parent plant.
6. Irrespective of the direction in which one moves, one finds oneself in that particular place.
7. Your harsh, abrupt canine utterance is directed upward at the incorrect tall, woody plant.
8. A single complete movement of a threaded needle when accomplished within a certain amount of passing time prevents nine such movements.
9. Human beings who inhabit dwellings fashioned from transparent material ought not to hurl projectiles consisting of earthy or mineral matter.
10. It is futile to make inarticulate sobbing sounds after whitish liquid falls out of its container.

45f Try to please the ear

Although most writing is meant to be read silently, many readers sound out words as they read. Such readers will respond unconsciously to the sound pattern of your writing and will appreciate sentences with a nice rhythm, without heavy rhyming, repetition, or alliteration (repetition of an initial sound).

AUDIO

Read your draft to hear your sentences out loud.

> UNRHYTHMIC   A ban on cloning would be a poor plan, mollifying maybe those whom cloning horrifies but not doing anything else, I think.
>
> BETTER   A ban on cloning would do little, I think, but reassure those who fear it.

The first version of this sentence suffers from distracting attempts at rhyme (*ban/plan, mollifying/horrifies*), alliteration (*poor plan, mollifying maybe*), and repetition (*cloning/cloning*). The revised version avoids these problems, making the sentence easier to read.

45g Use figurative language thoughtfully

Figurative language uses words in nonliteral, creative ways to enhance the reader's understanding. Such nonliteral uses of words are called **figures of speech.** Two of the most common figures of speech are simile and metaphor, both of which attempt to explain the unfamiliar by comparing it to the familiar.

1 Similes

A **simile** is the explicit use of one thing (called the *vehicle*) to describe another (the *tenor*). In the following example, scientist Carl Sagan uses similes to explain how the two hemispheres of the brain work:

> The left hemisphere processes information sequentially; the right hemisphere simultaneously, accessing several inputs at once. The left hemisphere works in series; the right in parallel. *The left hemisphere is something like a digital computer; the right like an analog computer.*
>
> —Carl Sagan, *The Dragons of Eden*

Assuming that readers are more familiar with computer technology than with neuroscience, Sagan uses the former to explain the latter.

Similes are created in the space of a single sentence, normally using the word *like* or *as* to make a simple, straightforward comparison. When a simile extends beyond one sentence, it is called an **analogy.**

2 Metaphors

A **metaphor** is an implicit simile. It draws the reader's attention to a surprising similarity between otherwise dissimilar things, but it does so without using *like, as,* or other explicit markers. Metaphors are much more common than similes. In fact, some scholars claim that most of our everyday language is metaphorical in nature. When you say "Her ideas *cast some light* on the subject" or "I *fell* into a deep depression," you are speaking metaphorically. Feel free to use metaphors in your writing, as Gretel Ehrlich does in this passage describing springtime in the Wyoming plains:

> Spring weather is capricious and mean. It snows, then blisters with heat. There have been tornadoes. They lay their elephant trunks

out in the sage until they find houses, then slurp everything up and leave. I've noticed that melting snowbanks hiss and rot, viperous, then drip into calm pools where ducklings hatch and livestock, being trailed to summer range, drink. With the ice cover gone, rivers churn a milkshake brown, taking culverts and small bridges with them.

—Gretel Ehrlich, *The Solace of Open Spaces*

Ehrlich's use of metaphor gives us a vivid picture of Wyoming spring weather. She describes tornadoes in terms of elephants, melting snowbanks in terms of snakes (*viperous*), and rivers in terms of milkshakes. In using words such as *capricious* and *mean,* she gives the weather a distinct human personality. This is an example of the use of **personification,** in which inanimate objects or abstractions are described as having human traits.

You can use different metaphors in a single piece of writing, as Ehrlich does, so long as you do not put them too close together. Otherwise, you will have what is called a **mixed metaphor.**

MIXED METAPHOR The idea was hatched two years ago, but it didn't catch fire until last month, when the school principal decided to jump on board.

—Adapted from Richard Lederer, *Anguished English*

This sentence mixes three incompatible metaphors: newborn chicks, fires, and boats.

3 Clichés

When they are still fresh, metaphors add sparkle to writing. But over time, if they are used heavily, they become worn out and lose their charm. An overused metaphor is called a **cliché.** Clichés are especially common in political discourse, because when politicians discover a catchy phrase that scores well with the public, they like to use it over and over. In a 1996 television appearance, presidential candidate Ross Perot used the term "a giant sucking sound" to describe the thousands of American jobs being transferred to Mexico via the North American Free Trade Agreement. It went over so well with the viewing audience that other politicians and media figures began using it. Soon, however, it had lost its freshness and was just another hackneyed expression.

WEBLINK

http://www.westegg.com/cliche/

A fun-to-use site with 3,300 clichés indexed

WC

How do clichés differ from ordinary idiomatic expressions such as *take a close look at, take someone for a ride,* and *learn the nuts and bolts of something,* which are also used frequently (see 45c-2, 63c)? Clichés are simply more noticeable, either because they evoke extremely vivid images (*white as a ghost, climbing the ladder of success*) or because they are repeated so frequently (*It's the real thing, Just do it*). They draw attention, which makes them more effective at first but also causes them to wear out quickly.

Clichés are generally less irritating in conversation than they are in writing because, like idiomatic expressions, they help speakers cope with the moment-to-moment pressure of putting ideas into words. When you have time to *plan* your thoughts—as you do when writing— you should make an effort to be original or at least use less hackneyed expressions.

Advertisers and headline writers sometimes use clichés and other idiomatic expressions in creative ways. For example, an ad for a dual-processor computer was headlined "Two brains are better than one," a catchy twist on the cliché, "Two heads are better than one." Such playfulness is less common in academic writing.

WWW

45.4
Examples of catchy head-lines and ads.

(**Grammar Checker Alert**) Most grammar checkers are programmed to identify certain clichés and overused expressions. But this means that they do *not* identify *other* clichés and overused expressions. Thus, your grammar checker is probably not entirely reliable in highlighting such expressions. You'll have to be vigilant yourself and try to develop an "ear" for detecting overused expressions.

(**EXERCISE 45.7**)

Think of five clichés and write them down. Where have you heard them? What does this tell you about your customary sources of infor-mation? Just for fun, imagine that you are a subversive graffiti artist. How would you alter these clichés to make them interesting or truth-ful? (For example, instead of the advertising slogan "Come to where the flavor is," you might write "Come to where the *cancer* is.")

EXER
Identify clichés and other dic-tion errors.

(**EXERCISE 45.8**)

Revise the following sentences (from Richard Lederer, *Anguished English*) to get rid of the clichés and mixed metaphors.

1. I wouldn't be caught dead in that movie with a ten-foot pole.
2. In our school, freshmen are on the lowest rung of the totem pole.
3. Flexibility is one of the cornerstones of program budgeting.

4. He was a very astute politician with both ears glued to the ground.
5. Many cities and towns have community gardening programs that need a little more help to get off the ground.
6. The slowdown is accelerating.
7. The sacred cows have come home to roost with a vengeance.
8. The bankers' pockets are bulging with the sweat of the honest working man.
9. When we get to that bridge, we'll jump.
10. It's time to grab the bull by the tail and look it in the eye.

CHAPTER 46

Language and Power

FAQs

▶ What variety of English is used in US colleges and universities? (46a)

▶ What is *bias,* and how is it expressed? (46b)

▶ What is sexist about a sentence such as "Everyone should pay attention to his spelling"? (46c-2)

▶ How can I avoid stereotyping? (46c-3, 46f)

Language is arguably the single most powerful tool we humans have. It is what sets us apart from all other species. It helps us think through problems. It allows us to explore and understand highly nuanced, abstract ideas. It lets us record complex information for future use. And every day, it routinely lets us communicate with other people near and far.

For all these things to happen, our use of language must satisfy two conditions. First, it must *conform to certain conventions or norms.* If you're stopped at an intersection and your friend says, "The light's green," you make sense of her utterance by knowing that "light" probably refers to the traffic light, that "green" refers to its color, that "'s" is a contraction of "is," and that the utterance as a whole constitutes a statement about the color of the traffic signal. These understandings are all based on conventions of word meaning and word order in English. Indeed, knowing English means knowing such *conventions of language.* Furthermore, you need to know certain *conventions of culture,* in this case the fact that a green traffic light in the United States authorizes drivers to proceed ahead. Finally, you need to know certain *conventions of situated meaning,* whereby in a case such as this you interpret your friend's remark not simply as a description of the traffic signal but as a suggestion to drive ahead.

Second, our use of language must be *flexible and creative* enough to accommodate changing circumstances and communicative needs. As we go through life, each situation we encounter is different, with its own demands. Sometimes, the best way to deal with such situations is to be creative and "bend the rules" of language. This kind of creative adaptation is commonplace in society. When new technologies, ideas, events, and so on occur, we often invent new names for them: *spyware, blog, Weaponsgate*. If we move to a new geographic area, we may have to adapt our language to regional differences: a *cooler* in one part of the country might be called an *ice chest* in another. Even in the course of a day, as we move from one context to another, we may alter our use of language in subtle, unconscious ways. "The light's green," for example, could have a different meaning in a different context. If your friend knows you have a romantic interest in a new acquaintance, and she discovers he's unattached, she might say "The light's green" to give you encouragement.

These two qualities—conventionality and flexibility—are in opposition to each other, creating a productive tension. We need to observe conventional norms so as to communicate with each other—this is a basic requirement. But by "bending the rules" at times, we can also adapt to new situations and needs. Furthermore, by being flexible we can inject creativity and playfulness into our interactions with other people, adding spice to these interactions and enhancing our social identities.

46a "Correctness"

Many students begin a writing course thinking that there is only one "correct" type of English, that all others are "incorrect." It's true that in US colleges and universities one style of writing, Standard Edited English, is considered the norm. Standard Edited English is the variety of English used not only in academia but in virtually every profession and occupation that requires higher education. It is the variety used by broadcasters and newspapers across the nation, giving it widespread influence and prestige in our media-saturated society. Therefore, to help prepare you both for college writing assignments and for your future career, your writing instructor will

46.1

Correctness: writing vs. speaking.

no doubt insist on adhering to Standard Edited English. In other words, Standard Edited English is the correct style to use in the context of a college-level composition class, and the guidelines laid down in Parts 6–12 of this book are designed accordingly.

Bear in mind, though, that correctness of language use is always relative to a context and purpose. In an informal setting, such as chatting with other students or sending a casual email message to your best friend, you may prefer to use an informal style sprinkled with slang or accentuated with dialect (see 45d). In the workplace or on the playing field, you may find it most comfortable to use a style of speech with lots of technical or sports jargon (45d). In situations such as these, you are interacting with a small group of "insiders" who share a common purpose or background. Using slang, jargon, or dialect may be more appropriate than using Standard Edited English in these contexts because it enables you to convey ideas faster and more efficiently and it reinforces the cultural bond you have with your audience. Indeed, the power of language is maximized to the extent that you have *mastery* of different styles (or norms) and can *shift* from one style to another as the situation requires.

46b Language and identity

As suggested above, language not only conveys information about some topic, it also conveys information about you and your audience. That is, your use of language in a particular situation reveals much about your social identity, or *persona* (3b-2), how you view the world, and how you perceive the relationship between you and the person(s) you are speaking or writing to. If you want to promote personal rapport between you and your audience, one way to do it is by adopting a style of language that you and your audience are comfortable with, a style that indicates shared experiences and shared beliefs.

The power of language can be used negatively, however, as well as positively. One of the main ways in which language can cause harm is through bias, the one-sided (usually negative) characterization of an entire group. Bias can be either direct ("All Catholics are _____") or indirect ("Jody's a southerner, so she tends to _____"). It can arise from a single discriminatory term, an ill-conceived sentence, or a poorly chosen example or illustration. Bias is so endemic to all human societies that people often are not even conscious of it. That, however, does not make it acceptable. Writers should try at all times to avoid bias in their writing, in ways that the following sections suggest.

46c Avoid biased gender references

In the past, men and women had distinctly different roles in society. The tasks performed primarily by men were considered high-status jobs, and the work done mostly by women was considered low-status. Language developed accordingly. The head of a committee was called a chair*man,* the work done by the labor force was known as *man*power, and humanity itself was referred to as *man*kind or just *man.*

> **WEBLINK**
>
> http://www1.umn.edu/
> urelate/style/
> language-bias.html
> A sensible discussion of
> nonsexist language usage,
> from the *University of
> Minnesota Style Manual*

> **WEBLINK**
>
> http://owl.english.purdue
> .edu/handouts/general/
> gl.nonsex.html
> Good advice on nonsexist
> language, following guide-
> lines from the National
> Council of Teachers of
> English

46.2
An online guide
to avoiding sex-
ist language.

A doctor was presumed to be male; in the relatively few cases where a woman happened to be a doctor, she was referred to as a *woman doctor.* A nurse, on the other hand, was presumed to be female; gender was indicated only in those relatively few cases involving a *male nurse.* And the default pronoun for secretaries, elementary school teachers, or flight attendants was *she.*

Today, women are pursuing career paths long dominated by men, participating in what were once considered male sports, and challenging the myth of male superiority in other ways. Also, men are following career paths once thought for women only. To acknowledge and encourage this trend, we all need to rethink our use of gender references. Since language is our primary means of communicating, we need to be more conscious about how we use it.

1 Gender-specific nouns

Many nouns in the English language implicitly discriminate against women because they emphasize one gender over another. If you use a word like *chairmen* to refer to a group of men and women, you are discriminating against the women in the group; a better choice would be *chairpersons* or just *chairs*. Likewise, female-marked terms such as *poetess* and *hostess* unnecessarily highlight the gender of the person involved; unless you think the person prefers such a term, use *poet* and *host* instead. In general, do not use gender-marked terms in situations where a person's gender should not be of any relevance. Fortunately, it is relatively easy to find nonsexist equivalents for such words. Your grammar checker should be helpful.

Sexist	*Gender-neutral*
businessmen	businesspersons
chairmen	chairs, chairpersons
congressmen	representatives
foremen	supervisors
mankind	humanity, humankind
manpower	personnel, staff
policemen	police officers
salesmen	salesclerks, salespersons
stewardesses	flight attendants
workmen	workers

2 Generic pronouns

Pronouns are more of a challenge, because the English language lacks a gender-neutral pronoun in the third-person singular. Traditionally, *he, him,* and *his* were used as **generic pronouns** to refer to all members of a group, regardless of sex. A sentence such as "Everyone should pay attention to his spelling" would (in theory) apply to both males and females. But studies have shown that when people are asked to visualize the meaning of such a sentence, they usually think of a male. Thus, the so-called generic pronoun is actually discriminatory in its psychological effects.

(**Grammar Checker Alert**) Most grammar checkers will flag gender-specific nouns such as those listed in 46a-1. However, they will not flag generic pronouns. Thus, you will have to deal with this problem yourself.

There is no simple way around this problem. How to Avoid the Generic Pronoun Problem lists four techniques, all of which are employed by expert writers.

> ## How to Avoid the Generic Pronoun Problem
>
> 1. *Pluralize the antecedent and use* they/their: "All writers should pay attention to their spelling."
> 2. *Restructure the entire sentence to get rid of the pronoun:* "Spelling deserves careful attention." This often works, but it lacks the vividness of the personal pronoun.
> 3. *Keep the singular antecedent and use* he or she (*or* his or her, *or* him or her): "Everyone should pay attention to his or her spelling." This is a cumbersome solution and should be used sparingly.
> 4. *Use the passive voice to get rid of an antecedent subject:* "Spelling should be paid close attention to." This solution produces an indirect statement that is less forceful than an active-voice statement; it too should be used sparingly.

AUDIO

Strategies to avoid generic pronoun problems.

3 Stereotyping in examples

Stereotyping can arise unwittingly through the careless use of examples and illustrations. If you use examples that consistently portray women as homemakers and men as breadwinners, you will be reinforcing a longstanding stereotype. Try to vary the roles of men and women in your examples, thereby broadening the spectrum of possibilities for both sexes.

46d Avoid biased language about race and ethnicity

Just as offensive as gender stereotyping is language that either intentionally or unintentionally discriminates against people because of their race or ethnicity. Obviously this type of language includes slurs, which are clearly a form of deliberate verbal aggression. But it also includes the sort of disparaging stereotyping evident in ethnic jokes and in statements like "_____ would do better if they just worked harder."

Terms such as *inner-city residents* and *illegal immigrants* also can be discriminatory if they are consistently linked to a specific ethnic or racial group. Although such terms do have legitimate uses, they are often used as indirect labels, or "code words," to refer only to certain kinds of inner-city residents or illegal immigrants. Do not let yourself be drawn into this kind of stereotyping.

Like sexism, ethnic and racial stereotypes can be reinforced by poorly chosen examples and illustrations. If you are writing about welfare recipients, for instance, and you use a single, teenaged African American mother as your main example, you will be perpetuating a longstanding, discriminatory myth. (Most welfare recipients in the United States are, in fact, white.)

Understandably, people are sensitive about the names used to describe their ethnic or racial identity because of the connotations that invariably attach to them. Since ethnic and racial labels often change over time, the issue can be confusing: should you use *American Indian* or *Native American? Hispanic* or *Latino? African American* or *black?* The best rule of thumb is to call people by whatever term they prefer, just as you should pronounce their personal name however they want it pronounced. If you are unsure of what name to use to describe a certain group of people, just ask members of that group.

46e Avoid biased language about age

In our youth-oriented culture, it is not uncommon to hear demeaning references to age. Indeed, the adjective *old* often is used gratuitously as a way of denigrating others, as in "When the first President Bush lost reelection, people said that was the end of the line for old George." (This is the same man who, five years later, took up skydiving!) Although it is true that people undergo certain changes as they age and that some of these changes are undesirable, other changes are for the better. Avoid focusing on the negative aspects of aging and assuming that anyone beyond a certain age is unworthy of respect. Do not use expressions like *old fogey, one foot in the grave,* and *over the hill,* and avoid age-related stereotypes in examples and jokes.

46f Avoid biased language about other differences

Occupational, religious, political, regional, socioeconomic, sexual-orientation, and disability-related groups are among the many other

www

46.3

Examples of biased language.

groupings in our society that are subject to stereotyping. As with ethnic groups, it is generally best to refer to such groups in ways that they themselves prefer. For example, most people with physical disabilities prefer to be called *physically disabled* rather than *handicapped*, and most people who clean buildings prefer the title of *custodian* rather than that of *janitor*. Political *conservatives* usually do not like being called *right-wingers*, nor do *Pentecostals* appreciate the label *holy rollers*. Sometimes people invent new labels just to exalt themselves, as in the case of one airline's flight attendants who decided to call themselves *personal service managers*. Most of the time, however, relabeling is driven by a desire to cast off undesirable connotations. This is a legitimate desire, worthy of respect.

EXER

Avoiding biased language.

EXERCISE 46.1

Remove the biased language from the following sentences, and replace it with more acceptable terminology.

1. The newly revised cookbook would be a welcome addition to any woman's library.
2. Orientals are good at math.
3. A professional nurse has a responsibility to keep up with developments in her field.
4. The old man must be pretty senile to believe that!
5. The church held a food drive to make sure that no little black children went hungry.
6. We await the day when man discovers a cure for the common cold.
7. Old people are not able to look after themselves.
8. The physical education teacher told the two boys not to speak Puerto Rican in her class.
9. We must pay attention to the needs of the deaf and dumb.
10. The shrewd Jewish businessman made a handsome profit.

EXERCISE 46.2

Revise the following passage to make it bias-free.

The clear superiority of the Anglo-American culture placed great pressure on the wretched immigrants to blend into this better way of life. Poor immigrant urchins learned more quickly than the old people to drop their backward ways and language for the more progressive customs of English-speaking Americans. In fact, just a few short years after their forefathers had arrived poverty-stricken, illiterate, and disease-ridden from the slums of Europe, the grandsons of immigrants had embraced a new American identity and way of life.

(FOR COLLABORATION)

Share your revised versions of the passage with your group.

CHAPTER 47

Building a Powerful Vocabulary

FAQs

▶ How can I improve the vocabulary in my writing?

▶ Word definitions are always referring to meanings from ancient languages like Latin and Greek. Why should I pay attention to those meanings? (47a)

AUDIO

Chapter overview.

Writing, in its simplest definition, is "putting words on paper" (or on a computer screen). Words are the nuts and bolts, the essential ingredient, of the entire enterprise. In order to write well, writers need to know lots of words—a large vocabulary means more tools to work with.

In general, the best way to learn the sort of vocabulary needed for academic and professional writing is through reading. Reading exposes you to a greater variety of words than does television, radio, conversation, or any other form of communication. Reading—whether of course textbooks, news magazines, a Toni Morrison novel, or online discussions—is the best way to develop a strong vocabulary.

As you come across new words in your reading, you can accelerate your learning of them by employing some basic strategies. This chapter describes those strategies.

47a Learn roots, prefixes, and suffixes

Sometimes when you encounter an unfamiliar word, you can make an educated guess at its meaning by looking closely at its parts—

its root and whatever prefixes or suffixes it may have. The **root** (or **stem**) of a word is its core, the part to which prefixes and suffixes are attached. A **prefix** is a word part that precedes the root; a **suffix** is one that follows it. Thus, in the word *renewal*, *-new-* is the root, *re-* is the prefix, and *-al* is the suffix. By recognizing that *re-* sometimes means "again," *-new-* means "new," and *-al* marks a noun form, you can guess that *renewal* is a noun meaning something like "making new again."

This kind of educated guesswork can be very productive in enlarging your vocabulary, especially the vocabulary needed for academic and profes-

WEBLINK

http://webster.commnet.edu/grammar/vocabulary.htm
An excellent guide to building a better vocabulary, with links to online resources and activities

www
47.1
How to build your vocabulary.

sional writing and reading. Most of the specialized terms found in academic and professional discourse were created from Latin and Greek roots, prefixes, and suffixes. *Introvert, counterintuitive, antibiotic,* and *hypothesis* are typical of words formed from Latin and Greek parts. By recognizing the parts and then noting the context in which the words are found, you can narrow down the possible meanings. With multiple exposures to a word—and perhaps some help from a dictionary—you can gradually learn the exact meaning of the word and how it should be used.

Some Common Roots

VIDEO
Using roots to build vocabulary.

Root	Meaning	Examples of words
-audi- (L)	to hear	audible, audience, auditorium
-bene- (L)	good, well	benefit, benevolent, benefactor
-bio- (G)	life	biology, biography, biosphere
-chrono- (G)	time	chronological, chronometer, synchronic
-cogni- (L)	know	cognition, recognize, incognito
-dict- (L)	say, speak	diction, dictaphone, predictable
-duc- (L)	lead, make	ductile, production, reduce
-fac- (L)	make, do	factory, facsimile, manufacture
-gen- (L)	kind, class	gene, generalization, genesis
-graph- (G)	write	graphic, photography, geography
-jur-, -jus- (L)	law	jury, perjure, justice
-log- (G)	reason, speech	logic, sociology, dialog
-luc- (L)	light	lucid, elucidate, translucent

Root	Meaning	Examples of words
-manu- (L)	hand	manuscript, manual, manufacture
-mis-, -mit- (L)	send	mission, transmit, emit
-path- (G)	feel, suffer	pathetic, pathology, sympathy
-phon- (G)	voice, sound	phonetics, phonograph, telephone
-port- (L)	carry	port, portable, transport
-prim- (L)	first	prime, primary, primitive
-scient- (L)	know	scientific, science, omniscient
-scrib-, -script- (L)	write	scribble, prescribe, description
-sens-, -sent- (L)	feel	sense, sensation, sentiment
-spect- (L)	see	spectacle, inspect, circumspect
-terr- (L)	earth	terrain, territory, inter
-therm- (G)	heat	thermal, thermometer, thermodynamics
-vert- (L)	turn	convert, diversion, versatile
-vid-, -vis- (L)	see	video, visible, envision
-voca- (L)	call	vocal, vocation, provoke

Some Common Prefixes

Prefix	Meaning	Examples of words
anti-	against, opposite	antibiotic, anticommunist, antithesis
co-, con-	together, with	cooperate, collaborate, conspire
dis-	do the reverse	disagree, disable, disappear
e-, ex-	out of	emit, evoke, export
hyper-	excessive(ly)	hypercorrect, hypersensitive, hyperbole
il-, im-, in-	not	illegal, immoral, inactive
im-, in-	in	immigrate, inaugurate, invade
inter-	between	intermission, intercept, international
intra-	within	intramural, intravenous, intracellular
intro-	inside	introduce, introverted, introspection
mono-	one	monologue, mononucleosis, monotony
neo-	new	neo-Nazi, neocolonialism, neoconservative

Prefix	Meaning	Examples of words
omni-	all	omnipresent, omniscient, omnivorous
out-	to surpass	outshine, outperform, outclass
over-	excessive	overworked, overexcited, overenthusiastic
re-	again	redesign, renew, reload
syn-	same	synonym, synchronize, syndrome
trans-	across	transmit, translate, transcontinental
uni-	one	uniform, unicycle, unisex

Some Common Suffixes

Suffix used to create a noun	Meaning	Examples of words
-al	act of	portrayal, dismissal
-ance	process of	acceptance, maintenance
-ism	practice of, belief	Taoism, activism
-ment	process of	government, atonement
-ness	state of being	kindness, dampness
-ship	condition	hardship, fellowship
-tion	action of	pollution, abstraction

Suffix used to create a verb	Meaning	Examples of words
-ate	cause to become	activate, irritate
-en	cause to become	strengthen, lessen
-ize	cause to become	memorialize, minimize

Suffix used to create an adjective	Meaning	Examples of words
-able, -ible	capable of being	desirable, edible
-al	relating to	national, political
-ful	having or promoting	powerful, useful
-ous, -ious	characterized by	monstrous, fictitious

Suffix used to create an adverb	Meaning	Examples of words
-ly	in this manner	quickly, suddenly

EXERCISE 47.1

Using the roots, prefixes, and suffixes listed in this section (and others that you know), try to determine what the following words mean. Keep in mind that the task is not simply a matter of decoding, as word meanings often change over time.

1. transcribe
2. synchronize
3. convocation
4. omnipotent
5. hyperconscientiousness
6. inducement
7. vertex
8. audiologist
9. omniscient
10. remission

EXERCISE 47.2

Identify the common root in each of the following sets of words, and try to determine its meaning. Also try to determine the meanings of any of the words you do not already know.

1. paternal, paternalism, patriot
2. congregate, gregarious, integration
3. fluid, effluent, confluence
4. emerge, immersion, merger
5. distend, tensile, extensive
6. agitate, agenda, action
7. astronaut, astrology, disaster
8. unicorn, cornea, cornet
9. pedal, pedestal, pedigree
10. sedentary, reside, session

47b Learn denotations and connotations

As you develop your vocabulary, try to learn both the exact dictionary meanings of words and the associations attached to them. The **denotation** of a word is its standard dictionary meaning—that is, what it means to anyone who knows the word (see 45a). Many words have more than one denotation. For example, *sanitize* means "to make sanitary" or "to make more acceptable by removing undesired features (as in a document)." The **connotations** of a word are the additional, often emotive, meanings it has for some people due to its association with certain contexts (see 45b). For example, the word *lawyer* denotes a person whose profession involves advising clients on legal rights and obligations and representing them in a court of law. However, for some, *lawyer* may connote someone who files inappropriate lawsuits or otherwise abuses the legal system. Such negative connotations have led many legal practitioners to call themselves *attorneys*.

Using words accurately is a vital part of writing. The best way to learn how to use words correctly is through extensive reading, because reading allows you to encounter words in their natural contexts. You will find that two words such as *heinous* and *infamous,* though they have similar basic meanings, differ somewhat in nuance and usage. If you encounter such words often enough, you will figure out how they should be used, primarily by using other nearby words and phrases as *context clues* to the meaning and usage of the target word. Common types of context clues include informal definitions, synonyms, contrasts, and examples. The following passage from a medical guide illustrates three of these.

> Allergic rhinitis, commonly called hay fever, is similar to asthma except in one respect. In asthma, an airborne substance causes an allergic, or hypersensitive, reaction in your lungs and chest. In allergic rhinitis, the reaction occurs in your eyes, nose, and throat.
>
> —*American Medical Association Family Medical Guide*

This passage twice uses synonyms to clarify the meaning of less common terms (*hay fever* for *allergic rhinitis* and *hypersensitive* for *allergic*), it contrasts allergic rhinitis to asthma, and it contains an informal definition: "Allergic rhinitis [is a disease in which] an airborne substance causes an allergic reaction in your eyes, nose, and throat."

Be aware, however, that context clues are not always reliable. If you are not certain about the meaning or usage of a word, consult a good dictionary (see Chapter 48).

47c Learn related words

Although a word can be seen in isolation, as a thing unto itself, readers normally experience words in relation to other words, as part of a word system. All words are related to certain other words. Knowing these relationships helps you as a writer, because it

WEBLINK

http://www.linguarama .com/ps/392-7.htm

A variety of strategies for learning new words

allows you to choose just the right word to express your meaning. There are three important ways in which words are related: in collocations, as synonyms, and as antonyms.

1 Collocations

Words often occur in combination with certain other words. These word relationships are called **collocations.** Some collocations, such as *bread and butter, cease and desist,* and *reinvent the wheel,* are so common as to be formulaic. Just hearing the first part of such a collocation allows you to fill in the rest: *beat around the _____, make a mountain out of a _____, leave someone holding the _____.* Other collocations are less predictable. The word *rumor,* for example, is commonly used with at least five different verbs: *spread, circulate, deny, confirm,* and *hear.* The sentence "I heard a rumor the other day" sounds like normal everyday English; "I absorbed a rumor the other day" does not. So, the words *hear* and *rumor* commonly go together, or collocate, whereas *absorb* and *rumor* do not. To learn to speak and write well, you should familiarize yourself with as many collocations as possible. Such knowledge will make it easier for you to construct idiomatic, or natural-sounding, sentences. It also will serve you well on those occasions when you want to create a humorous or stylish twist on a timeworn expression.

Be careful, though, not to overuse collocations. If you depend exclusively on common word combinations, your writing will lack originality and may be laden with clichés (see 45g-3).

AUDIO

The best way to learn collocations.

(ESL Note) Collocations are especially troublesome for non-English speakers (see 63b).

(**E X E R C I S E   47.3**)

Each of the following sentences contains a word that does not quite fit. Replace it with a suitable collocating word.

1. My family is probably one of the closest families anyone could come around.

2. The best way to learn is by doing mistakes and learning from them.

3. Education is important to me because it is my only hope to gain my goals.

4. To be creative in the food industry you need to have an open mind and a feeling of adventure.

EXER

Practice learning collocations.

5. Children aren't born knowing how to decipher right from wrong, so they must be taught by their parents.
6. Traffic was stalled because of a mishap involving several cars.
7. Contrary to myth, the Pilgrims did not solemnize Thanksgiving.
8. Many latent supporters are watching the gubernatorial candidate as she campaigns.
9. The referee called far fewer infractions in last night's game than he has called in previous games.
10. The pirate distinguished the spot where the treasure was buried.

2   Synonyms

Synonyms are words that mean essentially the same thing: *dreary/gloomy, fury/rage,* and *injure/damage* are all synonymous pairs. If you know lots of synonyms, you can use them to avoid the sort of heavy repetition that makes for an irritatingly dull style. Bear in mind, though, that there are almost no perfect synonyms in English (or in any other language). That is, there are very few cases where two words can be freely substituted for each other with exactly the same meaning in all possible contexts. Consider the words *injure* and *damage.* Although they have similar meanings, *injure* is used only with reference to humans and animals while *damage* can refer to inanimate objects. It would sound odd to say "I injured my computer." An important part of building your vocabulary is learning these subtle differences among synonyms. Consulting a thesaurus, or book of synonyms, can be a big help in this respect. Remember, however, to choose carefully among the synonyms listed; each one has its own particular uses and nuances of meaning. Better dictionaries often contain cross-references and usage notes that explain the differences among common synonyms (see Chapter 48).

3   Antonyms

Antonyms are words that have opposite meanings: *wrong/right, tall/short,* and *hate/love* are examples. Antonyms are useful in creating humor, irony, sarcasm, and other special effects. For example, a well-chosen antonym can be used effectively in tongue-in-cheek fashion to ridicule someone you do not want to accuse directly: "Senator _____ is the most *undefiled* [read *corrupt*] public servant we are privileged to know." Antonyms also can help you learn new words. By knowing the opposite of a word, you can get a better sense of what the word itself means.

Each of the following sentences contains an italicized word or phrase that is not quite right for the context. Consult your thesaurus, and then substitute an appropriate synonym.

1. Efforts to *fulfill* economic growth in Latin America have been hindered by overpopulation.
2. Political *confusion* in Latin America, as elsewhere, has often led to violations of human rights.
3. The United States strongly opposed the *diffusion* of communism in the Western Hemisphere.
4. For several decades, Brazil *fantasized* about entering the twenty-first century as one of the world's industrial giants.
5. Relations between the United States and Latin America have been *branded* both by friendship and by tension.
6. He *infracted* the city's ordinance that bans the feeding of birds on public property.
7. She *conveyed* her application in plenty of time to meet the deadline.
8. The rotten meat *issued* a sickening odor, which could be smelled throughout the house.
9. I made a list of ten *intentions* on New Year's Day.
10. The body of the *inanimate* president lay in state for three days.

EXER

Using
synonyms.

Bring some examples of unusual words, and their definitions, to your group. Discuss some ideas for continuing to build a more powerful vocabulary.

CHAPTER 48

Using a Thesaurus and a Dictionary

FAQs

▶ Do I really need a thesaurus? (48a)

▶ How can I get help if I am thinking of a certain concept but cannot remember the word for it? (48a-1)

▶ If a dictionary gives several different meanings for a word, how can I tell which one is the most common? (48b-4)

A writer needs tools, and two of the best are a good thesaurus and a good dictionary. A thesaurus such as *Roget's International Thesaurus*, 6th ed. (New York: HarperCollins, 2002), *Bartlett's Roget's Thesaurus* (Boston: Little Brown, 2003), or *Random House Webster's College Thesaurus*, revised ed. (New York: Random House, 1997) can be of great use in selecting appropriate words. A dictionary such as *The American Heritage College Dictionary*, 4th ed. (Boston: Houghton Mifflin, 2002), *The Random House Webster's College Dictionary*, 2nd ed. (New York: Random House, 1997), *Merriam-Webster's Collegiate Dictionary*, 11th ed. (Springfield: Merriam-Webster, 2003), or *Webster's New World College Dictionary*, 4th ed. (New York: Macmillan, 1999) can provide indispensable information about spelling, pronunciation, meaning, usage, word division, and etymology (word origin). These reference works are especially useful in describing Standard Edited English, the kind of English you are expected to use in college and in most professional careers (see 44d).

AUDIO
Chapter overview.

(ESL Note) If you are a non-English speaker, consider getting one of the specialized dictionaries that contain information about count and noncount nouns (see 60a), phrasal verbs (see 61a), verb complements (see 61b), and collocations (see 63b) and offer many sample sentences. (See Chapter 62 for specific references.)

48a Use a thesaurus to find the exact word

Part of being a good writer is choosing words that accurately express your thoughts (see Chapter 45). Do you ever find yourself thinking of a concept and knowing that there is a word to describe it, yet not being able to come up with the word? Do you find yourself wanting to vary your word choices to avoid excessive repetition (see 44c), yet not knowing exactly which substitute words to use? These are situations in which a thesaurus is of great help. A **thesaurus** is a book of synonyms and antonyms that allows you to zero in on the exact word you are looking for.

WWW

48.1

Access the Merriam-Webster Thesaurus online.

AUDIO

Getting maximum use out of a thesaurus.

WEBLINK

http://www.m-w.com/thesaurus.htm

The free, online WWWebster Thesaurus

A word of advice: Do not use a thesaurus just to find fancy words with which to dress up your writing. As synonyms often have special conditions of use and are not freely interchangeable (see 45b, 47c-2), substituting fancy synonyms for more common words just to impress your readers is likely to have the opposite effect.

1 Electronic thesaurus

Today, most word-processing programs have a built-in thesaurus, which you can use as you write. (It is usually on the same menu as the spell checker.) You can also find thesauruses on the Internet. Use *thesaurus* as your search term, and bookmark whatever good sites you find. One such site can be found at *<http://ecco.bsee.swin.edu.au/text/roget/search.html>*. Or, you can buy a thesaurus on a CD-ROM, either by itself or as a supplement to a dictionary.

With an **electronic thesaurus,** you have a great writing tool that is quick and easy to use. If you notice that a word you have written is not quite the word you want to use, all you have to do is select the word and then click on THESAURUS. You will get a listing of synonyms and, in some cases, antonyms and related words.

Sometimes, you quickly find the word you need; other times, the exact word does not pop up immediately. In these cases, you will have to be a little more inventive.

For example, when Jennie Lee was writing an essay called "Ride the Bus!" she used the thesaurus a number of times. At one point, she wanted to criticize students who think they have to own a car to get around. She wrote this sentence:

```
Many people have been tricked into believing that owning a vehicle is

the best means of meeting personal transportation needs.
```

At first this sentence seemed okay, but when Jennie was revising her draft she felt the word *tricked* was a little too strong. So she selected it with her mouse and clicked on THESAURUS. Figure 48.1 shows the computer screen that came up. Clicking on RELATED WORDS gave her the screen shown in Figure 48.2 on page 816. The only verb form listed here was *deceive*, which was not quite the word she was looking for, either. But she decided to click on it anyway, to see what it would bring up. She got the list of synonyms shown in Figure 48.3 on page 816.

Aha! *Mislead.* Yes, thought Jennie, *that* was the word she was looking for! "*Many people have been misled into believing that owning a vehicle is the best means of meeting personal transportation needs.*" Just to make sure, she examined all the synonyms listed and decided that although all of them conveyed a sense of deception, most, like *trick,* were too strong. Only *misinform* was close to *mislead* in its connotation. Briefly pondering the difference between these two words—and consulting her dictionary—Jennie decided that *misled* was indeed the word she wanted. It conveyed the idea of being deceived, but in a vague sense, without implying a specific agent of deception.

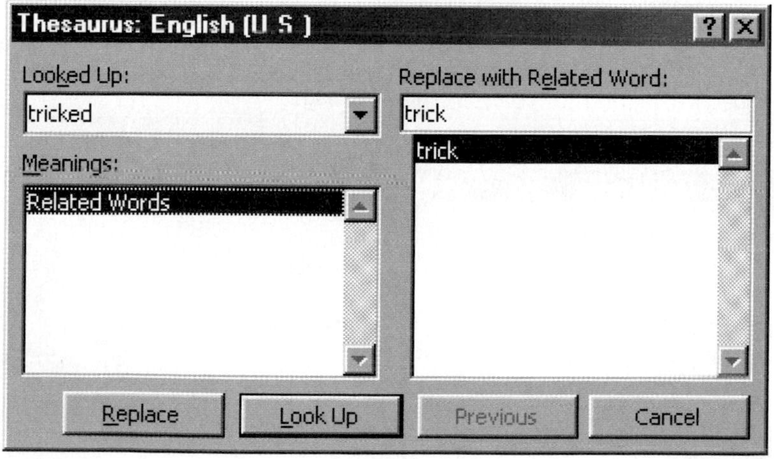

FIGURE 48.1 Thesaurus Screen for *tricked*

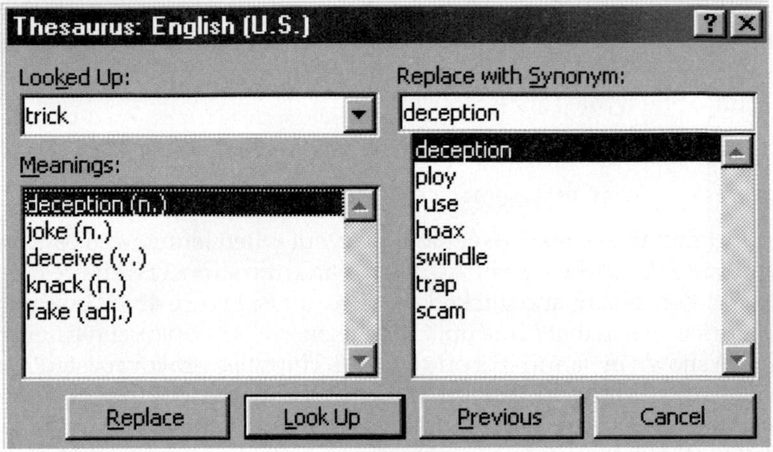

FIGURE 48.2 Thesaurus Screen Showing Related Words for *tricked*

What is the moral of this story?

- *Take advantage of your electronic thesaurus.* It will let you quickly search for the word you want. (This entire search took Jennie less than a minute.)
- *Be persistent.* If at first you don't succeed, do some exploring.

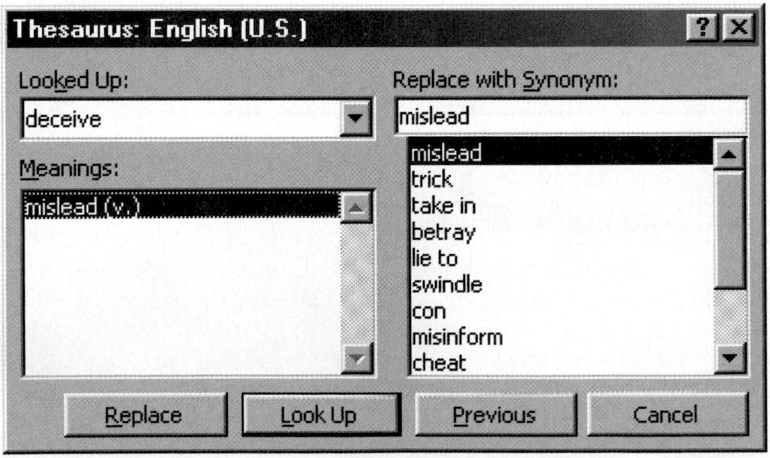

FIGURE 48.3 Thesaurus Screen for *deceive*

Using special electronic thesaurus features

Some of the newer electronic thesauruses offer special features that make it easier for you to find the word you're looking for. For example, one kind of program helps you when you have a certain concept in mind but can't think of the exact word for it. It works like a sort of "reverse dictionary": you enter a combination of keywords or concepts and the program suggests possible words. In Jennie's case, for instance, she might have benefited from this program by using a combination like *trick NOT cheat*, or perhaps *deceive AND error*. Either of these might have produced the word *mislead*. (See 9c-1 for tips on using the Boolean operators AND and NOT.)

Another program allows you to find words when you can think of only part of the word. For example, say you know that the word you are looking for starts with *for-* but you cannot remember how it ends. With this special program, you enter *for** and get a list of words all beginning with *for-*, including *forsake, forgo,* and *forget*. Or, if you are writing a poem and want to know all words that end in *-ette,* you just type **ette* and receive a list including *etiquette, diskette, corvette,* and *sermonette*.

2 Traditional thesaurus

You should also feel comfortable using a thesaurus in traditional book form. The pocket-size versions are handy for carrying around; larger, desk-size thesauruses are found in all libraries and many offices. In many pocket-size thesauruses, the words are arranged alphabetically, as in a dictionary. With most desk-size thesauruses, you first look up the word in an index at the back of the book and then turn to the most relevant sections indicated.

Whereas multiple clicks and extended searching are often required to find the word you are looking for in an electronic thesaurus, traditional thesauruses typically present a number of words in one place, allowing you to get a comprehensive look at the full set of synonyms for a word. For example, when we used our electronic thesaurus to look up the word *succinct,* we were presented with a screen containing nine synonyms. But when we checked in a modest traditional thesaurus, we were given seventeen: *concise, terse, short, brief, curt, laconic, pithy, trenchant, pointed, crisp, neat, compact, summary, condensed, short ened, abbreviated,* and *compressed*. Furthermore, unlike the electronic thesaurus, the traditional thesaurus gave us five antonyms: *verbose, prolix, loquacious, long-winded,* and *garrulous*. In short, the traditional thesaurus offered an immediate, more comprehensive sense of what the word *succinct* means.

Each of the following sentences contains an italicized word that does not quite fit with the rest of the sentence. Use a thesaurus to find a synonym that sounds better.

1. When I am bored, I like to go *observe* a movie.
2. A true New Englander enjoys a *segment* of pie for breakfast.
3. The Brothers Grimm were collectors of German fairy *narratives*.
4. The man playing third base is a very promising *neophyte*.
5. The couple went to the market to buy *comestibles*.
6. Most of us love to *vocalize* along with the radio.
7. Before starting the job, the teacher signed an employee *pact*.
8. We will need to measure the *girth* of the piano to see if it will fit through the door.
9. Ron and Sylvia have an *assignation* on Friday.
10. The board should *convoke* a special meeting of the leadership to review the current situation.

EXER
Using synonyms.

48b Use a dictionary to learn about words

WEBLINK

http://owl.english.
purdue.edu/internet/
resources/sourceofinfo
.html
Compilation of links to online dictionaries, the-sauruses, and style guides

Do you sometimes come across a new word in your reading and wonder what it means? Have you ever argued with a classmate about how a word should be pronounced? Have you ever had an instructor circle a word in one of your papers and write *usage* in the margin? Are you curious about where a word like *maverick* comes from? In using your thesaurus, do you find yourself trying to decide how the various words listed as synonyms differ? A good dictionary will help you out in all of these situations and more.

1 Kinds of dictionaries

Traditional, hardbound dictionaries come in two types: pocket size and desk size. The pocket size is handy, but the desk size contains more complete information. Electronic dictionaries usually have as much information as desk-size types.

There are two kinds of electronic dictionaries: those on CD-ROM and those on the Internet. Although the preferred method of using the CD-ROM type is to download it to your hard drive, you can play it directly from your CD-ROM drive. To use the Internet type of electronic dictionary, you log on to a Web site such as *WWWebster Dictionary* at *<http://www.m-w.com/dictionary.htm>*, the *Oxford English Dictionary* at *<http://www.oed.com>*, or *OneLook Dictionaries* at *<http://www.onelook.com>*. In some cases, you may have to pay a subscription fee.

A typical entry from a comprehensive dictionary, whether hard-bound or electronic, will look something like the one in Figure 48.4, from *The American Heritage College Dictionary*, 3rd ed.

Pronunciation   Part of speech   Word endings

Spelling and word division —

ha•rass (hăr′əs, hə-răs′)   *tr.v.*   **ha•rassed, ha•rass•ing, ha•rass•es. 1.** To irritate or torment persistently. **2.** To wear out; exhaust. **3.** To impede and exhaust (an enemy) by repeated attacks or raids. [French *harasser*, possibly from Old French *harer*, to set a dog on, from *hare*, interjection used to set a dog on, of Germanic origin.] —**ha•rass′er** *n.* —**ha•rass′ment** *n.*

Word senses (definitions)

Etymology

Related words

SYNONYMS: *harass, harry, hound, badger, pester, plague, bait.* These verbs are compared as they mean to trouble persistently or incessantly. *Harass* and *harry* imply systematic persecution by besieging with repeated annoyances, threats, demands, or misfortunes: *The landlord harassed tenants who were behind in their rent.* "Of all the griefs that harass the distress'd" (Samuel Johnson). *A gang of delinquents harried the storekeeper. Hound* suggests unrelenting pursuit to gain a desired end: *Reporters hounded the celebrity for an interview.* To *badger* is to nag or tease persistently: *The child badgered his parents to buy him a new bicycle.* To *pester* is to inflict a succession of petty annoyances: "How she would have pursued and pestered me with questions and surmises" (Charlotte Brontë). *Plague* refers to the infliction of tribulations, such as worry or vexation, likened to an epidemic disease: "As I have no estate, I am plagued with no tenants or stewards" (Henry Fielding). To *bait* is to torment by or as if by taunting, insulting, or ridiculing: *Hecklers baited the speaker mercilessly.*

Words having similar meanings, with examples

VIDEO
Using pronunciation guides.

USAGE NOTE: Educated usage appears to be evenly divided on the pronunciation of *harass*. In a recent survey 50 percent of the Usage Panel preferred a pronunciation with stress on the first syllable, while 50 percent preferred stress on the second syllable. Curiously, the Panelists' comments appear to indicate that each side regards itself as an embattled minority.

Authoritative opinions about correct usage

FIGURE 48.4 Entry from *The American Heritage College Dictionary*

2 Spelling, word division, and pronunciation

A typical dictionary entry begins with the main word, correctly spelled and divided into syllables: *ha•rass*. Knowing where to divide a word is helpful for typing if you do not use automatic hyphenation on your computer (see 59a). If a word has two correct spellings, they are both listed, with the preferred spelling first. A compound word is spelled according to its preferred usage, either hyphenated (*black-and-blue*), separated (*black magic*), or fused (*blackjack*).

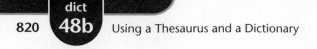

WEBLINK

http://writing.colostate
.edu/resources/page1.htm

Direct access to the best online dictionaries and thesauruses

The word's pronunciation is indicated next, in parentheses: (hăr´əs, hə-răs´). Most modern dictionaries have a pronunciation key at the bottom of the page to help you decipher the pronunciation. For words of more than one syllable, a heavy accent mark (´) indicates which syllable should receive primary stress; some words have a secondary accent (´) as well. Some electronic dictionaries allow you to click on a button and get a voice recording of the correct pronunciation of the word.

3 Parts of speech and word endings

Next come symbols describing some aspect of the word—for example, what part of speech it is (such as a noun, verb, or adjective) or whether it is singular or plural. (See Chapter 30 for an introduction to the parts of speech.) The most common abbreviations follow:

adj.	adjective	*intr.*	intransitive	*pron.*	pronoun
adv.	adverb	*n.*	noun	*sing.*	singular
aux.	auxiliary	*pl.*	plural	*suff.*	suffix
conj.	conjunction	*pref.*	prefix	*tr.*	transitive
interj.	interjection	*prep.*	preposition	*v.*	verb

Often an entry will include variants of the main word, showing different word endings. For verbs, for example, a comprehensive dictionary will give the principal tenses (see 32a). In the example shown in Figure 48.4, *The American Heritage College Dictionary* gives the past tense (*harassed*), the present participle (*harassing*), and the simple present tense (*harasses*). For other word types, you can expect to find other kinds of word endings. Adjectives, for example, will usually have their comparative and superlative forms listed. Nouns with irregular plural forms will have those listed.

4 Word senses

Many words have more than one meaning, or **sense.** Each sense has a separate listing, generally preceded by a boldfaced number. In some dictionaries, these senses are arranged historically, according to when they entered the language; in other dictionaries, senses are listed according to current popularity, with the most commonly used sense appearing first. (It is a good idea to consult the front of your dictionary to see which system it uses.) Sometimes the main senses are further divided into subsenses, generally indicated by a boldface lowercase letter.

5 Etymology and related words and expressions

Information about a word's origin, or **etymology,** is given in square brackets. This information can help you to learn the word and use it accurately. Sometimes, **related words**—words derived from the same root—are given as well. These might include related expressions such as phrasal verbs (see 61a) and idioms (see 63c).

6 Synonyms and usage notes

Some dictionaries list synonyms for certain words, along with explanations of the differences among them and examples. Also, some dictionaries provide **usage notes,** which typically represent the judgments of a panel of authorities about "correct" usage (see 44d). In many dictionaries, particular senses of a word may be given **usage labels** such as *Informal, Colloquial, Nonstandard, Slang, Vulgar, Obscene, Offensive, Archaic,* or *Obsolete.* You may want to check the front of your dictionary to see how the different kinds of usage are defined.

7 Field labels

If a word sense typically is used only in a certain field of study or activity, most dictionaries will label it accordingly. For example, a *genoa* is a type of sail on a sailboat, so it is labeled *Naut.* (for nautical). Some other common field labels are *Anat.* (for anatomy), *Biochem.* (for biochemistry), *Comp. Sci.* (for computer science), *Gk. Myth* (for Greek mythology), *Mus.* (for music), and *Phys.* (for physics). A full listing of field labels can usually be found in the dictionary's front matter.

EXER

More on synonyms.

(EXERCISE 48.2)

Select two interesting new words from your course readings. Go to a library or bookstore and look them up in three of the newest dictionaries. Take note of the differences among them. Write a two-page report describing these differences and recommending one dictionary over the other two.

(FOR COLLABORATION)

Share your conclusions with your group; is there a consensus on which dictionaries were preferred?

CHAPTER 49

Spelling

FAQs

▶ My spell checker is too slow. Can I make it go faster? (49a)

▶ Are there certain times when I should not depend on a spell checker for help? (49b)

▶ What are the most helpful spelling rules? (49d)

Modern English is a product of many other languages, including German, French, Latin, Greek, Scandinavian, and Spanish. One unfortunate result of this hybridization is an irregular system of spelling that causes problems for many users of the language. If you are one of those people, be assured that you are not alone. However, it is important that you work on your spelling and keep trying to improve it. Many readers, including employers and customers in the workplace, have little tolerance for bad spelling. In fact, studies have shown that even a few misspellings on a résumé can cause a job applicant to be eliminated from consideration.

AUDIO
Chapter overview.

49a Use a spell checker

A computerized **spell checker** makes it easy to review your work for spelling errors. If you are not already doing so, you should routinely run a final spell check on any important document you write. Some word processors allow you to set the spell checker so that it will identify possible misspellings either while you are typing or after you have finished. Although spell checking can be frus-

VIDEO
Recognizing spelling problems.

WEBLINK

http://www.asu.edu/duas/wcenter/spelling.html
Spelling rules and advice

WWW

49.1
View "Ten Rules for Better Spelling" online.

HELP

How can I speed up spell checking?

1. If you have already checked part of your document for spelling errors, you can set the spell checker so that it skips that part the next time you run it. (See the HELP menu in your word-processing program.)

2. If you are using a lot of specialized terms, consider customizing the spell checker by installing one or more specialized dictionaries. (The HELP menu in your word-processing program will explain how.)

tratingly slow, there are things you can do to speed it up (see the Help box above).

Spell checkers are far from perfect. Sometimes they flag words that are spelled correctly (especially names), and sometimes they fail to flag words that are spelled incorrectly. The first problem is particularly annoying, but it can be resolved. For example, suppose you are writing a paper on Hemingway and your spell checker keeps flagging the name *Hemingway*. Instead of clicking IGNORE every time, you can customize the spell checker so that it will recognize the name. With most spell checkers, you can customize as you write. You also can add special dictionaries to the one on your word-processing program. (Web sites such as *OneLook Dictionaries* at *<http://www.onelook.com>* and *CSEN Global List of Special Dictionaries* at *<http://www.csen.com/special-dictionaries>* allow you to download a special dictionary—as long as you are using it for educational purposes and do not publish it anywhere as though it were your own work.)

Identifying misspellings that the spell checker missed is a more difficult problem. Spell checkers will accept any word that happens to match a word form in its dictionary, even if the word is misused. For example, if you write *golf coarse*, the spell checker will not recognize the misspelling of *course* because the word *coarse* is in its dictionary. Thus, even with a spell checker, you must have the knowledge to prevent or correct misspellings. The most effective ways to gain such knowledge are by (1) mastering troublesome homophones, (2) guarding against common spelling errors, and (3) learning some general spelling rules and patterns. The remainder of this chapter is devoted to these topics.

(**E X E R C I S E 49.1**)

Create a document called "Personal Spelling Demons" on your word processor, and enter any words that you have trouble spelling.

49b Master troublesome homophones

Homophones are words that sound alike but are spelled differently and have different meanings. They are one of the most common causes of misspelling in English and cannot be detected by a spell checker. For this reason, you should study them and learn their differences, especially those listed below.

(**Grammar Checker Alert**) Although homophones slip past a spell checker, some of them are flagged by a grammar checker. But most homophones are overlooked, even by the best grammar checkers. For example, the grammar checker in *MS Word 2002* identifies only about one-fourth of the homophones listed below.

AUDIO
Use pronunciation differences to learn homophones.

affect	verb: "to have an influence on"
effect	verb: "to bring about"; noun: "result"
its	possessive pronoun
it's	contraction of *it is*
loose	adjective: "free, not tightly secured"
lose	verb: "to fail to keep"
their	possessive form of *they*
there	adverb: "in that place"
they're	contraction of *they are*
to	preposition
too	adverb: "also"
two	adjective and noun: "2"
who's	contraction of *who is*
whose	possessive form of *who*
your	possessive form of *you*
you're	contraction of *you are*

Some other frequently confused homophones and near homophones include the following:

advice	recommendation
advise	to recommend

all ready	fully prepared
already	by now
all together	everyone or everything in one place
altogether	completely
allude	to refer to
elude	to avoid or escape
allusion	reference to
illusion	misleading appearance
brake	to stop
break	to reduce to pieces, destroy
breath	air inhaled and exhaled
breathe	to inhale and exhale air
choose	to select
chose	past tense of *choose*
cite	to quote as an authority
sight	vision
site	place, location
clothes	garments
cloths	pieces of fabric
coarse	rough
course	path, track; academic class
conscience	sense of right and wrong
conscious	aware
dairy	place where milk is produced
diary	personal daily journal
desert	dry, barren area
dessert	sweet food at the end of a meal
device	apparatus, tool
devise	to plan or invent
dominant	controlling, ruling
dominate	to control, govern
elicit	to call forth, evoke
illicit	illegal
eminent	distinguished
immanent	existing within, inherent
imminent	about to happen

envelop	to surround
envelope	flat paper container
fair	equitable, permissible, acceptable
fare	transportation charge
formally	in a formal manner
formerly	previously
forth	forward or onward
fourth	in position 4 in a countable series
gorilla	ape
guerrilla	irregular soldier
heard	past tense of *hear*
herd	group of animals
hole	opening
whole	entire, complete
human	referring to people
humane	compassionate
lead	to guide or direct
led	past tense of *lead*
may be	might be
maybe	perhaps
miner	someone who works in a mine
minor	underage person
patience	perseverance, endurance
patients	doctor's clients
peace	absence of war
piece	fragment, part
personal	individual, private
personnel	employees
plain	ordinary, simple, clear
plane	flat surface; airplane
presence	being in attendance
presents	gifts
principal	leading person; a capital sum; most important
principle	rule or guideline
quiet	silent
quite	completely; somewhat

rain	water drops falling to earth
reign	period of rule
rein	strap to control a horse
respectfully	with respect
respectively	in that order
right	correct; opposite of left
rite	ceremony
write	to put words on paper
sense	reason, feeling
since	because, subsequently
stationary	standing still
stationery	writing paper
than	in comparison with
then	at that time
threw	past tense of *throw*
through	in one side and out another
thorough	complete
waist	midsection of body
waste	useless byproduct; to use needlessly
weak	opposite of strong
week	seven days
weather	atmospheric conditions
whether	if it is the case that
were	past tense of *are*
where	at or in what place

EXERCISE 49.2

In the following sentences, choose the correct spelling from each pair of words in brackets. Add any words you get wrong to your Personal Spelling Demons document. (See Exercise 49.1.)

1. The doctor [who's, whose] license was revoked by the medical [bored, board] is no longer allowed to treat [patients, patience].
2. The television [diary, dairy] is one of the [devices, devises] used by A. C. Nielsen to research the programs people choose.
3. The [peace, piece] of [advice, advise] Ann Landers gave was simple, practical, and [fare, fair].

4. The poster [sighted, cited] Jesse Jackson, who said, "Your children need your [presents, presence] more than your [presents, presence]."

5. Because he is an excellent magician, he always allows the audience a [through, thorough] inspection of his props before he creates his wonderful [allusions, illusions].

6. More than once last [weak, week], the tardy student managed to [allude, elude] the [principal, principle] as she entered the building.

7. At a gorgeous [site, sight] atop a hill, the women gathered for a bonding [right, rite], calling forth the [immanent, eminent] wisdom from each person present.

8. The [personal, personnel] department's intense search for a [principle, principal] engineer to [led, lead] the department [led, lead] to the promotion of a woman [who's, whose] talent had [formally, formerly] gone unrecognized.

9. When the camouflaged [gorilla, guerrilla] [herd, heard] something moving in the underbrush, he tried to determine [weather, whether] it was an enemy soldier.

10. The small craft carrying [elicit, illicit] drugs encountered bad [whether, weather] that night and traveled far from [it's, its] intended [coarse, course].

49c Guard against common spelling errors

Although a spell checker can flag many spelling errors for you, it is still worth learning the correct spelling of the most commonly misspelled words. Some of these words follow.

Commonly Misspelled Words

accidentally	develops	occasionally
accommodate	environment	occurred
achieved	exaggerate	parallel
address	exceed	quantity
apparent	February	receive
appropriate	government	recommend
argument	heroes	seize
basically	lose	separate
beneficial	maintenance	success
calendar	manageable	therefore
committee	misspell	truly
definitely	necessary	until
dependent	noticeable	without

WWW

49.2

A guide to British/American spelling differences.

If you find your spell checker flagging the same misspelled words over and over, add them to your Personal Spelling Demons document and study them from time to time. Most spell checkers will allow you to enter such words into a file with just a single mouse click.

Many words include letters or syllables that are not pronounced in casual speech (or even, in some cases, in careful speech). Here are examples of such words; try to "see" the silent letters or syllables as you visualize these words.

ad<u>d</u>ress	gove<u>rn</u>ment	quan<u>t</u>ity
can<u>d</u>idate	int<u>e</u>rest	recog<u>n</u>ize
diff<u>e</u>rent	lib<u>r</u>ary	rest<u>au</u>rant
dum<u>b</u>	paral<u>l</u>el	surprise
enviro<u>n</u>ment	<u>p</u>neumonia	therefo<u>re</u>
Feb<u>r</u>uary	priv<u>i</u>lege	tomato<u>e</u>s
for<u>ei</u>gn	prob<u>ab</u>ly	We<u>d</u>n<u>e</u>sday

If you are unsure about a certain letter in a word, try to think of a related word; it may provide a clue. For example, suppose you are wondering whether *gramm<u>a</u>r* or *gramm<u>e</u>r* is correct. If you think of *gramm<u>a</u>tical*, you will spell *grammar* correctly. Here are some other examples:

	Think of
competition or compitition?	comp<u>e</u>te
democracy or democricy?	democr<u>a</u>t
mystery or mystry?	myst<u>e</u>rious
relative or relitive?	rel<u>a</u>te

(EXERCISE 49.3)

In the following paragraph, choose the correct spelling from each pair of words in brackets. Add any words you get wrong to your Personal Spelling Demons document.

EXER

Choose the correct spelling.

On the second [Wensday, Wednesday] in [Febuary, February], those running for various positions in town [government, goverment] gathered for a [Candidates', Canidates'] Night. At the event, the two [canidates, candidates] for school [comittee, committee] expressed [diffrent, different] opinions about how to [accomodate, accommodate] the new state education standards without having to [excede, exceed] the available amount of money. Mr. Smith believes that the state legislature is right to make [forein, foreign] language a required course. He also pointed out that an up-to-date school [libary, library] is [neccessary, necessary] for student [sucess, success]. Ms. Jones, on the other hand, [basically, basicly] believes that, although beneficial, both [forein, foreign] language courses and school [libaries, libraries] are less important than other things, such as regular school building [maintainance, maintenance]. The [canidates, candidates] then had an [arguement, argument] about building [maintainance, maintenance], Ms. Jones [reccomending, recommending] that the town [seize, sieze] the opportunity to repair current buildings and Mr. Smith stating that the [maintainance, maintenance] budget is [exagerated, exaggerated] and proposing that the town defer some of the repairs in order to spend more on educational programming. Because the debate highlighted [noticeable, noticable] [diffrences, differences] between the [canidates, candidates], the voters who attended the event were well served.

49d Learn general spelling rules and patterns

Although English is not the simplest language in the world to learn when it comes to spelling, it does have a number of general rules and patterns that make things easier.

1 Prefixes

Prefixes are small word parts, like *re-, anti-,* and *pre-,* placed at the beginnings of words (see 47a). Prefixes do not change the spelling of the root word: *anti-* added to *-freeze* becomes *antifreeze.* In some cases, though, a hyphen is required: *anti-* plus *-intellectual* is spelled *anti-intellectual* (see 59a).

> **WEBLINK**
>
> http://www.io.com/~hcexres/tcm1603/acchtml/twspell.html
> Reviews the most common spelling problems

    mis + spell = misspell

    un + necessary = unnecessary

    re + entry = reentry

    dis + service = disservice

2 Suffixes

Suffixes are small word parts, like *-age, -ence, -ing,* and *-tion,* placed at the ends of words (see 47a). By adding suffixes to a root word such as *sense-,* you can create different meanings: *sensitive, sensual, sensory, senseless.* In doing so, however, you must observe the following spelling rules.

1. If the word ends in a silent *e* and the suffix starts with a vowel, drop the *e*.

imagine + ation = imagination

debate + able = debatable

pure + ist = purist

perspire + ing = perspiring

There are some exceptions. Some words need to retain the *e* in order to be distinguished from similar words (*dyeing/dying*), to prevent mispronunciation (*mileage, being*), or to keep a soft *c* or *g* sound (*noticeable, courageous*).

2. If the word ends in a silent *e* and the suffix starts with a consonant, do not drop the *e*.

require + ment = requirement

spine + less = spineless

hate + ful = hateful

definite + ly = definitely

Some exceptions are *argument, awful, ninth, truly,* and *wholly.*

EXERCISE 49.4

Combine the following words and suffixes, keeping or dropping the silent *e* as necessary. Add any words that you spell incorrectly to your Personal Spelling Demons document.

1. complete + ly
2. grace + ious
3. grieve + ance
4. wholesome + ness
5. exercise + ing
6. trace + able
7. continue + ous
8. sole + ly
9. argue + ment
10. sedate + ive

3. When adding a suffix to a word that ends in *y*, change the *y* to *i* if the letter preceding the *y* is a consonant.

study + ous = studious

joy + ous = joyous

comply + ance = compliance

pay + ment = payment

Exceptions are words with the suffix *-ing*, which keep the *y* in all cases: *studying, carrying, drying, paying.*

4. In creating adverbs from adjectives, add *-ly* to the adjective unless the adjective ends in *-ic*, in which case use *-ally.*

silent + ly = silently

hopeful + ly = hopefully

vile + ly = vilely

wild + ly = wildly

terrific + ally = terrifically

basic + ally = basically

An exception is *publicly.*

5. In choosing between *-able* and *-ible,* use *-able* if the root word can stand alone; otherwise, use *-ible.*

understand + able = understandable

change + able = changeable

agree + able = agreeable

vis + ible = visible

ed + ible = edible

aud + ible = audible

Some exceptions are *resistible, probable,* and *culpable.*

6. Double the final consonant of the root word if (a) the root word ends with a single accented vowel and a single consonant and (b) the suffix begins with a vowel.

drop + ed = dropped

slim + er = slimmer

occur + ence = occurrence

begin + ing = beginning

laugh + ed = laughed   [Root word does not end with a single consonant.]

sleep + ing = sleeping   [Root word has two vowels.]

commit + ment = commitment   [Suffix does not start with a vowel.]

happen + ing = happening   [Root word does not end with an accented vowel.]

(**EXERCISE 49.5**)

In each case, combine the root word and the suffix so as to form a single, correctly spelled word. Add any words you get wrong to your Personal Spelling Demons document.

1. room + mate =
2. hesitant + ly =
3. shop + ing =
4. control + (able or ible?) =
5. plaus + (able or ible?) =
6. cool + er =
7. drastic + (ly or ally?) =
8. quiet + est =
9. thin + ness =
10. public + (ly or ally?) =

(**FOR COLLABORATION**)

In your group, share your lists of Personal Spelling Demons. How many words appear on more than one person's list?

3 Plurals

English has several different ways of forming plurals from singular nouns. Following are some rules for forming plurals.

1. For most words, add -s.

tool, tools   minute, minutes
window, windows

2. For words ending with s, sh, ch, x, or z, add -es.

bus, buses   sandwich, sandwiches
crash, crashes   fox, foxes
quiz, quizzes   [Note the doubled final consonant.]

3. For words ending with a consonant followed by y, change the y to i and add -es.

enemy, enemies   strawberry, strawberries
mystery, mysteries   theory, theories

4. For some words ending with *f* or *fe*, change the *f* or *fe* to *v* and add *-es*.

calf, calves   life, lives
half, halves   thief, thieves
knife, knives   yourself, yourselves

Some exceptions are *belief, beliefs; chief, chiefs; proof, proofs;* and *motif, motifs.*

5. For compound nouns written as single words, add the plural ending as you would to an ordinary noun.

laptop, laptops   database, databases
workstation, workstations

6. For compound nouns written as two or more words or hyphenated, add the plural ending to the noun being modified.

video game, video games   [The noun being modified is *game.*]

word processor, word processors [The noun being modified is *processor.*]

sister-in-law, sisters-in-law   [The noun being modified is *sister.*]

Irregular plurals must be learned individually. Sometimes, an internal vowel must be changed to make a noun plural:

woman, women   mouse, mice
tooth, teeth

With some nouns derived from Latin or Greek, a final *us, um,* or *on* must be changed to *i* or *a:*

syllabus, syllabi   curriculum, curricula
alumnus, alumni   medium, media
stimulus, stimuli   criterion, criteria

Some nouns have the same form for both singular and plural:

deer, deer   species, species
sheep, sheep

(**EXERCISE 49.6**)

Make the following words plural. If necessary, check your dictionary.

1. device   2. memorandum

3. church
4. goose
5. moose
6. kiss

7. sky
8. syllabus
9. mailbox
10. mouse

4 The "*i* before *e*" rule

The rule you had to memorize in elementary school is worth keeping in mind: "*i* before *e* except after *c* or when sounded like *ay*, as in *neighbor* or *weigh*."

I BEFORE *E*

achieve   field
believe   friend
brief   piece

EXCEPT AFTER *C*

ceiling   deceive
conceive   receive

OR WHEN SOUNDED LIKE *AY*

eight   vein
neighbor   weigh

Some exceptions are *ancient, caffeine, conscience, counterfeit, either, foreign, height, leisure, neither, seize, science,* and *weird.*

(**EXERCISE 49.7**)

EXER
More spelling practice.

Insert the correct form (*ei* or *ie*) in the following words:

1. exper___nce
2. perc___ve
3. h___ght
4. ch___f
5. v___n

6. dec___t
7. for___gn
8. th___f
9. b___ge
10. anc___nt

CHAPTER 50

End Punctuation

▸ Which is correct, *FBI* or *F.B.I.*? (50d)

▸ Should the question mark go inside or outside quotation marks? (50e-1)

▸ What is an "indirect question," and how do I punctuate it? (50f)

It is important to end sentences with proper punctuation so that readers know what types of statements are being made and what kinds of silent intonation to give each one. There are three ways to punctuate a sentence: with a period, a question mark, or an exclamation point.

AUDIO

Chapter overview.

The Period

The period is used for several purposes: to indicate the end of a statement, to punctuate initials and abbreviations, and to mark basic divisions in units and computer names.

50a Use a period to mark the end of a statement

Sometimes called a "full stop," the period is most commonly used to mark the end of a sentence. Just make sure before you place the period that the words form a *complete grammatical sentence,* or else you will be creating a sentence fragment (see Chapter 35).

If the sentence ends with a quotation mark, place the period *inside* the quotation mark (see also 55e):

One commentator said that "rainforest destruction, overpopulation, and the global arms trade are problems for the entire world."

If the sentence ends with a parenthesis, place the period *outside* the parenthesis unless the entire sentence is a parenthetical comment (see also 56a–56c):

> Mexicans voted Sunday in elections that could weaken the power of the world's longest ruling political party, the Institutional Revolutionary Party (PRI).

50b Use periods to punctuate initials and many abbreviations

Initials that stand for middle names or first names take periods:

Mary W. Shelley   O. J. Simpson   F. Scott Fitzgerald

Leave one space after each period when punctuating initials in names.
Most abbreviations ending in lowercase letters take periods. Some such abbreviations are

Ms.	a.m.	St.	Jan.
Mrs.	p.m.	Ave.	i.e.
Mr.	etc.	Rd.	Jr.
Dr.	e.g.	apt.	Inc.

For further discussion of abbreviations, see Chapter 58.

50c Use periods to mark basic divisions in units and computer names

Basic divisions in money, measurements, email addresses, and file names all take periods:

$99.50   3.2 meters   13.5 gallons
English.paper.doc   michael.okiwara@u.cc.utah.edu

50.1
Examples of
European
punctuation
conventions.

50d Avoid common misuses of periods

1. *Do not use a period to mark just any pause.* If you insert a period whenever you want readers to pause, you run the risk of creating sentence fragments. Consider this example:

Attempts to challenge reactionary political views are often branded as "politically correct" by those same reactionaries. Who support only their own versions of "free speech."

The second statement is a fragment (see Chapter 35), because the writer has incorrectly set it off as a separate sentence. The correct way to signal a pause is to insert a comma (see Chapter 51), thus turning the fragment into a relative clause:

Attempts to challenge reactionary political views are often branded as "politically correct" by those same reactionaries, who support only their own versions of "free speech."

2. *Do not use periods with acronyms and other all uppercase abbreviations.* The recent trend is not to use periods with common abbreviations for states, countries, organizations, computer programs, famous people, and other entities, such as

CA	NJ	USA	UN	FBI
NOW	NAACP	MS-DOS	CD-ROM	COBOL
MIT	NBA	JFK	FDR	AAA

3. *Do not use periods at the end of stand-alone titles or headings.* The title of this chapter and its numbered headings are examples of stand-alone titles and headings, respectively.

4. *Do not use periods at the end of sentences within sentences.* Here is an example of a sentence within a sentence:

The famous statement "I think, therefore I am" originated in an essay by the French philosopher Descartes.

5. *Do not use periods after items in a formatted list (except for full sentences).* The table of contents for this handbook is an example of a formatted list. Only when the items in the list are full sentences is it acceptable to have periods after the individual items.

The Question Mark

Question marks are placed after direct questions, whereas periods follow indirect questions. Do not use a comma or a period after a question mark.

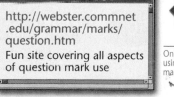

WEBLINK

http://webster.commnet
.edu/grammar/marks/
question.htm
Fun site covering all aspects
of question mark use

50.2

Online help for
using question
marks.

50e Use a question mark after a direct request

REQUESTING
INFORMATION

Who wrote *Jesus Christ, Superstar?*

ASKING FOR
CONFIRMATION

It's a complicated situation, isn't it?

MAKING A POLITE
REQUEST

Could you please be a little quieter?

1 Using question marks with quotation marks

If the quotation is a question and it is at the end of the sentence, put the question mark inside the quotation marks.

The police officer asked me, "Do you live here?"

If the quotation is a statement embedded within a question and it comes at the end of the sentence, put the question mark outside the quotation marks.

Who said, "Those who forget history are condemned to repeat it"?

(See Chapter 55 for more on quotation marks.)

2 Using question marks in a series

It is acceptable to put a question mark after each independent item, even if it is not a full sentence.

Will our homeless population continue to grow? Stay about the same? Get smaller?

If the question is an either/or type, put a question mark only at the end of the sentence.

Are you coming with us or staying here?

50f Do not use a question mark after an indirect question

AUDIO
Punctuating
indirect
questions.

An indirect question is the writer's rewording of a question posed by someone else.

A tourist asked me where the Lincoln Memorial was.

The Exclamation Point

Exclamation points are used to show strong emotion, including amazement and sarcasm. Do not use a comma or a period after an exclamation point.

50g Use an exclamation point to signal a strong statement

The statement marked with an exclamation point does not have to be a full sentence.

AN OUTCRY OR COMMAND	Oh! Watch out!
STRONG EMPHASIS	People before profits!
ASTONISHMENT	Imagine reading this news report and not getting upset!
SARCASM	And the cigarette companies claim that smoking is not addictive!

WEBLINK

http://www.uottawa.ca/ academic/arts/writcent/ hypergrammar/endpunct .html

All about end punctuation

1 Using exclamation points with quotation marks

If the quotation itself is an exclamation, put the exclamation point inside the quotation marks.

It is not a good idea to go into a crowded movie theater and shout "Fire!"

Otherwise, the exclamation point should be placed outside the quotation marks.

Can you believe that he said, "Alice doesn't live here"!

2 Avoiding overuse of exclamation points

Exclamation points are rarely used in college papers, essays, and other kinds of formal writing. Try not use them except in highly unusual circumstances. Any kind of writing—even informal writing—

that has too many exclamations sounds juvenile. There are better ways to express your enthusiasm (see Chapter 43).

EXERCISE 50.1

VIDEO
Exploring end
punctuation.

The following email message contains a number of errors in end punctuation. Make the appropriate corrections.

Guess what

I just found the Web site for NoF.X. Which I have been meaning to search out. It's NoF.X.@anyservercom.

I just got their new C.D. it was a real deal At WEJones Music downtown—$12 99 I'm listening to it now—it rules.

That's it for now I have to write a paper (yuck) due Tues It's on F.D.R. and W.W.II Got to go

Later :)

EXERCISE 50.2

EXER
End
punctuation.

The end punctuation marks have been deleted from the following paragraphs. Supply the appropriate punctuation marks.

1. How long have human beings been concerned about population growth If you believe the warnings, we have long been on the verge of overpopulating the earth In a warning written around AD 200, a Roman writer named Tertullian lamented that "we are burdensome to the world and the resources are scarcely adequate to us" The population at the time is believed to have been 200 million, barely 3 percent of today's 5.8 billion He thought *he* had reason for concern

2. Can a program ever be believed once it stages an incident Sometimes it can NBC's *Dateline* was not the first network to fake a car crash when it used igniters in its dramatization of the hazards of GM trucks; all three networks had done the same Unfortunately, the public was not told that program personnel "helped" ignite the fire Why did the network do it They did it because of competition for viewers The line between entertainment and news was badly blurred What was the reason for the media error *Dateline* anchor Jane Pauley replied, "Because on one side of the line is an Emmy; the other, the abyss"

CHAPTER 51

The Comma

FAQs

▶ Should I use a comma before *and* and *but?* (51b)
▶ How should I punctuate a series of items? (51c)
▶ In addresses, is there a comma between the state and the zip code? (51g-2)
▶ Should I put a comma after *such as?* (51j)

The comma is the most common and most useful punctuation mark in the English language—and also perhaps the most difficult to master. Commas are used essentially to interrupt the flow of a sentence, to set off certain parts of it and thereby enhance the sentence's readability. This chapter provides some *guidelines* (not rules) for the use of commas. In most cases, these guidelines will help you clarify meaning and follow conventions for separating confusing elements. But there are occasional situations where it is helpful to look beyond the guidelines to see what separations may be needed to clarify meaning. Practice (and reading lots of expert writing) will give you the intuition and confidence required to use commas appropriately and effectively.

AUDIO

Chapter overview.

51a Use a comma to set off an introductory phrase or clause

When readers start to read a sentence, one of the first things they do (unconsciously) is try to locate the grammatical subject. Help them do this by setting off with a comma any potentially distracting words that *precede* the subject. In the following excerpt, note how the commas allow the reader to identify easily the sentence subjects that follow them: *cultural relativism, most US citizens,* and *bullfighting.*

> *Because we tend to use our own culture to judge others,* cultural relativism presents a challenge to ordinary thinking. *For example,* most US citizens appear to have strong feelings against raising bulls for the sole purpose of stabbing them to death in front of crowds shouting "Olé!" *According to cultural relativism, however,* bullfighting must be viewed strictly within the context of the culture in which it takes place—its history, its folklore, its ideas of bravery, and its ideas of sex roles.

51.1

A guide to the use and abuse of commas.

> **WEBLINK**
>
> http://owl.english.purdue
> .edu/handouts/grammar/
> g_comma.html
> A discussion of the main
> uses of the comma, accompanied by good proofreading strategies and exercises

The writer has put a comma after an introductory subordinate clause (*Because we tend to use our own culture to judge others*), a transitional phrase (*For example*), and a prepositional phrase and conjunctive adverb (*According to cultural relativism, however*). In each sentence, the comma marks off everything preceding the subject, allowing the reader to locate the subject easily.

Using a comma after an introductory element is sometimes necessary to prevent possible confusion.

CONFUSING   Soon after starting the car began making funny noises.

CLEAR   Soon after starting, the car began making funny noises.

Exception: If the introductory element is short and unemphatic, you do not need to insert a comma.

> *Today* I have class from 9:00 a.m. to 1:00 p.m.

> *On most days* the mail does not get here until late afternoon.

51b Use a comma before a coordinating conjunction to separate independent clauses

The combination of a comma and a coordinating conjunction (*and, but, or, nor, for, so, yet*) is one of the most common ways of connecting independent clauses.

> Members of a mainstream culture often feel threatened by a counterculture, *and* they sometimes move against it in the attempt to affirm their own values.

Conflict theorists acknowledge that social institutions were originally designed to meet basic survival needs, *but* they do not see social institutions as working harmoniously for the common good.

Using a comma before a coordinating conjunction to separate independent clauses, as in these examples, clarifies for the reader that each clause is making a separate statement.

When the two clauses are closely linked, however, you may want to omit the comma, as in this example.

> It was very hot and the men had marched a long way. They slumped under the weight of their packs and the curiously black faces were glistening with sweat.
>
> —George Orwell, "Marrakech"

When you are using a coordinating conjunction to link phrases rather than clauses, you generally do not insert a comma.

INCORRECT Acupuncture has proved effective for treating chronic pain, and for blocking acute pain briefly.

CORRECT Acupuncture has proved effective for treating chronic pain and for blocking acute pain briefly.

However, writers sometimes insert a comma to create more separation between the two parts.

Acupressure is similar to acupuncture, but does not use needles.
[The contrastive phrase is separated with a comma.]

51.2
Using the comma for rhetorical effect.

Here the writer has put a comma between the two verb phrases in order to emphasize the contrast in meaning between them. (See 30d, 35b, and Chapter 36 for more on using phrases and clauses in sentences.)

EXERCISE 51.1

Correct the comma errors in the following sentences:

1. In comparison with ordinary soap the production of detergents exerts a more intense environmental impact.
2. Three out of four Americans claim to believe in God and four out of ten go to church regularly.
3. If a typical book contains 500 pages the information content of a single chromosome corresponds to some 4,000 volumes.
4. There are numerous private daycare centers in the US but the employees are often underpaid and weary from looking after too many children.

5. In many countries people cannot conceive of themselves apart from the family or group they belong to. In America on the other hand self-reliance is the fundamental virtue.
6. The English language surrounds us like a sea and like the waters of the deep it is full of mysteries.
7. Of all the world's languages (which now number some 2,700) English is arguably the richest in vocabulary.
8. For most people body temperature drops at night, and then rises in the morning.
9. Enjoyment and appreciation are related terms but they are not synonymous.
10. Although one can enjoy music without understanding it appreciation of music requires some knowledge.

51c Use commas between items in a series

A series of three or more items should have commas after all but the last item.

My super-patriotic neighbor says *red, white, and blue* are his favorite colors.

Each day, cigarettes contribute to over 1,000 deaths from *cancer, heart disease, and respiratory diseases.*

Many writers, however, drop the final comma (or **serial comma**), especially in fields such as journalism, advertising, and business.

My uncle used to work for *Pierce, Fenner and Smith.*

Using the serial comma is never wrong, however; and sometimes it helps clarify the meaning of a sentence.

UNCLEAR The three balls were colored red, blue and white and green.

CLEAR The three balls were colored red, blue and white, and green.

OR

CLEAR The three balls were colored red, blue, and white and green.

51d Use commas to separate coordinate adjectives

When the adjectives in a series could be arranged in any order or could be (but are not) strung together with the use of *and,* they are termed **coordinate adjectives.** To show their loose relationship and to avoid confusion with adjectives that cumulate in a particular order to modify each other, separate coordinate adjectives with commas (see 51j).

A *rusty, dented, broken-down* car was left behind.

In this example, each adjective modifies the word *car,* and the string of adjectives could be rearranged:

A *broken-down, dented, rusty* car was left behind.

(See Chapter 62 for more on word order.)

51e   Use commas to set off nonessential elements

A **nonessential element,** or **nonrestrictive element,** provides an extra piece of information that can be left out without changing the basic meaning of the sentence. Always use punctuation to set off non-essential or nonrestrictive elements from the rest of the sentence. (By contrast, elements that are essential or restrictive are always integrated into the sentence without separating punctuation; see 51j.) Non-essential elements are most commonly set off with commas; however, dashes (56d) or parentheses (56a) may also be used.

Lung cancer, *the leading cause of cancer deaths in the United States,* kills more than 153,000 Americans each year.   [A nonessential appositive is set off with commas.]

Many other illnesses, *like the common cold and even back strain,* are self-limiting and will improve in time.   [A nonessential phrase is set off with commas.]

Universal health care, *which guarantees every citizen at least basic medical benefits,* is found in every industrialized country in the world except the United States and South Africa.   [A nonessential clause is set off with commas.]

In each of these sentences, the writer could have omitted the italicized elements without affecting the basic meaning of the sentence. She could have said,

Lung cancer . . . kills more than 153,000 Americans each year.

Many other illnesses . . . are self-limiting and will improve in time.

Universal health care . . . is found in every industrialized country in the world except the United States and South Africa.

HELP

How do I identify punctuation errors in my writing?

1. Open the grammar checker.
2. Click on the OPTIONS feature.
3. Select the CUSTOM setting.
4. Open the customization feature.
5. Deselect all grammar and style features except the one called something like PUNCTUATION ERRORS.
6. Run the program on your document. For extra speed, turn off the spell checker.

Instead, she chose to insert extra information to help the reader.

Unless the nonessential element ends the sentence, be sure to use *two* commas to set it off, not just one.

INCORRECT	Alzheimer's disease, *a progressive impairment of the brain* strikes over 4 million older Americans every year.
CORRECT	Alzheimer's disease, *a progressive impairment of the brain,* strikes over 4 million older Americans every year.

When should you use commas instead of dashes or parentheses to set off nonrestrictive elements? Commas represent less of a break in the flow of thought, so the elements they enclose are a bit more closely attached to the main part of the sentence. Dashes (see 56d) give more emphasis to the nonrestrictive element, while parentheses (see 56a) can make the nonrestrictive element seem almost like an afterthought.

EXERCISE 51.2

EXER
Correct comma errors.

Correct the comma errors in the following sentences.

1. The antitax group collected 65,202 signatures, on a petition, in support of an immediate tax cut.
2. Although this is more than the required 64,928 signatures it still may not be enough.
3. Because of duplications, illegible signatures and people improperly signing for other family members a minimum margin of at least 2,000 is usually needed, to withstand challenges experts say.

4. At one time many states often barred the sale of contraceptives to minors prohibited the display of contraceptives or, even, banned their sale altogether.

5. Today condoms are sold in the grocery store and some television stations, even air ads for them.

6. The capital campaign which was off to a great start, hoped to net $1.2 million.

7. When we shop we want to get the most for our money.

8. Herbalists practice herbal medicine which is based on the medicinal qualities of plants or herbs.

9. Economically and culturally overshadowed by the United States Canada has nonetheless managed to carve out a feisty independent identity since World War II.

10. The participants who had been carefully chosen by Akron's political and community establishment expressed a range of views.

51f Use commas to set off conjunctive adverbs

Conjunctive adverbs include the words and phrases *however, therefore, consequently, thus, furthermore, on the other hand, in general,* and *in other words* (see 41b). They serve as useful transitional devices, helping the reader to follow the flow of the writer's thinking. By enclosing conjunctive adverbs in commas, you give them more prominence, clearly marking a shift in thinking.

> Over eighty million people in the United States suffer from chronic health conditions. Their access to health care, *however,* is largely determined by whether or not they have health insurance.

> Resistance training exercises cause microscopic damage to muscle fibers, which take twenty-four to forty-eight hours to heal; *therefore,* resistance training programs require at least one day of rest between workouts.

51g Use commas with dates, place names and addresses, titles and degrees, and numbers

1 Using commas with dates

When writing a date in the traditional American format of month, day, and year, set off the year by placing a comma after the day.

John F. Kennedy died on November 22, 1963.

Do not use a comma if only the month and year are given.

John F. Kennedy died in November 1963.

Do not use a comma when writing the date in inverse order (day, month, year).

John F. Kennedy died on 22 November 1963.

2 Using commas in place names and addresses

Use commas after all major elements in a place name or address. However, do not put a comma before a zip code.

Aretha Franklin was born in Memphis, Tennessee, on March 25, 1942.

Alfredo's new address is 112 Ivy Lane, Englewood, NJ 07631.

3 Using commas with titles and degrees

Use commas to set off a title or degree following a person's name (see 58a).

Stella Martinez, MD, was the attending physician.

Ken Griffey, Jr., will never break Barry Bonds's home run record.

4 Using commas in numbers

Use a comma in numbers of five digits or more, to form three-digit groups. In a number of four digits, the comma is optional.

2,400 OR 2400

56,397

1,000,000

Exceptions: Do not use commas in street numbers, zip codes, telephone numbers, account numbers, model numbers, or years.

51h Use commas with speaker tags

If you are quoting someone and using a speaker tag (such as *he said*, *according to Freud*, or *notes Laurel Stuart*), put a comma between the tag and the quotation.

Thomas Edison said, "Genius is 1 percent inspiration and 99 percent perspiration."

"The only thing about the fishing industry that has not changed much," *she writes,* "is the fishermen themselves."

Note that if a quote ends in a comma, the comma goes *inside* the quotation mark (see 55e).

A comma is not used if the quote ends in another punctuation mark.

"What a marvelous performance!" exclaimed the Queen.

A comma is not used if the quotation is introduced with *that*.

Rush Limbaugh claims that "the poorest people in America are better off than the mainstream families in Europe."

51i Use commas with markers of direct address

Put commas around words that indicate that you are talking directly to the reader: words such as *yes* or *no,* the reader's name (*Bob*), question tags (*don't you agree?*), or mild initiators (*Well, Oh*).

Yes, the stock market is likely to turn around.

Do you really think, *Grace,* that Professor Wilson will postpone the test?

Intelligence is impossible to measure with just one type of test, *don't you think?*

Some people say we should all have guns to protect ourselves. *Well,* I do not agree.

EXERCISE 51.3

Correct the comma errors in the following sentences.

1. One fictitious address used by advertisers is John and Mary Jones 100 Main Street Anytown USA 12345
2. We are a nation of shoppers aren't we?
3. Easy access to birth control however, was not always the case.
4. "It would be good to have this question on the ballot" the governor said.
5. Dr. Martin Luther King Jr. often quoted lines from the Bible.
6. For example, he would sometimes say "Let justice roll down like the waters."

EXER

More comma error correction.

7. A Renoir exhibition organized and first shown by the National Gallery of Canada in Ottawa Ontario opened at the Art Institute of Chicago, on October 21 1997 and ran through January 4th, of the next year.

8. Much to the irritation of its neighbor, for instance Canada keeps friendly ties with Fidel Castro's Cuba.

9. Lee surrendered to Grant at Appomattox Court House Virginia on April 9 1865.

10. According to the police there were more than 10000 protestors at the rally.

51j Avoid misuse of commas

1. *Never use a single comma between the subject and predicate.* When a complex subject begins a sentence, writers sometimes feel inclined to add an inappropriate comma that splits the subject and predicate.

AUDIO
Do not insert a comma between subject and predicate.

INCORRECT	Numerous psychological and social factors, have a strong influence on how people age.
CORRECT	Numerous psychological and social factors have a strong influence on how people age.

WEBLINK

http://webster.commnet
.edu/grammar/commas.htm

An excellent illustrated guide to commas, with quizzes

This mistake arises only if you insert a *single* comma between subject and predicate. A nonrestrictive element between the subject and the predicate may be set off by two commas.

Police discretion, the decision as to whether to arrest someone or even to ignore a matter, is a routine part of police work.

2. *Never put commas around essential elements.* Essential (or **restrictive**) **elements** are phrases or clauses that help define some other element in the sentence. Unlike nonessential elements (see 51e), they should not be set off with commas.

INCORRECT	Consumers, who are considering using a hospital or clinic, should scrutinize the facility's accreditation.
CORRECT	Consumers who are considering using a hospital or clinic should scrutinize the facility's accreditation. [Omitting the commas makes it clear that the writer is referring only to those consumers who are considering using a hospital or clinic.]

INCORRECT	Be sure to use a filtration system, which will destroy all harmful bacteria in the water.
CORRECT	Be sure to use a filtration system which will destroy all harmful bacteria in the water. [Omitting the comma before the modifying phrase makes it clear that the writer is referring only to a certain type of filtration system, not just any filtration system.]

Essential elements include names that come immediately after a common noun and define what the noun refers to:

The film *Citizen Kane* is an all-time classic. [The name *Citizen Kane* serves as a restrictive appositive, identifying a specific film.]

The Chilean novelist Isabel Allende is an acclaimed defender of human rights. [The name *Isabel Allende* is a restrictive appositive, identifying a particular Chilean novelist.]

Guidelines for Comma Use

Use commas to separate

Introductory phrases or clauses, especially if they tend to obscure the subject (51a)

Independent clauses connected with a coordinating conjunction (51b)

Three or more items in a series (51c)

A string of adjectives that could be rearranged or linked by *and* (51d)

Nonessential phrases or clauses that add to but do not restrict the sentence's basic meaning (51e)

Conjunctive adverbs used as transitional devices (51f)

Speaker tags (51h)

Markers of direct address (51i)

Do not use commas to separate

Subjects and predicates that would be split with a single comma

Restrictive phrases or clauses that are essential to a sentence's basic meaning

Adjectives that depend on their order to show modification in meaning

Items in a series of only two items

Phrases beginning with *than*

Subordinating conjunctions

Independent clauses that are not connected with a coordinating conjunction (36b, 51b)

3. *Avoid using commas with cumulative adjectives.* Adjectives that accumulate before a noun, each one modifying those that follow, are called **cumulative adjectives.** Their modifying relationships, which depend on their order, are likely to be confused by the separating commas that are common with adjectives in a coordinate series (see 51d).

INCORRECT   The suspect was seen driving a *small, new, Italian, luxury,* car.

CORRECT   The suspect was seen driving a *small new Italian luxury* car.

Cumulative adjectives follow a certain order (see 62b). Therefore, one way of identifying cumulative adjectives is to see whether they can be reordered. If the result sounds awkward (*a luxury Italian new small car*), the original ordering is cumulative.

Coordinate adjectives are different. Instead of modifying the following adjectives, they each modify the head noun directly. Therefore, it is appropriate to separate them with commas (see 51d).

4. *Avoid putting a comma before* than. Resist the urge to heighten a comparison or contrast by using commas to separate the *than* clause from the rest of the sentence.

INCORRECT   Beating our arch rival was more important, than getting to the state playoffs.

CORRECT   Beating our arch rival was more important than getting to the state playoffs.

5. *Avoid using a comma after a subordinating conjunction.* A comma should not be used to separate a subordinating conjunction from its own clause.

INCORRECT   Although, the car is fifteen years old, it seems to be in good shape.

CORRECT   Although the car is fifteen years old, it seems to be in good shape.

6. *Never use a comma before parentheses or after a question mark or exclamation point.* A comma is superfluous with an opening parenthesis, a question mark, or an exclamation point, unless the punctuation mark is part of a title.

INCORRECT   Muhammad was born in Mecca, (now in Saudi Arabia) and founded the religion of Islam around AD 610.

CORRECT   Muhammad was born in Mecca (now in Saudi Arabia) and founded the religion of Islam around AD 610.

INCORRECT	"Where are you going?," he asked.
CORRECT	"Where are you going?" he asked.
BUT	According to the book *Culture Shock!*, 57% of Americans are Protestants.

7. *Do not insert a comma before a list.* Resist the urge to punctuate before a listed series. (For suggestions on rewriting sentences to handle a list, see 53a.)

INCORRECT	Some countries, such as, Holland, Sweden, and Denmark, have very compassionate welfare systems.
CORRECT	Some countries, such as Holland, Sweden, and Denmark, have very compassionate welfare systems.
INCORRECT	My toughest subjects are, math, biology, and physics.
CORRECT	My toughest subjects are math, biology, and physics.

8. *Do not use a comma in a two-item series.* While commas are needed to separate three or more items in series, separating two items with a comma is unnecessary and distracting.

INCORRECT	Her outfit used strong contrasts between red, and blue.
CORRECT	Her outfit used strong contrasts between red and blue.

(**EXERCISE 51.4**)

Remove commas where necessary from the following sentences.

1. Tiger Woods has more competition, than he did three years ago.
2. My favorite sports are team sports such as, basketball and football.
3. Anyone, who appreciates classic art, would enjoy a visit to the Prado museum in Madrid.
4. The cues of daylight and darkness, help to keep plants and animals synchronized with the environment.
5. Someday, when we begin to assemble a kind of time map of the body's various rhythms, everyone will be surprised and perhaps delighted to recognize rhythms already observed in themselves.
6. Although, they often find Americans welcoming, and friendly, this is not altogether an easy country for foreigners to travel in.

7. Rodney gave his girlfriend a necklace with a beautiful, large, black, gemstone in it.

8. I normally use the Internet portal, *Yahoo!,* but my mother prefers *Excite.*

9. The objective of the American school system, is to bestow a broad education on every youngster.

10. Unless, they frequently trade in their car for a new one, people normally search for a car, that will last many years.

EXERCISE 51.5

Insert or remove commas where appropriate in the following sentences.

1. Length area and volume, are properties that can be measured.

2. Many plants are poisonous and others can be toxic if used in high doses.

3. We spend more on health care than does any other nation yet, unlike the rest of the industrialized world we do not provide access to health care for our entire population.

4. Stereotypes concerning inevitable intellectual decline among the elderly, have largely been refuted.

5. Classified advertisements are lists of ads set in small, type sizes, that advertise jobs items for sale and garage sales.

6. Long detailed explanations, can put a listener to sleep.

7. People, who are good shoppers, spend many hours planning their purchases.

8. They check sale circulars, from the newspaper and use the telephone to compare prices.

9. When they, finally, find an item at the best possible price they make their purchase.

10. Celebrations, marking the year 2000, were held in cities and towns across the continent.

EXERCISE 51.6

The following passage contains a number of comma errors (not in the original). Make the appropriate corrections.

To survive on the Earth human beings require the stable continuing existence of a suitable environment. Yet the evidence is overwhelming, that the way, in which we now live on the Earth is driving its thin life-supporting skin, and ourselves with it to destruction. To understand this calamity we need to begin with a close look, at the nature of the environment itself. Most of us find this a difficult thing to do for there is a kind of ambiguity, in our relation to the environment. Biologically human beings *participate* in the environmental system as subsidiary parts of the whole. Yet, human society is designed to *exploit* the environment as a whole to produce wealth. The paradoxical role we play in the natural environment—at once participant, and exploiter—distorts our perception of it.

Among primitive people a person is seen as a dependent part of nature, a frail reed in a harsh world governed by natural laws, that must be obeyed if he is to survive. Pressed by this need primitive peoples can achieve a remarkable knowledge of their environment. The African Bushman lives in one of the most stringent habitats on earth; food and water are scarce and the weather is extreme. The Bushman survives, because he has an incredibly intimate understanding of this environment. A Bushman can, for example return after many months, and miles of travel to find a single underground tuber noted in his previous wanderings when he needs it, for his water supply in the dry season.

—Barry Commoner, *The Closing Circle*

FOR COLLABORATION

Share your corrected paragraphs with a friend or member of your group. Notice which revisions do the most to improve the paragraphs.

The Semicolon

AUDIO

Chapter overview.

There are three ways to show a close relationship between independent clauses: with a *comma* and coordinating conjunction (see 51b), a *colon* (see 53b), or a *semicolon*. A semicolon is used when the two clauses have a coordinate relationship—that is, when they convey equally important ideas (see 41b)—but do not have a coordinating conjunction (*and, but, or, nor, for, so, yet*) between them.

 52a **Use a semicolon to separate independent clauses not linked by a coordinating conjunction**

WWW

52.1

Six guidelines for using semicolons.

WEBLINK

http://www.wisc.edu/writetest/Handbook/Semicolons.html

A complete guide to semicolons

When there is no coordinating conjunction, related independent clauses should be connected with a semicolon rather than a comma.

The first panacea for a mismanaged nation is inflation of the currency; the second is war. Both bring a temporary prosperity; both bring a permanent ruin.

—Ernest Hemingway,
Notes on the Next War

52b Use a semicolon to separate independent clauses linked by a conjunctive adverb

If you separate two independent clauses with a conjunctive adverb like *however, therefore,* or *nevertheless* (see list on page 755), you must use a semicolon (see 36c):

> More than 185 countries belong to the United Nations; *however,* only five of them have veto power.

> Japan and Germany are now among the five most powerful nations in the world; *therefore,* they would like to have veto power, too.

52c Use semicolons in a series with internal punctuation

A **complex series** is one that has internal punctuation. Normally, commas are used to separate items in a series (see 51c); however, if the individual items contain commas, it can be difficult for readers to determine which commas are internal to the items and which commas separate the items. In these cases, semicolons are used to separate the items.

> I have lived in Boulder, Colorado; Corpus Christi, Texas; and Vero Beach, Florida.

52d Place semicolons outside quotation marks

Semicolons are always positioned outside quotation marks.

> Those who feel abortion is not a woman's prerogative say they are "pro-life"; those who feel it is say they are "pro-choice."

AUDIO
Using a semi-colon between balanced clauses.

52e Avoid common semicolon errors

Most errors with semicolons occur as a result of confusing semicolons with commas (see Chapter 51) or with colons (see Chapter 53).

1. *Do not use a semicolon between an independent clause and a dependent clause or phrase.* Dependent clauses or phrases are linked to independent clauses most often by commas, not semicolons (see Chapter 51).

HELP

How can I spot places where I need a semicolon with a conjunctive adverb?

1. Open the SEARCH (or FIND) program in your computer.
2. Enter *however* in the SEARCH field, and run the search.
3. Wherever your computer flags the word *however*, see whether there are independent clauses on both sides of the word.
4. If there are, insert a semicolon before *however* and a comma after it (see 36c).
5. Do the same with *therefore, for example, nevertheless,* and other conjunctive adverbs.

52.2
Online help
for using
semicolons.

> **WEBLINK**
> http://www.uottawa.ca/
> academic/arts/writcent/
> hypergrammar/semicoln
> .html
> **Abbreviated help with use
> of semicolons**

INCORRECT   When we say that a country is "underdeveloped"; we imply that it is backward in some way.

CORRECT   When we say that a country is "underdeveloped," we imply that it is backward in some way.

INCORRECT   In *MS Word,* you can remove several items from a document and then insert them as a group into another document by using the Spike; a scrapbook-like feature.

CORRECT   In *MS Word,* you can remove several items from a document and then insert them as a group into another document by using the Spike, a scrapbook-like feature.

2. *Do not use a semicolon to introduce a list.* Use a colon instead of a semicolon to introduce a list (see 53a).

INCORRECT   Utah has five national parks; Arches, Bryce, Canyon-lands, Capitol Reef, and Zion.

CORRECT   Utah has five national parks: Arches, Bryce, Canyon-lands, Capitol Reef, and Zion.

EXERCISE 52.1

Correct the punctuation errors in the following sentences.

1. Socrates disliked being called a "teacher," he preferred to think of himself as an intellectual midwife.

2. Tests will be given on the following dates; Monday, November 2, Friday, November 20, and Monday, December 7.

3. The scientific naming and classification of all organisms is known as *taxonomy,* both living and extinct organisms are taxonomically classified.

4. A single category of a species is called a *taxon,* multiple categories are *taxa.*

5. Since laughter seems to help the body heal; many doctors and hospitals are prescribing humor for their patients.

EXER

Using the semicolon.

6. Beethoven was deaf when he wrote his final symphonies, nevertheless, they are considered musical masterpieces.

7. Some people think that watching a video at home is more fun than going to a movie, movie theaters are often crowded and noisy.

8. The lifeguards closed the beach when a shark was spotted, a few hours later some fishermen reported seeing the shark leave; so the beach was reopened.

9. The feeling of balance is controlled by the ears, inside each ear are three small tubes filled with fluid.

10. Since its opening in 1955; Disneyland has been an important part of American culture, it has the ability to reflect and reinforce American beliefs, values, and ideals.

CHAPTER 53

The Colon

FAQs

▶ How does the colon differ from the semicolon? (53b)

▶ What punctuation mark should I use to introduce a quotation? (53c)

AUDIO
Chapter overview.

In formal writing, the colon is used mainly after a general statement to announce details related in some way to the statement. These details may be a list of items, a quotation, an appositive, or an explanatory statement.

53a Use a colon to introduce a list or an appositive

WEBLINK

http://www.uottawa.ca/academic/arts/writcent/hypergrammar/colon.html
An introduction to using the colon

In creating a macro, you can assign it to any one of three places: the toolbar, the keyboard, or a menu.

One principle should govern your choice: which one is most convenient?

In using a colon to introduce a list or an appositive, be sure that the introductory part of the sentence is a grammatically complete clause.

AUDIO
When to use a colon to introduce a list.

FAULTY COLON USE

The four main parts of a memo are: header, introduction, summary, and details.

FAULTY COLON USE REVISED

A memo has four main parts: header, introduction, summary, and details.

OR

There are four main parts to a memo: header, introduction, summary, and details.

In academic writing, the phrase *as follows* is often used. It directly precedes the colon.

There are four main parts to a memo, as follows: header, introduction, summary, and details.

53b Use a colon to set off a second independent clause that explains the first

Rock climbing is like vertical chess: in making each move up the wall, you should have a broad strategy in mind.

(Note) You may begin the clause after the colon with either an uppercase letter or a lowercase letter.

Although both the colon and the semicolon can be used to separate independent clauses, they cannot be used interchangeably. A semicolon is used when the two clauses are balanced (see 52a); a colon is used when the second clause is a specification of the first.

COLON   Blessed are the pure in heart: for they shall see God.

SEMICOLON   And the earth was without form and void; and darkness was upon the face of the deep.

53.1
Instructions for how to avoid overusing colons.

53c Use a colon to introduce a quotation

When a colon is used to introduce a quotation, the part of the sentence that precedes the colon should be grammatically independent (see 53a).

In *Against Empire,* Michael Parenti states his concern about American foreign policy: "We should pay less attention to what US policymakers profess as their motives—for anyone can avouch dedication to noble causes—and give more attention to what they actually do."

If the part introducing the quotation is not an independent clause, use a comma instead of a colon.

> In *Against Empire,* Michael Parenti states, "We should pay less attention . . . ."

(Note) If the quotation serves only as an example and is set off from the sentence that introduces it (as in the two examples above), no colon is used.

53d Use colons in titles

Colons are often used in the titles of academic papers and reports. The part of the title that follows the colon is called the subtitle. It usually provides a more explicit description of the topic than does the title.

> Nature and the Poetic Imagination: Death and Rebirth in "Ode to the West Wind"

53e Use colons in business letters and memos

In business letters and memos, colons are used in salutations (*Dear Ms. Townsend:*), to separate the writer's initials from the typist's initials (*TH:ab*), and in memo headings (*To:, From:, Date:, Subject:, Dist:*). (See Chapter 25 for more on business writing.)

53f Use colons in numbers and addresses

53.2
A guide to punctuating with colons.

WEBLINK

http://leo.stcloudstate.edu/punct/colon.html

A comprehensive discussion of all uses of the colon

Colons are used in Biblical citations to distinguish chapter from verse (*Matthew 4:11, Genesis 3:9*), in clock times to separate hours from minutes and minutes from seconds (*5:44 p.m.*), in ratios (*3:1*), and in Web site addresses (*http://www.fray.com*).

(EXERCISE 53.1)

Correct the punctuation errors in the following sentences.

1. There are several steps involved in writing an effective summary; read the original carefully, choose the material for your

summary rewrite the material in a concise manner, identify the source of the original text.

2. We need to buy several ingredients in order to bake the cookies, brown sugar, chocolate chips eggs, and milk.

EXER
Using colons.

3. In *Becoming a Critical Thinker,* Ruggiero states, "Truth is not something we create to fit our desires. Rather, it is a reality to be discovered."

4. There are three important characteristics that all critical thinkers possess; the ability to be honest with themselves, the ability to resist manipulation, and the ability to ask questions.

5. Experts say swimming is one of the best forms of exercise, it burns as many calories as running but is low-impact.

6. The hacker apparently logged on to *<http//www.au.org>* at 9.03 a.m.

7. There are four qualities of a diamond that a prospective buyer should be aware of, color, clarity, cut, and carat weight.

8. In *The Language Instinct,* Steven Pinker discusses the inherent nature of language, "We are all born with the instinct to learn, speak, and understand language."

9. There are six major speech organs which are used to articulate sounds; the larynx, soft palate, tongue body, tongue tip, tongue root, and lips.

10. Denise titled her paper "Howls of Delight; Reintroduction of the Wolf into Yellowstone National Park."

The Apostrophe

▶ What is the difference between *it's* and *its?* (54a-1)

▶ How do I show possession with two names, like *Maria and Roberto?* (54a-2)

▶ Should I write *1990's* or *1990s?* (54c-2)

AUDIO

Chapter overview.

VIDEO

How to recognize apostrophe problems

The apostrophe is used to indicate possession, to alert the reader to contractions and omitted letters, and to form certain plurals.

54a Use apostrophes with nouns to indicate possession

In its grammatical sense, *possession* refers to ownership, amounts, or some other special relationship between two nouns. With singular nouns, possession is usually indicated by attaching *'s* to the end of the noun.

Sue Ellen's jacket	everyone's dream
my mother's photo	yesterday's bad weather
the club's treasurer	Gandhi's place in history
Ahmad's smile	a week's worth of work
Mr. Linder's class	

There are two exceptions to this rule:

1. If the rule would lead to awkward pronunciation, the extra *s* may be omitted: *Euripides' plays, Moses' laws, Mister Rogers' Neighborhood.*

2. In names of places, companies, and institutions, the apostrophe is often omitted: *Robbers Roost, Kings County, Starbucks, Peoples Republic.*

For plural nouns ending in *s*, form the possessive by just adding an apostrophe at the end:

WEBLINK

http://www.salon.com/news/col/huff/2002/12/17/apostrophe/

A popular commentator bemoans "America's apostrophe catastrophe"

54.1

A guide to the apostrophe, with exercises.

the Browns' car   the Yankees' star pitcher   my parents' friends

For plural nouns not ending in *s*, form the possessive by adding *'s*:

women's rights   children's section   sheep's wool

1 Avoiding apostrophes with possessive pronouns

Pronouns never take apostrophes to indicate possession. They have their own possessive forms: *its, his, her/hers, your/yours, their/theirs, our/ours, my/mine* (see 31e).

Be careful not to confuse *its* and *it's.* The former is possessive; the latter is a contraction for *it is.*

POSSESSIVE   The university has revised its policy on hate speech.

CONTRACTION   If you fall way behind in your studies, it's hard to catch up.

2 Showing possession with multiple nouns

With multiple nouns, use apostrophes according to your intended meaning. If you want to indicate joint possession, add an apostrophe only to the last of the nouns:

AUDIO

Confusion between *its* and *it's.*

Bill and Hillary's wedding

Siskel and Ebert's recommendations

If you want to show *separate* possession, put an apostrophe after each of the nouns:

Julie's and Kathy's weddings

Omar's, Gretchen's, and Mike's birthdays

54b Use apostrophes to indicate contractions and omitted letters

In casual speech, syllables are sometimes omitted from common word combinations. For example, *cannot* becomes *can't*. In formal writing, such contractions are generally inappropriate. In much informal writing, however, such as email messages and personal letters, contractions are quite common. Just be sure to punctuate them correctly with an apostrophe.

will not → won't	should not → shouldn't	it is → it's
I am → I'm	you have → you've	they are → they're

The apostrophe also can be used for less common contractions, especially if you are trying to create a colloquial, slangy tone.

the 1990s → the '90s	magazine → 'zine
underneath → 'neath	neighborhood → 'hood

54c Use apostrophes to mark certain plural forms

When a letter or symbol is used as a noun, the usual way of pluralizing nouns (adding an *-s* or *-es*) does not work well: "There are four ss in *sassafras*." In such cases, an apostrophe can help out.

1 Forming the plurals of letters, symbols, and words referred to as words

54.2

Basics on apostrophe use.

WEBLINK

http://owl.english.purdue
.edu/handouts/grammar/
g_apost.html
A discussion of all uses of the apostrophe, accompanied by proofreading strategies and exercises

Adding *'s* instead of *s* clarifies the plural forms of unusual nouns.

There are four *s*'s in *sassafras*.

How can she have two *@*'s in her email address?

My instructor said I have too many *there*'s in my paper.

2 Forming the plurals of numbers and abbreviations

Both the Modern Language Association and the American Psychological Association recommend omitting the apostrophe in forming plurals like the following:

the 1990s   several IOUs
a pair of 6s   a shipment of PCs

54d Avoid misusing the apostrophe

Be careful not to use apostrophes where they do not belong. The following box lists some of the most common apostrophe errors.

(Grammar Checker Alert) Your grammar checker should flag most of the apostrophe errors described in this chapter, including all three of the common errors listed in the box below. However, it may not tell you exactly how to fix the problem. For example, in the sentence "TV news reporting *seem's* like yet another form of entertainment," our grammar checker identified *seem's* as problematic but offered five different alternatives, only one of which was correct. You will have to exercise your own judgment in such cases. The guidelines in this chapter should help you.

Common Apostrophe Errors

1. Do not use an apostrophe for the possessive form of it.

   NO   Her dog lost *it's* collar.

   YES   Her dog lost *its* collar.

2. Do not use an apostrophe with nonpossessive nouns.

   NO   This report discusses four major *features'* of modern mass media.

   NO   This report discusses four major *feature's* of modern mass media.

   YES   This report discusses four major *features* of modern mass media.

3. Do not use an apostrophe with present-tense verbs.

   NO   TV news reporting *seem's* like yet another form of entertainment.

   YES   TV news reporting *seems* like yet another form of entertainment.

Each of the following sentences contains at least one error involving apostrophes. Make the appropriate correction(s).

EXER

Apostrophes mark contractions and omissions.

1. Its unfortunate that Bobs' birthday falls on February 29.
2. I wanted to go to Maria's and Roberto's party, but I wasnt able to.
3. The snake sheds it's skin many times during its life.
4. Does the mens' group meet here?
5. No, its a womens' group that meets in this room on Thursdays.
6. I can't wait til my vacation comes!
7. Im taking my lawyers advice on such matter's.
8. All of the orchestra member's instruments seemed to be out of tune.
9. The driver and passenger's airbags both deployed after the accident.
10. Kevin's and Lauren's older sister is in high school now.

FOR COLLABORATION

Take note of apostrophe errors that you see on campus or in your neighborhood; share your examples with your group.

CHAPTER 55

Quotation Marks

FAQs

▶ Should I use quotation marks if I am only paraphrasing someone's words? (55a-1)

▶ Should a comma go inside or outside the quotation mark?
(55e)

▶ How do I introduce a quotation? (55e)

The primary use of quotation marks is to acknowledge other people's words and statements. Using quotation marks is especially important in academic writing, which puts a premium on the ownership
of ideas.

AUDIO

Chapter
overview.

55a   Use quotation marks for exact direct quotations

Quotation marks should be placed around any words, phrases, or
sentences that you have borrowed from someone else (unless the quotations are so lengthy that you prefer to set them off as an indented
block).

In *The End of Work*, Jeremy Rifkin said, "In the years ahead, more
than 90 million jobs in a labor force of 124 million are potentially
vulnerable to replacement by machines."

One reviewer called it "a very readable and timely book."

Some years ago, a group of artists designed a "space bridge"
between Los Angeles and New York.

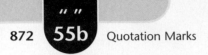

1 Paraphrasing or quoting indirectly

A summarization, restatement, or paraphrase of a statement made by someone else is a form of **indirect discourse,** and quotation marks are not used. Putting quotation marks around words that were not those of the speaker or writer would be extremely misleading.

> Rifkin argues that in the future more than two-thirds of the American workforce could be displaced by automation.

2 Setting off long quotations in block form

A long quotation (more than four lines) should be set off as an indented block without quotation marks.

> Rifkin sees this reduction of the workforce as having profound social effects:
>
>> The wholesale substitution of machines for workers is going to force every nation to rethink the role of human beings in the social process. Redefining opportunities and responsibilities for millions of people in a society absent of mass formal employment is likely to be the single most pressing social issue of the coming century. (Rifkin xv)

(For an example of such indentation in a student paper, see 14c-2.)

55b Use quotation marks to suggest skepticism about a term

Sometimes you may find yourself writing about a concept that you think does not deserve the respect other people are giving it. In such cases, you can convey your skepticism by putting the concept name in quotation marks.

> Although many people consider the family the foundation of American society and talk about a return to "family values" as a desirable objective, it is clear that the modern American family looks quite different from families of previous generations.

In this example, the quotation marks around *family values* suggest that the writer has a skeptical view of the term.

This application of quotation marks (sometimes referred to as "scare quotes") should be reserved for cases where you believe that a term is being misused by others. In a sense, you are quoting others (see 55a), though not directly. Only on rare occasions should you use quotation marks simply to make ironic or sarcastic comments.

INCORRECT   Action films are very "intellectual," aren't they?

CORRECT   Action films are not very intellectual, are they?

55c   Use quotation marks to indicate shifts of register

Quotation marks can be used occasionally to set off a colloquial term from the more formal discourse surrounding it.

One should always try to avoid an inflexible, "cookie-cutter" approach to rhetorical criticism.

(Note) Colloquialisms should be used sparingly in formal writing, even when punctuated with quotation marks.

55d   Use quotation marks when citing titles of short works

When referring by title to short stories, book chapters, poems, essays, songs, and other brief works, enclose the titles in quotation marks.

I will never forget the first time I read Shirley Jackson's short story "The Lottery."

"Smells Like Teen Spirit" has become a '90s classic.

Chapter 20, "Design Principles and Graphics," talks about the functionality and aesthetics of formatting.

Titles of longer or more encompassing works are italicized or underlined (see 57e).

55e   Follow standard practice in using other punctuation with quotations

Quoted material is commonly combined and mixed with a writer's original material. Here are common guidelines for using other punctuation with quotations.

1. *Put commas and periods inside the end quotation mark.* Standard American editorial practice calls for commas and periods to be placed as shown in the following passage:

WEBLINK

http://webster.commnet
.edu/grammar/marks/
quotation.htm
A description of all uses of
quotation marks, with links
to exercises and related
topics

55.1

A guide to using quotation marks.

"The definition of community implicit in the market model," argues Patricia Hill Collins, "sees community as arbitrary and fragile, structured fundamentally by competition and domination."

(Note) Readers of British publications may see exceptions to this rule, as the British style is to place commas and periods outside quotation marks. When quoting from British sources, you should standardize punctuation for consistency with modern American usage, placing periods and commas inside quotation marks.

2. *Put colons and semicolons outside the end quotation mark.*

One critic called 1990 "the year in which rock and roll was reborn": the fusing of metal and rap by groups like Living Colour and Faith No More broke down racial barriers in a way reminiscent of early rock and roll.

One of the things that distinguished Snoop Doggy Dogg from other rappers was his style, which was described in the *New York Times* as "gentle"; "where many rappers scream," said *Times* reporter Touré, "he speaks softly."

3. *Put other punctuation marks inside the end quotation mark if they are part of the quotation; otherwise, put them outside the end quotation mark.* Question marks, exclamation points, dashes, parentheses, and other punctuation marks should be positioned according to meaning.

PART OF QUOTED TITLE

Whitney Houston's "How Will I Know?" entered the pop charts at number one.

PART OF SENTENCE

What do you think of controversial songs like "Deep Cover" and "Cop Killer"?

AUDIO

Using quotation marks with question marks.

4. *Use single quotation marks (' ') for quotation marks within quotation marks.*

Garofalo notes that "on cuts like "JC" and "Swimsuit Issue," Sonic Youth combined an overt sexuality with uncompromisingly feminist lyrics about women's issues."

5. *Introduce quotations with the punctuation standard grammar calls for.* The sentence or phrase you use to introduce a quotation should be punctuated according to the grammatical relationship between the introduction and the quotation. If the introduction is not a grammatically complete sentence, do not use any punctuation.

> The conservative Parents Music Resource Center maintained that heavy metal was "the most disturbing element in contemporary music."

If the introduction is a quotation tag such as *she said* or *he notes,* use a comma.

> As *Rolling Stone* noted, "Beneath the 'save the children' rhetoric is an attempt by a politically powerful minority to impose its morality on the rest of us."

If the introduction is a grammatically independent clause, use a colon.

Common Quotation Mark Errors

1. Do not use quotation marks just to call attention to something.

> NO   Pete Sampras won the Wimbledon championship "seven" times.

> YES   Pete Sampras won the Wimbledon championship seven times.

2. Do not use quotation marks for indirect discourse (see 39f).

> NO   President Bush said "he was a compassionate conservative."

> YES   President Bush said he was a compassionate conservative.

3. When presenting the title of your paper on a title page or at the head of the paper, do not put quotation marks around it. If your title contains within it the title of *another* short work, that work's title should be enclosed in quotation marks. (See 20a for an example.)

Nelson Mandela indicated his understanding of the power of mega-concerts when he thanked the performing artists backstage for their efforts: "Over the years in prison I have tried to follow the developments in progressive music. . . . Your contribution has given us tremendous inspiration."

WWW

55.2

Entertaining examples of misused quotation marks.

55f Avoid misusing quotation marks

Be careful not to use quotation marks where they do not belong. The box on page 875 lists some common errors to avoid.

EXERCISE 55.1

Correct the punctuation errors in the following sentences.

1. The question is not "why some rappers are so offensive, but rather, why do so many fans find offensive rappers appealing"?

2. "When you hear your record company has been sold for 20 or 30 times its earnings", said Tim Collins, Aerosmith's manager, "you think, "I want a piece of that"."

3. According to critic Anthony Kiedis, the 1992 Lollapalooza summer tour was, "way too male and way too guitar-oriented."

4. Garth Brooks's songs challenged some of country music's most "sacred cows." In 1991, TNN refused to air the video of The Thunder Rolls, which ends with a woman shooting her abusive husband. We Shall Be Free was written as a response to the Rodney King beating and includes lines supportive of gay rights.

EXER

Using quotation marks.

5. PMRC's Pam Howar expressed the concern that Madonna was teaching young girls: "how to be porn queens in heat".

6. In announcing that US superskier Picabo Street will miss the World Cup races because of a knee injury, her coach told the press", When the mind is ready but the body is not [. . .] there is danger of another injury".

7. The citation for the 2002 Nobel Peace Prize given to Jimmy Carter reads, in part: In a situation currently marked by threats of the use of power, Carter has stood by the principles that conflicts must as far as possible be resolved through mediation and international co-operation based on international law, respect for human rights, and economic development.

8. There are people who really enjoy line dances like "YMCA" and "The Electric Slide", although there are others who think those dances are silly.

9. Older people are often labeled "old and sick", "old and help-less", old and useless, or old and dependent:" in fact, the general image of old age is negative.

10. The Celtic tune "Greensleeves" is the melody used for the carol "What Child Is This"?

CHAPTER 56

Other Punctuation Marks

FAQs

▶ When should I use dashes instead of parentheses? (56d–56e)
▶ How should I use brackets and ellipses in quotations? (56g–56i, 56k, 56m)

VIDEO

Exploring other punctuation marks.

AUDIO

Chapter overview.

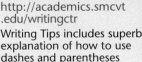

WEBLINK

http://academics.smcvt
.edu/writingctr

Writing Tips includes superb explanation of how to use dashes and parentheses

Parentheses, dashes, brackets, ellipses, and slashes can all be used, in moderation and in the proper contexts, to clarify meaning and add interest to writing. (See 24a-5 for a discussion of punctuating with email diacritics.)

Parentheses

Parentheses are indispensable to formal writing. Be sure, though, not to overuse them.

56a Use parentheses to insert parenthetical comments

Usually, parenthetical comments—clarifications, asides, examples, or other extra pieces of information—are embedded within sentences. They can be as short as a single word or as long as an entire clause.

Many components of biological diversity (biodiversity) are dwindling, and attempts to conserve them in the United States through the Endangered Species Act (ESA) and other policies affecting land use and aquatic resources sometimes conflict with the short-term economic goals of individuals, firms, industries, or political entities.

For most right-handed people, the left hemisphere of the brain controls manual skills and language (and vice versa for most left-handed people). . . . The fact that manual skill (i.e., the skill associated with tool-making and tool-using) is usually localized in the same hemisphere as speech has led some anthropologists to speculate that tool-making either necessarily preceded or developed concurrently with language.

Sometimes parenthetical comments comprise one or more sentences.

The worst release of radioactive substances in US history was during a deliberate experiment in 1949. . . . The experiment, called "green run," released into the atmosphere some 5,500 curies of iodine 131 and a still-classified inventory of other fission products, secretly measured by the AEC, in a 200-by-40 mile plume. There was no public health warning. (By contrast, when the 1979 Three Mile Island nuclear accident released 15 to 24 curies of radioactive iodine into the countryside, people around Harrisburg were evacuated and milk was impounded.)

Another common use of parentheses is in documentation. The scientific reference style calls for inserting reference citations in

HELP

How do I find out whether I have a "parenthesis habit"?

1. Select several pages of your writing.
2. Open the SEARCH (or FIND) feature of your word-processing program.
3. Enter a left parenthesis in the SEARCH field, and have the program search your document.
4. Record how many times you have to click FIND NEXT.
5. Using your grammar checker, determine how many sentences are in your document.
6. If you have more than one parenthesis for every four or five sentences, you may have a parenthesis habit.

parentheses within sentences. This parenthetical style is the pre-ferred method of the MLA, APA, and CBE (see 13a, 14a-1, 15a-3).

56b Do not overuse parentheses

Parentheses are so handy that you may be tempted to overuse them. Resist the temptation. Too many parentheses can make it diffi-cult for readers to follow the main train of thought. If you find yourself developing a "parenthesis habit" (see the Help box on page 879), look for ways to rewrite some of the parenthetical comments as modifiers (see 30c) or as subordinate clauses (see 41c).

56c Use parentheses around letters or numbers to set off embedded lists

Listed phrases or clauses embedded in a longer sentence may be itemized with numbers or letters placed within parentheses.

Socialism has three essential components: (1) the public ownership of the means of production, (2) central planning, and (3) distribution of goods without a profit motive.

EXERCISE 56.1

The following passage has too many parentheses. Rewrite it, using the suggestions given in 30c and 41c.

Abatement of water pollution in the United States (like that of air pollution) has been largely a success story. It also is one of the longest running (its legislative origins go back to the turn of the century). Until the 1970s, most legislation addressed public health issues and included provisions for helping communities build treatment plants (specifically, for water and sewage). With passage of the Water Pollu-tion Control Act in 1972 (later called the Clean Water Act), the federal government turned its attention to cleaning up the nation's water-ways (they had become badly polluted from industrial effluents and inadequately treated sewage).

FOR COLLABORATION

If you feel that you have a "parenthesis habit," give a sample piece of writing to a friend or member of your group, and ask him or her for suggestions for revision.

Dashes

Dashes are an informal kind of punctuation, with several uses and some misuses. You can create a dash either by typing two hyphens, which some word processors will then convert into a solid dash, or by opening the special character or symbol feature on your word-processing program and selecting the full-length dash (called the "em dash").

56d Use dashes to highlight extra informational comments

Dashes set off internal, informational comments in a more emphatic way than parentheses do.

> Public decision makers have a tendency to focus mostly on the more obvious and immediate environmental problems—usually described as "pollution"—rather than on the deterioration of natural ecosystems upon whose continued functioning global civilization depends.

Dashes are particularly useful for setting off an internal list of items:

> As costs have climbed, resistance to increased pollution controls by some business and industry groups has also risen, contributing to the environmental backlash. Particularly hard hit have been small businesses in California—paint dealers, gas stations, and dry-cleaning establishments—which the state began regulating in 1990.

56e Use dashes to set off important or surprising points

If not overused, dashes can be a dramatic way to set off an inserted comment.

> While the Marshall Islanders continue to wrestle with the consequences of nuclear testing, a new proposal is on the table that will make the islands a dumping ground for American garbage—literally. An American waste disposal company, Admiralty Pacific, proposes to ship household waste from the west coast of the US to the Pacific islands—an estimated 34 billion pounds of waste in the first five years of the program alone.

56f Confine yourself to one pair of dashes per sentence

56.1

Three ways to
punctuate
asides.

Dashes, like parentheses, can be overused. If you need to add more than one informational comment to a sentence, use commas (see 51e) or parentheses around the other comments. Too many dashes in a paragraph are a sign of poorly integrated ideas.

(Grammar Checker Alert) If you suspect that you have a "dash habit," check your writing for dashes, using the SEARCH process described for parentheses.

(E X E R C I S E 56.2)

Insert appropriate punctuation if needed (parentheses, dashes, or commas) in the places marked in the following sentences.

1. In 1987, officials in the Guatemalan government and the US Drug Enforcement Agency__DEA__entered into an agreement to defoliate vast areas of Guatemala's north and northwest__a region that contains a wildlife refuge and the largest area of unplundered rainforest remaining in Central America.

2. On the Internet are thousands of Usenet newsgroups, made up of people who communicate about almost any conceivable topic__from donkey racing and bird watching to sociology and quantum physics__.

3. People look forward to communicating almost daily with others in their newsgroup, with whom they share personal, sometimes intimate, matters about themselves__even though they have "met" only electronically__.

4. There is no theory that would have led anyone to expect that after World War II, Japan__with a religion that stressed fatalism, with two major cities destroyed by atomic bombs, and stripped of its colonies__would become an economic powerhouse able to turn the Western world on its head.

5. Although the distinction between race and ethnicity is clear__one is biological, the other cultural__people often confuse the two.

6. The United Nations defines seven basic types of families, including single-parent families, communal families__unrelated people living together for ideological, economic, or other reasons__, extended families, and others.

7. By the late 1980s, the proportion of adult Americans who were single by choice or by chance__often after failed marriages__had

EXER
Practice punc-
tuation.

increased to slightly over 25 percent of adult men and over 20 percent of adult women.

8. If you were to go on a survival trip, which would you take with you__food or water__?

9. The key to a successful exercise program is to begin at a very low intensity, progress slowly__and stay with it__!

10. The three branches of the US government__the executive, the legislative, and the judicial__ are roughly equal in power and authority.

Brackets

Brackets are an important editorial device for providing proper context for the quoted or cited material used in research writing.

56g Use brackets to insert editorial comments or clarifications into quotations

Quotations represent someone's exact words. If you choose to alter those words (because of a misspelling in the original quotation or to add explanatory information, for example), you must indicate that you have done so by putting brackets around the alterations.

> "One of the things that will produce a stalemate in Rio [the site of the 1992 UN conference on the environment] is the failure of the chief negotiators, from both the north and the south, to recognize the contradictions between the free market and environmental protection."

The reference to "Rio" in this quotation might not be understood out of context, so the author has inserted a brief clarification between brackets.

Whenever you insert a quotation from your reading into your writing, be aware that you may need to give the reader important information that was located in the sentences immedi-

WEBLINK

http://webster.commnet.edu/grammar/marks/marks.htm

Excellent coverage of a range of punctuation marks, from the common to the rarely used, with illustrations and exercises

56.2

Review punctuation with the "Punctuation Tree."

ately preceding or following it in the original. Any necessary clarification may be added either outside the actual quotation or within it, in which case it should be in brackets. Say, for example, that you have come across this passage in your reading and want to quote the final sentence:

Sea snails are the source of highly refined painkilling chemicals now being tested for human use. One scientist describes these as "little chemical factories" that are in essence doing what drug companies are trying to do. They have created thousands of chemical compounds and refined them to be exquisitely sensitive and potent.

If you just quoted the final sentence word for word, readers would not know what *They* referred to. Therefore, you should write the sentence in one of the following two ways:

Sea snails "have created thousands of chemical compounds and refined them to be exquisitely sensitive and potent."

OR

"[Sea snails] have created thousands of chemical compounds and refined them to be exquisitely sensitive and potent."

56h Use brackets with the word *sic*

The Latin word *sic* (meaning "so" or "thus") indicates a mechanical error—for example, an error of grammar, usage, or spelling—in a quotation. You may want to use it to show both that you recognize an error in a quote and that you did not introduce the error when transposing the quote into your writing. Place it in brackets in the quotation, immediately following the error.

"Any government that wants to more and more restrict freedoms will do it by financial means, by creating financial vacums [*sic*]."

If you frequently quote Internet messages like this one, you may have many opportunities to use *sic*. Overusing it, though, may make your writing sound snobbish.

56i Use brackets to acknowledge editorial emphasis within a quotation

When you quote a passage, you may want to emphasize a certain part of it that is not emphasized in the original. You can do so by underlining or italicizing that part and then, at the end of the passage, acknowledging the change by writing *emphasis added* or *italics mine* between brackets.

Brown states,

Whereas in the past the world has relied primarily on fishers and farmers to achieve a balance between food and people, it now depends more on family planners to achieve this goal. *In a world where both the seafood catch and the grain harvest per person are declining, it may be time to reassess population policy.* For example, in such a world, is there any moral justification for couples having more than two children, the number needed to replace themselves? If not, then political leaders everywhere should be urging couples to limit themselves to two surviving children. [Emphasis added.]

56j Use brackets for parenthetical comments within parentheses

If one parenthetical comment is nested within another, the inner one should be punctuated with brackets to distinguish it from the outer one.

The spectacular palace that King Louis XIV built at Versailles (which is located 19 kilometers [12 miles] west of Paris) required 35,000 workers and 27 years to construct.

Ellipses

An **ellipsis** (plural: *ellipses*) is a series of three periods, used to indicate a deletion from a quotation or a pause in a sentence. An ellipsis consists of three *spaced* periods (. . .), not three bunched ones (...). The *MLA Handbook for Writers of Research Papers,* 6th edition, recommends placing brackets around the ellipses points you add if necessary to a quotation already containing ellipses to distinguish your ellipses from the author's (see 56m). If you end a quoted sentence with an ellipsis, use a fourth period to indicate the end of the sentence.

"The notion of literature as a secular scripture extends roughly from Matthew Arnold to Northrop Frye. . . ."

56k Use an ellipsis to indicate a deletion from a quotation

The sentence with an ellipsis should not be significantly different in meaning from the original sentence, nor should it be ungrammatical.

"Practically any region on earth will harbor some insect species—native or exotic—that are functioning near the limits of their temperature or moisture tolerance."

An ellipsis can be used to mark a deletion from either the middle or the end of a sentence, but not the beginning of a sentence.

56l ▶ Use an ellipsis to indicate a pause in a sentence

To mark a pause for dramatic emphasis in your own writing, use an ellipsis. When you use an ellipsis in your own writing, you will not need to enclose the ellipsis points in brackets (see 56m).

I was ready to trash the whole thing ... but then I thought better of it.

Beware, however, of overusing ellipses to indicate pauses.

> (EXERCISE 56.3)
>
> Reduce the following passage to a two-sentence quotation, using at least one set of brackets and one ellipsis.
>
> Preserving the planet's remaining natural areas is one of our most urgent responsibilities. Such places are fundamental to every economy in the world, no matter how divorced from "nature" it might appear to be, and no conceivable development will lessen that dependence. There is no substitute for a stable hydrological cycle, healthy pollinator populations, or the general ecological stability that only natural areas can confer. We need these places in ways that are direct enough to satisfy even the most hard-nosed economist, but we also need them for reasons that are harder to quantify.

56m ▶ Use brackets around ellipses in quotations to differentiate them from the author's ellipses

MLA style (see 13a) recommends that you place brackets around your ellipsis marks if necessary to differentiate them from ellipsis marks the original author used. One space should be inserted before the opening bracket and one space after the closing bracket, unless it is followed by another punctuation mark. There should be no space between a bracket and the ellipsis mark itself. Thus, someone quoting the example sentence in 56l above might insert additional ellipsis marks as follows:

"The writer states: 'I was ready to trash the whole thing . . . but [. . .] thought better of it.'"

Note that this bracketing applies only to quotations. It is *not* done with statements of your own:

I was ready to trash the whole thing **...** but then I thought better of it.

Slashes

Slashes serve a variety of purposes in both formal and informal writing.

56n Use slashes to separate lines of poetry quoted within a sentence

If you are quoting lines of poetry without setting them off in separate lines as they appear in the poem, put a slash (surrounded by spaces) between the lines.

> Gerard Manley Hopkins's poetry features what he called "sprung rhythms," as can be heard in these lines from "The Windhover": "No wonder of it: sheer plod makes plow down sillion **/** Shine, and blue-bleak embers, ah my dear, **/** Fall, gall themselves, and gash gold-vermilion."

56o Use a slash to show alternatives

Slashes are used in expressions such as *either/or, pass/fail, on/off, win/win,* and *writer/editor.* Readers may object, though, if you overuse them. The expressions *he/she, his/her,* and *s/he* are admirable attempts at gender neutrality, but many people dislike their phonetic clumsiness. We suggest you use *he or she* and *his or her* or find other ways of avoiding sexist pronouns (see 16a-2).

56p Use a slash to indicate a fraction

Fractions that would be set in formal mathematics on separate lines also can be shown on one line, with a slash dividing the numerator from the denominator:

$1/3$ $3/8$ 2-$2/5$

Your word-processing program may automatically convert fractions into more elegant versions like ½ and ¼, but first you have to type them with slashes. (Check under AUTOFORMAT to see whether your program will format fractions for you.)

EXER
Other punctuation marks.

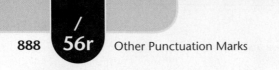

56q Use slashes in Internet addresses

Slashes are indispensable components of URLs (Web site addresses), for example, *<http://mediachannel.org/views/>*. Include the last slash if it brackets a directory, but not if it brackets an actual HTML file. (Tip: If your browser automatically adds a final slash to the address, that tells you the final term names a directory, not a file.)

56r Use slashes in writing dates informally

Instead of writing out a date like June 16, 1999, you can write the date informally: 6/16/99. (Note: In many other countries, this date would be written 16/06/99.)

CHAPTER 57

Capital Letters and Italics

FAQs

▶ Should I capitalize the first word of a sentence in paren-theses? (57a)

▶ Should I capitalize directions like *east* and *northwest?* (57b)

▶ Do I need to capitalize email addresses? (57d)

▶ If I cite a URL, should I put it in italics? (57f)

▶ Should all foreign words be italicized? (57h)

Capital Letters

Capital (uppercase) letters are used to indicate the start of a new sentence. They are also used for proper names, proper adjectives, and some abbreviations.

AUDIO
Chapter overview.

 Capitalize the first word of all freestanding sentences

Sentences like the one you are now reading should always start with a capital letter. Sentences that are embedded in other sentences, however, may or may not start with a capital letter, depending on the situation.

If a sentence follows a colon or dash, capitalization is optional:

Some employees have strong objections to mandatory drug testing in the workplace: They believe that their civil liberties are being violated.

OR

Some employees have strong objections to mandatory drug testing in the workplace: they believe that their civil liberties are being violated.

You should be sure to pick one capitalization style for this situation, however, and use it consistently throughout your writing.

If a sentence occurs in parentheses within another sentence, the first word of the parenthetical sentence should not be capitalized:

Major league baseball no longer seems to enjoy the civic loyalty it used to (For example, several teams have threatened to leave their cities if new facilities are not built).

If, however, the parenthesized sentence is set off as a separate sentence, the first word should be capitalized:

Major league baseball no longer seems to enjoy the civic loyalty it used to. (For example, several teams have threatened to leave their cities if new facilities are not built.)

If a sentence occurs as a quotation within another sentence and is set off by a colon, comma, or dash, the first word should be capitalized:

Rush Limbaugh once said, "vegetarians are a bunch of weaklings who wouldn't be able to bench press 50 pounds after one of their meals."

However, if the quotation is not set off by a colon, comma, or dash, the first word should be lowercase:

Rush Limbaugh once said that "Vegetarians are a bunch of weaklings who wouldn't be able to bench press 50 pounds after one of their meals."

Question fragments can also be capitalized.

Will the stock market keep booming? Level off? Take a dive?

If you are quoting a poem, capitalize the first letter of each line (if the original did so).

> Long as the heart beats life within her breast
>   Thy child will bless thee, guardian mother mild,
> And far away thy memory will be blest
>   By children of the children of thy child.
>
> —Alfred, Lord Tennyson, 1864

57b Capitalize all names, associated titles, and proper adjectives

Capitalize the first letter of any name, title, or proper adjective referring to a particular person, place, or thing.

1. *Capitalize names and associated titles of people.*

Ralph Nader	Aunt May
Ruth Bader Ginsburg	Dr. Harris
Professor Mixco	Ken Griffey, Jr.

(Note) Professional titles and family relationships are *not* capitalized if they are not used as part of the person's name:

My aunt is a doctor specializing in internal medicine.

2. *Capitalize place names.*

San Diego, California	the Rockies
Lake Michigan	Maple Street
the Great Northwest	Apartment 34
Long Island	Yellowstone National Park
the Mississippi River	Africa

(Note) Compass points (*north, southwest*) are capitalized only when they are incorporated into a name (*North Carolina*) or when they function as nouns denoting a particular region (*the Southwest*).

3. *Capitalize the names of historic events.*

World War II	the Boston Tea Party
Reconstruction	the My Lai Massacre
the Middle Ages	the Cold War

4. *Capitalize the names of days, months, holidays, and eras.*

Monday   the Reagan Era
April   Thanksgiving
the Gilded Age   Veteran's Day

(Note) Seasons of the year usually are not capitalized:

last fall   winter sports   spring semester

5. *Capitalize the names of organizations, companies, and institutions.*

Common Cause   the Central Intelligence Agency
the National Rifle Association   Digital Equipment Corporation
Time-Warner, Inc.   New York University
the United Nations   Alameda Community College

6. *Capitalize the names of certain objects and products.* In most cases, only the first letter of each word in an object or product name is capitalized:

the Power Mac   the *Titanic*
the Plymouth Voyager   the North Star
the Hope Diamond   the Boeing 767

57.1

Rules for
internal
capitalization.

Some manufacturers, however, especially in the computer industry, use intercaps:

WordPerfect   *QuarkXPress*
HotJava   *GlobalFax*

Many objects and products have abbreviated names in all uppercase letters: *HDTV, AOL, RISC* (see 58d).

7. *Capitalize religious, national, and ethnic names.*

Catholicism   Passover
the Koran   the Prophet
Buddha   Holy Communion
the Bible   the Ten Commandments
Korean   African American
Chicana   Polynesian

8. *Capitalize adjectives based on proper nouns.*

American football   Jewish literature
French history   Southern hospitality
Newtonian physics   Islamic tradition

57c Capitalize all significant words in titles

In titles of books, poems, articles, plays, films, and other cultural works, every word except articles (*a, an, the*), conjunctions, and short prepositions should be capitalized. The first word of the title and of the subtitle should be capitalized, even if it is an article, conjunction, or short preposition.

WEBLINK

http://webster.commnet.edu/grammar/capitals.htm

A brief guide to capitalization

57.2

Online help with capitalization.

For Whom the Bell Tolls　　"Ode to the West Wind"
The Joy Luck Club　　　　　"Learning in Context: A Qualitative Study"
Death of a Salesman
Pulp Fiction

(Note) The APA reference style calls for capitalizing only the first word of the title and of the subtitle and any proper nouns (see 14b).

57d Follow the owner's preferences in capitalizing email addresses and URLs

Although most of the Internet is not case-sensitive, there are two important reasons for writing email and Internet addresses exactly as the owners do. First, some parts of Net addresses, such as the URL pathnames that follow the first single slash, *are* case-sensitive. Second, some Netizens use uppercase and lowercase letters to make important distinctions in their addresses. For example, Holli Burgon uses upper case and lowercase letters to help users make sense of her email name. As the middle child in her family, she came up with *HbMidKid*, which is easier to decipher than *hbmidkid*.

(Grammar Checker Alert) Your grammar checker will probably flag—and in some cases automatically correct—errors of capitalization involving names of people, days, months, countries, major cities, religions, and so on. But it will miss many other proper names, especially names that resemble common nouns. For example, when we wrote *boston tea party*, our grammar checker flagged *boston* but let *tea* and *party* go. So you should not count on your computer to identify all errors of capitalization.

(EXERCISE 57.1)

Correct the capitalization errors in the following sentences.

1. On july 17, 1996, a Trans World airlines passenger plane crashed into the atlantic ocean, killing all 230 people aboard.

2. Bound for paris, france, the boeing 747 disappeared from Radar screens at 8:48 p.m.

3. The plane was about fifty miles East of the Airport when it plunged into the Ocean about ten miles South of East Moriches, long island.

4. The US coast guard conducted a futile rescue effort, and the national transportation safety board carried out a long investigation.

5. Meanwhile, rumors circulated on the internet and a well-known Politician claimed, "the plane was shot down by a US navy missile."

EXER
Practice with
capitals.

6. I logged on to <*HTTP://WWW.cbpp.org/pa-1.htm*> and found a report called "Pulling apart: a State-by-state analysis of income Trends."

7. The report, published by the center on Budget and policy priorities, says that "in 48 States, the gap between the incomes of the richest 20 percent of families with children and the incomes of the poorest 20 percent of families with children is significantly wider than it was two Decades ago." (only Alaska and north Dakota bucked the trend.)

8. Individual states could counteract this National trend (Few, however, have done so).

9. My Nephew, Julius Evans, jr., is a Junior at San Francisco state university.

10. [The first stanza of a poem by Doug Downs:]
   So, we'll sit no more a'writing
      so late into the night,
   though our minds be still a burning,
      and our thoughts be still as bright.

Italics

In published documents, *italic* type is used for a number of purposes, which will be described in the sections that follow. Although most word processors permit the selection of an italic type, many instructors prefer that students use <u>underlining</u> instead of italics in their papers, as underlined letters and words stand out more than italicized ones. If you are a student and wish to use italics rather than underlining, we suggest that you check with your instructor first.

57e Italicize titles of independent creative works

Titles of books, magazines, digital magazines ("e-zines"), newspapers, and other creative products that are independently packaged and distributed to a public audience should be written with italics or underlining (see Chapter 13). Here are some examples:

> **WEBLINK**
> http://webster.commnet.edu/grammar/italics.htm
> A brief guide to using italics and underlining

BOOKS	*The Scarlet Letter* or The Scarlet Letter
MAGAZINES	*National Geographic* or National Geographic
E-ZINES	*Salon* or Salon
NEWSPAPERS	*Los Angeles Times* or Los Angeles Times
LONG POEMS	*Paradise Lost* or Paradise Lost
MOVIES	*Dead Man Walking* or Dead Man Walking
PLAYS	*The Iceman Cometh* or The Iceman Cometh
TV PROGRAMS	*The X-Files* or The X-Files
PAINTINGS	*Nude Descending a Staircase* or Nude Descending a Staircase
SCULPTURES	Rodin's *The Kiss* or Rodin's The Kiss
CDS	*Cracked Rear View* or Cracked Rear View
MUSIC VIDEOS	*Binge & Purge* or Binge & Purge
COMPUTER GAMES	*Mortal Kombat* or Mortal Kombat
ONLINE WORKS	*Encarta* or Encarta

(Note) The names of personal or commercial homepages should not be underlined or italicized.

57f Italicize URLs and email addresses

When writing an Internet or email address in the body of a text, use underlining or italics.

Helpful information about current Congressional legislation can be found at <*http://thomas.loc.gov/*>. The email address is <*thomas@loc.gov*>.

57g Italicize names of vehicles

Names of particular vehicles, not types of vehicles, should be underlined or italicized. These include the names of spacecraft, airplanes, ships, and trains.

Voyager 2 or <u>Voyager 2</u>

Spirit of St. Louis or <u>Spirit of St. Louis</u>

Titanic or <u>Titanic</u>

Wabash Cannonball or <u>Wabash Cannonball</u>

57h Italicize foreign words and phrases

In general, it is best to avoid using foreign words and phrases when writing in English. However, if you need to use a foreign expression (for example, because there is no good English equivalent), write it with underlining or italics and, if possible, provide a brief English explanation.

One of the nice things about Brazilian culture is the custom of giving a *jeitinho*, or helping someone work things out.

My Dutch friends say they like being in a *gezellig* environment, one that has a lot of human warmth.

Latin names for plants, animals, and diseases should be underlined or italicized.

The sandwich tern (*Sterna sandvicensis*) is slightly larger than the common tern.

If foreign words and phrases have been so thoroughly assimilated, or Anglicized, that they are commonly recognized, however, they do not need underlining. Here are some examples:

machete (Spanish)	judo (Japanese)
sauerkraut (German)	coffee (Arabic)
pasta (Italian)	data (Latin)
cologne (French)	criteria (Greek)

The richness of the English language comes from borrowings like these, and they can all be found in a standard English dictionary. The best rule of thumb is to underline or italicize only truly foreign expressions. If the expression can be found in a standard English dictionary, do not underline or italicize it.

57i Italicize words, letters, and numbers referred to as such

When you write a word, letter, or number so as to talk about it as a word, letter, or number, use underlining or italics.

Many people misspell the word *misspell;* they write it with only one *s.*

The witness said the license plate had two *5*s in it.

Underlining or italics is also appropriate for a word you are about to define. (Alternatively, boldface type can be used.)

Before starting up a cliff, rock climbers sometimes like to get *beta*— advice from someone who has already done the climb.

AUDIO
Underlining versus quotation marks.

57j Italicize words for emphasis

You can use underlining or italics to emphasize a certain word or phrase (see 43e).

Unfortunately, those who cannot remember the past tend to repeat it, which explains why U.S. officials continue to repeat the propaganda strategies of the 1950s. Rather than changing the way we actually *relate* to the people of the Middle East, they still dream of fixing their image through some new marketing campaign cooked up in Hollywood or on Madison Avenue.

—Sheldon Rampton and John Stauber, *Weapons of Mass Deception*

But be sure that you do not overdo it. If you use this kind of underlining too often, you may irritate your readers. It is better to rely on word choice and syntactic structuring to create emphasis (see Chapter 43).

EXERCISE 57.2

In each of the following sentences, add underlining to those words and phrases that need it.

EXER
Practice with italics.

1. My favorite poem in Robert Creeley's book For Love is "A Wicker Basket."

2. Juan says the new drama teacher is very simpático.

3. Of the fifty people interviewed, twenty-two said that 13 is an unlucky number.

4. You can keep track of the spaceship NEAR's progress at <http://spacelink.nasa.gov/>.

5. Smoking also contributes to platelet adhesiveness, or the sticking together of red blood cells that is associated with blood clots.

6. She's an easy teacher—she gives all A's and B's.

7. For me, the best track on Fleetwood Mac's Greatest Hits is Rhiannon.

8. The flower that does best under these conditions is the prairie zinnia (Zinnia grandiflora).

9. For further information, email us at <johnsonco@waterworks.com>.

10. The term dementia implies deficits in memory, spatial orientation, language, or personality. This definition sets it apart from delirium, which usually involves changing levels of consciousness, restlessness, confusion, and hallucinations.

CHAPTER 58

Abbreviations and Numbers

FAQs

▶ Is it okay to use acronyms in formal writing? (58d)
▶ When should I spell out numbers? (58f–58j)

Abbreviations

Abbreviations include shortened versions of words (*Mr., Rev., fig.*), initialisms formed from the first letters of a series of words (*FBI, NBC, IBM*), and acronyms, or initialisms that are pronounced as words (*OPEC, NASA, RAM*). In formal writing, abbreviations should be used sparingly. If you are not sure that readers will know what a certain abbreviation stands for, spell out the word the first time it is used and put the abbreviation in parentheses right after it:

VIDEO
Exploring abbreviations.

> The Internet uses a domain name system (DNS) for all its servers worldwide.

AUDIO
Chapter overview.

58a Abbreviate titles, ranks, and degrees only before or after full names

Title before full name
Ms. Yuko Shinoda
Mr. Steven D. Gold
Dr. Teresa Rivera

Degree or rank after full name
Jan Stankowski, DDS
Derek Rudick, CPA
Teresa Rivera, MD

Prof. Jamie Smith-Weber   Young-Sook Kim, PhD
Rev. Martin Luther King, Jr. James Norton, PFC
Rep. Richard A. Gephardt   Chris L. Miller, DSW

When titles or ranks are followed by only a surname, they should be spelled out:

General Clark   Senator Lott   Professor Davis

58b Use abbreviations after numerical dates and times

The following abbreviations are commonly used in writing dates and times:

124 BC ("before Christ") OR 124 BCE ("before the common era")

AD 567 (*anno Domini,* or "year of our Lord") OR 567 CE ("common era")

9:40 a.m. (*ante meridiem*) OR 0940 hrs (military or international 24-hour time)

4:23 p.m. (*post meridiem*) OR 1623 hrs

Avoid using *a.m.* or *p.m.* unless it is adjoined to a specific number:

The package arrived late in the a.m. *morning.*

Avoid abbreviating the names of months, days, and holidays in formal writing:

This year Xmas fell on a Thurs. *Christmas* *Thursday*

58c Use Latin abbreviations sparingly

The following abbreviations, derived from Latin, are appropriate in academic writing. Be careful, however, not to overuse them.

58.1
More examples
of scholarly
abbreviations.

Abbreviation	Latin term	English meaning
cf.	*confer*	compare
e.g.	*exempli gratia*	for example
et al.	*et alii*	and others
etc.	*et cetera*	and so forth
i.e.	*id est*	that is
N.B.	*nota bene*	note well

58d Use acronyms and initialisms only if their meaning is clear

An **initialism** is an abbreviation formed from the first letters of a name—for example, *FBI* (for *Federal Bureau of Investigation*). Usually the letters are all capitalized. An **acronym** is an initialism that is pronounced as a word—for example, *ASCII, PAC, AIDS*. Some abbreviations, such as *JPEG, MS-DOS*, and *DRAM*, are **semiacronyms:** part of the term is pronounced as one or more letters, the rest as a word (for example, "jay-peg"). Some initialisms and acronyms have "morphed" into verbs, gerunds, and participles. In such cases, use uppercase letters only for the abbreviated part: *ID'd, MUDding, CCing, BBSes, ATMs, AOLer.*

AUDIO
Acronyms and periods.

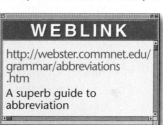

WEBLINK

http://webster.commnet.edu/grammar/abbreviations.htm

A superb guide to abbreviation

Because they are so convenient and economical to use, initialisms and acronyms tend to be overused. But in many cases, especially in the computer world, they are virtually indispensable. As long as your audience knows what they mean and as long as you do not overdo it, there is nothing wrong with using such abbreviations where appropriate.

58e Avoid most other abbreviations in formal writing

Place names, including the names of states, countries, provinces, continents, and other localities, should not be abbreviated except in addresses and occasionally when used as adjectives (for example, in *US government*). Organization and company names should not be abbreviated unless they are extremely familiar: *IBM, CBS, UPS, UCLA, NYU.* Many official company names, however, include one or more abbreviations, which should be kept as is: *Canon, Inc.; Braun AG; Mac Pro.* Fields of study should not be abbreviated. Write *political science* (not *poli sci*) and *psychology* (not *psych*).

WEBLINK

http://www.ucc.ie/cgi-bin/uncgi/acronym

The *Abbreviation and Acronym Server*

WWW

58.2

Access "The Acronym Database" online.

In formal, nontechnical writing, most units of measure should be spelled out: *inches, yards, meters, square feet, gallons*. In technical and scientific writing, abbreviations are standard: *m, kg, bps, dpi, mips, GB, rpm*.

Symbols such as @, #, &, +, and = should not be used in the body of a paper. They can be used, though, in graphs, tables, and email addresses and for other similar purposes.

EXERCISE 58.1

In the following sentences, correct any abbreviations that are not in the proper form and write out any expressions that are not appropriately abbreviated in academic writing.

1. Dr. Ernesto Garcia, M.D, is a specialist in the treatment of A.I.D.S.
2. There has always been a friendly rivalry between people who live in N.H. and those who live in Mass.
3. The Girl Scouts of Tr. 76 visited Representative Harriet Stanley at the Mass. State House.
4. Among the questions the girls asked Rep. Stanley were several about a proposal to extend the school year into July and Aug.
5. The G.O.P. and the Dems have very different positions on that bill.
6. Many colleges have a phys. ed. requirement.
7. When I drive to work in the a.m., my usual radio station is 1030 a.m.
8. The unit of blood one gives at a blood drive measures 450 ml.
9. It was a dramatic advance in science when DNA was 1st used to clone a sheep.
10. HTML is the fundamental language of the WWW.

EXER
Abbreviations.

Numbers

When you are writing text and need to cite a number, keep in mind the following guidelines.

58f Use figures with abbreviations and conventionally numerical references

Time

7:00 a.m.	0700 hrs	seven o'clock in the morning
2:45 p.m.	1445 hrs	two forty-five in the afternoon

Dates

65 BC (or BCE)   AD 126 (or 126 CE)   the 1890s   May 15, 1996
from 1996 to 1998   1996–1998   1996–98

Money

$23.4 billion $12,566 $7.99   45¢   forty-five cents   one dollar

Rates of speed

55 mph   33.6 bps
200 MHz   3000 rpm

Decimals and percentages

.05   5 percent (or 5%)

> **WEBLINK**
>
> http://owl.english.purdue
> .edu/handouts/esl/
> eslnumber.html
> An excellent guide to the
> use of numbers

Telephone numbers

617-555-1284 [US]   +1 (617) 555 1284 [International]

Addresses

233 East 19th Street   PO Box 45   Route 66
New York, NY 10011

Divisions of books and plays

volume 2, chapter 11, pages 346–55

King Lear, act II, scene i, lines 5–7 OR *King Lear* II.i.5–7

The Alchemist, act 2, scene 1, lines 5–7 OR *The Alchemist* 2.1.5–7

58g Write out other numbers that can be expressed in one or two words

One to ninety-nine

fifteen   twenty-two   eighty-four

Fractions

two-thirds   one-fourth   five-sixteenths

Large round numbers

thirteen hundred   four thousand   thirty million

Decades and centuries

the eighties (or the '80s)

the twenty-first century (or the 21st century)

VIDEO

Exploring
numbers.

58h Write out numbers that begin sentences

FAULTY   18% of Americans believe that career preparation should begin in elementary school.

REVISED   Eighteen percent of Americans believe that career preparation should begin in elementary school.

When a number is too large to write out (more than two words), keep the numerical form but rearrange the sentence so as to avoid beginning with a number.

FAULTY   240,183 people could be fed for one year with the food we Americans waste in one day.

REVISED   We Americans waste enough food in one day to feed 240,183 people for one year.

58i When one number modifies another, write one as a figure and the other as a word

We bought fourteen $25 tickets.

There were 75 twelfth-graders at the dance.

58j Write related numbers alike

When comparing two or more numbers in the same sentence or paragraph, make the comparison easy to see by putting the numbers in the same form, as either words or figures.

It takes nine~~hundred~~ *900* hours of training to become a licensed hair braider in New York City but only 117 hours to become an emergency medical technician.

(EXERCISE 58.2)

EXER
Practice using numbers.

Correct the use of numbers in the following sentences.

1. 200 prayers are sent to the Wailing Wall each day by email.
2. 1998 is the year in which Hong Kong was turned back to the Chinese government.

3. Some workers now work two eight-hour jobs back to back.

4. In 1582, Pope Gregory the 13th instituted the calendar we still use today.

5. At one time, mathematicians were able to work only with the 3 dimensions they can visualize, but now they have analytic methods which allow them to deal with 4, 5, or more dimensions.

6. Much has changed over the years, but the price of Boardwalk remains $200 in Monopoly.

7. The long passage of 16th notes in that piece makes it a difficult one for a beginner to play.

8. Abraham, patriarch of Christianity, Judaism, and Islam, probably lived in about 1800 B.C.E.

9. The university hopes to increase its endowment by 50% over the next 5 years.

10. In the early 80's, home mortgage interest rates were as high as 16 or 17%.

CHAPTER 59

The Hyphen

FAQs

▶ Should I hyphenate a term like *third grader?* (59b)
▶ What are the rules for hyphenating a word at the end of a line? (59e)

AUDIO
Chapter
overview.

The hyphen (-) is typed as a single keystroke, with no space before or after. It differs from a dash, which is typed as two consecutive hyphens (--) and then usually converted by the computer into what looks like a long hyphen (—). The hyphen has two main functions: punctuating certain compound words and names (*self-destruct, fifty-fifty, Coca-Cola*) and dividing a word at the end of a line.

59a Consult your dictionary on hyphenating compounds

A **compound** is a word made up of two smaller words. Sometimes these smaller words are connected by a hyphen (*screen-test*), sometimes they are separated by a space (*screen pass*), and sometimes they are fused (*screensaver*). Many compounds start out as two separate words (*data base*), become hyphenated for a while (*data-base*), and then, if they are widely used, evolve into a single word (*database*). There are no firm rules for determining how to write a particular compound, so it is best to check your dictionary. *Wired Style* says, "When in doubt, close it up," giving examples like *email, homepage,* and *offline.*

(Grammar Checker Alert) A grammar checker will consult the computer's dictionary for you, to determine whether a compound should be hyphenated. But most computerized dictionaries lack full coverage of compounds, and therefore grammar checkers are limited in what they can do. For example, after we deliberately mishyphenated the compounds in the previous paragraph, our grammar checker failed to detect all but two of the erroneous compounds.

59b Hyphenate compounds acting as adjectives before nouns

When you place a compound in front of a noun to act as a modifier, you usually hyphenate the compound.

I teach *seventh-grade* algebra.

Notice that the same compound, when *not* put before a noun, is *not* hyphenated.

I teach algebra to the *seventh grade.*

Hyphenate only compounds that *precede* nouns, not those that follow.

She goes to a *little-known* college. The college is *little known.*

Exceptions to this rule include everyday compounds like *science fiction, long distance,* and *zip code,* which can be used as modifiers without hyphens.

Do you have a *zip code directory?*

There's something wrong with my *floppy disk drive.*

Complex compounds are compounds made up of three or more words, like *cut-and-paste, ultra-high-density,* and *up-to-date.* When you hyphenate a complex compound, be sure to hyphenate all its parts—put hyphens between all the terms.

I do a lot of *cut-and-paste* revising.

My boyfriend needs a more *up-to-date* computer.

In cases where two or more hyphenated compounds occur before a single noun, a recurring part of the compound can usually be "factored out," as in this example:

Martha teaches *seventh-* and *eighth-grade* English.

59c Hyphenate spelled-out fractions and numbers from twenty-one through ninety-nine

one-half   three-eighths   forty-four
two-fifths   twenty-six   seventy-nine

59d Hyphenate to avoid ambiguity and awkward spellings

Some words, especially those with the prefix *re-*, *pre-*, or *anti-*, require hyphens to prevent misreadings, mispronunciations, and awkward-looking spellings:

Now that Professor Muller has complicated the problem, we will

have to ~~resolve~~ *re-solve* it.   [Without the hyphen, *re-solve,* "to solve again," would be read as *resolve,* "to deal with successfully."]

~~Preemergent~~ *Pre-emergent* weedkillers are best used in springtime.   [Without the hyphen, some readers might see *preem* as a single, unrecognizable syllable.]

Hyphens can be used in series to indicate the omission of repeated words.

My neighbor has both first- and second-generation satellite dishes for his TV.   [The hyphen after *first* helps the reader understand that the writer is referring to *first-generation.*]

59e Use hyphens for end-of-line word division

In general, it is best to avoid dividing a word at the end of a line. But there are situations where word division is desirable. For example, if you are trying to arrange text in columns (in a brochure or résumé, for instance), end-of-line hyphenation may provide valuable extra space. (Note: You should be able to turn your hyphenation program on or off.) General principles for end-of-line word division follow.

1 Dividing words only between syllables

If you are using a computer, you can have the hyphenation program divide words for you. Otherwise, consult a dictionary to find

Checklist for Using Automatic Hyphenation

1. Can the document have a ragged right margin?
   a. If so, you can disable your word-processing program's automatic end-of-line hyphenation without running the risk of having large gaps, or "rivers," in the middle of lines. Rivers reduce readability (see 20b-4).
   b. If the document is a brochure or newsletter, for example, and requires block-justified text, activate the hyphenation program so as to avoid internal rivers.
2. Does the justified text have too many hyphenated lines? If so, further steps are needed, as excessive hyphenation can interfere with readability.
   a. You may want to adjust some of the hyphenated lines manually.
   b. You might consider changing the width of your columns.

out where the syllable breaks are. (In most dictionaries, a dot indicates a syllable break.) For example, the entry **den • si • ty** means that the word can be hyphenated as either *den-sity* or *densi-ty*.

2 Avoiding a second hyphen in a hyphenated word

Words with prefixes like *self-*, *ex-*, and *all-* and complex compounds should not be hyphenated anywhere else.

Jimmy Carter has set a new standard for civic activism by ex-presi-
presidents.
~~dents.~~

3 Leaving at least two letters on a line

Do not divide a word so that a single letter is left hanging either on the first line or on the second line.

emo-
Stress management requires an examination of one's e-
tional
~~motional~~ responses to others.

If you have to divide a name that includes two or more initials, keep the initials together.

In the movement for racial equality, few stand taller than ~~W. E.~~ *W. E. B.*

~~B.~~ Dubois.

4   Avoiding consecutive lines ending in hyphens

Ending three or more lines in a row with hyphens draws attention and looks ungainly.

Admitting to your feelings and allowing them to be expressed through either communication or action is a stress-
management technique that can help you through many difficult situations.

In a word-processing program, you can prevent such situations by clicking on the LIMIT CONSECUTIVE HYPHENS feature in the hyphenation program and setting the maximum number of hyphens in a row at two. Alternatively, you can widen the hyphenation zone (which determines the range in the width of the characters on the line).

VIDEO
Understanding word-division problems.

Either way, however, you run the risk of creating another problem—extreme raggedness in left-justified text or large internal gaps in block-justified text. One of the main reasons for using end-of-line hyphenation is to have attractively filled-out paragraphs and blocks of text. If you are using a ragged right (left-justified) text style, you do not want the text to look *too* ragged. If you are using block justification, you do not want to have large gaps in the middle of lines (see 20b-4). Although you can avoid these extremes by making the hyphenation zone narrower, you are then increasing the odds of producing an excessive number of hyphens. You may have to experiment with your word-processing program until you get the right balance.

WWW
59.2
Examples of special cases for using hyphens.

(E X E R C I S E   5 9 . 1)

Correct the hyphenation errors in the following paragraphs.

EXER
Using the hyphen correctly.

1. Stress-management calls for the development of positive self esteem, which can help you cope with stressful situations. Selfesteem skills are instilled through learned habits. Stress management also requires that you learn to see stressors not as adversaries but as exercises in life. These skills, along wi-th other stress management techniques, can help you get through many difficult situations.

2. Smoke-less tobacco is used by approximately 12-million Americans, one fourth of whom are under the age of twenty one. Most users are teen-age and young adult males, who are often emulating a professional sports-figure or a family-member.

3. In a consumer oriented environment, many hospitals are making efforts to improve patient care. Many are now designated as trauma-centers. They have helicopters to transport victims, they have in house specialty physicians available around-the clock, and they have specialized-diagnostic equipment. Though very expensive to run, trauma-centers have dramatically reduced mortality-rates for trauma-patients.

4. Hispanics made up the fastest growing segment of the US-population during the 1990s. However, Hispanics constitute diverse groups, having come from a variety of Spanish speaking countries at different times in the nation's history-Because the United States at one time seized large amounts of land from Mexico- the largest group of Hispanics are of Mexican-descent. Newspapers serving these descendants are called the Chicano-press and are printed in Spanish, English, or sometimes both languages.

5. Felice Schwartz (1989) suggested that corporations off-er women a choice of two parallel career paths. The "fast-track" consists of high powered, demanding positions that require sixty-or-seventy hours of work per week, regular responsibilities, emergencies, out of town meetings, and a briefcase jammed with work on week-ends. The second track, the "mommy-track," would stress both career and family. Less would be expected of a woman on the mommy-track, for her commitment to the firm would be lower and her commitment to her family higher.

(**FOR COLLABORATION**)

Exchange your corrected paragraphs with another member of your group for checking. See what types of hyphenation errors are particularly troublesome for you.

CHAPTER **60**

Tips on Nouns and Articles

FAQs

▶ Why is it necessary to use articles?

▶ How do I know whether to use *a* or *the?* (60a–60c)

▶ When is it okay to use no article at all? (60e)

AUDIO

Chapter overview.

　　Articles (*a, an, the*) are important in the English language because they clarify what nouns refer to. There is a significant difference in meaning between "I found *a* new Web site" and "I found *the* new Web site." The first sentence introduces new information, while the second sentence implies that the new Web site is something the reader or listener already knew about. Articles can be used to mark other subtleties as well. Because many other languages do not use articles in this way, though, many nonnative speakers of English have trouble with articles.

60a **Use the plural only with count nouns**

　　To use articles (and other determiners; see 60f) correctly, you first need a clear understanding of the difference between count nouns and noncount nouns. **Count nouns** refer to things that have a distinct physical or mental form and thus can be counted, such as *book, apple, diskette, scientist,* and *idea.* Count nouns can be enumerated and pluralized—for example, *eight books, three apples, several diskettes, two scientists,* and *many ideas.*

Common Examples of Two-Way Nouns

As a count noun

a *wine* (a type of wine)

a *cloth* (a piece of cloth)

a *thought* (an idea)

a *beauty* (a lovely person or thing)

a *hair* (a single strand of hair)

As a noncount noun

wine (the fermented juice of grapes)

cloth (fabric made by weaving or knitting)

thought (mental activity, cogitation)

beauty (loveliness)

hair (filamentous mass growing out of the skin)

Noncount (or **mass**) **nouns** are words such as *air, rice, electricity, excitement,* and *coverage* that do not have a distinct form as a whole. (Though each grain of rice may have a distinct form, rice as a mass quantity is variable in form.) Noncount nouns are neither enumerated nor pluralized. No one would say *eight airs, three rices, several*

WEBLINK

http://leo.stcloudstate
.edu/grammar/countnon
.html

Help with count and non-count nouns

electricities, two excitements, or *many coverages.* Noncount nouns can be quantified with expressions like *a lot of, much, some,* and *a cup of*—for example, *some air, a cup of rice, much excitement,* and *a lot of coverage.*

Some nouns can be used as either count or noncount nouns. In such cases, the countable sense is more specific than the uncountable sense. For example, *reading* as a noncount noun refers to the general activity ("I enjoy *reading*"), while *reading* as a count noun refers to a particular type of reading—for example, a text ("We were assigned a collection of *readings*"), an interpre-

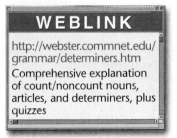

WEBLINK

http://webster.commnet.edu/
grammar/determiners.htm

Comprehensive explanation of count/noncount nouns, articles, and determiners, plus quizzes

tation ("I made several *readings* of the data"), or a performance ("We were invited to a public *reading*"). See the Common Examples of Two-Way Nouns. (See also 30a-1 for more on count and noncount nouns.)

EXERCISE 60.1

Decide whether each of the nouns listed below is countable, non-countable, or both (depending on context). If the noun is countable, write its plural counterpart next to it. If the noun can be either countable or noncountable, explain in what context it would be appropriate to pluralize the noun.

EXER
Distinguish count and non-count nouns.

1. idea
2. money
3. math problem
4. government
5. party

6. memorization
7. computer program
8. silence
9. tobacco
10. movie

60b Use *the* for specific references

In deciding whether to use *the, a, an,* or no article at all, keep in mind the concept of specificity. Does the noun refer to some particular thing or set of things, or does it refer to something general? As mentioned in the introduction to this chapter, "*the* Web site" refers to a specific, unique Web site, whereas "*a* Web site" refers to any Web site.

> **WEBLINK**
>
> http://owl.english.purdue
> .edu/handouts/esl/
> eslcount2.html
> A discussion of the use of articles, with links to count vs. noncount nouns and exercises

There are many types of situations in which nouns refer to specific things and must be preceded by *the*. In all these cases, the writer assumes that the reader knows *which* thing or set of things is being referred to. If you are using a noun that names something unique and specific, use the definite article *the* with the noun, whether or not the noun is countable. (Note: This guideline applies to common nouns only, not to most proper nouns.)

1 Using *the* with superlative adjectives

Adjectives like *best, worst,* and *most interesting* single out one particular thing among many.

Pete Sampras is *the best tennis player* in the world.

2 Using *the* with unique things

The past, the present, the sun, and *the solar system* all have unique identities. There is only one past, only one present, only one sun (in our solar system anyway).

Thirty minutes after boarding, the plane was still on *the ground.*

3 Using *the* with nouns followed by a modifier

Many nouns are followed by a phrase or clause that restricts the noun's identity.

The theory of relativity was developed by Einstein.

The girl in the corner is in my physics class.

4 Using *the* to refer to a previous mention

Once something has been mentioned, it becomes part of the reader's knowledge. If you refer to it again, use *the* so that the reader knows that you are talking about the same thing.

I went shopping today and bought some beans, rice, and *chicken.* We can cook *the chicken* for dinner.

(Note) For clarity or emphasis, the demonstrative adjective *this, that, those,* or *these* may be used instead of *the* if the second mention occurs closely after the first.

5 Using *the* to draw on shared knowledge

If you and your reader can draw on shared experience to identify something in particular, use *the* to mark it.

Please shut down *the computer* when you are done with it.

6 Using *the* for contextual specificity

Sometimes the context of a situation allows you and your reader to identify something as unique. Consider, for example, the word *printer.* There are many printers in the world, but if you are writing about a computer and you want to mention the printer attached to it, use *the* to indicate that it is the only printer in this particular context.

> I was using my friend's computer and could not get *the printer* to work.

7 Using *the* to denote an entire class of things

The can be used with a singular count noun to denote an entire class or genre of things.

> *The earthworm* is one of nature's most valuable creatures.

> *The personal computer* has revolutionized modern life.

(Note) This generic use of *the* to refer to an entire class of things applies only to singular count nouns, not to plural count nouns or noncount nouns.

EXER

Using *the*.

(EXERCISE 60.2)

Study the following paragraph, and insert *the* where appropriate.

_____ physical fatigue is _____ result of overworking our muscles to _____ point where _____ metabolic waste products—carbon dioxide and lactic acid—accumulate in _____ blood and sap our strength. Our muscles cannot continue to work efficiently in _____ bath of these chemicals. _____ physical fatigue is usually a pleasant tiredness, such as that which we might expect after playing a hard set of _____ tennis, chopping _____ wood, or climbing a mountain. _____ cure is simple and fast: we rest, giving _____ body a chance to get rid of _____ accumulated wastes and restore _____ muscle fuel.

60c Use *the* with most proper nouns derived from common nouns

Proper nouns are names of things such as persons, places, holidays, religions, companies, and organizations. Most proper nouns, even though they uniquely identify somebody or something, do not take the definite article:

Muhammad Ali	Mother Theresa	New York	China
Christmas	Ramadan	Catholicism	Microsoft
September	Greenpeace	*Hamlet*	

Many proper nouns, though, do take the definite article:

the Rolling Stones	the United States
the Panama Canal	the International Red Cross
the Vietnam War	the Golden Gate Bridge
the Himalayan Mountains	the University of Chicago
the Fourth of July	*The Grapes of Wrath*

Do you see a general pattern that distinguishes these two kinds of proper nouns? Those that take the definite article have a head noun derived from a common English noun: *stones, states, canal, cross, war, bridge, mountains, university, fourth,* and *grapes.*

There are many exceptions, however, to this pattern. Many common-noun names do not take the definite article: *Elm Street, Salt Lake City, Carleton College, Princeton University, Lookout Mountain, Pine Creek, Walden Pond, Capitol Hill, Burger King.* And a few names not derived from a common noun nonetheless do take the definite article: *the Vatican, the Amazon, the Congo, the Hague.* In general, major landmarks tend to take the definite article, while lesser ones do not: *the Pacific Ocean* vs. *Walden Pond, the United Kingdom* vs. *Burger King.* This is not an absolute rule, however: Michigan State University and the University of Michigan are of comparable size, yet only one is referred to with the definite article. We suggest that you pay close attention to each proper name you encounter and note whether it is used with *the.*

> **WEBLINK**
>
> http://owl.english.purdue
> .edu/handouts/esl/eslcount
> .html
> More help with count and
> noncount nouns and articles,
> plus exercises

www
60.1
Situations
requiring the
use of *the.*

(Note) English uses the definite article with titles, place names, and other proper nouns less consistently than Spanish does. For example, *El señor Lopez (está enfermo)* in English is simply *Mr. Lopez . . . ,* without an article. *La Suecia* is simply *Sweden. El catolicismo* is simply *Catholicism.*

60d Use *a* or *an* in nonspecific references to singular count nouns

Nonspecific nouns refer to *types* of things rather than to specific things. With nonspecific singular count nouns, such as *shirt, jacket, belt,* and *hat,* you must use an indefinite article (either *a* or, if the next sound is a vowel sound, *an*) or some other determiner (for example, *my, your, this,* or *each*).

EXER
Practice select-
ing correct
articles.

I bought a shirt and an overcoat.

60e Use no article in nonspecific references to plural count nouns or noncount nouns

With nonspecific plural count nouns, such as *shirts, jackets, belts,* and *hats,* no article is used. You may use, however, determiners like *our, some, these,* and *no.*

There were *socks* and *shorts* on sale, but *no belts.*

WWW
60.2
A thorough guide to determiners, with quizzes.

> **WEBLINK**
>
> http://a4esl.org/q/h/grammar.html
>
> A great collection of self-study quizzes for ESL students

Nonspecific noncount nouns, such as *clothing, apparel,* and *merchandise,* do not take articles either. They can, however, take determiners like *some, much, enough, your, their, this,* and *no.*

> *People* were buying *lots of clothing,* but I did not have *enough money* to get everything I needed.

EXERCISE 60.3

EXER
Using articles correctly.

Study the following sentences, and insert *a, an,* or *the* where appropriate.

1. Sarah used to play _____ soccer for her high school team, and she was _____ star player.
2. He gave me _____ good advice.
3. _____ anecdote is _____ type of illustration.
4. You should give credit to _____ people who did _____ work.
5. _____ professor surprised _____ students with _____ quiz.
6. All of _____ dogs in _____ neighborhood started to bark when _____ power went out.
7. Vera bought _____ new pink dress for graduation, but, unfortunately, _____ dress was too big.

EXERCISE 60.4

Study the following paragraphs, and insert *a, an,* or *the* where appropriate.

1. In _____ different societies, _____ gift giving is usually ritualized. _____ ritual is _____ set of multiple, symbolic behaviors that occurs in _____ fixed sequence. Gift-giving rituals in our society usually involve the choosing of _____ proper gift by _____ giver, _____ removing of _____ price tag, wrapping of _____ gift, timing _____ gift giving, and waiting for _____ reaction (either positive or negative) from _____ recipient.

2. In _____ latter part of _____ nineteenth century, _____ capital-
ism was characterized by _____ growth of _____ giant corporations. Control of most of _____ important industries became more
and more concentrated. Accompanying this concentration of industry was _____ equally striking concentration of _____ income in
_____ hands of a small percentage of _____ population.

60f   Use other determiners correctly

Articles belong to the class of **determiners.** A determiner is a word
or phrase that begins a noun phrase. Other determiners include quantifiers (such as *many, some, no*), demonstratives (*this, these, that, those*),
and possessive adjectives (such as *my, your, their*). Do not use more than
one determiner with any one noun phrase.

1. Quantifiers indicate some amount of a noun. Some quantifiers are used only with count nouns, such as *many, several, few, a few,
a couple of, every,* and *each.* Other quantifiers are used only with noncount nouns, such as *much, not much, little,* and *a little.* Still others are
used with either count or noncount nouns, such as *some, no, enough,
any,* and *a lot of.* Note: *few* and *little* have negative connotations, while
a few and *a little* have positive connotations.

60.3

Tips on using
quantifiers.

> *few*
> Loners have ~~a few~~ friends.

> *little*
> A poor person has ~~a little~~ money.

2. Demonstratives specify the person or thing referred to. *This*
and *these* indicate something nearby or just mentioned; *that* and *those*
indicate something more distant.

> *This* book should help you with your English.

> *That* computer you bought five years ago might be outdated now.

This and *that* are used with noncount nouns and singular count nouns.
These and *those* are used with plural count nouns.

3. Possessive adjectives indicate ownership. They resemble possessive pronouns (*mine, yours, theirs,* and so on) but differ in function
and location. Possessive adjectives occur in the determiner position,
initiating a noun phrase. Possessive pronouns substitute for noun
phrases; they do not initiate noun phrases.

POSSESSIVE ADJECTIVE   *Your* book is on the chair.

POSSESSIVE PRONOUN   This book is *yours.*

Note that *yours*, like other possessive pronouns, is spelled without an
apostrophe (see 54a-1).

CHAPTER 61

Tips on Verbs

FAQs

▶ I have a lot of trouble with verbs like *look out for* and *look over*. Do I need to learn them? (61a)

▶ If it is okay to say "I like to read," what's wrong with "I dislike to read"? (61b–61c)

▶ What is wrong with "The program is consisting of four parts"? (61f)

▶ What are the correct verb tenses for *if* sentences? (61i–61k)

AUDIO

Chapter overview.

If you are having trouble with English verbs, take heart: verbs often pose a problem for speakers of English, both native and non-native. The main features of the English verb system are discussed in Chapter 32; subject-verb agreement in 33a; and tense, mood, and voice in 39b. This chapter addresses aspects of the verb system that may present special difficulties: phrasal verbs, verb complements, verbs of state, modal auxiliary verbs, and conditional sentences.

Phrasal Verbs

Phrasal verbs are made up of a verb and one or two particles (prepositions or adverbs)—for example, *pick over, look into, get away with*. For this reason, they are sometimes called **two-word verbs** or **three-word verbs.** Phrasal verbs are common in English, especially in informal speech. Some phrasal verbs mean something quite different from their associated simple verbs. For example, if a friend of yours says, "I just *ran into* Nguyen in the library," the encounter probably had nothing to do with running. *To run into* means "to encounter unintentionally." Other phrasal verbs are used merely to intensify the meaning of the simple verb. For example, *fill up* is a more emphatic version of *fill*.

Some phrasal verbs are **transitive** (that is, they have direct objects), while others are **intransitive.** For example, *dig up* (meaning "find") is transitive ("I *dug up* some information for my paper"), but *speak up* (meaning "speak louder") is intransitive ("Please *speak up*"). Some phrasal verbs have both transitive and intransitive meanings.

> **WEBLINK**
>
> http://www.gsu.edu/ ~wwwesl/egw/three.htm
>
> Three rules for distinguishing phrasal verbs from verb + preposition combinations

For example, *show up* can mean either "expose or embarrass (someone)" or "appear," depending on whether it is used transitively or intransitively: "He tried to *show up* the teacher" (transitive) versus "He never *shows up* on time" (intransitive). (See 30a-4 and 32f for more on transitive and intransitive verbs.)

Some transitive phrasal verbs are **separable,** meaning that the particle may be placed after the object of the verb: "I quickly *looked over* my paper" or "I quickly *looked* my paper *over*." Other transitive phrasal verbs are **inseparable,** meaning that the verb and the particle must be kept together: "I quickly *went over* my paper," not "I quickly *went* my paper *over*."

61.1

A list of phrasal verbs and their meanings.

 **61a** Note phrasal verbs as you listen and read

AUDIO

Phrasal verbs in spoken English.

To master idiomatic English, you must learn hundreds of phrasal verbs. The best way to do so is by listening to and reading as much informal English as you can and noting the phrasal verbs. Also consult a good pocket dictionary of phrasal verbs, such as the *Handbook of Commonly Used American Idioms,* 3rd ed., by A. Makkai, M. Boatner, and J. Gates (New York: Barron's, 1995). A good Web site to visit is Dave Sperling's *Phrasal Verb Page* at <*http://www.eslcafe.com/pv/*>.

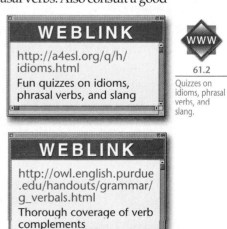

> **WEBLINK**
>
> http://a4esl.org/q/h/ idioms.html
>
> Fun quizzes on idioms, phrasal verbs, and slang

61.2

Quizzes on idioms, phrasal verbs, and slang.

Verb Complements

> **WEBLINK**
>
> http://owl.english.purdue .edu/handouts/grammar/ g_verbals.html
>
> Thorough coverage of verb complements

Verb complements include gerunds (*swimming*), *to* infinitives (*to swim*), and unmarked infinitives (*swim*). English verbs differ in the kinds of verb complements they can take.

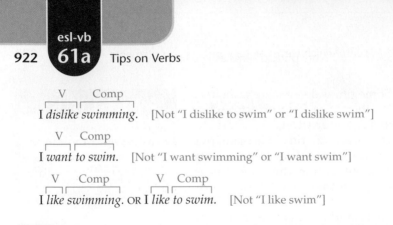

I *dislike swimming*.   [Not "I dislike to swim" or "I dislike swim"]

I *want to swim*.   [Not "I want swimming" or "I want swim"]

I *like swimming*. OR I *like to swim*.   [Not "I like swim"]

61b   Learn which verbs take gerunds as complements

The following verbs take gerunds (verbals ending in *ing*), but not infinitives, as complements, as in "Maria *acknowledged skipping* class."

acknowledge	deny	give up	put off
admit	depend on	have trouble	quit
advise	detest	imagine	recommend
anticipate	discuss	insist on	regret
appreciate	dislike	keep	resist
avoid	dream about	miss	result in
cannot (can't) help	enjoy	object to	risk
consider	escape	plan on	succeed in
consist of	evade	postpone	suggest
delay	finish	practice	talk about

61c   Learn which verbs take *to* infinitives as complements

The following verbs take *to* infinitives, but not participles, as complements, as in "Kim cannot *afford to buy* a car."

afford	decide	intend	offer	seem
agree	demand	learn	plan	struggle
ask	expect	like	prepare	tend
attempt	fail	manage	pretend	threaten
claim	hesitate	mean	promise	wait
consent	hope	need	refuse	want

61d   Learn which verbs take both gerunds and *to* infinitives as complements

The following verbs can take either a gerund or a *to* infinitive as a complement: "He *began learning* English as a small child" or "He *began to learn* English as a small child."

begin	dread	like	stop*
cannot (can't) stand	forget*	love	try
continue	hate	remember*	

For those verbs marked with an asterisk, the meaning of the sentence depends on the type of complement: "He *forgot to go* to the store" means that he didn't go to the store, while "He *forgot going* to the store" means that he did go to the store but didn't remember going there.

61e Learn which verbs take only unmarked infinitives as complements

There are four verbs that, when followed by a noun or pronoun, take an infinitive without *to*, as in "She *let him pay* for dinner." These verbs are

have   help   let   make

(Note that *help* can also take a *to* infinitive as a complement.)

EXERCISE 61.1

In the following sentences, fill each blank with the correct form of the verb in parentheses.

1. Professor Adams refused (change) _____ the student's grade.

2. The student believed that (change) _____ the grade was the only fair course of action.

3. The student also insisted on (discuss) _____ the matter with the dean of the college.

4. The student hoped (convince) _____ the dean that the professor was being unjust in her refusal to change the grade.

5. The dean, however, decided (side) _____ with the professor, so the student's grade was never changed from a B to an A.

6. The famous scientist offered (speak) _____ at the university graduation ceremony.

7. Most students dislike (study) _____ for final examinations.

EXER

Practice using correct verb forms.

Verbs of State

Many English verbs depict states or conditions rather than events or actions. These verbs are called **verbs of state.**

61f Do not use the progressive tense with verbs of state

Verbs of state generally cannot occur in the progressive tense, which indicates continuous action rather than a static condition (see 32d). For example, *consist of* is a verb of state and therefore cannot occur in the progressive tense, which is comprised of some form of the verb *be* and the *-ing* form of the main verb.

> *consists*
> The program ~~is consisting~~ of four parts.

The following verbs do not occur in the progressive tense:

appear	contain	know	result in
believe	correspond	mean	seem
belong	differ from	need	suppose
consist of	exist	possess	understand
constitute	involve	represent	want

Modal Auxiliary Verbs

The **modal auxiliary verbs** include *can, could, may, might, must, will, would,* and *should* (see 30a-4, 32c). They are used to express a variety of conditions including possibility, necessity, ability, permission, and obligation. Each modal auxiliary has at least two principal meanings, one relating to social interaction and the other to logical probability. For example, the word *may* in a sentence like "*May* I sit down?" requests permission, an aspect of social interaction, while the word *may* in a sentence like "It *may* rain today" denotes logical possibility. Within these two general categories, the modal auxiliaries carry different degrees of strength, as shown in the following box. Modal auxiliary verbs have certain distinct grammatical features that can cause problems for nonnative speakers.

61g Use only a base verb form immediately after a modal auxiliary

Any verb immediately following a modal auxiliary must be in the base, or simple, form (for example, *teach, have, go, run*), not in the *to* infinitive or gerund form.

NO   History *can to teach* us many good lessons.

YES   History *can teach* us many good lessons.

Modal Auxiliaries Ranked by Strength

Modal verb	Social interaction meaning	Logical probability meaning	Strength
will	intention	certainty	**Strong**
must	obligation	logical necessity	↑
would	conditionality	conditional certainty	
should	advisability	probability	
may	permission, possibility	possibility	
can	permission	possibility	↓
might/could	very polite permission, possibility	low possibility	**Weak**

NO   The UN *should done* more to help stop the Rwandan civil war.

YES   The UN *should have done* more to help stop the Rwandan civil war.

61h   Do not use more than one modal at a time

NO   If I study hard, I *might could* get an A.

YES   If I study hard, I *might get* an A.

YES   If I study hard, I *could* get an A.

If you want to combine a modal auxiliary verb with some other modal meaning, use a modal phrase such as *be able to, be allowed to,* or *have to.*

YES   If I study hard, I *might be able to* get an A.

(EXERCISE 61.2)

Some of the following sentences have verb tense errors. Make the appropriate corrections.

1. A formal academic essay usually is containing an introduction, the main discussion, and a conclusion.
2. My parents must will send me some money.

3. A thesis statement should to present the main idea of the essay.
4. Right now, Marinela studies in the library for a test in her one o'clock class.
5. Yuka could not imagining to miss even a day of her ESL conversation class.
6. Many students enjoy to study in small groups.
7. Many students are not understanding that the organization of an essay is as important as its content.

Conditional Sentences

Conditional sentences have two parts: a subordinate clause beginning with *if* (or *when* or *unless*) that sets a condition and a main clause that expresses a result. The tense and mood of the verb in the subordinate clause depend on the tense and mood of the verb in the main clause. There are three main types of conditional sentences: factual, predictive, and hypothetical.

61i   In factual conditionals, use the same verb tense in both parts

Factual conditional sentences depict factual relationships. The conditional clause begins with *if, when, whenever,* or some other condition-setting expression; the conditional clause verb is cast in the same tense as the result clause verb.

If you don't *get* enough rest, you *get* tired.

When we *had* a day off, we *went* hiking in the mountains.

61j   In predictive conditionals, use a present-tense verb in the *if* clause and an appropriate modal in the result clause

Predictive conditional sentences express future possible conditions and results. The conditional clause starts with *if* or *unless* and has a present-tense verb; the result clause verb is formed with a modal (*will, can, should, may,* or *might*) and the base form of the verb.

If we *leave* now, we *can be* there by five o'clock.

She *will lose* her place in class unless she *registers* today.

61k

In hypothetical conditionals, use a past-tense verb in the *if* clause and *would, could,* or *might* in the result clause

Hypothetical conditional sentences depict situations that are unlikely to happen or are contrary to fact (see 32h). For hypothetical past situations, the verb in the conditional clause should be in the past perfect tense and the verb in the main clause should be formed from *would have, could have,* or *might have* and the past participle.

> If we *had invested* our money in stocks instead of bonds, we *would have gained* a lot more.

For hypothetical present or future situations, the verb in the conditional clause should be in the past tense and the verb in the main clause should be formed from *would, could,* or *might* and the base form.

> If we *invested* our money in stocks instead of bonds, we *would gain* a lot more.

(**E X E R C I S E   6 1 . 3**)

Choose the correct verb in the following sentences.

1. If Frank studied harder, he (*got, would get, will get*) better grades.
2. Whenever Suzy turns on her computer, she (*gets, would get, will get*) an error message.
3. If we plan ahead, we (*finish, should finish, would finish*) the project on schedule.
4. You will disappoint your parents unless you (*call, may call, should call*) them soon.
5. If the rain (*stopped, has stopped, had stopped*) sooner, there would not have been so much flooding.
6. If Agassi retires, tennis (*loses, should lose, will lose*) one of its most exciting players.
7. Just when you think things can't get worse, they sometimes (*do, might, would*).
8. Unless the price of oil comes down, world financial markets (*are, will be, would be*) in trouble.
9. If you like good art, you (*go, will go, should go*) to the Guggenheim Museum in New York.
10. If Mozart had lived a full life, he (*composed, had composed, might have composed*) much more music.

WWW

61.3

Tips on using conditional sentences.

Tips on Word Order

AUDIO

Chapter overview.

Unlike many other languages, English depends on word order to convey meaning. A change in word order often produces a different meaning. For example, "Kevin likes Maria" means something quite different from "Maria likes Kevin." Basic sentence patterns like these are discussed in 30b. This chapter discusses some other word-order patterns involving strings of adjectives, compound nouns, and adverb placement.

62a   Use inverted word order in sentences

Normal word order in English sentences follows a subject-predicate pattern (see 30b):

Subject	Predicate
Your roommate	has missed a good opportunity.
Dallas	is a large city.
The bus driver	made a wrong turn.

Inverted word order is commonly used for direct questions and exclamations. In such cases, if the predicate includes an auxiliary verb, the auxiliary verb is placed before the subject:

	Auxiliary verb	Subject	Rest of Predicate
QUESTION	Has	your roommate	missed a good opportunity?
EXCLAMATION	Has	your roommate	missed a good opportunity!

Note If the predicate includes more than one auxiliary verb, only the first auxiliary is placed before the subject.

If the predicate consists of only a simple verb and it is a form of *be*, this verb is placed before the subject.

	Form of be	Subject	Rest of Predicate
QUESTION	Is	Dallas	a large city?
EXCLAMATION	Is	Dallas	a large city!

If the predicate consists of only a simple verb and it is not a form of *be*, the auxiliary verb *do, does,* or *did* (according to the tense and number of the simple verb) is placed in front of the subject and the main verb is changed to its base form:

	Auxiliary verb	Subject	Rest of Predicate
QUESTION	Did	the bus driver	make a wrong turn?
EXCLAMATION	Did	the bus driver	make a wrong turn!

Inverted word order should be used only with direct questions, not indirect ones. An indirect question is preceded by a phrase like *He asked if, She wants to know whether,* or *They wondered how.*

He asked if your roommate missed a good opportunity.

She wants to know whether Dallas is a big city.

They wondered how the bus driver could make a wrong turn.

62b String adjectives in the order preferred in English

Usually, adjectives either directly precede the nouns they modify or follow a linking verb (see 30b, Chapter 34).

The fence is *broken.* The *broken* fence will be repaired.

In general, adjectives should be used only one at a time, as in these examples.

> **WEBLINK**
>
> http://cctc2.commnet.edu/grammar/adjective_order.htm
>
> Good stuff on ordering adjectives, with exercises

www

62.1

All about ordering adjectives.

Occasionally, though, you may want to string two or more adjectives together; in such cases, you will have to put them in the appropriate order.

FAULTY   The *wood old* fence will be repaired.

REVISED   The *old wood* fence will be repaired.

The following list shows the preferred ordering of adjectives in English:

1. Article or determiner: *the, a, an, my, our, Carla's, this, that, those*
2. Ordinal expression: *first, second, last, next, final*
3. Quantity: *one, two, few, many, some*
4. Evaluation: *beautiful, delicious, interesting, unfortunate, ugly*
5. Size: *tiny, small, short, tall, large, big*
6. Shape: *square, oval, cylindrical, round*
7. Condition: *shiny, clean, dirty, broken*
8. Age: *new, young, old, ancient*
9. Color: *black, red, yellow, green, white*
10. Nationality: *Mexican, Chinese, Vietnamese, Japanese*
11. Religion: *Catholic, Confucian, Buddhist, Muslim*
12. Material: *cotton, stone, plastic, gold*
13. Special use or purpose (may be a noun used as an adjective): *carving, carrying, sports, medical, computer*
14. The noun being modified

Here are some expressions created by following the preferred ordering:

1	2	3	4	5	6	7	8	9	10	11	12	13	14
The	first			small		shiny	new		Japanese			sports	car
A	few						young			Buddhist			monks
Her			favorite		long			yellow			silk		flowers

EXERCISE 62.1

Create three strings of your own, using at least three adjectives in each.

FOR COLLABORATION

Share your adjective strings with a friend or member of your group, and ask for suggestions for revision or improvement.

62c String nouns for easiest recognition

Stringing nouns together to form **noun compounds** is common in English (see 34b). Terms like *bike lock*, *keyboard*, *houseboat*, *picnic table*, and *bookmark* were formed by putting two ordinary nouns together. And it is easy to add a third noun to make them more descriptive: *combination bike lock*, *keyboard cover*, *houseboat community*, *picnic table leg*, and *bookmark program*. In theory, you can make noun strings as long as you want. However, if you use more than three nouns in a row, the reader may have trouble figuring out what you are trying to say.

In all noun compounds, the rightmost noun is the **head noun** and the nouns preceding it serve as modifiers. These modifier nouns can modify either the head noun or another modifier noun.

Modifier	Head		Modifier	Head
noun	noun		noun	noun

combination bike lock   mountain bike lock

When you create a noun compound, be sure to build it from familiar parts. For example, say you wanted to buy for your bicycle a lock that included a cable. If you were calling a local store to ask if the store carried such a lock, what name would you give it? Three nouns are needed—*bike*, *lock*, and *cable*. The head noun, *lock*, should go at the end. But what about the other two nouns? Should you call the lock a *bike cable lock* or a *cable bike lock*? The latter term is better. Because *bike lock* is a more recognizable term than *cable lock*, you should use *cable* as a modifier of *bike lock*. In effect, you are talking about a *bike lock* with a *cable*.

AUDIO

Hyphenating a three-noun compound.

In creating noun compounds, bear in mind that nouns used as modifiers typically lose any plural endings they might have. Someone who loves movies is a *movie lover*, not a *movies lover*; the juice from cranberries is *cranberry juice*, not *cranberries juice*. (Exceptions to this pattern include *claims adjuster* and *weapons manufacturer*.)

EXERCISE 62.2

Convert the following expressions into noun compounds. The first one has been done for you.

1. An institute that does research in marketing is called ___*a marketing*___
   research institute.

2. A car that uses fuel generated in cells is called a
    _____.

3. A computer device that uses a touchpad for pointing (instead
    of a mouse) is called a _____.

4. An electronic program for taking notes is called an
    _____.

5. A program feature that allows you to send attachments with
    email is called an _____.

6. A baseball player who is designated to hit for the pitcher is
    called a _____.

7. Someone who provides daycare in his or her home is called a
    _____.

8. A service that prepares tax returns is called a
    _____.

9. Someone whose job it is to control airplane traffic is called an
    _____.

10. A module designed to land on the moon is called a
    _____.

62d Use meaning to place adverbs that modify verbs

Adverbs can modify verbs, adjectives, other adverbs, or entire
sentences (see 34c). Adverbs that modify verbs can be placed at either
the beginning, the middle, or the end of a clause, depending on their
meaning.

1 Placing adverbs of frequency

EXER
Practice placing
adverbs.

WWW

62.2
All about Eng-
lish adverbs.

Adverbs of frequency (*usually, seldom, always, never*) are usually
placed directly before the main verb (and after the auxiliary verb, if
there is one).

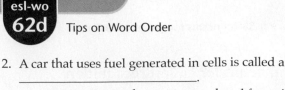

WEBLINK

http://webster.commnet.edu/
grammar/adverb.htm
Fun discussion of adverb
placement, with exercises

Tim says he *usually* writes his
papers on time, yet he is *always*
turning them in late.

Some adverbs of frequency (*often, twice,
many times*) can also be placed at the
end of the clause.

He has missed class *quite often*.

2 Placing adverbs of time when

Adverbs of time when (*yesterday, at eight o'clock, last year*) are most often placed at the end of the clause, though some can also occur in other positions.

The exhibit will open *next month.*

Will they be there *after dinner?*

He *recently* had an accident.

Tonight there will be a full moon.

3 Placing adverbs of place

Adverbs of place (*upstairs, in the park, under a tree*) usually follow the verb. However, they should not intervene between the verb and an object.

Mike went *inside* to escape the heat.

She took her dog *to the park.*

4 Placing adverbs of manner

Single-word adverbs of manner (*gently, hurriedly*) can occur in any of the three main clause positions:

Gently the nurse adjusted the patient's pillow.

The nurse *gently* adjusted the patient's pillow.

The nurse adjusted the patient's pillow *gently.*

EXER
More adverb placement.

Phrasal adverbs of manner (*with care, in a rough manner*) occur most often at the end of a clause, or occasionally at the beginning:

The drill sergeant spoke to the recruits *in a rough manner.*

With great care the ranger approached the wounded bear.

62e Place adverbs directly before adjectives or adverbs that they modify

An adverb that modifies an adjective or another adverb should be placed directly before the word it modifies.

Jose is an *unusually quick* learner. He concentrates *very intensely* on his studies.

62f · Place adverbs before sentences or clauses that they modify

An adverb that modifies a whole sentence or clause is usually placed at the beginning of the sentence or clause.

> *Unfortunately,* his younger brother Ramon does not follow his example.

Less commonly, it is placed after the grammatical subject or at the end of the sentence.

> His younger brother Ramon, *unfortunately,* does not follow his example.

> His younger brother Ramon does not follow his example, *unfortunately.*

EXER

Watch adverb positioning.

62g · Do not put an adverb between a verb and its object

Nonnative speakers sometimes make the mistake of positioning an adverb between the verb and its object or objects.

HELP

How do I check my placement of adverbs?

Using the fact that most adverbs end in *-ly,* you can often have your word-processing program flag the majority of the adverbs in a passage.

1. Open the SEARCH (or FIND) feature of your word-processing program.
2. Type *ly* in the SEARCH FOR (or FIND WHAT) field, and then have your program do the search.
3. Inspect each word. If it is an adverb, use the guidelines given in this chapter to determine whether it has been properly placed.

FAULTY   Javier writes *often* letters to his family.

REVISED   Javier *often* writes letters to his family.

EXERCISE 62.3

The following sentences contain adverbs that have been incorrectly placed. Make the appropriate corrections.

1. Hanna has seen twice the movie *The Lost World*.
2. Princess Diana was only thirty-seven when she died sadly.
3. She swims usually laps in the afternoon.
4. I twice sent the fax before my brother received it.
5. Never Guillermo stops working.
6. Downstairs he went to do the week's laundry.
7. The sponge cake recipe is difficult quite to follow.
8. The string orchestra played last night a very difficult program.
9. The skater misses seldom her required jumps.
10. Around the curve coasted smoothly the car.

CHAPTER 63

Tips on Vocabulary

FAQs

▸ Are there Internet resources that would help me expand my vocabulary? (63b)

▸ Can I use idiomatic expressions in academic writing? (63c)

AUDIO

Chapter overview.

Many nonnative speakers of English feel that they just do not know enough words to express their thoughts as fully as they would like. Knowing enough words, and knowing them well, is a challenge for almost all nonnative speakers of English; indeed, it is a challenge for many native speakers, too. This chapter covers some of the most common vocabulary problems for nonnative speakers—those related to cognates, collocations, and idioms.

63a Look for cognates, but watch out for "false friends"

Cognates are words that have a formal relation to similar words in another language. They are usually quite recognizable. For example, the English *telephone* and Spanish *teléfono* are cognates, and it is easy for speakers of either language to recognize this word when learning the other language. Cognates are either derived from a common ancestor language or borrowed by one language from another. Sometimes the borrowing process involves minor alterations, as in *telephone/teléfono*; sometimes it involves more significant changes, as in the English *northwest* and Spanish *noroeste*.

If your native language is closely related to English, cognate recognition is a good strategy for learning new words. In most cases, you can trust a cognate to carry more or less the same meaning in your

Some Spanish/English False Cognates

Spanish	Meaning	English	Meaning
bonanza	fair weather	bonanza	a treasure
coraje	anger, rage	courage	bravery, valor
desgracia	misfortune	disgrace	dishonor
eventual	possible	eventual	final, ultimate
falacia	deceit, fraud	fallacy	false reasoning
informal	unreliable	informal	casual
lunático	temperamental	lunatic	insane
particular	private, personal	particular	specific
sensible	sensitive	sensible	reasonable
voluble	moody, fickle	voluble	talkative

63.1
Some false cognates from other languages.

second language as it has in your first language. Of course, there are often subtle differences that you should pay attention to. For example, although the word *collar* is used in both English and Spanish to refer to the band around the neck of an animal, in Spanish it is also used to mean "necklace."

Sometimes, however, words that look similar in two different languages have entirely different meanings. These words are called **false cognates.** An example of a false cognate is the English *jubilation* and Spanish *jubilación.* The English word means "happiness," while the Spanish one means "retirement, pension (money)." You should always be on the alert for false cognates. Never assume that two words mean the same thing just because they look similar.

(**EXERCISE 63.1**)

If your native language is related to English, create a special document on your word processor called "False Cognates." Set up a table like the one above, and enter as many false cognates as you can think of. Use this document as an ongoing resource for vocabulary building.

63b Try to get a feel for collocations

Collocations are words that commonly occur together (see 47c-1). For example, the word *advice* commonly occurs with the verbs *give, get,*

WWW

63.2

Take a quiz on
collocations.

WEBLINK

http://www.better-english
.com/strongcollocation/
collocations.htm

The Better English quiz on
collocations

and *receive* and with the adjectives *good,*
bad, and *sound.* This is why the sentence
"She gave me some good advice"
sounds like normal American English,
while the sentence "She presented me
some nice advice" does not.

An intermission allows theatergoers
to ~~extend~~ *stretch* their legs.

A steep ~~upshoot~~ *rise* in grain prices could topple many governments in
the Third World.

On Christmas Day, the children were bubbling ~~up~~ *over* with excitement.

Lazy thinkers tend to make ~~wide~~ *broad* generalizations about things.

EXER

Practice using
collocations.

The best way to develop your knowledge of collocations is to pay
attention to them in the English you see and hear around you. In this
way, you will develop a feel for which words go with which. Another
good strategy is to consult collocational dictionaries such as the
COBUILD English Language Dictionary, 4th ed. (New York: Harper-
Collins, 1996), which is based on a 500-million-word corpus of actual
written and spoken English. By logging on to the Web site at
<http://titania.cobuild.collins.co.uk>, you can access the corpus directly
and take advantage of the concordance program, which will give you
forty random samples of actual usage for any word in contemporary
English.

You can also get help with collocations through a specialized
English learner's dictionary that provides plenty of example sen-
tences. Good choices include the *Longman Dictionary of Contemporary
English,* 4th ed. (London: Longman, 2003), the *Longman Dictionary of
American English,* 2nd ed. (Reading: Addison-Wesley, 2002), and the
Oxford Advanced Learner's Dictionary, 6th ed. (New York: Oxford Uni-
versity Press, 2000). On the Internet, try *OneLook Dictionaries* at
<http://www.onelook.com>.

EXER

Vocabulary
choices.

EXERCISE 63.2

In each of the following sentences, replace the underlined word to
form a collocation. You may want to consult an appropriate dictionary for help. The first sentence has already been done.

1. *highest*
   Kenya has one of the ~~tallest~~ standards of living in sub-Saharan Africa.
2. Gone are the days when a doctor would make <u>house visits</u>.
3. Let's all give the winner a <u>volley</u> of applause.
4. The students were on their <u>promise</u> not to cheat.
5. She was the first woman to <u>achieve</u> the finish line at the Boston Marathon.
6. The young actor had to learn his lines <u>to</u> heart.
7. I just got an A on my English paper, and things are <u>seeing</u> up.
8. He told the waiter that he would <u>eat</u> the specialty of the house.

63c   Learn idioms in their entirety

A special type of collocation, an **idiomatic expression,** or **idiom,** is a fixed phrase whose meaning cannot be deduced from the meanings of its parts. For example, even if you know the words *kick* and *bucket,* you may not know what the idiom *kick the bucket* means (it means "die"). Because of their unpredictability, you have to learn idioms in their entirety, one at a time. And you have to use them in exactly the right form. If you said *kick a bucket* or *kick the pail,* many listeners would not know what you meant.

The best way to learn a language's idioms is by listening to native speakers. Some good Web sites can also be of help: Dave Sperling's *ESL Idiom Page* at *<http://www.pacificnet.net/~sperling/idioms.cgi>*, *The Monthly Idiom* at *<http://www.comenius.com/idioms>*, and *Vocabulary on the Internet* at *<http://ec.hku.hk/vec/vocab/vocint.htm>*.

Because most idioms are colloquial, you should generally avoid them in formal written English (see 45c). They are most often used for casual communication, as in ordinary conversation, email correspondence, or chat groups. Some idioms, though, are quite acceptable in more formal uses.

> **WEBLINK**
> http://www.eslcafe.com/idioms/
> An interactive site for learning colloquial idioms

AUDIO
Using idiomatic expressions.

> **WEBLINK**
> http://a4esl.org/q/h/idioms.html
> A great collection of self-study quizzes for ESL students

EXER
An extra vocabulary quiz.

Glossary of Grammatical and Rhetorical Terms

absolute phrase   A subject and an adjective phrase (often a participial phrase) used to modify an entire clause—for example, *"Her curiosity satisfied,* she left the meeting." (30c-2)

abstract noun   A word that names an idea, emotion, quality, or other intangible concept—for example, *beauty, passion, despair.* (30a-1, 45a-2)

acronym   A pronounceable word formed from the first letters of a multiword name and usually written in uppercase letters—for example, *UNESCO, ASCII, RAM.* (58d)

active form   *See* active voice.

active voice   The form a transitive verb takes to indicate that the subject is performing the action on the direct object. Also called the *active form.* (30a-4, 32g)

adjective   A word that modifies a noun by qualifying or describing it—for example, *new, interesting.* (30a-3, Chapter 34). *See also specific types of adjectives.*

adjective clause   A dependent clause, usually introduced by a relative pronoun, that modifies a noun or pronoun. Also called a *relative clause.* (30c-3)

adverb   A word that modifies a verb, adjective, clause, sentence, or other adverb—for example, *quickly, well.* (30a-5, Chapter 34, 62d). *See also specific types of adverbs.*

adverb clause   A dependent clause that begins with a subordinating conjunction and answers the question when, where, how, or why. (30c-3)

agreement   The grammatical requirement that a verb and its subject have the same number (either plural or singular) and that a pronoun and its antecedent have the same number and gender. (Chapter 33)

analogy   A simile that extends beyond one sentence. (45g-2)

analytical writing   Writing that examines the whole of a work in relationship to its component parts. (17a-3)

annotating   Making summary notes in the margin, as well as underlining or highlighting important words and passages. (2b-3)

antecedent   The noun that precedes and is replaced by a pronoun. For example, in the sentence "David is proud of himself," *David* is the antecedent of *himself.* A pronoun should agree in number and gender with its antecedent. (30a-2, 33b, 37a)

antonyms   Two words having opposite meanings—for example, *love* and *hate.* (47c-3)

appositive   A special type of pronoun-noun pairing in which a pronoun is conjoined with a noun—for example, *we students.* Also, a noun that is placed next to the subject to give it extra characterization. *See also* appositive phrase. (31c)

appositive phrase   A noun phrase, placed next to another noun, that describes or defines the other noun and is usually set off by commas—for example, "Sammy Sosa, *my favorite baseball player,* may someday break the home run record." Also called an *appositive.* (30c-2)

argument   A course of reasoning that puts forth a claim and supports it with evidence. (7)

article   A word that precedes a noun and indicates definiteness or indefiniteness. Standard Edited English has three articles: *a, an, the.* (30a-3, Chapter 60)

aspect   *See* verbal aspect.

auxiliary verb   A verb, such as *has, be,* or *do,* that combines with a main verb to form a simple predicate—for example, "The guests *have* left." Also called a *helping verb.* (30a-4, 32c)

base form   The main form of a verb, given as the headword in the dictionary—for example, *run, ask, consider.* Also called *simple form.* (30a-4, 32a)

bibliography   Any listing of books and articles on a particular subject. (8d)

Boolean operators   Specific words (AND, NOT, OR) that are combined with other words or phrases to allow you to focus your search terms during a database search. (9c-1)

brainstorming   Generating random ideas or fragments of thought about a topic. (3c-1)

case   The form a pronoun takes to indicate its grammatical relation to other words in the sentence. (Chapter 31). *See also* objective case, possessive case, subjective case.

clause   A group of words that has a subject and a predicate. (30c-3). *See also specific types of clauses.*

cliché   An overused expression—for example, *sick and tired, climbing the ladder of success.* (45g-3)

clustering   A prewriting technique that helps a writer see relationships among ideas. (3c-4)

cognates   Two words, from different languages, that are similar in form and meaning—for example, the English *disaster* and the Spanish *desastre*. (63a)

coherence   The characteristic of writing that makes it "stick together" from sentence to sentence and paragraph to paragraph. (5a-2)

collective noun   A singular word that names a group—for example, *team, band, trio*. (30a-1)

collocation   The relationship between two or more words that frequently occur together—for example, *write* and *check*. (47c-1, 63b)

comma splice   Two independent clauses joined only by a comma. Comma splices are not acceptable in formal English. (Chapter 36)

common noun   A word that names one or more persons, places, things, concepts, or qualities as a general category—for example, *flowers, telephone, determination*. Common nouns are lowercased. (30a-1)

complement   *See* object complement, subject complement, verb complement.

complete predicate   The simple predicate plus any objects, complements, or adverbial modifiers. (30b-2)

complete subject   The simple subject of a sentence, plus all modifiers. (30b-1)

complex compound   A word made up of three or more words. (59b)

complex sentence   A sentence that has a single independent clause and one or more dependent clauses. (30d-2, 44b)

complex series   A series in which individual items contain internal commas, necessitating the use of semicolons to separate the items. (52c)

compound   A word made up of two smaller words. (59a)

compound antecedent   A noun phrase consisting of two or more terms joined by *and*—for example, *Kim and her brother*. It is usually considered plural; therefore, if it is referred to later by a pronoun, the pronoun should be plural. (33b)

compound-complex sentence   A sentence that has two or more independent clauses and one or more dependent clauses. (30d-2, 44b)

compound predicate   A predicate containing two or more verbs with the same subject. (30b-1)

compound sentence   A sentence that has two or more independent clauses and no dependent clauses. (30d-2, 44b)

compound subject   A sentence subject consisting of two or more simple subjects. (30b-1)

concrete noun   A word that names something that can be touched, seen, heard, smelled, or tasted—for example, *automobile, music, cloud*. (30a-1, 45a-2)

conditional sentence   A sentence composed of a subordinate clause (usually beginning with *if*) and a main clause—for example, "If I'm late, please start the meeting without me." (61i-k)

conjunction   A word that joins two sentences, clauses, phrases, or words—for example, *and, or, but.* (30a-7). *See also specific types of conjunctions.*

conjunctive adverb   An adverb that modifies an entire sentence or clause while linking it to the preceding sentence or clause—for example, *however, therefore.* (30a-5, 51f)

connotation   Extra meaning that a word has, beyond its basic meaning. (45b, 47b)

contraction   A reduced form of a word or pair of words—for example, *can't* for *cannot, I'll* for *I will.* (45c-2)

coordinate adjectives   A series of adjectives, separated by commas, that could be arranged in any order—for example, a *rusty, dented, broken-down* car. (51d)

coordinating conjunction   A conjunction used to connect sentences, clauses, phrases, or words that are parallel in meaning—for example, *and, but, or, nor, yet.* (30a-7)

coordination   The pairing of equivalent sentences or sentence elements by putting them in the same grammatical form and linking them via a coordinating conjunction, conjunctive adverb, or semicolon. (41b)

correlative conjunctions   Conjunctions that are used in pairs—for example, *both/and, either/or, neither/nor.* The two elements connected by such conjunctions should be in parallel grammatical form. (30a-7)

count noun   A word that names something that can be counted and pluralized—for example, a *book,* some *friends,* three *dollars.* (30a-1, 60a)

cumulative adjectives   A series of adjectives, each one modifying those following it—for example, *a small new Italian luxury* car. These adjectives must follow a certain order, and commas are not used to separate them. (51j)

dangling modifier   An introductory verbal phrase that does not refer to the subject of the sentence. Dangling modifiers are unacceptable in formal English. (38e)

debating   A prewriting technique that helps writers to examine arguments for and against a controversial issue. (3c-5)

declarative sentence   A sentence that makes a statement about something. In most writing, declarative sentences predominate. (30d-1)

deductive reasoning   Argumentation that starts with some general rule or assumption and then applies it to a specific fact to arrive at a logical conclusion. (7a-2)

demonstrative adjective   An adjective that singles out a specific noun—for example, *this* book, *those* promises. (30a-3, 34a)

demonstrative pronoun   A pronoun that points to its antecedent noun—for example, *this, those.* (30a-2)

demonstratives   Short for demonstrative pronouns and/or demonstrative adjectives.

denotation   The basic dictionary meaning of a word. Compare with *connotation*. (45a, 47b)

dependent clause   A clause that cannot stand alone as a sentence but must be attached to a main clause. A dependent clause typically begins with a subordinating conjunction or relative pronoun. The three types of dependent clauses are adjective, adverb, and noun clauses. Also called a *subordinate clause*. (30c-3, 35b)

determiner   A word such as *the, this,* or *her* that initiates a noun phrase. (30a-3, 60f)

development   The depth of coverage given to particular topics in a piece of writing reveals its development. (5a-2)

dialect   Speech that is identified with a particular social, ethnic, or regional group. (45d)

diction   A writer's choice of words. (Chapter 45)

direct discourse   Language that is taken word for word from another source and is enclosed in quotation marks. (39f)

direct object   A noun, pronoun, or noun phrase that completes the action of the verb in an active sentence—for example, "Our neighbor plays *the piano.*" (30b-2)

disciplinary discourse   The language conventions and genres typically used by a particular academic discipline, e.g., the discourse of political science or the discourse of physics. (Chapter 16)

disjunctive antecedent   A noun phrase consisting of two or more terms joined by *or* or *nor*—for example, *the wife or the husband*. If the disjunctive antecedent is referred to later by a pronoun, the pronoun should agree in number with the last term in the phrase. (33b)

disjunctive subject   A sentence subject consisting of two nouns or pronouns joined by *or* or *nor*. (33a-4)

ellipsis   Three spaced periods marking the omission of a word or phrase. (11b-2, 56j)

end-weight   The emphasis that falls naturally on the words located at the end of a clause or sentence. (43a)

enthymeme   A syllogism with one of the premises unstated. (7a-2)

etymology   Information about a word's historical development. (48b-5)

exclamatory sentence   A sentence that expresses strong emotion and is punctuated with an exclamation point. (30d-1)

exemplification   The use of examples to make difficult concepts understandable. (6b-8)

expletive pronoun   An introductory word (*it, there*) that opens a sentence but carries little meaning. Expletives are sometimes overused. (30a-2, 40c)

fallacy   A false statement or line of reasoning. (7g)

false cognates   Two words, from different languages, that resemble each other but have different meanings—for example, the Spanish *compromiso* and the English *compromise*. Also called *false friends*. (63a)

false friends   *See* false cognates.

faulty predication   An ungrammatical sentence in which the subject and the predicate are not consistent with each other. (39e)

figure of speech   A figurative, or nonliteral, use of language such as a metaphor or simile. (45g)

final bibliography   The final listing of sources you actually used in writing the research paper, formatted according to a particular documentation style. (8d)

focus   Refers to how well a piece adheres to its topic and purpose. (5a-2)

format   (*n*) The way a piece of writing delineates its subtopics and parts through headings, typeface, typestyle, and so forth. (*v*) To set up a piece of writing's visual style. (5a-2)

fragment   *See* sentence fragment.

freewriting   Writing down thoughts in connected sentences as they come to mind. (3c-2)

functional résumé   A résumé in which certain skills are emphasized through the use of categories such as "Computer Skills" and "Language Skills." (25c)

fused sentence   *See* run-on sentence.

future perfect progressive tense   A verb tense formed by combining *will have been* and the *-ing* form of the main verb. It emphasizes the continuous or repetitive nature of the action—for example, "Next month, my father *will have been teaching* for 30 years." (32d-3)

future perfect tense   A verb tense formed by combining *will have* and the past participle of the main verb. It describes an action that will occur in the future but before some specified time—for example, "Soon I *will have completed* all the requirements." (32d-3)

future progressive tense   A verb tense formed by combining *will be* and the *-ing* form of the main verb. It expresses action that will be continuing or repeated in the future—for example, "My daughter is on vacation now, but she *will be going* back to school in the fall." (32d-3)

future tense   A verb tense formed by combining the modal auxiliary *will* and the base form of the main verb. It expresses actions or conditions that will occur in the future—for example, "The final exam *will be* hard." Also called *simple future tense*. (32d-3)

gender   Classification of a noun or pronoun as masculine, feminine, or neuter. (33b)

generic pronoun   A pronoun used to refer to all people regardless of gender. (46a-2)

genre   The kind of writing form used, such as an essay, poem, song lyric, or report. *See also* literary genre. (3b-3)

gerund   A verb form that ends in *ing* and functions as a noun—for example, "We went *skiing* last week." (30a-9)

gerund phrase   A phrase consisting of a gerund and any modifiers, objects, and/or complements—for example, "*Running a business* can be difficult." (30c-2)

head noun   The rightmost noun in a noun compound. (62c)

helping verb   *See* auxiliary verb.

homophones   Words that sound alike but are spelled differently and have different meanings—for example, *brake* and *break*. (49b)

idiom   *See* idiomatic expression.

idiomatic expression   A phrase whose meaning differs from that of its individual words—for example, *kick the bucket*. Also called an *idiom*. (45c-2, 63c)

imperative mood   A grammatical form of a verb used to express a command or a strong request and give instructions. Imperative sentences are always addressed to an understood subject *you*, which is usually omitted. (30a-4, 32h, 39b)

imperative sentence   A sentence that expresses a command, a request, or a suggestion, usually with an understood subject *you*—for example, "Don't fret!" "Try using the toolbar buttons." (30d-1)

indefinite adjective   A nonspecific adjective—for example, *some* people. (30a-3, 34a)

indefinite pronoun   A pronoun that refers to one or more nonspecific persons, places, or things and does not require an antecedent—for example, *anybody, anything*. (30a-2)

independent clause   A group of words that includes a subject and predicate and can stand alone as a sentence. Also called a *main clause*. (30c-3)

indicative mood   A grammatical form of a verb used to make assertions, state opinions, and ask questions. (30a-4, 32h, 39b)

indirect discourse   A summarization, restatement, or paraphrase of a statement made by someone else. (39f, 55b-1)

indirect object   A noun, pronoun, or noun phrase that is indirectly affected by the action of the verb—for example, "My boyfriend gave *me* a present." (30b-2)

inductive reasoning   A pattern in which the writer states the main claim for an argument late in the work, in order to first present a skeptical audience with supporting evidence. (7a-2)

infinitive   The base form of a verb preceded by *to*. It can function as a noun, adjective, or adverb. (30a-4, 30a-9). *See also* perfect infinitive, present infinitive.

infinitive phrase   A phrase consisting of an infinitive and any modifiers, objects, and/or complements—for example, "Kevin said he wanted *to make his own way.*" (30c-2)

initialism   An abbreviation formed from the first letters of a multiword name and usually written in uppercase letters—for example, *FBI, CPU.* (58d)

inseparable verb   A transitive phrasal verb whose particle must be kept together with the verb—for example, "I quickly *went over* my paper." Compare with *separable verb.* (Chapter 61)

intensive pronoun   A pronoun that consists of a personal pronoun plus -*self* or -*selves* and is used for emphasis—for example, "They did it *themselves.*" (30a-2)

interjection   A word or short phrase that expresses an emotional outcry and is punctuated with an exclamation point. (30a-8)

interpretive writing   Writing that discusses another person's intended meaning or the impact of a work on an audience. (17a-2)

interrogative adjective   An adjective that raises a question about a noun—for example, "*Which* way do I go?" "*Whose* hat is this?" (30a-3, 34a)

interrogative pronoun   A pronoun that introduces a question—for example, *who, what, whose.* (30a-2, 31d)

interrogative sentence   A sentence that raises a question and is punctuated with a question mark. (30d-1)

intransitive verb   A verb that does not take a direct object—for example, "My driver's license *has expired.*" (30a-4, 32f, Chapter 61)

invisible writing   A computer freewriting technique designed to release writers from inhibitions created by seeing their own words onscreen. (3c-3)

irregular verb   A verb whose past tense and past participle are not formed through the standard pattern of adding -*d* or -*ed* to the base form—for example, *run (ran, run); know (knew, known).* (30a-4, 32b)

jargon   Specialized, technical language used by a professional or special interest group. (45d)

keywords   Words that are used to identify the subjects found in electronic databases. Also called *descriptors* or *identifiers.* (8e-2)

linking verb   A verb that joins a sentence subject to a subject complement, indicating a condition, quality, or state of being—for example, "They *will be* late." (30a-4, 30b-3)

literary genre   Type of literature, such as poetry, fiction, or drama. (17a-1)

main clause   *See* independent clause.

mass noun   *See* noncount noun.

metaphor   A figure of speech in which the writer describes something in a way normally reserved for something else, thus presenting it in a new light. (45g-2)

mixed construction   An ungrammatical sentence that starts out one way but finishes in another. (39d)

mixed metaphors   Two different metaphors put close together in a piece of writing—for example, "Milwaukee is the golden egg that the rest of the state wants to milk." Mixed metaphors should be avoided. (45g-2)

modal auxiliary verb   A special type of verb that indicates necessity, probability, or permission—for example, *may, might, should, can*. Also called a *modal verb*. (30a-4, 32c, 61f). *See also* auxiliary verb.

modal verb   *See* modal auxiliary verb.

modifier   A word, phrase, or clause that adds detail to another word, phrase, or clause. (30c, Chapter 38). *See also* dangling modifier, split infinitive.

mood   Classification of a verb according to the type of statement made—indicative, imperative, or subjunctive. (30a-4, 32h, 39b)

narrative   A type of writing that tells a story in a time-ordered sequence. (6b-7)

nominalization   A noun derived from a verb—for example, *removal* (derived from *remove*) and *fascination* (derived from *fascinate*). The frequent use of nominalizations results in a noun-heavy style. (40f)

noncount noun   A word that names something that typically is not counted or pluralized—for example, *milk, generosity, rain*. Also called a *mass noun*. (30a-1, 60a)

nonessential element   *See* nonrestrictive element.

nonrestrictive element   A phrase or clause that provides extra information in a sentence. A nonrestrictive element can be omitted without changing the basic meaning of the sentence; it is set off with commas, dashes, or parentheses. Also called a *nonessential element*. (51e)

noun   A word that names a person, place, thing, quality, idea, or action. (30a-1). *See also specific types of nouns.*

noun clause   A dependent clause that begins with a relative pronoun and functions as a sentence subject, object, complement, or appositive. (30c-3)

noun compound   A sequence of two or more nouns, with the rightmost noun being the head noun and the other noun(s) serving to modify it—for example, *income tax form*. (34b, 62c)

number   Classification of a noun, pronoun, or verb as singular or plural. (33b, 39a)

object   *See* direct object, indirect object, object of the preposition.

object complement   A noun, noun phrase, adjective, or adjective phrase that elaborates on or describes the direct object of a sentence—for example, "The film made me *angry*." (30b-2)

object of a preposition   A noun or pronoun in a prepositional phrase—for example, "He was on the *boat*." (30a-6)

objective case   The form a pronoun takes when it is used as a grammatical object. (Chapter 31)

organization   The plan that a piece of writing follows, typically based on the thesis and opening paragraphs. (5a-2)

paragraph   A sentence or group of sentences, presented in a text as a unit, that develops a main idea. (Chapter 6)

parallel form   *See* parallelism.

parallel structure   *See* parallelism.

parallelism   The use of similar grammatical form for words or phrases that have a coordinate relationship. Also called *parallel structure* or *parallel form*. (6e, Chapter 42)

participial phrase   A phrase consisting of a present or past participle plus any objects, modifiers, and/or complements—for example, "I saw someone *running down the street*." (30c-2)

participle   A verb form that can serve as an adjective—for example, *earned* income or *earning* power. (30a-9). *See also* past participle, present participle, present perfect participle.

particle   A preposition or adverb that, when attached to a verb, creates a phrasal verb—for example, look *into*, see *through*, knock *out*. (30a-6)

parts of speech   The different categories in which words can be classified according to their grammatical function: nouns, verbs, adjectives, adverbs, pronouns, prepositions, conjunctions, verbals, and expletives. (30a)

passive form   *See* passive voice.

passive voice   The form a transitive verb takes to indicate that the subject is being acted upon. Also called the *passive form*. (30a-4, 32g)

past participle   A verb form that can be used by itself as an adjective or can be combined with some form of the auxiliary *have* to form perfect tenses or with some form of the verb *be* to create passive-voice sentences. With regular verbs, it is similar in form to the past tense—for example, *picked, opened*. (30a-4, 30a-9, 32a, 32e-4)

past perfect progressive tense   A verb tense formed by combining *had been* and the present participle of the main verb. It puts emphasis on the continuing or repetitive nature of a past action—for example, "By the time he crossed the bridge, Roy *had been running* for two hours." (32d-2)

past perfect tense   A verb tense created by combining *had* and the past participle of the main verb. It is used to describe a past action that preceded another past activity—for example, "Before she injured her knee, Beth *had hoped* to become a top ski racer." (32d-2)

past progressive tense   A verb tense formed by combining the auxiliary verb *was* or *were* and the present participle of the main verb—for example, "I *was* just *starting* to cook when our guest arrived." (32d-2)

past tense A verb tense that indicates past action—for example, "World War I *started* in 1914." With regular verbs, the past tense is formed by adding *-d* or *-ed* to the base form. Also called *simple past tense*. (30a-4, 32a, 32d-2)

perfect infinitive A verb form consisting of *to have* plus the past participle of the verb—for example, *to have changed, to have stopped.* It is used for an action that occurs prior to the action expressed by the main verb. (32e-3)

person Classification of a pronoun based on whether it refers to the speaker (first person: *I, me, us*), the person spoken to (second person: *you*), or someone or something spoken about (third person: *she, him, it, they*). (39a)

persona A writer's presentation of him- or herself through a piece of writing. (3b-2)

personal pronoun A pronoun that refers to one or more specific persons, places, or things—for example, *she, it, they.* (30a-2)

personification A type of metaphor in which an inanimate object or abstraction is described as having human traits. (45g-2)

phrasal verb A verb consisting of a verb and one or two particles—for example, *pick over, look into, get away with.* Also called a *two-word verb* or *three-word verb.* (30a-6, 61a)

phrase A group of related words that does not have both a subject and a complete predicate (compare with *clause*). Phrases can function as nouns, verbs, or modifiers. (30c-2). *See also specific types of phrases.*

plagiarism Unauthorized or misleading use of the language and thoughts of another author. (11a-3)

possessive adjective An adjective that indicates possession—for example, *my* coat, *their* country. (30a-3, 31e, 34a, 60f)

possessive case The form a pronoun takes when it is used as a grammatical possessive. (Chapter 31)

possessive pronoun A pronoun such as *mine, yours,* or *hers* that stands by itself—for example, "This seat is *mine.*" (31e)

predicate The part of a sentence that contains the verb and makes a statement about the subject. (30b-2)

predicate adjective An adjective that follows a linking verb and refers back to the noun subject. (30a-3)

prefix A word part, such as *anti-, re-,* or *dis-,* that is attached to the beginning of a word—for example, *anti*freeze, *re*new, *dis*cover. (47a, 49d-1)

preposition A word that indicates a relationship between a noun or pronoun and some other part of the sentence—for example, *to, in, at, from, on.* Also called a *particle* in phrasal verbs. (30a-6)

prepositional phrase A group of words consisting of a preposition plus a noun or pronoun and its modifiers. (30a-6, 30c-2)

present infinitive   A verb form consisting of *to* plus the base form of the verb—for example, *to go, to hesitate*. It is used for an action that occurs at the same time as or later than the action expressed by the main verb. (32e-3)

present participle   A verb form created by adding *ing* to the base form—for example, *sewing, writing*. It can be used by itself as an adjective or noun or can be combined with some form of the verb *be* to form the progressive tenses. (30a-4, 30a-8, 32a, 32e-4)

present perfect participle   A verb form consisting of *having* plus the past participle of the verb. It is used to express an action occurring prior to the action of the main verb—for example, "*Having changed* my PIN number, I cannot remember it." (32e-4)

present perfect progressive tense   A verb tense formed by combining *have been* or *has been* and the present participle of the main verb. It typically emphasizes the ongoing nature of the activity—for example, "People *have been complaining* about the working conditions for years." (32d-1)

present perfect tense   A verb tense formed by combining the auxiliary verb *have* or *has* and the past participle of the main verb. It is used to indicate action that began in the past and either is continuing or has continuing effects in the present—for example, "The United Nations *has served* many purposes." (32d-1)

present progressive tense   A verb tense formed by combining the auxiliary verb *am, is,* or *are* and the *-ing* form of a main verb. It is typically used to indicate present action—for example, "Mike *is taking* a heavy load of classes this term." (32d-1)

present tense   The verb tense used to express a general statement, make an observation, or describe a habitual activity—for example, "Geese *fly* south in autumn." Also called *simple present tense*. (30a-4, 32a, 32d-1)

primary research   Generating information or data through processes such as interviewing, administering questionnaires, and observing. (8a-1, 8f-6)

principal parts   The major forms of a verb: base form, present tense, past tense, past participle, and present participle. (30a-4, 32a)

process description   A type of writing that depicts a step-by-step procedure. (6b-7)

pronoun   A word that substitutes for a noun and always refers to a noun. (30a-2, 33b). *See also specific types of pronouns.*

proper noun   A word that names a particular person, place, institution, organization, month, or day—for example, *Anne, New York City, Monday*. Proper nouns are almost always capitalized. (30a-1)

quantifier   An adjective such as *many, little,* or *every* that indicates some amount of a noun. (60f)

reciprocal pronoun   A pronoun that refers to the separate parts of a plural antecedent—for example, "They made promises to *one another.*" (30a-2)

redundancy   The use of words that could be left out without changing the meaning of a sentence. (40b)

reflexive pronoun   A pronoun that consists of a personal pronoun plus *-self* or *-selves.* It refers back to the subject to show that the subject is the object of an action—for example, "Katy cut *herself.*" (30a-2)

register   The overall degree of formality of a piece of writing, including its identification with a particular field or community of users. (45c)

regular verb   A verb that forms the third-person singular present tense by adding *s* or *es* to the base form, forms the present participle by adding *ing* to the base form, and forms the past tense and past participle by adding *d* or *ed* to the base form. (30a-4, 32a)

related words   Words derived from the same root. (48b-5)

relative clause   *See* adjective clause.

relative pronoun   A pronoun that introduces a dependent clause—for example, *that, which, whom.* (30a-2, 31d)

restrictive element   Information essential to the precise meaning of a sentence and thus not set off with commas. Compare with *nonrestrictive element.* (51j)

résumé   A concise summary of an individual's accomplishments, skills, experience, and personal interests. (25c). *See also* functional résumé.

rhetorical classification   *See* functional classification.

rhetorical stance   A writer's approach to his or her topic, encompassing purpose, persona, and audience. (3b-2)

root   The main part of a word, to which prefixes and suffixes can be attached—for example, the root of *telephonic* is *phon.* Also called a *stem.* (47a)

run-on sentence   Two independent clauses fused together without any intervening conjunction or punctuation. Run-on sentences are not acceptable in formal English. Also called a *fused sentence.* (Chapter 36)

secondary research   Finding information in secondary, or previously published, sources. (8a-1, 8f-1 to 8f-5)

semiacronym   An abbreviation where part of the term is pronounced as a word, the rest as one or more letters—for example, "jpeg" (pronounced "jay-peg"). (58d)

sense   The meaning of a word. (48b-4)

sentence   The basic unit of written language for expressing a thought. All sentences except commands have a stated grammatical subject and a predicate. (30b). *See also specific types of sentences.*

sentence fragment   A grammatically incomplete sentence. (Chapter 35)

sentence subject   *See* subject.

separable verb   A transitive phrasal verb whose particle may be placed after the object of the verb—for example, "I quickly *looked* my paper *over*." Compare with *inseparable verb*. (61)

sequence of tenses   The time relationship among verbs in a block of text, expressed by verb tenses. (32e)

serial comma   In a series of items, the comma that separates the items. (51c)

signal phrase   The introductory phrase that signals a quotation to follow. (11b-2)

simile   A figure of speech in which the writer uses one thing to describe another. Similes typically employ the word *like* or *as*—for example, "The brain is somewhat *like* a computer." (45g-1)

simple form   *See* base form.

simple future tense   *See* future tense.

simple past tense   *See* past tense.

simple predicate   A main verb plus any auxiliary verbs. Also called a *verb phrase*. (30b-2). *See also* predicate.

simple present tense   *See* present tense.

simple sentence   A sentence that has a single independent clause and no dependent clauses. (30d-2, 44b)

simple subject   The noun or pronoun that constitutes the heart of a sentence subject. (30b-1)

slang   Nonstandard language characterized by short-lived, colorful expressions. It is most commonly used by teenagers and tight-knit subcultures. (45d)

split infinitive   A *to* infinitive with one or more words between *to* and the verb—for example, *to quickly retreat*. (38d-2)

stative verb   *See* verb of state.

stem   *See* root.

subject   A noun, pronoun, or noun phrase that indicates what a sentence is about and typically precedes the main verb of the sentence. (30b-1, 33a-1, 39b). *See also specific types of subjects.*

subject complement   A noun, noun phrase, adjective, or adjective phrase that elaborates on the subject of a sentence and usually follows a linking verb—for example, "Joanne was elected *student body president*." (30b-2)

subjective case   The form a pronoun takes when it is used as a grammatical subject. (Chapter 31)

subjunctive mood   A grammatical form of a verb used to express hypothetical conditions, wishes, and other uncertain statements. Verbs in subjunctive mood often appear in dependent clauses beginning with *if* or *that*. (30a-4, 32h, 39b)

subordinate clause   *See* dependent clause.

subordinating conjunction   A conjunction that is used to introduce a dependent clause and connect it to an independent clause—for example, *although, because, if, since.* (30a-7)

subordination   In a sentence containing two ideas that are not equal in importance, making the lesser idea into a subordinate, or dependent, clause. (41c)

suffix   A word part, such as *-ful, -ship,* or *-ness,* that is attached to the end of a word—for example, boast*ful,* fellow*ship,* kind*ness.* (47a, 49d-2)

syllogism   A form of deductive logic consisting of a major premise, a minor premise, and a conclusion. (7a-2)

synonyms   Words that are similar in meaning—for example, *desire* and *want.* (47c-2)

tense   *See* verb tense.

theoretical writing   Writing that examines individual works or events to determine how they exemplify broader trends. (17a-3)

thesaurus   A collection of synonyms and antonyms. (48a)

thesis statement   A sentence or two that concisely identifies the topic and main point of a piece of writing. (3e-2)

three-word verb   *See* phrasal verb.

tone   The tone of a piece of writing, including the attitude a writer conveys toward the subject through language choices. (5a-2, 39c)

topic sentence   A sentence, usually at the beginning of a paragraph, that gives readers an overview of the paragraph. (6a-1)

transitive verb   A verb that acts on an object—for example, *carry, show.* In the active voice, a transitive verb acts on the direct object of the sentence. In the passive voice, it acts on the subject. (30a-4, 32f, Chapter 61)

two-word verb   *See* phrasal verb.

unified paragraph   A paragraph that focuses on and develops a single main idea. (6a)

usage label   In dictionaries, a notation indicating a particular sense of a word—for example, *Informal, Archaic.* (48b-6)

usage note   In dictionaries, an expert judgment about the correct use of a word. (48b-6)

verb   A word that expresses action, occurrence, or existence. (30a-4, Chapter 32). *See also specific types of verbs.*

verb complement   A participial or infinitive phrase attached to a verb—for example, in the sentence "I like to swim," *to swim* is the complement of the verb *like.* (61b)

verb of state   A verb that expresses a condition or state, rather than an action or event—for example, *involve, need, consist of.* Verbs of state do not have progressive tense forms. Also called a *stative verb.* (32d-1, 61f)

verb phrase   A main verb plus any auxiliary verbs. Also called a *simple predicate.* (32c)

verb tense   The form a verb takes to indicate the time of the action or the state of being. (32d, 39b)

verbal   A verb form that functions in a sentence as a noun, adverb, or adjective. There are three types of verbals: participles, gerunds, and infinitives. (30a-9, 30c-2)

verbal aspect   The particular form a verb takes, within its tense, to indicate duration or completion of the verb's action or state of being. Standard Edited English has three verbal aspects: perfect, progressive, and perfect progressive. Also called *aspect.* (32d)

voice   The form a transitive verb takes to indicate whether the subject is acting (*active voice*) or being acted upon (*passive voice*). (32g, 39b) Sometimes used to refer to the tone of a piece of writing. (See12a-3.)

warrant   An assumption in the form of a general statement or rule (often unstated) that logically connects the evidence or data a writer is using to the point he or she is making. (7e-2)

working bibliography   A listing of all the sources you encounter in your research. May not be in final citation format. (8d)

Glossary of Usage

a, an   Use *a* before words beginning with a consonant sound: *a program, a uniform.* Use *an* before words beginning with a vowel sound: *an open book, an uncle.*

accept, except   *Accept* is a verb meaning "to receive gladly." *Except* is usually a preposition meaning "with the exclusion of."

adapt, adopt   *Adapt* means "to adjust" or "to make suitable." *Adopt* means "to take as one's own." *If you adopt a child, you will have to adapt to it.*

adverse, averse   *Adverse* means "unfavorable." *Averse* means "opposed to." *I am averse to anything that has adverse consequences.*

advice, advise   *Advice* is a noun meaning "guidance." *Advise* is a verb meaning "to guide." *I advised her to take my advice.*

affect, effect   *Affect* is usually a verb meaning "to influence." *Bad weather seems to affect my mood. Effect* is usually a noun meaning "result." As a verb, *effect* means "bring about." *The new policy will effect important changes.*

aggravate   "Make worse." *Donna's asthma was aggravated by the polluted air.* Also commonly used to mean "irritate," though some experts consider this incorrect.

ain't   Nonstandard. *Am not, is not, are not,* or *have not* are preferred in standard English.

all ready, already   *All ready* is an adjective phrase meaning "all prepared." *They were all ready to go. Already* is an adverb meaning "by this time." *They have already left.*

all right   Should be spelled as two words. An adjective phrase meaning "satisfactory."

all together, altogether   *All together* means "in unison; as a group." *Altogether* means "completely." *The witnesses spoke out all together. They were altogether happy to get the chance.*

allusion, illusion   *Allusion* means "indirect reference." *Illusion* means "false perception of reality."

a lot   Spelled as two words, not *alot* or *allot.* Informal. In formal writing, use *much* or *many* instead.

among, between   See *between, among.*

amongst   British equivalent of *among.*

amoral, immoral   *Amoral* means "neither moral nor immoral"; to some, it connotes "not caring about right and wrong." *Immoral* means "not moral."

amount, number   *Amount* is used with noncount nouns; *number* is used with count nouns. *A number of people said they had a large amount of money to give.*

an, a   See *a, an.*

and etc.   Redundant. Use *etc.* or *and so on.*

ante-, anti-   *Ante-* is a prefix meaning "before." The broker asked us to *antedate* the check. *Anti-* is a prefix meaning "against." Our planes encountered *anti-aircraft* fire.

anxious, eager   *Anxious* means "uneasy, worried." We were *anxious* about the weather. *Eager* means "having a strong desire." We were *eager* to see the show.

anymore   Should be used only in negative sentences. *She doesn't live here anymore.* In positive sentences, use *nowadays. I have many friends nowadays.*

anyplace   Informal for *anywhere.*

anyways, anywheres   Nonstandard for *anyway* and *anywhere.*

as   Be careful when using *as* as a substitute for *because* or *since. As I fell asleep, I lost track of the time.* Does *as* in this case mean "because" or "while"?

as, like   See *like, as*

assure, ensure, insure   These words have the same basic meaning of "to make certain." However, *assure* has a more personal orientation, "to set someone's mind at ease." *Ensure* and *insure* both mean roughly, "guarantee"; the latter carries a financial connotation.

at   Redundant when used with *where.* The colloquial *Where is he at?* should be shortened in formal writing to *Where is he?*

at this point in time   Wordy. Use *now, at present,* or *currently.*

averse, adverse   See *adverse, averse.*

awful, awfully   Avoid using these to mean "very," except in informal communication.

bad, badly   *Bad* is an adjective and *badly* is an adverb; avoid mixing these functions, as in *I feel badly* or *He plays bad.*

because of, due to   Use *because of* after a clause. *She had a headache because of stress.* Use *due to* after a noun. *Her headache was due to stress.*

being as, being that   These phrases are colloquial when used in sentences like *Being as the roads are icy, we should drive carefully.* In formal writing, replace them with *because* or *since.*

better, had better *Had better* is an idiomatic expression meaning "should." *You had better leave.* It is acceptable in formal writing. *You better leave* is too colloquial.

between, among Use *between* when referring to distinct individuals, especially two of them. *Let's divide it up between you and me.* Use *among* when referring to a mass or collectivity: *Let's divide it up among our friends.*

bring, take *Bring* suggests motion toward the writer or speaker; *take* suggests motion away from the writer or speaker. You *bring* something here, but you *take* something there.

but May be used to begin a sentence. Be aware, however, that some traditionalists may disagree with such usage.

calculate, figure, reckon Colloquial expressions for "guess" or "suppose," as in *I calculate we'll have a losing season again.* In formal writing, use *suppose, surmise,* or *imagine.*

can, may *Can* is preferred when expressing ability; *may* is preferred when requesting permission. *May I have another piece? Can she walk without crutches?*

can't hardly, can't scarcely Nonstandard. In formal writing, use *can hardly* or *can scarcely. Even accountants can hardly make sense of the tax code.*

censor, censure *Censor* means "to remove objectionable ideas from." *Censure* means "to condemn." *Church authorities censored the film and censured the film's producers.*

center around In formal writing, *center on* is preferred. *My paper will center on hate speech.*

cite, site *Cite* is a verb meaning "to quote." *Site* is a noun meaning "place."

climactic, climatic *Climactic* is the adjective form of *climax. King Lear's death is the climactic event of the play. Climatic* is the adjective form of climate. *Global warming could be a climatic disaster.*

complement, compliment A *complement* is something that completes a whole. *The flowers beautifully complemented the table setting.* A *compliment* is an expression of praise. *She complimented me on my dancing.*

compose, comprise *Compose* means "to make up, constitute." *Comprise* means "to consist of." *Seven days compose one week; one week comprises seven days.*

conscience, conscious *Conscience* is a noun meaning "a sense of right and wrong." *Conscious* is an adjective meaning "aware" or "intentional." *Todd made a conscious decision to clear his guilty conscience.*

continual, continuous *Continual* means "repeated at intervals." *Continuous* means "without interruption." *The flow of time is continuous, but a heartbeat is continual.*

could of Nonstandard for *could have*. *He could have tried harder.*

council, counsel A *council* is an assembly of people who advise or regulate. *Counsel* means "advice or guidance." *A council can give counsel.*

criterion, criteria *Criterion* is singular, meaning "standard of judgment." *Criteria* is the plural form.

data Traditionally, *data* was used only as the plural form of *datum*. However, it is now also (and more commonly) used as a singular form meaning "numerical information."

device, devise *Device* is a noun meaning "small machine" or "scheme." *Devise* is a verb meaning "to plan or invent."

different from, different than In formal writing, use *different from* when the comparison is between two persons or things. *My opinion is different from hers.* Use *different than* when the object of comparison is a full clause. *The party turned out different than I wanted it to be.*

discreet, discrete *Discreet* means "tactful" or "modest." *Discrete* means "distinct" or "separate."

disinterested, uninterested *Disinterested* means "neutral, unbiased." *Uninterested* means "unconcerned, indifferent to." *Although good judges are always disinterested in the case before them, they are not likely to be uninterested in it.*

due to, because of See *because of, due to*.

eager, anxious See *anxious, eager*.

effect, affect See *affect, effect*.

elicit, illicit *Elicit* is a verb meaning "to call forth." *Illicit* is an adjective meaning "illegal."

emigrate, immigrate, migrate *Emigrate* means "move permanently away from." *Immigrate* means "move permanently to." *Migrate* means "move temporarily from one place to another."

eminent, immanent, imminent *Eminent* means "distinguished." *She is an eminent scholar. Immanent* means "inherent." *God's spirit is immanent in nature. Imminent* means "about to occur." *A stock market crash is imminent.*

ensure See *assure, ensure, insure*.

enthused As an adjective, *enthused* is nonstandard. In formal writing, use *enthusiastic*.

especially, specially *Especially* means "deserving of special emphasis" or "particularly." *I am especially happy about my math grade. Specially* is the adverb form of special; it means "exceptionally" or "for a particular reason." *Today is a specially designated holiday.*

-ess A noun suffix used to denote a female, as in *lioness* or *hostess*. In cases where gender is irrelevant, use of this suffix has sexist connotations. Instead of terms like *poetess* and *sculptress*, use *poet* and *sculptor*.

G-21 Glossary of Usage

et al. Abbreviation for Latin *et alia* ("and others"). Should be used only to avoid repeated reference to three or more authors of a single work. *Johnson et al. make the same argument.*

etc. Abbreviation for Latin *et cetera* ("and the rest"). Should not refer to people and should not be used in formal writing. Instead of *She likes Cezanne, Matisse, etc.,* write *She likes artists such as Cezanne and Matisse* or *She likes Cezanne, Matisse, and other such artists.*

everyone, every one *Everyone* is an indefinite pronoun. *Everyone is here.* In *every one, one* is a pronoun and *every* is a quantifier. *Every one of the guests has been seated.*

except, accept See *accept, except.*

expect Verb meaning "anticipate." In formal writing, should not be used to mean "presume" or "suppose."

farther, further *Farther* refers to physical distance. *She hit the ball farther than anyone else. Further* refers to time or degree. *Should we go further with our research?*

fewer, less Use *fewer* with items that can be counted. Use *less* with general amounts. *He had fewer problems and less anxiety than I did.*

figure See *calculate, figure, reckon.*

firstly, secondly, thirdly Common in British English, but considered pretentious in American English. Use *first, second, third.*

get Informal in most uses, especially idiomatic expressions such as *get cracking* or *get around to.* In some cases, your thesaurus will suggest more formal alternatives.

good, well *Good* is an adjective, *well* is an adverb: *I feel good. I write well.*

gorilla, guerrilla A *gorilla* is a large ape. A *guerrilla* is a member of a rebel army.

had better, better See *better, had better.*

hanged, hung Use *hanged* for executions, *hung* for all other past-tense meanings. *The prisoner was hanged at dawn. The flag was hung from the railing.*

hardly, scarcely These adverbs have a negative meaning ("almost not at all"); using them with *not* creates a double negative, which is nonstandard in English. Instead, omit the not: *It hardly matters* (not *It doesn't hardly matter*).

he, him, his Using this singular masculine pronoun generically, that is, to refer to a mixed-gender group of people, is considered sexist by many. For ways around this problem, see 46c-2.

he/she, him/her, his/her These forms can be used to avoid the sexism of generic *he, him,* or *his.* Use them sparingly, however. (See 46c.)

heard, herd *Heard* is the past form of hear. *Herd* is a group of animals; also sometimes a verb, as in *to herd animals.*

hisself Nonstandard for *himself. He shot himself in the foot.*

hole, whole *Hole* is a noun meaning "gap" or "cavity." *Whole* is an adjective meaning "complete" or "entire."

hopefully Used widely as a sentence adverb, as in *Hopefully, the war will soon be over.* Although this usage is grammatically correct, some readers object to it.

hung, hang See *hang, hung.*

if, whether Although both of these conjunctions can be used to express an alternative, *whether* is clearer. *She doesn't know whether she can go.*

illicit, elicit See *elicit, illicit.*

illusion, allusion See *allusion, illusion.*

immanent See *eminent, immanent, imminent.*

immigrate See *emigrate, immigrate, migrate.*

immoral, amoral See *amoral, immoral.*

imply, infer *Imply* means "to suggest indirectly." *Infer* means "to draw a conclusion from what someone else has said." *The owner implied that I didn't have enough experience. I inferred that she would not offer me the job.*

incredible, incredulous *Incredible* means "unbelievable." *His performance was incredible. Incredulous* means "disbelieving." *He was incredulous when he heard the news.*

individual, person *Individual* is overused as a substitute for *person. Individual* should be reserved for situations emphasizing a person's distinctiveness. *Elizabeth Cady Stanton was a remarkable individual. Person* can be used in all other cases: *The person who stole my laptop will be caught sooner or later.*

infer, imply See *imply, infer.*

ingenious, ingenuous *Ingenious* means "inventive, clever." *Ingenuous* means "unsophisticated, candid."

in regards to Nonstandard. Use *in regard to, regarding,* or *as regards.*

instill, install *Instill* means "to implant." *A good parent instills good character in a child. Install* means "to set in position for use." *I should install new brakes in my car.*

insure See *assure, ensure, insure.*

irregardless Nonstandard for *regardless.*

its, it's *Its* is the possessive form of *it. It's* is the contracted form of *it is. It's important that a company give its employees a sense of security.*

kind of, sort of, type of Be careful to observe number agreement with these modifiers. Use *this kind of book* (all singular) or *these kinds of books* (all plural), not *these kind of books, these kinds of book,* or *this kind of books.*

lay, lie *Lay* takes a direct object. *They want to lay a wreath at his grave. Lie* does not take a direct object. *I think I'll lie down for a while.*

lead, led   *Lead* is a noun referring to a certain type of metal. *Led* is the past form of the verb to lead. *Our efforts have led to nothing.*

leave, let   *Leave* means "go away." *She plans to leave tomorrow. Let* means "allow." *Let me pay for this.*

lend, loan   These verbs both mean "to give something temporarily." But *loan* is used only for monetary transactions, while *lend* can be used for more figurative meanings, such as *lend someone a hand.*

less, fewer   See *fewer, less.*

lie, lay   See *lay, lie.*

like, as   In formal writing, use *like* as a preposition before a noun phrase and *as* as a conjunction before a clause: *She looked like her mother* versus *She looked as I thought she would.*

loan, lend   See *lend, loan.*

lose, loose   *Lose* is a verb meaning "fail to keep." *Loose* is an adjective meaning "not fastened."

lots   Informal. Use *many* or *much.*

man, mankind   Avoid these terms in situations where gender-inclusive terms such as *people, humanity, humans, humankind,* or *men and women* can be used instead.

may, can   See *can, may.*

might of   Nonstandard for *might have.* They *might have* left.

migrate   See *emigrate, immigrate, migrate.*

moral, morale   A *moral* is a lesson taught in a story. *Morale* is a state of mind regarding confidence and cheerfulness.

must of   Nonstandard for *must have. They must have lost their way.*

number, amount   See *amount, number.*

okay, OK, O.K.   Informal. In formal writing, use more precise terms such as *enjoyable, acceptable,* or *pleasing.*

person, individual   See *individual, person.*

personal, personnel   *Personal* is an adjective meaning "private" or "individual." *Personnel* is a noun meaning the people employed by an organization. *The personnel office keeps personal files on all the company's employees.*

phenomenon, phenomena   A *phenomenon* is "a perceivable occurrence or fact." *Phenomena* is the plural form.

plus   Colloquial when used in place of *moreover. We had gone past the deadline; moreover* (not *plus*) *we were over budget.*

precede, proceed   *Precede* means "come before." *Proceed* means "go ahead."

pretty   In formal writing, avoid using *pretty* as an adverb. *JFK was a very* (not *pretty*) *good writer.*

principal, principle   *Principal* is an adjective meaning "foremost." *Principle* is a noun meaning "rule" or "standard." *Our principal concern is to maintain our high principles.*

raise, rise   *Raise* is a transitive verb meaning "lift" or "build." *He raised his hand. Rise* is an intransitive verb meaning "stand up" or "ascend." *She rose from her chair.*

real, really   *Real* is an adjective; *really* is an adverb. In most cases, both of these terms should be avoided in formal writing. *The economy is doing very* (not *real* or *really*) *well.*

reason . . . is because   Colloquial. Use *reason . . . is that* in formal writing. *The reason the Yankees won is that they had better pitching.*

reckon   See *calculate, figure, reckon.*

respectfully, respectively   *Respectfully* means "with respect." *Respectively* means "in the order given." *The teacher called on Bart and Juana, respectively.*

rise, raise   See *raise, rise.*

set, sit   *Set* is used most often as a transitive verb meaning "place" or "arrange." *Set the table. Sit* is an intransitive verb meaning "take a seat." *Sit down over here.*

shall, will   In American English, *shall* is used only for polite questions in the first person (*Shall we sit down?*) and in legalistic writing. Otherwise, *will* is the standard modal verb for future tenses.

should of   Nonstandard for *should have.*

site, cite   See *cite, site.*

somewheres   Nonstandard for *somewhere.*

sort of   See *kind of, sort of, type of.*

specially, especially   See *especially, specially.*

stationary, stationery   *Stationary* is an adjective meaning "not moving." *Stationery* is a noun meaning "writing materials."

take, bring   See *bring, take.*

than, then   *Than* is a conjunction used to introduce the second part of a comparison: *Donna is taller than Jo. Then* is an adverb meaning "at that time."

that, which   As a relative pronoun, *that* is used only in essential clauses. *The storm that* (or *which*) *everyone talks about occurred ten years ago. Which* can be used with either essential or nonessential clauses. *The storm of 1989, which I'll never forget, destroyed part of our roof.*

their, there, they're   *Their* is the possessive form of *they. They retrieved their car. There* is an adverb of place; it is also used in expletive constructions. *There is someone at the door.* (See 33a-9, 40c.)*They're* is a contraction of *they are. They're too young to drive.*

theirselves   Nonstandard. Use *themselves.*

threw, through/thru   *Threw* is the past form of the verb *throw. Through* is a preposition, as in *walk through the house.* Do not use *thru* in formal writing.

till, until, 'til   *Till* and *until* are both acceptable in formal writing. *'Til* is informal.

type of   See *kind of, sort of, type of.*

uninterested, disinterested   See *disinterested, uninterested.*

unique   "The only one of its kind." In formal English, *unique* should be used without any degree modification. *Tiger Woods is a unique (not very unique) athlete.*

until   See *till, until, 'til.*

use, utilize   In most cases, *use* is the better choice. *Utilize* means "to make practical use of" and should be used only with this meaning.

weak, week   *Weak* is the opposite of strong. *Week* is a period of seven days.

weather, whether   Use *weather* as a noun meaning "atmospheric conditions." Use *whether* as a conjunction meaning "if" or "either."

well, good   See *good, well.*

whether, if   See *if, whether.*

will, shall   See *shall, will.*

which, that   See *that, which.*

whole, hole   See *hole, whole.*

who, whom   *Who* and *whom* are used as interrogative or relative pronouns. *Who* stands for a grammatical subject; *whom* stands for a grammatical object. (See 30a-2.)

who's, whose   *Who's* is a contraction for *who is. Whose* is the possessive form of *who.*

would have   Should not be used in the *if* part of a conditional sentence. *If I had (not would have) started sooner, I would have finished the paper on time.* (See 61k.)

would of   Nonstandard for *would have.*

your, you're   *Your* is the possessive form of *you. You're* is a contraction of *you are. You're loyal to your friends.*

Credits

Adbusters Reprints. Reprinted by permission.

American Heritage College Dictionary, The. 3rd ed. Boston: Houghton, 1993. Copyright © 1997 by Houghton Mifflin Company. Reproduced by permission from *The American Heritage Dictionary, Third Edition.*

AP Photographs. Courtesy of AP/Wide World Photos.

Barlow, John Perry. "Crime and Puzzlement." *CyberReader.* Ed. Victor Vitanza. Boston: Allyn, 1996. 92–115.

"B.C." By permission of John L. Hart FLP, and Creators Syndicate, Inc.

Beebe, Steven A., and Susan J. Beebe, *Public Speaking: An Audience-Centered Approach.* 5th ed. Boston: Allyn, 2003.

Beers, Burton F. *World History.* Englewood Cliffs, NJ: Prentice, 1990. 719.

Bishop, Elizabeth. "One Art" from THE COMPLETE POEMS: 1927–1979 by Elizabeth Bishop. Copyright © 1979, 1983 by Alice Helen Methfessel. Reprinted by permission of Farrar, Straus and Giroux, LLC.

Briggs, Barrett M. "Resuscitating Trigger." Online posting. Writing Program Administrator Listserv. 1 Dec. 1997.

Cassity, Jeri. *Brochure Writing: Examining the Rhetorical Situation.* Logan: Utah State University, 1993. 6–7.

Chaika, Elaine. *Language: The Social Mirror.* Cambridge, MA: Newbury House, 1989. 90.

Claywell, Gina. *The Allyn and Bacon Guide to Writing Portfolios.* Boston: Allyn, 2001. 77–78.

Climate Change. 2003. World Wildlife Fund (WWF). 1 Nov. 2003. <http://www.panda.org/about_wwf/what_we_do/climate_change/index.cfm>.

Cole, K.C. *The Scientific Aesthetic.* New York: Discover, 1983. Reprinted by permission of the author.

Commoner, Barry. *The Closing Circle.* New York: Bantam, 1974. 11–12.

Corel® WordPerfect for Windows®.

Cousins, Norman. *Human Options.* New York: Berkley, 1981. 41–42, 63, 90.

Deja News [Online]. 12 Sept. 2000 and 3 Feb. 2001 <http://www.dejanews.com>.

Dominguez, Joe, and Vicki Robin. *Your Money or Your Life.* New York: Viking, 1992. 13.

Donatelle, Rebecca J. *Access to Health.* 8th ed. San Francisco: Benjamin Cummings, 2004. © 2004 by Benjamin Cummings. Reprinted by permission.

Easterbrook, G. "The sincerest flattery: Thanks, but I'd rather you not plagiarize my work." *Newsweek.* July 19, 1991. 45–46.

"Effects of the Bush Tax Cut, 2004–2010," Children's Defense Fund and Citizens for Tax Justice. <http://www.ctj.org./html/gwb0602.htm>.

Ehrlich, Gretel. *The Solace of Open Spaces.* New York: Viking, 1985. 7.

Eisler, Riane. *The Chalice and the Blade.* San Francisco: Harper, 1987. 12.

Environmental Periodicals Bibliography. Citation taken from *Environmental Periodicals Bibliography* database (copyright, International Academy at Santa Barbara). This database is available on CDROM and on the Internet. Subscription information is available on the Academy's Website at <http://www.iasb.org>.

Excite NewsTracker [Online]. 23 June 2000 <http://www.excite.com>. Excite and the Excite logo are trademarks of Excite, Inc., and may be registered in various jurisdictions. Excite screen display copyright 1995–1998 Excite, Inc.

Farb, Peter. *Living Earth.* New York: Harper, 1959.

Garofalo, Reebee. *Rockin' Out: Popular Music in the USA.* Boston: Allyn, 1997. Copyright © 1997 by Allyn & Bacon. Reprinted by permission.

General Motors Corp. Used with permission. GM Media Archives.

Hardgrave, Robert L., Jr., *American Government.* Orlando: Harcourt, 1986. 477.

Hemingway, Ernest. "Notes on the Next War: A Serious Topical Letter." *By-Line: Ernest Hemingway.* Ed. William White. New York: Scribner's, 1967. 206.

Henslin, James M. *Sociology: A Down-to-Earth Approach.* 6th ed. Boston: Allyn, 2003. Copyright © 2003 by Allyn & Bacon. Reprinted by permission.

Hopkins, Gerard Manley. "The Windhover." *Collected Poems.* London: Oxford UP, 1918.

Hopper, Vincent F., and Bernard D. N. Grebanier. *Essentials of European Literature.* Vol. 2. Great Neck, NY: Barron's, 1952.

Hotbot [Online]. <http://www.hotbot.lycos.com>. © 1998 Lycos, Inc. Hotbot® is a registered trademark of Carnegie Mellon University. All rights reserved.

Hult, Christine. *WebCT* [Online]. Discussion forum for English 405. 10 Nov. 2000. Used by permission.

Internaut Capt. Jack. "A 'Livable Minimum Wage' Is a Bad Idea." 8 Nov. 1997 <www.mindspring.com/!bumpy1page4.htm>.

Ivins, Molly. "Truly Happy News to Look For: Better 'Doug Jones' Average," syndicated column, published by Creators Syndicate; appeared in *Salt Lake Tribune,* Feb. 27, 2000.

Kaniss, Phyllis. *Making Local News.* Chicago: U of Chicago P, 1991. 88–89.

Kantorowitz, Barbara. "Men, Women, and Computers." *Newsweek.* May 16, 1994.

Kingsolver, Barbara. *The Bean Trees.* New York: Harper, 1988. 1.

Kirkpatrick, Judith. *WebCT* [Online]. Opening screen for English 100. 10 Nov. 2000. Used by permission.

Lederer, Richard. *Anguished English.* New York: Wyrick, 1987. 115, 150–153. Excerpts from *Anguished English,* copyright 1987 by Richard Lederer. Published by Wyrick & Company.

Lycos [Online]. <http://www.lycos.com>. ©1998 Lycos, Inc. Lycos® is a registered trademark of Carnegie Mellon University. All rights reserved.

Martini, Frederic. *Fundamentals of Anatomy and Physiology.* Englewood Cliffs, NJ: Prentice, 1989. 3.

Meyer, Michael, with Anne Underwood. "Crimes of the 'Net'." *CyberReader.* Ed. Victor Vitanza. Boston: Allyn, 1996. 63–65.

Microsoft Corporation. Screen shots from Microsoft Windows Explorer®, Internet Explorer®, Microsoft Word 2000®, and Windows ftp® reprinted by permission from Microsoft Corporation.

Miller, Kenneth R., and Joseph Levine. *Biology.* Englewood Cliffs, NJ: Prentice, 1991. 76.

My Virtual Reference Desk. Ed. B. Drudge. 1985–2000. 16 Jan. 2001 <http://www.refdesk.com>.

Netscape. Portions Copyright Netscape Communications Corporation, 1997. All Rights Reserved. Netscape, Netscape Navigator, Netscape Composer, and the Netscape N logo are registered trademarks of Netscape in the United States and other countries.

New Book of Knowledge, The. New York: Grolier, 1998.

Niethammer, Carolyn. *Daughters of the Sky.* New York: Macmillan, 1997. 96.

Orwell, George. "Marrakech." *A Collection of Essays.* Garden City, NY: Doubleday, 1957. 186–192.

Rifkin, Jeremy. *The End of Work.* New York: Putnam, 1995.

Rutz, Carol. Director, Writing Program, Carleton College. Used by permission.

Sacks, Glenn. "Title IX Lawsuits Are Endangering Men's College Sports." Reprinted by permission.

Sagan, Carl. *The Dragons of Eden.* New York: Ballantine, 1977. 177.

Science & Technology Review, Jul./Aug. 2003, Lawrence Livermore National Laboratory.

Sen, Amartya. *Inequality Reexamined.* Cambridge, MA: Harvard UP, 1992. 21.

Social Sciences Abstracts [Online]. November 1997. Reprinted with permission of H.W. Wilson Company and Utah State University Libraries.

Sternberg, Robert J. *Pathways to Psychology.* 2nd ed. Fort Worth: Harcourt, 2000. 14.

SyllaBase [Online]. Class calendar. File sharing. © 3GB Group. Used by permission.

Tannen, Deborah. *You Just Don't Understand.* New York: Morrow, 1990. 136.

Taylor, Todd. "The Persistence of *Difference* in Networked Classrooms: *Non-Negotiable Difference* and the African American Student Body." *Computers and Composition* 14 (1997): 169–178.

Terkel, Studs. *Working.* New York: Avon, 1972. xix.

Thomas, Lewis. *Lives of a Cell.* New York: Viking, 1974. 107.

U.S. Bureau of the Census, Current Population Reports, P60–103, *Money Income in the United States: 1995,* U.S. Government Printing Office, Washington, DC, 1996. xii.

U.S. Energy Information Administration. "Annual World Energy Consumption, 1992-1995." *International Energy Annual,* U.S. Government Printing Office, Washington, DC, 1996.

Utah State University Libraries.

Woolfolk, Anita E. *Educational Psychology.* 9th ed. Boston: Allyn, 2004. 122. Copyright © 2004 by Allyn & Bacon. Reprinted by permission.

Yahoo! [Online]. Text and artwork copyright © 1998 by Yahoo! Inc. All rights reserved. YAHOO! and the YAHOO! logo are trademarks of Yahoo! Inc.

Index

F

M

O